Management Development and Training Handbook

Management Development and Training Handbook

Editors: Bernard Taylor (UK)
and
Gordon L. Lippitt (USA)

McGRAW-HILL Book Company (UK) Limited

London · New York · St Louis · San Francisco · Auckland
Bogotá · Düsseldorf · Johannesburg · Madrid · Mexico
Montreal · New Delhi · Panama · Paris · São Paulo
Singapore · Sydney · Tokyo · Toronto

Published by McGRAW-HILL Book Company (UK) Limited

MAIDENHEAD · BERKSHIRE · ENGLAND

Library of Congress Cataloging in Publication Data

Taylor, Bernard (Date)
 Management development and training handbook

 "Bibliography on management development and training [by] N. R. Hunter": p. 615.
 1. Executives, Training of—Addresses, essays, lectures. 2. Organizational change—
 Addresses, essays, lectures. I. Lippitt, Gordon L., joint author. II. Title.

 HF5549.5.T7T295   658.4'07'124   74-13384

 ISBN 0-07-084446-1

2 3 4 5 JWA 7 9 8 7
PRINTED AND BOUND IN GREAT BRITAIN

Contents

Part 1. Management Development

1. Management Development: The International Perspective   3
   H. C. de Bettignies
2. Top Management's Role in Management Development   12
   Jan Kreiken
3. The Role of the Central Management Development Service   23
   D. S. Markwell
4. Identifying Executive Potential: Methods of Testing and Assessing   40
   Esther C. Lawton
5. The Use of Assessment Centres in Management Development   63
   William C. Byham
6. Management Selection and Recruitment   84
   G. A. Randell
7. Developing Managerial Understanding of the Younger Generation   99
   Leonard Nadler
8. Developing Resourceful Managers   109
   John Morris
9. The Role of the External Consultant   126
   Alan Mumford
10. Identifying and Developing the Entrepreneur   135
    Gerald F. Smyth
11. Management Development in the Developing Countries   149
    Shyam B. L. Bharadwaj

Part 2. Management Training Methods

12. Management Education—A Conceptual Framework   169
    Bohdan Hawrylyshyn
13. The Case Method in Management Training   182
    Donald D. Simmons
14. The Use of Syndicates in Management Training   191
    John Adams
15. Action Learning Projects   204
    R. W. Revans
16. The Construction, Operation, and Evaluation of Management Games   217
    Clive Loveluck
17. Guidelines for the use of Sensitivity Training in Management Development   240
    Gordon L. Lippitt
18. The Use of Audio-Visual Aids in Management Training   260
    Jørgen Roed
19. Management Training by Teletuition   275
    Georg Marais

Part 3. Management Training Programmes

20. Training for Communicators 293
Thomas J. Attwood
21. Creativity Training Comes of Age 310
W. J. J. Gordon
22. Training in Decision Making 317
Jerome Rhodes
23. Developing Planning Skills in Managers 328
Edward J. Green
24. Life Goals Planning for Managers 342
Donald H. Swartz
25. Training Managers in Industrial Relations Negotiations 359
Arthur Marsh

Part 4. Organization Development

26. The Contribution of Behavioural Sciences to Organization Development 371
Meyer Feldberg and John D. Simpson
27. Managerial Grid in Practice 385
Robert R. Blake and Jane S. Mouton
28. Management by Objectives in Practice 399
Peter Hives
29. Job Enrichment in Practice 428
W. J. Paul
30. Action-Centred Leadership 442
Edwin P. Smith
31. The Organization Renewal Process in Practice 454
Frank T. Laverty
32. Organization Development in the Small Business 470
Philip J. Sadler
33. The Role of the Consultant in Organization Development 485
Geoffrey Morris

Part 5. Planning and Organization

34. Organization Change and Organization Planning 503
Wilbur M. McFeely
35. Manpower Forecasting: Estimating the Supply and Demand for Managers 527
A. R. Smith
36. Management Manpower Planning 542
Derek Walker
37. The Organizational Review: Assessing the Business and its Management 551
Neville Osmond
38. The Establishment and Organization of a Company Training Centre 564
R. A. Godsall
39. Developing Management Development Trainers 573
John E. Henriksen
40. The Analysis and Costing of Management Training 584
John Talbot
41. The Use of Attitude Surveys in Management Development and Training 603
Robert M. Worcester

Appendix

Bibliography on Management Development and Training   615
Neil R. Hunter

Index   629

Preface

Throughout the world, trained, experienced managers are being seen increasingly as a 'resource', the supply of which is critical to the survival and future development of an organization or a nation. It is becoming apparent that the differences in performance between countries, and the competitive advantages of business enterprises, rest not so much on their supply of natural resources—or even on technological expertise—but on the ability of their people to manage these resources and to utilize new technology through efficient and innovative organizations. It is not, therefore, surprising to find that senior managers and administrators are now paying more attention to 'the management of human resources'.

As this handbook demonstrates, the technology for the selection, appraisal, training, and development of managers, and for the assessment, restructuring, and development of whole organizations, is readily available, though in a fairly unsophisticated form. However, as is often the case with management, the problem lies not so much in identifying problems and producing concepts, techniques, and procedures to cope with them, but in the implementation of what is already known; particularly in finding the time and energy to prepare for the medium- and long-term development of an organization in spite of the pressures involved in managing the day to day operation.[1]

Studies of long-range planning suggest that planning for manpower is much less advanced than planning for finance or marketing. Personnel statistics are often poor and it is not unusual to find corporate plans in which the personnel figures appear simply as totals with no breakdown by type or grade. It is common for large multinational companies to discover, following a reorganization, that they have no succession plans for their most senior management—one of the resources which is most crucial to the future of the firm.[2]

If manpower planning and management development are relatively unsophisticated compared with planning for other areas of activity in large organizations, in small organizations there is virtually no provision for management training and development. Recent studies of management development and training in Europe suggest that organizations with less than 500 personnel rarely engage in management training and development and rely mainly on buying trained management from larger organizations.[3]

In various parts of Europe, e.g., Britain, France, and Ireland, national governments are using the force of law and all kinds of financial incentives to encourage firms to establish management development and training schemes. If Britain's experience is any indication, the results of government intervention are likely to be disappointing in the field of management, although there may be substantial progress in other fields, e.g., the establishment of apprentice-training schemes. In Britain today, despite the efforts of the industrial training boards, only about 15 per cent[4] of companies have management development schemes and, in any one year, only 7 per cent of managers take part in a formal management course (internal or external) lasting one week or more. Management development and training is still regarded as a luxury in which only large firms indulge—and then only in good times.[5] During the 1970–71 recession, even the largest firms cut their management training budgets by as much as half, and some stopped management training entirely.

It is nevertheless true that, during the past decade, there has been a rapid growth of interest in management development and training on a worldwide basis. The symptoms are all there:

(a) a plethora of conferences, seminars, books, and articles on the subject (see Bibliography, p. 615);
(b) government legislation and the formation of industrial training boards;
(c) the emergence of a new generation of behavioural science consultants specializing in:
    (i) selection and appraisal of managers;
    (ii) 'organization development' programmes;
    (iii) or in-company training aimed at improving 'creativity', 'planning', or 'decision making';
(d) the establishment of central executive development functions in most bluechip companies;
(e) increasing use of techniques for manpower planning and manpower forecasting.

Many of these innovations originated in the US, which probably still accounts for 90 per cent of the world's research and development investment in management. But the movement is becoming multinational. In the last ten years, indigenous university business schools have appeared in most industrialized countries, and they have now formed faculties and research teams of their own. In the developing world, and in the Communist countries, there is also growing interest in management, as it has become obvious that investment in technology is often very wasteful unless it is properly managed. Governments in the emerging economies are naturally anxious that their economies should not be entirely dominated by huge multinational companies, and interesting experiments are being made to try to identify and develop entrepreneurs in the local community. The consequence, as de Bettignies points out, is that management and management development are now seen in a multinational context. Management is not seen as a homogeneous activity but as a process which varies with the cultural context.

The Handbook

This handbook is designed as a standard work of reference on the latest thinking and practice in management development and training, with the senior manager or administrator and the personnel manager or management development specialist in mind. The book consists of a symposium of original articles specially commissioned from recognized authorities in various parts of the world. There are more than forty contributors from a dozen countries, in North America, Europe, and the developing world. The authors include senior managers from major companies, personnel specialists from the Civil Service in the US and Britain, academics from the world's leading business schools and management colleges, and consultants who have pioneered highly successful programmes for in-company training and organization development. The Handbook is divided into five parts:

Part 1, Management Development, starts with a definition of the concept, and looks at various aspects of the process—the role of top management; the function of a central management development service; the identification and assessment of executive potential; management selection and the use of 'assessment centres'; career planning; and the role of the external consultant. There is a fascinating chapter about the 'generation gap' in management; also, two articles of special interest in an international context—one on identifying and developing the entrepreneur, the other concerned with management development in the developing countries.

Part 2, Management Training Methods, provides an authoritative briefing on the principal teaching methods at present in use: case studies, syndicates, projects, management games, and T-Groups, together with a classic evaluation of the contribution which each of these approaches can make in the education process. This section ends with a look at more recent developments in audio-visual aids, and in training by correspondence and television.

Part 3, Management Training Programmes, is concerned with in-company training. The chapters are written by specialists who have pioneered training courses in basic management skills, e.g., communications, creativity, and decision making. The section includes details of new programmes recently developed in three important areas: industrial relations negotiation, managerial planning, and motivation. The penultimate chapter has the fascinating title 'Life Goals Planning for Managers'.

Part 4, Organization Development, starts with an assessment of the contribution of the behavioural sciences to 'OD'. This is followed by an exposition of the different approaches to OD by some of the leading figures in the movement. The chapters are concerned less with theory than with the practical problems of organization and implementation, and the approaches considered include: Managerial Grid, Management by Objectives, Job Enrichment, Action-centred Leadership, and Organization Renewal. The section ends with a description of OD in a small business, and a consideration of the function of the internal and external consultant in introducing and facilitating the process.

Part 5, Planning and Organization, begins with a study of how organizations change and what happens when new structures are introduced. This is particularly topical at a time when it seems that every kind of organization in the public and private sector is being reorganized. The other chapters are concerned with planning, organizing, evaluating and controlling the management development and training process. The topics covered include:

(a) estimating the supply and demand for managers;
(b) assessing the enterprise and its management;
(c) organization planning;
(d) establishing and organizing a company training centre;
(e) developing management trainers;
(f) the analysis and costing of management training;
(g) the use of surveys to measure the effectiveness of training courses.

This handbook has been prepared in remarkably short time. This has required a great deal of effort on the part of the contributors, all of whom are extremely busy people. We would like to thank everyone who has contributed to this volume. We would also like to thank, personally, Mrs Valerie Alasia and Mrs Jean Carter, who have been responsible for ensuring that all the various parts of the book arrived at the publishers on time.

We would appreciate hearing from readers about new developments which might be referred to in future editions.

Bernard Taylor
Administrative Staff College
Henley-on-Thames

Gordon L. Lippitt
George Washington University

1974

References

1. See E. K. Warren, *Long Range Planning: The Executive Viewpoint*, Prentice-Hall, Englewood Cliffs, New Jersey, 1966.
2. See B. Taylor and P. Irving, Organised Planning in Major UK Companies, *Long Range Planning*, **3,** 4, 1971; K. A. Ringbakk, Organised Planning in Major US Companies, *Long Range Planning*, **2,** 2, 1969; J. K. Brown *et al.*, Long Range Planning in the USA—a NICB Survey, *Long Range Planning*, **1,** 3, 1970; and Planning in West German Industry, *Long Range Planning*, **3,** 1, 1970.
3. See B. Taylor, A Seller's Market for Management Education, *Management Decision*, summer 1967; B. Tomlin, *The Management of Irish Industry*, Irish Management Institute, Dublin, 1966; and H. Rose, *Management Education in the 1970's: Growth and Issues*, NEDO, HMSO, 1970.
4. See Report on Management Training Survey, Orr Boss and Partners, April 1973 (unpublished confidential report); B. Taylor, A Seller's Market for Management Education in Britain, *Management Decision*, summer 1967; and H. Rose, *Management Education in the 1970's: Growth and Issues*, NEDO, HMSO, 1970.
5. See A. Mant, *The Experienced Manager: A Major Resource*, British Institute of Management, London, 1969.

Contributors

JOHN ADAMS (UK) is deputy principal of the Administrative Staff College, Henley. He graduated from Oxford University in 1933 and was a Commonwealth Fund Fellow at the University of Chicago and the Brookings Institution, Washington, DC, from 1933–5. From 1935–9, he was Director of the Tyneside Council of Social Service. After war service, he joined the University of Sheffield where, from 1946–56, he was Warden of Crewe Hall, lectured on the history of economic thought and on political theory and institutions, and started a business studies course. He joined the Administrative Staff College in 1957 to work with syndicates, with special interests in organization and the relations between industry and government, and has contributed to programmes in India, East Africa, and Australia. (Chapter 14)

THOMAS J. ATTWOOD (UK) is chairman of London based international management consultants Cargill, Attwood & Thomas Ltd. As management communication specialists, Cargill Attwood International conducted the first ever management development programmes for the United Nations at Geneva. He has broadcast on communication and addressed the World PR Congress; he has attended Harvard and INSEAD business schools. (Chapter 20)

SHYAM B. L. BHARADWAJ (India) is the Director of Studies at the Administrative Staff College of India, Hyderabad. He obtained his PH.D. in industrial and organizational psychology at Lucknow University and pursued postdoctoral studies in social, industrial, and clinical psychology, at New York University. Before taking up his appointment at the Administrative Staff College, he was assistant professor at Gorakhpur University, visiting professor of psychology at New York University, and senior defence scientist to Ministry of Defence, New Delhi. He is currently engaged in teaching, research, and consultancy in the areas of management development and organization development. (Chapter 11)

ROBERT R. BLAKE and JANE SRYGLEY MOUTON (US) began a long collaboration in behavioural science applications in 1952 as professors at the University of Texas. They have published many research-based books and articles, developed the Managerial Grid system, and were the originators of the concept of organization development. Drs Blake and Mouton are, respectively, president and vice-president of Scientific Methods Inc., of Austin, Texas, an applied behavioural science consulting and training firm operating throughout the world. (Chapter 27)

WILLIAM C. BYHAM (US) started the assessment centre programme at the J. C. Penney Company, where he was responsible for all selection, appraisal, and general management programmes. He claims, in fact, that he has probably helped more organizations set up assessment centres than has any other individual. As a consultant in this field, Dr Byham has helped organizations such as Kodak, Ford Motor Company, Shell Oil, Owens, Illinois, Merill Lynch, Pierce, Fenner and Smith, South Africa Mutual Life Insurance, Northern Electric, Steinberg's, and Roche Laboratories. He is cofounder, with Dr Douglas Bray, of AT and T, of Development Dimensions, a company specializing in providing exercises and tools for management assessment and development. (Chapter 5)

H. C. de BETTIGNIES (France) is associate professor and chairman of the Organizational Behaviour area at INSEAD. He graduated from the Ecole de Psychologues Practiciens (Paris) and is Licencié ès Lettres (psychology, sociology) from the Sorbonne, where he received his Doctorat d'Etat, following the publication of his book *The Process of Change in Managerial Practices in Modern Japan.* He was a research assistant at the University of California, Berkeley, and for three years that he spent in Japan, was Visiting Lecturer at Rikkyo University and at several management development centres. He spent a year at the Harvard Business School (International Teachers Programme). Professor de Bettignies is a consultant for several international organizations and has written several papers for academic and management journals. (Chapter 1)

MEYER FELDBERG (South Africa), B.A. (Rand), M.B.A. (Columbia), PH.D. (University of Cape Town), was born in Johannesburg in 1942. In January 1972, Professor Feldberg was appointed to the first full chair of management at the University of Cape Town. In May of that year, he was appointed director of the Graduate School of Business. He has been a visiting professor of business administration at Northwestern University, Graduate School of Business, Chicago; the Cranfield School of Management in England; the Institute of Business Administration, in Paris and the Massachusetts Institute of Technology in Boston. A keen sportsman and former Springbok swimming champion, Professor Feldberg was one of the recipients of the Jaycee 'Four Outstanding Young Men of the Year Award' (1972) for his work in management education and development. (Chapter 26, *see also* John D. Simpson)

R. A. GODSALL (UK) is director of the Dunchurch Industrial Staff College, one of the largest post-experience management training centres in the UK. He has held this appointment since 1969, having spent the previous ten years in academic appointments at a number of colleges and universities, where he specialized in industrial management. He continues as a visiting lecturer at some of the leading UK business schools. Throughout his academic career, an industrial consultancy practice has helped him to maintain experience gained in earlier years of production management in manufacturing. He is recognized as a leading authority on the development and use of business simulation as a training medium. (Chapter 38)

W. J. J. GORDON (US) is president of Synectics Education Systems. His work in the field of creative process led to the metaphorical basis of Synectics: a word which has become generic since coined by him in 1955. Today, most of his time is devoted to educational research, and work with graduate students in the US and abroad. As well as his work in social science, William Gordon has to his credit more than 100 patents in various technical areas, and his fiction has earned him the O. Henry Short Story Award and the Science Fiction award. His educational experience has ranged from responsibility for a group of children who 'could not play' to being a member of the Harvard Faculty, as well as chancellor of a highly experimental college. He is the author of many articles, both technical and for the layman, and nine books, of which the best known are *Synectics* and *The Metaphorical Way of Learning and Knowing*. (Chapter 21)

EDWARD J. GREEN (US) is chairman of Planning Dynamics, a firm of management counsellors devoted primarily to helping clients develop and implement programmes to increase management effectiveness. Also vice-chairman of Babb, and a director of several corporations, he has, during the past eight years, provided counsel and assistance to the top management of more than 100 organizations—corporations, institutions, associations, and government agencies. Before establishing Planning Dynamics, Mr Green was vice-president (planning and marketing) for Westinghouse Air Brake Company, and vice-president and director of Westinghouse Air Brake International Corporation. He is a member of the Marketing and Planning Councils of the American Management Association and a member of the Advisory Council of the Long Range Planning Service for Stanford Research Institute. (Chapter 23)

BOHDAN HAWRYLYSHYN (Switzerland) is director of the Centre d'Etudes Industrielles (CEI), Geneva. Born in the Ukraine, he is a Canadian citizen. He started at the CEI as a faculty member, then became director of studies before taking up his present post as director. He has taught production management, economic growth, and management of international operations and has acted as consultant to international organizations and multinational corporations. Dr Hawrylyshyn has lectured at universities and at international conferences in more than twenty countries and has written articles in various languages, on creativity and management education. (Chapter 12)

JOHN E. HENRIKSEN (Denmark), manager of the Management Consultancy in BP Olie-Kompagniet A/S, came to the company from the Psycho-Technical Institute of Copenhagen. He studied psychology at the University of Copenhagen. He was president of the Danish Association of Commercial and Industrial Education from 1967 to 1972 (the association's members are professionally concerned with management development. (Chapter 39)

PETER HIVES (UK), who died recently, was until the time of his death a senior consultant with Urwick, Orr and Partners. He read mechanical sciences at Cambridge University and obtained industrial experience with Rolls-Royce. In 1957 he became a management consultant, and was closely associated with the development of Management by Objectives in a wide range of industries. He published a number of papers on MbO, task force management, and managerial manpower planning. (Chapter 28)

NEIL R. HUNTER (UK), B.A., A.L.A., has been librarian at the University of Bradford Management Centre since August 1970, having joined the staff of the main university library in 1968. Before entering librarianship, he spent two years planning hospitals, followed by three years as a university administrator. (Bibliography)

JAN KREIKEN (Holland), fellow of the International Academy of Management (CIOS), is the Chancellor of the THT University of Technology, Enschede. He is director of two major Dutch companies, and an adviser to Dutch and British industry. As president of the IUC, he was cofounder of the European Foundation for Management Development in Brussels and is a member of the Board of Trustees. Dr Kreiken is a board member of three Dutch institutes for management development. In 1966, after chairing the CIOS World Management Congress in Rotterdam, he was presented with the NIVE annual award. From 1950 until 1968, he held executive posts in South Africa, France, and Holland, and has been president of the executive board of Sitos NV, one of the largest Dutch food groups. Dr Kreiken has also served as chairman of government commissions. He is a life member of the American Management Association, and honary board member of IUC. (Chapter 2)

FRANK T. LAVERTY (Canada) is president of Management Renewal. Formerly, he was chairman of business, Cambrian College, and chairman of management, Algonquin College. He holds degrees from Carleton University and George Washington University. Mr Laverty specializes in organization renewal, Management by Objectives, creative management, and the effective utilization of human resources. He emphasizes the practical application of processes on a continuing basis in real work situations. He has consulted with, and conducted training sessions for, 3000 Canadian managers from more than 150 government, industrial, service, and educational organizations. He has also introduced and conducted continual organization renewal activities with more than 1000 participating managers. (Chapter 31)

ESTHER C. LAWTON (US) is the deputy director of personnel in the US Treasury Department. She is the recipient of several awards, notably the Federal Women's Award, the Office of the Secretary of Honor Award, and Professional Woman of the Year (1970 and 1972). Her distinctions include B.A. Cum Laude, M.A. with distinction, and election to Phi Beta Kappa. She was the only woman president of the Society for Personnel Administration and is on a number of executive committees of organizations in her field. She has completed two terms as president of the Classification and Compensation Society and has been president of a number of women's organizations. She was recently made an honorary life member of the International Personnel Management Association. (Chapter 4)

GORDON L. LIPPITT (US) is professor of behavioural sciences at the George Washington University. He also serves as president of Organization Research, a nationwide consulting and training organization. He served as President of the American Society for Training and Development in 1969. He is the author of more than 200 articles and books in the field of leadership, management, and organization behaviour. (Chapter 17)

CLIVE LOVELUCK (UK) is director of the Ulster Management Centre. Formerly director of studies at the School of Management Studies, North London Polytechnic, and a senior consultant with the PE consulting group, he is a graduate of the London School of Economics and of the Harvard Business School International Teachers Programme. Recognized internationally as an expert on management games, Clive Loveluck has written many for organizations such as Ford, Vauxhall, and General Electric, for hospital boards and for more general use by universities and companies, e.g., his Small Business Game, Snibbo, and Exmark. He worked on the BBC TV series *You Are the Boss* and has appeared in many TV programmes. (Chapter 16)

GEORG MARAIS (South Africa) is director of the School of Business Leadership and professor of business policy at the University of South Africa. He obtained his Bachelor's and Master's degrees in commerce at the University of Stellenbosch and continued his studies on a government scholarship at the University of Wisconsin, where he obtained his PH.D in economics in June 1956. In 1961, at the age of 29, he was appointed professor in business economics at the University of South Africa, after five years' service at the Department of Commerce and Industries and the Board of Trade. Professor Marais has published two books and thirty-one articles. (Chapter 19)

D. S. MARKWELL (UK) is senior manager in the management development section of Unilever, in London, where he is responsible for management education and training in Unilever internationally. Born in New Zealand in 1930, Dr Markwell read psychology at Victoria University, Wellington, and joined Unilever New Zealand, at which time he was also deputy director of the New Zealand Administrative Staff College. He is coauthor of *The Organization of Management Development Programmes* and *Business Planning for the Board* and a number of professional articles. He is a visiting speaker to the Administrative Staff College, Henley, CEI in Geneva and Graduate School of Management, Northwestern University. (Chapter 3)

ARTHUR MARSH (UK) is senior research fellow in industrial relations, St Edmund's Hall, Oxford. He has been researching and teaching industrial relations for more than twenty years and, in the 'sixties, having a special interest in the engineering industry, developed techniques for teaching negotiation in the motor and other industries. He is currently researching into staff relations in engineering and in industrial relations, generally in the steel industry. His *Dictionary of Industrial Relations* was published in 1973. (Chapter 25)

WILBUR M. MCFEELY (US), who died recently, was on the staff of The Conference Board and worked for many years on organization planning. His chapter is reprinted by permission from *The Conference Board Report* 1972: *Organization Change: Perceptions and Realities.* (Chapter 34)

GEOFFREY MORRIS (UK) is a director of European Manpower Advisory Services (EMAS) and Eurocontact. Before joining EMAS, he worked for Birds Eye Foods, first as training development manager and then as company training manager, during which time he devised and implemented an organizational effectiveness programme involving all levels of management and supervision. Subsequently, he assisted Unilever, France, in applying a similar programme. As director of EMAS, he has acted as consultant to well-known companies in the areas of organization development, strategic planning, industrial relations, and the management of human resources. He has worked in various countries in western Europe and was a member of the BACI/IPM/ITO delegation to the EEC. He has broadcast on legal, industrial, educational, and sociological subjects and presented the BBC TV series 'Training for work'. (Chapter 33)

JOHN MORRIS (UK) is professor of management development at the University of Manchester Business School. He has been responsible for developing new programmes of joint development activities with a number of organizations in the public and private sectors. He has written extensively on management development and the psychology of learning and has participated widely in executive education and training programmes. (Chapter 8)

JANE SRYGLEY MOUTON (US). See entry under Robert R. Blake. (Chapter 27)

ALAN MUMFORD (UK) is senior manpower development consultant with International Computers (ICL) and was vice-president (training and development) of the Institute of Personnel Management from 1971 to 1973. His first major experience in the field of management development was with the construction firm John Laing and Son, as training manager and management development adviser; later, he was with IPC (magazines). As deputy chief training adviser at the Department of Employment he was responsible for two major surveys on the work of industrial training boards, the first reviewing management development, the second the advisory role of the training boards. He is the author of *The Manager and Training.* (Chapter 9)

LEONARD NADLER (US) is professor of adult education and human resource development, School of Education, George Washington University, Washington, DC. He has worked with a variety of organizations in both the public and private sectors. He has travelled, lived, and worked in twenty-seven countries. In addition to his university position, Dr Nadler provides consultation and other assistance to organizations in the area of human resource development, i.e., training, education, and development. Before joining the university, he served as training director in a variety of organizations, and was a member of the President's Task Force on the War Against Poverty, where he designed training for the Job Corps staff. (Chapter 7)

NEVILLE OSMOND (UK) read economics at Cambridge, and served as a district officer in Tanganyika. In 1960, he joined Clarks, the shoemakers, and held positions in production, personnel, and customer services, involving re-organization and management development. He then moved to Thomson Publications, where he was responsible for organization review, training needs, assessment, and personnel development. Between 1968 and 1972 he was a consultant with the MSL group, concerned with executive selection and organizational change. After a period as a principal consultant with TEAM (management consultants), he joined the Johnson Matthey Group of Companies in 1974. (Chapter 37)

W. J. PAUL (UK) is a director of North Paul and Associates. An American, resident in the UK, he has worked in American industry as a consultant and was formerly research colleague to Professor Frederick Herzberg. His work has included a study of the motivational attitudes of US Air Force officers, observations of the job attitudes of Russian and American workers, and studies of job enrichment in ICI, Shell UK, and other British companies. He was awarded first prize of the American Psychological Association Cattell Fund in 1969, for research related to psychological consultancy. Dr 'Bill' Paul is coauthor, with Keith Robertson, of *Job Enrichment and Employee Motivation* and is author of numerous articles in magazines and journals in the UK and Europe. (Chapter 29)

GERALD RANDELL (UK), B.SC., M.SC., PH.D., is senior lecturer in occupational psychology at the University of Bradford Management Centre, where he is also director of the Human Resources Research Group and head of the General Management Programme. He is an assessor to the British Civil Service Selection Board, chairman of Independent Assessment and Research Centre, London, director of Wharfedale Management Services, Harrogate, and a member of the editorial board of *European Training*. In 1965–6, Dr Randell was chairman of the Occupational Psychology Section of the British Psychological Society. He has worked previously as an industrial chemist, in personnel selection of aviation staff, in operations research, and at Birkbeck College, London. (Chapter 6)

R. W. REVANS (UK) was formerly research fellow, Emmanuel College, Cambridge, Guy's Hospital Medical School, London, and the European Association of Management Training Centres, Brussels. He has also been professor of industrial administration, University of Manchester; visiting professor, Southern Methodist University, US. He is now a consultant to several organizations, including The International Labour Office; The Foundation for Industry and the Universities, Brussels; and The Organization for Economic Cooperation and Development. Professor Revans is the author of *Standards for Morale, Cause and Effect in Hospitals, The Theory of Practice in Management, Science and the Manager,* and *Developing Effective Managers.* He described (at the time) the management education of the 'sixties as 'an academic Klondyke' and 'an impudent fraud' which, 'now that its tinselled bandwagon has collapsed under the weight of the self-dramatizing nonentities who fought their way aboard', he considers as two gross understatements. (Chapter 15)

JEROME RHODES (UK), M.A., DIP. ED., M.I.P.M. is managing director of Kepner-Tregoe. Born in 1930, he took his degree and diploma at Oxford University. After several years in teaching, he gained commercial experience from sales management with Hoover, then general management experience with Guest Keen and Nettlefolds. For some years, he has been deeply involved in management education on a number of fronts: as education and training manager, Rank Xerox UK; management development adviser, the Rank Organization; and then to his present position with Kepner-Tregoe. His experience thus ranges from line management through staff specialist to external consultant, and his association with Kepner-Tregoe includes three years as a client. (Chapter 22)

JØRGEN ROED (Denmark) is managing director of Scanticon, a-s, Scandinavian Management and Conference Centre. After qualifying as a teacher and economist, he took up teaching. In 1961, at the age of twenty-five, he began his management career, as managing director of the newly established Danish subsidiary of Northern Europe's biggest printing group, Esselte, Sweden, which produces and markets school supplies and undertakes total furnishing of educational establishments from kindergarten to university level.

In 1968, he was appointed managing director of Scanticon a-s, Scandinavian Management and Conference Centre, Denmark, over a year before it opened. He has been president of Round Table Denmark, and is a member of The Danish Council for Scientific Management, and The Presidents Association. Born 1935. (Chapter 18)

PHILIP SADLER (UK) is principal of Ashridge Management College. He studied sociology at the London School of Economics, 1950–54, and has been mainly concerned with organization research and the development of management education. In recent years, his research interests have concentrated on the problems of management organization in smaller enterprises. He is a Fellow of the British Institute of Management and a member of the executive committee of the Long Range Planning Society. (Chapter 32)

DONALD D. SIMMONS (UK) is director of the Case Clearing House of Great Britain and Ireland. Beginning his career as a management trainee in the manufacturing industry, he subsequently worked for a number of international companies, eventually becoming involved in consultancy. This led him into management teaching in British and North American universities. In a recent research appointment he developed a casebook on the management of education, following which, he took up his directorship of the Case Clearing House. (Chapter 13)

JOHN D. SIMPSON (South Africa) is assistant director of the Graduate School of Business, University of Cape Town. He holds a B.SC. in psychology, an M.B.A., and a PH.D. in consumer behaviour. He instructs mainly in consumer behaviour and marketing, and human relations and organization. Much of his work is centred on organization development: he has undertaken a two-year research project into organization development in the South African Navy. He subsequently designed an organizationwide training programme for a large retail chain. He recently developed a study into the effectiveness of management development programmes in South Africa. Dr Simpson acts as a consultant to South African companies in the marketing and organization development areas. (Chapter 26, see also Meyer Feldberg.)

A. R. SMITH (UK) is Under Secretary (director of statistics) in the Civil Service Department. He graduated from the London School of Economics and joined the Admiralty as a Civil Servant in 1950. He worked in several areas of naval and civilian personnel management before becoming head of a Naval Manpower Division, in 1964, and of the Defence Manpower Studies Unit in 1967. He transferred to the Treasury in 1968, and hence to his present position. He has been concerned with a number of NATO conferences on manpower and is an OECD consultant. He is a member of council of the Manpower Society and the Institute of Manpower Studies, a member of the Institute of Personnel Management, and a Fellow of the Royal Statistical Society. (Chapter 35)

EDWIN P. SMITH (UK) is head of member relations with the Industrial Society and acts as organization and leadership adviser to the Bishop of Southwark. He has had thirty years' industrial experience as an analytical, development and production chemist, much of it in management positions. He is a management graduate and one-time member of the Management Studies Department, Slough College, and is the author of several articles on leadership and of *The Manager as a Leader* and *The Action-Centred Leader: Tutor's Manual*. (Chapter 30)

GERALD F. SMYTH, (Ireland) B.E., M.B.A., is executive director of programmes for smaller businesses at the Irish Management Institute. He has organized a wide range of short programmes for smaller engineering, furniture and retail motor firms, and longer development programmes for the owners of smaller firms in Ireland and Kenya. These development programmes integrate need achievement with general management training. The objectives are to get the participants to identify opportunities for their businesses, to establish goals, and to draw up plans to reach the goals. (Chapter 10)

DONALD H. SWARTZ (USA) President and founding member of the Effectiveness Resource Group, professional consultants who specialize in helping individuals and organizations increase effectiveness. He is senior organization effectiveness consultant for the Weyerhauser Company. In his work with Weyerhauser, Mr Swartz has led innovative efforts in productivity improvement, communication effectiveness, career and personal growth planning, and improved organization effectiveness. These efforts have been recognized in articles appearing in journals such as the *Harvard Business Review* and the *Wall Street Journal*, and in a report on job enrichment by The National Conference Board. (Chapter 24)

JOHN TALBOT (UK) has been director of European Manpower Advisory Services since its foundation in July 1971. Before this, he was principal training adviser to the Food, Drink and Tobacco Industry Training Board, and previously he spent eight years as a training manager in the Unilever Group. He has a wide range of practical and consultancy experience, particularly in the fields of training, organization development, and manpower policies. An area of special interest has been the financial aspects of human resource management, and he is coauthor of *Analysis and Costing of Company Training*. (Chapter 40)

BERNARD TAYLOR (UK) has been closely associated with the development of corporate planning in Britain. He is editor of two international journals: *Long Range Planning* and the *Journal of General Management*. He has written numerous articles and produced eight books dealing with various aspects of business strategy and planning. He lectures widely in Britain and on the continent, and in 1971, completed an assignment for the United Nations, in New Delhi, with the National Council for Applied Economic Research. He has held responsible positions in marketing, and education and training with Proctor and Gamble and Rank Xerox. He founded the post-experience programme at the University of Bradford Management Centre and is now Professor of Business Policy and director of planning and development at the Henley Administrative Staff College. (Editor)

DEREK WALKER (UK) is personnel controller of the Rank Organization, one of Britain's leading companies, with 35 000 employees. He is a member of the Industrial Tribunal and a council member of the Institute of Manpower Studies, and vice-president of the Institute of Personnel Management. (Chapter 36)

ROBERT M. WORCESTER (UK) is managing director of Market Opinion Research International, an associate of the NOP group of companies. An American, resident in the UK, he is a graduate of the University of Kansas. Mr Worcester has contributed papers to ESOMAR, WAPOR, and the Market Research Society conferences, and articles to a number of journals. He is a member of the editorial staff of the *Journal of Marketing* and editor-in-chief of McGraw-Hill's *Consumer Market Research Handbook*. (Chapter 41)

Part 1. Management development

1. Management development: The international perspective

H. C. de Bettignies

We know more about management development techniques and tools than about their effectiveness, and in any case, little is known about application in an international perspective. As a process of change, management development must have clearly defined objectives, as operational as possible and specific in an international management development situation. A proposal is made for an integrated learning system, specifically designed for the development of international managers, while the need to place management development efforts within an organizational development model is stressed.

Whether or not tomorrow's business environment will be made up of a few hundred huge corporations, expanding fast all over the world in giant multinational conglomerates, can be left to the speculation of international futurologists. This much is certain; business is less and less limited to geographic boundaries, and—through concentrations, mergers, joint ventures, and financial participations—firms are becoming less parochial in defining their markets and are entering more complex systems of operations. Though the conceptual differences between foreign, international, and multinational operations are useful—beyond academic circles—in each of the three there is a common element: managing people from different environments. Academics still spend a lot of time in trying to identify what international management is about, and attempt to define it as a separate field of study, either in nature or degree.[1] The literature on international and multinational management is flourishing,[2] and it seems that the academic who likes travelling feels compelled to write a book on international management.

We talk of internationalizing the business curriculum,[3] and a graduate school which has not labelled some courses 'international marketing', 'international finance', or even 'international management', must not expect

3

a competitive edge in management education. Does this mean that we all know well what international management is about? Furthermore, does it imply that we have a fair understanding of the kind of man needed for 'international management'?[4] If so, we would be able to offer international management development programmes specifically designed for the new brand of men needed in international organization. Do we, in fact, really know what 'management development' is? Would it not be useful to define management development prior to giving it the international perspective? We can then attempt to identify the components of management in an international perspective, since this is a prerequisite to designing specific management development programmes for international managers. Following such an identification, we shall define objectives and describe a systematic process for the management development of international managers, as has been used in Europe recently.

The Nature of Management Development

Today, management development is not a choice left to the goodwill of top management, a luxury of profitable corporations, a fringe benefit of large organizations. It is a 'must', a requirement of the economic system, a process imposed on the company as a result of organizational growth, changing technology, and a changing competitive environment in its broadest sense. The systematic development of managerial talent is one of the primary tasks of any organization, for its own survival in an increasingly changing environment.

Management development can be defined as *the attempt to improve managerial effectiveness through a planned and deliberate learning process.* It is part of 'organizational learning', a process through which the organization develops its capability to understand its own behaviour, and, more specifically, the interdependent parts of its decision-making process in multiple environments. Management development is therefore one of the tools of organization development and is conceived as a planned change involving the whole organization as a complex system, and aimed at increasing the effectiveness of the organization, thus its health.

As such, management development is a social influence process of change, dealing with change of attitudes and understanding to affect managerial behaviour, job performance, and operational results. Any management development effort aims—through learning—to increase change, but change is a process which is oriented towards desirable goals, and management development efforts, if they are a necessity, are in no way an insurance against organizational ineffectiveness. Apart from the work of House,[5] only limited studies have taken place to assess systematically the impact of management development efforts. There is ample evidence that management development efforts have by no means been universally successful; not only have some had no demonstrable or measurable effects, but frequently, management development programmes have been known to cause problems,

4

e.g., lower morale among participants,[6] increased managerial turnover due to dissatisfaction,[7] undesirable behaviour by participants,[8,9] and conflict between participants and their superiors.[10]

Paradoxically, we know more about management development techniques and tools than about their impact, in many organization environments. Among the reasons for this unfortunate situation is the frequent lack of clear definition of the management development effort's objectives. Most management development programmes are still not thought of systematically, relying on a sound assessment of organizational and individual needs; nor are they integrated within a long-term plan for human resources development, or accorded a thorough definition of 'input' as well as 'output variables'. Given the lack of operationality of the output-variables definition, a cost-benefit analysis of many European management development efforts would probably bring pretty grim results—apart from the methodological difficulties it would imply. It would sadden corporate executives watching their return on investment, and could be a painful process. Management development does not constitute the dispatching of managers to a variety of well-packaged executive development programmes which promise to turn anyone into a manager in one to four weeks, or turn a plant engineer into a marketing executive in a fortnight.

Management development is a planned effort to generate learning—well defined in its scope—to help the organization as a whole to monitor more effectively its change process; it cannot therefore be the unplanned, punctual dispatching of individuals to a variety of training courses. Individualized development plans, well meshed into organizational development efforts, are a prerequisite to long-term organizational effectiveness.[11] Individual, as well as organization, development strategies should be designed in terms of outcomes as clearly defined as possible.

Management Development for International Operations—or the Relativity of Management Principles

After these preliminary remarks to stress the youth of management development and the current unsophistication of its use, we shall explore the area of international activities, beyond the national boundaries of business—a field in which little research has been undertaken.

Many corporations still assume that the manager who is successful at home will also be a success abroad, and 'not many companies have formal development plans and programmes designed specifically for their international executives. In general, the executives are included in overall corporate programs or in international programs patterned after those that are national'.[12] In his survey, Chorafas was struck by the lack of attention paid to specific management development for international executives. He observed a number of dysfunctional consequences in terms of communication, adaptability and effectiveness, and also noted a general belief

5

that an effective manager within domestic operations will carry his effectiveness in his briefcase, worldwide.

Whether management is the science that academics would like it to be, or an art as practitioners would prefer to see it, or both, in today's environment, management principles are not universal. As Hagen put it, fifteen years ago: 'Principles of business administration are not absolute, they are relative to the culture of the society'.[13]

Is there a better illustration of this remark than Japan? Today's third economic power, Japan relies for her success on management principles, methods, and practices which often have little resemblance to the so-called modern management principles which are the credo of American business schools. However, using their *own* ways, are not the Japanese fairly effective in managing their economy? Everyone knows about the originality of the Japanese managerial system and its unorthodox features, puzzling to the Western manager. Nevertheless, the Japanese have so far been very articulate corporate builders, and quite dynamic managers.

Beyond technology, structure, task, and a number of other parameters, managerial behaviour is contingent upon a broader range of variables: the cultural ones. Beyond the functional similarities which managements reveal—and which have led many to believe that, as a profession, management has a universal set of principles—it must be acknowledged that, if management wishes to apply certain principles of organization to any society, these principles or doctrines must be the product of that society's way of thinking, values, and goals. Managers, like everyone else, are subject to activities which are the product of a particular way of life, of a specific culture. As part of the environment in which they have been brought up, their motivation and goals, for instance, are influenced by that specific culture. The decision-making process in German, French, and Japanese firms differs, and the concept of power and authority is also defined differently in each of these cultural environments.

By its very nature, international management—whatever the technical definition we give—needs the ability to cope with cultural differences. This requirement is indeed the challenge of international business. The very effective American manager in Chicago might be a loser when running a Bordeaux plant, while the promising French controller may prove inadequate in operating an Osaka joint venture. Not everyone has the knack for successful international business operations. Only when we have identified the specific attitudes, skills, and knowledge needed for operating in a foreign environment, then—and only then—can we hope to enter successfully into management development for international operations.

If management is a process of influence, its success or failure internationally rests ultimately on the ability of the manager to influence the behaviour of his foreign colleagues, and to be influenced by them. To influence others, one has inevitably to accept their influence, since the process of influence is, by its very nature, a reciprocal one.[14]

Management development as a planned and deliberate learning process should be, for the international executive, a process through which he will develop a certain number of particular attitudes and skills and a certain amount of knowledge, each carefully defined, if possible operationally, in order to permit an assessment of its effectiveness. While objectives remain undefined, no one can assess the effectiveness of an action—including training.

The process of learning being a process of change, a manager who has learnt is expected to behave differently afterwards than he did before. The output variables of the management development effort in an international perspective can be divided into three different areas:

a. *Attitudes.* A change in the motivational, emotional, or intellectual make-up of the participant which is likely to enhance the effectiveness of his response to a variety of environmental stimuli. Attitudes of openness towards himself and others, of tolerance to cultural differences, of trust and confidence in himself and others are examples.

b. *Skills.* A change in the intellectual and interpersonal abilities of the participant which can enhance the effectiveness of his operation in foreign environments: listening, communicating, decision-making, motivating, and dealing with uncertainty are some of the abilities specifically useful when working abroad.

c. *Knowledge.* A change in the level of information that the manager can understand, process, and utilize. As well as language, and knowledge about a culture, we think—for instance—of understanding the dynamics of the intercultural process of communication or environmental analysis. In this, we are at the cognitive level, which may need to be preceded by change at the attitudinal level; thorough knowledge is far from being enough, especially in international business.

Change in any of the three areas will then be assessed in terms of job performance (as perceived not only by the manager himself but by his direct professional environment), and the operational results will be assessed in terms of overt behaviour, and organizational output.

It seems, then, that management development for international operation is firstly an attempt to increase the intercultural competence of an individual. This intercultural competence is not something that can be developed merely by reading books or listening to lectures. If one accepts the definition of intercultural competence as the ability to cope effectively (achieving one's own objectives) with a variety of sometimes contradictory, environmental stimuli, then the development of this competence must involve the manager as a whole, not only his cognitive capabilities. This has pedagogical implications, and as we will see, requires an experimental approach.

This intercultural competence has a number of elements, and it is a complex task to develop them. To cope with the challenge of operating in foreign environments, the manager must first become aware of the motivating values and goals which condition his *own* behaviour. The more he knows about himself, about who he is, about his strengths and weaknesses, his biases, stereotypes, and prejudices, the more effectively will he be able to monitor his behaviour to cope with the uncertainty of cultural differences. Working in a foreign environment must increase uncertainty for the individual, confronted, as he is, with unfamiliar working conditions, languages, and behaviour. An international management development programme beyond an attitude of openness towards oneself and of self-understanding, must also aim at developing tolerance toward others' viewpoints, values and behavioural patterns. It must then develop an attitude of flexibility, to adjust to behavioural differences in working with foreign colleagues.

But the management development process for international executives cannot aim exclusively at modifying attitudes and promoting new ones through the unfreezing–moving–freezing process which I have described in this context elsewhere.[15] Without entering into the endless chicken and egg controversy of the social scientist, as to whether or not change in attitudes must precede behavioural change, we should record that behavioural skills must also be a prime target in management development programmes for international executives. Among the skills necessary to the objectives of the programme are those of listening, not only to words, but to non-verbal cues; those of communicating, communication being the transmission of emotions and attitudes, as well as information; those of analysing the network of dynamic interdependencies among parameters making up behaviour; and those of dealing with uncertainty. The development of such skills cannot be achieved by mere transmission of knowledge but requires an experimental approach which relies on 'learning by doing', in an international training situation in which participants try out new behaviour, and within a learning design conducive to experimental behaviour; sensitivity groups could be one of the approaches used.

The relevance of knowledge is nevertheless, unambiguous. It provides conceptual frameworks to assess the cultural dimensions of the environment, and is a critical step in the learning process to relate experience during the management development programme to other experiences in a professional situation—on the job, and vice versa. Knowledge will also provide tools for understanding oneself and others, for environmental analysis, and for theoretical inputs to help the international manager to have a better grasp of causal relationships cross-cultural situations.

Management Development for International Operations: From Objectives to Design and Process

Such a concept of management development, with its three interrelated dimensions (attitudes, skills, and knowledge), should be sufficiently comprehensive to define specifically the content of each dimension, the mix to be given within the set of three, and this in terms of objectives, measurable whenever possible. To have carefully defined objectives is only a first step in the complex learning system.

The next step is to design the learning methodology, to choose the pedagogical tools effective to achieve the above objectives, given the particular characteristics of the population with whom the manager will work. We know from Hawrylyshyn that, today, pedagogical tools have a wide range of effectiveness depending on objectives for which they have been selected.[16] The selection of the appropriate management development design and tools can be made *only* after a thorough definition of the individual or group characteristics.

Once objectives have been carefully defined, the learning situation will be designed to blend a variety of pedagogical tools into an integrated design, each pedagogical instrument chosen to achieve the objective for which its effectiveness is optimized. The learning situation in a very successful two-week programme which we have offered at INSEAD for the last five years[17] combined a multicultural group of participants, an international faculty, and multinational teaching materials. However, these three factors are only *environmental* conditions of the learning process. The programme is designed to produce a genuine cross-cultural situation in which participants can experience cultural differences, and learn through them, while confronted with real managerial problems, initially taken 'out there' (with actual organizational cases involving intercultural conflicts and decision making), and soon becoming the 'here and now' within the management of the learning process itself. The staff, then, function as 'enablers' and 'encouragers', serving as resources for the managers in their searching process for discovering alternative ways to deal with themselves and others in intercultural situations often loaded with much uncertainty. The staff help the participants to learn how to learn, and have the difficult role of catalyst in a learning process whose monitoring is given over to the participants themselves. The make-up of the participant's groups, and the climate created, are designed with the overall objective of improving the intercultural competence made up of attitudes, skills, and knowledge—the components which we referred to before.

In such a learning experience, participants are confronted with the obsolete character of some of their traditional behavioural models (flight, dependency, flight), while working in a highly uncertain foreign environment. They then have to discover alternative ways of behaviour, new models, an uncharted territory to explore, with professional colleagues often bringing with them a considerable amount of international experience.

In such a management development programme, it is not the imparting of information or technical knowledge (e.g., in international finance or marketing) which is the objective—for which other programmes might bring whatever is known in those promising fields—but the development of the learning ability of the manager in a foreign environment (foreign people or foreign methods).

9

In such a programme, participants should be chosen carefully, each according to his individual characteristics, and also in view of the intended make-up of the group, itself a significant part of the process.

Here, management development becomes the monitoring of a learning process—through the design of an original experiential learning environment—defined in terms of a complex system, where attention is paid not only to the transformation process but also to the inputs and outputs. The assessment of the development effort is carried out not only through a post-experience instrument—often of limited use—but also through a follow-up, becoming systematic over time, to measure as far as possible the actual transfer which takes place 'back home', in behavioural terms.

In searching for the few individuals able to cope successfully and quickly with cross-cultural problems, the international organization—be it a multinational corporation, a foreign agency, or the diplomatic service (though, here, there might be professional norms less congruent with some values implicit in our learning process!)—will have to go beyond its investment in developing the technical expertise of its human resources. Management development effort in the increasingly international perspective of today is an increasingly significant problem for which there is no ready-made solution, few answers available, and much research needed. What has been outlined here is a systematic proposal for a learning process, specifically designed to help individuals to improve their competence while working with cultures different from their own. Through an increased awareness of the cultural basis of behaviour (from very explicit to implicit), the individual improves his sensitivity to himself and to his environment, is able to input more information into his own system, and use his limited processing capabilities to relate his objectives more effectively to the environment— through a better use of himself as his main resource. In such a development process, we are not interested in behavioural prescriptions, in a list of do's and don'ts; we do not want to draw up a list of behaviour emphasizing what is desirable or what is taboo. The aim is to help the individual to draw, from within himself, and in cooperation with others, the potential capacities which his professional experience has left untapped.

To conclude, we must add that such a management development approach for international operations is, as described here, an effort at the individual level and not on the organizational plane. Here, we touch the limits of management development, which, be it in an international perspective or not, is too often limited to the development of people, individually or in groups. Individual, as well as group behaviour, is deeply inbred in the cultures of the systems to which a person belongs. Once through the management development process, the individual comes back to his former organizational culture, which affects his behaviour as much as he, himself, does. So long as we do not integrate the management development process within an 'organizational' development framework which is a *systematic* and *strategic* influence on the overall system, including its structure and processes, we run the risk that the organization will remain a slow 'learner'. A great deal of time would then be needed for the management development process to produce results. By the time that enough people have been through the process, the first group of them will be obsolescent unless the management development process has aimed at learning how to learn, rather than at more learning. This ideal is still, unfortunately, far from what traditional management development courses offer today. But things are changing, even in management education!

References

1. FAYERWEATHER, J., BODDEWYN, J., AND ENGBERG, H. *International Business Education*, Workshops in International Business, New York University, Graduate School of Business Administration, 1966, pp. 5–6.
2. ROBINSON, R. D. *International Management*, Holt, Rinehart and Winston, New York, 1967.
   FARMER, R. N. *International Management*, Dickerson Publishing, Belmont, California, 1968.
   PRASAD, S. B. *Management in International Perspective*, Appleton Century, New York, 1967.
   HECK, H. J. *The International Business Environment*, American Management Association, New York, 1969.
   VERNON, R. *Managers in the International Economy*, Prentice-Hall, Englewood Cliffs, New Jersey, 1968.
   BROOKE, M. Z., AND REMMERS, L. *The Strategy of Multinational Enterprise*, Longman, 1970.
   KAPOOR, A., and GRUB, P. D. (Eds.) *The Multinational Enterprise in Transition*, Darwin Press, Princeton, 1972.
3. OTTESON, S. F. (Ed.) *Internationalizing the Business Curriculum*, Indiana University, Graduate School of Business, Bureau of Business Research, 1968.
4. CHORAFAS, D. *Developing the International Executive*, American Management Association Research Study 83, 1967, pp. 19–25.
5. HOUSE, R. J. *Management Development: Design, Evaluation, and Implementation*, Bureau of Industrial Relations, Ann Arbor, 1967; includes extensive bibliography.
6. FORM, W. H., and FORM, A. L. Unanticipated Consequences of a Foreman Training Program, *Personnel Journal*, **32**, 6, 1953.
7. SYKES, A. J. M. The Effects of Supervisors' Training Course in Changing Supervisors' Perceptions and Expectations of the Role of Management, *Human Relations*, **15**, 1962.
8. HARITON, T. Conditions Influencing the Effects of Training Foremen in New Human Relations Principles, Ph.D. thesis, *Dissertation Abstracts*, **11**, 1951, pp. 734–5.
9. FLEISHMAN, E. A. Leadership Climate, Human Relations Training and Supervisory Behavior, *Personnel Psychology*, **6**, 1953, pp. 205–22.
10. HOUSE, R. J. op. cit., p. 472.
11. GOODSTEIN, L. D. Management Development and Organization Development, *Business Quarterly*, winter 1971.
12. CHORAFAS, D. N. op. cit., p. 10.
13. HAGEN, E. E. Foreword to J. Abegglen's book: *The Japanese Factory*, Free Press, Glencoe, Ill., 1958.
14. TANNENBAUM, A. *Control in Organizations*. McGraw-Hill, London, 1968.
15. de BETTIGNIES, H. C. and RHINESMITH, S. H. Developing the International Executive, *European Business*, 1970, p. 24.
16. HAWRYLYSHYN, B. Preparing Managers for International Operations, *Business Quarterly*, autumn 1967.
17. Managerial Skills for International Business: a two-week programme for forty executives from fifteen countries.

2. Top management's role in management development

Jan Kreiken

Management development demands an investment in the long-term potential of the total organization which may depress the immediate results of a division or department in the short term. Operating management will only make the necessary sacrifices of time and money if top management make it clear that they give a high priority to management development and are prepared to assess the performance of management in this area, as well as through the budget, and if they take a personal interest in management development programmes.

Long before management was considered to be a profession or a science, top managers were engaged in management development. Pioneers like Robert Owen (1771–1858) in England, Ernest Solvay (1838–1922) in Belgium, Henry R. Towne (1844–1924) in the US, Henri Fayol (1841–1925) in France, and many others soon after, were entrepreneurs and top managers of large industrial firms propagating and practising management development inside and outside their own organizations. They were active in this field at a time when there were no didactic specialists of adult education, personnel officers and psychologists available, and separate management institutes or faculties were completely unknown.

Nowadays, specialized knowledge and experience in the field of management training abound in almost embarrassing choice; its science has developed to a high level, and its research and applications are backed by hundreds of institutes the world over. Large corporations have set up their own departments of management development, and some have even built their own (international) schools. In medium-sized organizations, special groups in personnel administration have been formed for this purpose, and still smaller firms can make liberal use of the outside services of consultants and management training centres. All kinds of courses are offered—

general and specialist, long and short, international and cross-cultural, courses spanning one or more industries, language courses—and in many instances, outside centres provide custom-made in-company training.

Today, no firm or organization is without access to these facilities, and there should be no excuse for not using them. But, from a more critical viewpoint, it could be said that many firms use them as an easy solution to their management development problems. Management development is on its way to becoming a product supplied to top management, rather than being a product of top management. It is relevant to ask whether such a trend—though interesting and, to a large extent, welcome—does not isolate top management from one of its most essential functions. Lawrence A. Appley, whose ideas I have always found to be of fundamental value in a wide variety of applications, has said that 'management is not the direction of things, but the development of people'.

The Development of People

If management is the development of people, what then is management development and what is top management's role therein? It is the management of developing managerial ability, in all functions, at all levels, and in all departments of the organization. It is, therefore, first and foremost the *responsibility of the highest unifying level of management*, i.e., of top management. Top management can fulfil this responsibility in three ways. Firstly, by creating the climate, structure and procedures which foster the development of people in, and for, managerial functions. This is the creation of a permanent condition, and is, primarily, a line (not a staff) management responsibility at every level. Secondly, by periodically making appraisals of present and forward assessments of future management talent, in quantity and in quality. Thirdly, by organizing internal and/or external programmes to accelerate—not replace—the autonomous, 'natural' management development within the organization as such. This third activity is mostly a staff management function; it is a specially organized 'rapid' in the normal stream of development.

In this way, the responsibilities of top management and of the management development programmes can be put in their right context. In many instances, however, actual practice deviates far from this 'ideal' situation.

Three Aspects

In this chapter, I shall deal with three aspects:

(a) The underlying causes for the trend in management development to become isolated from top management, and for the re-entry problems of participants;

(b) the ways and means of integrating top management with specific management development programmes, and the dilemma of specific versus general training;

(c) the creation, by top management, of a climate for continuous and autonomous management development at all levels and in all functions.

The application of these principles is not limited to any specific type of business or public organization in any specific type of social or cultural environment. So far as I can survey the international scene, the fundamentals of this problem and its solutions are universal.

Trends Towards Isolation from Top Management

There are three main reasons why management development programmes may tend to become isolated from top management. The first is the high degree of scientific specialization, the second lies in the often secluded location of the training centres, and their teaching staff, and the third concerns the fallacies in management thinking on management development as such.

Isolation through Specialization

Like so many other fields of activity within the modern enterprise, management development has become an operation of such magnitude and specialization in study and research, that it has, understandably, become the domain of high-calibre experts. It is, of course, a good management principle to delegate special activities such as these to the most competent staff available, although, in an increasing number of instances, this delegation goes so far as to include almost complete freedom in planning, executing, and appraising the entire development programme. Moreover, those with responsibility for management development become more and more active in the selection and appraisal of participants, a role in which they may come into conflict with line management for obvious reasons.

Specialists are likely to attract other specialists into their department, and when it comes to outside help, it is quite natural that they have their own ideas about whom to select as consultants and as training institutes. The management development department tends to become a 'world on its own' with its own idiosyncrasies, sometimes even 'stale' in its programmes and outside relationships, and rather far away from top management. This can, of course, be true of any specialized department in any organization. But, in the case of management development, these trends must be watched with care because the department deals with the most valuable people in the organization, the new and potential managers of the future, and because it holds a key position in influencing the 'climatic' conditions in the company, and the prevailing management philosophy. A situation could arise in which rather serious divergences develop between top management and the departments.

Isolation through Location

The frequently secluded location of management training centres, far from the hub of business activity, affects the teaching staff at the centre—especially

14

when they are also living on, or nearby, the premises—more than it does course participants. Unless they have 'visiting' teachers, outside management institutes may suffer the same disadvantage, even though their directors may be leaders in industry and public administration. If isolated from the mainstream, management teaching, texts, cases, and subjects in general tend towards scientific complication, and at the same time, towards practical simplification; towards the assumption of too many variables and too few constraints; towards a too easily assumed availability of timely, exact and relevant information; towards teaching models rather than modelling, and towards rather lightly defined system boundaries. Only close and frequent contact with actual operations and research of the 'live organization' can guarantee an optimal blend of theory and practice in producing realistic, yet scientifically advanced management training.

A secluded environment is ideal to engender participants' concentration, and should certainly not be changed. But, at the same time, top management should watch for certain pitfalls which can be inherent in the geographical isolation of the training centre. In general, management training and development centres should be concentrated in one centre as much as possible, such as has been done by several large international companies in recent years. Such centres encourage after-work social mixing between company participants of all ranks, functions, departments, and nationalities. Management development programmes which are fragmented and scattered over a larger number of centres require the attention of top management, as the degree of isolation may be high in programme content and otherwise.

Isolation through Misconception

The most dangerous cause of isolation lies with top management itself, in the serious fallacies and misconceptions of its own thinking. Sometimes, these misconceptions are fed by scientific or semiscientific theories, especially in countries where both education and social systems have been built on 'disciplines' rather than pragmatic, problem-solving approaches. These theories produce scientific support to concepts such as specialist 'committee management', centralized decision making, and the assignment of management development as a purely staff management responsibility which sounds good. Such well-entrenched ideas—and even official policies—can be found in many government and other public administrations, but they also exist in large industrial organizations, e.g., in continental Europe. Further misconceptions may prevail in regard to the boundaries of management development's domain, e.g., by limiting its activity to certain functions or levels only.

It may therefore be of some use to amplify my earlier definition, which I shall develop further in later sections. Management development is the programmed and non-programmed continuous development of the managerial ability of people, at all levels, in all executive and supervising functions, and in all departments. It is fundamentally a line responsibility, and one of the most essential functions of top management. Only the 'technical' parts of management development's planning, organization, and control, its selection and appraisal of participants, its evaluation of courses and programmes, their timing and duration can be delegated as staff functions; the lion's share of all these aspects remains the responsibility of line management.

So far as courses are concerned, top and other line management should not shy away from being speakers and from participating in discussions. Although some theories claim that freedom of discussion is impaired when line management is present (if, at all, their time permits), this depends on the subject being debated. Future-oriented themes, new research subjects, and discussions on fundamental concepts and values in management and policy can only foster mutual respect and team spirit throughout the organization, irrespective of the rank and function of the speaker. Integration, not isolation, builds communication and creates the living entity that an organization should be.

Isolation Causes Re-entry Problems

The causes of management development's isolation from top management are ever present, because they are endemic in a highly developed specialized organization. For other reasons, they are equally present in smaller companies, where programmes are necessarily run by outside institutes. There is no reason to condemn any of these tendencies, nor the high-calibre specialists who devote all their knowledge, experience, and talents to this work. There is simply reason for care, and for stressing the fundamental principles of good top management in this activity.

Otherwise, isolation will lead to re-entry problems when participants come back to the operating organization, and may even cause frustration, when they find that the philosophies of their training clash with those prevailing in the company, and when their newly learned techniques seem impractical in view of insurmountable constraints. Eventually, participants may be lost to the company as they seek out other directions and organizations where they believe their talents can be more fruitfully used—but where they may meet the same difficulties. Isolation, therefore, produces a contrary effect, and neither contributes to the success of the organization nor to the happiness of individuals. Only top management can, and should, prevent this.

Top Management and Programmed Management Development

As in any other field of activity, management development requires the 'management process'. This means, that line management—and top management in particular—must formulate the specific objectives of its management development in the company; it has to weigh various courses of action to reach this aim; from these alternatives, it has to decide on a plan and programme; it has to choose the structure of its organization, either inside or outside the company, or both; it has to provide the necessary communication and motivation to make this programme and structure work; and finally, it has to evaluate the results and make timely corrections, wherever and whenever necessary.

One of the first requirements for well-integrated management development is *management*. There is no greater danger than to have randomly chosen participants haphazardly taking part in management development programmes. All authors and practitioners in this field agree that at least a certain degree of policy and planning, as well as a minimum of criteria and procedures for selection and appraisal, are conditions *sine qua non*. Clearly, these conditions can only be fulfilled in companies where modern Management by Objectives has been, at least, introduced. *Management development and Management by Objectives are interdependent*, but if a choice of sequence must be made, then the *objectives* come *first*.

Planning

The detailed planning of management development is dealt with in other chapters. Here, the relevant fact is that management development derives from the overall strategic plan, and that it must take account of envisaged technological and social changes, of prognosticated expansion or contraction, and of diversification, internationalization and innovation. This, in itself, illustrates clearly that management development is essentially a long-term affair, and that it is, therefore, one of the prime responsibilities of top management. No management training department or programme can ignore this premise, nor can it operate without continuous support from management. Not only in this longitudinal time dimension, but also in the transverse direction this responsibility of top management applies. Only at this high level is the equally necessary *interdepartmental* view available for making the right decisions towards the planning of management development in a company.

There is another aspect of management development planning and top management that needs attention at this point—the dilemma between the planning of specific versus general training. When the system boundaries in which management development is planned are drawn rather narrowly, the tendency towards a specific programme content increases. This may be necessary for training specialized managers in specific fields, but in general, it may have an impoverishing effect on broader managerial abilities. This is the more so, as specialist manager training depends much more on an accurate forecast of the specific social and technological future than does the training for a broader management context. The same applies to management training within just one department or division of a company. Specialist management training, therefore, can afford, or even needs(!), a shorter time span and a narrower planning system. The dilemma of specialist versus general management development does not really exist; apart from having different aims and different types of participants, the two *operate in different system boundaries and have different relationships with top management*. It could be advisable for top management to withhold to some degree its participation in management development programmes, lest they frustrate, by 'accurate', narrow, long-term forecasts, unpredictable creative forces.

For, although management philosophy should not have to compromise in formulating development programmes, it would be foolish to think that all future situations of management can be expressed in exact terms. This is particularly true in respect to the formulation of future functions and the quantitative assessment thereof. Although planning is an absolute necessity, top management should guard against too presumptuous claims of accuracy; space for development and flexibility must be kept open. This is the more necessary, since talented people dislike being 'engineered' in their careers. Between the requirements of planning and the need for flexibility, management development must steer through Scylla and Charybdis. Top management must be known to be fully conversant, and in agreement, with the planning and programming by the management development staff.

Selection

Closely related to this problem is the selection of participants for the various courses. Classification into levels and functions, specialists and non-specialists will usually require other measures or refinements, by which, criteria such as age, mobility (within, or possibly outside the company), loyalty, and indispensability play important roles. Staff management can assist expertly in all these questions; they can supply the scientific analysis and careers records, and can help in many ways where line management may fall short. On the other hand, they will have to overcome many obstacles in the understandable resistance of line management to the temporary moving around of their 'best people'; arguments such as their being 'irreplaceable' in their department, or division, concern most the very best candidates for further management development. Again, it is clear that the participation of top management is required; no other level of management has the capacity to weigh up conflicting interests and view the organization as a whole. Even the most tactful handling of such matters by management development staff cannot suffice without support from the chief executive and his board.

Duration

Top management has a similar role to fill in making the final decisions as to the duration and form of programmes. Choices between training 'off' or 'on' the job, in internal or in external centres, in short, long, or intermittent schedules, are not just 'scientific' and 'objective' choices which can be made by staff management only. These choices affect line management duties. If they are made in isolation, the management development staff tends to avoid controversies with line management by selecting programmes which depend as little as possible on the cooperation of line management. This natural tendency may lead, in the end, towards the isolation which I have indicated earlier. The prediscussion between the several parties could best be guided by members of the board; this is a basis for all successful programmes, participation and application, and is as important as the quality of programme contents and of instructors.

Where outside centres are used, there is the danger that the participant may be too long away from his work. When coming back, he may find either a desk overloaded with a backlog of work, or a near-empty one if others have taken over his duties. This re-entry aspect can be so grim that it may induce aversion rather than motivation; in certain cases, this can be manipulated by line managers who try to avoid supplying candidates for further training if they are to be away for fairly long periods. Again, this is an aspect which may need the direct attention of higher management.

Organization

Top management's involvement with management training is not limited to aspects of policy, planning, programming, selection, and motivation. It also concerns organization and control. Although the organization and contents of development programmes should be delegated, as much as possible, to specialists in management education, it can be important for top management to make some contribution. Whatever its form, this contribution should not be limited to a welcoming speech at the beginning of a major course or seminar. Such high-level pep talks may contrast unfavourably with the efforts of other speakers and have an adverse effect. It is much better, even if only in a limited number of cases for top and line management to take part in discussion sessions with a speaker; this stimulates participants to believe that their superiors are themselves interested and attach great value to the contents of the programme. It also stresses the idea of 'developing together', rather than 'being developed' or 'being improved' for the sake of higher management.

Some large concerns have even gone further in integrating top management with the organization and contents of management training programmes. In these cases, one or two members of high-level line management are relieved of their usual duties for six or twelve months so that they can join the specialist training staff of a training centre. In this position, they do not function as the 'head' of the centre, but as one of the senior colleagues. This set-up improves mutual understanding and coordination, especially when the person involved returns to his or her high-level executive position. The presence of such a temporary 'colleague' usually makes a refreshingly realistic and critical impact on the centre's operations. It also facilitates the smooth re-entry of participants, and improves communication and application after the course.

Control

Finally, it is obvious that appraisal and control of both participants and programmes must concern top management. Appraisal of participants should be a function carried out by specialist staff *and* line management together. It is not always possible to do so at the same moment; the former appraisal will precede that of the line manager. But such reviews are intertwined, which is both fair for the participant involved, and necessary for the control of the programmes. In any case, appraisals should not be made in isolation of each other—not only in the individual's interest, but to prevent programmes from continuing for years unchecked, and unchanged, in an almost automatic sequence. The periodic role of top management in this matter is obvious, the more so as appraisals will normally be of an interdepartmental nature.

Top Management and Autonomous Management Development

So far, I have discussed the subject of structured management development work and top management's role therein. I have referred to the concept that management development and Management by Objectives are interrelated, indicating a connection between structured management development programmes and *the style of management within a company or organization*. When there is need to decide which comes first, then it is Management by Objectives which does so.

This is not the place to discuss modern decentralized management at length. However, I must stress that the most important development of managerial talent does not take place through courses or seminars, nor through job rotation or any other method of acquiring knowledge and a certain amount of skill. *Managerial talent is best developed by actually managing* in an environment where talents can develop. Management is the development of people. Top management must create the climate, i.e., the structure and the procedures which foster the development of managerial talent of people at all levels and in all functions. This is the greatest 'programme' of all. It is the environment for continuous and autonomous management development throughout the organization.

Self-Development

People, unlike machines, are not engineered, or built or rebuilt. People are living creatures, developing themselves, when given the right mental climate, the right intellectual means, and the right measures and structures for self-appraisal. All development is fundamentally self-development, no matter whether activated by 'programmes' or not. The circumstances in which this can happen is created by and from top management downwards, and is not only a *sine qua non* for management development as such; it is also important in view of the limited degree of accuracy in planning future talent requirements. In other words, it is a matter of foresight to create continuously a *general reserve of managerial talent*, to meet unpredictable needs as they arise. An industrialist in the Netherlands once called this 'the theory of the trout basin'. A system of Management by Objectives, of truly decentralized management, is surely the best contribution that top management can make towards such a reserve of autonomously developed talent.

It is useful to expound the conditions which top management should create. For self-development, the mental climate should leave opportunity for creativity; this means that people are stimulated towards innovation, rather than judged against established methods and traditions. Objectives, in this context, are more important than methods and techniques. It also means the provision of the right intellectual environment and resources, the availability of counselling and training, the free contact and orientation with colleagues inside and outside the 'system', and time allowance for the study of new concepts and techniques relevant to the work.

As there are always 'natural' obstacles mitigating against these opportunities, especially when operations are strained, top management must create these conditions at certain planned intervals.

Management Structure

The right stucture and procedures form a permanent condition for self-development. These include the establishment of clear objectives, the exact definition of system boundaries and their input and output measurements (e.g., profit centres), the availability of timely, precise, and relevant information (for self-control), and the responsibility and authority over complete management cycles of planning, organizing, and control. Any dilution of these conditions, e.g., by inaccurate transfer values between subsystems, or by splitting the management cycle into 'planners', 'organizers' and 'controlling inspectors', will diminish the opportunity for autonomous management development. A system of centralized decision making, with split management cycles at several levels, with vague objectives and late, inaccurate, or too much irrelevant information, produces barren, sterile organizations in which managerial talent is starved. Such a system can hardly be helped by structured management development programmes organized by expert staff; no matter how high the quality of training, after re-entry the participants will become even more frustrated than before.

Success or failure of both structured and autonomous management development therefore depends largely on the quality and 'intensity' of top management.

It is an illusion that management development can be started 'overnight', or that it can be delegated to specialist staff alone. In essence, management development should not be a product supplied to top management, but a product and a feature of good top management. May this principle be realized, for the sake of organizations and individuals, and the specialist staff who assist them.

Suggested Reading

APPLEY, L. A. *The Management Evolution*, part 7, American Management Association, New York, 1963.

BENNET, W. E. *An Integrated Approach to Management Development*, Executive Selection, Development and Inventory, American Management Association, New York, 1957.

BRECH, E. F. L., *The Principles and Practice of Management*, parts 3 and 5, Longmans, Green, 1963, chapter 8.

DRUCKER, P. F. *The Practice of Management*, Heinemann, 1955, chapter 17.

FERGUSON, L. L. Better Management of Managers' Careers, *Harvard Business Review*, Mar.–Apr. 1966.

HUMBLE, J. W. *Improving Business Results*, American Management Association, Management Centre Europe, Brussels, 1968.

KREIKEN, J. Three Dimensions of the Management Task: An Analysis and its Consequences for Management Education, *Proceedings IUC Congress*, Brno, USSR, 1971.

MANT, A. *The Experienced Manager: A Major Resource*, British Institute of Management, 1969.

ODIORNE, G. S. *Training by Objectives, an Economic Approach to Management Training*, Macmillan, New York, 1970.

SINGER, E. J. and RAMSDEN, J. *Human Resources*, McGraw-Hill, New York, 1972.

SOFER, C. *Men in Mid-Career, a Study of British Managers and Technical Specialists*, Cambridge University Press, 1970.

3. The role of the central management development service

D. S. Markwell

In recent years, it has become advantageous for large companies to establish a central department to administer an executive development service. Dr Markwell discusses the role of such a central department in interpreting and influencing corporate strategy and corporate planning, participating in the development of a coordinated programme for organizational change, and making the optimum use of the human resources within the enterprise.

Within the context of the company, there is only one reason for a management development programme. Expressed very simply, this is to improve the effectiveness of the management and the business. Any business, organization, company, corporation, government department, or local authority can have as a major objective an improvement in the quality of their service and its cost effectiveness, or the improvement of profit—sometimes it will be both. The role of management development as a staff service is not, therefore, primarily educational development; nor is it even necessarily related to the needs of the individual. It is to improve the effectiveness of the business or organization to enable it to achieve its immediate and longer-term goals and to maximize utilization of its human resources to this end. Management development is primarily a tool of top management concerning itself with the supply and effectiveness of managers. In addition, it will take into account many other parameters, such as the expectations of the individual, the social responsibility of the organization, the way in which people are used and services provided, but will, nonetheless, focus on the availability of effective human resources to achieve goals and objectives. Within this context, the word 'managers' needs to be interpreted broadly: as all those who, by virtue of their line operation or specialist contribution to a business, are among the critical mass of people whose individual and collective contribution is vital to the success of an organization.

In this context, management development is a growth task, unlike the role of the auditor in a fiscal environment. It is not merely concerned with what is happening, or has happened, but very much more with what should be happening in the future, and the opportunities for growth that can be provided both for the individual and the organization—the 'business organism'; and emphasis always lies on development.

A part of the machinery of any management development activity will be to establish the current experience, needs, and facts of a situation, but its main emphasis will be on future plans and the way in which they are to be met, rather than looking at needs, failures, or other historic data. Hence, any management development service that is provided is a forward-looking activity. It is a part of the business plan of any organization, closely related to its strategic objectives, and integrated into its operating plans. In such a context, management development as a central service is one of the strategic tools of a business, along with its cash, assets, and other economic resources. This integration can only be achieved if those responsible for management development are, themselves, a part of the corporate strategy team of the business, not just in terms of its manpower statistics, plans, and human resource development and utilization, but in terms of using management development to provide an opportunity for organizational review and organizational development.

There are, therefore, three essentials for a central management development service:

(a) its integration into the corporate strategy of a business;
(b) its concern with the optimum utilization of human resources;
(c) its effective role in organizational development.

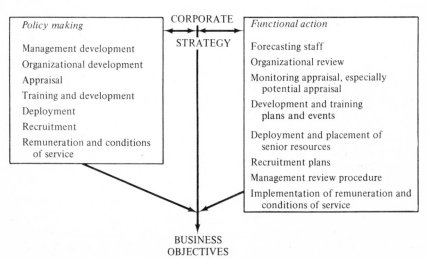

Fig. 3.1. A simple model of central management development for effective human resource utilization.

37044

There are many different aspects to the role of a central management development service, and these can be dealt with under separate headings, although, in doing so, the danger is that they will be seen as fragmented, whereas they are intrinsic facets of the whole management development process.

Policy

A central management development service has a basic responsibility for determining the management development policy of an organization. It is within the framework of such a policy that the organization will execute its management development plans. A policy provides the guidelines within which the different parts of the organization can operate in matters of management development. The resources of such a service department should therefore include people capable of developing a conceptual framework in order to be able to consider issues and provide guidelines on a whole range of subjects, e.g., the extent to which a company wishes to develop its own people or to recruit from outside. Other headings are:

(a) performance appraisal;
(b) potential appraisal;
(c) selection;
(d) remuneration;
(e) termination;

BUSINESS OBJECTIVES

Fig. 3.2. Tasks of the central management development service.

(f) training;

(g) organization review;

(h) placement;

(i) career planning;

(j) the type of communication structure and its degree of consultation and involvement.

In addition to the specific type of issues raised above, general questions—such as those related to the sort of work culture that the business wishes to provide for its managers—fall within the concern of the management development service.

The purpose of the policy developed within a central service is to provide guidelines within which creative management development can occur and to provide a springboard for the growth in effectiveness of individuals, organizational groups, and the business as a whole. Viewed in this way, policies tend to be the minimum starting points rather than prescriptive barriers to growth. They should be not so much the way that things are done in a particular situation, i.e., barriers to change, but starting points for progress—opportunities not constraints—and can be interpreted as areas from which to grow, rather than as limitations to further development.

Advisory

The central management development service, once established, will find its major task in the area of constructive advice. It will be much less concerned with policing the system than with helping operational management achieve their corporate objectives, particularly in relation to improving the effectiveness of individuals and groups by means of suggestions about placement, secondment, varieties of career experience, and education and training. Even if a central service has either explicit or implicit executive powers, its success is more likely to be measured in terms of the utility of its advice, and its persuasive capacity, than in terms of its ability to enforce.

The advisory role of the central department will normally be marked by a high degree of interdependent relationship and an interactive process with those whom it is seeking to help. Relationships of counterdependence, or simply dependence, will be much less creative and constructive than interactive interdependence. The synergy of this relationship commends it above all others. Even if the central service has mandatory authority, its capacity to achieve its defined objectives will be the product of this creative relationship rather than a product of any authoritarian executive role.

The building of a relationship of an advisory sort is a delicate and time-consuming operation. Nonetheless, it is probably the most useful single component of effective management development. The staff service function will perhaps, above all, have a highly creative 'listening role' to fulfil. Its utility will be a function of its ability to listen and respond relevantly and creatively to what it hears. Experience teaches that advisory roles cannot be

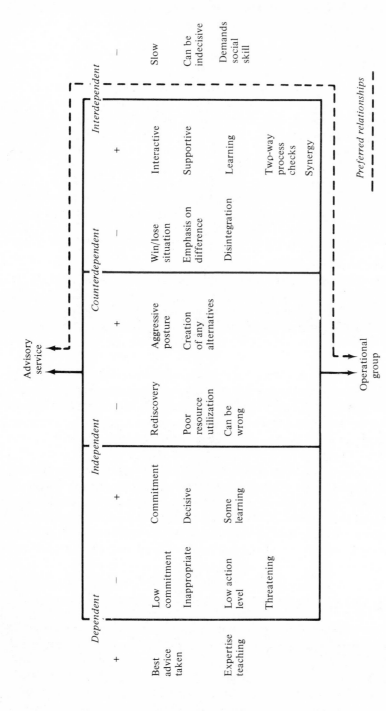

Fig. 3.3. Modes of relationship for a central service.

27

imposed. However, the right to give advice can be earned, and a relationship in which asking for advice will become a norm can painstakingly be developed if care and consideration is given to the process.

Operational Role

There are many aspects of the operational role of a central management development service. By and large, they stem from the criteria of supportive activities to the operational parts of a business. The service department can provide resources and develop activities, e.g., central training or placement, which may be more effectively centralized in some instances than if allowed to develop haphazardly in a disintegrated way. The sorts of reason that make operations worthwhile will be questions of cost effectiveness, optimizing resource utilization, and providing information for top management about the human possibility of achieving their operational goals. The demands of top management for information of this sort will also lead to an operational task for the central service. This operational task, however mandatory its establishment, is more significantly based on the logic of the situation, and may even be threatening to the operational parts of the business unless there is an implicit and accepted logic in this responsibility being held by a central service. Hence, any operational responsibility that a management development service may have is most likely to be successful when it is seen and understood to be of genuine use, and not an imposed system of control.

This implies, even in the operational aspects of its role, that there is an on-going interaction between a central management development service and the operational parts of a business; this has many implications, not least of which will be the continuing dialogue between the management development service and those for whom the service is provided, even the latter's close involvement in many aspects of the service.

The logic of this concept of dialogue and interaction would also indicate that staff movement be maintained between the management development services and the operating parts of an organization. Populating a management development service solely with specialists may increase, rather than decrease, the capacity for misunderstanding between the two, and disregard the stimulating value of interaction between operators and specialists on a basis of mutual respect.

Environmental Awareness

Central management development services are of relatively recent origin in most organizations, and, even where they have been well established, many are still at the developmental stage themselves. Like other parts of a business, they run the risk of becoming complacent, and one of their essential tasks—both for their own growth and development and for that of the organization as a whole—must lie in their continuing dialogue with the external environment: professional, academic, and collegiate. There is no ideal model for management development, since the needs of management itself and business are dynamic and changing. To respond to this, the management development model must, therefore, also be dynamic and changing. External contacts will be an important function of a central services department, not only to stimulate itself but to interpret the external environment to the operational parts of the organization. In this sense, the central management development service can fulfil a very useful function as the interpreter of external development and change to the organization as a whole, and be the 'bridge builder' of appropriate external links. In this way, the central service department acts as one of the vital 'link functions' of the organization and the environment.

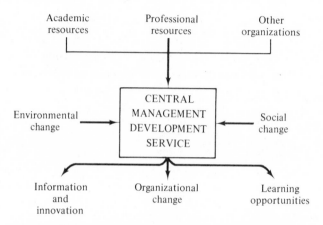

Fig. 3.4. Bridge-building role of the central management development service.

It may act more as a developer of management development than a basic research unit, and is likely to have an adaptive rather than a seminal role. No business can rely on purely internal resources to re-create itself, nor can it be unresponsive to environmental change. If it is to achieve significant adaptation and growth itself, the importance of this link function must be both recognized and implemented.

Coordination

Any central management development service has a prime responsibility to ensure the effective coordination of activities, to make the best use of resources. Independent management development in different parts of an organization will not provide this. While logical adaptation is important in the parts of an organization, a central service should be able to avoid the rediscovery of things which have already been validated in other environments or other parts of the organization. The importance of providing an opportunity for management to avoid having to rediscover concepts, systems, methods, and approaches that have already been well thought out in other places is an important part of the central services function. The central service can therefore aim to see that the right sort of development, appropriate to the resources available, is being carried out in given situations. This does not mean that the central service should constrain individual initiative, but that initiatives which are logically taken have the benefit of the experience of other parts of the organization or environment.

There will be occasions when the circumstances indicate that complementary initiatives can be profitable, but there is usually a point beyond which they can become unprofitable, and central coordination would be more effective.

Information

Closely linked with the coordination role of the central service is that of the dissemination of information. Without dissemination of information into the organization, disintegrated development and repetitive rediscovery are likely to occur. To overcome this, the centre has a very important resource function to fulfil, both by propagating information and acting as an information resource which can be used by the business as a whole. Unless this information is systematically available, it will probably fail to overcome problems of repetition in the organization and, perhaps more important, to act as a stimulus to progressive thinking. The obvious danger is that information for its own sake can become a norm of a central management development service. The central service must constantly check, therefore, that the information it provides and promulgates is relevant, usable, and directed to the problems of operational parts of the organization.

In an environment in which information pollution is one of the major problems facing operational management, the central management development service should have the capacity and ability to screen the material that is available or can be developed and supplied and, sometimes, to sharpen that material to the needs and goals of the operational functions.

Motivation

One of the basic reasons for the existence of a central service will undoubtedly be the stimulation that it provides for on-going management development to occur. Any system will cease to be effective if it does not also provide for the sort of stimulation which will encourage people to continue with the management development task at an operational level. The very fact that the service exists and operates will provide a motivational force for line management constantly to review and implement their own management development activities. This motivation factor is less of an auditing function than a stimulating role. The existence of a management development service that is asking questions, stimulating ideas and seeking to work with line management will provide an on-going stimulus for management development to occur without recourse to a mandatory policy or directive.

Corporate Resources

Corporate resources can be described in many different ways and, certainly, many of them are purely economic, e.g., capital assets, cash, and market capability. Today, it is commonly recognized that people, and especially management, are also important corporate resources, and a central management development service could be seen as guardians of this resource. Hence, their role is not so much one of caring for people in statistical terms, although that may be an important part of their information role, but as a stimulator of continual thinking about the use of people, the way in which they are deployed, and the organizational work culture. This is particularly important since management resources, unlike economic resources, have a capacity for self-utilization as well as organizational utilization. Assets in money can be placed, people cannot unless they are willing to be placed. Hence, emphasis is not only on the placement of human resources, in this sense, but on the understanding of those resources since their capacity to frustrate placement should they wish to do so is high, unlike that of economic resources. It must be a concern of the central services not only to see that the resources are optimally utilized in placement terms, but that the work culture enables their potential for use to be realized in the operational situation. A management development service must be very much concerned with human resource deployment, but, at the same time, by appreciating the work culture, also with that resource's needs for change and the expectations of its members for appropriate recognition and utilization.

Monitoring

In a sense, a management development service is both the stimulator of a management development activity within the organization, and the monitor of organizational and managerial well-being. In industrial anthropology, this could be described as a continuing process of reviewing the health of the work culture. As such, the central management development service is a listening post—particularly for top management of the organization—as to the feelings, attitudes, and expectations of the managerial cadre of the organization, and the morale levels of the business. Although the central service will have a responsibility for monitoring the management development systems of the organization and assuring their standards, more important, it will be aware of the danger signals of managerial or organizational ill health, which may be imperceptibly arising within the organization. Unless these signals are sympathetically perceived and carefully and systematically monitored, the organization can find itself in a problem situation before it knows it has reached the point where a 'turn-about' is possible. Then, as Likert has illustrated, the time lag for reactive change in this area is substantial. It is a part of the central management development service's responsibility, therefore, to be aware of the dynamic symptoms of organizational ill health before the illness reaches the dimensions of crisis, and to interpret danger signals to ensure the continuing effectiveness of the organization. These signals are often not obvious and require special social skills both to perceive them and to react to them in the work environment. The central service should have those social skills among its resources, and the opportunity to use them in a positive and constructive way.

Standardization

It has been constantly suggested that the success of a central management development system depends more on its capacity to influence than to require. But even in an organization, particularly its operational division, individual standards of effectiveness will vary in things like selection, appraisal, salary policy implementation, and general work culture. The role of the central service must in part be to see that approximately uniform standards are maintained across the whole spectrum of the organization. The capacity of some top managers to see, for example, a large proportion of their managers as being of high potential should be challenged against the view of those who see few in this category. While statistical techniques and normal distribution expectations can assist in this process, in the end the simple challenge, plus the broad view of the central service, will be one of the best guardians of uniformity. Uniformity for its own sake may have little merit but, where a business or organization is trying to make the best use of its management resources and possibly move them from place to place, uniformity can be important.

Similarly, in the human environment in which this management development is operating, there is an expectation in today's world that relative justice is not only done but seen to be done. To achieve this, an element of uniformity and perhaps standardization is necessary, though not at the expense of effectiveness. Such uniformity may be ensured by the involvement of a more neutral third party—in this case, the central service—which can be of great importance to the morale levels and managerial health of the organization.

Innovation

Much of what has been said about the role of the central management development service has been concerned with the establishment and maintenance of such a function. There is one important respect, stimulation for creativity, in which the central service should also be the innovators and the developers of conceptual thinking at managerial and organizational levels within the concern. In this way, some of the traps of bureaucratic centralization can be avoided, and the central service be not only reactive to the needs of the business but create some of those resources to meet the needs that will arrive from the areas of activity into which the business may be moving. Stimulation for creativity may be generated within the organization itself, or within the central service. It is most likely, however, to be the product of the interaction of the central service with its external environment, particularly its professional environment. As such, it is part of the innovative resources both for achievement of corporate strategy and for providing some of the parameters for determination of that strategy. The central service will therefore have, in some respects, a close relationship, and indeed involvement, in the creative and innovative aspects of the organization both in terms of its use of the human contribution to the business and in terms of the integration of human needs into corporate development.

Evaluation and Review

Any central management development system that is going to achieve its objectives in real terms will be a self-monitoring process. Not only has it a stimulating and monitoring role in relation to the business to which it is providing a service, but it will act as its own internal evaluation and review agency. Simply because it is set aside for a particular task, it is provided with a unique opportunity to question, evaluate, and re-create policies, procedures, and systems. Its degree of constructive dissatisfaction with its own performance will, in some measure, be the hallmark of its success—not only in relation to the evaluation of its own activities within the organization but in relation to its own activities against those going on in its external and professional environments.

Staff

It has already been implied that needs rather than power are the key to the success of a central management development service. The staffing of such a management development central service is, therefore, a matter of prime importance. Since it is based on a model which has two main links—one with the external professional environment, the other with the internal operational environment—the central management development service should itself represent these two facets of its activity. It will therefore be most appropriately staffed by a mixture of both professional expertise and operational experience. Staff should thus come from experienced line management and academically experienced specialists, among whom the common elements will be their sensitivity for human situations, organizational culture and its development, and their capacity to persuade and influence. The proper use of these people within the central staff service is important. Their combination of expertise and operational experience can increase the logic of the systems and their acceptability. In turn, it will provide, for the service, recognition of its pragmatic excellence.

Experience tends to show that psychological separation between operational experience and expertise, even within the same department, leads to the suboptimization of effectiveness on the part of the operator, and unused resources on the part of the specialist. Advisers who wait to be consulted are rarely used, and functional responsibility—albeit, of the 'influence type' already described—should be part of the method of operation of both experts and operational management engaged in the management development service.

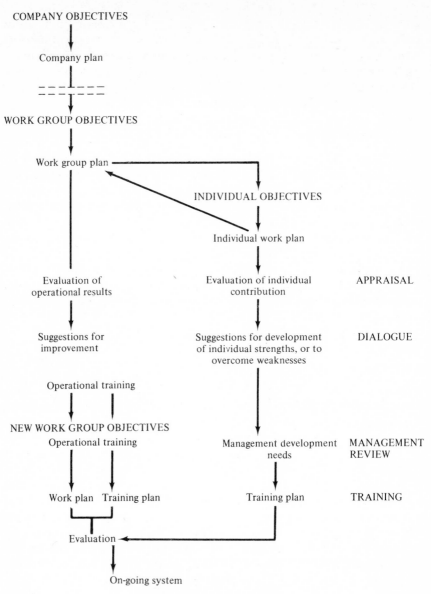

COMPANY OBJECTIVES

Company plan

WORK GROUP OBJECTIVES

Work group plan

INDIVIDUAL OBJECTIVES

Individual work plan

Evaluation of
operational results

Evaluation of individual
contribution

APPRAISAL

Suggestions for
improvement

Suggestions for development
of individual strengths, or to
overcome weaknesses

DIALOGUE

Operational training

NEW WORK GROUP OBJECTIVES

Operational training

Management development
needs

MANAGEMENT
REVIEW

Work plan   Training plan

Training plan

TRAINING

Evaluation

On-going system

Fig. 3.5. Training in the company.

The same sort of pattern of objectives, work plans and specified tasks appropriate to line management can, at least in broad terms, be defined for all those involved in providing a management development service.

The establishment and maintenance of such a central management development service will be much more related to growing needs than to the mandatory imposition of such a service and its costs, which in the end have to be borne by the operational sectors of the business. Value will be measured in terms of a genuine feeling of service obtained.

Function / Job Class	Establishment — 1.1.1972					Establishment — Expected 1.1.1977					Increases/(Decreases)					Recruitment Target	
	A	B	C	D	Total	A	B	C	D	Total	A	B	C	D	Total	1972	Next Five Years
General Management	1	—	—	—	1	1	—	—	—	1	—	—	—	—	—		1
Marketing	1	3	4	—	8	1	3	5	—	9	—	—	1	—	1		
Sales	1	1	3	8	13	1	1	3	9	14	—	—	—	1	1		
Tech./Production	1	2	4	—	7	1	2	4	—	7	—	—	—	—	—		
Engineering	—	1	1	—	2	—	1	1	—	2	—	—	—	—	—		
Finance/Accounts	1	1	2	2	6	1	1	2	2	6	—	—	—	—	—		
Buying																	
Personnel		1			1		1			1		1	(1)				1
Others		1			1		1			1				1			2
Totals	5	9	15	10	39	5	10	15	11	41		1		1	2		2

Fig. 3.6. Five-year forecast.

Note: After considering current vacancies, known retirements, estimated wastage, anticipated transfers within the concern, and promotables, the company is requested as shown in Fig. 3.9 to present its conclusions on likely shortages or surpluses of management in the various functions and job levels.

Basic Components of the Management Development System

Forecasting (Fig. 3.6)

(a) managerial;
(b) organizational requirements.

Appraisal (Fig. 3.7)

(a) individual performance;
(b) individual potential;
(c) organizational review.

Development and Training (Fig. 3.8)

Individual and group needs and plans.

Deployment

(a) placement of the most suitable managers in the job;
(b) providing opportunities for promotion, development, and experience.

Recruitment

(a) to fill forecasting shortfall;
(b) to attract potential management talent.

Management Review or Audit (Fig. 3.9)

The methodology for highlighting the continuous review process systematically and ensuring that forecasts for management and organizational development are integrated into the forward business plans.

Remuneration and Conditions of Service

Concerns the organization's ability to attract and retain executives with talent and potential.

Country	Company	Location	Year 1972

Whether expatriate　　Nationality

Name

Present position

Age	Years in organization	Experience	Years	Job	Job class	% Job value	Developmental potential

Acad./prof. qualifications	Languages:	Major training

Overall performance

Potential:

Own wishes:

Comment:

	Action		
Recommendations:	Subunit	Unit	Central MDS
Promotion/Lateral transfer:			
Attachments/Visits (excl. courses):			
Courses:			
Special:			
No action:			

Name

Fig. 3.7. Management development schedule (summary of information and appraisal).

Senior external courses					Senior internal courses					Other training or attachments			
Course suggested	Name	Age	Job class	Year	Course suggested	Name	Age	Job class	Year	Name	Age	Job class	Year
Stanford INSEAD	Jones	38	A	1974	General management course	Brown	39	C	1973	*HO Attachment* Smith	30	C	1973

Note: Under each of the above headings the entries should be in order of priority. Additional course titles can be inserted as required.

Fig. 3.8. Nominations for major courses attachments.

| Job | | | Present holder | | Name(s) of possible successor(s) | Remarks |
Title	Job class	When vacant	Name	Job to which moving		
Marketing director	A		Jones	Retiring	Brown and Black	Although not due to retire until 1978, may well go early; not too soon to think of successor
Transport manager	C	1975	Smith	Retiring	None within XYZ Company	Job will be restructured, and successor likely to be JCB

Fig. 3.9. Vacancies and succession table.

4. Identifying executive potential: Methods of testing and assessing

Esther C. Lawton

The first half of this chapter discusses a variety of testing and assessing techniques to identify potential executives. It discusses the advantages and disadvantages and relevant statistical information. The second part describes two systems: the overall US Government executive assignment system, and a particular application in the Internal Revenue Service of the US Treasury Department.

Techniques

There is no absolutely reliable method for testing and assessing potential of any kind, especially where executive potential is concerned. If this statement appears too positive, that is precisely its intent, since man has not as yet developed a crystal ball which will precisely predict the effect of particular events on an individual, an organization, or on any other event. This has to be my conclusion, based on personal observation, professional insight, and corroborative statistical, and narrative documentation.

However, the prospect is not altogether bleak because all other things being equal—which they seldom, if ever, are—some testing and assessment methods have proved to be at least satisfactory, if not always completely accurate, and some methods are basically better than others. Before discussing these, however, I would like to establish the framework for my comments.

Among the many books on the subject of executives and executive behaviour, one stands out by virtue of its comprehensiveness. In *Managerial Behavior, Performance and Effectiveness*, by John P. Campbell *et al.*, a detailed analysis is made of predictive manager-identification techniques. The book explores the matter of assuring effective managerial behaviour through the proper selection, training, and development of 'potential' managers or executives. The authors not only describe various testing and assessment techniques used to predict executive behaviour but also analyse the value of the various techniques in terms of their intrinsic nature and their application in a variety of organizations and situations. The book was published in 1970, though some of the reported statistical information dates back to the 'fifties and 'sixties. I am convinced that the volume and diversity of variables which are referred to by the authors are the factors which militate against the complete reliability of tests which attempt to predict the unpredictable future behaviour of any person, much less an executive whose behaviour can—and does—change.

Any one thing, or combination of things, can cloud the judgement, and hence the effectiveness, of an executive in his job. For example, domestic problems, health problems, interpersonal relationships at home, at work and at large, labour–management relations, organizational difficulties, new technologies and unprecedented situations—to name only a few—can, and do, affect and even upset the behaviour of an executive. The authors of the book cited above identify such factors in general terms backed up by statistical data, indicating that 'something' only too often has the effect of upsetting expectations of executive potential.

Standardized selection tests or techniques which can be used in more than one organization are even more vulnerable than 'tailor-made' tests or assessment techniques. The reason is obvious: the number of variables which can influence results is multiplied. Yet, for some jobs, the success of certain testing methods in some organizations justifies their continued use, if for no other reason than that they are likely to be more objective and, therefore, potentially more reliable than the personal decisions of one or a few people.

Need for Identification of Potential Executives

First, in a day of dynamic change, it is more important than ever to make careful selections of the persons who will manage the office, the store, industry, or government agency. It is not enough to have a manager or an executive able to use manpower, money, machines, and materials effectively: in today's world, the manager must be able to cope with the 'future shock' described by Alvin Toffler in his book of that title. That is, the manager of tomorrow must be much more alert to rapid technological and ideological changes than the manager of today is. And his own ideology must embrace matters beyond his own immediate environment, on social and political levels, as well as on the particular economic level affecting his organization.

But even if there were no desperate need for competent, resourceful managers with insight, the scarcity of such persons, the rate of obsolescence of present-day executives in the face of accelerated changes, and the disinterest of current students to enter managerial fields of study, make it more urgent than ever to have systematic ways to identify and/or develop the person, or persons, who can take over tomorrow in the most efficient way possible.

Determination of Selection Techniques

To determine the best method of identifying executive potential, a number of preliminary steps are necessary. First, it is essential to make an inventory of existing or proposed executive jobs and of the short- and long-term plans for assuring their occupancy by the best-qualified persons. A concurrent inventory of potential and current executives should also be made.

Second, each job must be *carefully* described in terms of the qualities most needed currently to perform it effectively. This has to be done in terms of the *results* required, and not on the basis of traditional qualities of past executives, because jobs change, the environment changes, and other things change, so that the qualities needed yesterday for the head of an office are not the same as those needed tomorrow. The qualifications of a job must be so clearly defined that the task of finding an appropriate executive to fill it will be facilitated.

Third, the decision must be made as to whether or not the job can be performed best by someone from the organization or by someone from outside, since additional, and possibly different, testing methods may be required for an outsider. As a general rule, promotions, i.e., selections for executive positions from within the organization, can usually be made in less time and with less effort than hiring someone from outside.

Fourth, executive training must be provided. If the training is provided before the need for an executive to occupy a particular job, the training process itself can serve as a means to identify potential executives within the organization. If it is done after a selection is made, either within or outside the organization, the training can be of two kinds: training on the specific executive job itself, or grooming for the job to be occupied, through education and indoctrination in a variety of areas needed in executive jobs generally. Results attained during the training process can serve as a basis for selecting executives. In any case, the training or development of a future executive must be carefully planned and systematically executed.

The fifth step in the preliminary selection process is the determination of the method, or methods, of selection to be used.

Description of Selection Methods

The terms 'selection' and 'identification' have so far been used interchangeably. As a practical matter, the 'identification' of potential executives is a general process that may involve a number of candidates; 'selection', on the other hand, usually refers to the choice of one of several candidates.

Techniques for identifying potential executives are primarily of two types, traits oriented or results oriented. In the first, the person's personal qualities are the prime consideration; in the second, the person's performance on past and current jobs are the main factor. Most selection programmes combine both types of techniques.

An alphabetical list follows of major testing and assessing methods for identifying and selecting potential executives.

a. *Assessment Technique or Assessment Centre Approach.* Among users of this technique are the American Telephone and Telegraph Company, International Business Machines, the Caterpillar Co., General Electric, Sears, Westinghouse Electric Corporation, and Macy's Department Store in New York. Most users are comparatively large companies. Although details vary from one organization to another, the basic ingredient of this technique is to expose an employee, in a structured environment, to a variety of exercises, tests, simulated situations, and the like. His reactions are observed and evaluated by current managers, or others, in terms of potential effective managerial behaviour in a particular job of the particular organization. The centres can be on the site of the jobs for which candidates are being assessed, or at a remote retreat or some other facility.

The principles involved in this technique are both traits oriented and results oriented and have proved useful ever since its limited use prior to and during the Second World War in the training of officers and in studies in personality. Its use in assessing manager potential is comparatively recent, and not too extensive because of the costs involved. Hence, there is not enough data to validate its overall or long-term effectiveness, and what data there are indicate mixed results. Suffice it to say that it has been more successful in identifying executive potential than has virtually any other technique, or combination of techniques, in those large companies where it has been tried.

The primary reason for the comparative success of the assessment centre technique is its high degree of objectivity, i.e. in most of the centres, all participants are assessed on the same basis by the same assessors who do not know the participants but relate performance at the centre to the specific job requirements, without any 'built-in' biases.

Most individual assessments at the centres are supplemented by job ratings on current and past jobs, and also by supervisory recommendations, before final selections are made for a particular job.

A comprehensive analysis of assessment centres has been made by Barry M. Cohen, University of Florida; Joel L. Moses, American Telephone and Telegraph Company, and William C. Byham, University of Pittsburgh, in their monograph *The Validity of Assessment Centers: A Literature Review,* which comments on the validity, as well as the nature of assessment centres.

In general, assessment centres include multifold techniques that have been used in part, in combination, or as a single method of identifying and selecting executives. For example, in-depth interviews have frequently been the sole basis for selection but they are only a part of the eclectic approach used in assessment centres. The interview technique is usually derived from inventories or autobiographical questionnaires prepared by candidates. The inventories and questionnaires are frequently used *alone,* without interviews.

The assessment centre approach has other uses than identifying future executives. Components of the approach also provide the opportunity to determine progress, plan careers, identify training needs, furnish needed training, and evaluate performance. Some of the components include: in-basket exercises, role playing, individual and peer evaluations, group evaluations, group discussions, work group exercises in fact finding and problem solving, questionnaires, intelligence tests, problem-solving exercises, analysis of educational records, and written psychological tests.

In the monograph cited above, the authors present an excellent summary of the benefits and faults of assessment centre techniques. However, as objective as they are, they, too, would seem to allow subjectivity to creep into assessor appraisals, either because of the assessor's own predelictions or the biases built into job requirements initially. Another common fault is in the interpretation of assessment results. The chief benefit, of course, is the highly predictive accuracy experienced by companies that use this technique, compared with other techniques. For example, in a study of American Telephone and Telegraph's assessment centre predictions, 42 per cent of the people seen as material for middle management attained that level within five years, while only 7 per cent of low-rated persons progressed to that level. The technique is clearly more valid than pen and paper tests, which have been subjected to much criticism in recent years for *their* built-in biases. The American Management Association, in its literature describing its own assessment centre programme states: 'A survey of 20 companies revealed 22 studies that clearly demonstrated assessment to be more effective than other approaches in identifying managerial potential.'

In summary, the assessment centre approach is at least more systematic, certainly more objective, and surely more comprehensive in its insight into the candidates under consideration than any other approach to date.

b. *Experience and Seniority.* The validity of these techniques as indicators of executive potential is highly questionable. Work experience in other jobs or other organizations is not *per se* a determinant of effective past performance or effective potential performance; nor is seniority *per se* an indicator of effective performance. Indeed, as one personnel wag has put it, twelve years' experience could mean twelve experiences of one year each instead of one experience lasting twelve years; the former implies superficiality, the latter could mean in-depth assimilation of occupational knowledge.

Yet many organizations depend greatly on a candidate's experience, as a determinant in hiring and promoting employees. In fact, much attention is paid to personal inventories which require extensive details on past positions held. While it is true that the very exposure to jobs implies at least some acquisition of knowledge, too much weight is given to it when considering employees for new jobs. This is unfortunate when executive positions are in question, since effective performance in any number of non-executive positions is no guarantee of effective performance in a position which entails a different relationship with one's superiors, peers, and subordinates. Too often, a highly competent technician is put into a position of directing others only to find that directing others, and being responsible for a programme, is not the same as independently carrying out a project.

Seniority, like experience, leaves much to be desired, whether taken in the physical sense or used as an indicator of executive potential. It is, however, a very sensitive matter in many organizations because of the emphasis placed on it by employees, employee unions, and officers themselves. There is a 'sentimental' attachment to the tradition that the senior person—not necessarily in age, but in service—must be 'rewarded' by being given a particular executive position. The unfortunate thing is that the employee may be the least qualified of available candidates to assume the post. He may have reached the stage of surfeit or his highest level of incompetence, or may long ago have gone beyond his capacity to perform effectively. Seniority, as a *sole* determinant of potential is dangerous; if all other things are equal, and the existence of two outstanding candidates makes a decision on their selection difficult, then, and only then, should seniority be a deciding factor. Even so, before a senior person, whose ideas may be still in the Dark Ages, is selected over another candidate who is *au courant*, interpersonal relationships in the organization should be very carefully weighed. Fortunately, in the larger organizations at least, there has been enough experience with bad selections on this account that this method of selection, if used at all, is tempered with other techniques which attempt to bring to light other information such as adaptability and some of the other characteristics that may be needed in a specific executive position.

c. *Forms: Application Blanks and Biographical Data Forms.* These are 'inventory' forms which furnish background information on the education, training, experience, and biographical data of the potential executive. As a matter of fact, inventories are kept of all employees, executives and non-executives alike.

This method of identification is the easiest, and most widespread, of all techniques used for identifying potential employees of all types. It could also be the most misleading. Its basic defect lies in the fact that people interpret even the best-constructed forms differently whether they are preparing the form or reviewing it. Thus, errors in selection may well be compounded. Certainly, its validity as a positive means of identifying executives is questionable.

What the form does do is provide a quick review of an employee's career, and from this, other facts can be deduced. For example, the form may yield information that indicates a need for certain additional training or education in order for the employee to meet the requirements of a particular executive job.

If the inventory is used in conjunction with other techniques, it is a time saver. In any event, it provides some biographical information which may give a clue to certain kinds of behaviour. The horror is that, only too often, it is the sole basis for initial selection or screening of employees who may later become executives for want of other available persons.

d. *Interviews.* Interviews are primarily traits oriented and are, perhaps, the most widely used technique for identifying executives, although they are frequently combined with other techniques. For example, they supplement the use of tests or they may follow an analysis of employee autobiographical questionnaires and inventories. The interview may be a 'sizing-up' interview or merely a form of polite introduction; it may be with a single interviewer or with a panel; it may be structured or unstructured, and it may be relatively short, or in-depth; the interviews may be used to obtain specific answers or to supplement other facts about personality, performance, or behaviour. In fact, some interviews may be only one in a series of multiple interviews.

Dunnette and Bass state in their article 'Behavioral Scientists and Personnel Management' (*Industrial Relations* **2,** 3, 1963, pp. 115–30) that:

> The personnel interview continues to be the most widely used method for selecting employees, despite the fact that it is a costly, inefficient, and usually invalid procedure. It is often used to the exclusion of far more thoroughly researched and validated procedures. Even when the interview is used in conjunction with other procedures, it is almost always treated as the final hurdle in the selection process.

The trouble with interviews is that reactions of the interviewer tend to be subjective and patterned in his own image. The blustery executive is likely to react negatively to an equally dominating interviewee, either out of instinctive fear of competition or because of his need to 'rule the roost'.

A useful addition to the interviewing technique by lay persons is the interview with a psychologist or psychiatrist. Here, too, however, the atmosphere of the interview process may not be conducive to completely objective results, but, even if it is, it is still no guarantee of the person's behaviour once he is in an executive position, and is actually faced, for example, with a serious personality conflict between himself and one of his superiors, peers, or subordinates.

e. *Performance Evaluation.* This technique is obviously results oriented, but only too often it reflects the traits of the evaluator rather than the candidate. Although most organizations use this technique—according to reports and studies on the subject—few systematic approaches have been tried or validated. Indeed, few records have been maintained from which to report results.

The evaluation process varies in details from organization to organization. For example, some companies rank their employees by merit, i.e., performance rather than making systematic evaluations. Where there are no specific criteria for the ranking, the results are of course inconsistent, subjective, and consequently misleading if taken at face value in identifying executive potential.

As a practical matter, a superior's estimate of his employee is frequently based on estimates of potential rather than on past job performance, and the estimates are without a solid basis for the prognostication. Furthermore, superiors who evaluate performance are prone to evaluate in terms of their own performances and frequently, therefore, make evaluations which seem to reflect on themselves rather than their subordinates. Finally, since evaluations are made at different times without benefit of established measurement devices, evaluations from the same supervisor can vary for the same employee.

In summary, most persons concerned with such matters agree that past performance is the best predictor thus far devised, but the technique is so full of holes that past performance evaluations should be used only in combination with other techniques and should be derived from more than one source to be a reasonably reliable indicator of past, much less potential, performance.

f. *References and Recommendations: Consultant's Appraisals.* These can be obtained from or made by superiors, peers, and subordinates and from persons outside the organization. Even references and recommendations on those who make references and recommendations are not infrequent— and I can appreciate why: recommendations and references are not intrinsically objective but, most important, are based on varied criteria and, if considered together, may prove inconsistent. Furthermore, since standards and patterns of behaviour vary from one organization to another, what is acceptable in one is anathema to another.

Another basic defect of this method is that the anxiety to disengage oneself of an undesirable, inefficient, or incompetent employee frequently brings about an unwarranted eulogy on his behalf. Fortunately, bad experiences in this regard have diminished the importance of recommendations and references as a means of selecting employees.

A related method of identifying potential executives is the use of employee appraisals made by consultants; i.e., consultants in residence, or hired on a part-time basis, appraise the behaviour and performance of employees through observation and analysis of the employee's work and through discussions with the employees themselves, their superiors, peers, or subordinates. This is usually supplemented by analysis of autobiographical inventory forms. But such appraisals are as defective as references and recommendations in that, for the most part, they are not systematically structured, and they tend to be too subjective because they are based on personal reactions rather than concrete criteria.

Consultant's appraisals can be just as biased as those of non-consultants. Furthermore, because of personal biases acquired by or reported to consultants, their appraisals have lacked uniformity as well as validity. Where they are used at all, there appears to be a particular insightful consultant who is accepted on faith.

g. *Tests: Psychological Tests, Interest Tests and Others.* Tests of one kind or another have been used for selecting leaders since time immemorial. From the skirmishes among competing cavemen to tournaments among medieval knights, to intelligence tests among students, tests have been used to identify those who stood out as leaders.

The variety of tests in use today to measure almost any characteristic is voluminous. Those used specifically to identify potential executives include psychological tests. Normally, tests are used in combination with other selection methods before final personnel decisions are made. While widespread, tests are not used by all organizations, and certainly not for all jobs.

Usually the higher the level of the job, the smaller the use of tests is.

Among the standardized psychological tests in use are personality tests, interest tests, intelligence tests, and mental ability tests. They test cognitive, verbal and arithmetic ability as well as personality, interest, and projective qualities. Combinations of these tests are also used. Usually, the tests have been developed by psychologists for research studies. They are sometimes adapted for particular organizations but, in many instances, are not specifically related to the jobs for which executives ase being sought. Nevertheless, the tests are used as indicators of traits which are required for some jobs.

Among the standardized tests most commonly used are: the Wonderlic Personnel Test, the Shipley-Hartford Test, the SRA Verbal Test, the DAT Abstract Reasoning Exam, the Watson-Glaser Critical Thinking Test, the Davis Reading Test, the Kuder Preference Record and the Guilford-Zimmerman Temperament Survey, the Primary Mental Abilities Test for the SRA Verbal, the Strong or Kuder Interest Measures, and the Early Identification of Management Potential (EIMP) battery of tests.

As indicated, some of these tests are adapted, or interpreted, in terms of specific jobs in a particular organization. Because the tests are clearly traits oriented, they are not considered to be completely predictive of behaviour, however, and so their use is primarily for the initial hiring of employees rather than for identifying them for high-level executive positions. Nevertheless, research is growing in this field because the tests are fairly inexpensive to administer. Certainly, they can at least serve as initial screening devices and weed out those who do not meet minimal attitudinal or aptitudinal qualifications for executive jobs.

h. *Training and Development of Executives.* The training and development of executives has become almost a routine practice in all organizations of any size. Practices vary from organization to organization. Some training is done to improve skills and knowledge already possessed, and some to acquire such qualities. Some are geared to certain general categories of positions, some to specific occupations, some to specific skills, some to general knowledge—in fact, training and development have become almost as varied and important in organizations as are the functions for which the organizations were established.

Training varies not only in its general nature but in its details. It may be highly formalized, with classroom instruction and courses either on the site of the organization where the job occurs or at universities or other facilities; or training may take the guise of informal coaching by someone in the unit where the job occurs; it may consist of on-the-job training where explanations are given as assignments are carried out; some training consists of applied cognitive programmes directly related to the jobs for which executives are being sought—this includes simulation exercises and role playing, in addition to or instead of formal courses, as well as on-the-job training, coaching, and job rotation assignments. In short, training may be generalized or particularized, applied or theoretical; it may include cognitive programmes or substantive training in the field of work involved; it may mean training in special skills or techniques, and it may involve training courses in human relations, psychology, and behaviour patterns. In other words, training or developmental programmes can consist of anything that a particular organization feels inclined, or is induced, to do.

Unfortunately few, if any, training and development programmes have been scientifically validated, and many of them do not even have the distinction of having been developed systematically. Too many management training programmes have been adopted with little regard for their real value or application in the organization. They are nevertheless extensively used, they are costly, and they are increasing both in cost and volume and variety. New training fads seem to spring up daily and are used without assessments of their validity.

Yet, despite the criticism that can be rightfully directed against many training programmes, a word should be said about those that have appeared to be successful. Later, I shall describe one such programme which has had some measure of success because it was developed in direct relationship to the executive jobs to be filled. However, much more research needs to be done in the whole area of what is needed in executive jobs in general, and then what is specifically needed for a particular executive job. Then, and only then, can training programmes really be effective if not completely valid.

Training and development programmes have been listed here among the techniques to be used in identifying executive potential because, frequently, achievement in programmes is an indicator closely related to performance on the job itself. This is particularly true when the programme is directly related to the jobs to be filled. For example, when executive training is to groom likely candidates for executive positions and consists of carefully selected special or rotating assignments, performance on such assignments can readily be used as an indicator of future executive performance. This method is at least as reliable for identifying potential as any other single selection method, provided that interpersonal and organizational relationships to be met in the future are part of the training programme. Indeed, this method of identifying and selecting executives is the commonest, and among the most reliable, of the testing and assessment techniques despite its occasional lapses of accurate prognostication. As Robert Desatnick says, in his publication *A Concise Guide to Management Development* (American Management Association, 1970, p. 27): 'The best predictor of future performance is past performance.' Further, he says (p. 30): 'While it is recognized that superior accomplishment as an individual contributor does not *guarantee* success as a manager, it is the best indicator we have to date.' (my italics).

i. *Combined Testing and Assessing Methods.* Because they recognize that it is essential to provide for the future, organizations have adopted one or more of the methods described above, for testing and assessing their employees—and also outsiders—to identify those who may carry on the business of the organization in the years to come. Variations and combinations of the methods described have been individualized to become the particular technique used by a particular organization for particular jobs. The assessment centre approach, for example, is gaining ground as a composite technique which combines a variety of techniques for assessing individuals and their capacity to carry out executive assignments. As an indication of how even one method can be adapted, the simple method of performance appraisals has undergone a number of variations. For example, ratings may be made not only by superiors but by peers and subordinates. Appraisals may be single or multiple. Multiple appraisals may be made orally in discussion or may be written and then summarized and weighted; inconsistencies can be resolved through follow-up with the appraisers. The appraisals may be narrative (and therefore likely to be objective) or they may be in accord with specific criteria or specific items. Finally, performance appraisals may be used not only for executive selection or promotions but to determine needs for training.

As a further example, combinations of specific tests can be made so that questions or exercises can be combined in one test to assess general intelligence, verbal ability, numerical ability, perceptual speed and accuracy, inductive reasoning, spatial relations ability, mechanical knowledge or comprehension, personality, and vocational interest.

In the book by Campbell *et al.*, the following statement appears (pp. 38–39):

> Influences on managerial effectiveness are diverse and complex, involving the interaction of individual characteristics and motivational and organizational environment variables. How should predictors be combined to reflect the complexity of these interactions? Simply adding them by means of equations or statistical rules seems too mechanistic and seems to depart from our aim of individualized prediction. But combination by purely clinical inference also seems precarious. Such predictions may be individualized but they also seem haphazard and overly conjectural. Granted that certain predictors may be better than others, the questions still remain of how they should be combined to yield accurate predictions about managers' job behavior.
>
> The safest thing to do at this point would probably be to conclude with the statement that there are wide individual differences among firms in the use of selection instruments.

The authors then make the observation that interviews are extensively used in hiring recent college graduates, with tests and 'weighted' biographical forms being increasingly used. On the other hand, 'internal' selections depend primarily on experience and evaluated performance, with the assessment centre approach on the upsurge. In any case, most selections are made on the basis of judgement 'rather than on the basis of any carefully developed and validated pattern or configuration of predictor information'. They conclude, after analyzing statistical results from a large number of firms, that intellectual ability, perceptive accuracy, personality, and interest tests are the best indicators.

Application

The rest of this chapter is concerned with a discussion of the application of some of the techniques described above, in a programme used in the Internal Revenue Service of the US Treasury Department, together with a discussion of the broad umbrella that covers this programme, in the form of the so-called executive assignment system used in the Federal Government service.

Executives in the US Government Service

There are several kinds of executives in the Service. This section deals only with executives in the executive not the legislative or judicial, branches. The basic distinction is that some of them are career executives and some are non-career executives. Career executives are primarily those who entered the service and were competitively ranked and selected in accord with the requirements of the US Civil Service Commission. These are based on the results of written and/or oral examinations in some occupations; in other occupations, inventory forms indicating education, experience, training, accomplishments, and so forth are analysed, rated, and ranked by psychometricians and others.

Career executives normally have certain claims on the executive jobs they have been appointed to, although they can—theoretically—be subject to dismissal in certain circumstances. On the other hand, non-career executives do not go through a competitive selection process and are subject to changes in political administration or other changes. Normally, non-career executives do not have claims on executive jobs to which they have been appointed.

There are four major systems involving the pay of executives in the executive branch of the Federal Government. The four basic systems are: the Federal Executive System, the General Schedule System, the Foreign Service System, and the system for selection of medical staffs. The last two are very specialized, and applicable to only a small number of positions comparable to executives: they will not therefore be discussed in detail. A description of the others follows:

a. *Federal Executive System.* This provides for a separate pay scale consisting of five fixed levels of pay, e.g., level I, $60 000 per annum to level V, $36 000 per annum. It includes, primarily, positions at the highest echelons in the executive branch, as, e.g., all Cabinet Secretaries, Under Secretaries, and Assistant Secretaries. Primarily, jobs in this system are occupied by political appointees whose selection method is political party affiliation. However, the system does include some positions below the top echelons where the executives are selected and appointed to their positions on a competitive ranking basis such as described above. Positions in this system are included by statute or by Executive Order and, hence, are fairly fixed in number.

b. *The General Schedule System.* This includes the largest number of Federal Government executives, who are 'graded' in three levels—each having a different range of pay and familiarly known as a 'supergrade'. The system was established for a number of purposes, but most important, to do away with automatic selection of 'internal' candidates, to provide a wide range of choices for selection of candidates, to identify potential candidates readily, and to control the number and use of supergrade positions.

Basically, the system consists of the completion of a detailed inventory form by all persons already in supergrade positions or in the grade level immediately below. The form contains biographical, educational, and work-experience data and is prepared in triplicate, a copy for the employee himself, a copy for the particular government agency, and a copy for the Civil Service Commission.

The Civil Service Commission transfers the data received to computer machines and tapes which store the information. Three important additional forms are used in this system, namely, the notice of a vacancy in an executive position, the notice of intent about the future nature and use of a supergrade job, and a form outlining the specific duties and responsibilities of a job, together with the qualifications of a particular candidate.

Thus, whenever an executive is needed, the government agency is supposed to ask the Civil Service Commission to 'search' the data files to identify possible candidates who match the job requirements. If no likely candidates are found, the agency may perform an outside search (outside the government, that is) and obtain likely candidates. A number of potential candidates are then 'analysed' within the agency, and a selection made. Usually, this process consists of a review of the data on the inventory form; obtaining evaluations from prior superiors; oral interviews; 'ranking' the candidates (with subjective judgement often the only criterion); and recommending a selection to the Civil Service Commission. The Commission then approves the selection officially. There are variations to this process, but this is how most executives under the General Schedule System are identified.

Theoretically, the system is sound; practically, it has been less than successful in meeting its goals. For one thing, the inventory data is not always current; the search and screening process consumes a lot of time, e.g., hundreds of names could be 'spewed' up by the computer, yet it is not guaranteed to come up with names of all or the best-qualified persons because the initial data may be incorrect; the screening process is haphazard in some agencies; job criteria have not always been clear or specific enough; evaluations of previous superiors may have been subjective and unsystematic with the result that they are inconsistent with each other; but the worst criticism is that, despite the search and referral system with its thousands of potential candidates, most selections are made from within the same organization and are substantially the same selections as would have been made without the system. But the system itself is not to blame; theoretically it provides a broad base for the identification and selection of potential executives. The fault lies not so much with the Civil Service Commission as with the agencies who have prostituted the system through loose ways of applying it.

This system has three basic methods for testing and assessing potential executives: the inventory form, supervisory evaluations, and 'consultant' appraisal, i.e., Civil Service Commission occupational analysts who act on agency recommendations. Other methods are supplementary, are performed by the agencies themselves, and vary from agency to agency. The agencies use one or more, or a combination of methods, and the assessment centre approach is increasingly being used.

The Executive System in the Internal Revenue Service of the US Treasury Department

The Internal Revenue Service (IRS) has programmes to identify supergrade executives, and executives or managers at various organizational and lower-grade levels. Programmes for the lower-grade executives use various methods, such as performance appraisals, self-appraisals, career guidance through supervisors and others, inventories, technical training, formalized courses, and special assignments to identify potential managers. One such programme is described in detail by Dugan Laird in his article 'They Manage Very Well at IRS', (*Training*, August 1970).

An article in *Training and Development* (September 1970), entitled 'The Supervisory Assessment Center' describes one of the latest approaches which the IRS has adopted to identify and select highly technical specialists, namely, the assessment centre. The authors of the article, Frank DiCostanzo and Thomas Andretta, state that:

> The purpose of the Center is to put individuals selected for certain positions through a series of individual and group exercises, interviews and tests designed to simulate the conditions of the job and to show if they have the skills and abilities necessary to perform that job . . . [it] looks primarily at what a man can do in a new position, not what he is doing or has done in his present one. It gathers performance information relevant to the new job rather than making predictions based on present job performance.

These comments confirm what has already been said about assessment centres.

However, in this discussion, my concern is with the supergrade executive identification and selection programme in the IRS because it is integrated with the governmentwide system. The Revenue Service has one of the best executive identification and assessment programmes in the government because it is custom tailored to that agency and because it includes combinations and variations of various testing and assessing techniques. The programme comes under the jurisdiction of the governmentwide General Schedule System for selecting supergrade executives but there are a few exceptions. For example, certain IRS positions are exempt from a search in Civil Service Commission inventory files. The selected candidates for these particular positions still require 'official' Commission approval before assignment to the position can be made, but this approval is usually perfunctory. The programme is described in a booklet entitled *The Executive Selection and Development Program*. The following account is abstracted or adapted from this booklet.

At the end of the Second World War, the Bureau of Internal Revenue was hampered by 'an organization developed for less than a fourth of the new workload, and a staff grown approximately two and one-fifth times'. After the reorganization of 1952, one of the first problems faced by the Internal Revenue Service (as it was now called) was that of filling its new District Directorships, Regional Commissionerships, and other executive positions created and brought under the merit system by the reorganization.

'At the time of reorganization and in the years immediately following, the Service attempted to staff these positions through civil service examinations announced to the public at large. This practice was adopted in order to give incumbent Collectors of Internal Revenue an opportunity to compete for the new jobs and also to assure the widest possible competition. While a few outstanding executives from outside the Service were attracted and appointed by this method, results were generally disappointing. For one thing, the examination procedure itself proved to be expensive and time consuming as it was necessary to allow at least a month for filing applications and several months for the required investigations of all the applicants' experience. More seriously, however, the examinations simply did not attract the kind of candidates from outside the Federal service that had been hoped for. The reason appeared to be that candidates well placed in private employment did not find enough inducement in Federal salaries to warrant their making the transition to Government. In addition to these practical difficulties, it was obvious that the Service could never become a true career organization unless it systematically developed executives from within its own organization.

Thus, Internal Revenue directed its energies to the creation of a system that would assure a continuing supply of executives from the more than 50 000 employees then constituting its work force. Early in 1955, a small committee of IRS career officials was appointed to survey existing practices and consider the need for a formal executive selection and development system in the Service. In its report, the committee noted a number of deficiencies:

1. The Service lacked a comprehensive long-range plan for identifying and developing men of ability and potential.

2. In the absence of a regular system for filling vacancies, key positions often remained vacant for extended periods or were filled hastily with no clear assurance that the best candidate had been selected.

3. Generalist 'line' positions, such as Assistant District Director and District Director, were typically filled by men who had gained all of their experience within a given function (Audit, Collection, Intelligence, etc.), were unfamiliar with the managerial demands of the other functions, and had no specific preparation for their higher responsibilities.

4. Finally, there was no system for obtaining periodic, comprehensive, and objective evaluations, both to help the executive improve his performance and to provide reliable information on which to base selections for advancement to higher level positions.

As its primary recommendation, the Committee proposed that the Service establish a Corps of General Administrators, consisting of officials in its top field executive positions. For their initial selection and training recommendations they focused on the Assistant District Director position because the ADD is the first Service official responsible for multi-functional management, and is the logical source from which to select District Directors and, ultimately, Regional Commissioners. In the words of the Committee: '... It is at this point that we would divide our total supply of potential executives between those who will continue within their respective functions and those who will be pulled out of this functional progression and placed in the 'general' management promotion ladder.' The Committee's approach was approved and action was begun immediately to place into effect the recommended selection and training program.

On June 4, 1956, the first announcement was sent to Internal Revenue Service employees, describing the new program and the procedures for applying. Eleven candidates were selected in that first year, given 6 months of training, and assigned to Assistant District Director positions. Though the program met, as expected, with some initial misgivings, the outstanding performance of most ES and D graduates gradually convinced even the most hardened skeptics.

In the years that followed, while the basic approach remained the same, experience and research brought about changes in the details of selection and training. From time to time, specialists from outside the Service were brought in to observe the program and provide a fresh and unbiased point of view. This was done most recently in 1964 when Internal Revenue invited a number of experts from education, industry, and the government to explore improved methods of measuring executive potential. The participants were highly impressed with the IRS program and their ideas and suggestions provided a basis for continuing refinements.

Over the years ES and D has developed into a strong and respected instrument of IRS policy. Today, its graduates are the basic source of candidates for Internal Revenue's Assistant District Director and Assistant Service Center Director positions and the primary reserve for all of the Service's 234 key executive jobs.

But the program has benefited the Service ... in still another way. It has dealt a death blow to any traces of the 'spoils system' in Internal Revenue —the practice of attempting to obtain political support for advancement. One of the results of political selection of Collectors of Internal Revenue was that employees in the organization, though under civil service, were tempted to solicit political sponsorship for advancement. The reorganization of 1952 and the placing of all Revenue positions in the Civil Service generally put an end to this practice... The program has thus played an important role in keeping the Internal Revenue Service absolutely free from considerations unrelated to merit in appointments, advancements, and the determinations of tax matters.

a. *Qualification Requirements and Application Procedures.* As the first step in identifying best qualified candidates, Internal Revenue periodically conducts a nationwide competition. This is normally held annually, and is open to all those who meet basic eligibility requirements.

To publicize this competition, an announcement is prepared outlining the purposes of the program, eligibility requirements, the nature of the training, and procedures for applying. Management officials are responsible for seeing that these announcements are given wide distribution and for encouraging their best qualified people to apply. In a typical year, approximately three to four hundred persons enter competition.

Because Division Chief and Assistant Division Chiefs in IRS districts and service centers are the group from which Assistant District Directors and Assistant Service Center Directors would most logically come, they are automatically considered. All other Service employees must, of course, apply to the head of their office, providing data on their experience, qualifications, and availability.

Although ES and D is intended primarily as an internal career system for the development and advancement of IRS employees, to avoid inbreeding and capitalize on outstanding talent available in other agencies, the Service some years ago opened up the program to applicants from outside sources. Candidates from outside IRS are obtained in the following ways:
(a) Other employees of the Treasury Department may be recommended by the head of their bureau.
(b) Government employees of other agencies may be recommended either by a high-level official of the Internal Revenue Service or by the Civil Service Commission, and
(c) Candidates from private industry may be considered through referrals from professional organizations or the use of appropriate Civil Service registers.

To be eligible a candidate must be able to meet Civil Service requirements to occupy a position in the competitive service and have had at least a year of significant management experience. Geographic mobility, though not an absolute eligibility requirement, is an important consideration for selection into the program. A candidate's chances of selection diminish to the extent he places limitations on availability.

b. *The Selection Process.* The purpose of selection for executive positions in the Internal Revenue Service begins long before a man becomes a candidate for the ES and D Program. A basic element in the Service's concept is the early identification and development of talent through carefully structured career programs and through training of first-line supervisors and middle-managers. The ES and D Program may be thought of as the final step in this process.

A key characteristic sought in candidates for all the Service's management positions is potential to assume responsibilities beyond those of the position for which the selection is being made. In the nationwide ES and D competition, therefore, selections are guided by an estimate of the candidate's demonstrated competence and his potential for advancing to senior level executive positions. The selection process comprises three phases.

Initial Nominating Phase. The first (Initial Nominating) phase is conducted in districts, service centers, regions, and in the National Office for candidates from these offices. During this phase, at least three evaluations are obtained from persons most familiar with the candidate's work and ability. These evaluations cover personal traits, job performance, potential executive ability, strengths and weaknesses.

A written test of administrative judgement and learning ability serves as a second source of information on each candidate. The score made on this test is one factor considered in making selections for the program, but no candidate is selected or eliminated solely on this basis. It is used as an indicator which is checked against other available data.

After considering test results along with the candidates' background and work experience and information obtained through written evaluations, the head of office then obtains more detailed evaluative information on those candidates who are being recommended for second phase screening. This information, obtained through personal interviews with evaluators and key executive officials, is intended to resolve differences in evaluations and to give the head of office a sharper view of each candidate. On this basis, he then determines those individuals he judges best qualified for further consideration and forwards their names for Intermediate Screening.

Intermediate Screening Phase. Intermediate Screening (the second phase of the selection process) is conducted by regional screening committees, chaired by the Regional Commissioners, and by a special committee, designated by the Deputy Commissioner, to consider candidates from the National Office. Candidates from outside the Revenue Service enter competition during this phase, and are considered (depending on their geographical location) by a regional or National Office Committee.

These intermediate screening committees review all the information gathered during phase screening—written evaluations, test results, experience and training. In addition, they obtain further bases for evaluation by conducting group and individual interviews. Usually, about 40–60 candidates are chosen in this second round. Their names are forwarded to the National Office, where the Executive Resources Board conducts the final phase of screening.

Final Screening Phase. The Executive Resources Board, consisting of the Deputy Commissioner, as Chairman, and the Assistant Commissioners with functional responsibilities in the field as members, conducts the final phase of the ES and D competition. As a part of their larger responsibility for the overall planning, supervision, and evaluation of all executive personnel and development programs, they evaluate candidates for the Service's executive corps and recommend to the Commissioner those whom they believe to be of the highest potential for executive assignment. The Commissioner makes the final selections.

Finalists in this last phase of the competition are further appraised through the use of an Executive Assessment Center. The assessment center consists of simulation exercises to test candidates' responses to executive problem situations. Information from the first phases along with assessment center reports and the results of individual interviews of candidates by the Board are considered in this final phase.

The number of applicants selected is based on the number of vacancies expected to occur in Assistant District Director, Assistant Service Center Director, and Assistant Regional Commissioner positions during the coming year. In a typical year, about 12 to 15 persons are finally selected for Executive Training.

c. *Executive Training.* The ultimate goal of the entire ES and D Program is to transform a select group of managers, with backgrounds in a single function, into executives responsible for the overall direction of several functions. The objective of the Service's executive training course itself, however, is more immediate and limited.

Formal executive training in IRS consists, initially, of a six month pre-assignment program of seminars, discussions, and coaching by experienced executives which may be supplemented, by a period of on-the-job training in a special interim position. The specific objective of this training is to help the candidate make the transition to an entrance-level executive job where he will assist, for the first time, in directing a multi-functional organization. While the primary focus of the course is on the trainee's first executive assignment, the development of the individual over the range of his entire career is also given strong emphasis.

As presently structured, IRS executive training is designed to meet the needs of each candidate in four general areas. These are:

1. The duties, responsibilities, and problem solving techniques of the District and Service Center executive.

2. The operations and problems of the functions he will be responsible for directing, particularly those in which he has no previous experience.

3. The new relationships he will have e.g., with the press and other communications media, community and professional organizations, legislative groups, and other executives both in government and in business.

4. Areas of broad management interest and significant issues of national concern pertinent to the job of a Federal executive.

In the course of his six months training, each candidate is assigned for short periods of time to an IRS Region, District, and Service Center. The emphasis during this phase of the program is on a close tutorial relationship between the trainee and key field officials. As much time as possible is spent with the head of each office and his principal assistants, to provide a first-hand view of the day-to-day techniques used and problems encountered in managing a complex multi-functional organization. Discussions are open and frank, and problem areas are explored as well as achievements.

Complementing the training received at various field offices are two sessions at the National Office—the first at the beginning of the program and the second at the end.

During the first weeks of the program, candidates assemble in Washington for an orientation and view of Internal Revenue as seen by the Service's top executives, the Commissioner, Deputy Commissioner, and the Assistant Commissioners. These officials discuss Service policy, how programs are developed and evaluated, and field officials' responsibilities for implementing programs.

An important phase of training occurs at the end of the program when the candidates return to Washington from their various field assignments. During these final weeks, IRS invites eminent people from many fields to meet with and address the group. Discussion leaders are distinguished persons in Government and the private sector, who can broaden the participant's view of a Federal executive's responsibilities. Speakers usually include, for example, the Deputy Secretary of the Treasury, Chairman of the House Appropriations Sub-Committee, an Assistant Attorney General, a State Director of Revenue, a tax practitioner, and the President of a large corporation. In addition, a program would typically include such topics as:

'Taxation and the National Economy'
'Trends in the Labor Force'
'New Trends on the Status of Women'
'Executives' Responsibilities for Equal Employment Opportunity'
'Change in the Urban Environment'
'How the White House Coordinates the Efforts of Agencies'

These sessions play a valuable part in shaping the future careers of trainees. All are being groomed for important positions throughout the country. Many are destined to become the senior Federal executives in their areas. They must, of necessity become familiar with the political, social, and economic institutions that form the society in which they will carry out their responsibilities.

At the National Office, as in the field, a certain amount of time is set aside for individual development. A variety of activities may be undertaken, including reading in the fields of management, economics, taxation and other subjects pertinent to Service work. Some participants visit government and non-government organizations, researching such topics as recruitment techniques or management control systems. Others attend seminars on a variety of subjects designed to enhance their effectiveness. These individual activities, like the more formal training, are oriented toward a single end— IRS leadership that is broad gauged, skilled at managing, and technically proficient.

Initial Placement. During the last weeks of training, the Executive Resources Board discusses placement possibilities for the ES and D trainees with

Regional Commisioners and meets with each member of the class in considering potential assignments. The Chairman of the Board then discusses the placement proposals with the Commissioner, who makes the final selection decisions.

Placements are made with the needs of the Service and the individual in mind. Most graduates will be placed in vacant Assistant District Director or Assistant Service Center Director positions. Indeed, some of these positions are developmental only and serve as training assignments for graduates of the program.

Graduates of the program, at some point in their development, may be assigned to an appropriate National Office position to provide them with a well-rounded perspective of Service management.

d. *The Corps of General Executives.* Upon successful completion of Executive Training, the candidate becomes a member of the Corps of General Executives. This places him in a singular position among IRS employees for, as pointed out earlier, it is from this corps alone that selections are made for the Service's Assistant District Director and Assistant Service Center Director positions (which are the normal channels to District Director, Service Center Director, and Regional Commissioner jobs). It should be noted, however, that completion of the course does not, in itself, guarantee appointment to an executive position. Graduates are assigned when they have clearly demonstrated, either during the Executive Training Course, or in temporary training assignments afterwards, that they are fully ready for advancement to executive responsibilities. Nevertheless, aside from the usual dropouts for personal reasons (e.g., health or desire to stay put), there are few graduates who do not, ultimately attain executive status. This is so, primarily, because of the highly selective nature of the screening process, but also because the size of each class is determined by a careful forecast of vacancies which prevents an oversupply of potential executives in the pool.

A measure of the program's success in providing the Service with a corps of skilled and effective executives may be obtained by examining the record of its graduates.

Of the 157 candidates who have completed the program since its beginning in 1955, 105 continue to serve IRS in key executive positions.... Of this group, 65 have received two or more promotions. Twenty-four have received three or more. Although none began the program in supergrade positions (grades GS-16, 17, and 18), 70—about two thirds—are now in such positions. Out of 32 Assistant District Directors, 30 (including incumbents) have completed ES and D training. The other two came in before the program began.

After their initial permanent appointments, graduates of ES and D are in competition with other Assistant District Directors, Assistant Service Center Directors, District Directors, and Service Center Directors for higher level positions.

Selections for these positions are made by the Commissioner on the recommendation of the Executive Resources Board. The Board, a continuing body, maintains current evaluative information, consisting of supervisory appraisals and personal data, on each member of the corps.

An individual can progress by various routes, and assignments cover a great diversity of levels of difficulty and responsibility. There are some District Director positions in grade GS-15, some in GS-16, and some in GS-17. Similarly, there are Assistant District Director positions in grades GS-14, GS-15, and GS-16. An ES and D graduate might serve at some point in his progress as an Assistant Regional Commissioner, or in a National Office position, or as a Service Center Director, Actually many career patterns can be and have been followed by graduates of the program.

The IRS organization of 1990 may very well be different from today's. A different organization will call for different requirements in numbers and kinds of executive positions. Nonetheless, the basic human factor will remain a constant. Internal Revenue will continue to require talented and dedicated Civil Servants to staff its high level executive positions. Selection and training methods may change, as may course content, but the goals of ES and D will remain the same—a continuing supply of able administrators to cope with the management problems of a complex and viable organization.'

Summary

From the above discussion, it is obvious that the validity of testing and assessing techniques to identify potential executives is *not* clear. Analyses and studies of results and records are neither voluminous nor definitive. Much remains to be done that can reasonably be done, to 'predict' behaviour, even remembering that many variables can negate the best predictions.

Certainly, the art of prediction is better now than thirty years ago ; perhaps that is the trouble—we are just catching up to thirty years ago.

In any case, it should be remembered that a combination of methods is likely to be more effective than one method, but that no method or combination can be truly successful without the other requirements for effective executives, such as : a good working climate, recognition of efforts, systematic career planning, an effective communications and reporting system in the organization, opportunities for exposure to new challenges, 'refresher' training, and, most important, support from top management.

But, even before that prophylactic list, it should be remembered that 'no man is an island' and if an executive lacks the 'common touch' that relates him to other men around him, he is not an executive but an executioner.

Suggested Reading

CAMPBELL, J. P., DUNNETTE, D., LAWLER, E. E., III, and WEICK, E., Jr. *Managerial Behavior, Performance and Effectiveness*, McGraw-Hill Series in Psychology, 1970; includes extensive bibliography.

COHEN, B. M., MOSES, J. L., and BYHAM, W. C. *The Validity of Assessment Centers: A Literature Review*, Development Dimensions, 767 Colony Circle, Pittsburgh, Pennsylvania, 1972; includes extensive bibliography.

DESATNICK, R. L. Developing Managers, *American Society of Training and Development Journal*, **24**, 8, 1970.

DESATNICK, R. L. *A Concise Guide to Management Development*, American Management Association, 1970.

DiCOSTANZO, F. and ANDRETTA, T. *Training and Development Journal*, The Supervisory Assessment Center in the Internal Revenue Service, September 1970.

FRITZ, R. J. Management Development Is Your Responsibility, *Personnel Journal*, **47**, 8, 1968.

LAIRD, D. They Manage Very Well at IRS, *Training*, **7**, 8, 1970.

ROBERTS, T. J. *Developing Effective Managers*, Institute of Personnel Management, 1967.

SCHEER, W. E. *Personnel Directors' Handbook*, Dartnell Corporation, Chicago and London, 1969.

TOFFLER, A. *Future Shock*, Bantam, New York, 1972.

ZALEZNIK, A. The Human Dilemmas of Leadership, *Harvard Business Review*, July–Aug. 1963.

5. The use of assessment centres in management development

William C. Byham

By simulating the problems and challenges that a candidate will face if promoted, before the promotion takes place, management is able to get a valid indication of both the potential for advancement and the specific training and development needs of the individual. In addition, participation as an assessor is an extremely powerful learning experience for the manager who observes and evaluates the candidates. More than 500 organizations on five continents have already applied the method, which has proved valid in both large and small organizations and in vastly different cultures.

One of the hottest ideas in the management development field is the assessment centre method of identifying and developing management potential. Why? Assessment centres are superior to any other technique in identifying management potential, and, at the same time, taking part in a centre is a powerful management training experience for both the participants and their higher management assessors. Not a place, but a method, which is available to all sizes of organizations, assessment centres are being used at all levels of management, from the first level of supervision to top corporate management. Organizations using centres can be found in every major industry and in government, in almost all the industrialized nations of the world.

In a typical centre, twelve first-level manager participants are nominated by their immediate supervisors as having potential for middle-level management positions, based on their current job performance. For two days, participants take part in exercises developed to expose behaviours deemed important in the particular organization. A participant may play a business game, complete an in-basket exercise, participate in two group discussions and in an individual exercise, and be interviewed. Six line managers, two levels above the participants act as assessors, observe the participants' behaviour and take notes on special observation forms. On completion of the exercises, participants go back to their jobs, and the assessors spend two more days comparing their observations and making a final evaluation of each participant. A summary report is developed on each participant, outlining his or her potential and defining development action appropriate for both the organization and the individual. (See appendix 5.1, for a description of typical assessment centre exercises.)

The level of candidate to be assessed usually dictates the duration of the centre. Centres for identifying potential in non-management candidates for foreman positions often last only one day while middle-management and higher-management centres can last as long as two-and-a-half days, including evenings.

The Use of Assessment Centres as an Aid in Identifying Management Potential

A doctor would never prescribe a drug for a patient without first diagnosing the illness, yet many management development courses and internal moves are prescribed every year with little or no diagnosis of the actual development needs of the manager in question. The assessment centre is a method of diagnosing, with great accuracy, individual training and development needs so that more precise prescriptions of training and development actions can be made. The result is more effective training and more effective expenditure. An assessment centre can aid in determining the following:

(a) which employees have potential for higher management positions;
(b) individual training and development needs of those assessed;
(c) appropriate prescriptions for correcting the training and development needs observed.

Accuracy of Assessment Centres

The greater accuracy of an assessment centre compared with management appraisals and tests has been proved in a number of well-controlled studies in organizations such as the International Business Machines Corporation, American Telephone and Telegraph, General Electric, Sears Roebuck, and the US Internal Revenue Service. However, assessment centres are not intended to replace these methods but, rather, to supplement them, thereby giving an organization a more rounded look at its employees.

Assessment centres are more accurate than supervisory judgement in predicting potential because the exercises used provide a means of observing the behaviour needed at higher levels before a person is put on the job. The selection of a sales manager is a good example of the superiority of the assessment centre method. A supervisor asked to nominate a salesman for supervision can judge his men only in terms of their sales performance. Usually the best salesman is nominated. However, because many other skills are needed in management, the man often fails and the company loses both a manager and an excellent salesman. If an assessment centre were used, the unique abilities needed for management would be determined, and their presence or absence observed through simulations before the individual is promoted.

Assessment centres are more accurate than personnel tests in predicting potential because they sample actual behaviour not what the applicant says he would do, or says he has done. For years, managers have observed that applicants can often tell a story better than they can perform. The assessment centre checks actual performance.

The accuracy of assessment centres results from a number of factors:

(a) Candidates are observed by line managers who have been specially trained to perform their tasks of observing behaviour and who are giving this function their full attention rather than trying to observe behaviour while subjected to other on-the-job pressures which often prevent them from observing accurately.

(b) The managers usually come from above the level of the candidates' immediate supervisors and have a broader perspective of the skills and abilities needed than does an immediate supervisor nominating people for his own level.

(c) Line-management assessors bring to the task a thorough knowledge of the whole company—its mores and its idiosyncracies. They know the skills needed now, and those that will be needed based on projected changes.

(d) Where possible, assessors who have no direct management contact with the candidates are used to make the evaluation, thus decreasing bias.

(e) The use of exercises exactly consistent for all candidates means that comparative judgements can be made on large numbers of candidates working for different bosses in vastly different circumstances.

(f) The format of the assessment centre method forces the assessors to spend time and effort in seeking information about the applicant before they make a decision. Even though research has constantly shown that the more a person 'fact finds', the more accurate the decision, most managers jump too quickly to a decision about people. They are 'turned on' or 'off' by some aspect of the individual, and jump to an immediate decision. They then only seek information that will reinforce the decision. Fact finding and decision making are separated in assessment centres.

(g) Group decisions about individuals, such as are obtained in an assessment centre, have constantly been shown to be more accurate than individual decisions. Perceptions can be compared, biases can be challenged.

(h) Managers are more likely to make effective use of assessment centre results than they are with psychological test results, because they understand the sources of the findings better. Assessment centres look valid and make sense to management. Most organizations using centres now systematically rotate the managers who will receive the reports, through assessor assignments, so that they are fully familiar with the entire process—a situation seldom encountered with test results.

Use of Assessment Centres as a Training Experience

Participation in an assessment centre has a positive training impact on both the participants (assessees) and the management observers.

Training Impact on Assessors

An assessor in an assessment centre benefits more than the participant in terms of direct training. Between assessor training and participation as an assessor in a centre, the assessor benefits in the following ways:

(a) improvement in interviewing skills;
(b) broadening of observation skills;
(c) increased appreciation of group dynamics and leadership styles;
(d) new insights into behaviour;
(e) strengthening of management skills through repeated working with in-basket case problems and other simulations;
(f) broadening of the repertoire of responses to problems;
(g) establishment of normative standards by which to evaluate performance;
(h) development of a more precise vocabulary with which to describe behaviour.

While many on-the-job uses can be made of these improved skills, perhaps the greatest impact is in the performance appraisal process. Extensive self-report data from assessors indicate a vast improvement in both the accuracy of evaluating behaviour and the success in changing subsequent behaviour. Organizations such as General Electric feel so strongly about the many benefits from assessor training that they have increased the ratio of assessors to participants in their programmes in order to expose more assessors to the experience.

Assessor training comes from a formal training programme prior to the centre, but principally, from application of the procedures as an assessor in an assessment centre. It is a unique opportunity for managers to focus on observing behaviour without the normal interruptions associated with business. After observing the behaviour, the assessors can compare their observations with those of other assessors, and sometimes have the opportunity to repeat the observation via video tape recording. The procedures learned in assessor training are put into practice and thus stamped into the assessor's memory.

The principal focus of assessor training is usually on interviewing, observing behaviour, and handling the in-basket exercise. All exercises in an assessment centre usually call for some combination of these skills. In addition, practice in all the exercises to be observed in the organization's assessment centre is usually provided. Any number of assessors can be trained at once, with assessor training for as many as twenty-five individuals not uncommon. Many organizations starting assessment centres initially train large numbers of managers as assessors, to establish a pool from which to draw them. This plan has a number of other benefits which include provision of a large number of management people with a quick orientation to the programme so that they can most effectively use the reports generated. It also allows the opportunity for a rough screening of the assessors so that the most skilled assessors can be used in the subsequent assessment centre programmes.

In most centres run by large corporations, assessors serve only once. The exception is American Telephone and Telegraph, where assessors work on six-month assignments in centres. In smaller companies, assessors must by necessity be used more often. In all situations, assessors must be trained, but, naturally, more training is committed to the person who will serve for twenty weeks than for one week. Training for new, short-service assessors usually takes from three to five days, depending on the complexity of the centre, the importance of the assessment decision and the importance which management gives to assessor training. (See Appendix 5.2, for an example of an assessment centre summary report.)

Training Impact on Participants

Participation in an assessment centre is a development experience. As can be quickly recognized, many assessment exercises such as the in-basket exercises, management games, and leaderless group discussions have been used for years as training exercises. Thus, to the extent that performance feedback is provided, participation in an assessment centre is a developmental experience. In most centres, above the lowest level of management, considerable performance feedback is provided during the assessment programme. A good example of the kinds of feedback provided is the assessment centre programme of the parts division of the Ford Motor Company. After many group exercises, participants take part in professionally led critiques of their performance or they watch their performance in the groups by means of video tape. After individually taking the in-basket exercise for assessment purposes, they meet in small groups to share their decisions and actions with each other, to evaluate their reasoning and to broaden their repertoire of responses. Even without special feedback opportunities built in, there is a great deal of evidence that most participants gain in self-insight from participating in assessment exercises, and that this insight is fairly accurate.

While self-insight gained from assessment centre exercises is important, it is secondary to the insights gained from receiving feedback of the assessor observations. Almost all assessment centres provide feedback to participants. The amount and detail of the feedback vary greatly but are largely related to organizational level. Career counselling and planning discussions are often combined with assessor feedback for higher-level participants. Many feedback interviews end in a written commitment to developmental action on the part of the participant and, sometimes, the organization.

Other Training Benefits

Passing through an assessment centre has a positive influence on morale and job expectations. Candidates see the centre as a chance to show their ability in fair and realistic situations. They also obtain a realistic idea of the requirements of the positions for which they are being considered. After doing an in-basket exercise, for example, some candidates from the ranks have withdrawn from consideration because of their new understanding of the volume of paperwork involved in a manager's job.

By designing the exercises carefully, it is possible to improve candidates' understanding and attitude subtly while they are being assessed. For example, one company which, as routine, assessed service technicians for management potential designed a group discussion exercise which concentrated the candidates' attention on a service facility's staffing problem. This exercise was structured to lead the candidates logically to the conclusion that management sometimes has no alternative but to schedule overtime on Saturdays.

Costs

Costs vary dramatically among centres, depending on the objectives of the centre, the number of participants and assessors, its duration and location, and, most of all, what is included in costs. Organizations have produced cost figures for their programmes ranging from $5 per head to $500. The figures, however, cannot be compared and may be vastly misleading because costs for different companies may include quite different elements. The cost of assessors' time (including training), participants' time, and administrators' time (including preparing for the centre and writing reports) are sometimes included, but frequently are not. Costs are always greatly dependent on the duration of the centre, and the amount of training given assessors.

Costs of meals and facilities can be calculated on the basis of the organization's experience in conducting training programmes. Programmes on company premises can cost as little as $50, while those at resorts can cost as much as $3000 for twelve participants, six observers, and one administrator.

Exercise costs depend on the length of the programme and the nature of the exercises. They generally run between $15 and $25 per participant. There is usually a once-only investment in reusable supplies, which is around $1000. These costs assume that all exercises are bought commerically. In fact, many organizations develop at least one unique exercise for their centre, and some organizations prefer to have all exercises unique.

The remaining cost considerations are initial costs which depend on the organization's needs for consulting help. Many organizations acquire information from articles, etc., such as this, then order exercises and start the assessment centre. Other organizations send their potential assessment centre administrators to workshops on assessor training. Many others use consultants to aid in planning, assessor training, administration of several pilot programmes, the initial writing of assessment centre reports, and the planning of feedback interviews. Consultants can make their greatest contribution in planning a centre and in assessor training.

The out-of-pocket costs of the assessment centre are not usually the determining factors as to whether, or not, the organization will use a centre. The major consideration holding back companies is the large amount of management time that must be devoted to the process. At the minimum, a number of managers have to be freed for one week of assessor training and one week of assessment activity. Often, a second or even third week of assessor time is needed over a period of a year. Obviously, this is a large management commitment and cannot be taken lightly.

If the only result of the assessment centre were the final assessment report, perhaps this large commitment of management time could not be totally justified in many situations. But this is not so. The major benefit of the management training derived from the participation of managers in assessor training and in being an assessor in a centre is thought by most organizations to be, alone, worth the cost. Thus, a certain amount of the cost of assessment centres and, certainly, of the assessors' time should be allocated to a management development budget.

Use of Assessment Centres by Small Organizations

The assessment centre method may not be appropriate for many companies, even where the cost of operation is manageable. Particularly at higher-level positions, most companies do not have enough candidates to warrant the operation of an assessment centre. For these companies, a possibility may be participation in multicompany centres where a number of companies send one or two individuals to a centre operated by a consultant, a university, or another company.

Such centres are offered in the US with good results. Some centres use psychologists and other professionals as assessors, while others rely on managers from the participants' organizations. The latter seems preferable because it trains the managers, orients them to the proceedings, and helps them understand the use of the assessment centre report.

The Assessment Technique for Individual Assessment

While the assessment centre technique is usually thought of as appropriate only for groups of people, the exercise and interviewing techniques developed for centres are increasingly being offered on an individual basis as a supplement to multiple interviews. In the past, companies typically collected applicant information from application forms, reference checks, and interviews—with the latter being by far the most important source. An applicant might have been interviewed by five or more men during the selection process. The problem was that the applicant did not receive five different interviews. He repeated the same interview five times. Interviewers tended to ask the same questions and make their judgements on the same restricted fund of information.

Accuracy of selection can be dramatically improved by restructuring the interview situation and using assessment exercises. A schedule for selecting a salesman is given overleaf.

Day 1

10.00–12.00. Interview by executive 1 (could be sales manager) on product knowledge, sales experience, and sales skill. (Also a chance to sell the company.)

12.00–1.30. Lunch with selected company management.
1.00–2.30. Fact-finding/decision-making exercise given by executive 2.

2.30–4.30. Interview concerning applicant's motivation and need for achievement. Interviewed by executive 3 (could be general manager). (Interviewer assumes that applicant has all technical qualifications.) Homework assignment:

(a) analyse a case and prepare a ten-minute presentation of recommendations;
(b) complete an in-basket exercise.

Day 2

9.00–10.00. Applicant gives his presentation of case recommendations and defends decisions. Executive 4 observes (also executive 1, 2, and 3, if available).

9.00–10.00. Executive 5 goes through the in-basket and prepares to conduct a follow-up interview.

10.00–11.00. In-basket interview conducted by executive 5.

11.00–12.00. Applicant can go home. If he seems to be a good prospect, he can be sent out for a tour and lunch while the interviewers meet.

11.00–12.00. Executive 1, 2, 3, 4, and 5 meet to compare observations and reach a decision.

Depending on local requirements, the steps can be shortened or rearranged over different time periods. The number of executives needed can be cut by having some executives responsible for more than one portion of the selection procedure.

With the exception of the first interview on the first day, the various exercises can be accomplished by people not directly concerned with sales, e.g., the general manager, production manager, or personnel manager.

Steps in Starting an Assessment Centre

Determining objectives for a non-supervisory or non-managerial assessment centre is usually fairly easy. The objective is to determine whether or not the person will be successful in the job for which he is being considered, i.e., the scientist, for a scientific position, etc. Determining objectives for a super-visory–managerial centre is somewhat more difficult. The objective or objectives might be one, or all, of the following:

(a) assessment of supervisory or management potential for selection purpose (finding the best man or men from nominees);

(b) assessment of strengths and weaknesses to aid in developing individualized training and development programmes;

(c) developing self-insight for participants into their strengths and weaknesses.

Any, or all, of these objectives can be met by the same centre but there are definite trade-offs. The second option requires more assessment time, more exercises, more highly trained assessors, and more dimensions. The third option requires even more time during the centre, and special administrator and assessor skills in handling the training aspects of the programme.

Determining Job or Job Level For Which Assessment Is To Be Used

The assessment centre technique has been of proven value in determining management potential for all levels of management, from supervisor to president, and also for specialized positions such as salesman, personnel interviewer, personnel manager, executive secretary, etc. In reality, the technique can be used to evaluate potential or training needs for any position where behavioural dimensions can be identified, e.g., interpersonal interaction, interpretation and processing of data, etc. There are many characteristics which can be evaluated in a less expensive way and, thus, the method is usually used to identify those characteristics which are difficult or impossible to get at with any other method.

Assessment centres are best applied in situations where performance data about a person's future performance is lacking. If a person is being promoted to a grander version of his current job, the insights from an assessment centre are less valuable than if the job is different, i.e., requires performance dimensions that cannot be adequately evaluated in the current job. The more different the job, e.g., salesman to sales manager, supervisor to middle manager, the more the need for an assessment of how the individual will perform in his future job. The greater the management component of the job, the more accurate the assessment centre will be, if its objective is to identify management potential. Points to remember in determining the appropriate job level are:

(a) availability of enough participants at the level, to make the centre economic;

(b) availability of assessors; at least one or, preferably, two levels above the participants;

(c) possible future need to evaluate the assessors in the assessment centre by the assessment centre method. Once a person has been trained as an assessor, the accuracy of putting him through an assessment centre programme is questionable, and thus, long-term use of the assessment centre method must be considered in initial planning;

(d) status problems. Experience has indicated that there is no difficulty in mixing participants of different sex, race, age, or experience in the assessment centre, but potential problems do arise when participants with different organizational status are mixed. Organizational status leads to

71

potential differential treatment of some individuals in group exercises, allowing them to assume leadership because of status rather than performance.

Multiple use of the assessment centre technique within a management hierarchy is becoming increasingly popular. A number of companies are using the method to identify candidates for first-level supervision from internal and external sources, and later, are using another variation of the technique to determine middle- and higher-management potential.

Most companies starting an assessment centre initially plan only one application. Multiple applications come after the pilot project proves its worth. The site of the first centre should be the area of greatest need for additional information—the area where current methods of making selection decisions or development plans are least effective. The decision about the appropriate job or job level at which the assessment centre technique should be used is mostly a function of the specific organizational needs.

For many organizations, there is no alternative but to assess for a level of management rather than for a specific job. These organizations do not have a sufficient number of people in any particular job to warrant an assessment centre programme. In addition, there are other advantages in using a job level as an objective for the assessment centre:

(a) interdepartment and divisional transfer is facilitated as participants are exposed to management representatives from various departments and divisions acting as assessors. Assessment centre findings become recognized as an indication of management potential in general, rather than potential for a specific job;

(b) even for large companies, great efficiencies can be obtained by having centres every week or every two or three weeks. Scheduling, staffing, and organization are easier if a common centre can be regularly scheduled, rather than running several centres of different types;

(c) assessors can be brought in from different parts of organizations. It is thus easier to obtain assessors who have no personal knowledge of participants.

It is possible to run an assessment centre for several different jobs with different dimensions at the same time, so long as the organizational background and educational levels of the applicants are fairly constant. Take the situation where fifteen dimensions are identified for position A, fifteen dimensions for position B, and that ten of the identified dimensions for the two positions are the same. It is possible to run an assessment centre assessing for twenty dimensions. While all twenty dimensions are observed and evaluated by assessors, candidates for position A are only evaluated on the appropriate fifteen dimensions; and candidates for position B are only evaluated on the appropriate fifteen dimensions.

One of the best ways to determine whether a single assessment centre covering a number of jobs, or multiple assessment centres, each aimed at a particular job, are needed is to go through the process of determining dimensions independently for each of the jobs. After the dimensions are identified, the overlap in dimensions can be observed and the decision based on the findings.

Determining Who will be Assessed and for What

Often, when a crucial or difficult promotional decision can be isolated, such as 'the problem of obtaining good merchandizing managers in a store', the proper assessee seems obvious—and in most cases they are. Salesmen are obvious candidates for sales-manager positions. Yet there are three additional factors to consider:

(a) How early should potential be identified so that training can be given to shore up the weak spots of even the best candidates? From a developmental viewpoint, it can be strongly argued that it is wise to identify potential for positions far enough in advance for the organization to have time to do something about strengthening the weaknesses, once they are identified. This would argue for dropping down further in the organization than the immediate subordinate level.

Another way of looking at this is to consider, when we are assessing an individual at x level, for what level he should be assessed $x + 1$, $x + 2$, $x + 3$, etc. Some companies with a strong promotion-from-within policy, such as AT and T, have elected to look at candidates for first-level management positions not only in terms of their suitability for that level but with heavy emphasis on possible promotion above that level. Other organizations believe that, once they have a person in the management ranks, they can assess their abilities through ordinary appraisal procedures, and are only concerned with first-level potential. There is no right answer. There are problems and benefits associated with both decisions.

(b) Are all possible candidates being considered? Are there staff from other departments who might be potential candidates and would bring in some unique information and skills? The assessment centre is an ideal way to discover such latent potential and many organizations have been pleasantly surprised.

(c) If development insights are a goal, should current incumbents be considered as participants? Many organizations have included incumbent employees in order to assess them relative to certain dimensions which are hard to guage by other methods. Sales managers have been assessed for sales-management jobs, etc. More often, such insights come as extras while managers are being considered for higher jobs, but not in all cases. It is increasingly popular to put an entire level of management through centres over a period of time.

Determining Dimensions to be Assessed

The entire assessment centre process depends on the accurate determination of the behavioural dimensions of the job or job level for which the participants will be assessed. It is absolutely essential that the identification be accurate and comprehensive.

A dimension is a distinct, measurable, behavioural portion of individual behaviour and is associated with success or failure on a job or at a job level. Successful managers are successful because they are high on certain job dimensions. Unsuccessful managers are unsuccessful because they are low on certain dimensions. These dimensions can be thought of as personal characteristics of those successful or unsuccessful on the job, e.g., leadership, sensitivity, etc.

The task of identifying dimensions important to success or failure is one of defining the areas in which a person should be evaluated. It is not defining a profile of a perfect candidate. The dimensions identified are almost always interrelated and interdependent. Thus, it is possible for two successful individuals to have quite different constellations of strengths and weaknesses in the dimensions. The purpose of identifying dimensions is to identify those areas about which the assessment process should be concerned. It is up to the assessors, when they meet to compare observations on the participants in the latter stages of an assessment centre programme to make judgements about the relative importance of the evaluations of the dimensions in relation to the particular job or job level under consideration. In other words, no one would expect an individual to be high on all the dimensions developed for a job or job level. It is the combination of dimensions that is important.

Steps in Obtaining Dimensions

There are a number of ways in which the behavioural dimensions of a position or job can be identified. A step by step process will be given, with variations discussed.

Identify Job or Job Level to be Assessed (see above)

If potential for several jobs is to be assessed, e.g., various positions at a level of management, the dimensions for each job should be identified independently.

Conduct a Job Analysis of the Position

This should include:

(a) a review of current organizational information on the job (job description, personnel-department job analyses or man specifications);
(b) a review of published research on dimensions of similar jobs;
(c) an interview with current incumbents to determine 'how they spend their time', 'most difficult decisions', etc. For some positions, it is suggested that the person developing the dimensions gain experience in doing the job itself, e.g., by going on calls with an insurance salesman or going with a district manager as he visits stores in his district. The purpose of the personal contacts with the incumbents is to identify critical incidents

74

of behaviour which are associated with the job, and particularly associated with success or failure on the job. It also provides a 'feel' for the level of difficulty of material and problems handled;

(d) an interview with executives at various levels above the level of the job to be assessed to determine critical incidents of job success or failure. Questions such as, 'Think about a person who was unsuccessful in this job and tell me what he did that made him unsuccessful', should be asked. Executives should also be asked how they see the job changing in the future so that the dimensions finally developed are appropriate both for the job as it is currently defined, and for the future.

An efficient method of interviewing executives is to hold brainstorming meetings to develop critical incidents. In this way, the executives stimulate each other's thinking, and acquire some idea as to how frequent the various incidents are. Group meetings are also a good time to check out the critical incidents identified in individual interviews with the incumbents.

Define the Dimensions

The consultant or person charged with obtaining the dimensions studies, the critical incidents, and the other information obtained above must cast them into dimensions along with appropriate definitions. He needs to identify the basic dimensions behind, or causing, each incident. It is very useful to use tested definitions as an aid and guide, e.g., those available from Development Dimensions, which are the results of considerable research, and have proved themselves understandable to assessors. Often, the definitions in the Development Dimensions catalogue need to be expanded with illustrative examples pertinent to the particular organization, in order to increase the clarity of the dimensions. When needed, new dimensions and definitions should be carefully framed and should follow the same general style.

The number of dimensions needed is an important consideration. Two rules of thumb generally apply:

(a) the higher the assessed job is in an organization the more dimensions are needed (jobs are more complex, therefore, it takes more dimensions to describe them);

(b) increased emphasis on identification of training needs more dimensions. (Centres for making go–no–go decisions, such as salesmen selection, can have relatively few dimensions—the key areas of success or failure. As the need to identify training needs increases, the need for a more precise diagnosis increases. It is no longer satisfactory to say a person is not a leader. The things he does, and does not do, in a group situation must be defined so that a more precise prescription of learning and development recommendations can be given.)

A major error of companies starting assessment centres is to have too many dimensions. This:

(a) decreases the precision with which all the dimensions can be assessed;
(b) substantially increases the work of assessors;
(c) lengthens the time for assessor discussion.

Basically, an organization should have all the dimensions that are truly needed in the job, but no 'extras' which would be just 'nice to know'.

Develop a Questionnaire

This should further determine the importance of the dimensions and the clarity of the definitions. The questionnaire should also allow the opportunity to determine which dimensions can be adequately assessed in the candidate's current job. This knowledge is a great aid in selecting exercises, as more stress can be put on those dimensions which are important, but difficult to assess, in the current job—as opposed to those dimensions that are important but assessable in the current job. The questionnaire should be distributed to appropriate levels of management concerned with the job or job level.

Refine Dimensions

Dimensions can be further refined during the assessor training and initial assessment centres.

Selecting Exercises

Three things must be known prior to exercise selection:

(a) objectives of the centre;
(b) dimensions to be assessed;
(c) basic abilities of applicants (reading level, business sophistication);
(d) time constraints.

Figure 5.1 is a guide to choosing exercises which will bring out the dimensions sought. It indicates which of the common dimensions are observable from each type of assessment exercise. Many other dimensions of possible interest to organizations may also be observable.*

Training Assessors

Assessor training is extremely important. Minimum training for a typical centre would include:

(a) joining in as a participant in all exercises in the assessment centre;
(b) practice in observing, recording behaviour, and writing reports on at least one group exercise;
(c) practice in pre-planning and conducting a background interview;
(d) discussion of various methods of handling each item of the in-basket;
(e) familiarization with the procedure for reaching final assessment decisions.

---

* A catalogue of exercises appropriate for various levels of assessees, which offers a choice of exercises in each category, is available from Development Dimensions Inc., 767 Colony Circle, Pittsburgh, Pa. 15243, USA. (Exercises are available in many languages and adapted for various countries.)

Categories of exercises →	1 Interview	2 Management game	3 In-basket and interview	4 Leaderless group discussion (assigned)	5 Leaderless group discussion (non-assigned)	6 Fact finding and decision making	7 Analysis/presentation (If group discussion, see also column 5)	8 Interview simulation	9 Writing exercise
Dimensions									
1. Impact	(✓)	✓	(✓)	✓	✓	✓	✓	✓	
2. Energy	(✓)	✓	(✓)	✓	✓	✓	✓	✓	
3. Oral communication skill	✓	✓	✓	✓	✓	✓	✓	✓	(✓)
4. Oral presentation skill				(✓)			✓	(✓)	
5. Written communication skill	✓		(✓)					(✓)	(✓)
6. Creativity	✓		✓	✓					✓
7. Range of interests	(✓)								✓
8. Stress tolerance		✓		✓	✓	(✓)	✓		
9. Motivation	(✓)								
10. Work standards	(✓)								✓
11. Career ambition	(✓)								
12. Leadership	✓	(✓)		(✓)	(✓)				
13. Salesmanship				(✓)	✓	✓	(✓)	(✓)	
14. Sensitivity	✓	✓	(✓)	✓	✓	✓	✓	(✓)	
15. Listening skill		✓		✓	✓	(✓)		✓	
16. Flexibility		✓		(✓)	✓	(✓)	✓	(✓)	
17. Tenacity	✓	✓		✓	✓	(✓)	✓	✓	
18. Risk taking	✓	(✓)	✓		✓				
19. Initiative	✓	✓	✓	✓	✓				
20. Independence	✓	✓		✓	✓	✓			
21. Planning and organization	✓	✓	(✓)				✓	✓	✓
22. Management control	✓		(✓)						
23. Use of delegation	✓		(✓)						
24. Problem analysis	✓	✓	✓	✓	(✓)	(✓)	✓	✓	✓
25. Judgement	✓	✓	(✓)	✓	(✓)	(✓)	✓		✓
26. Decisiveness		✓	(✓)		(✓)	(✓)			

Note: The ticks indicate those categories of exercises which usually bring out a particular dimension. Parentheses indicate that an exercise is particularly good at bringing out the dimension.

Fig. 5.1. Guide for selection of exercises. (Reproduced with permission of Development Dimensions, 767 Colony Circle, Pittsburgh, Pennsylvania. © 1973.)

Conducting Centres

Centres can be run in an organization's own facilities or a conveniently located hotel or other location. They can be from one to three days in length.

Conclusion

There are many potential problems with the assessment centre technique. They include the fact that centres not only identify those who have potential for advancement but also those who do not. Morale and turnover problems can result if those who do poorly are not handled delicately. The image of the centre in the eyes of both the potential employees and their supervisors is important, and potentially a trouble spot—particularly in the centre's relationship to current job performance. The nature, speed, and quality of the feedback of results is a perennial problem, and delay in feedback is the most common error made in starting a programme. Yet hundreds of organizations have proved that these potential problems can be overcome. The secret is complete planning of the programme before its commencement. If proper planning is undertaken, no problems should develop.

While the effectiveness of an assessment centre has not been proved beyond doubt, all the research—both published and unpublished—seems to indicate that the method has more validity than other existing methods. It is in this comparison that the strength of an assessment centre lies. Granted that it is not perfect, it seems that use of an assessment centre for identifying management potential is a sounder and fairer method than those traditionally used by management.

Appendix 5.1 Common Assessment Centre Exercises

Background Interview

A participant completes a background interview form which covers education, work history, major accomplishments, plans for the future, values and attitudes. After considerable training, and following detailed directions in an 'interview guide', the assessor uses the information from the background information form to prepare a patterned interview designed to bring out the desired predetermined dimensions. After the interview, the assessor completes a specially designed evaluation form.

B and B Electronics Game

The B and B Electronics Company buys electrical components and assembles them into simple appliances for resale. In groups of four, participants must make decisions concerning allocation of resources, purchase of capital equipment, inventory control, manufacturing, scheduling, and marketing. In three twenty-minute periods, and using real electrical components, the group attempts to maximize profits through investment and good management.

Section Managers' In-Basket

Administrative, organizational, leadership, and communication problems are but a few of the challenges that await the potential middle manager who takes this exercise. Newly appointed to the section-manager position, the participant is in his office on Saturday with no opportunity to make phone calls or to seek other advice. He must go through his predecessor's in-basket, solving problems, answering questions, delegating, planning, and making decisions just as he might do if he were promoted to the position.

Management Problems

Four short cases calling for various forms of management judgement are presented to teams of participants. In one hour, the team—acting as consultants—must resolve the problems and submit written recommendations of appropriate actions. Observations of dimensions such as problem analysis, judgement, sensitivity towards others, decisiveness, and creativity can be made from a participant's handling of the discussion. Observations of dimensions such as leadership, salesmanship, reaction to time stress, flexibility of thinking, etc., can be obtained from observing his role in the group.

Compensation Committee Assigned Role Group Discussion

The compensation committee of a hypothetical organization is meeting to allocate $8000 in discretionary salary increases among six managerial employees. Each member of the committee (participants) is instructed to 'do the best he can for one of the employees'. Information about his candidate is provided to help him in his task. The exercise provides opportunity to bargain and so some quick thinking.

Financial Analysis

The ability to sift through data, come to a conclusion, then present a logical argument to back up the conclusion, can be observed in this exercise. The participants are given financial data on the C. F. Pretzel Company and are asked to recommend appropriate courses of action for the company. At least two hours' preparation time is allowed. The participant then makes a seven-minute standing oral presentation of his position; this is followed by the opportunity to meet several other participants, to come up with the best solution to the problem.

Research Budget Individual Fact-Finding and Decision-Making Exercise

The participant is told that he has just taken over as a division manager, who is faced with a request to continue a research project turned down by his predecessor. The participant is given fifteen minutes to ask any questions he can think of relative to the facts in the case. Following the questioning period, he must present his decision orally, with supportive reasoning, and defend it under challenge.

Appraisal Interview Simulation

The participant assumes the role of a supervisor recently assigned to a new position. He is scheduled to conduct an appraisal interview the next day and must do so entirely on the basis of the personnel file of the subordinate. The task of the participant is to reinforce the 'employee's' strengths while helping him to see, and overcome, his weaknesses.

Appendix 5.2   Example of Assessment Centre Summary Report

Smith's overall performance in the Management Development Centre (MDC) was average or below average on most exercises. He showed strengths in energy and initiative.

Observers saw him as having some potential for a middle-manager position but as requiring a great deal of development. The odds of his actually being a middle manager were seen as slim.

In the background interview, Smith was extremely open in discussing his problems and hopes in detail. He came across as a loyal, hard-working, highly motivated person who had a strong desire to do a good job, but he was weak in creativity, initiative, independence, and leadership skills. He appeared to be tenacious and have a high stress tolerance but to be weak in problem analysis. He struck the assessor as being overwhelmed by his job, where his efforts are not bearing the fruit he would like. He may well have feared for his job, given the division's performance. Delegation seemed weak, as was subordinate development. He felt the only way to train was to teach by example. Sensing poor morale, he did not know how to improve it.

Smith participated energetically in the exercises and appeared to be intent on doing well. In the group discussion exercises, he showed initiative in starting the group on its task and providing initial organization. His oral communications were somewhat hampered by his use of slang, but, in general, he spoke in a clear, articulate, fluent manner. His voice was low in volume. On the negative side, he tended to be repetitive in speech and have a great need to summarize and then resummarize. He did not seem over stressed by MDC.

Unfortunately, Smith's impact on exercise groups was fleeting. Others quickly took control, with usually only a minor fight from Smith. Peer and self-ratings indicate he was never recognized as the group leader. His overall contribution was usually in the middle. His principal difficulty in group exercises came from his inability to convince the group. Rather than pursue an argument until he won, he would give in too quickly.

Smith's financial analysis presentation was excellent, but he had several flaws in his analysis. His presentation in the group discussion was weak, and he was unable to convince the group. He was an effective secretary for the group.

Questioning in the 'research budget' fact-finding exercise was not well organized, but effective. He appeared to find decision making difficult, but once the decision was made, he stuck to his idea. Slightly nervous, he was not stressed by the resource person.

Writing seemed to be a weak area. Smith's financial presentation was hard to read and disorganized. Similar observations were made about his creative writing assignment, and his in-basket.

In the in-basket exercise, Smith did poorly, failing to organize material or set priorities. He did not handle all the material and, on several occasions, displayed poor judgement.

Strengths

Work Standards. Tried hard in every exercise; worked very hard on job; did not want to settle, personally, for less than the best. Was disappointed by own performance, as indicated by his self-evaluation.

Intelligence. Fast reader, caught on fast.

Corporate Thinking. A company man, very loyal.

Integrity. Will not compromise convictions, e.g., copy-machine discussion.

Energy. Active in all exercises.

Stress Tolerance. Except for management game, showed little stress.

Interest in Self-Development. Welcomed help, worked his way through college, willing to move. (While interest seemed very high, there was some doubt about strength of drive for self-development.)

Level of Aspiration. Seemed to be unhappy without winning or doing the best possible.

Weaknesses

Creativity. Not seen in approach to current job or in exercises—nothing shown in creative writing exercise.

Leadership. After an initial positive impact, he could not influence group.

Independence. In present job, seems to do what his boss wants; same attitude expressed in in-basket where he tended to delegate up and to follow 'what boss wants'.

Salesmanship. Except for the formal financial presentation, showed little salesmanship; in the salaries exercise, he tried for too much money, didn't convince peers; in group situations, could not sell under opposition.

Sensitivity. Assessors described him variously as sensitive, very sensitive, too sensitive, and insensitive during the centre. There was a general feeling that he might be soft, e.g., his delay in firing one of his subordinates, whom he admitted should have been fired sooner. He seemed less sensitive to people, problems in in-basket, and cases than to the needs of individuals in discussion groups, where, on several occasions, he showed good sensitivity and understanding.

Tenacity. When ego was involved, or he felt there was an ethical problem, Smith could be very tenacious, e.g., fighting for doing right by customer regarding the photocopier. On the other hand, he did not follow up on points in group discussions.

Management Style. Seemed to tell a story better than he practised, or than could be determined from the interview. Expressed concern for 'subordinate training', but assessor wondered how effective he was, tended to delegate up—lets people overlead him. Realized need to be more 'tough-minded'.

Planning and Organization. Attempted to organize most groups but did not attempt to maintain organization. In-basket organization of work and priorities poor.

Use of Delegation. Not effective on job, average in in-basket. He reported he did a lot of work that should be done by subordinates.

Problem Analysis. Did not understand 'conglomerate'; did not see many of the major problems in in-basket; background interview indicated a lack of problem definition in job; did not see all facets of Pretzel Company problem.

Financial Analytical Ability. Below average on financial problems, e.g., missed opportunity to change product mix.

Range of Interest. Seemed to be restricted to marketing.

Flexibility. Seemed to approach every case and every situation in the same way (was flexible in accepting ideas of others).

Temper. When he did not get his way in discussion, he became obstructive to leader.

Mixed Findings

Impact. Good first impression—after that, would not stand out in a crowd.

Oral Communication Skill. Fluent, articulate, talked too much, did not sell.

Oral Presentation Skill. Formal presentations good, e.g., financial presentation; informal poor, e.g., group discussion situations. Seemed to depend on preparation.

Written Communication Skill. English ability adequate, very hard to read writing.

Management Control. Interview indicated some weaknesses in this area; showed that Smith would have a tendency to overcontrol too far down, but in in-basket he did an above-average job of controlling, using due dates, etc.

Judgement. Showed good judgement in marketing and related problems; weak in judgement in other areas.

While Smith did poorly in many areas, it was felt that he was definitely trainable. He was seen as needing a lot of support and guidance and a

82

supportive, understanding, fatherly supervisor, and one that would force him to make decisions. It was thought that he would develop best in a highly-structured job with slowly increasing planning and organizing responsibility as his skills developed. An assignment at Homewood, as a product manager, might be good.

Some priority development challenges:

(a) management through others;
(b) problem analysis;
(c) organization;
(d) administrative skills.

Smith should be easy to communicate with, regarding his assessment. He was extremely open and was accurate in his self-appraisals. A potential difficulty could be his insecurity, causing him to view 'help' as a threat.

Suggested Reading

BRAY, D. W. and GRANT, D. L. The Assessment Center in the Measurement of Potential for Business Management, *Psychological Monographs*, 1966.

BRAY, D. W. Increased Opportunities for Women Through Management Assessment Centers, *Personnel*, Sept.–Oct., 1971, pp. 31–34.

BRAY, D. W. Formative Years in Business. Wiley Interscience, 1974.

BYHAM, W. C. The Assessment Center as an Aid in Management Development, *Training and Development Journal*, December 1971.

COHEN, B., MOSES, J., and BYHAM, W. C. *Validity of Assessment Centers: A Literature Review*, Development Dimensions, 767 Colony Circle, Pittsburgh, Pennsylvania, 1972; includes extensive bibliography.

KRAUT, A. I. A Hard Look at Management Assessment Centers and their Future. *Personnel Journal*, May 1972, pp. 317–326.

6. Management selection and recruitment

G. A. Randell

After discussing various ways by which organizations acquire and develop their managers, the chapter sets out the various policy implications for management selection. It then identifies three main selection strategies—the 'basic' the 'pragmatic', and the 'systematic'. The various parts of a management selection procedure are described and related to the three strategies. The chapter contains checklists and diagrams aimed at helping senior managers to design and develop the appropriate management selection procedure for their organization.

Every organization has to acquire its human resources somehow. Personnel selection is an on-going and continuous source of concern to all managers. When it comes to acquiring its managerial staff, organizations are faced with a serious policy problem concerning how they should go about obtaining the managers they need. In practice, personnel selection policies are rarely thought out and made explicit; even when they are, they are more likely to reflect a managerial philosophy rather than any deliberate planned approach to the acquisition of human resources. So organizations need a clearer idea of their strategy for acquiring the appropriate management resources. This strategy must take into account their existing state of development as an employer of managers, and their forecast needs.

In practice, the difference between acquiring people for managerial posts from inside or outside the organization need not be as different as it sometimes appears. Both activities attempt to predict managerial behaviour; both try to reduce the chance of managerial failure; both have to make use of the people that are available, or who apply; both present the organization with a forced-choice decision problem, either to choose from who is available or not to choose—and start the process over again. Consequently, there are similarities between the material in this chapter and that by Lawton on identifying executive potential. These similarities can be seen in even more detail when comparing the methods described by Lawton and those described in the Davies Report[1] on the system of selection to the British Civil Service.

The theme of this chapter is to stress that what an organization needs to do about its selection and recruitment problems is to go about it in a knowing, thorough, and repeatable way. So-called 'scientific selection' is a misnomer, the problem of predicting human behaviour is too complex for it to be explained completely—or understood why some managers are more successful than others—in terms of a 'general theory of managerial behaviour'. Certainly, some managers are more effective than others, so at least it is possible to attempt to reduce the chances of failure or even increase the chances of selecting the more successful. This can be achieved through various levels of effort and expenditure. This chapter identifies three levels of attack on this problem of selecting managers; they will be called the 'basic', the 'pragmatic', and the 'systematic'. Their similarities and differences will emerge as we proceed with the chapter.

Some senior managers do develop their own 'theories' about what it takes to be successful in their organization. For example, membership of a certain social class or educational group may be believed to be associated with managerial ability. An international oil company has identified a trait which they call the 'helicopter quality' and relate to capacity for senior management posts. They define this quality as *the ability to look at one's problems from a higher vantage point and shape one's work accordingly on the basis of a personal vision. The urge and ability to place facts and problems within a broader context, by immediately detecting relevant relationships with systems of wider scope'.*

Other organizations believe that the behaviour of people in 'trial' situations is the best predictor of effective managerial behaviour, and look for the evidence of high intellectual attainment, or outstanding results in other organizations, as predictors of senior management performance.

It is not necessary to have any theory at all, about management behaviour, before setting up a management selection procedure. By eschewing theory, all the problems and arguments concerning the nature of 'leadership' or 'management potential' can be set aside. Whether or not they are traits; or behaviour in specific situations; inherited or acquired; or whether or not they grow or can be trained for, can all be treated as interesting fringe issues. For these are scientific questions which beg the need to explain a particular phenomenon. From an organization's point of view, what is required is some *technological* system that enables the organization to achieve what it is that it wants to achieve; the whys and wherefores are more of concern to academics than senior managers.

Consequently, the approach taken in this chapter is to treat management selection as a predictive problem and to set out some ideas and procedures which will be helpful to managers setting up their own managerial resource acquisition system. It will not attempt to embroil the reader in some of the controversial issues, of which there are many, surrounding the whole topic of the nature and identification of management potential. Other chapters in this book touch sufficiently on these problems.

Selection Policies

Management selection is essentially a problem of prediction. Certain work of a managerial kind has to be done and this has to be performed by people. The need for such work can be foreseen, and plans can be made in advance, so that someone is ready to do it when the time comes. Alternatively, a need may present itself suddenly to the organization, and consequently, somebody must be obtained as quickly as possible to do the work that has to be done. This is the first selection-policy issue facing an organization. It can be stated as—how far ahead should preparations be made for the need to recruit managers?

The various approaches to this problem can be identified and grouped under four headings. The first approach can be called the *jungle method*. An organization usually waits to see what managerial work has to be done, and who is around and wanting to do it. Then, either the next person in line or the person who pushes himself forward, and perhaps shifts others out of his way, is appointed to the vacant managerial position. After this, the managers below may move up one, and the process begins again. This approach usually leads to a great deal of jockeying for position and in-fighting among the staff. It is undoubtedly the cheapest way to go about solving a managerial acquisition problem. The principles begins its working are those of 'natural selection', 'survival of the fittest', 'seniority', and 'promotion to a level of incompetence'. The policy of the organization is to allow these principles to apply, and wait to see who emerges as the strongest claimant for the vacant managerial position. Although it is the cheapest method, it is probably the most costly in terms of psychological health, human well-being, and wasted effort.

The next approach can be called the *agricultural method*. Here, the organization acquires high-quality 'seed' materials with potential for growth, 'plants' them in a supportive environment, 'nurtures' them over a period of time, and watches the managers 'grow'. This approach obviously takes time, and, as in all agricultural methods, some 'plants' fall by the wayside, but others grow strong, and even multiply. This approach works through the principles of producing a surplus, letting things take their time and, more specifically, through planned training and career development. There are often various safety devices in the background, e.g., personal counselling. Often associated with this method is a reward structure providing just adequate financial rewards for the staff who are being so carefully nurtured, and who look forward to the fruits of their own steady growth being given to them at some time in the future.

The next approach can be called the *manufacturing method*. Here, the organization buys in partly experienced managers, tries them out on a range of its own problems, and attempts to adapt what it has acquired to its own needs. The principles behind this approach are those of 'sequential selection', 'personnel auditing', and applying special courses and trial postings to the managers being 'manufactured' by this method. Often associated with this approach are reasonably powerful rewards, not only in terms of promised positions but in financial and perquisite terms.

The fourth approach can be called the *purchasing method*. This is where organizations buy their managers 'ready-made'. They reward them generously, but also are pretty quick to fire them if they turn out to be inadequate. The relevant technique here is 'head hunting' through the use of management selection consultants who specialize in extracting successful managers from other organizations. This purchasing approach can be very costly both in terms of cash and its effect on the morale of existing employees. However, it is a particularly useful approach for shaking up an organization which is getting sluggish or running into difficulties, or, because of previous managerial activities, has been denuded of all the managerial talent that it may have had.

The point now needs to be made, very strongly, that each of the above approaches could be right for an organization at its present stage of development and in the light of its current needs. It is obviously for the senior management of an organization to choose the most appropriate policy to meet its managerial acquisition needs. Clearly, there are advantages and disadvantages in each approach, and these must be weighed by the personnel policy makers—and the appropriate decision made.

Techniques for Management Selection

Once policy towards management development has been decided, the next decisions concern the use of various techniques which can be applied to the task of selecting managers. Three levels of effort are classified below.

The *basic*, as the name implies, involves the minimum effort likely to result in selection decisions being made which are better than those that would have been made by chance. This entails a certain amount of effort in understanding the job that needs to be done, and the kind of person who would be best suited for it. This is then followed by interviewing a range of applicants, and offering the job to that person who 'looks best'.

The *pragmatic* goes beyond this, mainly in detail, and attempts to collect more information about the organization, the job, and the applicants. It can make use of many techniques, on the assumption that the more information that can be applied to a selection decision, the more probable it is that a good decision will be made.

The *systematic* level may not use as much data as the other methods, but what it does use is known, through research, to be relevant to the selection decisions. Its essence is follow-up information, where the 'predictors' of managerial behaviour which are used have been checked against measures of that behaviour.

Again, a policy decision needs to be made by the senior management of the organization as to what level of effort will be applied to management selection.

The Start—Organization Specification

The start to management selection is the preparation, or at least the discussion, of an organization specification. The senior management involved should get together and decide what type of organization they are, and what they would like to be. As a result, it could be that they decide there is no need to appoint any managers other than themselves.

Such an analysis should at least help them to understand and agree what kind of organization they are in terms of their real area of business; their reward structure; their technology; their style of management; and their balance between production, sales—and just making money. Wherever possible, the outcomes of such an analysis should be set down on paper. Hopefully, this encourages some kind of agreement among the senior staff as to their aims. Selection at managerial levels is more often fitting people to organizations rather than to jobs. This aspect of management selection is a critical, and often ignored, one. It is often the role of an external consultant, with his knowledge and experience, to sum up the kind of organization that his client actually is, and then to carefully describe the nature of the organization to the job applicants, so that the individual knows what he is letting himself in for. This effort towards some kind of self-selection by job applicants is often a sign of maturity in a selection procedure.

Job Specification

Once some kind of organization specification has emerged, the next task is to produce a description of the actual managerial job that needs to be done, and the kind of person who should be doing it. This kind of job specification opens up the key issue—that of just what is meant by 'effective managerial behaviour'. It is as difficult to be precise about the content of managerial jobs as it is difficult to be precise about what it takes to be a good manager. More often than not, organizations do not make explicit exactly what they require from their managers. The requirement is often put in general terms, such as 'making a lot of money', 'reviving an ailing company', 'producing high morale', 'high output', 'superior service', and so forth. Exactly what is required in terms of personal attributes is not made explicit because it is difficult to do so. However, saying that a problem is exceedingly difficult is no excuse for not attempting to do anything about it. The cornerstone of any successful management selection procedure is the strength and quality of the information collected and assembled about the job and the people who should be doing it. The more precise and comprehensive the information, the more probable that the person selected will be successful at the job, or at least, not fail.

In theory, it should be possible to get a great deal of information about the kinds of behaviour associated with being an effective manager in a particular organization from an analysis of their staff appraisal forms. If the staff appraisal procedure is of the person-centred, data-based kind described by Randell,[2] it is probably generating useful information of relevance to a job specification. However, more often than not, such forms tell the reader more about the nature of the organization, and the style of management that it is fostering, than about the actual behaviour of the appraised managers. Consequently, it is often necessary to make a separate study of what it takes to be effective in a managerial position in a certain organization. The first line that could be followed is actually to study the successful managers and compare what they do with what is done by the less successful ones. A development of the critical incidents technique, such as that described by Campbell,[3] provides a useful approach to this task. A problem is to discriminate between the 'successful' and the 'less successful' managers, and Ghiselli and Dunnette[4] illustrate just how difficult this is. This is where a Management by Objectives scheme could be useful. This would at least reduce the dependence on subjective judgements made about managerial effectiveness by senior managers. A particularly useful source of information are exit interviews. If the managers leaving the organization are skilfully interviewed to reveal their difficulties and distastes about work in the organization, this provides some key information for the job specification.

When a larger sample of managers is available for study, an alternative technique is to use a statistical approach, and attempt to find the discriminating characteristics between the less successful and the more successful managers, in terms of identifiable and measurable psychological and biographical attributes. The argument would then follow that selection of managers with more of the desirable characteristics, and less of the un-desirable ones, would probably lead to more successful managerial behaviour in the organization. In practice, a blend of the critical incidents and statistical approaches is probably the most useful way to go about the task of trying to develop a specification for the kind of person who should be doing a managerial job.

Once the method of job analysis has been agreed, the first information that needs to be recorded is *exactly* what capacities are required to perform the work that has to be done. These can be listed under four headings: the essentials, the desirables, the disqualifiers, and the undesirables. (See Fig. 6.1.)

Then, the inclinations required in the man who is going to be appointed need to be known. These can be grouped under three headings, depending on whether they are sources of alienation, conflict, or motivation—as shown in Fig. 6.1. This approach follows from the view that it is a waste of time for an organization to appoint someone to a post who can apparently do the job, but who then discovers that his psychological needs are not being met by the work opportunities or rewards that the organization provides, and consequently, then leaves. This puts the organization back to where it started and increases its expense through the need to search again.

Job capacity and job inclination analysis can be combined, as a decision structure (Fig. 6.2), which can guide the preparer of a job specification

From a study of a job that has to be done, first write a brief description of the job and follow it by *capacity* and *inclination* statements about the person who should be doing it, under the following headings:

1. *JOB CAPACITY ANALYSIS*

(a) *Essentials*

These are usually very few, of the kind:
Minimum educational or professional attainments
Minimum previous experience
Minimum age, height, sight, and mobility
Minimum scores on a *valid* test

(b) *Desirables*

These usually dominate contemporary job specifications, and frequently indicate the wish to employ paragons of industrial virtue, with high 'intelligence', 'integrity', 'drive', and 'leadership', all of which are impossible to define precisely. They should be in terms of experience, attainments that are known to *aid* learning or performance of the job, etc.

(c) *Disqualifiers*

Experiences or attributes known to be directly related to failure on the job. Their presence or absence indicates a *certain* inability to do the work, or a quick resignation from it.

(d) *Undesirables*

Experience or attributes known to cause difficulty to people on the job, and lead to expressions of dissatisfaction by supervisors, and complaints by the incumbents. Can be too much of an 'essential', or not enough of a 'desirable'.

2. *JOB INCLINATION ANALYSIS*

(a) *Sources of Alienation*

These are usually areas of frustration which could have an immediate *blocking* effect on the inclination to work. They are often of a job context kind, such as pay, status, etc. and relate to an individual's current occupational needs.

(b) *Sources of Conflict*

These are usually aspects of the work that may emerge after a little time and could have a *braking* effect on the inclination to work. They often arise from lack of job opportunities, such as feelings of insecurity, poor training, and inadequate equipment.

(c) *Sources of Motivation*

These usually develop once a person gets deeper into his job and the organization, and can have a *boosting* effect on the inclination to work. They are often of a job content kind, such as recognition, power, responsibility, and even special bonuses, and are usually associated with an individual's long-term needs.

Fig. 6.1. Checklist of steps in preparing a job specification.

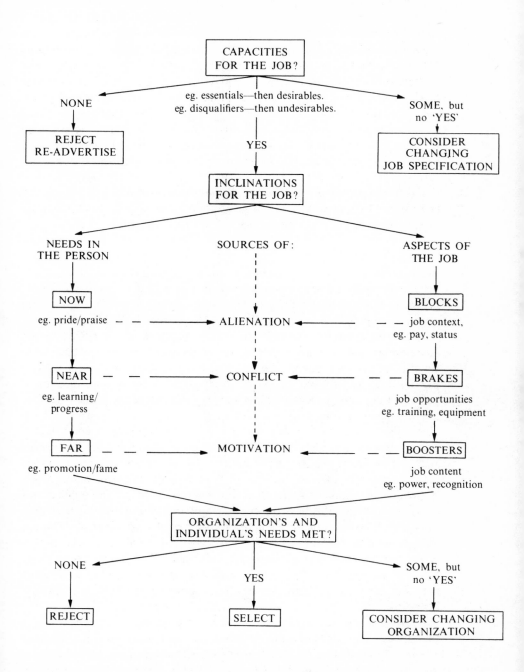

Fig. 6.2. Decision structure for personnel selection.

through the first stages of setting up a management selection procedure, and provide an outline for an interview record form.

The above remarks about the managerial job and the kind of person that should be doing it are far easier said than done. Many organizations assess the workload and expertise required, and then decide to employ consultants to assist them. Others shy at the expense, and seek an easier and cheaper approach. Such methods usually involve recruiting people with the highest level of educational and managerial attainments obtainable, who are then put to work on creating their own job content. This approach is based on the assumption that, as high-calibre people are very adaptable, they will respond to the demands of a situation, learn from their experiences, and so become effective at their tasks. As this approach does work on some occasions, this is taken as sufficient evidence that it will always work. However, to leave things to chance is risky; hence, the methods described here aim at reducing the effects of chance. How far to go beyond a 'basic' level in studying an organization or job is a difficult practical decision to take.

Getting Applicants

Once all the necessary information about the organization and the job has been assembled, the next task is to match it against data from, and about, people who are thought likely to be able to do the job—this requires the appropriate people to apply for the job. This can be achieved by advertising, both internally and externally; the use of agents who are skilled in job advertising; and perhaps, too, the use of specialist executive-search consultants or 'head hunters'. All these ways may have to be considered. Encouraging appropriate people to apply to work for an organization is part of a long-term, public-relations activity. Much depends on the organization's general standing in the world of work, and the kinds of publicity—both favourable and unfavourable—that it is currently enjoying. A good public-relations image considerably helps the recruiting of high-quality managerial staff; a poor image can seriously hamper it. Job advertising is a highly skilled activity, where a specialist can be of great help in a selection procedure. A great deal of money is spent on advertising job vacancies, and much of this expense could probably be better spent. Many rules of thumb exist concerning the content, layout, position, and appropriate media for advertisements for managerial jobs. Such guidelines have mainly been developed by experience, rather than systematic research, but at least they help selectors not to make the obvious mistakes in job advertising. This is where the job advertising specialist can be useful in helping to attract suitable applicants, at little or no extra cost.

In Britain, organizations are now able to recruit their managers through the government administered Professional and Executive Recruitment Service (PER). This is based on a new classification of occupations and a directory of occupational titles, CODOT.[5] This is similar to the International Labour Office classification and that used in the Office of Population Censuses and Surveys, in that it classifies an occupation by its work content and not

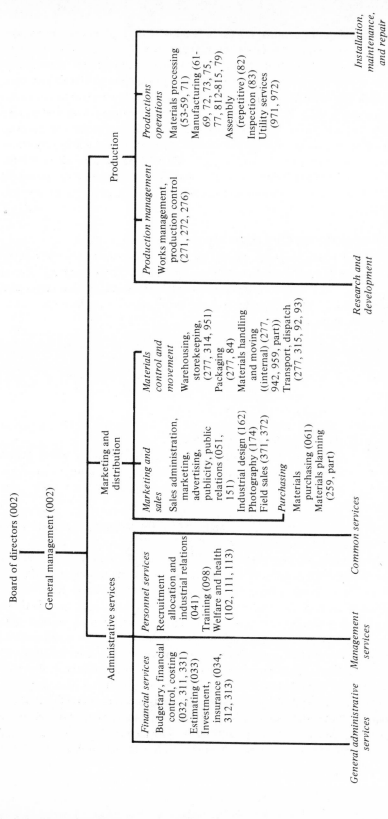

Fig. 6.3. CODOT (classification of occupations and directory of occupational titles) in relation to company organization (manufacturing). CODOT minor or unit group reference numbers are shown in parentheses. (Reproduced with acknowledgement to the Department of Employment.)

93

on the basis of qualifications, status, or level of skill. It gives each job a five-digit occupational number with provision for two-digit 'may' items to allow for more precise job content information. A diagrammatic representation of managerial jobs in manufacturing, and their appropriate CODOT numbers, is set out in Fig. 6.3. Once a job has been classified, it can be submitted to the computer-based PER register, and a match is attempted with the people currently available in the 'candidate bank'. It is then up to the employer to decide whom he wishes to call to the next stage of his selection procedure from the list provided to him by the PER office. The employer pays a fee for this service, no charge falling upon the applicant. The British Government hopes that this will become a financially self-supporting agency over the next few years.

Information Gathering From Applicants

Now comes the difficult issue of deciding on the structure and content of the actual data-gathering procedure that will be used. This can range from a single, simple, face to face interview, through interview boards, tests and questionnaires, to very elaborate data-gathering activities, spread over many days. The methods commonly found can be listed as follows:

(a) scrutiny of application forms, academic and other qualifications, references and confidential reports;
(b) interview; face to face, or boards of two or more interviewers;
(c) written tests. These can be intelligence, aptitude, or interest tests, or attempts to measure other personality traits;
(d) exercises and practical tests. These can be such things as the in-basket test and other problem-solving situations;
(e) groups tasks. This could either be in leaderless groups, or where group members have specific roles such as group leader or committee chairman, and are observed managing a group of other applicants under test situations.

These methods are further described in Lawton's chapter on identifying executive potential, and in Anstey *et al.*[6]

Other activities are sometimes used. These include handwriting analysis, body movement analysis, and special stress situations designed to display the responses of an individual to the strains of managerial work. Rubenowitz and Silberer[7] provide a useful review of the use of various selection methods across a range of 845 companies throughout Europe, and emphasize that there has yet to emerge any standard set of techniques for selecting managers.

The basic psychometric standards of reliability, validity, and utility apply to all these data-gathering methods. What is also common to them is that they all need highly skilled staff to administer and interpret the data that they yield. There is a great deal of controversy about the usefulness of all the above techniques. Often, the less reliable the data-gathering technique, the more pertinent the information is thought to be. The face to face interview is the prime example of this: it is strongly criticized for its lack of reliability but is widely used because of its utility. Similarly, the most psychometrically reliable of the data-gathering methods—the standardized aptitude test— often falls into disfavour because it is thought only to measure a very narrow range of human attributes which are likely to be relevant to a manager's job.

All the techniques grouped in (a) to (e) above may have their place in a selection procedure. Perhaps, no single method would be sufficient, but to use them all in conjunction is not necessary. In a basic selection procedure, probably only those techniques in groups (a) and (b) would be used. In a pragmatic procedure, the more data collected, the better the procedure is thought to work. Obviously, there are social and ethical constraints limiting the amount and kind of information that can, and should, be collected from job applicants. The prevailing culture and employment situation can strongly influence the kind of data regarded as socially acceptable for selection purposes. A data-gathering procedure lasting more than two days is not uncommon. The British Civil Service uses a two-day data-gathering procedure which has been investigated by an independent committee,[1] and found to be technically sound and socially acceptable. When it is considered that a selection procedure is trying to predict worker behaviour over twenty to thirty years, it is not unreasonable to spend two days in gathering data on which to base that prediction.

Decision Making

Once all the data have been assembled, a decision has to be made as to whether or not any of the applicants matches the job specification sufficiently well to be considered. If not, the decision is 'not select', and perhaps, too, to consider redesigning the job, or even restructuring the organization.

If there seem to be possibles among the applicants, the shortlist which emerges must be closely scrutinized. The decision structure in Fig. 6.2 that has been derived from the job specification format should help in making the appropriate selection decision by guiding a decision maker through the steps which need to be taken when analysing all the relevant information that has been gathered.

The applicants should be informed of the decision that has been made about them as quickly and as humanely as possible. Then all the data needs to be filed, ready for the final stage in a selection procedure.

Control and Development

A further policy decision now needs to be made, as to whether it is necessary to check that the selection procedure is actually working in the way required by the senior management of the organization.

A basic selection procedure provides, and requires, relatively little opportunity for evaluating its worth. It is usually cheap and quick to operate, and so long as it is providing people to do the work, it is doing its job. In a pragmatic selection procedure, it is usually considered self-evident that the people appointed are more or less carrying out the jobs to which they have been appointed. Perhaps an occasional read through the selection files is all that is necessary to convince the selectors that they have made the correct selection decisions.

However, in a systematic selection procedure, special effort is made to discover whether or not the procedure is increasing the probability of appointing more effective managers.

The process of attempting to discover how well a selection procedure is working is termed *validation*. This term literally means how strong the evidence is that the procedure works. The basic technique of validation is to collect data about the subsequent performance of people who have been through the selection procedure and to compare it with the data about them collected during the procedure. The statistical technique most frequently used is that of correlation. This provides a measure of association between data collected at the selection stage—now termed the 'predictors'—and that collected by following up the applicant's job performance—now called the 'criteria'. When these two sets of data are correlated, the resulting statistic is called the 'validity coefficient'. This indicates how well the predictors are associated with the criteria. Tables in statistical textbooks indicate, for differing sizes of groups studied, how well the validity coefficient differs from a chance result.

Such an activity is the crucial aspect of any systematic selection procedure. It is far easier described than, in practice, carried out. Problems exist in collecting criteria data comparable for all the people appointed so that it can be merged into a sufficiently large sample on which calculations can be made.

If validity coefficients can be calculated, not only for predictors that are being used, but for data-gathering devices that are being proposed, the selection procedure can be developed in the light of data rather than by assertion. This is the essential difference between a systematic selection and the others. It is not only data-based decision making, but also uses data which have been demonstrated, statistically, to be relevant to the decisions that have to be made.

Summary

This chapter has described the kinds of policy decisions and procedures that need to be established in setting up an effective management selection activity. A checklist of all the steps that need to be considered is given in Fig. 6.4. The letters 'B', 'P', 'S' indicate, at each stage, the kind of selection procedure to which they apply, i.e., basic, pragmatic, or systematic.

Each of these procedures can be effective in meeting an organization's needs to acquire managerial staff. The task facing the senior management of any organization is to decide on the appropriate management selection strategy, then ensure that it is carried out.

P   S

Organization specification

Agree the type of organization, and
in what ways it is required to be developed.

Make sure that selectors have some skill
in selection methods.

If they do not, see that they are given
training.

P   S

Job description ──────────────→ **Control data** S

Ensure that a full and accurate job
description, written in operational
terms, is available for use in the
selection process.

Check to establish whether or not
performance criteria are available.

If they are not, take steps to see that
they are made available.

B P S

Job specification

Infer from the job description what previous
behaviour and/or personal characteristics are
likely to be associated with satisfactory
managerial performance.

B P S

Advertisement

S

Design an attractive advertisement which
gives enough information to ensure that ──────→ Analyse effectiveness
unsuitable candidates do not apply. of advertisement.

B P S

Application form

Design an application form which is easy to
complete and easy to read. It should include ──────→ Check the effect of
essential details plus any other items thought, the form on a sample
or known, to be relevant to the job. of applicants.

B P S   P (S)

Interview ←──────────────── **Selection devices**

Check to see that all interviewers are trained
in selection interviewing techniques. If they
are not, arrange to have them trained.

Have someone trained in the use of other
data-gathering methods and psychological
tests, if no one on the staff is already
suitably qualified.

Circulate the job description and make sure
that all staff concerned with the selection
procedure are fully acquainted with it.

Decide on the nature of the exercises/
instruments/questionnaires/tests to be
used, and record all the information
derived from them.

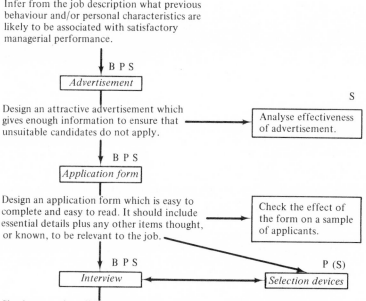

Fig. 6.4. Checklist for setting up a management selection system.

97

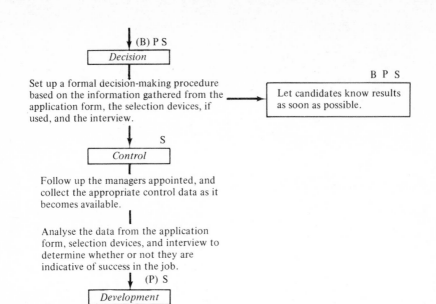

Fig. 6.4. (continued)

References

1. DAVIES, J. G. W. *et al. The Method II System of Selection*, HMSO, 1969.
2. RANDELL, G. A., PACKARD, P. M. A., SHAW, R. L., and SLATER, A. J. *Staff Appraisal*, Institute of Personnel Management, 1972.
3. CAMPBELL, J. P., DUNNETTE, M. D., LAWLER, E. E., and WEICK, K. E. *Managerial Behaviour, Performance and Effectiveness*, McGraw-Hill, 1970.
4. GHISELLI, E. E. and DUNNETTE, M. D. *Assessing Managerial Performance*, Independent Assessment and Research Centre, 1971.
5. *Classification of Occupations and Directory of Occupational Titles (CODOT)*, HMSO, 1972.
6. ANSTEY, E., HANDYSIDE, J. D., DUNNETTE, M. D., HARRELL, T. W., and MULLAN, C. *Assessing Managerial Potential*, Independent Assessment and Research Centre, 1971.
7. RUBENOWITZ, S. and SILBERER, P. Organisation de la fonction du personnel chez quelques sociétés européennes, *International Review of Applied Pscyhology*, **17,** 2, 1968.

Suggested Reading

DENERLEY, R. A. and PLUMBLEY, P. R. *Recruitment and Selection*, Institute of Personnel Management, 1968.
DUNNETTE, M. D. *Personnel Selection and Placement*, Wadsworth Publishing, 1966.
GUION, R. M. *Personnel Testing*, McGraw-Hill, 1965.
UNGERSON, B. (Ed.) *Recruitment Handbook*, Gower Press, 1970.

7. Developing managerial understanding of the younger generation

Leonard Nadler

Being young in today's world is different from having been young at any other time. The rapidity of change makes us no longer able to understand the life style and experience of the young. Younger workers are a resource for any organization, but there may be clashes with their life style and expectations as contrasted with those which exist in the organization. In the US, until at least 1985, almost half the work force will be between 16 to 34 years of age. To utilize this work force effectively, management must explore and develop new, and more appropriate, responses.

Each of us has been young, and consequently, we tend to generalize from our own youth as to how other young people should behave and what they should understand. At one time, this may have been possible. Today, to repeat an often cited, but less often understood, phrase, 'We live in a constantly changing world.' The difficulty with fully understanding this statement is our inability to realize the impact of this change on many aspects of the organizations in which we work and live.

Managers are usually drawn from older members of society (above 35 years of age). With work forces being younger (as will be illustrated later in this chapter), the manager of the next decade will be working with a younger work force than ever before. This may vary from country to country, but the worldwide trend is obvious from the population figures available.

These younger workers represent a tremendous resource for any organization. They have vitality, education, and, frequently, are highly motivated. But they can be expected to clash with those already at work in the organization. This is not new. The numbers of younger workers will be much greater than in the past. Also, the younger people will bring different life styles (or microcultural behaviours) than have been seen recently in the established work force.

Definitions and Misconceptions

For the purposes of this chapter, young persons are those of 35 years in age and under. For the most part, they were born in the post-Second World War era, sometimes after 1945.

They do not present a single homogeneous group. Sociologists prefer the term 'cohort' to the more common term 'generation'. The rapidity of change is reflected in this usage of terms. Cohort refers to those of approximately the same age. We usually think of generations as reflecting a span of twenty years. Yet, we are finding that as little as two or three years can separate the 'generations'. In the US, in the early 'seventies, the conceptual differences between an incoming freshman class in college, and the seniors in the same institution, represent a gap. The moves, from being an activist, to accepting, to withdrawing, occur within each few years.

It is dangerous to generalize about young people, even in one country and of the same age group or cohort. There are many influences at work which produce vast differences even among those born at the same time. Hence, age alone is not a factor. Managers must be sensitive to the vast variations in dress, language, motivations, and goals of the various groups of young people entering the organization.

Managerial Understanding

The need for managerial understanding of the younger generation is the same need for any managerial understanding of a significant part of the work force. Two dimensions suggest the greater need for managerial understanding:

(a) the younger work force;
(b) different life styles.

The Younger Work Force

To be specific about the implications of the young people in the work force, we must look at statistics. For this purpose, we shall deal only with those of the US, but I would urge readers from other countries to review these same statistics within their own countries. The implications may be even more far-reaching.

As can be seen in Table 7.1, the age pattern of the labour force in the US is slowly getting younger, and will not change until after 1980. In 1970, some 44 per cent of the work force was less than 34 years in age. By 1980, the proportion will be 49 per cent of the work force. Extremely important is the drop in the 45 to 54 age group. Until 1985, there will be a slowly decreasing percentage of this group in the work force, and yet this is the group from which we frequently draw our upper-level managers. Similarly, the middle-management group, frequently in the 35 to 44 age group will also be declining in available numbers, until at least after 1980. These changes in the work force have serious implications for some of our traditional patterns in developing the middle-manager and upper-level executives.

Age	1950	1960	1970	1975*	1980*	1985*
16–24	19	18	23	23	23	21
25–34	24	21	21	24	26	27
35–44	22	23	20	18	19	22
45–54	(30)	20	20	19	16	15
55–64	(30)	13	13	13	13	12
65+	5	5	4	3	3	3
	100	100	101†	100	100	100

* Projected
† Due to rounding
Source: *Manpower Report of the President*, March 1972, US Government Printing Office, Washington. Based on statistical tables, p. 253 and 256.

Fig. 7.1. Total labour force in the US (as percentages).

Each country must bring these statistics to the attention of those involved in manpower planning. In many countries of the world, the rapid increase of the birth-rate since the Second World War will make the trends even more pronounced. The impact on the labour force is largely due to those who were born eighteen years ago or more. In most countries, these young people are now entering the labour force in great numbers. In some countries, their impact on the labour force was felt earlier than the eighteen years after their birth.

Numbers alone are not a factor in viewing the make-up of the work force. These young people represent some significant changes, related to their age. In India, we are now finding young people emerging into the labour force who never knew their country under foreign leadership. They tend to be critical of their own countrymen and are not prepared to accept excuses based on earlier periods of British domination. In Japan, the young people entering leadership positions never knew the old absolute imperial status of the Emperor, and the ancient Bushido religion with its *giri* and *on* forms of obligation. They are Japanese, they are not imitating anybody else, but these young people have a different set of values than those who are currently in high managerial positions.

Different Life Styles

The tendency in past years has been to project the life styles of adults to the developing generation. In slowly changing societies, this is not only possible, but also appropriate. Given that change is rapid in much of our world today, such projection is no longer an appropriate practice.

Margaret Mead points out[1] that we are passing into a totally new situation. In the past, it was possible for an older person to say to a younger one: 'I have lived your life. I have been young. You have not yet been old, so I can tell you what is ahead.' Today, the younger person can respond: 'But you have never been young in my kind of world.' The reality is, most managers in the 40+ age group have not been young in this rapidly changing world.

The new employee today, particularly the young manager, has probably had a more solid grounding in management theory than the practitioner who learnt only by experience. The younger person has had the benefit of more advanced learning methods. His learning experiences will have been spiced with liberal doses of research so that he has been able to learn from the experiences of many.

Even in lesser developed countries, we find a rising flood of expectations, based on communication with other parts of the world, which was not readily available to the older brothers/sisters and parents of today's young people. Even the use of the term 'lesser developed countries' can engender hostility as being demeaning and a memento of earlier, imperialist days. Many of the young leaders in these countries prefer to label themselves, when labels are necessary, as part of the Third World. They are not lesser anything, though they are certainly willing to recognize their differences and their need for growth.

The younger members of the work force have grown up with media which were either unknown or unavailable some ten years ago, in many countries of the world. Today, there is television, and it is slowly becoming a nationally oriented medium. In 1972, Malaysia had a thriving television station (supplemented by one from Singapore) which reached a large portion of the population. There were some programmes in English, but a large number of news, discussion, and dramatic features were in the Malaysian language. The new thrust was to replace 'foreign' commercials with those designed specifically for the Malaysian people. It was more than just translating the foreign commerical into the language of the country. The attempt was to depict the life style of the Malaysian people, most of whom were and still are young.

In many parts of the world, the tendency had been to emulate the dress of the major foreign powers. The younger people have not accepted this. Rather, they have rediscovered their national dress and have made it a point of honour to be seen wearing it. This is an amazing identification with the past, but does suggest that older people must recognize this groping for identification, and searching for roots. It appears to be a contradiction, that younger people promote the reappearance of ancient dress, language, and even customs; to older persons, it seems outdated. Yet, in the US today, a young person wearing a beard is modern. Ten years ago, he would have been called a 'freak'.

Differing life styles do not have the same significance in all countries. In some, it may be a rejection of the trend of the current political leaders. In others, it may be a search for relevance to the past which has been lost in the rush to the future. Whatever the reasons, it becomes important for management to try to understand the differences in life styles which are emerging among younger workers. With the rise in multinational companies today, management must also be sensitive to what happens to a young person who is selected to go to another country as part of his training programme. The young worker, returning, may bring with him more than

102

what was actually communicated in his training programme. He will have interacted with other young people who are experimenting with various life styles. The problem of re-entry will be a joint one and should not be viewed negatively. The new insights into a variety of life styles can be healthy if the young worker is not received back into a punitive environment.

Any meaningful management training programme contains units concerned with change, and bringing about change. To the older manager, change may still be theoretical. He recognizes the need, and may even have been part of a change situation as experienced in an organization development experience. However, this manager has only rarely been a significant element in himself bringing about change. By contrast, in the US, we are now having college graduates entering the work force who were part of the campus movements of the 'sixties. They do not philosophize about change. They recall having brought about change. They do not see change as a threat, and have had some significant experiences in dealing with resistance. So far, they have not reacted as violently as had been predicted, and there is evidence that they have not given up their goals for change—to improve the organization and make it meaningful for all the employees.

Current Practices

Too many of our current managerial practices are based on an understanding of the way young people were—the way 'we' were when we were young. The practices are based on experiences which were valid with a different kind of young person, in different societal arrangements, with much more limited transport and communication. These factors all contribute towards the need for new managerial understanding of young people—their experiences and their aspirations.

Generally, management has not been punitive, but has tried in many organizations to understand and to work with the younger work force. Sometimes, this has led to confrontations, and frustration on both sides. Management, having the power, has tended to resist the efforts of the newer and younger members of the organization.

Despite the differences, forward-looking managements have sought ways of encouraging younger people to assume broader roles. Too often, these have been directed from above without involving the younger persons in the change process. As would be expected, resistance developed. Among the current practices, we find:

(a) increased use of management intern programmes;
(b) attention to orientation;
(c) provision for internal mobility.

Increased Use of Management Intern* Programmes

To date, the use of management intern programmes for developing new, young personnel has been subjected to insufficient study. It is generally

* Intern Program = Induction Programme. (Editors)

agreed to be a good idea by all concerned, yet many companies report almost a 100 per cent turnover within six years! This raises questions as to the efficacy of the programme.

Management intern programmes are generally of two kinds. The first is used in the US, and the common practice is to select bright college seniors and/or graduates. They are enrolled in a programme usually for two years. The employing organization offers them the opportunity to move rapidly through managerial ranks in an organized manner. The US Government makes extensive use of this approach, with movement through the employment levels at almost rocket-like velocity.

Why, then, is there such a rate of turnover? Research is lacking, but if one listens to some of the former interns, the reasons become clear. The company sees the two-year MI programme as one devoted to preparing the new employee for later and significant positions in the organization. The trainee having spent almost all of his prior life in a learning posture, is anxious to test the reality of his ability to make the kinds of decisions for which he has been preparing. He seeks specific job assignments and the opportunity for achievement. The organization wants him to keep on learning. This lack of mutual expectations dooms most such programmes to failure. Management thinks that it is contributing to the growth and future productivity of the MI. The MI sees the whole affair as just another attempt of older people to keep him from becoming influential in the organization.

Among blue-collar workers (non-college graduates), there is somewhat the same phenomenon. It has contributed to the re-examination of traditional apprenticeship programmes and a reduction in the length of such programmes. Apprenticeships which formerly took four years have been reduced to 18 months. US Steel is proud of its reassessment of the apprentice programme, and the changes it has made to reduce the time allotted without decreasing the proficiency level of the apprentice.

The second type of MI programme uses much longer periods of time for movement within the organization. An MI will be given a job assignment which lasts a year or two. During this time, he will be producing. But he knows that he is not going to stay in that job. Indeed, if he does stay there longer than is customary in the company, he is likely to have given up the possibility for future promotions. In the US, in some of the larger organizations, this is a common practice. For example, an MI will be assigned to a personnel function for about a year. After that, he may be transferred to purchasing, sales, or some other unrelated component of the organization. This may be viewed, by the organization, as preparing the MI for future and greater responsibility. For the MI it can mean frustration, for just as he gets to know the job and can begin to produce, he is whisked away to a new assignment.

In Japan, the similar schedule for new managers (younger workers) usually utilizes a three- to five-year reassignment programme. In the past, this was readily accepted as being the pattern. Stanley M. Davis gives us a case study entitled 'Yamada's Dilemma',[2] which explores the problem confronting a young Tokyo executive who is being transferred to a remote branch. In earlier years, such a transfer would not have been questioned in Japan. Today, many younger workers are not moved so easily, either physically or emotionally.

Today, in some parts of the world, many of the larger organizations are moving towards these MI models, though with some variations. The traditional specialist is being replaced very early by the generalist. The younger manager faces many more challenges and changes earlier in his career than his older brother did.

Attention to Orientation

Orientation of all new employees is a constant challenge. Where there is mobility in the external labour market, i.e., outside the employing organization, there can be a tendency to lessen the resources committed to orienting new employees. Anticipated turnover precludes such an expenditure. However, managements are tending to recognize that improved orientation can lessen turnover among new, younger workers.

For those just entering the labour force, there is a significant difference in the US from former days. Before 1950, it was common for a new member of the labour force to come to the world of work with some knowledge of it. With the growth of suburbia, i.e., with people living far away from the regular world of work, we now have employees on their first job who know little about appropriate behaviours in the office or the factory. They are not antagonistic—they may just be unknowledgeable. The school system, and possibly appropriately so, does not prepare them for a specific job or a particular type of employment. Therefore, the employer must bridge the world of school and the world of work.

Cooperative education programmes are expanding at the junior and community college level (two-year institutions beyond secondary school), to prepare students more readily for their work environments. This requires the cooperation of management to make the necessary provisions for cooperative programmes with schools.

In countries which have been predominantly agricultural, the move towards industrialization brings about much the same problem. The new employee knows far too little about the new behaviours expected of him. He has not had role models. It becomes necessary for the employer to provide a more comprehensive orientation both to lessen turnover and to shorten the period between hiring a new employee, and the time he attains the expected level of proficiency.

For a variety of reasons, some organizations have sensed the need among new employees for some further learning about the economic system. In some countries, where the government controls the school system, this is not necessary. Indoctrination in the underlying concepts of the economy of the country are part of the regular schooling. In other countries, such as the US, this is not so. As a response, General Electric has developed a series of films and session outlines to be used with technical and engineering recruits to help them understand the economic system of the US.

Provision for Internal Mobility

Transfers within an organization are sometimes referred to as movement within the internal labour market, i.e., internal within one employing organization. The larger the organization, the more possibilities there are for a well-developed internal labour market. Some organizations use a post-and-bid system, i.e., when a vacancy occurs, it is posted on previously designated bulletin boards. Sometimes, the posting takes the form of companywide memos, or other internal communication systems. The requirements for eligibility are made known to all, and those employees who think that they are qualified and are interested in the available position can submit a request to be considered.

Younger workers tend to distrust this system, despite the good intentions of management. For younger workers, this is not the usual method of position filling which they are familiar with. They tend to think that the system is fixed or 'rigged' (as it sometimes is), and so they withdraw from competition. Accordingly, their mobility within the organization is hampered. Management has not fully communicated the benefits of such a system to these younger workers.

Where there is an informal system, younger workers tend to be sceptical about movement within the organization. They are not usually familiar with the unwritten patterns of mobility. Where management proposes a change which is to the benefit of the new employee, he may resist leaving the relative security of his present position for something far less known. It is not that the younger employee fears change or new challenges; the reverse is true. But he is still not sure of the ground-rules within the organization and may not view the change as a positive one. Management must develop more effective mechanisms to take the basis for personnel changes out of the realm of such privileged information that it engenders hostility rather than support.

Trends

The trends that one can observe in managerial understanding of younger workers are a combination of too many factors which are insufficiently identified and understood. The size of the younger work force, its impact on a particular organization at a point in time, the economy of the country—all these contribute to developing and reinforcing trends. Uppermost is the willingness of management to recognize that these newer workers are not just younger—they are also different. The range of differences varies. In some countries, the new workers have had more schooling than those currently in the work force. In othes situations, they have an agricultural background while their older coworkers have been in industry for several years.

Among some of the trends, the following can be identified:

(a) increased internal labour force mobility;
(b) provision for counselling;
(c) training sessions for existing management.

Increased Interior Labour Force Mobility

Given that unplanned change engenders fear, some managements have tended to overreact to the young. They have moved the younger worker quite rapidly through the organization without recognizing the damage that can result.

Generally, the younger worker can make the necessary adaptations to rapid change, but he also seeks fulfilment. This is not too dissimilar from other members of the work force. But the younger workers have had much less opportunity to achieve the satisfactions that have become part of the work experience of the older members of the work force. Management, in the future, must seek to build in these possibilities for success. It is not suggested that artificial situations be contrived to provide success for those who are not able. But the new worker wants to achieve as soon as possible. In working with the 'hard core' new employees, i.e., those who had never held a regular job for any significant length of time, organizations found that it was helpful to identify some immediate and very visible goals. When these could be achieved, and seen by all, the new worker reached a satisfactory level of performance with less difficulty.

Mobility, then, must be coupled with sufficient success at each stage. Some organizations are recognizing this by using younger workers as members of task forces or project groups. They mingle with older workers, but are encouraged to participate as equal members, receiving equal recognition for the success of the group.

Provision for Counselling

It is not new for an organization to provide counselling for employees. Any adequate career development plan must contain such a provision. Managers who are sensitive to the differences within their work force know that provision for counselling reduces the waste of preparing an employee for a position for which he is not suited, but would accept anyhow, in order to conform to the wishes of the organization.

The difference is in the focus. We generally seek to find out where the employee would like to be, say, in the next five years. This means a label, e.g., department manager, division head, which indicates a specific position or a general area of endeavour. Among the new younger workers, there is a different focus. It is not that they are not achievement oriented. They are, but the achievement is in accomplishments rather than in titles. Counselling now introduces the question: What would you like to accomplish within the next five years? This leads to much more realistic goal setting. It also allows for exploration of the goals of the younger worker as compared with the directions planned by management.

Training Sessions for Existing Managers

The full impact of the younger workers has still not been felt. Yet too few organizations are making appropriate provisions. In the US, when employing organizations became involved in the National Alliance of Businessmen, and similar programmes, the training of supervisors and foremen was an important activity. The younger workers present a similar challenge to management, and call for specific responses. It is necessary to facilitate communication and understanding, and this cannot come about without some organized opportunities—which are readily provided in training sessions.

The sessions should not be limited to orientation. It is not the objective for the younger workers to conform to the existing organization. Rather, there is an accommodation necessary among the younger workers, the older workers, management and organizational objectives. If organizations are not to lose the vitality and contributions which can come from the younger workers, carefully organized and conducted training sessions for existing managers are a necessity.

There are many models and approaches. David A. Nadler, at the time a younger worker, told us that we should focus on the manager.[3] He cited his own experience with IBM, where, as a young trainer, he was called upon to provide contact, as a younger person, in a learning situation for middle managers. He urged such contacts and the development of appropriate responses by management, through a series of organized training experiences.

Managerial understandings will vary, but the need remains an ever-constant concern. Management must develop appropriate responses, and the process of developing these can contribute to the growth of the organization and its employees.

References

1. MEAD, MARGARET, *Culture and Commitment*, Doubleday, 1970.
2. DAVIS, S. M. *Comparative Management*, Prentice-Hall, 1971.
3. NADLER, D. A. *The NOW Employee*, Gulf Publishing, Houston, 1971.

Suggested Reading

BENNIS, W. G. and SLATER, P. E. *The Temporary Society*, Harper and Row, 1968.
CHALOFSKY, N. Experience May Not Be The Best Teacher, *Training and Development Journal*, **26,** 8, 1972.
DAVIS, S. M. *Comparative Management: Organizational and Cultural Perspectives*, Prentice-Hall, 1971.
NADLER, L. *Developing Human Resources*, Gulf Publishing, Houston, 1970.

8. Developing resourceful managers

John Morris

Professor Morris argues that the increasing uncertainty of the manager's environment, both inside and outside the organization, places a premium on the development of resourcefulness. He fears that recruitment and training programmes—together with the growth of career planning as a specialism—may pay lip-service to resourcefulness but often serve, in practice, to foster and reward predictable, measurable, stable qualities of performance. Seven qualities that appear to be particularly relevant to resourcefulness are briefly described.

A distinction is drawn between four aspects of organization—(a) keeping things going, (b) doing new things, (c) coping with breakdown and failure, (d) pulling the first three aspects together into a manageable whole, responsible to the larger society. The types or styles of management that one finds in each of these aspects are discussed in relation to the qualities of resourcefulness.

Finally, two methods of providing relevant experience are discussed: individual assignments and group development projects.

Career planning, in the formal sense used by personnel specialists, has been coming under increasing attack as an outgrowth of rational, bureaucratic control. Whatever the claims of bureaucracy to continuity and efficiency, it seems unsuited to satisfying many of the deeper and more significant human needs, such as the needs for love, freedom, and adventure. The question has clearly emerged: What kinds of career planning and development are feasible and acceptable both to the individual and the organization, not merely the organization alone? Also, Who is best placed to do the planning? Even a cursory examination of the attempts of enlightened organizations to relate individual and organizational needs brings out, quite clearly, that it is easier to raise important questions than to answer them.

Many career planners, working under pressure and with meagre resources, have felt forced into staying close to organizational continuities, inferring trends from inadequate information, and tentatively projecting them into the next five years. They have worked step by step with conservative procedures, rather than looking for fundamental changes of pattern and then envisaging the forms of work that may become the careers of the future. Yet recent management writers such as Schon, Toffler, and Bennis have stressed that we have moved into an 'age' of discontinuity', to use a phrase made famous by Peter Drucker.[1]

In a turbulent environment, quickwittedness and flexibility of response seem to be valuable managerial qualities. For want of a better term, we shall call the set of qualities that seem appropriate for dealing managerially with continuing uncertainty, 'resourcefulness'. Resourceful managers are people who can, among other things:

(a) cope decisively with new situations with the required degree of skill and self-confidence;
(b) use whatever information is obtainable in order to develop broad, but practical plans, with plenty of room for contingencies;
(c) work as managers—operating with and through other people—rather than as self-sufficient individualists.

In these respects, resourceful managers are in contrast to the stable but readily manipulated 'human resources' who appear so frequently in textbooks of personnel planning and control.

Resourceful managers prefer to plan for themselves, rather than to fit into other people's plans. Since they have a lively sense of contingency, they are often sceptical of formal, long-term plans and see them as both unrealistic and a source of personal constraint. They like to think of their careers as nothing more or less than their own working lives in progress, rather than as a standardized string of jobs within a single specialism or organization. They are of considerable and growing value to organizations and are usually the first to recognize this. They are interested in their own development. How can this be enhanced, without falling into the trap of treating such managers as compliant fodder for existing training programmes? First, it may help to try and identify the elements of resourcefulness.

The Nature of Managerial Resourcefulness

There is a certain paradox in trying to outline the anatomy of the resourceful manager. Resourcefulness is nothing if not variable, mercurial, and individual. It does not stand still to be measured and dissected. Yet some qualities of resourcefulness can be recognized, and often form the centre of appreciative discussion among those who enjoy such qualities. Seven that seem particularly significant, because all of them can be improved by selective experience, are:

(a) flexible intelligence;
(b) technical abilities;
(c) social abilities;

(d) emotional resilience;

(e) drive for continued effectiveness;

(f) effective judgement in situations of uncertainty;

(g) commitment to fundamental values.

Flexible Intelligence

This is a linked set of information-handling abilities, rather than a single ability. It relates to the rapid assessment of changing events and activities, using the recognition of emerging patterns; focusing on a promising issue in order to gain a detailed understanding; gathering new information, where appropriate, and relating it economically to the matter in hand; and moving from one level or area of knowledge to another, without marked effort or loss of clarity and balance. These abilities go well beyond the straightforward problem-solving skills of intelligence tests, and have more in common with the qualities discerned in senior managers by Muller,[2] and dubbed the 'helicopter mind'.

Technical Abilities

Resourceful managers need to do more than merely handle information. They need to cope with the physical world—the world of tools, machines, materials, and instruments. No doubt some of the other characteristics of resourcefulness, such as intelligence and drive, play a part in the development of technical abilities, but their distinguishing aspect is the capacity for making physical discriminations and coordinating movements in relation to a three-dimensional world of physical objects. One of the great attractions of the physical world, for the practitioner, is that it lends itself readily to experiments and manipulation. The results of successful practice can be effectively standardized and communicated to others.

It is no accident, therefore, that management training has always tended to use the model of technical training as an ideal. This tendency is disturbing when one reflects that managers are increasingly required to work in a world permeated with values. Even the physical world is now being seen as being in need of care, respect, and even love, rather than manipulation in the interests of instrumental efficiency.

Social Abilities

Much of the job of the manager consists of working with and through other people. Resourceful managers, who are working in constantly changing situations, particularly need to develop sensitivity to changing relationships. By no means all these relationships will be cooperative. Many will be competitive, and even hostile.

The patterns of social relations that are required of a resourceful manager include such diverse skills as negotiating, bargaining, collaborating, competing, influencing, persuading, exhorting, and many other modes of social activity. It is becoming increasingly clear that people can develop far greater

111

flexibility in their social relationships by focusing on their own social behaviour, and practising new ways of behaving in experimental settings.

Emotional Resilience

The first three qualities of resourcefulness are all forms of ability, and can be judged as more or less effective. But they need the support of deep and sincere feeling. Emotional resilience is closely linked with openness to one's feelings and to the inner lives of others. But without some form of self-control, openness can become oversensitivity and lead to emotional breakdown.

Drive for Continued Effectiveness

Aspects of this tendency could be called 'initiative' or 'ambition'. It is on-going commitment to bring about effective outcomes to action rather than commitment to keep things running smoothly under stable conditions. Like the other qualities discussed here, drive is continuously variable. At its most intense, it can take on the characteristic of an obsession, such as a compelling drive to perfection.

Effective Judgement in Situations of Uncertainty

If drive is very intense, it may threaten emotional resilience and effective judgement. So the seven qualities have to be brought together into some coherent pattern. The clearest indication of balance in the individual is that he is capable of making sound judgements. A sound judgement, in general terms, is one that reflects the realities of the situation and meets the interests of the participants accurately and fairly.

Commitment to Fundamental Values

A manager who is highly resourceful, but lacks grounding in fundamental values, could well be a social menace. Entrepreneurs are resourceful, almost by definition, but often use their flexibility and energy to undermine the security and welfare of others. The 'entrepreneurial approach' is therefore not only celebrated, but notorious. The qualities of character that link a manager with deeper values can, however, be threats to resourcefulness, since they often emphasize stability. There seems to be a continuous tension between commitment to such values as sincerity, integrity, and loyalty and the restless pursuit of effectiveness in constantly changing conditions. In short, resourcefulness and fundamental values are often uneasy bedfellows. But let us note, at this point, that we are nevertheless, including value commitments in our 'formula' for the resourceful manager.

Resourcefulness and Career Development

Resourcefulness requires exercise through expression. The most effective place for its expression is through work. But, here comes a vital problem. Whenever one looks at organizations, work is seen to be packaged into 'jobs'.

This is perhaps a convenient point at which to consider the difference between a job and a career.

Jobs are sets of working activities performed at a given time by a single person. The career is a sequence of jobs, particularly the jobs that are held one after another by people in a particular line of work. Many people do not really achieve a career; they are job holders. Their level of skill and the technology in which they work does not offer a substantial sequence but only one job, which the same person may hold throughout his life, if he is not displaced by a younger person who can do it better. Managers, however, do achieve some sort of career.

It seems useful to distinguish between three kinds of career:

(a) the specialist career;
(b) the organizational career;
(c) the personal career.

The first is a sequence of jobs linked together by specialized knowledge and skill, such as a production manager, sales manager, or finance manager. The second is a sequence of jobs within a single organization, whether it is a giant multinational corporation or a small family firm. These two kinds of career have dominated the scene in traditional thought and practice in career choice, education, and planning. But the growing significance of the resourceful person, seeking coherent and meaningful work in an increasingly turbulent world, begins to shift the balance of careers from the impersonal work system to the working life of the individual. *Personal* careers are valued by individuals, for whom they are a central part of their lives. The disruption of well-trodden career paths in organizations and vocations has its tragic side in the displacement of reliable, worthy people; but it offers great opportunities to the individual to see his own plans and values as the appropriate source of coherence in his personal life, rather than the standardized careers offered by the world of work up to this point in time.

The change is merely beginning—much official thinking about careers is still deeply traditional. But there are increasing signs of new attitudes: job changes initiated by the person rather than by his employers; demands for changes in jobs to make them more interesting and responsible; the emergence of new sequences of jobs, many of them so diverse that observers who are wedded to the older concept of career are forced to talk about two-career or three-career working lives.

Of course, outstanding gifted people have always blazed their own trails. Lord Franks, for example, the distinguished founder of British business schools in their modern form, has been in turn a university professor, an ambassador, a senior Civil Servant, a bank president, and chairman of many working parties and Commissions of Inquiry. Lord Beeching has moved to his present industrial eminence through diverse jobs in many organizations, mostly working as a trouble-shooter and development manager. Their idiosyncratic career paths are likely to remain exceptional in their distinction, but the variety of work will probably become increasingly commonplace.

The change of emphasis to be discussed here is simple, but profound. Instead of jobs being seen as the rightful possession of vocations and organizations—which are thereby given a superhuman status—they are seen as a phase of an individual working life. Work is the living activity of an individual, belongs to him, and is his or her responsibility. Careers, therefore, are lives in progress—working lives—rather than a string of jobs put together by strangers for someone else to perform. But if we think of managerial careers in these terms, what are the elements out of which a career can be realistically developed? Is there a simple classification of management tasks that would serve as a guideline?

A Model of Organizational Tasks in Relation to Management

There are many classifications of managerial jobs. Some simply take the established functions, such as marketing, sales, distribution, production, engineering, purchasing, finance, accounting, personnel, and administration, and point out that all these diverse activities need to be run properly by managers. Others analyse the different phases of managerial activity, such as planning, controlling, organizing, and leading others. These distinctions are all useful. The model briefly described here starts from a quite fundamental distinction between three organizational activities which need to be brought together by a fourth. I believe that these four activities form a natural basis of differentiation in every type of organization, especially in times of rapid change. The three basic activities are:

(a) keeping things going;
(b) doing new things;
(c) coping with failure (often called trouble-shooting or fire-fighting).

The fourth, integrative activity is 'pulling things together'. These labels deliberately use plain words, in order to bring out their essential quality. But, in large organizations, they become specialized and acquire an array of formal titles, e.g., pulling things together becomes 'corporate strategy', doing new things becomes 'the management of innovation'. Another advantage of homely labels is that it becomes clear that the activities exist not only at the organizational level, but also within working groups, and even within single jobs. From now on, we shall discuss these four sets of tasks in relation to jobs and careers, but with particular reference to the three specialized aspects which need to be pulled together.

When one comes to look at each of these three basic organizational (and, therefore, managerial) activities, it quickly becomes clear that each of the three can be split into two segments. There is nothing surprising about this. If the tasks are as basic, as we claim, they will split into many subactivities, especially in large-scale organizations. But differentiation usually proceeds by splitting into two parts (such as internal and external relations, continuity and discontinuity, people and things). These particular splits are most interesting and relevant to our tasks of developing resourceful managers who can handle the most essential parts of their own career planning.

First, the central region of activities—keeping things going—divides into those managerial activities that continue under stable conditions, and those that are concerned with the task of continuing under unstable conditions. I have sought to find a non-technical term that memorably expresses a key quality, or cluster of qualities, of managers in each of the six sets of activities which we are about to discuss and which are shown in Fig. 8.1. The two here are 'solid' and 'fixer'. The 'solid' style of management develops as a result of having stable conditions to deal with, and the task of keeping a stream of effective work going under these conditions. It could be argued that this style of management is almost non-managerial, especially if we regard management as the handling of uncertainty and change. Perhaps this is so. Certainly the 'solid' style of management turns the activity of the manager into a set of predictable routines and rituals.

The 'fixer' stands in strong contrast to the 'solid' style. The manager using this style is constantly devoting his skill and qualities of character to keep a steady stream of work emerging from difficult and changing conditions. No wonder the manager using this style often has mingled envy and contempt for those using the 'solid' style. From the embattled perspective of the 'fixer', the solid approach seems so easy. On the other hand, the manager who spends most of his time using the 'solid' approach is inclined to make severe judgements on the 'fixer' style of management, seeing it as wasteful and devious. The first of these criticisms refers to the fact that keeping things going under changing conditions often uses extra resources. The second refers to the rapid changes that the 'fixer' needs to make in order to keep things going when he cannot anticipate the situation in which he and his workers will have to work.

Turning to the area of doing new things, the two most readily recognized styles of managerial behaviour are the *handling of ideas* and the *exploitation of opportunities*. The first deals with possibilities, the second turns them into actualities. The names of these styles of management are various, 'ideas man', 'entrepreneur', 'scientist', 'inventor'. Obviously, some of these are not limited to managers. It might be questioned whether an inventor need be a manager at all, though there are distinguished inventor-managers such as Alec Issigonis and Edwin Land. The distinction is well recognized in such widely used labels as 'research and development'. Many studies, e.g., Carter and Williams,[3] bring out the difficulty that British enterprises have experienced in developing the excellent ideas of British research workers, and, in 1962, the National Research Development Corporation was established to deal with this problem.

Two convenient labels for the two styles are 'light' and 'bright'. The first implies the insubstantial nature of the work. Its critics talk of 'cloud 9', 'waffle', 'airy-fairy' to refer to their clear awareness of the difference between ideas and practice. But 'light' can also be seen from the positive side—'lucid', 'brilliant', 'illuminating' often apply to research work.

The third category has been somewhat neglected in discussions of management development, though managers themselves will always testify to their

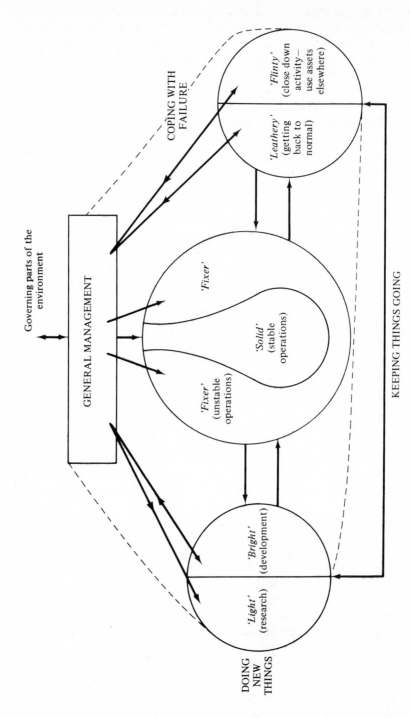

Fig. 8.1. Types of organizational activities and related types of management.

continuous involvement in its activities, namely, coping with failure. The two subdivisions here are:

(a) bringing a serious breakdown back to the desired level of activity;
(b) making the hard decision to close down a set of activities, scrap some resources, and use others elsewhere.

I call the first style, 'leathery', and the second, 'flinty'. 'Leathery' catches the element of thick-skinned urgency, and even ruthlessness, that is common in 'trouble-shooting', while 'flinty' refers to the coolness and detachment traditionally attributed to those who make hard decisions to close things down. Figure 8.1 sets out these managerial styles.

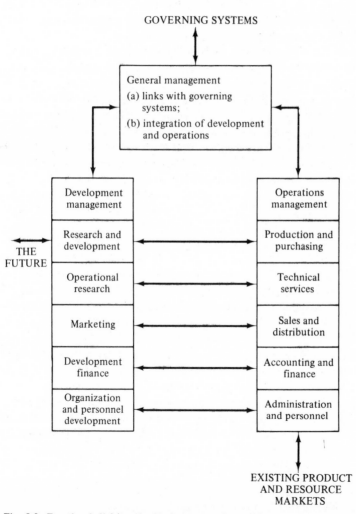

Fig. 8.2. Functional divisions in development and operations, as they occur in a manufacturing enterprise.

117

Two of our three basic categories are concerned with the effective handling of major uncertainties: doing new things and coping with failure. These are *prime areas for developing resourcefulness*. But the role of 'fixer' has many opportunities, especially for the young manager, since it brings him into close touch with 'solid' managers and their attitudes and experience. Even more important, the development of all-round resourcefulness needs experience of managing effectively in *all six* forms of activity. In my view, it is the integration of these six into a set of abilities and values appropriate for the situation in which he is working, that makes the general manager.

How do these forms of activity relate to the familiar functional specialisms such as production, sales, and accounting? This is shown in Fig. 8.2, which spells out some of the functional divisions commonly found in two of the three basic sets of activities. The functional breakdown of manufacturing enterprises has been used as an example because these functions have tended to provide the model for organizational analysis.

Figure 8.2 brings out the tendency of operational functions to grow their own development specialisms. These often start modestly, with one or two people brought in to test the feasibility of some development work, whether it be marketing, development finance, research and development, or other activities. If their value is demonstrated to the satisfaction of the senior managers who made the original experiment, the core of newcomers is enlarged, and the new development becomes a specialism in its own right. In some instances, an unusually successful development function takes over the operational function from which it grew: marketing is the best example of this. Such a situation is only likely to occur if the new activities to be dealt with rise to a steady flow, with continuous inputs to mainstream operations.

From long, and sometimes bitter, experience, the operational functions have learned to work together, however reluctantly. No such imperative leads the development functions to work together. Despite the slow emergence of posts for development managers in go-ahead enterprises, there is not yet much evidence that the development functions have begun to work effectively together, as, what rather fancifully, can be called the 'organization of the future'.

Yet surely this change will occur. Vast funds are being channelled into the development of new products and processes. Able and well-educated young managers have high expectations of contributing to the development of the enterprise rather than to its maintenance. Change must occur or the development functions, lacking the discipline of well-established procedures and work habits, will become hopelessly diffuse and self-indulgent.

What should happen in the organization of the future? General management should be seen to be working to bring together four sets of concerns:

(a) the continuing well-established operations of the enterprise;
(b) the development activities of the enterprise;
(c) the failures of maintenance and development;

(d) the external opportunities and constraints, in so far as these are not yet allocated to one or more of the first three concerns.

Recent organizational theory, e.g., Lawrence and Lorsch,[4] and Beer,[5] reminds us that differentiation in an organization or its environment can only be managed effectively by a control system that is at least as complex (in the respects to be managed) as the system which it is to manage. Thus, general managers can only manage the four functions mentioned above (which are our three basic functions plus the relations with all those other matters of organizational concern that can be lumped together as the 'governing system') if these are represented, in some sense, in their own general management structure and organization. The task of pulling things together requires people who are individually or collectively skilled in development, maintenance, and breakdown. More to the point, general management must find ways of integrating these aspects of organization into a coherent pattern for which they are accountable, both inside and outside the system they are managing. In some ways, this is the ultimate test of resourcefulness, making heavy demands on intelligence, resilience, and social ability, but, above all, on sound judgement.

Two Approaches to Resourcefulness in the Context of Careers

The first approach, and in some ways the simplest and best, is to use existing jobs in the organization, but to look for unusual connections between them, so that the organization has richer and more diverse paths for resourceful individuals to follow (we must beware of the term 'follow'; one exciting task is for resourceful managers to establish the paths for others to follow). Career planning can do much to provide information about possible paths. This depends, in turn, on good models of organizational tasks and requisite skills and values. The second approach is more challenging. It is concerned with the invention of new jobs, both for individuals and groups. Often, such jobs are thought of as temporary, but this is an assumption that needs testing. After all, every job was once new and had to be invented (or perhaps discovered).

Development and breakdown are ideal activities for the invention or discovery of new jobs and the connecting paths that constitute new careers. In the operations, or the maintenance, area, a lot of rationalization has usually taken place, with intelligent and zealous specialists in work control setting up 'specifications' and 'evaluations'. It is in this part of the organization that one sees managers standing firmly within their well-defined territories, and engaged in routine or, perhaps ritual, transactions over the boundaries, with even minor changes being attacked as empire-building, or politics. This is hardly the place for establishing new jobs. Within the second approach, I have only space to discuss two types of activity:

(a) individual assignments;
(b) group development projects.

Individual Assignments

The very existence of assignments—as special postings of able managers to do a necessary task—is a reminder of the rigidity of most managerial careers. The 'beaten track' moves step by step up a functional ladder: in accounts, production, engineering, personnel, or sales. All the work being done in jobs is part of on-going operations, or so it would seem, because organizations develop a life of their own, based on keeping things going as they have done in the past.

Organizational inertia is nothing new. Assignments are a way of getting necessary work done without disturbing the equilibrium of the existing system of jobs. Many assignments are given to people without altering their job title, the work they 'should' be doing is spread over a number of their colleagues or subordinates. Sometimes, more disturbingly for those who like to know exactly what is in store for them, a manager will be shifted to a special assignment, perhaps to handle a piece of trouble-shooting. His job title may be vague—'special assistant to . . .'—and he will be uncomfortably aware of being moved from one well-defined track, with a place in the running, to a point which may lead nowhere. Since organizations are known to be places where people can sometimes be lost, the assignment may be the cause of some anxiety unless it is seen as conferring an accolade on the person selected.

All these points are obvious enough. One could turn them around and say that the existence of assignments is an indication of the ability of most organizations to devise special arrangements for special circumstances. We are really testing two things when we assign a manager to a special task: we are testing his ability to do a job under unusual circumstances and we are testing his confidence in his ability to do a job under unusual circumstances, and avoid being 'locked' in a blind alley in the organization. From this point of view, one could argue that the resourceful manager will clearly indicate to his seniors that he is not going to accept being placed at a disadvantage because he has been selected for special service.

It is commonplace in modern business organizations to find a critical attitude towards the armed forces and the Civil Service. Both systems are seen as rather authoritarian (or, paternalistic—to use another current term of abuse). But both of these forms of organization have long used assignments (and a related activity, secondments) as ways of developing able people, as well as useful devices for getting a temporary need met.

Again, in the services, a number of posts are recognized as development posts, devised to give a good deal of information and experience in the shortest possible time, all under the immediate eye of a senior man. Industry and commerce, obsessed (often, understandably) with making a profit and cutting costs, have frequently been inclined to axe these posts, even when they exist. Finally, simulation activities and intensive development courses, both rather new even in enlightened industrial and commercial enterprises, have long been established in the services.

The experience of those in industry and commerce who have used assignments as development opportunities brings out some of the difficulties in making effective judgements of individual performance in unfamiliar situations. As the use of assignments grows, these difficulties tend to decline. Two problems are extremely common. First, an able manager is not likely to develop well if his assignment is lightweight. He needs to have real work to do. There are dangers that, if real work is lacking, he will seek to arrogate some of his senior's work, or that he may be seen as rather ineffectual by the very manager who is depriving him of the chance of doing anything worth while. The 'personal assistant' role offers frequent teething troubles to organizations which have introduced it as a convenient development position.

Second, and clearly more likely to happen when the assignment is set up to meet an urgent need, the manager carrying out the assignment should be given ample support. Such assignments are associated with heavy workloads whose weight can sometimes prove crippling. Perhaps this point sounds rather fussy and overprotective. Indeed, a policy of support could be taken to extremes and interpreted by a resourceful manager as an indication of lack of trust in his energy and ability. This would be disastrous. But equally disastrous is the assumption that able men are somehow capable of meeting anything that arises. This is sheer complacency and can lead to breakdown of managers whose only fault is their fear that demand for more support would be interpreted as a sign of ineffectiveness.

Group Development Projects

Most forms of organization have used project teams, working parties, or study groups as the means to concentrate a set of specialized resources on an issue that seems important enough to deserve special investigation. Sections of the organization that are concerned with research, development, or trouble-shooting may conduct most of their work in project teams. The kind of development group that I have in mind here, though, is one especially devised for management development purposes. This kind of group has been the particular interest of the 'organization development' approach. Unfortunately, because of the great difficulty of setting up and running such groups, there has been a marked tendency for them to be limited to education and training projects, often focused on simulation activities (such as business games) in a training centre.

The form of group that I shall discuss here, because I have personal experience of it, is the joint development programme of the Manchester Business School. This was pioneered in 1969–70, with a well-known engineering organization, and became an established part of the School's offerings to the world of management, in autumn 1971. The organizations taking part in the programme include some of the best known in Britain, all with a reputation for close interest in education, development, and training of managers. Plessey and Tarmac are both leading companies in their fields: Plessey in electronics and communications, Tarmac in road surfacing and construction, especially civil engineering. The National Freight Corporation and the Post Office are large industrial corporations in the public sector. Some work has also been done with a medium-sized firm in the foods industry: Warburtons of Bolton. It has good previous contacts with the School through its top management, both of them British alumni of top American business schools.

Despite the enormous differences between these organizations in scale, type of activity, and history, they all have one thing in common—a desire to bring about change in management effectiveness within the organization, with the willing participation of the managers concerned. The design of the joint development activities is simple enough, but proves complex in practice.

The work focuses on the activities of a project of able managers of high potential. They select a project from a carefully composed list with which they are provided by a steering group of senior managers (sometimes their immediate seniors; more often, two levels up). The topics have been chosen to provide two opportunities: first, and more important, an opportunity for the managers in the project group to develop themselves in the context of their own organization, thus learning to work effectively together as a team and to make recommendations that are feasible and useful. Second, and vitally important as a motivating factor, an opportunity of working on a significant issue in real time, rather than a hypothetical exercise aimed solely at providing some learning for the group members.

The problems of setting up project groups within the organization, particularly if their level and numbers make it impossible to free them all for a full-time assignment, are legion. Organizations are for the most part based on maintaining continuity ('keeping things going'), and there are strong defences against people wandering around the system, detached from their usual roles. Strong mechanisms of defence and attack are set in motion: the project group are seen as a 'Mafia', as 'hatchet men', or 'whizz kids'. Isolated from their normal bases of skill and authority, the members make slow progress, if any, and assume that project work is rather like committee work, a fiendish device for wasting the time of good managers who have better things to do.

To help with these difficulties, the School provides support facilities, in the form of a small number of staff members who work closely as consultants to the joint development activity, and draw on their colleagues for specialized support as necessary. The main job of the consultant group is, in an important sense, achieved when the project team has been set up, provided with a steering group and a set of viable projects; selected the topic they want to work on; and set themselves up in a working group with an initial plan of campaign.

These three corners provide stability for the activity: ultimate authority and funding from the steering group; the work itself, from the project team who are also intended to be the main beneficiaries of the development; and support from the School consultants and tutors. Stability is very necessary in these innovative activities because of inherent tendencies towards breakdown. Even when the initial project topic has been chosen, and the project team has got its basic plan, there are many difficult days ahead. In our experience at the School (though we are still in the very earliest days of working on these joint activities), many of the most serious problems are 'political'. When managers from an organization are within their normal occupational roles, they have a reasonably well-understood set of relationships above, sideways, and below, leaving them a reasonably well-established and well-defined territory within the organization. Moving into a project team, unless these are a very firmly established part of the working life of the organization, means that new conventions have to be established with fellow managers. This is particularly important when the work of the team includes looking at the relative effectiveness of some of the existing activities within the organization. We strongly feel that—at this stage in joint development activities—the area of innovation is very much safer than the breakdown area, which is inevitably beset with strong defences. But, as we have seen, the line between innovation and breakdown is often difficult to draw. The project-group members, therefore, have to go extremely carefully in their establishment of new relationships with their colleagues, seniors, and subordinates. This is particularly important when one comes to consider the action implications of project work. It is easy enough to gather a body of information and make recommendations—the traditional role of some of the less effective consultants to organization, but it is quite another matter when these recommendations have to be translated into organizational action.

The steering group is able to help members of the project team to avoid issues that are too hot to handle. But steering groups themselves, although composed of people with a considerable amount of experience of the political problems of the organization, often make serious misjudgements about how activities are organized at several levels below them. It is not cynical to comment that, in most organizations, there are powerful controls on information flowing upwards. Subordinates let their seniors know what they think is 'appropriate' for them to hear. This may include gross distortion of the truth, but much more often involves selection from the available information, so that a manager preserves some freedom of action at his own level. Some project groups lack skills in entering these delicate networks of relationships and understandings. Perhaps one of the most important requirements, therefore, is to gain some knowledge and skills about the communications systems of organizations, especially from the social and psychological aspects.

Here, we have run into a difficulty with the Manchester Business School projects. We have been so eager to avoid the activities becoming 'just another course' that we have lost a number of opportunities for enabling project-team members to gain a good deal of formal, as well as informal, understanding of how organizations handle information and control, both as opportunities and as constraints. The Revans model, used in Belgium and Egypt, has very much more emphasis on lengthy preliminary training before the members of the project team start their work. Possibly, some kind of compromise will need to be achieved between long, formal inputs, (which, in the hands of a business school, could lead to the programme becoming overstructured), and no inputs until the end of the project, when some of them may be too late.

A question that inevitably arises is the nature of the distinction between project groups engaged in a joint development activity, and normal study groups, working parties and project teams within the organization as a whole. The clear distinction (not so clear, however, in practice) is between the use of people's existing specialist strengths in the normal form of project teams, and the opportunity for people to develop skills in unfamiliar areas that is a characteristic of joint development activities. Of course, if the projects on which people are working as part of their development have considerable substantive importance for the organization, there will be some stage at which people will be dragooned into operating in the area of existing specialist skills, rather than being encouraged to operate in areas of ignorance.

In these brief notes, we have focused mainly on the difficulties of management development groups, but they are nevertheless immensely fruitful as an opportunity of enabling people to grow within their organizations, in areas of organizational growth. If this sounds a little like a play on words, it is nevertheless a very important play. We are arguing that the levels of competence within established posts make it difficult for people to come into them to acquire skill. If, on the other hand, one focuses on the areas where the organization is learning, then that is a splendid opportunity for individuals and groups to learn as well.

Summary

This chapter began with what purported to be an argument, but was more like an assertion. Career planning, it was claimed, often takes a conservative line, focusing on the supposed needs of an organization or a specialism at some future time. A turbulent environment, generating discontinuity, often makes a nonsense of conservative plans based on projection of existing trends. We have, therefore, a need for resourceful managers. These people were then described, with sympathy, and an organizational model was presented, which was designed to distinguish between continuity, in the form of keeping things going, and discontinuity, in the forms of doing new things and coping with failure. The rest of the notes did no more than elaborate on the theme of using discontinuities that the organization is already committed to dealing with as the development ground (arena? battleground? stage?) for resourceful managers.

A few points seem worth restating: some in a slightly different form. Industrial and commercial organizations have become overcommitted to rationality, which implies high levels of knowledge and control. They can learn much from organizations that have learned the hard way about the non-rational and the irrational elements in life. Antony Jay[6] has stated the case for taking politics seriously but the message is too novel to have sunk home yet. The armed services have taken resourcefulness very seriously, especially when at war. The Church is sometimes seen as a dreadful example, yet where did 'charisma' originate from?

Specialist careers and organizational careers are almost certainly here to stay, even in a turbulent world. But personal careers should be taken more seriously; and not merely after death or retirement—by way of biographies.

The close links between resourcefulness and fundamental values have only been indicated, not explored. Career development without integrity, courage, humour is little but the shell of development. Once we slough off the constraining shell, we find that development is a deeply human activity, and is closer to fundamental values than to techniques of organizational control.

References

1. DRUCKER, P. F. *The Age of Discontinuity: Guidelines to our Changing Society*, Heinemann, 1969.
2. MULLER, H. *The Search for the Qualities Essential to Advancement in a Large Industrial Group: An Exploratory Study*, Carel von Bylandthaan, 30, The Hague, 1970.
3. CARTER, C. F. and WILLIAMS, B. R. *Investment in Innovation*, Oxford University Press, 1958.
4. LAWRENCE, P. and LORSCH, J. *Organization and Environment: Managing Differentiation and Integration*, Harvard University Press, 1967.
5. BEER, S. *Brain of the Firm*, Allan Lane, 1972.
6. JAY, A. *Management and Machiavelli*, Hodder and Stoughton, 1967.

Suggested Reading

MORRIS, J. F. and BURGOYNE, J. G. *Developing Resourceful Managers*, Institute of Personnel Management, 1973.
SCHON, D. A. *Beyond the Stable State: Public and Private Learning in a Changing Society*, Temple Smith, 1971.
TOFFLER, A. *Future Shock*, Bodley Head, 1970.

9. The role of the external consultant

Alan Mumford

This chapter considers some of the reasons for using a consultant and the types of role carried out. The difficulties arising from meeting the client's statement of a required solution—'run me a course'—are discussed, as are some of the implications in terms of solutions being centred on the consultant's expertise. It is suggested that an approach which is both problem solving and client centred may often be more effective. The consultant's role is seen as being to assist learning instead of to prescribe.

At least since the time of Alexander the Great, who said: 'I am dying with the help of too many physicians', the role of the consultant has been associated with fear and irritation on the part of the client. It may help readers to understand this chapter if I define it as being concerned with ways of reducing fear and irritation. It may also help if I offer some working definitions:

Role. Defined by the British Association of Teachers of Management as: 'A set of expectations of how the occupant of a particular position in an organization ought to behave.'

Consultant. At one end of a scale, the training consultant can be a person who provides a specific service to meet an already identified need, e.g., a course on financial accounting for managers. At the other end of the scale, he is someone capable of diagnosing management problems and helping to identify, where appropriate, management development solutions.

External. Normally, the external consultant is a visitor from another organization (if not another management planet), and paid a fee rather than a salary; a training specialist from the head office of a large organization might have much the same opportunities and problems.

I also offer a statement made by Colonel L. Urwick in 1961.[1]

The only work that is really worth doing as a management consultant is that which educates: which teaches clients and their staffs to manage better for themselves.

The consultant may suggest schemes to help a client cut costs and so on, but if the consultant has not done the basic job of re-educating and altering the outlook of the client's staff, he can go back in two years' time and blush for the fees he has drawn for a job he has not done.

I presume from the practice of many consultants that they do not agree with him.

Types of Consultant Work

The major advantages offered by a consultant to an organization are his knowledge and skill, and a view about the organization which may not be objective but is, at least, not politically oriented within the organization in the same way as a member of that organization might be. He brings with him an element of challenge to existing experience, which is often not only unwelcome but seen positively as a threat. His justification for existence is that he helps to resolve problems, hopefully without creating new problems.

The problems and opportunities in the types of service provided by a consultant can be illustrated by looking at a particular area of management development—methods of reviewing performance. These illustrations show not only the services provided by a consultant, but also comment on the willingness of the client to seek outside help:

(a) the consultant can provide a resource to carry out an answer already prescribed by the client. The client might say: 'We have decided that we ought to review the performance of managers formally, and we want you to design an appraisal scheme for us.'

(b) the client may identify a problem, and go to a consultant who is known to have a package answer to that kind of problem. The client might say: 'Our opinion survey shows that managers are not doing performance reviews very well.' The consultant's answer might be his well-known and successful two-day course on methods of appraisal;

(c) the consultant can provide a unique non-packaged answer to a problem identified by the client. His answer to the problem identified above might be to propose to assess what is lacking in the conduct of performance reviews, to provide a special course to meet those needs, and then to do follow-up;

(d) the client might say to the consultant: 'We are not very satisfied with the way in which our performance review system is working; we would like you to investigate and propose solutions.' The consultant might produce a report showing that what is lacking is not the skill of conducting appraisal sessions but motivation by managers, and a failure to follow through on the results of performance review;

(e) the consultant can assist the client to understand and define his own problems. In answer to a statement from the client such as: 'Help us find out what is wrong with the appraisal scheme', he might ask questions such as: 'Why are you doing performance review? What are your objectives?' A client might be brought to understand that the problem was that managers were not getting any personal benefit from the appraisal scheme. The firm has a system, not a method, of helping managers to do their jobs.

Choice of Role

The role of the consultant must obviously vary according to the situation and his own personal abilities. Any of the consultant activities described above can be helpful. He can help to provide justification for a solution already recognized by a client, who does not wish to impose that solution without external support. He can help the client to test proposed solutions, or identify a wider range of options. He can act, with more or less dramatic skill, the role of the wise expert. However, in carrying out the first three of the types of work suggested above, there are few special characteristics except his externality to distinguish him from an internal training specialist, and the ways in which he could work are described elsewhere in this book. The problems faced by a consultant in doing this kind of work may be:

(a) the fact that too often these activities relieve symptoms rather than dealing with causes;
(b) the work is too often centred on the skills and needs of the consultant rather than on the wants of the client;
(c) the economics of consultancy tends towards dealing with managerial units, systems, and large numbers of managers rather than with the individual personal needs of single managers;
(d) the method of work often creates dependence on the consultant, rather than resolving problems in a way which helps managers to learn how to solve problems better;
(e) as Mark Silber has said,[2] line managers too often see the training specialists as trying to turn their departments and themselves into experimental objects rather than seeing the training professional as a producer of results which line management needs.

I repeat, that despite these comments, the appropriate role for a consultant might be that of a provider in the sense mentioned in (a) to (d) above; that role ought to be chosen, however, as a result of full consciousness on the part of both client and consultant, of what the consultant can provide. It is certainly for the client to know whether he wants to identify and solve problems, or whether he wants something different. Some management courses are not intended to be an answer to problems, but to be an answer to questions of the status of the firm, the wish of the managing director that something should be seen to be done, or a belief in the beneficial results of management education. These may all be quite legitimate reasons for what the organization asks of a consultant, so long as both it, and the consultant, are clear on what is being attempted—and why.

I shall concentrate on work centred on the client, his problems, and his wants because this seems to me both more specifically the work of an external consultant and also more unusual.

The Client-Centred Approach

Argyris[3] has said that the role of the consultant is:

(a) to enable valid information to be generated;
(b) to enable the client to make a free, informed choice;
(c) to enable the client to be committed to the choice he makes.

The emphasis in his definition, and the difference from the practice of many consultants, is on the client making a choice and being committed to it. I take his definition as being useful in this context, and preferable to Schein's model of process consultancy, in which he says that the consultant in this role should not be an expert resource, in the sense of suggesting solutions to management problems. The training consultant is certainly in the business of suggesting solutions, and he is an expert resource. He has skill and experience in excess of those possessed by his client, and will deploy them both to help the client by making appropriate inputs of knowledge outside the range possessed by the client. The consultant's commitment to improvement, however, presses him towards defining and answering the client's needs. Consultants sometimes act like missionaries in search of converts, sometimes with as much immediate success. They often share, too, with the missionary a positive desire to make people uncomfortable. A concern with perfection and revolution within an organization may lead to a greater satisfaction for the consultant in the system he has invented than for the client in the results of the system.

The client may also be committed to improvement, but improvement to him means greater efficiency, productivity, and profitability, or the avoidance of complaints. He sees improvement in terms of work problems rather than improvement in planning methods. Yet, although the client may have a commitment to improvement, he rarely has any commitment to change. More frequently, he is opposed to change and frightened of new styles of management. In his Reith Lectures, Donald Schon said: 'Organizations are dynamically conservative—they fight like mad to remain the same—and resist change with an energy that is roughly proportional to the radicalness of the change that is threatened.' Managers tend to be extremely sceptical of the benefits involved in changes, and particularly sceptical about the new styles of management with which so much of management development is concerned. To most managers, change is agony, and advisers wanting to introduce change are angels of death not mercy.

The client will probably be willing to talk about his wants in terms of his current problems but will not respond, in most cases, to a definition of needs provided by an adviser, however accurate these might be in the abstract. There have been considerable benefits derived from the analytical approach to defining training needs with which so much of the training movement has been concerned over the past ten years. There have, however, been unfortunate consequences in the rigid application of this technique—drawn originally from operator training—to management development. The approach to training needs through a preparation of a job description is one example of this. This approach has been specified by many influential bodies in Britain, particularly by the Central Training Council and, subsequently, by the industrial training boards. A survey on management development[4] carried out for the Central Training Council found, however, that job descriptions were often seen as irrelevant by managers, where the intended result was a definition of training needs. Simply, this approach is seen as too lengthy and too far removed from what the manager understands the problem to be. (I am not, incidentally, opposed to job description in principle, and, indeed, believe some version to be essential when looking at problems of managerial performance.) The method of defining needs is crucial because the client is the only person who can make answers work; if the helper defines what is needed, then the client has little motivation to accomplish the helper's task.

In the field of management development, I believe that the most effective consultants are those who use their skill, knowledge, and experience to help the client illuminate his problems and produce his own answers. Given that the consultant knows a wider range of answers than the client, these answers should be produced only to the extent that the client can be helped to ask the right questions. The client's answers will often be less thorough, less precise, and produce a lower level of results than the answers the consultant would produce; they are more likely to be implemented. One example of this approach is the self-assessment questionnaire developed by Hawdon Hague, of Context Training. He asks managers to look at their jobs, their skills and their needs. One interesting result of this kind of approach is that managers often identify for themselves what might be called skills of self-management, e.g., the organization of their working time, methods of working effectively with colleagues and subordinates, and decision taking. These are, of course, aspects of managerial performance which might well be identified by a consultant as 'needs', but training consultants, of all people, ought to be aware of the advantages of self-motivation secured through self-analysis.

Aspects of Client-Centred Consultancy

Client-centred consultancy is concerned to help the manager recognize problems, rather than to sell him solutions. The skills which the consultant needs to deploy are certainly more sophisticated than those possessed by a salesman. In an unpublished survey for the Central Training Council, a team of which I was the leader spoke to a variety of consultants and advisory bodies, including industrial training boards, about the skills required by an adviser. We found that these skills included:

(a) ability to give advice without creating long-term dependence;
(b) removing defensiveness in the relationship between adviser and advised;
(c) sensitivity to situations and people;
(d) the ability to get managers to define their own solutions;
(e) the ability to establish methods of checking the pay-off from advice;
(f) listening skills.

130

Of these, listening is probably the most significant; listening for the real problems of a client, and listening for his definitions of his wants, rather than listening for a clue in his activities which gives the consultant an excuse to provide a solution which he happens to be good at. Consultants may too often be concerned to sell performance review, or succession planning, or a five-day course in man management, instead of dealing with the more personal issue of concern in the individual manager to whom they should be speaking.

Clients may, of course, be more used to dealing with consultants who provide prescriptions rather than with consultants centred on a client's wants. If the client expects to be provided with neat little packages, he will find it disturbing to find that the consultant does not, in the end, provide neat little packages. It might be logical to say that a client-centred consultant dealing with the client's wants will provide packages if that is what the client wants. It would be more appropriate to say that the client should be given a reasonable choice between an approach to a redefinition of the client's problems, as compared with a neat package.

Both the consultant and the client ought to be aware of the different motivations involved for them. The consultant must consider carefully his personal requirements for power and achievement, and relate these to the desirable role for him in relation to the client. In addition, the consultant must be seen to respond to these organizational variables rather than to the prescriptions of the organization to which he himself belongs, e.g., the prescriptions of his firm of consultants or of a training board.

I have inferred, so far, that the skills, and experience required of the consultant relate to the processes of management development. I have found, both in my direct personal experience and in the surveys which I have carried out on the work of training boards, that a knowledge of the industry, area of commerce or public service is an important, and probably essential, contributor to the ability of the consultant to be centred on the wants of the client. The size, type, and objectives of the organization involved are also significant. Many consultants would not agree with this viewpoint, and it may indeed be the case in management development that these are not objective requirements. Discussions with many organizations take me to the view that there is, in effect, an emotional requirement that the consultant knows by direct experience the problems of the organization in which he is working. However similar the management development problems are in ice-cream manufacture and detergents, the initial contract of sympathy between manager and consultant depends a great deal on ability to talk soap or ice-cream effectively.

Consultants and clients have another bond in the sense of the arrangement made between them about the nature and purpose of the consultant's work: the consultant's responsibility not merely to meet deadlines but to consider the ethics of the intervention he is making, and the implications of the changes he is encouraging.

The consultant will be more concerned to help to develop an attitude of mind, and to encourage appropriate behaviour by managers, rather than to set up a neat, written system of management development. Of course, there are benefits in a wholly systematic approach, and benefits in having a coherent unified policy of management development within one organization. Carefully constructed systems of performance review or succession planning certainly have their place. One of the problems with training specialists, however, has been that we have become too much concerned with training systems, and not enough with how people learn and continue to learn. I remember a manager whom I was responsible for advising on the development of his senior staff. The answers he gave to development questions on the formal appraisal system were not particularly helpful and, indeed, in some cases positively inappropriate; he did not like the system and did not know how to use it effectively. He was, however, very concerned to develop his staff, and personal discussions with him were very fruitful. I did not have the courage then or perhaps the realism to suggest that we should abandon the system in his part of the company, and agree to meet once a year to have a prolonged discussion on his people. In his case—and, I believe, in that of many other managers—the system did not help him to learn how to deal with his own problems better. Consultants ought to ask whether a system is necessary, whether the forms and charts involved really achieve anything for managers, and what alternative methods are available.

Rather than challenge the client's attitude and experience directly, the consultant is helping the client to challenge them himself. The consultant listens and diagnoses through asking questions. 'What is the background to that problem? What do you expect to achieve?' In essence, client-centred consultancy means that the consultant must get his satisfaction from helping others rather than from directing them. In common with certain other burgeoning professions, consultancy has perhaps geared itself too strongly to the traditions of the legal and medical professions in terms of role. Advice in law and medicine is authoritative and rarely drawn from the client; it is often only called 'advice' in an attempt to conceal the arrogance of power. It is almost a definition of a profession that you pay the professional for his skilled services, not for results. In management development, the more appropriate professional analogy is with what is delicately called the oldest profession of all, where concern for the client outweighs personal satisfaction.

What Should a Consultant Provide?

Whether he is providing courses or helping to diagnose problems, the consultant should be providing reassurance to the organization he is serving that the solutions developed have been checked against best practice, although best practice itself may not be appropriate to the client. The consultant should be helping to map the feasible path between the ideal solution and the solution which the reality of the situation in the client organization will allow. This means that, for example, he will know when it is appropriate for a company to engage in the sensitive areas of training for interpersonal skills, and how to undertake such training.

132

He will be as expert in identifying and developing opportunities to learn from live business situations as he is at creating off-the-job simulations of managerial experience. Alistair Mant's report 'The Experienced Manager'[5] insisted that this learning from real experience would be the crucial change in management development; it remains an area of potential rather than actual achievement, presumably because it is both difficult to arrange, and expensive. The consultant has the difficult role of being initially a coach to the client while being able, nonetheless, to withdraw coaching support eventually. The essential element in effective coaching is that the man being coached should be helped to improve his capacity to accept the help being offered.

The consultant is inevitably involved, to some extent, in a challenge to existing practices. He has to provide that challenge in a way which enables the client to evolve new practices without feeling himself involved in an unacceptable revolution of outlook or behaviour. The fact that the consultant is relatively objective and uninvolved is part of his strength.

The consultant should provide a practical illustration of management development by his demonstrated skills in managing the consultancy operation, and also by his development of the client's own resources.

Problems in Client-Centred Consultancy

Many clients are used to receiving prescriptions and solutions, and think that is what they are paying for. Client-centred style of working may create uncertainty and a feeling of ambiguity in the client, who may initially prefer the feeling of dependency, relying on the father-figure involved in the more familiar style of consultancy. The more successful the consultant in helping the client to identify his own problems and to draw out his own solutions, the more he may be creating a situation in which the client thinks that he is doing all the work himself but paying a consultant expensively to listen to the client's solutions.

There are, therefore, considerable risks involved for the consultant in client-centred work of this kind. A client may not see the dramatic results which he expects, or wants, early enough; I remember a case in sales-management training where the attempt of the consultant to get the client to look at his problems was met by growing irritation at the failure of the consultant to produce the one-week sales-management course which the client was quite convinced he needed.

For the client, there is the difficulty that the greater his involvement in identifying his own problems, determining his own solutions and being committed to the implementation of those solutions, the less he is able to blame a failed solution on a consultant.

Conclusion

If consultancy really is about learning, and not about systems, managers may actually acquire from it better equipment to handle their problems, rather than being persuaded to buy the equipment that a consultant has to sell. If it is suggested that the role I have described is too modest, I would reply that this kind of modesty, in the face of real managers with real profit and loss problems, is a desirable attribute. I started with one statement about doctors, and conclude with another; obstetricians do not produce babies, they help them to emerge.

References

1. URWICK, L. F. The Part Played by the Management Consultant, talk to FBI Conference, April 1961.
2. SILBER, M. Are You a Failing Training Manager, Training and Development Journal, Aug. 1972.
3. ARGYRIS, C. *Intervention Theory Method*, Addison-Wesley, Reading, Mass., 1970.
4. *Survey on Management Training and Development*, HMSO, 1971.
5. MANT, A. 'The Experienced Manager', British Institute of Management, 1969.

Suggested Reading

HARRISON, R. Choosing the Depth of Organisational Intervention, in *Personal and Organisational Effectiveness* (Ed. R. Hacon), 1972.
KOLB, D. and BOYATZIS, R. On The Dynamics of the Helping Relationship, *Journal of Applied Behavioural Science*, **6,** 3, 1970.
LIPPITT, G. Criteria for Selecting, Evaluating and Developing Consultants, *Training and Development Journal*, Aug. 1972.
SCHEIN, E. *Process Consultation*, Addison-Wesley, Reading, Mass., 1969.

10. Identifying and developing the entrepreneur

Gerald F. Smyth

This chapter illustrates the action which the Irish Management Institute has taken in order to stimulate the growth of a significant sector of the Irish economy, namely small industrial and distribution businesses.

The characteristics of an entrepreneur, and the typical problems faced by owners of small businesses, are identified. The Irish Management Institute has designed a development programme to give drive and confidence to an owner-manager to overcome his problems and to transform his firm into a dynamic unit working to clearly identified objectives.

There are descriptions of examples of action taken by owners as a result of various elements of the programme. The programme is a process of attitude change to make the owner think beyond his day to day problems. It gives him an opportunity to practise managing his business and to review his performance in the manner of a high achiever.

With larger corporations tending increasingly to become multinational firms there is a concentration of productive and distributive resources in the hands of an ever-decreasing number of giants. Small companies meet the demands for goods and services which cannot be economically supplied by the larger firms. The small firm is a necessary part of the infrastructure, and is continually changing its role in the developed and developing economies.

A review of the size structures of firms throughout the world shows that about 90 per cent of all industrial firms have fewer than 100 employees. This is true of the United States and the EEC. In countries like Japan, the figure is more than 95 per cent. This vast block of small firms gives significant employment. For instance in Germany, 29 per cent of the industrial employees are employed by firms with less than 100 people employed.

Identifying Entrepreneurs

In our work at the Institute we do not screen the applicants for our courses into entrepreneurs and non-entrepreneurs. Instead, we define entrepreneurial behaviour and train our participants to behave in this manner. The model we use is that developed by Professor D. C. McClelland of the University of Harvard. In simple terms, this model selects from the many needs which spur a man to take action that will result in self-satisfaction. The successful businessman has a need to achieve, and his consequent actions are directed towards satisfying this need. A businessman has many other needs which, if dominant, will result in a modification of his behaviour and may lead him to behave in a manner which will reduce his effectiveness.

'A need to achieve what?' you may say. We are talking about achieving economic success in business by growth in sales and net assets, and by growing efficiently or with profits, in order to be able to reduce the time taken to achieve significant results and provide a better life for the employer and the employed. Profits are a means to an end and not the end in itself.

We do not select entrepreneurs for our programmes. We believe that the people who come willingly* on our 'development programmes for the smaller businessman' are behaving in an entrepreneurial way, and that they have a higher need to achieve than the average owner-manager, but research is needed to prove this belief.

The characteristics of the successful businessman which derive from Professor McClelland's motivation theory are:

(a) he actively seeks out opportunities to do new things. This may vary from developing new products to seeking out new methods to reduce the costs of his existing processes;
(b) he quantifies the results that he is attempting to achieve. Besides enabling him to realize he has reached his goal, this helps him to plan;
(c) he takes moderate risks, which naturally enhances his chances of success. This means planning in detail the steps to be taken to achieve the goal;
(d) he does research, to find new opportunities, to reduce the risks and to obtain information on his progress towards his goal;
(e) he uses profit as necessary, both as a feedback on progress and a means of reaching further goals;
(f) he calls in experts to help solve problems;
(g) he gets himself into relationships with people where the outcome benefits both;
(h) he takes personal responsibility for the achievement of results.

The Problems of Small Firms

Research into the operations of small business have indicated a range of problems. Some of these can be tackled during a training programme;

* Certain industrial sectors have been levied by the Government to 'encourage' training. Attendence on some of our programmes qualifies some firms to recover a major portion of their levy.

others need a different approach. The problems occurring in small businesses are as follows:

(a) There is a lack of clear overall direction or objectives for the business. Small firms must, by nature, be adaptive and flexible, but the owners of many small firms have no objective other than survive the present problems.
(b) The business depends on one man who makes all the decisions. There is a high mortality rate in infant firms. The owner's total assets are frequently committed to the business in its early years, and the owner makes all the key decisions in the period of high risk. This conditions the firm to the habit of centralized decision making.
(c) The dynamic nature of the firm changes with the age of the owner. This problem is a direct consequence of its dependency on one man.
(d) There is a succession problem. Many small firms die with the owners, not just because he may have married later in life than the average man, but more often, because of the centralized decision-making policy and lack of clear objectives.
(e) The owner-manager frequently has a very poor understanding of finance.
(f) Profits are lost due to lack of knowledge of hidden costs, and low product profitability frequently occurs. Many small firms work without an information system, and costs are estimated by rule of thumb.
(g) Small firms are frequently undercapitalized. This is due to the loss of profits and the overtrading which occur through ignorance. Because of the risk, small businesses do not attract commerical investors, who find it easier to watch their investments in a small number of larger firms and who are worried by the lack of financial planning in small firms and by the quest for loans based on questionable product-costing systems.
(h) Apart from some specialism of the owner, the small firm frequently lacks the specialist staff to be found in large firms. This means that the owner has to have a good general knowledge of all areas of activity of the business and the interrelationships that exist. This is generally not the case, and decisions taken to correct problems in one area often create problems in other areas.
(i) The small firm frequently finds it difficult to recruit staff. There are many reasons for this, which include lack of opportunity for advancement and development in family businesses, less attractive conditions of employment, and reduced security.
(j) Inflation affects costs more rapidly. Because of its non-capital-intensive nature (and its shortage of capital), the small firm's major inputs of cost are direct materials and direct labour. The shortage of capital means that little stock is carried, so inflation rapidly affects the cost of goods sold.
(k) The small business has low purchasing power. Because of the low usage rates and the shortage of working capital, the small firm cannot take

advantage of the bulk discounts available to the larger consumer, and it must frequently buy from the middle man (wholesaler or distributor) and not from the primary source of supply.

(l) Keeping up to date with the technology of both products and processes is very difficult for the owner-manager because of the demands on his time. This is a major problem in some cases where the key to success in the early years depended on the founder's knowledge of a new product or process.

(m) The owner-manager has little skill in setting targets. It is our experience on programmes that when owner-managers first set a monthly target for themselves, less than 40 per cent of the targets are achieved. The failure rate on targets over extended periods would be much larger.

(n) Owner-managers frequently do not manage their time. In fact, it is the main reason why the monthly targets mentioned above are not met. The managers spend their time solving problems rather than anticipating obstacles and planning to eliminate many of the problems.

(o) Many owner-managers exhibit a low level of motivation to develop their businesses. Many never think of why they are in business or what their resources are, and never look for opportunities which could put their business on a sound growth path.

The problems listed above are not interdependent, nor are all found in all small firms, but many of them are present to a greater or lesser extent in the firms of the owner-managers who come on our development programmes. These are designed to help solve many of these problems and to train the owner-manager to modify his behaviour.

Developing the Smaller Firm

On the basis of the many problems which exist in smaller firms, and using the model of the successful businessman as the basis of how the owner-manager should behave, the Irish Management Institute has developed a series of programmes for the owners and managers of smaller businesses.

The major programme is of eight days' duration, but eight consecutive days does not always suit the owner-manager, since his business may depend on his presence to solve day to day problems. It was therefore decided that the course should be held on two consecutive days every month for a period of four months. This not only meets the needs of the owners, but suits the method of training being used. The core of the programme is concerned with identifying opportunities; goal setting, deciding on action steps to achieve goals, self-management and product analysis. A six-day extension to this programme, which is also held on two consecutive days each month, enables those who have attended to prepare plans for their firm for the following twelve-month period. The objectives of the development programmes are to stimulate in the owner the desire to achieve, help him to understand the potential and limitations of his total resources and understand the interrelationships that exist in his business so as to improve his ability to set realistic targets. These programmes have been instrumental in helping many firms to achieve a significant improvement in performance and, out of one group of sixteen participants, three people who were employed managers had set up their own business within a year of attending the programme.

Other courses, usually of two to three days' length, concentrate on basic management techniques such as cash planning, costing, production control, and marketing techniques.

An interesting new development has been the running of courses for supervisors and department managers of firms whose owners have been on the eight-day development programme. As a result of identifying the objectives of their firm, the owners were able to specify the training needs of their supervisors to match the needs of the 'changed' business. These courses have been organized for businesses in certain industrial sectors, such as engineering firms, retail motor trading, footwear, and clothings.

The Development Programme

Any attitude-change programme takes time, and, to the pragmatic owner-manager, the promise of success in the distant future is less helpful than concrete examples of the success of the new approach during the training programme. It is necessary that the owners experience an early success; the programme is designed with this in mind. As already stated, the objectives of the programme are to develop within the owner-manager a will to achieve in business, to train him to practise the behaviour of the high achiever and apply his knowledge to his new understanding of his business. The programme attempts to integrate a programme of work into the manager's normal routine. It is the intention that the manager does not feel that he is leaving his work to go on a course, but that he sees the course as his work. One frequently hears the remark, particularly after the extended fourteen-day programme, that 'we should continue meeting for two days every month'. The four- or five-week interval between sessions is useful in other ways. It enables the manager to set goals to be achieved between sessions. This practice at setting goals, and the subsequent review of performance, is a key to developing entrepreneurial behaviour in the manager and gives him skill which enables him to set realistic long-term goals for his business. The interval also gives the manager the opportunity to try to put into practice analytical, planning, or control techniques which are discussed. These are usually successful, and nothing succeeds like success. It encourages the manager to become even more involved in the process. If the attempt has been a failure, then the manager can discuss the problems during the next two-day session, and any difficulty can be ironed out so that he can try again in the next interval.

Usually, the managers are eager to talk about their success, and this develops the enthusiasm in the group. The close working relationship over a long period of time helps develop trust, even between competitors.

One notable success in this area was where there were two managers whose firms were in the same business sector but whose trading areas were 250 miles apart. At the end of the programme, they agreed to open their books to each other, and each would travel every alternate month to the other man's business to have a management meeting—a review of progress and a plan for the next two months. Both businesses performed extremely well with this arrangement.

The methodology for entrepreneurial training developed by McBer and Company, has been modified to suit the needs of our small business owner-managers.

The Content

The content of the eight-day programme is a blend of entrepreneurial training to give the manager the basic skill of business analysis—carrying

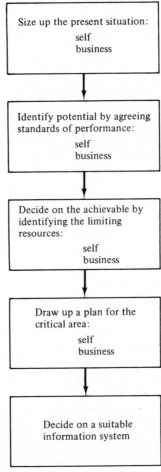

Fig. 10.1. Model of the development programme.

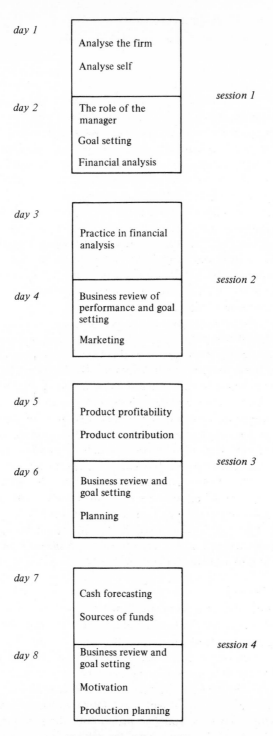

Fig. 10.2. The daily structure.

out the analysis and leading on to corporate planning. Figure 10.1 summarizes the approach, and Figure 10.2, the daily structure.

Analysing Self

The self-analysis looks at how the owner performs as a manager, and why he performs that way. The analysis of how he performs, which continues throughout the programme, begins with a look at the role that the owner sees himself as occupying the business. He then analyses how well he has played that role in the days immediately before the course—it seems that there is no such thing as a typical day. In subsequent discussion on business objectives, the key tasks he should perform as manager to achieve the business objectives are compared with the actual role played. One picture emerges time and again. It is of a man not doing what he ought to do, but doing either something he likes to do or is forced to do. The result is trouble. At various periods throughout the programme, the owner is asked to keep a record of how he spends his time and compare it to how he should spend it.

It must be emphasized that, in a small firm, there is a shortage of specialist staff and some of the key tasks to be performed by the manager would not fall within a definition of management.

Why does the owner-manager behave as he does? Answering this question is a critical part of the programme. Exercises in imagery are used by the participants to identify the strength of their need to achieve. The model of the successful businessman—high achiever—is illustrated by reference to some well-known entrepreneur, and a full discussion of the various elements takes place so that everyone present fully understands them. Finally, each participant compares his own characteristics with those of the entrepreneur.

The owner of a small engineering shop stated that this section of the programme was the most important experience in his life and he need not attend the rest of the programme. He did complete the programme but he did other things besides. For twenty years he had run his small business—twelve employees including members of his family—with little change. As a result of the programme, he looked at what business opportunities he could grasp in his area. In four years he has increased his sales eightfold, doubled his employment, and is investing his profits to ensure continued growth according to a business plan.

Analysing the Business

This is just a little different from the approach used by some management consultants, who examine the various functions of the business individually and then integrate the problems to find the 'total' picture. They then decide on a cure, and prescribe accordingly. We prepare a detailed questionnaire covering all the activities, resources and systems in the firm, and the analysis is carried out by the owners themselves. This questionnaire is contained in the planning folder, details of which are shown in Figure 10.3. The initial shock of realizing that they know so little about their business is nothing compared to the shock they get when they cannot find answers to obvious questions because their staff don't know; nor do they have a proper informa-

```
Section 1
Analysis of:
  Markets
  Products
  Profitability
  Productivity
  Management

Section 2
Summary of:
  Strengths
  Weaknesses

Section 3
The idea of the business

Section 4
Objectives
```

Fig. 10.3. Planning folder.

tion system. The revelation that major problems exist which they never thought about becomes a powerful tool in changing many owners' attitudes to their businesses. As one owner put it: 'It is bad enough having to break our backs every day but now we shall not be able to sleep at night.'

The analysis covers:

markets;
products;
marketing;
competition;
people;
selection;
training;
motivation;
communication;
organization;

financial performance over a three-year period;
present financial situation;
financial controls;

production resources;
production processes;
production planning and control;

technology;
effects of external factors.

One service engineering company found that it had far less customers than it had assumed. Many firms find that they do not know such basic things as their position in the market-place, the strength of the competition, or which products contribute the bulk of their profits, or losses in some cases.

We have listed many of the problems which face the owner-manager of a small firm. Telling him about his problems makes little impact—getting him to find out in detail his own problems is a learning experience which does not, alone, stimulate action leading to a cure, but the analytical process is one that he can pass on to his departmental managers and supervisors. One retail motor trader used the questionnaire in the following way. He found that he did not know all the answers so he gave the relevant sections to his department managers. Answering the questions and discussing the problems and interrelationships has become the agenda of monthly meetings of the management staff. The resultant improvement in interpersonal relations and profitability has been outstanding.

It should be noted that the business analysis questionnaire is answered, so far as possible, in private rather than in groups, and the tutor circulates to help participants with difficulties.

Identifying the Potential—Self

The sessions on the high achiever lead on to the goal-setting exercise. This exercise ties together self-management and the development of one of the characteristics of the high achiever, namely setting concrete goals. While the goal is the important thing in the exercise, it is the habit of setting stretching, but attainable, goals that we strive to develop in the manager. The exercise is continued throughout the eight-day programme.

The managers are given about forty minutes to select three tasks which they will have completed before they return on the next module. They may choose the application of techniques discussed, they may pick out projects that they have on hand, or they may select three from the 'list' that they have been putting off for many months. The tasks chosen are written in terms of results to be achieved. They are placed in envelopes which are collected by the tutor. On the next module the envelopes are opened by each individual, and a measure of group achievement is attained in terms of the percentage of total goals set that have been fully completed. Partial success is counted as failure.

Successful tasks are then examined before the entire group to see who set challenging and achievement-type tasks (innovation and improvement).

Tasks are examined in terms of the degree of quantification of results. Subjective standards are not acceptable initially. Reasons for failure are examined. The most common causes of failures cited by the managers are:

(a) shortage of time: poor self-management, or unreasonable objective;
(b) information not available;
(c) dependency on others within the organization;
(d) dependency on external agents;

(e) lack of planning;
(f) objective frustrated;
(g) other work and problems not foreseen.

You can see how this self-examination holds the mirror up to the manager. He soon realizes that if he cannot set four-week goals for himself he has little chance of setting realistic long-term goals for his business and his employees.

Goal setting helps the owner to identify his potential to perform in a variety of circumstances; also, how the output can vary depending on the degree of delegation practised. He realizes that time is required at the goal-setting stage, that planning is necessary, and that unless there is constant review, there is a high probability of failure. He looks at his dependency relations more closely and, last but not least, sees how little time he has been spending on those activities which help to achieve his objectives. The goal-setting exercises help to solve some of the major problems in small businesses, namely:

(a) poor self-management;
(b) unclear objectives;
(c) little delegation;
(d) the succession problem.

Problems (c) and (d) are closely linked. After about two attempts at goal setting, many managers realize that their problem is that they have been trying to do everything themselves. Delegation of some key activities commences, and this results in new life in the organization and the birth of possible successors with decision-making experience.

Identifying the Potential—Business

When carrying out the job of analysing how the business currently stands, owners must also examine the potential of the various areas of the business if all the opportunities for improvement were availed of by using the strengths of the company to take full advantage of the market-place. This is done, firstly, without regard to the interrelationships that exist and the limiting resources of the business. The summary of strengths and weaknesses is listed in the planning folder. Potential is usually expressed in economic terms in relation to sales, production, and utilization of resources.

The frequent lack of understanding of finance on the part of owner-managers, together with its resultant problems of loss of profits and frequent overtrading, is tackled on the programme.

The only functional area in which there is considerable input on knowledge and techniques is in the business-finance area. This business language is necessary to understand the situation of the business, identify the threats and opportunities in economic terms and to plan the future within the constraints of the limiting resources of the firm. The programme covers the understanding and use of financial accounts, costing, budgeting, and cash planning. Perhaps the most important aspect of business finance discussed is using marginal costing to identify those products or services which contribute highly to the fixed costs and profit of the business. In this way, the business potential can be seen.

The product-contribution analysis is proving to be a turning point in many businesses and gives some of the participants their first significant success on the programme. One company with sixty employees, making a range of stainless-steel tanks, found that there were certain sizes of tanks which were high contributors, and that others were low contributors. They found that they had been trying for a number of years to push the wrong products in the market-place.

Of course, product-contribution analysis should not be done until the potential to reduce the direct costs has been examined. To do this, statistics from similar businesses are discussed. Material-conversion rates, labour-, machine-, and space-productivity rates are discussed. On two programmes for retail motor dealers, we have carried out interfirm studies. The discussions on such topics are more usefully conducted among groups in similar industrial sectors for whom we run programmes, and even in a sector as broad as engineering, it is possible to find a number of common subgroups.

Exchanging Experiences

A valuable part of a development programme is the sharing of business experience. This is not left to chance in the after-dinner hours. Time is set aside to discuss the business sector, the current problems of some members present, and interesting things an owner may have tried out in his business. For example, one firm of coach builders with thirty-five employees had productivity problems. The coach-building industry is one of the traditional craft industries with centuries of 'custom and practice'. This firm introduced a modified form of the Scanlon plan, and the resultant increase in productivity has meant the survival of the firm, whose product was costing more than the market price. Another company analysed all their quotations to their customers over a two-year period and have drawn up a demand curve which helps them match their capacity with the market demand. This exercise might be followed by many large firms.

Experience exchange helps build trust relationships, and we have some indications from a small research project that a number of joint ventures have been established as a result of the programmes.

Deciding on the Achievable—Self

Having examined his potential in various areas, the owner is now asked to select areas in which he wants to specialize. This is a difficult part of the programme for the owner. He goes through a process of identifying his achievable life goals and he is brought back from his long-term goals to medium- and short-term goals for himself individually, and for his business.

Having identified the potential of the various elements in the business, it is now necessary to understand the interrelationships and identify limiting factors. This is done, initially, by applying the financial knowledge gained to finding solutions to a number of corporate-planning case studies.

In small businesses, limiting resources fall mainly under four headings:

(a) shortage of capital;
(b) shortage of skilled labour;
(c) shortage of management time;
(d) shortage of new ideas.

Shortage of capital can be indicated in several ways. The most frequent is the shortage of working capital—inability to give credit, carry stock, or take advantage of discounts for early payment. It is also expressed in terms of poor layout, shortage of working space, and obsolete plant. A major problem in firms which must be adaptive and flexible is inability to finance new products. On our programmes we invite commercial investors as after-dinner speakers, to talk about sources of loans and grants which can be drawn on by owners of small business.

The effective use of fixed and current assets is discussed but training in techniques in this area, and in that of labour productivity, is restricted to separate, short intensive courses.

Shortage of management time has already been discussed. We have asked several groups who have come on our programmes to identify the long-term problems facing their company. The one which is consistently being reported is the shortage of ideas for products to replace their existing lines. Survival means flexibility, shortage of cash means no investment in research and development, no turnover of management staff limits the flow of fresh ideas.

The solution to this problem is extremely difficult. Course participants are informed of suitable technical journals, advised on trade fairs and given names of our semi-state organizations who may be able to give assistance, but, more important, the continual review of its strengths and opportunities is emphasized as essential when a firm is faced with the problem. The idea of a business—as in part three of the planning folder (see Figure 10.3)—is not so much what the company makes, but a statement by the owner of the achievable results in the market it serves with the resources it commands.

Planning

In a programme as short as eight days, there are limitations on the inputs. The major planning work stems from an indentification of long-term personal and organizational goals. These are then reduced to subgoals to be achieved in the short term. These subgoals are entered in the fourth part of the planning folder. A method of drawing up a business plan for the next twelve months is covered, but generally there is only time for the manager to pick one key area of the business and draw up plans for that area. Where

147

programmes are extended to fourteen days, a considerable part of the final six days is spent in planning in detail the activities of the firm, the organization of the firm, the role of the management team, and the information system required by each manager and supervisor to control and coordinate activities according to plan.

The Information System

Small businesses require less detailed information systems than their big brothers. Because of the financial tightrope that the owner of a small business walks on, he is encouraged to introduce cash budgeting with monthly reviews. Cash budgeting is one of the financial techniques covered in the programme. If there is another area of his business which is limiting, such as a bottleneck in the production area, it is suggested that a planning and control system be set up to get maximum utilization of the scarce resource, but such systems are not covered in the programme.

Evaluation

A major research project is now under way into the effect of an extended programme on twenty manufacturing businesses. It is examining the changes in the businesses twelve months after the completion of the programme. Each manager indicates how many of the changes he attributes to the programme, and the results are now being compared with the original course objectives, the objectives for individual sessions, the evaluation carried out by participants after each two-day module, and the final end-of-course evaluation. Changes being measured include profitability, sale and number of people employed.

At the time of going to press, 60 per cent of businesses have returned the completed questionnaire. The results are very encouraging and will be published in December 1974.

Conclusion

We are not pushing the boundaries of knowledge. We are not developing new management techniques. What we are doing is giving drive and confidence to the owner-manager, helping him to identify the potential of his firm clearly, and directing him in an action-oriented approach to achieve clearly stated objectives.

Suggested Reading

CONNELLAN, L., EGAN, D., and GORMAN, L. The Use of Behavioural Science, Findings in the training of Entrepreneurs; paper presented to EAMTC annual conference, 1970.
DEAN, N. and McCONNELL, J. *Managing Finance in a Small Industry*, Irish Management Institute, Dublin, 1971.
DRUCKER, P. F. *Managing for Results*, Pan, 1964.
GORMAN, L. and MOLLOY, E. *People, Jobs and Organisations*, Irish Productivity Centre, 1972, chapter 8.
IRISH MANAGEMENT INSTITUTE, *Management*, xvii, 8/9, 1970; xviii, 7/8, 1971.
McBER and Company, *Performance Improvement Series*, 1970.
McCLELLAND, D. C. and WINTER, D. G. *Motivating for Economic Achievement*, Collier-Macmillan, London, 1969.
SMYTH, G. F. 'Going it alone—Managing a low technology business', *Technology Ireland*, 5, 10, January 1974.
WOOD, E. G. *Bigger Profits for the Smaller Firm*, Business Books, London, 1972.

11. Management development in the developing countries

Shyam B. L. Bharadwaj

Management development in the developing countries must be organically related to the development goals and ethos of these nations. It must meet rigorous criteria of relevance and utility; flexibility; national identity; responsiveness to socioeconomic and political realities; urgency; and vigorous pursuit of efficiency, cost consciousness, time consciousness; and generation of surplus. It should help the manager to understand and create an effective relationship between his organization and national purposes, and enable him to play his role as a developer, a change agent, a resource optimizer, and a resolver of differences and conflicts. It should foster an entrepreneurial climate of daring and excellence.

The present status of management development in eighteen developing nations of Asia and Africa has been examined within this framework; and certain basic dimensions of its evolution, along with some international influences have been identified. The author emphasizes the organic relationship between manager development, organization development, and national development, and notes the emergence of certain hopeful signs.

The past decade, both in the developed and the developing countries, has been one of intensive questioning and debate about the future of man and his institutions. The result of this scrutiny has been an alternation between hope and despair, and the tentative solutions that have been proposed range from the radical to the conservative. The educational system, as a vital means of preparation for the present and the future, has provided one of the hottest debating themes of the decade. Existing educational systems in different countries have been assailed on grounds of relevance, utility, flexibility, vision, methodology, scope, and output. Management development, as an aspect of formalized educational effort, today is being subjected to the same kind of severe but necessary examination.

The term 'management development' is used here in a comprehensive and generic sense. Although, in the course of this review, we shall confine our attention mainly to the formalized and institutionalized aspects of management education, we recognize that development is, or should be, a total and continuous process in the lifespan of a manager; and often, the less formal educative influences that impinge upon him contribute significantly to the growth of his ability to adapt and cope, and his effectiveness as a person, as a manager, as a member of his organization, and as a citizen of his country and the world. However, as a working definition for our purpose, management development may be taken to imply: *planned and institutionalized interventions which aim at helping a manager to play his managerial roles more effectively by acquiring broader perspective and 'cognitive maps'; clearer frames of reference and order of priorities; relevant information, concepts, and theories; updated professional and technical skills; creative and progressive attitudes relevant to his roles; and personal skills related to learning how to learn, and how to become an integrated, productive and 'growthful' individual.* Such definition is, however, more in the nature of a challenge and a hope than a description of the present state of affairs. The achievement of such comprehensive objectives of management development would imply an orchestration of purposes between the individual manager, his organization, the external educational agencies, and the national social institutions; this has rarely been attempted, even in the developed countries.

The term 'management' has been largely associated with business and industry, although it has clear relevance for many other forms of the organized sector. As a result, there has been a disproportionate bias in management education towards optimization of processes related to the manufacturing and trading organizations. This has led to a parallel, and often independent, creation of institutions dealing with the development of 'public administrators'.

Arguments have been advanced to emphasize the distinction between the manager and the administrator, and between industrial culture and bureaucratic culture. It has been stated that the *administrator* deals with relatively more structured situations, operates in a rational and hierarchical organizational system, tries to avoid errors and undue risks, lays greater emphasis on the procedures and propriety of the decision-making process rather than on its outcomes, is concerned more with workable compromises than the optimum solution of problems, and is heavily affected by political processes and considerations. On the other hand, it is claimed that the *manager* is involved in the process of production and generation of surpluses and profits, operates often in an environment of ambiguity, uncertainty and crises, works under heavy stresses and severe time pressures, frequently has to take calculated risks, has a pronounced 'achievement motivation', and is more concerned with arriving at effective, rather than proper, solutions. There may be some basis for the above distinctions, but there are administrators and administrators, and managers and managers, just as there is a wide range of structures and cultures both in business and industry, as well as the so-called administrative sector.

In the developing countries aiming at rapid evolution of a new society and a viable economy within the framework of social and economic justice, the difference between the roles of the manager and the administrator becomes less pronounced. This calls for an imaginative link between 'management development' and 'administrator development'. The realization of this has resulted in a series of reviews and studies sponsored by the United Nations and other agencies. As an illustration of a move in this direction, the Administrative Staff College of India has redefined its role, as: a contribution through training, research, and consultancy activities towards a better management of national affairs. Thus, apart from the familiar management courses for the practising manager-administrator, this institution is entering into such fields as educational administration, family-planning administration, transport administration, dissemination of science and technology, and management of research and development, etc. On the other hand, in many developing countries, where industrial activity is still marginal, institutes of public administration are expected to carry out the task of training public administrators, both for development administration and for industrial management. Examples of this are the National Institute of Development Administration, Thailand; the Centre for Economic Development and Administration, Nepal; the Philippine Executive Academy, University of Philippines; and similar organizations in some African countries.

The programmes conducted by many of these institutions are a blend of the traditional inputs of public administration and the new management subjects. Even if, for various historical reasons, there are separate institutions for training the public administrator and the manager, there is an urgent need in the developing countries to bring these two types of executives together, within the framework of programmes calculated to develop an understanding of each other's priorities, roles, and constraints. This is being attempted in a few countries, in the context of general management programmes for the practising administrators and managers.

For historical and political reasons, and for reasons of availability, in many of the developing countries of the world, managerial personnel for the newly established business and industrial enterprises in the public sector have been drawn from the Civil Service and the military. Hastily created management development programmes, often fragmentary and superficial, have sometimes been planned and pushed through for inducting the 'public servant turned manager' into the world of business and industry. This has been both a help and a hindrance. Some countries, e.g., India, have become aware of the limitations of such a strategy for staffing managerial positions in public-sector enterprises and have taken corrective steps by trying to instate the professional manager in place of the careerist public administrator.

There are certain other historical and political influences operating in the management development scene in the developing countries. In many newly independent nations, concepts and practices in management development have been heavily influenced by their association with former colonial powers. Thus, British and French models of managerial practices and management education systems seem still to be influencing some of their former colonies in Asia and Africa. The US, with its image of a colossus in the field of business and industry, has been a later, but often more powerful influence in the field of management education, in many developing countries of south and South-east Asia, Latin America, and, perhaps, Africa. The American influence has even permeated developed countries such as Britain, France, West Germany, and Japan. Certain influences in this direction also seem to be emanating from the USSR, Yugoslavia and the East European countries, and may gradually increase in the developing countries moving towards socialistic ideologies.

It would therefore seem that, in all its aspects, management education in the developing countries may have a serious identity problem. A number of private communications which I have received from people working in management development in countries such as the Sudan, Burma, and Turkey describe the management education efforts in their respective countries with diffidence, doubt, and even scepticism. There is some thinking emerging to the effect that, in matters related to management education, the developing countries should learn from one another. This may be inferred from visits of delegations from Ghana, Nigeria, the Sudan, Malaysia, and Bangladesh to other developing countries, to study their organization and content of management education.

Agencies such as UNDP, ECAFE, USAID, ILO, CIOS, the Asian Productivity Organization, and the Ford Foundation are evincing some interest in promoting the development of regional cooperation among the developing countries in the matter of management development, among other things. However, although the developing countries may look for management development models elsewhere, obtain foreign aid and advice, and learn from the successes and mistakes of the developed countries, and although they may pool their resources, and exchange information and experiences with other like-minded developing countries, in the ultimate analysis each developing country will have to find, for itself, the knowledge and resources to create plans and institutions of management development to suit its internal realities and its own aspirations, objectives, and priorities.

The developing countries can ill afford the luxury of accepting irrelevant fashions in management education. They cannot permit a *laissez-faire*, unplanned, and slow evolution of management development to arise in passive response to the domestic market. What they need is meticulous planning, bold new concepts, and an entrepreneurial plunge into management development activities, geared to an accelerated pace of national development. For both survival and growth, they have to have the courage of temporal compression: the developmental gap of centuries has to be leapt in decades, that of decades in years, that of years in months. The 'aspiration' explosion among the peoples of most developing countries, the population explosion in many countries, and the glaring contrast between hope and reality, between promise and performance, leaves these struggling nations with but little time, which they have to seize with faith, vigour, and a consuming sense of urgency.

In action terms, this means a heart-searching critique, an imaginative consolidation, lion-hearted planning for growth, a readiness to face the shockwaves of change, a dramatic breakthrough in strategies of investment and implementation, a rigorous attempt at institution building and organization development, and a massive effort at social engineering and transformation of attitudes. All these must be fully reflected in their management development programmes.

Developing a Nation

In order to understand the nuances of management development in the developing countries, it is necessary to take a look at the goals, prerequisites, processes, strategies, and means of national development. Much literature on developmental phenomena has appeared during the past two decades. But, often, the analysis suffers from disciplinary biases, narrow perspectives, and hasty prescriptions. Economists, sociologists, historians, philosophers, political scientists, anthropologists, and psychologists have vied with one another in propounding theories of economic, political, technological, and social development. The field is littered with untested assumptions and partial insights, valuable but limited. What is needed is an integration of the various theories into a dynamic system.

The price now being paid by the highly developed countries of the world in terms of alienation, protest and violence, neurosis and psychological insecurity, dehumanization, ecological crisis, and loss of purpose and relevance, has all been paid in the name of development and progress. Does development merely mean industrialization, technological revolution, urbanization, creation of a mass consumption society, and other phenomena lumped together under the dubious label of 'modernization'? Is this the model which is entirely relevant for the newly emerged nations of the world? These questions are difficult to answer with any degree of certainty; and the developing countries may not yet have any tangible alternative to the economist's and the technologist's versions of a happy world.

Someday, perhaps, man will acquire the wisdom to redefine his 'pursuit of happiness' in such a manner that it would not tend to threaten his very existence. Till then, we must seriously concern ourselves with problems of balancing agricultural growth against population growth; banishing poverty and disease; liberating the human mind and energy through education, nourishing creativity and innovation; creating means for transport and communication; bringing the insights and fruits of science and technology to the door of the common man; efficiently harnessing the means of production; building houses for the homeless; finding gainful employment for every citizen; ensuring social and economic justice to all; building humanized organizations; reconciling freedom with discipline; creating a human culture dominated by authenticity and trust; creatively handling differences and

153

conflicts; learning to use power and influence in an effective manner. These goals are tangible enough, for the developed and developing countries alike, but they are too many and too complex, and some of them appear to be mutually contradictory.

It is the complexity of these social, political, technological, and economic goals that makes the choice of priorities, means, and strategies difficult for the developing countries. The dilemmas of development are many: how fast do we want to develop; shall we attempt development on all fronts, or concentrate on raising GNP through production and commerce; what relative priorities shall we assign between agricultural development and industrial development; what balance shall exist between consumption and investment; shall we make or buy; what foreign aid and know-how should we seek, and from whom; what mix of public and private investment would be optimal for our goals of industrial development; shall we go into capital-intensive industries or labour-intensive industries; what protection and incentives can we offer to indigenous industry; what shall be the meaning and degree of self-reliance in our developmental effort; how much shall we invest in social overheads; how much of the gains of development must reach the common man, and how fast; how can we strike a balance between social, political, and technological development?

These, and a host of similar decisions, are being taken by the developing countries of the world in the context of their ideological and political development. Thus, developing countries may differ as much among themselves as they do from the developed countries, in their choice of goals and strategies of development. However, internal compulsions have often led them towards centralized planning for development, and creation of a large and influential public sector. The private sector in most of these countries is being increasingly regulated and controlled, and even progressively nationalized.

It is in this context of ferment, control, uncertainty and hope that management development has to seek its validation and relevance in the developing countries. What these countries require is managers to bridge the 'implementation gap', with vigour and commitment, effectiveness, and daring. If management development effort is to prove viable it must meet rigorous criteria of relevance and utility, flexibility, a sense of national identity, responsiveness to socioeconomic and political realities, clarity of purpose, a sense of urgency, and vigorous pursuit of efficiency, cost consciousness, time consciousness, social responsibility, and generation of surplus. Above all, management development activities must result in the creation of a unique managerial style rooted in the culture and aspirations of the country. The manager must not only swim with the socio-political tide, he must also have the skill and wisdom of bridging or diverting it into nationally productive channels. He must understand the relationship of his organization with national purposes, and have the skills needed to relate microlevel planning to macrolevel planning. He must overcome professional obsolescence and personal obsolescence. He must learn to be a developer, a change agent, an innovator and creator, a resource optimizer, a manager of differences and conflicts, and an entrepreneur.

Entrepreneurship

The concept of entrepreneurship may well prove to be one of the key concepts of management development in the developing countries. Numerous studies have attempted to understand the role and motives of the entrepreneur as a contributor to development. The entrepreneur has been described as an individual who perceives an opportunity, organizes an economic activity, takes risks, strives for profits, constantly and tirelessly struggles to achieve progressively higher standards of excellence, innovates, is highly 'achievement motivated', and is very often a 'social deviant'. Psychologists, sociologists, economists, and anthropologists have devoted much time and effort to studying his characteristics, and the conditions under which he emerges, flourishes, languishes, or declines.

Norman R. Smith[1] has distinguished between three types of entrepreneurs, and the corresponding patterns of organization that each type builds for himself. The 'craftsman-entrepreneur' has a technical orientation, both educationally and mentally, and perceives himself as a practical man. He is often a poor communicator, but a man of action. He builds a rigid organization, with unchanging production techniques, product mix, and markets. He does not like the large organization, because he is loath to delegate and relies on personal contacts to recruit staff or gain customers. He is paternalistic in his employee relations and is rooted in the past and the present. The 'opportunistic entrepreneur' has more formal education and work experience. He perceives himself more as a manager than a technician. He has high social awareness and involvement and is often a good communicator. He displays flexibility, and confidence in his own capacity to deal with the economic and social environment. He builds a flexible organization, delegates authority, uses multiple sources of capital, and various competitive strategies in addition to price and quality. He is future oriented and develops long-range plans for his organization. A third type of entrepreneur, the 'inventor-entrepreneur' seemingly has as his main goal to continue to invent and to have his inventions used by industry.

There are others, like Collins *et al.*,[2] who believe that in a highly developed country such as the US, the ambition to have one's own business may be on the decline, and that the entrepreneurial function is about to be built into the large organization.[3] Thus, a new type of manager emerges in the bigger organizations, who could be called a 'business hierarch', and who differs significantly from the typical, self-employed entrepreneur. The business hierarch focuses on specialized job activities and personal career interests. He seeks to find a niche in an established organization, and becomes an 'organization man'.[4] He concentrates on doing his appointed job well and tries to become a specialist and an expert within his occupational speciality. He relentlessly pursues his potential for advancement in the hierarchy.

The successful business hierarch has positive attitudes towards his boss, and works hard so as to be singled out for speedy advancement. He displays great ability to organize unstructured situations, to perceive relationships among isolated events, to predict the outcome of his decisions and actions. He is quick and clear in his choices and has the courage of his conviction.

It is perhaps legitimate to extend the meaning and application of the term 'entrepreneur' beyond that indicated above. If entrepreneurship implies innovation, pursuit of excellence, an urge to convert challenges into opportunities, and wisdom in the face of ambiguities, uncertainties and frustrations, then a truly developing nation has to be an entrepreneurial society, with entrepreneurial organizations and institutions, and entrepreneurial elites and workers. This spirit of entrepreneurship has to permeate social, political, educational, technological, and economic activities. The general educational system and the management education agencies have to be coordinated, and pressed into service, to bring about this revolution of values and ferment of purposive activity conducive to accelerated national progress.

Management development, in this context, becomes the development of entrepreneurial attitudes and skills. In order to nourish this climate of innovation and daring, management education in a developing country should be extended to all small, medium, and large organizations engaged in the challenging task of national development. Management development programmes must be designed to provide continuous opportuntities for growth and renewal to managers at all levels, and in all types of developmental enterprises. Such a concept of management development may be slowly emerging, but all developing countries have still a long way to go towards this goal. Material and human resources have yet to be found to tackle this gigantic task: till then, pragmatic improvizations have to be made, and new opportuntities for management development created.

Present Status

In the light of the above philosophy, the current realities of management development call for a brief review. Published literature on the subject is meagre, as there have been few attempts at systematic documentation. Although a start towards management development has been made in most developing countries of Asia, Africa, and Latin America, progress is generally inadequate and uneven. The effort has been disproportionately greater in the politically sensitive regions of south and South-east Asia, and Latin America. Foreign aid and attention to management development seems to have been concentrated in the Philippines, Thailand, and India in particular, and other South-east Asian countries in general, where there has been a dramatic resurgence of interest in regional cooperation in this field. Institutions and programmes with regional implications, in South-east Asia, include: the Asian Institute of Management (Philippines), the Asian Institute of Technology (Thailand), the National Institute of Development Administration (Thailand), the Asian Productivity Organization (regionwide), the Regional

Institute of Higher Education and Development (Singapore), and the advanced management programme sponsored jointly by the Singapore Institute of Management, the Malaysian Institute of Management, and the Thailand Management Association. A study of management development needs in South-east Asia, conducted in 1971–2 by a US management consulting firm[5] has recommended the founding of a Management Association of South-east Asia, whose functions would include regional research on management education and training needs; designing programmes in management education and training for participating countries, individually and collectively; developing collaboration among the universities of the region, through a council or consortium of schools of management education; its use as a point of contact between the programmes and institutions of the region and international and foreign organizations; and promotion of a professional management approach. However, as elsewhere, the regional approach to management development in South-east Asia, may have limited utility, because of differences in language, socio-economic status of the countries, differing systems of general education, and differing national priorities and political systems.

Emergence of indigenous management education and training activity seems to follow the following pattern in most of the developing countries of Asia and Africa:

(a) Foreign industries within the developing country become interested in training their 'native' managers, either abroad or locally.

(b) The government of the country becomes aware of the managerial manpower requirements for development, and initiates institutions and programmes in 'development administration' and 'management education', either independently or together. Institutional models for this purpose are formulated on the basis of those obtaining in the former colonial power with which the country had been associated. Ideas are later borrowed from other foreign countries.

(c) Advice and aid is sought from international agencies and management institutions abroad. Practising and potential teachers are sent abroad for training. Managers are also sent abroad for training, until local institutions develop.

(d) Institutions for public administration and business management are set up locally, either within the framework of the existing universities and institutes of technology, or as autonomous organizations wholly or partly financed by the government and/or industry. If the country can attract political attention, it begins to receive foreign aid for their maintenance.

(e) As industrialization progresses, other professional agencies, such as management associations, productivity councils, etc., begin to emerge, and help conduct training programmes. Later, individual entrepreneurs enter the scene.

(f) Industrial enterprises become interested in developing their own training establishments and programmes and become ardent consumers of external programmes, initially on a trial and error basis, later in a more enlightened and critical manner.

(g) Management consulting and research activity emerges, and becomes linked with management education and training. Professional literature, including books and journals, begins to appear, and gather momentum. Indigenous teaching material, including cases, begins to be developed.

(h) Various sectors of industry begin to create their own national or regional management institutions and programmes, e.g., those for banking, insurance, defence, iron and steel, textiles, petrochemicals, cooperatives, small businesses, etc.

(i) After management education and training come of age in a developing country, doubts and questionings begin. Problems of evaluating the activity attract attention. Issues are raised in terms of relevance, utility, costs, flexibility, coverage and content, faculty competence, methodology and teaching material, conceptual models, ideological implications, etc. A thorough review takes place, and modifications to the system are made.

The above is a 'polished' version of the *stages*, as well as the *dimensions*, of management education and training in the developing countries, although the sequence may differ from country to country. The emerging nations of Asia and Africa range all the way on the scale: from Morocco where there is hardly any management development activity, through the Philippines and Thailand, where reasonable progress has been made, to India[6-10] where the last-mentioned stage of evolution is rapidly being reached.

Systematic projections of managerial manpower needs are available for only a few developing countries, but have been estimated for those shown in Fig. 11.1. Such estimates are only possible for countries having a predictable rate of industrial and technological growth. The indications are that additional management education and training facilities (increased by 50 to 100 per cent) may be needed in 1980. This calls for a massive growth of management

Country	Estimated 1971	Projected 1980
Indonesia	173 000	263 000
Khmer Republic	8 900	19 600
Laos	600	1 200
Malaysia	125 000	190 000
Philippines	300 000	600 000
Singapore	21 500	35 000
Thailand	110 000	150 000
South Vietnam	9 700	15 100
India	99 074 (1969)	133 003

Note. The definition of 'manager' is much more rigorous for Indian estimates than those for countries of South-east Asia.
Source. Figures for India are based on S. Hajra and P. Ramakrishnan;[6] other estimates are based on Cresap.[5]

Fig. 11.1. Estimated managerial manpower needs for some developing countries.

development activity in these countries over the next ten years. Most of the countries, however, do not appear to be making commensurate effort towards the development of institutions and trained teaching staff to meet the needs of the future. Even existing staff seem to be inadequate in most countries, with a heavy reliance on foreign advice and expertise. Little attention is being paid to the renewal and updating of the faculty.

In many developing countries of Asia and Africa, management education and training seem to be largely confined to university departments of administration and/or business management, with hardly any link between the two. Courses seem largely to comprise economic and political theory, traditional organizational theory, managerial economics, quantitative and analytical techniques of data processing and decision making, finance, marketing, and industrial engineering. Inadequate attention seems to be paid to organization behaviour, human relations, organization development, and other aspects of management of human resources. Little importance seems to be attached to problems of personal growth. This description may apply to most developing countries, though not all.

Viable management associations have yet to be created in most developing countries, since an ethos of professionalism in management has not yet fully emerged. Productivity centres, however, have begun to be established and developed. In-company training programmes are in their infancy (with some exceptions, particularly in the case of foreign subsidiaries). The need for training public servants for 'developmental administration', however, seems to be appreciated in most developing nations.

Only in two or three countries has a strong indigenous management consultancy movement begun; the others seem to rely largely on foreign consultants. Management research and case development are rather inadequate in most developing countries of Asia and Africa, and, by and large, the links between training, research, and consulting remain tenuous. Professional journals and books of indigenous origin are either non-existent, or woefully inadequate.

Most effort seems to be concentrated on graduate programmes in business administration and management, and on basic programmes in public administration for entrants to the profession. In a few countries, brief courses in general management, functional specialization, and industrial engineering are being offered to the practising manager. However, the concept of continuous education and training, for the public administrator and the industrial manager alike, has not been fully developed. Training opportunities seem to be exploited more fully by the larger companies and a few medium-sized firms. Junior executives and top management levels have generally been neglected, as have first-line supervisors. Most family-owned enterprises are not enthusiastic about management training and education.

The greatest shortcoming seems to be that management development and training have not been perceived in relation to organization development; nor are the motivations and aspirations of the manager taken into account when sending him on training programmes. Links between career planning, appraisal of performance and potential, reward systems and promotion policies on the one hand, and management development on the other, are inadequate in most organizations.

Summary and Conclusions

This chapter began with an examination of the unique goals of management education and training in the emerging countries, engaged in the urgent task of development. It has been suggested that a spirit of entrepreneurship, in an extended sense of the term, must pervade management education and training in the developing nations. The manager/administrator should be trained to play the roles of developer, change agent, innovator and creator, resource optimizer, and manager of differences and conflicts, as well as entrepreneur. Management education and training effort in the developing countries must strive to build up its own national identity, although new ideas and help from other sources may well be helpful. Regional cooperation among like-minded countries may help, but has limitations.

Data regarding the present status of management education and training have been presented, based on a brief study covering South Vietnam, Laos, the Khmer Republic, Thailand, the Philippines, Malaysia, Singapore, Indonesia, Burma, Nepal, India, Iran, Morocco, Sudan, Ethiopia, Kenya, Nigeria, and Turkey. Nine dimensions and stages of evolution have been identified. Some of the shortcomings of management development effort are: inadequate planning and coordination at the national level; the limited number of institutions and agencies; inadequate faculty resources and teaching material; insufficient management consulting and research activity, with no links with training; inadequate interest in training for top management, junior executives, first-line supervisors, and self-employed entrepreneurs; insufficient attention to management training for small and medium-sized businesses; inadequate links between national development, organization development, and management development. In most developing countries, there seems to be hardly any training needs analysis at the national level, organization level, or individual level. Often, even the existing facilities for management development are not fully utilized. Evaluation of the effectiveness of management development activity is universally difficult.

However, there is a new awareness in this field in most developing countries. New institutions and coordinating agencies are being created. Links between general education and management education are being forged. New concepts and models in management education and training are being sought. Professionalism in management is emerging as a new ethos. A systems perspective is being increasingly adopted. Professional management associations and productivity centres are springing up. In-company programmes are being developed. The concept of continuous education for the manager/administrator has found acceptance. More developed nations and international agencies are coming forward with aid and advice to help the

160

developing nations in giving a new look to their development administration and 'business management'. The 'seventies have begun on a note of cautious optimism for the future of management development in the developing countries.

Sources

The author wishes to acknowledge the information provided in personal communications by the undermentioned:

H. C. Blaise, The Ford Foundation, Bangkok.
Dean, School of Business Administration, Thailand.
Director, Thailand Management Development and Productivity Centre, Industrial Works Department, Ministry of Industry, Bangkok.
First Secretary and Dy. Permanent Representative to ECAFE, Embassy of India, Bangkok.
Documentation Officer, Centre for Economic Development and Administration, Kathmandu.
First Secretary, Embassy of India, Baghdad.
Chargé d'affaires, Embassy of India, Tehran.
Dean, Faculty of Public and Business Administration, University of Tehran.
Principal, Kenya Institute of Administration, Lower Kabete.
Director, Management Development and Productivity Centre, Khartoum.
J. M. Ventura, C/O USAID/ADPA, APO San Francisco.
First Secretary (Commercial), Embassy of India, Addis Ababa.
Mrs F. Korun, Department of Management, Faculty of Administrative Sciences, Middle East Technical University, Ankara.
Chargé d'affaires, Embassy of India, Rabat.
National Manpower Board, Ministry of Economic Development, Lagos.
First Secretary, Embassy of India, Rangoon.

Institutions, Agencies, and Professional Bodies Concerned with Management Education and Training in Some Developing Countries of Asia and Africa.

Burma

The Institute of Economics, of the Arts and Science University, Rangoon.
Commerce Department, Faculty of Social Science, University of Rangoon.

Ethiopia

Centre for Entrepreneurship and Management, Addis Ababa.

India

Administrative Staff College of India, Hyderabad.
Indian Institute of Management, Ahmedabad.

Indian Institute of Management, Calcutta.
Universities: Aligarh, Allahabad, Andhra, Banaras, Bombay, Calcutta, Cochin, Delhi, Gujrat, Himachal Pradesh, Indore, Jammu, Jodhpur, Kurukshetra, Lucknow, Madras, Osmania, Poona, Punjab, Panjabi, Rajasthan, and South Gujrat.
Small Industries Extension Training Institute, Hyderabad.
National Institute for Training in Industrial Engineering, Bombay.
Institutes of Science and Technology at Bombay, Delhi, Kanpur, Kharagpur, and Madras.
All India Management Association, New Delhi (with twenty-seven local associations throughout the country).
National Productivity Council, New Delhi (with six Regional Directorates and forty-seven local Productivity Councils).
Institute of Defence Management, Hyderabad.
National Institute of Bank Management, Bombay.
Indian Institute of Public Administration, New Delhi.
National Academy of Administration, Mussoorie.
Vaikunth Mehta National Institute of Cooperative Management, Poona.
Railway Staff College, Baroda.

Indonesia

Faculty of Commerce, University of Indonesia, Djakarta.
Institute for Management Education and Development, Djakarta.

Iran

Iran Centre for Management Studies, Tehran.
School of Public and Business Administration, University of Tehran.
Iranian Management Association, Tehran.

Kenya

Kenya Institute of Management, Nairobi.
Kenya Institute of Administration, Lower Kabete.

Khmer Republic (Cambodia)

University of Phnom Penh.

Laos

A government-operated training programme for prospective Civil Servants is the only management training in the country.

Malaysia

University of Malaya, Kuala Lumpur.
National Institute of Public Administration, Kuala Lumpur.
Asian Centre for Development Administration, Kuala Lumpur.

Morocco

Hardly any facilities for management education and training. A few Moroccans are sent abroad.

Nepal

Tribhuvan University, Kathmandu.
Centre for Economic Development and Administration, Kathmandu.

Nigeria

Nigerian Council for Management Education and Training, Lagos.
Nigerian Institute of Management, Lagos.
Department of Management Studies, University of Nigeria, Enugu Campus, Enugu.
School of Administration, University of Lagos, Lagos.
Institute of Administration, University of Ife, Ile-Ife.
Institute of Administration, Ahmadu Bello University, Zaria.
Nigerian Chambers of Commerce and Industry, Lagos.
Nigerian Employers Consultative Association, Lagos.

Philippines

Asian Institute of Management, Manila.
The Philippine Executive Academy, University of the Philippines, Manila.
Sycip, Gorres, Velayo and Company.
Economic Development Foundation.
Institute for Small Scale Industry.

Singapore

University of Singapore.
Nanyang University.
Singapore Institute of Management.
Regional Institute of Higher Education and Development.

South Vietnam

Dalat University.
National Institute of Administration, Saigon.
Vietnam Management Association, Saigon.

Sudan

Management Development and Productivity Centre, Khartoum.
Business Administration Department, Faculty of Economic and Social Studies, University of Khartoum.
Department of Commerce and Business, Cairo University, Khartoum branch.
Institute of Public Administration, Khartoum.

Thailand

National Institute of Development Administration, School of Business, Bangkok.
Universities: Chulalongkorn, Thammasat, and Kasetsart, all at Bangkok.
Thailand Management Development and Productivity Centre, Bangkok.

College of Business Administration, Bangkok.
Thailand Management Association, Bangkok.
Asian Institute of Technology, Bangkok.
UN Asian Institute for Economic Development and Planning, Bangkok.

Turkey

Department of Management, Faculty of Administrative Sciences, Middle
East Technical University, Ankara.

References

1. SMITH, N. R. *The Entrepreneur and His Firm: The Relationship between Type of Man and Type of Company*, occasional paper, Michigan State University, Graduate School of Business Administration, 1967.
2. COLLINS, O. F., MOORE, D. G., and UNWALLA, D. B. *The Enterprising Man*, MSU Business Studies, Michigan State University, Graduate School of Business Administration, 1964.
3. HARBISON, F. Entrepreneurial Organization as a Factor in Economic Development, *Quarterly Journal of Economics*, **70,** August 1956, pp. 364–79.
4. WHYTE, W. H., JR. *The Organization Man*, Simon and Schuster, New York, 1956.
5. CRESAP, McCORMICK and PAGET, INC. *Management Development Needs in Southeast Asia*; and individual reports on Indonesia, the Khmer Republic (Cambodia), Laos, Malaysia, the Philippines, Singapore, Thailand, and South Vietnam, submitted to the respective governments of these countries in 1972. The study was endorsed by the Sixth Ministerial Conference for the Economic Development of South-east Asia, and financed by the US Agency for International Development Regional Economic Development organization for South-east Asia.
6. HAJRA, S., and RAMAKRISHNAN, P. *Managerial Manpower in Indian Industry*, ESRF Monograph no. 2, Economic and Scientific Research Foundation, New Delhi, 1971.
7. PHILIP, J. Development of Management Education in India and its Impact on Training in Organization, *ISTD Review*, 1(3), 1971, 25.
8. HILL, T. M., HAYES, W. W., and BAUMGARTEL, H. *Management Education in India*, 1971 (mimeo.).
9. DASGUPTA, A. *Management Education in India*, Delhi University, 1968.
10. CHANDRAKANT, L. S. Management Education and Training in India: Present Position and Future Needs, *Journal of Management Education*, 3(9–10), 6, 1971.

Suggested Reading

AGARWAL, A. N. *Education for Business in a Developing Society*, MSU International Business and Economic Studies, Michigan State University, Graduate School of Business Administration, 1969.
BELSHAW, C. S. The Cultural Milieu of the Entrepreneur: A Critical Essay, *Explorations in Entrepreneurial History*, **7,** 3, 1955, 146–63.
CARROL. J. J. *The Filippino Manufacturing Entrepreneur*, Cornell Press, Ithaca, N.Y., 1965.
CHAUDHURY, P. (Ed.) *Aspects of Indian Economic Development*, Allen and Unwin, 1971.
DERASSI, F. *The Mexican Entrepreneur*, OECD, Paris, 1971.
DESATNICK, R. L. *A Concise Guide to Management Development*, American Management Association, New York, 1970.
FRYER, D. W. *Emerging Southeast Asia: A Study of Growth and Stagnation*, McGraw-Hill, N.Y., 1970.
GALBRAITH, J. K. A Positive Approach to Foreign Aid, *Foreign Affairs*, April 1961.
HANDY, C. Exploding the Management Education Myth, *European Business*, **81,** 29, 1971.
HILL, P. *Towards a New Philosophy of Management*, Gower Press, 1971.
HIRSCHMAN, A. O. *The Strategy of Economic Development*, Yale University Press, 1958.

Hoong, Y. Y. *The Role of Universities in Management Education for National Development in Southeast Asia*, Proceedings of the workshops held in Singapore, 14–17 August 1972, Regional Institute of Higher Education and Development, Singapore, September 1972.

Hoselitz, B. F. *Sociological Aspects in Economic Growth*, Free Press, Glencoe, New York, 1960.

Kilby, P. (Ed.) *Entrepreneurship and Economic Development*, Free Press, Glencoe, New York, 1971.

Leys, C. (Ed.) *Politics and Change in Developing Countries*, Cambridge University Press, 1969.

Markwell, D. S. and Roberts, T. J. *Organisation of Management Development Programmes*, Gower Press, 1969.

McClelland, D. C. *The Achieving Society*, Van Nostrand, Princeton, 1961.

Myrdal, G. *Asian Drama: An Enquiry into the Poverty of Nations*, vols. 1–3, The Twentieth Century Fund, Penguin, 1968.

Nadler, L. *Developing Human Resources*, Gulf Publishing, Houston, 1970, pp. 40–42, 60.

Papanek, G. F. *Framing a Development Program*, International Conciliation, Carnegie Endowment for International Peace, March 1960.

Revans, R. W. *Developing Effective Managers: A New Approach to Business Education*, Longman 1971.

Richter, A. The Existentialist Executive, *Public Adminstration Review*, **30**, Jul.–Aug., 1970.

Rose, H. B., Clark, D. G., and Newbigging, E. *Management Education in the 1970s*, HMSO, 1970.

Rostow, W. W. *The Process of Economic Growth*, Cambridge University Press, N.Y., 1960.

Sayigh, Y. A. *Entrepreneurs of Lebanon*, Harvard University Press, 1962.

United Nations, *Appraising Administrative Capability for Development*, 1969.

United Nations, *Report of the Interregional Seminar on the Development of Senior Administrators in the Public Service of Developing Countries, Geneva, August 1968*, vol. 1 and 2, 1969.

Warr, P., Bird, M., and Rackham, N. *Evaluation of Management Training*, Gower Press, 1970.

Watanabe, S. *Entrepreneurship in Small Enterprises in Japanese Manufacturing*, International Labour Review, **102**, 6, 1970, pp. 531–76.

Wheatcroft, M. *The Revolution in British Management Education*, Pitman, 1970.

Part 2. Management training methods

12. Management education— a conceptual framework

Bohdan Hawrylyshyn

This article reviews the concepts underlying management education. It defines what management education is, in the context of other activities leading to improved managerial effectiveness. It explores how the needs for it can be established and objectives chosen; what the various approaches to management education have been. It then presents a model for the choice of objectives, the analysis of learning processes, and the selection of teaching methods.

Since determinants for managerial effectiveness vary from country to country, and since management across national borders requires special capabilities, key notions in international management education are also summarized.

Management education is but one of several related and overlapping activities aiming at improving the effectiveness of organizations. The other activities are: training, management development, and organization development. While all the above have complementary roles and use some of the same instruments, they are distinguishable as to objectives and methodologies. The definitions below attempt to bring this out.

Management education aims at developing a broad range of abilities, based on appropriate knowledge, attitudes and skills, to enable managers to cope with a large variety of tasks, often ill defined, in a large variety of organizational or situational contexts. It is not, therefore, task or organization specific. It is broader in scope and has a longer time scale of utility than has training. It is more man than job or task oriented. Since most of the things taught on educational programmes are of general validity, such programmes mostly are, and probably should be, external. People from many different organizations participate. Thus, they get an opportunity to compare practices in different companies and different organizations.

The objective of *management training* is to develop highly specific and immediately useful skills. It is intended to prepare people to carry out well-known tasks in well-defined job contexts. While management training can be given in external programmes, to develop skills common in many firms, training programmes are normally organized internally when company-specific practices must be taught. The whole activity can be described as being task oriented in so far as people are being prepared through it to accomplish specific tasks.

Management development encompasses the whole, complex process by which managers as individuals learn, grow, and improve their abilities to perform professional management tasks. It involves, first and foremost, learning on the job through experience. Management is a practice-oriented profession. The consecration of managers' activities lies in practical results. Learning must, therefore, be practice linked. Learning on the job can, and often is, enhanced and accelerated by a variety of instruments and activities, such as development-oriented performance appraisals, career planning, job rotation, participation in task forces, project teams, junior boards, and special assignments. Occasional participation in formal training or educational programmes should be an integral part of the overall management development. The responsibility for an individual's professional growth should be shared between him and his employing organization.

Most management training, education and development activities are focused on individuals. Managers, however, invariably work in an organizational context with other people. They cannot readily apply new knowledge or a new skill without somehow affecting other people. This generates the so-called transfer problem from individual learning to organizational doing. Therefore, more synchronized development activities are needed. Whole working groups, parts of the organization or, ideally, the organization as a whole, should share in a learning experience. This sharing makes possible the application of what is learned without undue friction, problems, and resistance.

The above considerations give rise to *organization development* activities. These normally focus on behavioural aspects. They aim to improve relationships, communication, effective team functioning, changes in the managerial styles, etc., rather than emphasizing the learning of new quantitative techniques and new scientific procedures in management. Sound organization development approaches, however, encompass and build on greater individual training, education, and development efforts, rather than ignoring them or going counter to them.

I shall now continue the discussion on management education exclusively.

Choosing Educational Objectives

As yet, there is no unified, all-encompassing theory of management. There is a variety of ways in which programmes are designed. These lead to different educational models. The main approaches are the following:

(a) schools of thought;
(b) survey of needs;
(c) analysis of tasks.

'Schools of Thought' Approach

Historically, three rather different philosophies have emerged as to what management is and, therefore, what management education should be. These main schools can be described as pragmatic, behavioural, and mathematical. While there is much overlap, they have a distinctive orientation.

According to the *pragmatic* school of thought, what matters in management are results. Desired results can be achieved only if correct decisions are made. The key activity of managers is, therefore, decision making. Decision making should be based on sound judgement. Sound judgement can normally be developed only through experience. Learning should, therefore, be practice based. It should thus be possible to simulate practice in a formal education setting by the study of real-life experiences described in so-called cases. This led to a very distinctive, widespread model of management education. The main argument for this model is that, in a relatively short time, it is possible to expose programme participants to a wide variety of situations. They have to extract from the descriptive data contained in the cases the information that is most relevant, analyse cause-and-effect relationships between different factors, and envisage the different action alternatives. In classroom discussions, participants can test their judgement against that of other participants, and improve it in the process.

The *behavioural* school of thought is somewhat more recent. Its key propositions are as follows. Management is the process of getting things done with and through other people. What one really has to be able to do in management, therefore, is to manage people. This calls for a series of human skills. These can naturally also be developed through observation and practice, but, in an educational setting, one can develop these skills by the study of human behaviour subjects, such as psychology, sociology, and applied anthropology. The purpose is to learn what motivates individuals, how they relate with others, how people work in small teams, in complex organizations. Other learning methods, such as sensitivity training, have emerged in recent years. They aim at the direct development of certain human skills, rather than first acquiring the knowledge from which, hopefully, these skills would flow. Some of the university-based management education programmes have a distinctive behavioural orientation, even though, naturally, they include other components of management know-how. Special institutions outside the universities have been created. They focus almost exclusively on the development of human skills required in management.

The most recent school of thought can be called the *mathematical* school. According to this school of thought the key task of managers is decision making. However, it is argued that the decision-making process should be a rational, logical one. What is rational and logical, is ultimately translatable into mathematical terms. These can be incorporated into quantitative models and processed with the help of calculating devices such as computers. The concern, therefore, is with the use of correct processes and correct, rational methods. The skills thought to be most important in management are the analytical skills, the abilities to quantify, to build models, to simulate alternatives, to assign probabilities, to evaluate, to choose rationally among various alternatives. It is further argued that such skills can be fully developed through formal educational processes, so that one can eliminate the need for practical experience. Practice allows application of analytical skills, but is not a precondition for the acquisition of such skills. While there is no teaching institution representing a pure mathematical model of management education, there are schools which are very heavily oriented in this direction. Figure 12.1 summarizes the above three educational models.

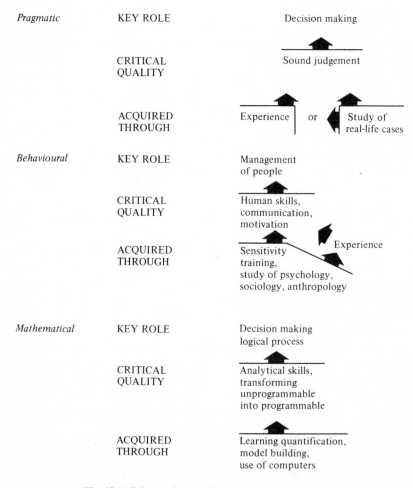

Fig. 12.1. Schools of thought in management education.

The 'schools of thought' approach could be described as 'production oriented' in management education. It is more characteristic of university-based and particularly, pre-employment management education. With the expansion of post-experience management education, some of it within firms, more concern has arisen for the assessment of needs. The result has been more 'market orientation' in management education.

'Survey of Needs' Approach

The objectives of programmes can be influenced, if not fully determined, by the studies of the perceived needs and wishes of prospective programme participants. Such needs can be distilled from questionnaires, interviews with managers, their superiors, their peers, or even their subordinates. Such data is often of low quality and difficult to aggregate into programme packages. Somewhat better data can be obtained by distilling educational needs from performance appraisals, particularly if they are linked to a good Management by Objectives scheme.

Another approach for determining educational needs is emerging. It is linked to corporate planning. The procedure is listed below:

(a) set corporate objectives;
(b) select strategy (product–market combinations);
(c) describe nature and scope of future operations;
(d) analyse future tasks and group them into jobs;
(e) design future organization structure;
(f) develop manning lists with job descriptions and qualifications;
(g) take inventory of present management;
(h) analyse gaps between present and required capabilities;
(i) plan gap-closing activities:
    (i) redeployment;
    (ii) hiring;
    (iii) training;
    (iv) education;
    (v) development;
    (vi) organization development.

Then, for education:

(a) determine criteria of effectiveness;
(b) allocate resources;
(c) select programmes;
(d) verify results;
(e) reiterate.

The above procedure seems very logical, but is difficult to practise. It is still in its infancy. As know-how evolves, the results of surveys of needs, as perceived by managers, will be compared with needs distilled from long-range plans.

'Analysis of Tasks' Approach

Educational needs vary greatly according to the nature of the responsibilities and tasks of managers. These, in turn, are strongly related to the position in the hierarchy. Some generalizations have emerged about the varying composition of skills required as managers move up the hierarchy. These skills are represented in Fig. 12.2.

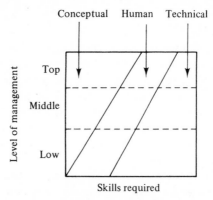

Fig. 12.2. Required skills throughout the hierarchy.

With the development of corporate strategy, a more rigorous analysis of tasks at various levels has become possible. Also, it is clear that hierarchy is not the only determinant. Required knowledge or skills vary also, according to the particular function, such as production management, finance. A matrix approach can now be used for the design of educational programmes, as in Fig. 12.3.

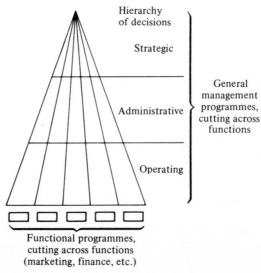

Fig. 12.3. Matrix approach to educational programmes.

Given the present state of knowledge of management and management education, what often carries more weight in the final design of a programme is what can be taught, rather than what needs to be taught. This applies, whatever the approach used in needs determination.

Integrative Model of Management Education

In the last few decades, several developments have taken place in parallel. Some convergence of views has been reached as to what management is. Management-related disciplines have matured. A whole range of new teaching methods has emerged. These methods make possible the simulation of various aspects of managerial activities and allow for a practice-based type of learning in educational programmes. These developments make it possible to prepare a synthesis of present knowledge, leading to a fairly comprehensive model of management education and answering the questions as to what should be taught, and how.

The thought process leading to the model is as follows. Management is the purposive use of resources. Effectiveness in management implies ability to achieve desirable results. It is rooted in an appropriate repertoire of knowledge, attitudes, and skills. Knowledge consists of retained observations, facts, and interrelationships and the ability to manipulate the various elements. It is rooted in our intellect. Attitudes are our predispositions to act and react in predictable ways. They are often emotionally rooted.

Skills are the ability to do things, to use the knowledge, to mobilize personality resources in order to carry out certain activities, to accomplish specific tasks.

The optimum combination of knowledge, attitudes, and skills varies according to the nature of the organization, and the level of responsibility or function. Matrix analysis, as in Fig. 12.3, provides some answers to this question. Knowledge, attitudes, and skills are interrelated and influence each other. Yet the process by which one acquires knowledge, attitudes, or skills varies greatly. Knowledge is acquired through a cognitive, intellectual process. Attitudes are acquired through experiential conditioning, i.e., through a more affective, emotional process. Skills are acquired through practice.

With the above learning processes, learning methods should be chosen to be compatible with learning processes for different learning categories. This is summarized in Fig. 12.4, which shows the skeleton of the integrative model, focusing on interrelationships between objectives, learning categories, learning processes, and teaching methods. Elements are listed in each of the above categories, not in an exhaustive fashion but by way of examples. To illustrate the full content of the model more effectively, some elaboration at the skill level is given below.

To decide what skills are required for effective management, the content of managers' work—the activities they have to carry out—are analysed. Managers go through certain cycles of activities in a repetitive, reiterative

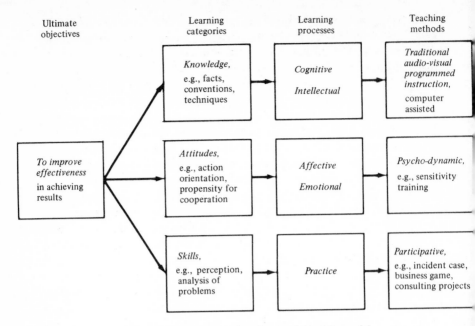

Fig. 12.4. Management education—an integrative model.

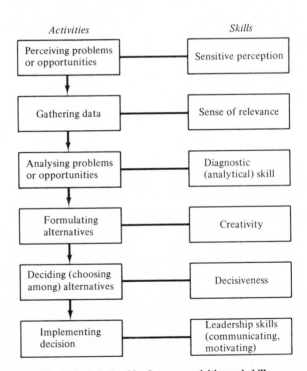

Fig. 12.5. Relationships between activities and skills.

fashion. These activities can be broken down into separate identifiable phases. Each may necessitate a range of knowledge and a variety of skills. Yet the successful accomplishment of each phase calls for a high degree of one of the skills. The relationships between activities and key skills are shown in Fig. 12.5.

There is, by now, a broad range of participative teaching methods, each permitting the simulation of some of the phases of the management activity cycle. This gives the programme participants an opportunity to practise, and to develop through practice, different skills. Each method has a comparative advantage *vis-à-vis* other methods. Each has a peak of effectiveness, even though each contributes to a varying degree to the development of other skills. It is therefore possible to make a rational selection of participative methods, once there is agreement as to what skills must be developed. This is shown in Fig. 12.6.

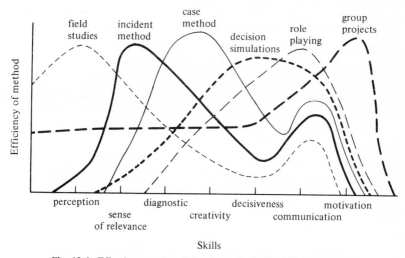

Fig. 12.6. **Effectiveness of participative methods for skill development.**

It must be borne in mind, however, that participative methods are multipurpose tools. They are flexible. Their use varies, depending on skills and preferences of teachers and on the composition of the participant body. Their effectiveness in contributing to the development of different skills varies accordingly.

International Aspects

With the internationalization of business, a need arose to develop special international management education programmes. Their objectives are to enable managers to work effectively in cultures other than their own, in teams of multinational composition, and to cope with problems that transcend national frontiers. Such programmes also accelerate the transplantation of successful practices from those parts of the world where they were developed to those where they can be applied. The conceptual foundations of international management education are as follows.

The management activity cycle, as described earlier, remains much the same. Also, much of the technology of management that permits managers to have a rational basis for their decisions, to optimize the use of resources, is universally valid. There are, however, great variations between different countries, political systems, economic structures, legal constraints, and, most importantly, social value systems. The above differences determine patterns of successful relationships between firms and public bodies, the market, organized labour, subordinates, superiors, and peers. They lead to great variations in managerial styles and personnel administration practices.

In addition to, or by building on, the already acquired know-how of management technology, international management education must lead to the development of special social and political know-how in management and to greater flexibility—a broader behavioural repertoire which enables managers to function effectively in a variety of situations with different rules of the game. This can be accomplished by giving managers, at the knowledge level, a broad understanding of differences in the business environment; by developing greater flexibility, adaptability, and learning orientation at the attitudinal level, and by developing skills to find the optimal behaviour between the extremes of blind adaptation to local ways ('going native') and determined disregard of them (isolation). These aims are summarized in Fig. 12.7.

The model for international management education is given only in its skeleton form. Its content can be illustrated by tracing through the acquisition of some knowledge about the cultural determinants of behaviour in different nations, by describing a way for testing attitudes towards learning and a method for the development of skills of perception in an international context.

At the knowledge level, a comparison can be drawn of US and Japanese management styles to illustrate how the different modes of behaviour can be highly effective in different cultures. This brings out the need for compatibility between values, management styles, and resultant personnel practices. The key elements of the analysis are as follows. Given the more individualistic value system in the US, the American management style is built on the individualistic and competitive behaviour of people, on merit, on individual rewards for differential performance. In Japan, on the other hand, values are more collectivist, leading to a greater propensity for cooperation. Hence, management style and personnel practices are built more on a group and cooperative approach to tasks, on interdependence, on seniority, on consensus building and conflict avoidance.

The American and Japanese management styles represent terminal points in a spectrum of values and consequent behaviours. Many of the west European countries fall between the two extremes. One finds elements of paternalism, of the seniority system. This means less sanctioning, but is also

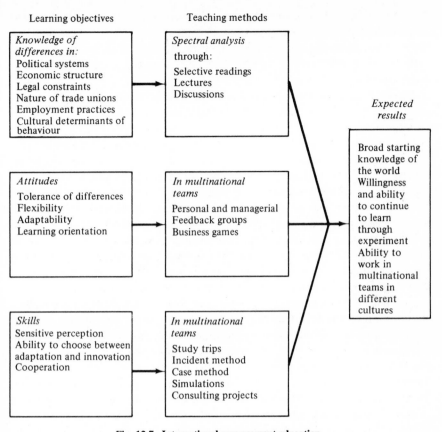

Learning objectives   Teaching methods

Knowledge of differences in: Political systems Economic structure Legal constraints Nature of trade unions Employment practices Cultural determinants of behaviour	Spectral analysis through: Selective readings Lectures Discussions	

Expected results

Broad starting knowledge of the world Willingness and ability to continue to learn through experiment Ability to work in multinational teams in different cultures

Attitudes Tolerance of differences Flexibility Adaptability Learning orientation	In multinational teams Personal and managerial Feedback groups Business games

Skills Sensitive perception Ability to choose between adaptation and innovation Cooperation	In multinational teams Study trips Incident method Case method Simulations Consulting projects

Fig. 12.7. International management education.

somewhat less rewarding for individual performance. These remarks illustrate the meaning of spectral analysis in Fig. 12.7.

It is impossible to give detailed knowledge of all countries. Therefore, in management education programmes, elements are selected which can provide the course participants with an analytical scheme for subsequent learning through reading, observation, and experiment on the job.

The approach at the attitudinal level is different. Seeing that the experience acquired in a domestic setting may be irrelevant abroad, and that it is impossible—even in an international educational programme—to give complete knowledge of all different environments, the international executive must have a positive attitude towards learning. He must not be over-reliant on the knowledge he already possesses, on experiences previously made. To enhance the learning orientation and the more experimental approach to decision making, which can facilitate learning, business games can be used to influence attitudes towards continuous learning. Such games should include a number of distortions of whatever reality they try to represent. These distortions can be used to represent a new or 'foreign' environment.

To succeed in such a business game, managers must design their decisions so as to find out, in the shortest possible time, the cause-and-effect relationships in the model in question. Through repetition, managers can focus on how to learn what works, rather than defending the validity of previous experiences.

Development of special skills calls for yet another approach. International executives have to learn how to differentiate between things they must adapt to in any given country, and areas in which they are free to bring with them their own practices and to innovate relative to the new environment. This calls for sensitive perception. For its achievement, the participants in an international educational programme can be put into consulting teams, composed of different nationalities, and sent to a country—normally foreign to them—to carry out a consulting project lasting several weeks. Members of such consulting teams must quickly observe the problem areas, select the data, carry out analyses, and present sets of action recommendations to teams of top managers. Given that the project teams are multinational in composition, the participants have ample opportunities to compare their individual observations and sort out which factors in the country concerned are of true significance to the problem at hand. They can test their skills in determining the happy medium between adaptation and innovation.

Several preconditions must be fulfilled for an international educational programme to be effective. The learning must take place under the guidance of a faculty which is itself composed of different nationalities. This is necessary to ensure the coexistence of different philosophies and value systems which lead to the understanding and acceptance of the fact that there is no one correct way of managing everywhere in the world. The second precondition is that there will be no one dominant nationality among the participants. This is important so that no one national set of management practices is used for comparison and evaluation of other people's ways. Also, the location is important. People on the programme must not feel the assimilative pressure of the country where the programme takes place.

International management education is based on the same fundamental notions as management education as such. The ultimate objective is effectiveness in achieving desired results. Such effectiveness is rooted in an appropriate inventory of knowledge, attitudes, and skills. The learning process at these three levels varies. Hence, teaching methods must be chosen accordingly. The primary difficulty lies in the proper selection of learning objectives. The conceptual framework exists. So does the understanding of the learning processes and teaching methods. Great progress, though, is still necessary in the proper implementation of available conceptual know-how.

Suggested Reading

Ansoff, H. I. *Corporate Strategy*, McGraw-Hill, 1965.
Bennis, W. G. *Organization Development: Its Nature, Origins and Prospects*, Addison-Wesley, 1969.
de Bettignies, H. C. Developing the International Executive, *European Business*, Jan. 1970.

CAMPBELL, J. P. *et al.* *Managerial Behavior, Performance and Effectiveness*, McGraw-Hill, 1970.

DRUCKER, P. F. What We Can Learn from Japanese Management, *Harvard Business Review*, **49**, 2, 1971.

HOUSE, R. J. *Management Development: Design, Evaluation, and Implementation*, Bureau of Industrial Relations, Graduate School of Business Administration, University of Michigan, 1967.

LIVINGSTON, J. S. Myth of the Well-educated Manager, *Harvard Business Review*, Jan.–Feb. 1971.

PAPALOIZOS, A. and NICHOLLS, J. R. An Approach to Measuring the Effectiveness of Participative Methods in Teaching Managerial Skills, *Training and Development Journal*, 1970.

REVANS, R. W. *Developing Effective Managers*, Longman, 1971.

TERPSTRA, V. *University Education for International Business: A Survey of American Business Schools*, Association for Education in International Business, 1969.

13. The case method in management training

Donald D. Simmons

As an aid to learning, the case study falls somewhere between a purely cognitive mode and real experience. Its use is greatly misunderstood, for there is no single case method but rather a multiplicity of methods depending on the nature of the case itself and the way in which it is presented. Thus, a particular case may be used to achieve a variety of educational objectives, making it an extremely flexible learning instrument. Such flexibility is at once a strength and a weakness, for an inexperienced leader may conduct a discussion which is most enjoyable for the participants, but from which little is learnt.

The use of the case study as an aid to management development was pioneered by the Harvard Business School, and case studies have been accepted as valuable instruments with which learning may be promoted. Nevertheless, there is still considerable misapprehension about the nature and use of the case study as a learning instrument. For example, reference is often made to the 'case method', as if there were a single approved technique for the use of cases, although the variations in content and format—to say nothing of the style of presentation used by the trainer—provide a wide range of 'methods' by which learning may be effected.

A case study is an account of situations and events drawn from real life. It is important to distinguish between a case study and a case history, for the material embodied in a case study has been selected and recorded in such a way as to provide a vehicle for planned learning, while a case history is merely a description which may be of interest, but which has not been designed specifically to promote learning.

Natural Learning

The major characteristic which differentiates man from the other animals is his greater ability to learn, i.e., to profit from experience. Throughout life, an individual constantly makes new discoveries about the environment in which he finds himself, and he assimilates the data obtained in this way in order that use may be made of it when an appropriate occasion arises. Learning consists of changes within the individual which only become evident to others through the behavioural changes which follow. Four types of change can be distinguished. Psychomotor changes involve the ability to interact with concrete objects; interpersonal changes are concerned with the ability to interact with people. Both these types of change may result from changes at a deeper level. Cognitive changes involve the ability to acquire and manipulate abstract concepts, while affective changes are concerned with the nature of emotional arousal about objects, concepts or people, including oneself.

In most learning situations, several of the four types of change are involved. For example, in a group situation, it is clear that changes in interpersonal skill may take place which would not happen in a solitary state; nevertheless, psychomotor and cognitive skills may be learnt with or without this interpersonal element. The most significant variable in any learning situation is the degree to which feedback can be obtained from the environment. When feedback is immediate and meaningful, the individual can be said to be involved in an experiential learning situation. At the opposite extreme is the cognitive process of reflective thought, in which the individual manipulates systems of concepts in detachment and, consequently, without feedback. Any learning which takes place under such conditions has little or no experiential component.

The features which distinguish natural day to day learning are that it is highly experiential, resulting from involvement rather than detachment; that it is largely unprogrammed, being directed by the intrinsic needs of the life situation as they arise from the need to cope with events or from curiosity, rather than being directed by some predetermined design; and that specific aspects of life are embedded in the complex total life situation, making them difficult to distinguish and comprehend. Maturation (other than in purely biological terms) is a summation of natural learning by experience through involvement, and this process may take a long time, due to the comparative randomness of such experience.

Contrived Learning

Because learning is of great value to the individual in helping him to comprehend and cope with the complexities of life, a need arises for the natural learning process to be made more efficient; from this need has sprung the education and training industry. To achieve the desired efficiency, the trainer seeks to contrive learning situations which follow a programme and therefore avoid the random happenings which take place in natural learning. If successful, this should lead to accelerated maturation of the learner.

The features of contrived learning are, then, that it requires a facilitator or programmer; that the learning situations should be largely determined by the facilitator, rather than by the learner himself; and that specific aspects of life should be dissected out from the complex of experience, so that they can be more easily distinguished and comprehended. Finally, this 'industrialization' of the learning process has resulted in it being often directed towards extrinsic needs, such as the need for qualifications, rather than towards the intrinsic need to cope more effectively with life.

There is no doubt that contrived learning has the potential to be more efficient than natural learning. However, contrived learning may produce unintended results which substantially lessen its efficiency. First, for reasons of economy, learners may have to be processed in bulk, so the planned learning situations cannot be precisely tailored to the needs or progress of the individual. Secondly, it is much easier to contrive learning situations of the cognitive type; therefore, traditional institutionalized programmes have used this type of learning almost to the exclusion of any other. The third consequence which follows is that the low level of experiential involvement, together with the apparent irrelevance of much cognitive learning to real life, results in a low level of learner motivation. Fourthly, the overwhelming cognitive element causes imbalance in the maturation of the learner so that, in the extreme 'academic' case, the attitudinal and interpersonal elements remain grossly underdeveloped in relation to the cognitive element. A final disadvantage is that much traditional contrived learning is so unlike real life that the transfer of learning to the real-life situation is difficult, if not impossible.

Training

It must not be inferred from the above that all institutionalized learning suffers from the disadvantages outlined. From very early times, the ideas of apprenticeship and of professional training have encompassed the use of experiential situations. Apprentices are subjected to a quasiwork environment, intending teachers practise in a real classroom, and medical students perform on real patients. In all these examples, the student is 'learning how to do it' rather than 'learning how it is done', gaining his knowledge as a result of the experience he receives through involvement, and developing the skills he will use later, when required to perform outside the training situation.

While the training of apprentices, teachers, and doctors is conducted by special arrangements in close association with those who are actually doing the job, it is not always possible to provide this sort of direct experience. However, it may be possible to provide synthetic experience of a very similar nature. An obvious example at the psychomotor level is the Link trainer, used to train aircraft pilots without the necessity for actually flying. This leads to the notion of providing experiential learning by simulations of real life, rather than by real life itself. If appropriate simulations can be devised, the degree of involvement and the consequent learner motivation can be increased, transfer of learning to real life can be made much easier, training can take place without disrupting the normal work of practitioners, and finally, the errors which learners necessarily make—and from which they learn—cannot have the possibly disastrous outcomes that they might have in real life. A consequence of this last feature is that, because there is less at stake, the learner feels free to experiment with a wider range of behaviour than he would otherwise employ.

Although cognitive learning must continue to play an important part in the development of a manager, in the past many teachers have relied on it to such an extent as to cause an imbalance in the total development of the learner. One might assert that the best way to learn to manage is actually to do the job, and this approach underlies many of the internal management apprenticeship schemes which have been devised. Such schemes are analogous to clinical, or classroom, training of doctors and teachers, but these arrangements are not always easily set up, and there is a need for something between a purely cognitive mode of learning and the real job.

Management Simulation

No simulation can ever be quite the same as the real thing. Management situations are often exceedingly complex, so the different forms of simulation which have been devised all exhibit a much simplified picture of a management situation and usually emphasize certain aspects only, leaving other aspects defined in outline, if at all. The most highly developed of such simulations are the so-called business games which, in their most sophisticated form, require the use of computer facilities and involve a relatively long playing time. The case study, in its various forms, provides an alternative type of simulation which is less costly, both in terms of time and facilities, but which may induce a considerable element of experiential learning.

Types of Case Study

A case study is an account of situations and events drawn from life and may take different forms but, whatever the form, each case embodies one or more definable issues. These issues may be broadly classified into those which provoke an examination of general theoretical principles and those which relate to the solution of specific problems. Of course, the first type has a more cognitive orientation than the second, which is essentially practice oriented. A case may vary from the relatively simple, where a single major issue is involved, to the more complex type which comprises a number of interdependent issues.

The content of a case study may provide an example of the successful handling of a situation for others to emulate, or it may show unsuccessful handling to provide an opportunity for criticism and the elaboration of alternative ways in which the situation might have been handled. Some cases call for the identification of an underlying issue in a complex situation, while others require judgement between alternative courses of action and the prediction of their associated outcomes. In using a case study to facilitate learning, the trainer may have in mind a number of objectives. For example, he may wish to impart information, to develop skills which may be intellectual or interpersonal, or to change attitudes. The following typology of case studies is based on the degree of learner involvement which can be induced. Of course, the suggested categories are not mutually exclusive, and many cases contain aspects of several types.

The Background Case

The primary purpose of the background case study is to impart information, to supply factual data or to familiarize the learner with the wider environmental circumstances of a specific situation. The advantage of doing this through the medium of a case, rather than by means of a reading, is that the learner absorbs the data more easily, since it relates to a real-life situation, than he would if the same data were presented *in vacuo*. It also has advantages for the older or more senior learner, who needs to acquire the data but might not be prepared to admit his ignorance if it were presented more formally.

The Exercise Case

In a similar way to the background case, the practice of certain techniques, particularly those involving quantitative manipulations, can be made more palatable if the data is provided in case form—so that the learner can see that it relates to an actual situation—rather than as a purely academic exercise.

The Situation Case

This is the type of case which most people envisage when the term 'case study' is used. It describes events which may be seen either as a success or a disaster. While the issues are usually fairly clear, they are often not those stated by the characters in the case. Those studying the case learn to examine critically such statements in the light of other evidence embodied.

The Complex Case

This is a situation case, where the problem is to diagnose the underlying issues. These are not easy to distinguish because they are submerged in a mass of data, much of which is often irrelevant, and because a number of more superficial issues are present as distractions. A further complication is that the issues, both superficial and underlying, tend to be interdependent.

The Decision Case

In contrast with the previously mentioned cases, the decision case requires the learner to go further than to acquire and manipulate data, or to provide an analysis of a situation. Here, the learner has to exercise judgement and state what he would do in the circumstances described. This requires the formulation of an action plan.

The In-tray Case

This type of case is a variation of the decision type and consists of a number of documents which the manager might find in his in-tray. Some background information is provided, and the learner is allowed a limited (usually inadequate) time in which to determine and record his action on each of the documents. This type of case approximates fairly closely to a real-life managerial function.

The Critical Incident Case

Here, the learner is presented with a small item of information about a situation. Further data is supplied only on request and may take the form of handouts or verbal descriptions. If the appropriate data is requested, the case situation can be comprehended, perhaps leading to suggestions for action. This type of case provides an opportunity to develop the skills of 'asking the right questions'.

The Sequential Case

The technique involved in this type of narrative case is to 'stop the action' at a critical point in the story, so that the learner can predict outcomes or suggest courses of action. The story is then continued, and an analysis made of the reasons for the divergence between the predictions and what actually transpired.

The Role Play Case

A role play is, in effect, a live case study. Role playing must be distinguished from acting, in which the action leads to a predetermined outcome. In role playing, each player receives an outline of the role that he has agreed to assume and is then free to develop the characterization of the role as he sees fit. Consequently, the outcome cannot be predetermined. While cases are specially written for role playing, it is possible to incorporate limited role play in conventionally written cases. For example, if the discussion leader detects a difference of viewpoint emerging between two members of the group about the behaviour of the characters in a case, he might ask the protagonists to assume the identities of the characters and play out an extrapolation of the situation as it might have developed. Where role playing is used, its function includes both the generation of a live case study for subsequent analysis and an opportunity for the players to experience the feeling of being themselves in the case situation, in which they can test their views for tenability.

Although most case studies are produced in printed form, it is possible, if time and facilities permit, to use audio taped cases, film or television. A number of cases in these formats are available, but are necessarily expensive and require special expertise in their use. Because a case study is drawn from real life, it rarely describes a simple situation, in that it mirrors the complexity of life itself. Many of these complexities have to be omitted from the case, or mentioned only by implication, so that, during the analysis, one invariably feels frustration and wishes for more information. However, in a real situation, one also suffers typically from insufficient information and is forced to make reasonable assumptions. Thus, in the analysis of a case, there is no objection to making reasonable assumptions provided the analyst declares what assumptions he has made, and his reason for making them.

Use of Case Studies

As an instrument to promote planned learning, the case study yields benefits from two sources, the content of the case itself and the method by which it is used. The content of a case may provide factual data, but it is more likely to generate a demand for data. Thus, the analysis of a case may impel learners to seek relevant information from other reference sources. If the analysis is conducted by group discussion, this information may be provided by a member of the group from his own experience, but, on many occasions, recourse to library or other facilities is essential, and it is most desirable that appropriate reference sources should be readily available. The content of a case is also of benefit as a means by which skills of analytical thinking, and powers of perception and judgement, may be sharpened.

While it is possible to study a case in solitude, this becomes a purely cognitive activity, whereas the use of cases in a group situation provides a degree of experiential involvement which increases motivation and provides an opportunity to practise interpersonal skills. Participants are encouraged to express their views clearly and concisely, but, perhaps more important, to listen with attention to the views of others and to make judgements and decisions under the conditions of uncertainty inherent in a case study. The verbalization of differing views enables participants to evaluate their own views in comparison with those of others, to cope with the emotional climate generated by these differences and, possibly, to modify their own views if these prove untenable. In the field of management, there is an abundance of concepts and principles which have a mythical origin but which prove insufficiently trustworthy to meet the needs of a real-life situation in a changing society. The interaction in a small group provides an environment in which participants can experience conceptual readjustments and replace mythological beliefs with more appropriate patterns of thinking.

Cases can be used in a number of ways, according to the time and facilities available, the experience of the learners, and the learning objectives. An essential prerequisite is that participants should have thoroughly assimilated the content of a case, and this is best achieved by individual study. At the same time, a preliminary analysis may be made, either in general terms or in response to specific questions set by the tutor. Posing questions in this way is somewhat directive but serves to focus thinking on particular aspects of the case. Those who are not accustomed to the analysis of case studies find this helpful, but with greater sophistication it should not be necessary.

Discussion of the case can now take place, either in small syndicates of up to ten participants, or in larger groups. If the latter method is employed, it is inevitable that a number of members will not contribute to the discussion unless they are encouraged to do so by the leader asking them for their views.

Such large groups do not exhibit the interpersonal action which is so marked a feature of the small groups.

If small groups are used, it is helpful for each group to prepare a summary of its conclusions, either in written form or by verbal report, so that a plenary session can be held in which the syndicates can examine the different approaches of the other groups. Where the participants are accustomed to the analysis of cases, the discussion in small groups can be very productive, but those who have not had experience of work with cases are likely to fail to perceive the issues embodied in the case and, therefore, to dismiss it with a perfunctory analysis only. The session may then degenerate into an anecdotal discussion barely relevant to the case. To avoid this waste of time, it is helpful to focus the thinking of the group, either by setting specific questions, or by leadership of the group.

To achieve the greatest productivity in group discussion, especially with inexperienced or newly formed groups, the assistance of a discussion leader is most desirable. The aims of the leader should be to facilitate the group learning process, rather than to direct the work of the group. This can be done by providing information sources where appropriate, by maintaining direction to the discussion through posing appropriate questions, and by inviting contributions from participants who appear to have difficulty in expressing their views. The use of the blackboard or similar equipment is invaluable so that points raised during the discussion can be noted and, thus, not overlooked.

As with all contrived learning, the facilitator must be clear as to his objectives—only then is he able to select a suitable case study. Some possible objectives are as follows:

(a) to sensitize to specific issues—follow the case with a theory session;
(b) to illustrate theory—precede the case with a theory session;
(c) to arouse a desire to acquire data or techniques—needed for analysis of the case;
(d) to impart information in an interesting way—background case;
(e) to apply techniques—exercise case;
(f) to improve analytical thinking—situation or sequential case;
(g) to improve perception and interpretation of data—complex case;
(h) to improve creative thinking and judgement—decision case, in-tray case;
(i) to improve skills of inquiry—critical incident case;
(j) to evaluate own attitudes—role-play case;
(k) to improve communication skills—talk, listen, convince and be convinced.

The planning of a case study session is as critical as the management of any other learning situation. Once the objectives are established, a suitable case must be selected, with the constraints of available time and the abilities and previous experience of the participants being borne in mind. A well-chosen case should utilize and build on the learner's existing store of knowledge.

It should be relevant to his experience, have credibility and provide a challenge. Under these conditions, interest and involvement will be maximized, but it is worth noting that the use of a case set in an alien environment is rarely successful, e.g., the use of industrial cases to train participants who come from the public services invites the comment that the case is not relevant to their experience. Adequate reference material must be available to aid the analysis, either through lectures, handouts or bibliographical references. Time for individual preparation must be allowed, and the size and composition of the discussion syndicate determined.

The case study is a valuable learning aid. Its purpose is to make the learning process more experiential, while retaining some of the cognitive aspects which have in the past dominated conventional learning methods. Cases provide information—or the desire to acquire it—intellectual exercise and the opportunity to re-examine attitudes. This is carried out in an environment which encourages experiment with new ideas and alternative interpersonal behaviours. To achieve the most useful experience, it is essential that the participants obtain feedback about their contributions. This may be provided by other members of the group, by the discussion leader, or by the review of an audio or video tape of the discussion. If an in-tray case has been used, feedback must come from a critical analysis of the decisions taken by the learners.

The case study is a highly flexible learning instrument because most cases can be used for a variety of purposes, depending on the objectives of the facilitator. This flexibility is both a strength and a weakness. In comparison with other learning methods, it imposes a greater responsibility on the facilitator or teacher with regard to his management of the learning situation. With appropriate management, case studies can have a powerful learning impact but, where the management is not appropriate, learning may be minimal. Unfortunately, such minimal learning occasions may not be apparent because the discussion of a case is usually in itself an enjoyable experience.

Suggested Reading

ROGERS, C. R. *Freedom to Learn*, Merrill Publishing, Columbus, Ohio, 1969.
TOWL, A. R. *To Study Administration by Cases*, Harvard University, Graduate School of Business Administration, 1969.
WILLINGS, D. R. *How to Use the Case Study in Training for Decision Making*, Business Publications, 1968.

14. The use of syndicates in management training

John Adams

The use of syndicates in management training and education is analysed, taking as a model the General Management Course at the Administrative Staff College, Henley. The syndicate is a form of small group, representing a variety of expertise and different types of enterprise. It serves as a useful base for exploiting the experience of its members, particularly in broad-based open-ended studies, but is also used for projects and case studies. It works as a management team, chaired for each study by one of its members, and so provides opportunity for the practice of management skills in the process of its work, an important part of which is to evaluate and improve its own effectiveness.

A syndicate is a form of small-group organization. Various small groups are often referred to as syndicates, e.g., discussion groups on a course or at a conference which are asked to report back to a plenary session. To illustrate a more comprehensive use of syndicates, I shall draw mainly on the experience of the General Management Course at the Administrative Staff College, Henley—a course of some 60 to 70 members working in six syndicates of 10 to 12 members for nine weeks. Though not the originator of the syndicate as a title for a learning group, Henley has been distinctively associated with this form of organization for management education and training and has been taken as a model by a number of colleges and programmes in Britain and overseas.

Syndicates were a feature of the military staff colleges on which, in its early days, Henley was largely patterned. In the military colleges, however, most of the members are drawn from one service; the directing staff are senior, trained staff officers in the same service; part, at least, of the aim is to train the members in the staff practices of that service, and this is reflected in the tasks of the syndicates and in the material for study; to pass through the Staff College is an essential step in progress to the higher positions in command or staff.

Henley was established to bring together and develop for higher management responsibilities men or women from many kinds of enterprise—companies, public corporations, government, trade unions, trade associations, and other administrative bodies. One of the objects of the College was to encourage managers from these different kinds of enterprise to learn from each other and foster understanding and collaboration between the different sectors of the economy in the national, as well as their particular interest. Managers drawn from such different sources do not share the common training or discipline of a service, and the enterprises from which they come differ greatly in their objectives, accountability, organization, and background. To attempt to inculcate standardized practices of organization and management would have been neither acceptable nor appropriate. Though government can learn much from business, and vice versa, there are good reasons why methods of management and administration should differ between these sectors.

When Henley started in 1948, there was little general agreement as to what should be contained in a management programme, and how it should be studied. The founders of Henley believed that higher management could best be studied with understanding by those who had considerable experience of management responsibilities. Comparing and evaluating with others this experience was an important starting point in the study of most problems of management.

From the start, this programme has been aimed at mid-career managers who have already proved themselves as managers in a functional or subordinate role and who are considered by their employers capable of assuming higher responsibilities. Their careers hitherto may have been mainly within the confines of a particular function, perhaps even in the same industry, company, government department, or other type of enterprise. They may have been general manager of a small company, or of a subsidiary in a larger group. In the future, they will need to encompass broader horizons and to test their judgement by reference to what goes on elsewhere, as well as within the environment of which they already have experience.

At this stage in the career of a manager or administrator, a substantial transition takes place. From working in an area in which his expertise is known and commands authority, he has increasingly to work with colleagues of different expertise, background, and outlook in a managerial group, e.g., a board of directors. The skills of managing or being an effective member of such a group, of persuading colleagues rather than ordering subordinates, of sizing up the important issues in an unfamiliar area, of using the expertise of others to bring relevant illumination to some problem, of formulating issues of policy clearly and simply, assume greater importance.

Despite the differences in circumstances from the military colleges, the carefully structured syndicate seemed a good instrument for building on experience. Members of a small group, considering many aspects of management over an extended period, get to know each other intimately and build up the confidence for frank exchanges. Working together as a team, under the management of one of their number in turn, they have to practise many of the skills of higher management—and learn about themselves and each other in the process. The development of each member as a person, as well as a manager, has always been a main aim of the programme.

Features

The characteristics of a Henley syndicate are that it is:

(a) composed of members with different expertise drawn from different types of enterprise;
(b) task oriented, in the sense that in each study a specified end-result is required by a stated time;
(c) self-managing, within the constraints of the programme, in that it is led for each study by one of its number as chairman, helped by another serving as secretary;
(d) expected, like any other alert managerial group, to evaluate and seek to improve its own effectiveness.

Composition

To ensure that each syndicate represents as wide a range of experience as possible, and also different types of enterprise and sectors of the economy, great care is taken over its composition. The major functions of management and types of enterprise are represented. Others are included as candidates available for a particular course. In practice, this means that each syndicate has representation from marketing, production, research and development, and finance, and also from central government, public corporations, banks, and—to bring in an outside view—from foreign companies or governments. Most members, however, are drawn from private-sector industry and commerce. Some syndicates have members with other expertise, such as personnel management, legal, secretarial or management services, or drawn from local government, the armed forces, police, hospitals, trade unions, or voluntary bodies. Members represent two kinds of experience—an expertise and a type of enterprise. A member with marketing expertise may come from a public corporation. A government scientist may represent the research and development component.

Tasks

To give purpose and provide a sanction for its work, a syndicate is always required to produce a definite end-product from its studies—be it a report, summary, questions for a conference, or an action plan for dealing with a particular situation presented in a project or case study. It is not just a discussion group, but a team which needs to be effectively managed to achieve the objectives set in the study. Its members are not role playing, except when specifically required to do so in an exercise or project, but taking part in real tasks.

Two main types of task are assigned to syndicates:

(a) to survey an area of management and formulate guidelines for action in this area;
(b) to do an exercise, project or case study.

In carrying out these tasks the syndicate has to study cooperatively a range of recommended reading, so that a much wider area is covered than any individual could manage in the time available. Its members go out as its representatives on field visits, from time to time, to report back information and observations on some aspect of a current study. It interviews visitors invited to meet it in the context of several studies. These activities help to develop capacities for observation and perception, for reporting back to colleagues briefly what is relevant to the task in hand and for getting the best out of an expert witness available only for a limited time, normally 45 to 90 minutes.

The discipline of surveying some general area of management concern is an open-ended deliberative activity for which managers usually have little time or opportunity in their normal work. It serves to:

(a) make members think about policy options and the basic issues in some area of management;
(b) give practice in the formulation of problems and guidelines for action at higher management levels;
(c) help clarify opinions and attitudes, which have to be explained and argued for with colleagues who may take very different views.

Managing the Team

Responsibility for managing the syndicate in each study is placed on two of its members—a chairman and a secretary, appointed by the College. In the belief that senior managers often have to look into matters in which they may have little personal knowledge, a member is usually appointed chairman for the study of some area with which he is not familiar. A research scientist, for example, may be required to chair the syndicate for a study of marketing. He thus has to size up the issues in an unfamiliar area, draw out the expertise of colleagues and see that they contribute relevantly to the task in hand.

The chairman, assisted by the secretary, manages the work throughout the particular study for which he is responsible. He has to plan the agenda and the use of time, which is always short; assign responsibilities for reading and other preparatory work, so that the maximum use is made of the co-operative effort of the syndicate; brief members going on field visits; guide the cross-examination of expert witnesses; see that conclusions are reached and embodied in whatever report or other end-product is required; and lead the syndicate in meetings with other syndicates. This challenges his capacity to plan, delegate, control, lead, and inspire. Important skills of management are being practised in the process of study.

Evaluating Performance

If a management team is to improve its performance, it needs from time to time to examine critically the way in which it works and to identify the factors and forces which are holding it back or helping it on, reducing the former and developing the latter. The syndicate, as a model of a management team, is thus encouraged to view itself as a workshop, analysing its effectiveness as a group, one factor in which may be the interpersonal relationships generated in the group as it goes ahead with its tasks. Its members have an opportunity to review and experiment with management styles away from the constraints of their job environment. So the problems of interpersonal relationships are explored within a group which gets to know itself very intimately. The members' perception and evaluation of themselves is stimulated and reinforced by exchanges within the group. In developing itself as a team and establishing criteria of effectiveness, the syndicate is engaging in a process of organization development on a small scale. Many of the concepts and techniques involved in the practice of organization development can be demonstrated and used to enrich this aspect of its activities.

Continuity and Variety

To maintain continuity, integrate the various studies, and forge an intimate understanding between a small group of members, the same ordinary syndicates need to continue throughout the programme. It is a demanding discipline to work intensively with the same colleagues over an extended period. Both the stayer and the sprinter have an opportunity to show their paces. Any long programme, however, needs to be varied and to give opportunity to establish intimate working relationships with as many other members as possible. So, from time to time, modified syndicates should be formed with a new mixture of membership for particular studies. This promotes a wider exchange of experience and views, and establishes a broader base of comparison for self-evaluation both by individuals and syndicates.

Size and Number of Syndicates

The appropriate size of a syndicate is determined partly by the requirements of the task and partly by the number of tasks in the programme. For an open-ended deliberative study, where representation of a wide range of expertise and types of enterprise is an advantage, the experience at Henley has been that a minimum of ten members is desirable. Intimacy is lost if this number is much exceeded. For exercises or projects where a broadly based group is less necessary, and more executive-type decisions are required, a smaller group of five to eight is more effective.

Since it is essential that each member should manage the syndicate on at least one, and preferably more occasions, the optimum size of the syndicate is affected by the number of separately assignable tasks in the programme. It needs twenty such tasks, if each member of a syndicate of ten is to have two duties as chairman and two as secretary.

The number of syndicates is also constrained by the requirements of intersyndicate activities. Plenary meetings tend to become tedious when more than five or six syndicates are reporting. Six is obviously a convenient number, if it is desired to arrange intersyndicate meetings of pairs or trios.

Inter-syndicate Activities

Competitiveness between syndicates, wider cross-pollination of ideas and experience, and practice in the skills of presentation to a wider group are promoted by intersyndicate meetings, either during or at the end of each study. There are a number of possible variations:

(a) a plenary meeting of all syndicates;
(b) meetings between pairs or trios of syndicates;
(c) meetings of smaller groups of two or more members from each syndicate.

Clearly, the smaller the intersyndicate meeting, the greater is the opportunity for more individuals to take part; the meeting can concentrate on the questions which are of special concern to those present. On the other hand, the range of interchange is more limited, which may be a serious loss when there are one or two members on a course who have distinctive experience or knowledge which should be shared with the whole body. Moreover, the smaller the group, the more it is like a normal syndicate meeting, and the less it provides opportunity for practising the somewhat different skills of communicating to a larger audience.

Syndicates as existing groups with a strong sense of loyalty are a useful basis on which to build intergroup learning situations, e.g., in negotiation exercises, where frequently loyalty to the group is in conflict with the need to reach a solution acceptable to both sides.

Role of the Staff

Emphasis on member initiative in managing the syndicate and in providing much of the input from their own experience or study requires a relationship between the staff and the syndicates different from the conventional teaching role, both in designing the various studies and in the contacts between the syndicate and the member of staff assigned to it as a general counsellor and guide.

A member of staff is responsible for setting up the work to be done in the particular areas in which he specializes, and is available for consultation by all syndicates. But the studies need to be set up in a form which a syndicate can handle. Not only must the objective of the study be clearly defined and the facilities explained, but the essential reading material must be of a character and quantity which can be absorbed and used by the syndicate working collectively in the time available, though optional further reading for members who want to pursue particular facets of the study in greater depth should be offered. In some studies the scene may be set by a verbal presentation by a staff specialist in a particular area, or by providing an introductory paper which gives essential information, outlines some of the main issues, and offers guidance for further study. The timetable of the study needs to be carefully designed so that the various other inputs, e.g., speakers, films, visits, syndicate visitors, case studies, come at a time when they are likely to be apposite. There must be suitable intervals between meetings for preparatory work. The designer of a study to be made by a number of self-managing groups needs, from the outset, to put himself in the mind of the user to a greater extent than necessary when planning a tutorial or seminar. There, the running is made by the tutor, who can readily vary the programme to meet the needs of the group. One danger is the temptation to overprogramme, leaving the chairman of the syndicate too little discretion and initiative in making a plan, though he usually has considerable latitude within the basic framework.

A member of staff is also assigned to work with each syndicate over the whole range of studies in the programme. To his syndicate, and the individual members of it, he is available as a consultant, adviser, friend, and resource man, in the sense that, even if he does not himself know the answer to some question, he usually knows where to look for it. He contributes to discussions from his own experience or knowledge, and asks awkward questions when the syndicate seems to be ducking some important issue. For convenience, the study of management has to be broken down into subjects or activities. The member of staff understands the design of the course, works with his syndicate over the whole range of subjects and activities, and can help the members to appreciate the interrelationship between them. In the syndicate's review of its activities and effectiveness, he takes a leading part, feeding back his observations of what is going on in the group, both during the various studies and at more formal evaluation meetings, and introducing them to concepts and techniques which will help to illuminate the process of evaluation.

The relationship between the syndicate member of staff and the syndicate, especially the chairman, calls for a delicate balance. The authority of the chairman should not be undermined by interventions from the staff. The members should do their own thinking, search out the information required, and be challenged to express their own views. It is easy for a member of staff who has seen most of the studies through on previous courses, to sort out the issues and suggest conclusions. To do so would destroy for the individual member the value of having to perceive and wrestle with the issues and argue his own views. In most studies, moreover, there is no one right answer.

197

Wrong information or misinterpretations must be pointed out, if they are not immediately corrected by the members themselves. Wherever possible, the aim is to encourage contributions to come from the members themselves. Advice and suggestions may often be offered more appropriately to individuals outside syndicate meetings. The role is that of a counsellor rather than an instructor. For this reason, he normally sits at the side in syndicate meetings rather than as a member of the group.

The syndicate member of staff also serves as a channel of communication between it and the College. The progress of studies is monitored continuously, deficiencies which can be put right quickly are recognized, and suggestions for improvement in the longer term are noted. He is thus a critic of his colleagues' work, looked at from the point of view of the customer, and in turn receives such criticism from his colleagues on the parts of the programme for which he is responsible. The management and internal evaluation of the programme by a group of staff, working with members over the whole range of subjects and activities, tempers the natural temptation of the subject specialist to fight for room for his own special area of interest.

Relevance to the Job Situation

Any training programme held away from the work situation of a particular enterprise must seem in some respects artificial. Yet freedom from the constraints of the work situation, and the opportunity to meet and work with other managers from different backgrounds and to experiment with ideas and behaviour, widens horizons and helps to develop the breadth of judgement required in senior managers.

To be relevant to existing or future job requirements, a training programme must meet the member's training and development needs as seen both by himself and his sponsors. Learning objectives need to be defined beforehand, and reviewed as the programme proceeds. Each individual then needs to relate what he is deriving from the programme to the problems of the work situation in his own enterprise. This is primarily a task for the individual, who can judge best what is appropriate to the particular circumstances with which he is faced in his job. The difficulties of transition from a work situation to an outside training programme and then back to the work situation can, however, be eased, and the relevance of what is being derived from the programme more thoroughly assessed, as a result of the frank exchanges for which the syndicate provides a base. Here also, the member of staff working with the syndicate can play a valuable role as an independent counsellor.

Syndicates in the Learning Process

Learning about management involves acquisition of knowledge and of skills in identifying, analysing, and solving problems and in leading people. Compared with individual study or lectures, tutorials or seminars under an expert instructor, the syndicate is not a particularly effective vehicle for the acquisition of knowledge. Techniques of analysis and problem solving also need to be demonstrated and then practised by individuals and in group work, for which the syndicate is a convenient base. Syndicate review of the application of knowledge and techniques to managerial situations may help the individual to see applications of which he had not personally thought.

The experience of a group of mid-career managers is an important first-hand source of knowledge on management problems and methods. The syndicate is a good forum for the exchange of experience, and works best when considering questions on which its members have substantial experience to contribute. It helps to develop the capacity to formulate experience and to evaluate and learn from the experience of others.

With the increasing differentiation of specialisms in modern management, an important requirement in a manager is to be a good leader or member of a team in which members have different expertise and come from different backgrounds. The syndicate also offers its members the opportunity to experiment in behaviour, free from the constraints of their normal job relationships, and to get feedback from a group of equals. Because it is a group of equals, the task of leading it is more than usually demanding. Its chairman has no more authority than he can earn, except that his colleagues will have to do the job in their turn.

A research study of mid-career development based on the experience of ex-Henley members showed that, while there was a demand for more detailed teaching, the process of development which stems from syndicate activities rated high in the assessments, and that this was particularly true of the more dynamic personalities described in the research as 'metamorphic' types who valued highly the 'active process of learning'. This is confirmed by less systematic feedback from past members who return to the College for various follow-up programmes.

Constructing a Syndicate

The process of constructing syndicates will depend on the purpose of the course and the amount and quality of information available about the members. In the Henley general management courses, the mix is designed first to get:

(a) a balance of the different kinds of expertise—marketing, production, finance, research, etc.;

(b) a balance of the different kinds of enterprise—private-sector business, public-sector business, government and other organizations;

(c) as broad a base of different kinds of industry and commerce as possible—therefore, only one representative of a particular industry or enterprise in a syndicate is acceptable;

(d) some representation of a non-British view—there should therefore be an overseas member in each group.

Second, to take into account the personality and abilities of the candidates. To see, for example, that aggressive personalities or quick thinkers have others to stand up to them, that they are balanced by slow-thinking and/or quiet types, who may be more profound but may need drawing out, so that each will learn from the others. The variables are too wide to be described briefly in general terms, but can be identified more closely in the specific situation. Third, to assign members to the syndicate of that member of the staff who in personality, knowledge, and experience seems most likely to be helpful to them.

Information is available from the record of the candidate's career and also from the notes made at an interview with the principal, or a senior member of the staff, during a visit to the College some time before the course assembles. The interview notes may include observations on the candidate's experience, knowledge, abilities, what he hopes to learn from the programme, and also general or specific guidance as to the studies for which he should be made responsible as a chairman. If such information is not available the process of syndication must, of course, be more mechanical.

An essential tool in the process of syndication is to prepare a card for each member, using colour and other codes to distinguish the variables to be taken into account. As syndication proceeds, codings are added to the cards to show the ordinary and modified syndicates of each member, to ensure that a satisfactory mix is being achieved.

In constructing syndicates, a start is naturally made with the members from the category in which the constraints are tightest. For example, there may be several from the same or related industries, who should be kept apart. Then take the category with the next largest number of constraints, finally balancing up with the categories where there are most individuals who could go anywhere. This would appear to be an operation which could easily be computerized, but the variables and constraints are complex and alter with the characteristics of the members of each course. Experiment with a computer program produced less satisfactory results, at more cost, than from manual sorting. With larger numbers, a computer program might be justified.

Chairmen and Secretaries

The other task is to allot the chairmanships and secretaryships in such a way as to give a fair balance of duties, eliminate overlaps, and ensure that in any one study all the chairmen are not drawn from the same category. It could produce an air of sameness if in one study all the chairmen were, for example, accountants. This can be handled by two simple forms. The first shows, on one axis, each member with any noted constraints, e.g., that he should not have an early chairmanship, and on the other, the various studies (see Fig. 14.1). From this, it is easy to check by inspection that there are no overlaps and no duties left uncovered, and that the same individuals are not working together twice in the same roles. On the second form (see

Members Studies					Names and particulars					
1	C				S					
2			C	S						
3		S				C				
4								S		C
5					C				S	
6	S						C			
7				C		S				
8			S					C		
9		C								S
10								S		C

Check horizontally that each study is covered. Check vertically that each member has appropriate duties. Check horizontally and vertically to see that roles are not repeated.

Fig. 14.1. Chairmen (C) and secretaries (S) in syndicate.

Syndicate Studies	A	B	C	D	E	F
1						
2						
3						
4						
5			Names and coded particulars of chairmen			
6						
7						
8						
9						
10						

Check horizontally to see that chairmen of each study represent a variety of expertise and enterprises.

Fig. 14.2. Chairmen of syndicates.

Fig. 14.2), the studies are entered on one axis, and syndicates on the other. The names of the chairmen, with a coding of their category, are then entered on the form. Any imbalance can easily be noted, and adjustments made.

Equipment

The physical equipment for syndicate work need not be elaborate. A table to sit round, blackboards and/or flip boards, and photocopying or duplicating facilities are essential. Tape recorders, video tape equipment, overhead projectors, or computer terminals may on occasion be useful. Whether their use justifies the investment will depend on the character of the studies to be undertaken. The table needs to be of a shape which makes it easy for each member to see the other. A coffin-shaped, round, or broad rectangular table meets this requirement.

Accommodation

Some of the rooms for syndicate meetings need to be large enough to hold two or three syndicates for intersyndicate meetings. A suitable room for plenary sessions is also essential (this is, in any case, required for other plenary occasions).

Future Developments

The syndicate as an instrument of management training was developed at a period when there had been relatively little research into the management process. The experience of practising managers was the most important source of information and guidance. While it is still an important source, systematic study and research is increasingly producing a much wider range of knowledge, concepts, skills, and methods with which the senior manager needs to be familiar. Some of these involve cognitive learning; some, as in the understanding of individual and group relationships, require activities which will enable members to experience the interactions involved. For some of these tasks, forms of group work other than the traditional syndicate will be appropriate. To make the syndicate's work more effective, two main developments, which have already been in train for a number of years at Henley, are required. The first is to improve the quality of input of information so that the increased range and bulk of management thinking is presented with as much rigour as possible, in a form which can be absorbed and understood by the practising manager in the limited time available. The second is to improve the activities through which group processes and interpersonal and intergroup relationships can be better understood so as to enhance the capabilities of members for teamwork in their present or future jobs.

Suggested Reading

HALL, N. F. *The Making of Higher Executives: The Modern Challenge*, New York University, 1958.

BRODIE, M. B. and LIFE, E. A. *Education for General Management: The Staff College Approach*, UNITAR monograph 1974.

RAPOPORT, R. B. *Mid-career Development*, Tavistock Publications, 1970.

TAYLOR, H. J. B. *The Administrative Staff Colleges at Home and Overseas*, Lyon, Grant and Green, 1968.

LLOYD, H. *Biography in Management Studies*, Hutchinson, 1964.

15. Action learning projects

R. W. Revans

The chapter opens with a theory of learning that assumes the cardinal need to try out new knowledge or new ideas in practical social situations before true learning can be achieved. In the author's view, there is no other form of learning—though there is abundant evidence of conditioning. Some examples are then given of how such a theory can be made operational by giving managers real problems (to which nobody knows the solution), both to act upon and to analyse with other managers. The illustrations open up the essential parameters of the management process and suggest what further academic or theoretical support the manager undergoing this process of autonomous development might need.

'Unless both doctor and patient become a problem to each other, no solution is found'—

CARL GUSTAV JUNG

'Before the mother can teach her infant to speak, the infant must first teach the mother how to talk'—

MARTIN LEWIS

The Essentials of Learning

Both the above observations suggest that learning is a social process: that is, learning should be regarded as the capacity to do new things, such as to cure (and be cured of) old diseases or to master the infinite complexities of human communication. If we examine how doctors and patients must work together to provide effective therapies, or what are the more fruitful exchanges between teachers and pupils in the classroom, we discover that successful achievement demands the following conditions:

(a) All parties, whether doctors, patients, teachers or pupils, must *want* to achieve. If patients do not want to get better or if children do not want to learn, it may be evident that there will be no lasting cure and no worthwhile learning; the patient may become more skilled in malingering, and the child find newer ways of evading work, but neither of these are to be taken as the set goals of the endeavours. But it may not generally be so obvious that the doctor must also want his patient to get better, and the teacher his pupil to learn, before either of them can help the processes of doing so. The nature of the doctor's interest may be simply to get rid of the patient who otherwise would continue to haunt his consulting room; the teacher may be motivated solely by the promise of a double fee if his pupil passes the examination. Their drives, on the other hand, may be quite different—and sometimes are. No matter; the point remains. Unless there is a will to achieve among all parties, nothing useful or lasting is achieved.

(b) The will to achieve is most commonly the desire to avoid, or escape from trouble, and the more threatening or pressing the problem, the greater is the will to be free of it. Jung may give a fresh emphasis to the cardinal role of involvement in the learning process when he observes that both doctor and patient must 'become a problem to each other before a solution is found', but we must not forget that it is to solve some other problem that the two are first brought together. Granted there is plenty of creative genius apparently inspired by needs other than to solve practical problems, and that many men have developed great talents to express their own imaginative ideas. Yet, to such men, their very efforts usually seem to be a struggle to solve all manner of problems: How to express this thought? How to achieve such-and-such an effect? How to prove this argument and to contradict that objection? How better to link the second variation with the first? All these are the highly specific problems of original composition, and there must be the technical skill to recognize them, and the emotional commitment to their conquest. From time immemorial, schoolmasters have complained that it is not intelligence—or the capacity to learn—that fails their charges; what eludes them is the relevance of their lessons to the goals that they set themselves in the world beyond the classroom.

(c) Given there is a will to master the challenges of reality, then progress is more quickly achieved (other things being equal) if the trouble is tackled by more than one person; learning is a social process in which two or more individuals act together to understand not only a problem, but how that problem is differently perceived. For an essential part of any problem-solving exercise is to know what that problem may be; it is particularly important to be aware of one's own part in creating the problem, even one's part in imagining it to exist. However, in this situation, it is generally helpful to have another person to comment on how one's behaviour or explanations or suggestions about the problem are seen by others, since in many cases, a deep involvement in a problem so distorts the view of what is causing it that even the most carefully thought-out measures to treat it are without avail; they may even give rise to a second situation worse than the first. Indeed, so many problems arise from subjective impressions, and from our personal misinterpretations of those impressions, that it is surprising that the world remains as peaceful as it does.

(d) After the willingness to learn, the problem-solving exercise to work on as a member of a group, the chance to try out one's suggestions is necessary. Any moderately lively children arguing among themselves as to how to do something—whether to answer the homework question they are tackling or to rescue a cat that has fallen into a coalhole—will soon produce a long list of answers to the question, or suggestions for getting hold of the cat. But unless these are tried out, how do they know if any of them are any good? Nobody can learn whether what he proposes is of any use unless it can be tried out in practice. The world is not short of ideas: places like mental hospitals and universities are seething with them; the difficulty is to identify those that can be used to answer questions and to solve problems. Any debate that goes on throwing up proposals that cannot be tested is not a debate from which constructive learning can emerge. It may well, as in many management case studies, teach clever men how to knock down the proposals of other clever men, but there is no true learning of how to master the outside world (rather than what other men say about it) unless the suggestions are both tried out and shown to work.

(e) A last refinement to the learning process consists in the detailed examination of the successful or 'insightful' idea. Just why did it work? How deep was the understanding? Was the black cat rescued from the black coalhole by the handle of the umbrella because that, too, was black—so bringing together three things of the same kind, because, as everybody knows, three is a perfect number? This is intended to be a serious argument, for there are many persons who go about the world with deep beliefs in the most bizarre ideas, which they have picked up by the most whimsical of former experiences. I knew an eminent mining engineer who would not use a particular kind of coal-transfer system known as a scraper conveyor, and who insisted on all of this type of equipment being removed from his collieries when he was given charge of a small coalfield. It was a long time before I discovered that he had once had charge of a colliery on the Northumberland coast, lashed by the biting salt sprays of every north-easterly gale; these had damaged all his outside gear, but nothing, it seemed, had suffered more than his scraper conveyors. On this account, he had developed a mania about them and was incapable of discussing the obvious merits which they have in the sheltered conditions of the normal coalface. Thus, when he lowers his defences far enough to admit a new idea, the prudent man should also do his best to see its wider dividends; misinterpretations of impressive events—like conveyor destruction by spray, or cat liberation by umbrella—may be the very denial of learning; the true learner is he who constantly examines his beliefs.

206

Theory into Practice

We can at once see why higher education is so ineffective a process; the normal student simply meets none of the conditions essential to true learning. He is in no position to decide whether or not he wants to learn, although he may want badly to be awarded a degree; this is not the same thing, and all some students learn is not only how to cheat at examinations, but how to cheat whenever it pays to do so. Secondly, he is not stimulated by the kinds of problems that he encounters in real life; he has to pit his wits against problems set for him by strangers, who, in turn, learnt to solve them from other strangers, or who may have read about them in books. Thirdly, students rarely work together on problems that equally concern them all; some universities even require their candidates for higher degrees to sign a declaration that they have not shared their labours with other students. Fourthly, the university student rarely tries out his supposed learning in practice; if he is studying one of the experimental sciences he is, from time to time, expected to go through a number of rituals, but they are not to test his own original inspirations, only to repeat the ceremonies of academic freemasonry. Finally, there is no opportunity for the average student to relate his new knowledge to the totality of his life beliefs or underlying values; he may learn the chemical engineering of napalm and never discuss the morality of using it, or he may take a degree in the history of Ireland and never give thought to the troubles of modern Belfast. It is striking, on the contrary, to hear some graduates in economics endlessly reasserting the arguments of their examination syllabus—even though they themselves must be able to see that these arguments now bear not the slightest relation to the most elementary facts of the world around us.

Our task is thus to construct programmes for the development of managers (and, for that matter, also for supervisors and workmen) so that the following conditions are observed:

(a) they are to be for volunteers (henceforth called fellows) sufficiently motivated to put themselves out, if necessary, or who, in other words, do not expect to get something for nothing, or to learn without needing to work in the process;

(b) they are to be based on the study of real problems, such as would be met in everyday life, and of a magnitude that presents a challenge;

(c) they are to enrol groups of fellows, who are given the fullest opportunity to work with each other, to support each other, to teach each other and to learn from each other, not only about their assigned problems but about each other and about themselves;

(d) they are to lead to action about the problems, so that any solutions or moves towards solutions suggested by the fellows are to have a reasonable chance of achieving the trials without which learning is impossible;

(e) they are to open up to the fellows the significance of their proposed actions—and any learning based on them—against their past experiences and their personal value systems.

The Belgian Inter-university Programme

In the autumn of 1968, a consortium of nineteen firms and five university management centres in Belgium staged the first Inter-university Programme. It is now being arranged for a fourth time. Two similar programmes have been organized in Egypt, and another is being planned for Syria.

The programme has three objectives:

(a) to give to a small number of future top managers (fellows) a structured view of how they change some complex system;
(b) to give a few enterprises an insight into their own dynamics or resistances to change;
(c) to offer the university staff the opportunity of studying, by responsible association, some industrial problems in real time.

The participating firms have genuine problems that they are ready to discuss before senior managers from other enterprises; the fellows are senior managers, exchanged full-time for almost a year, and concerned with general management problems rather than particular skills or techniques; the university staff are those willing to risk becoming operationally involved in real, but untidy business problems, in conditions liable to prove their most confident forecasts ignorantly misconceived.

After each of the nineteen organizations had defined what it thought was the problem that it would like investigated, the fellows moved between enterprises so that the total utility of their previous expert knowledge was a minimum. For example, a logistics analyst from an oil company studied the future strategies of a bank, a precision engineer studied the problems of creativity, a steel man examined the roles of part-time insurance salesmen (see appendix 15.1). Our first objective was to encourage the fellows to ask fundamental questions; the emphasis fell on question posing rather than question answering.

The fellows followed an introductory course in basic economic theory, the nature of systems, the processes of human communication and learning; they were made aware of the impacts they had on others. They then spent three months in their receiving enterprises, endeavouring to translate their problems into operational terms. These interpretations they then discussed at the Harvard Business School and at MIT. On their return from America, they spent four months back in their receiving enterprises, attempting to put their proposed solutions into practice.

While in their receiving enterprises, diagnosing and treating their problems, the fellows, allocated to the five university management centres, spent one day a week together, in small groups at the centres, where they discussed with academic staff their problems and progress. These weekly discussions, repeated for thirty weeks, were the cutting edges of the programme, for, in them, theory met practice and, more fruitfully, differing or conflicting perceptions of practice met each other. The programme was, in effect, a closely designed and highly interactive piece of research in which nineteen senior and action-oriented managers attacked, with the support of their colleagues, nineteen unstructured problems, each of such magnitude that everyone welcomed whatever help or advice his colleagues could give. Later several described how valuable it was to offer and accept help without thought of patronage or obligation. Men who, in their own firms, would never admit to being at a loss—much less seek help—learnt of their dependence on others, and so their own needs for development.

The success of each project was critically dependent on the coalition of power responsible in the receiving enterprise (see appendix 15.2). When the chief executive was interested in the solution of the problem, especially to nominate a powerful member of his own organization to work with the fellow, a great deal of progress was made. In Egypt, the chief executives were often more personally interested than those in Belgium. In Syria, even the Prime Minister has shown personal interest in the proposed programme and has asked that he should be kept closely in touch with its follow.

Further Guidelines for Programme Designers

It is instructive to ask what progress has been made by those who organized the Belgian and Egyptian managers, particularly in making their experience available to others who might wish to carry such action-oriented programmes into other fields. We found ourselves, not surprisingly, perhaps, rarely inquiring into the nature of economics, sociology, computer technology, accounting, inventory control, DCF, PERT, CPA, or other such themes. But we devoted much argument to the question: 'What kind of a man is a manager?' In broadest outline, our answers were:

(a) he is strongly moulded by his previous experience; behind the convictions of his present are the accumulated memories of his past;
(b) he prefers practice to theory, doing to talking; all his desire is to clear up his present troubles;
(c) he is ambitious to extend his field of action and responsibility; he sees ahead those who have succeeded, and whose example he is inspired to members.)

The promoter of any management programme should thus ask if these three qualities are, or could be, built into his operational design.

The Weight of Past Experience

It is useless to offer the average manager any idea that contradicts, or seems to contradict, his past experience of reality. The foundation for successful change in the manager is not, therefore, the brilliance of his teacher or the soundness of any new idea as such, but whether, if tried out, it helps the manager to reinterpret what he has already gone through. It is the responsibility of designers of management courses to help him make the greatest possible use of his existing arsenals of experience, and our first approach must be to encourage his unceasing evaluation of what these experiences mean in differing conditions. In a changing world, or in a manager moving towards new tasks, nothing does more harm than idolizing the past, whether cultural or personal; the manager, from whatever culture he may come, must be helped by his colleagues to match his experience against the problems that confront him now.

The Urge to Act

The second question raised by managers about any idea is its relevance to immediate action; after reluctantly accepting novelty, the practical man demands instant utility. But, just as Gresham's Law postulates that bad money drives out good, so does the imperative urge of the manager to solve the minor problem immediately beneath his nose often prevent him from perceiving the more distant storm clouds. Thus, the programme designer must transform the urge to hammer vigorously at today's known problems, into some disposition to anticipate those of tomorrow. This may demand exercises to trace the cause-and-effect relationships relevant to future action, to appreciate the concepts of model and of system, of transfer and of transformation, and so forth. (How, then to prevent the programme from becoming a gratuitous exhibition of academic erudition, not only operationally irrelevant, but discouraging, to non-mathematical developments.

The Appetite for Command

The ambition of managers, whatever the moralist may judge, cannot be omitted from the resources of any programme. Such ambition appears in two ways: first, identification with superiors judged successful; second, motivation, often unconscious, to keep control of all that is going on. Both can be disabling, however much they may help the manager in his career. For the first may lead him, in his admiration of the successful boss, to underestimate, indeed to despise, the hidden qualities of the subordinate— and these could often be very helpful to the superior manager had he but wit enough to value them. The second, the need of some men to keep all power over their own operations, not only makes them ineffective leaders; it often prevents them from knowing what, in fact, is going on, and so leads them to make serious mistakes. It is the strength of every successful manager to command the energies of other men: the jealous one cannot command even his own. Nor can any man employ fully the energies of another unless he can also first understand how the other perceives the world around him. Thus, our programme must help its managers to learn what knowledge and support they can gain from the less distinguished members of their enterprises. In some developing nations, where seniority is the culturally accepted criterion for respect, the future top manager must learn to appreciate his dependence on his staff, no less than he will expect that staff to demonstrate their subservience to him.

The Operational Model

The foregoing text suggests that our design should display the following features:

(a) it must constantly challenge each manager to review and to reinterpret his previous experience;

(b) it should apprehend and treat a real situation of the future rather than some emergency of the present;

(c) it must exploit the latent admiration of the manager for other successful managers;

(d) it should make the manager publicly aware of his dependence on subordinates, forcing him to work on equal terms with those whom he would normally consider unqualified either to carry responsibility or to display initiative.

We may now interpret these four conditions:

(a) Faced with the obligation to take, to promote or to encourage effective action within another enterprise exploiting an unfamiliar technology in an unfamiliar setting, the visiting manager must uninterruptedly question the relevance of his existing opinions and, hence, the meaning of his previous experience. In this, his new perceptions may be as often positive as negative, for he will read new value into what he had not previously seen as connected as often as he will learn to question what he had taken before as universal truth.

(b) He must disclose his arguments to other managers who have more knowledge than him; he must work closely with the directors of his receiving enterprise, for without their confident support he cannot know what he seeks. His task, moreover, is so great that he needs support from the other fellows; his dependence on these practical men amplifies the review and reassessment of his experience and beliefs.

(c) The fellow cannot take any immediate action; he must assess contradictory reports, trace the roots of conflict, elaborate interlocking plans for action, and engage in other deliberated moves, all demanding conjecture and debate long in advance of being tried out. In these exercises each must learn to observe before striking, to analyse before instructing, to forecast before ordering, and will need to re-examine the foundations of his theoretical or cognitive knowledge.

(d) The fellow must also unravel the many contradictions of opinion and judgement that flourish among his sponsors; he must try to find some correspondence between opinion and reality, and his search for what really goes on will take him into the depths of the enterprise, showing him problems unknown to the management; this will make him respect the simple competence of subordinate members of the enterprise, and, when he can weld together their many ideas, he will know more about the enterprise than does the president himself. The help of subordinates with his own assignment, will lead him to recognize his critical dependence on juniors. (This involvement is essential in developing countries, because there, traditionally, people listen only to those in authority.)

Schematic Representation of Programme

Our essential argument is set out in Fig. 15.1. This treats each project as a set of inputs transformed by action learning into a set of outputs. The managerial inputs are the personal qualities brought into the projects; the managerial outputs are the changes produced in these personal qualities.

Inputs	Processes		Outputs
Permanent qualities of managers	(i) Training operations exploited	(ii) Supporting academic subjects	Developmental objectives
Richness of previous experience (competence)	Confrontation with other managers in real tasks	Psychology of perception and defence mechanisms	Reintegration and reappraisal of own beliefs and approaches
Problem-solving drives (motivation)	Search for solution of intangible problem in unfamiliar environment	Expansion of cognitive knowledge; economics, operations research, etc.	Analysis of own decision processes, expecially towards future strategies
Respect for successful managers (data)	Dependence on information and support offered by subordinates	Sensitivity training and psychology of interpersonal relations	Avoidance of authoritarian attitudes and formation of leadership

Fig. 15.1. Relations between main elements of learning processes in action-oriented exchanges of responsible managers.

The manager must ask: 'Am I able enough? Do I care enough? Do I know enough?' Figure 15.1 shows how the underlying design of our action learning projects directs his attention to these very questions: 'What unused talents or abilities have I also got? How do I motivate myself to tackle the future? How do I make sure what is really going on?' Note that Fig. 15.1 reflects the general needs of all engineering systems, namely,

(a) materials on which to work;
(b) energy with which to work them;
(c) information as to the manager's goals and progress;

since a successful manager needs

(a) a fund of professional competence to deploy;
(b) the personal motivation to deploy it;
(c) adequate situational data about what to deploy it for.

Conclusion

Experiments in Belgian and Egyptian industrial and commercial enterprises suggest that managerial action may be improved by practical experiment supported by theoretical analysis. When action-oriented managers, in balanced groups, examine together the processes of effecting ordered change in complex organizations, we gain insight into their perceptions of how unstructured situations may be described, of how negotiations may be conducted to change those situations, and of how the managers themselves are changed by these efforts.

Appendix 15.1   The Belgian Inter-University Programme

Project number	Receiving enterprise	Main theme
1	An international fabric and paper company	To identify the main problems of innovation and of marketing policy
2	The world's largest producer of zinc	To examine critically the information network of the enterprise and to recommend accordingly
3	A major Belgian bank	To examine the changes taking place within the world of banking, and the consequent need for the bank to develop a marketing strategy
4	An international producer and seller of wire and of articles based on the technology of wire forming	To examine the potential of the computer in developing and controlling the operations of the enterprise
5	A major Belgian bank	To examine the incidence of change upon the staff of this bank, and to suggest the magnitude and causes of problems facing the introduction of new methods
6	An electricity generating and distributing corporation	To suggest an information service for management, adequate for effective decentralization of the enterprise

7	An international oil company	To help in introducing a scheme of management information useful for anticipating change and for controlling operations
8	A large insurance company	To improve the commercial services offered by the enterprise
9	An international producer of electronic apparatus	To examine the organizational problems of a complex assembly system and to suggest a set of procedures adequate for the procurement and stocking of many component parts
10	A large insurance company	To examine the human and social problems of automatic data processing
11	An international chemical company	To match the principal information streams of the enterprise with its main decision centres
12	An international company that makes, installs, and maintains commercial and marine telegraphy systems	To review the system of information now focused around the present computer and to ask how this should be developed
13	An international firm that makes and markets wood products of all kinds	To consider the information and organization useful in the development strategy of principal products
14	A refiner of non-ferrous metals, handling the largest annual tonnage of copper in Europe	To consider whether changes in the management structure (notably by increasing decentralization of decision making) is likely to improve the effectiveness with which middle management now uses its abilities
15	An old-established and world-famous steel company	To study the transfer and use of information about the needs and potentials of the enterprise for innovation

16	A major producer of steel sheet	To review in detail the conditions for defining, developing, and launching (or not launching) a new product
17	An international producer of photographic apparatus and materials of all kinds	To examine the relations between the departments of production, marketing, and finance with reference to the demand for, and supply of, light-sensitive products
18	A large Belgian bank	To examine the potential of the computer for this bank, and its probable impact on the organizational structure
19	A major international producer of large-scale civil-engineering materials	To examine the relations between the enterprise and its customers in the light of improved information services

Appendix 15.2   A Learning Experience

Many presidents were shocked by the reports that followed the projects. They discovered that serious problems passed undetected, or, if seen, were wrongly treated, often in the boardroom itself. Even these senior men become absorbed in day to day problems, thinking and working in terms of tactics rather than of strategy. Many of their exhausting conflicts could easily have been avoided had they had the courage, and had they found the time, to think about tomorrow's objectives instead always of hammering at today's troubles.

Thus, they were more than reluctant to believe what their visitors had to tell them: they bridled with hostility. When each of them first read the report on his particular enterprise, he saw it largely as an attack on his personal leadership, and each visiting fellow would have been in an impossible situation had he been un-protected from the indignation of his president. But the fellows as a group, unlike their presidents, knew very well that each among them had discovered much the same grounds for much the same criticisms; what they could see as a general weakness of Egyptian management as a whole—indeed, as a profession—each individual president read as a criticism of himself as a person.

But at the open presentation and review of the reports, held at the Nile Hilton, Cairo, in December 1970, the presidents found themselves becoming less hostile, more secure, and increasingly involved. As they saw themselves each the victim, not of their visiting fellow but of an inadequate management culture, so their attitudes were changed. A body of powerful men who came to protest about what they had first read almost as an organized defamation of their personal characters, left the hotel having resolved that the programme must at all costs be repeated and extended.

Translated from the Arabic by Professor Saad Ashmawy, Al Azhar University, Cairo
(Quoted from the Nile Project,
OECD, 94 rue Chardon Lagache, Paris 16e.)

Suggested Reading

Attitudes of Senior Public Service towards Changes of Roles and Tasks in Local Administration, Uitgave University Institute for Administration, Brussels, 1971.

Fire Brigades in Belgium: An Operational Approach to Organizational Psychology, Uitgave University Institute for Administration, Brussels, 1972.

MUSSCHOOT, F. Municipal Administration and the Prevention of Noise: An Organizational Case Study in Three Merged Municipalities, Uitgave University Institute for Administration, Brussels, 1972.

MUSSCHOOT, F. and WIELAND, G. Organizational Self-Surveys and Change, International Congress of Applied Psychology, Liege, 1971.

16. The construction, operation, and evaluation of management games

Clive Loveluck

The purpose of this chapter is to explain the main characteristics of management games; to outline their origin and development into a generally accepted educational method; to suggest some of their uses and their limitations; and to indicate some likely developments in the future.

Games of many different types are currently used in the educational programmes of a variety of educational institutions—from secondary schools to graduate schools of business administration. Their excitement and publicity value has given rise to national and international competitions, while their drama and visual appeal have brought them to the screen in several television programmes.

The proliferation of such activities suggests that it has become important to define more precisely what is meant by a management game. For our purposes, we shall define a management game as a *'dynamic teaching device which uses the sequential nature of decisions, within a scenario simulating selected features of a managerial environment, as an integral feature of its construction and operation'.* This definition takes into account the several features of management games particularly important to the training manager. Even excluding the technical aspects of game construction (which will be considered later), the training manager has to consider, in relation to his requirements, the validity of the scenario, the realism of the simulation, the relevance of the managerial environment, and the pressures induced by the decision processes involved in the game.

The Development of Management Games

Management games have a long list of antecedents, spread over centuries but beginning, as one would expect, with chess. Figure 16.1 indicates the

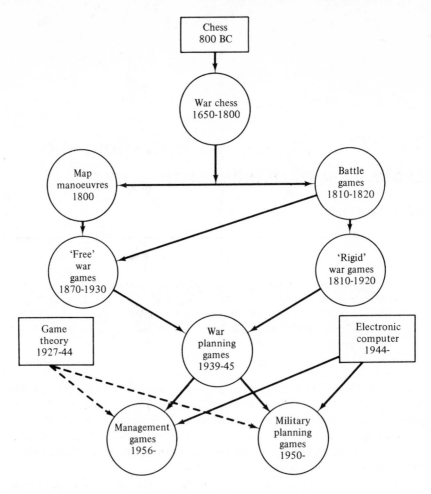

Fig. 16.1. Development of management games.

mainstreams in this development, with the main time periods of each development indicated.

Chess can easily be visualized as the major source of most competitive board games and, so far as is known, first emerged in recognizable modern form around 800 BC. Less well known, perhaps, is its modification, 'war chess' which appeared in Prussia in the middle of the seventeenth century, and linked the concepts of pieces and places in a simulation by physical representations of officers and men as figures on the board, with numbers and rules modified to enhance the realism of the game.

This change may have made chess more amenable to soldiers as a representation of war, but clearly represented only a small move towards realism. A stronger move in this direction came with two developments from war chess. These innovations came in two forms: 'map manoeuvres', developed by the French during the Napoleonic Wars, and 'battle games', developed in the Prussian forces by von Reissewitz. The former title is sufficiently descriptive but the latter represents a more important step towards modern gaming. Battle games, although in general limited to specific battles, involved a deliberate attempt to evaluate the relative importance of variance factors and to introduce these logically and realistically into a structured model.

The enthusiasm generated by battle games in military circles naturally led to the construction of more such games, but also to a dichotomy in the philosophy of game structure. On the one hand, the battle games developed into ever-more sophisticated models involving tables of fire-power, movement times, etc. These 'rigid *Kriegspiele*' were, however, criticized for their lack of flexibility and their implication of preconceived strategies and victories. Another development therefore emerged: the 'free *Kriegspiel*' in which human intervention, in the form of senior officers, determined the outcome of the conflict between alternative armies and strategies.

Both forms have, of course, advantages and disadvantages. They were, to a considerable degree, combined in the war-strategy games devised and used by the German Army in the design and planning of various activities such as the invasions of Britain and Russia and the Ardennes offensive.

Perhaps the greatest stimulus came in the immediate postwar years with the advent of electronic computers and the increasing impact of a new branch of mathematics—the theory of games. The former contributed the facility to formulate more complex models, compute results more accurately and speedily, and pre-programme a variety of optional strategies. The latter brought to business, via professional journals, an awareness of concept of strategy, outcome, etc., and the relevance of these to the business environment. Game theory has contributed little in the way of problem-solving techniques applicable to realistic business situations, but its attitude-forming influence has been considerable. It was the American Management Association's awareness and interest which caused them to visit the US Naval Academy to watch a war game in progress; it was the foresight of the AMA which led them to commission the construction of a management game in 1956.

The Educational Use of Games

The educational value of games is, of course, debatable. They have never been scientifically evaluated as a management teaching device so that their use really rests on the intuitive feelings of those who, experienced in using them, are convinced of their usefulness. The fact that games have never been *proved* to have real educational value is unimportant, since the same may be said of case studies and lectures, syndicate projects and role playing. In this section, the educational characteristics of all business games are considered, before looking at characteristics which a particular game may, or may not, possess.

One characteristic common to all games is the sense of involvement in the situation which the participants experience. There is a great sense of excitement and enjoyment in playing the game. This is undoubtedly of great value—particularly where the participants are students who are studying industrial administration in a compulsory and supplementary sense, e.g., the engineers' Higher National Certificate endorsement subjects.

All games force participants to realize the nature and importance of effective organization and intelligent cooperation. These are important virtues in the field of management, but they can be demonstrated by letting the participant play contract bridge. The virtue of a business game is that organization and cooperation are appreciated in relation to a businesslike situation and problem.

The participants must discover for themselves where the problems in this businesslike situation lie. They, alone, can discover how the choices they make, or can make, relate to the solution of these problems. There is no necessity here to include propositions of educational psychology but, clearly, for the student to discover for himself the nature of managerial problems is superior than for him merely to be told what these problems are.

A well-designed game provides a focal point for thought and discussion and establishes a common basis for communication between student and teacher. It is not uncommon for a teacher of management to have a class in which the industrial background of the students is different, and all are different from the experience of the teacher. In such a situation, a game—being based on general experience—provides the focal point for discussion on different aspects of the managerial process.

Arising from the previous point, it is clear that students of varied background may easily pick on certain aspects of a game as being unrealistic. They are, of course, correct—but this is a source of strength rather than weakness. The critical analysis of the specific assumptions on which the game is based is an exercise in analytical skills, and also a starting point for a consideration of the way in which 'real world' managerial problems evolve and impinge on one another.

Categories of Games

Functional Games

These are games covering only one (or, possibly, two or three) functions performed within the simulated company. The other functions which would exist if the entire operations of the company were simulated are ignored, or merely indicated. These games are much simpler than the types below and have the advantage that, for some of them, optimum solutions can be calculated.

Company Games

These are games where most of the functions of a company are simulated, but the participants are only concerned with the *internal* operations and consequences of decisions. There is no interaction between the companies in the game, and competition is on the same basis as that of teams in a darts match.

Management Games

These involve the simulation of competing—and interacting—companies. In American literature, such games are sometimes termed 'total enterprise' or 'top management' games. Most games developed so far come into this category where the decisions made by participants cover some of the broad policy decisions of a company. The difficulties which the participants must resolve refer to the overall competitive effects of the decisions rather than to the implementation and consequences of those decisions within the company structure. The title 'top management' is, however, misleading since no game really simulates all the problems of top management.

Society Games

Several experiments are in progress to develop games which simulate more general problems of economics and 'political warfare'. Of particular interest in this classification are those games designed to help in training public administration students, whose working environment excludes the profit motive and, therefore, the most commonly used method of game evaluation.

Branch Games

This is really a subsection of company games, but worth individual mention since several companies are developing games of this type. By a branch game, we mean a game of the 'company game' classification where the simulated company operates several divisions or branches. Competition between the branches can, for example, be induced by making only a limited amount of capital available to the company for expansion, and arranging the environment so that the branches can expand, but only at different rates and so that a choice must be made as to which branch will expand.

Abstract Games

The basic model of such games is *not* based on existing markets or companies. In some games, a real situation is vaguely indicated, but never in such detail that a student can readily transfer his real-life experience to the game. However, if the participant is to accept a game as a worthwhile educational device, even the most abstract game must possess a sufficient degree of verisimilitude, i.e., a degree of 'internal reality', so that, although the game does not mirror reality, it possesses a structure such that the participant will accept the relationships as intuitively reasonable.

Specific Games

In specific games, the model is based on the real situation in a company or market. The relationships, e.g., production functions, sales functions, etc., are realistic, and discovered by investigation into actual company operations. Games constructed by large companies, especially American ones, often fall into this category. Clearly, the development of games of this type requires very much more preparation than that of abstract games. They are, therefore, more expensive to produce and are used mainly in internal management development programmes.

Stochastic Models

A game with a stochastic model may demonstrate this property in two ways.

(a) The game is genuinely stochastic if the outcome of some decision is determined by the use of random numbers. Two such decisions frequently used as stochastic elements in a game are research and development expenditure, and sales made by salesmen's calls. The random element may of course, be an 'input' into the game, e.g., by the use of playing cards in a stock-control game.

(b) A game may appear to be stochastic if it is interacting, since, then, the state of the firm at a given moment is a resultant of decisions made by the firm and, also, of decisions and conditions outside the control of the firm. Thus—although in such a model the relationships are predetermined —to the firm, certain of them appear to be random variations. This is not, however, the same thing as actually being stochastic.

(Stochastic variables can be defined as variables with a definite range of values, each one of which, depending on chance, can be attained with a definite probability. A stochastic variable is defined if the range of its possible values is given and if the probability of attaining each particular value is also given.)

Non-Stochastic Models

Such games are completely deterministic both from the designer's view and the participants'. Random numbers for scoring systems do not enter into the game since all relationships are specified and completely defined in the underlying model.

Computer Games

Many games which are available use computers to calculate the consequences of the decisions made by the participants. The reason for this are that:

(a) Computer manufacturers have developed and utilized games as a method of demonstrating the facilities and virtues of computers.

(b) Computers can handle data extremely rapidly. This reduces the time between making decisions and receiving details of the consequences and has the great pedagogical virtue of retaining interest by keeping a fast pace throughout the playing of the game.

(c) A game designed for computer operation can be very much more realistic and complex than a hand-operated game, by virtue of (b).

Non-Computer Games

Non-computer games are those in which the calculation of decision results is done by hand. This technique has disadvantages corresponding to the advantages discussed above. The main virtue of hand-operated games is their economy in operation. A computer game is necessarily expensive and, for most colleges and firms, administratively inconvenient; for this reason, a game which can be operated without a computer has a clear attraction in the normal educational environment—although the rapidly decreasing cost of computer time may well change the balance of arguments.

There are, of course, other ways in which management games may be specified, but there is no virtue in multiplying this list. The criteria used here are sufficient to cover most purposes of the practising training officer or lecturer.

The relationship between the game and educational characteristics has been displayed most effectively by Kalman Cohen[1] in Fig. 16.2. This can be adopted by a training officer as a form of specification of a required game or as a form of description of an existing game (Fig. 16.3).

The Limitations of Games

It is not unusual for both the participant and the training officer to become euphoric about management games. Their sense of involvement, the excitement of the exercise, and the drama of the competitive situation can easily induce a false impression of the effectiveness of gaming as an educational process. The student may gain the impression that he has learned more than he really has; additionally, of course, the involvement which is so characteristic of games can also backfire and engender group feelings of such mutual ill will as to destroy whatever educational benefit might have been gained. For this reason, involvement must be carefully monitored and tactfully controlled.

All management games are simple compared with real life; they leave out many elements that are present in strength in every operating organization. In particular, games (by the very logic of their construction) overstress skills of numeracy: winning and losing are by simple measurable criteria, and underplay the qualitative aspects of business.

Most business games are structured in such a way that decision makers must choose from a restricted range of operations limited by the parameters determined by the game constructor. This limits the decision-making process to alternatives within a 'closed' list, whereas in real life, the imaginative businessman is more likely rewarded for creating new alternatives—an 'open' list. Games thus tend to discourage innovations, not because game designers wish to discourage such laudable activity but because they cannot, in the nature of things, construct a model which can cope with decisions that they cannot anticipate.

Course objectives:

Design characteristics	Analysis				Decision making			Organization		Environment		Educational characteristics				
	A	B	C	D	E	F	G	H	I	J	K	A	B (i)	B (ii)	B (iii)	C
	Enjoyment of game	Creating a problem situation	Systematic collection of information	Techniques for analysis	Inter-relations of functions	Conditions of uncertainty	Long-range planning	Solutions to organization problems	Creative behaviour in realistic situation	Credibility of results	Teaching institutional facts					
1. Complexity		−			+			+				−		−	+	+
2. Large teams (6 +)								+						+	+	+
3. Large number of moves (in real time)		−										+	+			
4. Considerable feedback of information			−									+	+			+
5. Possible to buy considerable information from umpires			+									+				+
6. Considerable random element						+						−				+
7. Long-range influence of decisions							+					−				+

Fig. 16.2. Game characteristics in relation to course objectives.

Game characteristics																	
9. Large amount of institutional information							+						+				
10. Multiple goals	−			+		+	−			+	+		−	+	+	+	−
11. Considerable time pressure				−	−		+						+	−	+	+	−
12. Results sensitive to decisions	+	+		+			+		+	+	+	+		+	+	+	+
13. Facilities for experimentation		+				+			+	+				+	+	+	+
14. Need to exchange information within the team					+		+			+	+			+		+	+
15. Subjective realism	+									+	+		+			+	+
A. Independent exercise	+									+	+		+	−	−	−	−
B. (ii) Functional		+	+		+	+								−	−	−	−
(ii) Interrelationship		+	+		+									−	−	−	−
(iii) Organization				+		+		+						−	−	−	−
C. Core of course	+	+		+		+	+	+						−	−	−	−

225

Administrative characteristics	1	2–4	5–8	9–15	16–20	21 +
Number of participants						
Number of teams		*				
Number of players in team			*			
Number of umpires						
Number of hours						

WEAK   STRONG

Educational characteristics	1	2	3	4	5	6
Interrelationship of functional areas			*			
Creating a problem situation	*					
Decision making under conditions of uncertainty		*				
Importance of systematic collection of information		*				
Use of techniques for analysis	*					
Organizational problems		*				
Importance of long-range planning	*					
Teaching institutional facts	*					
Decision making under time pressure	*					

LOW   HIGH

Design characteristics	1	2	3	4	5	6
Complexity		*				
Amount of information fed back to team	*					
Importance of random numbers		*				
Realism of game	*					
Use of 'free' element	*					

Fig. 16.3. **General business management simulation.**

The Operation of Management Games

The operation of a management game is highly dependent on the nature of a particular game. For example, it is obvious that a game which uses a computer as its calculating mechanism cannot be operated without a computer—this provides a basic factor for the operation of the game. It does not, of course, restrict the operation of the game as severely as this may appear: the computer can be accessed via a terminal, or used in an off-line manner, etc.

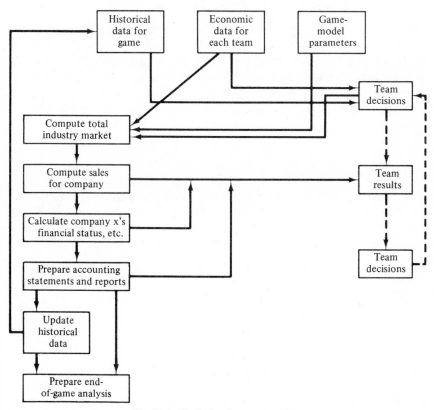

Fig. 16.4. The logic of game operation.

The logic of game operation is outlined in Fig. 16.4. As can be seen from this diagram, the starting point is the provision of 'starting point' data: historical data for the game and economic data for the team. The information on the game-model parameters is, of course, retained by the game administrator. Having made their decisions, the teams hand their results to an administrator who processes these to arrive at a set of results which are returned to the teams, who then begin to repeat the cycle. This, of course, is straightforward. The main problems in game operation are: the participants, the management of the game, and its evaluation.

The Participants

So far as most colleges are concerned, the characteristics of participants—including job experience, status, etc.—are outside the control of the game administrator. This is also true, though to a lesser extent, of the industrial training officer. This being so, there are two actions which the administrator may take:

Allocation of Participants to Teams. This should be done so that no team consists of any homogeneous professional group; all the engineers should not be in one team, all accountants in another, etc.

Allocation of Tasks within a Team. This may be determined completely by the game administrator or it may be left completely free to the teams. A useful 'middle way' is to leave the choice free to the teams, subject to the proviso that no participant should undertake the task, in a game, that he normally performs in his day to day work. If the game is particularly complex or is being used as the core of a course, it is a useful safeguard to select a strong, resilient personality as managing director of each team.

Management of the Game

This is a very difficult topic, since a great deal depends on the teams' experience of games, in general, and familiarity with the particular game being played. The following points are therefore merely indicative of some of the problems involved in the administration of games.

Introduction to the Game. Clearly, all games need some kind of introduction to the participants. It is impossible to state definitely how long, and into what depth, such an introduction should go, since it depends on the quality of the participants and on the complexity of the game. The following points should, however, always be covered;

(a) the reason why the game is being played;
(b) the general 'industrial' background to the game;
(c) the procedures of the game;
(d) the rules of the game;
(e) participants *must* be allowed a question and answer session on the previous points.

Operation of the Game. It is very important that the game should run smoothly and, therefore, that the computation of results should be performed as rapidly as possible and as accurately as consistent with the computing method chosen. The following points, in particular, should be noted:

(a) as the game proceeds, participants generally reduce the time taken to make decisions. It is very important that while this is happening, umpires should not increase the time which they take for computation;

(b) in general, when participants are doing nothing while awaiting results, there is little point in continuing the game with that group.

Evaluation of the Game. The time devoted to evaluation of results and performance is probably crucial to the success or failure of the game—from an educational point of view. The methods of evaluation are considered later, but the following points should be noted:

(a) the time devoted to evaluation is important. The writer's experience suggests approximately 25 per cent of the total game session as a proper minimum;
(b) the effectiveness of evaluation essentially depends on the quality and skill of the evaluator. He needs a broad grasp of the fundamentals of all aspects of management, although a detailed grasp of the tools of management is neither necessary nor (perhaps) desirable.

Note that the one thing without which all games collapse is a good relationship between the game administrator and participants *throughout* the session.

Information. For whatever purpose a game is designed, a key feature is that of information processing. It is, therefore, important that the provision— or lack of provision—of information should be carefully considered. The following notes indicate a few factors about the nature of information in management games.

(a) The amount and kind of information provided. The main decisions which the game designer must bear in mind in this context are:
    the amount of information provided for the initial period of the exercise, i.e., the starting point;
    how much, if any, information is to be provided during the game.
(b) Certain information which could be available may be provided automatically, that is at no 'cost' to the participants. The decision about the amount and kind of this information, which may be termed 'automatic feedback' must be made by the game administrator in the light of the educational objectives which he has in mind.
(c) Certain kinds—and quantities—of information relevant to managerial processes may be obtained, at a price, in real life. This situation can be simulated in a business game; thus, market research information (other companies' market shares, expenditures on advertising, etc.) may be made available, at a price, to competing companies. The problems facing the game designer or administrator are twofold:
    how much information can be bought?
    what price should be charged for such information?
        The solution to both these problems depends on:
    how sensitive the game is to availability of information;
    how sensitive the financial state of teams is to the (proposed) price of the information;
    what educational objective the game is designed to achieve.

229

It is important in this respect to realize that any given game can be adapted to serve a variety of educational objectives by varying:
the amount of automatic feedback;
the range of information available for purchase;
the price charged for this information.

(d) There are two other sources of information about the situation which may be available in a business game.

Information obtained during a trial run. The desirability of a trial run of a game depends on:
the complexity of the game—the more complex the game, the more desirable a trial run becomes;
the educational objectives of the game—the greater the emphasis (in the educational sense) on information gathering and processing, the less desirable is a trial run.

Information obtained from the other companies. Such information may be gained in two ways:
by an intensive study of all results;
by industrial espionage. This latter method is not unknown, particularly in view of the emotional intensity which games frequently induce.

Situational Stress. Frequently, the main claim made for business games is that they simulate the managerial position of making decisions under conditions of stress. This is quite true, unfortunately, stress is often confused with time pressure. Of course, most decisions made in what we have termed as 'management games' are, in real life, decisions of such importance that they are made after a considerable period of analysis and thought. The stress in major managerial decisions is not a stress of time but a stress involving the inadequacy of information, restrictions on courses of action, and inequality of company competitiveness.

(a) It is an essential part of any business game that all teams make decisions on inadequate information. It is a common experience in business games that practising managers become very annoyed at the absence of information which, in real life, they would not ask for. There is a clear educational gain here.

(b) Another characteristic of games in general is that the (necessary) existence of restrictions on the range of decisions available, and the constraints on action, frequently induces stress on the part of the players.

(c) With some games—and it is possible with all but functional games—teams may start with unequal market shares or opportunities for action. This also leads to stress although it may cause difficulties during the evaluation session.

(d) A characteristic common—to a greater or lesser degree—is the time pressure which is exerted on the teams. It is doubtful that this is invariably an advantage, but this point will be discussed later.

230

Decision Making. An important educational feature of business games, as we have seen, is that they stress a variety of problems related to decision making. The importance of decision making in a game depends on the model underlying the game; this may differ on the following points:

(a) The number of decision variables. In some games, a limited number of decisions are required, whereas in others, there is a wide range of decisions which must be made in each time period.
(b) The kinds of decisions to be made also vary. The model may be designed so that repetitive decision making is all that is required. On the other hand, the model may require both programmed and non-programmed decisions.
(c) Perhaps the most important way in which the model structure affects the decision-making content of a game is in the pattern of time available for formulating and considering policy. This should not be confused with time pressure; by the pattern of time available, we mean such things as:
   must each decision be made in each quarter?
   can the game be designed so that 'leap frogging' is possible? (By 'leap frogging', we mean a game in which the decisions for, say, period 7 are made while the umpires calculate the results of period 6; there is, therefore a period's delay between seeing results and making decisions.)
   has the time period in the game to be equal for each period?

Reports Required

It is necessary, when designing a game, to consider what kind of reports are to be made by the teams. The following list is clearly incomplete, but suggests the range available:

(a) reports by team on the objectives of the team;
(b) reports on the organization of the team;
(c) reports on administrative procedures designed and operated within the company;
(d) reports on, or to, such things as
   meetings of shareholders;
   meetings of boards of directors.

How far these reports are required, or utilized, depends on the model underlying the game, and the method of evaluation.

Special Assignments

In most games, it is possible to incorporate special assignments for students to complete. If the game is being designed from scratch, then it is certainly feasible to arrange for such assignments to be introduced, if desirable. Such special assignments may be split into two types:

(a) those dependent on the model structure. These include such things as:
   bargaining on wages;
   bargaining on loans;
   systems analysis of procedures;
(b) those independent of the model structure. These include such things as:
   choice of criteria for end-of-game results;
   design of variations on the game being played.

Composition of Teams

The way in which the teams playing the games are constructed is determined both by the design of the game and by the way in which the game is administered. The game designer can affect the structure and composition of games in three ways:

(a) the number of teams in the game;
(b) the number of participants in the team, which is determined by the complexity of the model underlying the game;
(c) the possibilities for division of tasks within a team, as determined by the extent to which the game constructor has structured the game in an organizational sense.

The Evaluation of Management Games

The evaluation of games can be interpreted in three ways: the assessment of games as a teaching device, particularly in comparison with other teaching methods; judgement of a particular game in relation to specific teaching objectives; and the evaluation of the performance of participants involved in the operation of the game chosen by the instructor. It is appropriate to consider the latter interpretation first, since it is the content and style of this type of evaluation which helps to determine the effectiveness of the game in meeting specified teaching objectives.

The Evaluation of a Game Session

It is the evaluation of the participants' performance during a game—and its feedback to those participants—which provides the greatest test of the instructor's teaching skills. The game 'constructor' has provided the scenario and the logical—mathematical—relationships which link the decisions with the results; the game 'administrator' has provided the physical environment, materials, and 'machinery' for linking decisions with results; the game 'teacher' must, by his skill and attitudes, build on these foundations to provide a positive learning experience. This is done by the evaluation session, without which any game is impotent to perform as a catalyst, and valueless as part of a training programme.

The task of evaluation is complex and demanding. This is due not only to the emotional tension likely to exist in participants at the end of a game, but also to the existence of two distinct, but related, elements in the evaluation process.

During the playing of all but the most significant games, participants are highly motivated, and interpersonal relationships become extraordinarily strong. Some of this social energy is absorbed in the problems of company organization, some into the problems of competitive strategy, and some must be dissipated by the instructors' attitude and skills in group teaching. The evaluation of social processes involved in organization and decision making can be an important learning experience but needs careful handling.

There are four major methods of evaluating the social processes involved in a game. The first is an informal discussion between instructor and participants; this is an intuitive approach which depends totally on the skills of the instructor and his attitude towards group processes. Its disadvantage rests on the scarcity of instructors as adept at the analysis of group dynamics as at the economic analysis which is an equally important element of the total evaluation. The second approach overcorrects for this: it involves using observers to analyse the dynamics of each group throughout the game. This means the concentration of considerable expertise on group processes but has corresponding problems: it is expensive in resources to assemble sufficient trained observers; it is very difficult to find such observers capable of appreciating the nuances of technical 'in jokes'; and it is a common experience that participants can rapidly become impatient with 'expert' discussion of group processes as they await an analysis of what are regarded, rightly or wrongly, as more important—results.

A third approach is similar to that of 'expert' observation, but avoids the resource problem by using 'non-expert' observers. This is done by equipping the observers with predetermined categories of behaviour provided by theoreticians such as Bales. The method has the apparent, but not real, advantage of economy, the temptation to spurious accuracy, and is built on the shifting sands of possibly outdated and irrelevant hypotheses. The writer's personal preference is for a fourth approach: the generation and measurement of the participants' own attitudes towards group processes. These sociometric techniques are not, of course, without their disadvantages and—indeed—their dangers, but they have two overriding advantages: they require no observers and can be used to produce statistics which, although debatable, can be used as a basis for discussion and a comparison with the more easily generated statistics of economic performance.

A useful technique is that in which the evaluation is able to focus on the individual's behaviour and group processes, and to link these with the economic results of the game. In this, an index—termed the consonance index—is devised, and used in the evaluation. The purpose of the index is to measure, by analysis of participants' own responses to a questionnaire, the extent to which group members perceive the influence structure of the group in the same way. This, clearly, can be used for comparing groups with each other and examining the variation in influence structures over the game-playing session, as well as in relating group processes to the economic results with which managers are more familiar.

The measure of consonance (derived from Festinger and Bach, 'Social Factors in Housing') is basically an analysis of the difference in perception by a group member, X, of who influenced him, and the perception of all other group members about who influenced X. Figure 16.5 shows the basic

---

Based on question 'who influences . . . .' (Circled numbers are read across the row and indicate response to question 'who influences you'.)

Player	1	2	3	4	Individual indices
1	×	②	1	0	$2/(3 + 1) = 0.50$
2	3	×	①	①	$1/(5 + 4) = 0.11$
3	①	②	×	0	$3/(3 + 3) = 0.50$
4	③	1	1	×	$3/(5 + 0) = 0.60$
Total					$9/24 = 0.375$

Fig. 16.5. Consonance index.

---

form of calculation as taken from an actual playing session. Look first at player 1. He says that he is influenced by player 2; two players say that he was influenced by player 2; and one player says that he was influenced by player 3. Our index for player 1 can now be calculated: the number in the circle is 2, i.e., two players agree with player 1 that he was influenced by player 2. This gives our numerator. Three 'votes' were cast altogether (two people thought player 1 was influenced by player 2 and one person that player 1 was influenced by player 3); in our example, we can see also that, since there were three players in addition to player 1, if that player had been completely right in his assessment, the figure circled would have been 3 rather than 2—a 'shortfall' of 1. This shortfall is added to the number of votes to give the denominator $(3 + 1)$ and our consonance index for player 1 is $2/4 \times 0.50$. The procedure is to calculate for each individual in each period of the game. The calculation for the team is made by summing the numerators and denominators to give the team consonance index.

The consonance indices have considerable power for generating group discussions and interpreting group behaviour. Thus, it is possible to follow changes in group and individual perceptions throughout the game, and also to link this with the economic performance of a team. Figure 16.6 is an example taken from a game session played with four groups of middle managers. Five points may be made concerning this diagram:

(a) for reasons connected with the particular game, the market share of each company was used as the key measure of economic performance;

(b) no consonance index was calculated for period 1, since these forms are normally disregarded due to their unfamiliarity to players and to the concentration on understanding the game;

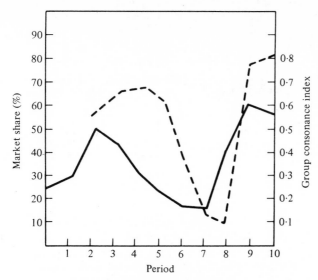

Fig. 16.6. Relationship between group consonance index and economic performance—team 1.

(c) there is a lag effect in the relationship between the consonance index and economic performance, since the sociometric forms are handed in with normal decision forms. For this reason, group attitudes in period n are formed mainly on the basis of results of period $n - 1$;

(d) the consonance index varies between 0 and 1; the higher the index the greater the degree of consistency within the team between individuals' perceptions of their influence, and other players' perception of that influence. In general, therefore, a high index indicates a more cohesive group;

(e) in the particular example, period 7 saw a change in leadership.

In the evaluation of a game session, the measurement of economic performance is very easy. Its precise form depends on the structure of the particular game but, in general, the measurement will be selected from:

(a) market share;
(b) profit;
(c) rate of return on capital;
(d) stock-market valuation;
(e) output as a proportion of capacity;
(f) average unit costs of production;
(g) increase in assets;
    etc.

One comment may perhaps be relevant. A sensible strategy for economic evaluation is to identify one factor from the preceding list as the key measure and to centre the discussion around this. Naturally, the more advanced

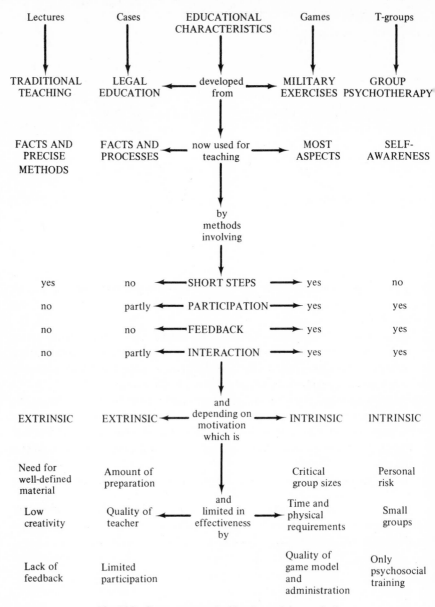

Fig. 16.7. Games compared with other training methods.

the participants, the greater is the advantage from demonstrating the inter-relationships between alternative measures of performance.

The comparison between games and other forms of management training is particularly difficult. The difficulty is basically common to all management training: how is the performance of a manager measured? This chapter is not concerned with such a basic question as this; instead we shall look subjectively at two aspects of the evaluation of games. Antoine Papaloizas and Rolf Stiefel[2] reported the opinions of a sample of European management teachers, and found that the use of games in teaching was thought to stress the ability to work with others, 'thus denoting the specific character of the business game which is always a competition between teams'. Respondents considered that the business game affects working with others, but does not affect to the same extent the 'understanding' or the attitudes towards others.

Figure 16.7 illustrates some differences and limitations on games compared with other methods of training.

Some Likely Developments

Anticipating the future uses of games is extraordinarily difficult. The one thing which seems assured is that games are no longer regarded as new, curious forms of training: games of many categories will be used in conjunction with other methods at the trainer's disposal. There would seem to be three major lines of development: an extension in the use of games, an increase in the complexity of games, and greater experiment in the structural forms underlying the decision processes involved in games.

The extension in games is likely to be twofold: using existing games in primary and secondary sectors of the educational system as well as in the tertiary and industrial sectors, and developing new forms of games in the tertiary and non-profit-oriented management. In this latter sector, we are likely to see games in which some form of social welfare function will replace profits as a criterion of game success. Once the concept of games as teaching methods is universally accepted, it seems likely that further experiment will lead to extension in both the character of players and the nature of the game.

An increase in complexity is likely once the use of computer facilities become cheaper. There is also likely to be a move toward computer-based games. Unfortunately, such games tend to use more complex models, partly to demonstrate programming virtuosity, and partly to increase the realism of the game. This is not necessarily an improvement, since complexity may improve realism in the sense of the correspondence between game model and the real world, but reduce the effectiveness of the game in a teaching sense.

Structural advances in games are likely in the decision-making mechanisms of games. In the main, the decision-making sequence involved in games is period by period. Participants make a decision, the umpires calculate results, return them to participants, who evaluate their results and make their decisions for the next period. This is not necessarily, however, a true reflection of real-life management decision making, where decision rules rather than *ad hoc* decisions are likely to be more common. It seems likely that 'programmed decision rules' are likely to be integrated into games, since this approach shifts attention away from period to period decisions to the determination of long-range strategy. The difference in procedures is illustrated in Fig. 16.8.

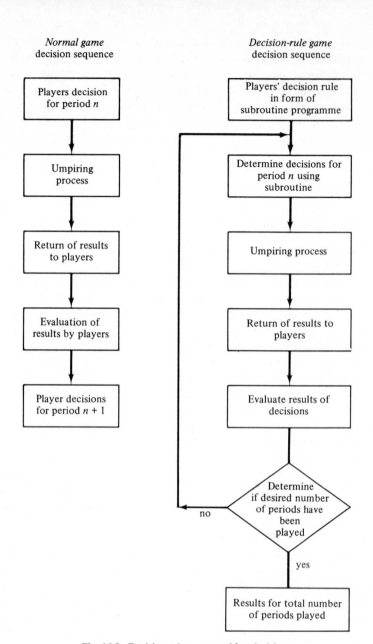

Fig. 16.8. **Decision rules versus** *ad hoc* **decisions.**

References

1. COHEN, K. J. and PHENMAN, E. The Role of Management Games in Education and Research, *Management Science*, **7**, 2, 1961.
2. PAPALOIZAS, A. and STIEFEL, R. The Effectiveness of Management Teaching Methods, *Management Decision*, **9**, summer 1971.

Suggested Reading

1. COHEN, K. J. and PHENMAN, E. The Role of Management Games in Education and Research, *Management Science*, **7**, 2, 1961.

GREENE, J. R. and SISSON, R. L. *Dynamic Management Decision Games*, Wiley, New York, 1959.

GREENSLAW, P. S., HERRON, LOWELL W., and RAWDON, R. H. *Business Simulation in Industrial and University Education*, Prentice-Hall, Englewood Cliffs, New Jersey, 1962.

KIBBEE, J. M., CRAFT, C. J., and NANUS, B. *Management Games*, Reinhold, New York, 1961.

ROCKHAM, N., *et al. Developing Interactive Skills*, Wellens Publishing, 1971.

RAIA, A. P. A Study of the Educational Value of Management Games, *Journal of Business*, **39**, 3, 1966.

17. Guidelines for the use of sensitivity training in management development

Gordon L. Lippitt[*]

Sensitivity training is no longer at the experimental stage. It is a valid, tested and professionally developed method of learning used in management development by numerous companies and organizations in many countries around the world. In this chapter, the authors offer guidelines to help managers in deciding on the kind, nature and appropriate resource for sensitivity training.

Some strong opinions have been expressed, pro and con, about laboratory methods of training for individuals, groups, and organizations. Douglas McGregor[1] says this kind of training can '... bring about significant improvements in the skills of social interaction', while George S. Odiorne[2] indicates that he believes that many human relations laboratories have become '... perverted into psychological nudist camps which end up mainly as self flagellation societies'.

Such strong opinions frequently cause confusion and concern by potential users and participants of laboratory methods. While much has been written and experienced about laboratory training, most of the literature is either too technical, or descriptive of individual experience. Sometimes, it appears in a rather flamboyant manner in popular magazines and stresses extreme applications of laboratory training. Such presentations are not helpful to the potential participant, training director, or administrator who wants to answer the pragmatic question: 'Is this kind of training desirable for me, or my organization, and relevant to my individual, group or organization's problems, needs, and objectives?'

When trying to get an answer of this kind of question, the interested individual usually consults someone who has been through a programme.

[*] This chapter is rewritten and updated by the author from an earlier article entitled 'Managerial Guidelines to Sensitivity Training' by Leslie E. This and Gordon L. Lippitt, which appeared in the *ASTD Journal*, April 1963. Selected portions are used by permission.

240

Almost inevitably he is told: 'Oh, I couldn't begin to tell you about it—you just have to experience it'. This is not helpful for effective understanding or decision making. The potential participant then may turn to a professional person who, usually, does not distinguish between the direct work-related benefits and the more complex areas of personality integration, social responsibility, self-fulfilment, and other person-oriented potential values of such training.

One key focus of laboratory learning is on skill development of individuals or groups. When certain approaches to encounter or confrontation groups lead to insight but non-action-related feedback for improving behavioural skills, the goals of laboratory education are not being completely fulfilled. Such dramatic types of experience make livid news stories that prompt the kind of comments made at the beginning of this chapter.

A person can learn about laboratory training in a variety of ways. A good counsellor experienced in laboratory training is well able to explain it to a client. A teacher can demonstrate to a class group the meaning of 'process examination' for learning about human relations. A number of excellent books and pamphlets have been written, and help managers, leaders, and others understand this method of education more effectively. In addition, there are video tapes and movies that have been made to help in the orientation to this kind of learning.

It seems desirable, in the context of a book on management development, to present some straightforward answers to a number of typical questions that are asked about laboratory training. One could ask and answer questions that would be appropriate for the professional trainer-educator. This is not my interest. One could also ask questions that pose theoretical arguments and then give the author's view. My goal is to list some of the typical questions that one is asked by management development planners interested in clarifying their thinking about this innovative process in education, and I shall focus on the level of inquiry that prompts these kind of potential questions by consumers.

What is Laboratory Education?

The expression 'sensitivity training' is an inadequate phrase popularly used in describing the laboratory learning theory and method used in human relations training. This kind of training usually includes the methods of unstructured group learning, individual feedback, skill practice, information sessions, and transfer of learnings to other life situations. The theory behind such methods is based on a laboratory concept of learning, which embodies the belief that individuals can best learn interpersonal and group skills through actual experience which is analysed for the benefit of the learner.

The words 'laboratory training' were first applied to this kind of learning in connection with the three-week human relations laboratories, sponsored by the National Training Laboratories at Bethel, Maine. Since those early years, beginning in 1947, this training has spread to many university-sponsored laboratories, in-house organization programmes, institutes in many countries, and the development of consultant services to provide this kind of training for specific clients.

Later, in 1957, the term 'sensitivity training' was used by Irving Weschler, Robert Tannenbaum, and colleagues. In the 'sixties, the term 'encounter group' was introduced by Rogers, Esalen, and other personal-growth-oriented laboratory educators.

How Can One Define 'Sensitivity Training'?

Charles Seashore wrote as follows about the sensitivity training approach to laboratory education:

> Sensitivity training is one type of experience-based learning. Participants work together in a small group over an extended period of time, learning through analysis of their own experiences, including feelings, reactions, perceptions, and behavior. The duration varies according to the specific design, but most groups meet for a total of 10–40 hours. This may be in a solid block, as in a marathon week-end program or two to six hours a day in a one or two week residential program or spread out over several weekends, a semester, or a year.
>
> The sensitivity training group may stand by itself or be a part of a larger laboratory training design which might include role playing, case studies, theory presentations, and intergroup exercises.[3]

Laboratory methods may vary, but the sensitivity training group-learning experience is at the core of the learning.

What are the Underlying Assumptions of This Kind of Learning?

It is natural to wonder if this kind of learning is based on solid learning theory and an understanding of the way that adults learn. Laboratory learning does use the experienced based concept of learning. As Seashore[4] points out, underlying laboratory training are the following assumptions about the nature of the learning process which distinguishes the laboratory method from other, more traditional models of learning:

Learning Responsibility

Each participant is responsible for his own learning. What a person learns depends on his own style, readiness, and the relationships he develops with other members of the groups.

Resource Person's Role

The staff person's role is to facilitate the examination and understanding of the experiences in the group. He helps participants to focus on the way the group is working, the style of an individual's participation, or the issues facing the group.

Experience and Conceptualization

Most learning is a combination of experience and conceptualization. A major sensitivity training aim is to provide a setting in which individuals are encouraged to examine their experiences together in enough detail for valid generalizations to be drawn.

Authentic Relationships and Learning

A person is most free to learn when he establishes authentic relationships with other people and, thereby, increases his sense of self-esteem and decreases his defensiveness. In authentic relationships, people can be open, honest, and direct with one another so that they are communicating what they are actually feeling rather than masking their feelings.

Skill Acquisition and Values

The development of new skills in working with people is maximized as a person examines the basic values underlying his behaviour as he acquires appropriate concepts and theory and as he is able to practise new behaviour and obtain feedback on the degree to which his behaviour produces the intended impact. The assumption underlying sensitivity training is that people learn best by self-discovery.[5] It does little good to read or to be 'spoken to' about many of the human behaviour kinds of learnings.

How Does this Training Differ from Therapy?

Laboratory groups are formed to help normal adults to improve their interpersonal skills. The line between a laboratory learning group experience and a therapy group may be hard to distinguish. One key difference is that a laboratory group usually deals with 'here and now' experience while a therapy group usually goes back to past 'there and then' type of data. In therapy, we are usually looking for pathology rooted in a person's or group's life history. As stated by the American Group Psychotherapy Association:

> Therapeutic groups are established for the purpose of treatment. The therapist is responsible for the effects of his practice and maintains responsibility for his patients. It is expected that he will: (a) have some way of screening prospective members, (b) have the group's goals clearly stated, (c) make a commitment to and contract with the group members, (d) indicate he has in mind the possibility that there may be a need to make provisions for helping group members who might find the group situation too upsetting, and (e) maintain interest in evaluation and follow-up of his group members and his group practices.[6]

Frank[7] has pointed out the major differences between the two techniques and points out there is a de-emphasis in the sensitivity training groups upon learning about internal dynamics of self. Others disagree, and point to the steady trend of de-emphasizing group processes in sensitivity training and focusing instead upon personal insight. Weschler *et al.*[8] have called this therapeutic focus in sensitivity training, 'psychotherapy for normals'.

An individual, group, organization, or community should not approach laboratory learning as therapy. The sponsors of laboratory training should not promise or imply therapeutic goals or results. The point at which learning stops and therapy begins cannot be accurately defined. The major point is the understanding, goals, focus, and orientation of the programme, resource person, and the participants.

Who Should Participate in this Kind of Management Development?

As one examines the thousands of participants in this kind of learning in the past thirty years, it would be hard to establish any typology. Instead, let us look at what the individual, group and organization might each receive from this kind of learning.

Individuals

A person might attend a laboratory learning experience as an individual. It might be a manager wanting to improve his own interpersonal skills; an administrator searching for new leadership skills; or a supervisor wanting to relate more effectively to groups.

Most individual participants gain a picture of the impact they make on other members of the group. A participant can assess the degree to which that impact corresponds with, or deviates from, his conscious intentions. He can also get a picture of the range of perceptions of any given act. It is as important to understand that different people may see the same piece of behaviour differently—e.g., as supportive or antagonistic, relevant or irrelevant, clear or ambiguous—as it is to understand the impact on any given individual. In fact, very rarely do all members of a group have even the same general perceptions of a given individual or a specific event.

Some people report that they try out behaviour in the T-Group that they have never tried before. This experimentation can enlarge their view of their own potential and competence and provide the basis for continuing experiment and skill development.

Groups

Sometimes homogeneous groups from an organization will plan a laboratory training experience. It might be a team building experience for a project group in the aircraft industry; a manager and his subordinates in a plant; a weekend retreat with a group of top executives; a classroom group in a school of education; or two staff-line groups resolving some intergroup relations.

The laboratory learning experience can focus on forces which affect the characteristics of the group, such as the level of commitment and follow-through resulting from different methods of making decisions, the norms controlling the amount of conflict and disagreement that is permitted, and the kinds of data gathered. Concepts such as cohesion, power, group maturity, climate, and structure can be examined using the experiences in the group to understand more easily how these same forces operate in the back-home situation. The group can improve its skills of problem solving.

Organizations

It would seem that laboratory training could be helpful as part of the organization development process. It would be helpful in serving three basic organizational concerns:[9]

a. *Employees and Managers Work in a Complex Organization System.* Organizations are more than the physical 'things' on their inventory lists. It is not possible to think of an organization without thinking of people— their functions and interrelationships. It is people that have organizational objectives: who need a division of labour; who do the work, or give the service; who need meetings, directives, policies, methods for delegating work, controls; and need to know how to get the most from other people.

One of the objectives of laboratory learning is to help the participant to see 'organizations', not as the eye sees the buildings, but as the informal, unseen or unnoticed functions, elements, characteristics, forms, authority, tradition, and interpersonal processes at work. The premise is that the more people understand the nature of the human encounter in the organization, the better equipped they will be to utilize, release, and control the organization for the attainment of organizational objectives.

b. *Organizations Accomplish Their Work as a Result of the Motivations of People.* Most managers or employees know their technical specialty quite well, and usually are quite well informed about the functions in their jobs, such as planning, reporting, controlling, etc. What they are less knowledgeable about is how to release the motivation of people. Through history, one of the precepts noted by successful leaders has been 'know thyself'. Whether a manager recognizes it or not, his behaviour, posture, gestures, tone of voice, ways of reacting to people and situations, silence—these, and many other personal factors—influence greatly how other people react to him.

It would follow that the more a person understands himself, and how a leader's behaviour, consciously or unconsciously, will affect others, the more effective that leader can be in relationships with other human beings. The objective is not to become an amateur psychiatrist, but to be more sensitive to the influence one's behaviour has on others, and vice versa.

Such sensitivity is not designed to make a person 'thin-skinned', but more aware of one's surroundings. The human organism has the 'radar' of its many senses which, frequently, are dormant or undeveloped. It is in the sharpening of these senses that laboratory learning can assist.

c. *Employees and Leaders Frequently Work in Groups.* A major share of today's work is spent in settings with two or more persons in an organizational work unit, conferences, institutes, planning groups, task forces, and similar groupings. Many of the factors at work in individual to individual contexts are also at work within groups. However, when a number of individuals are brought into a group setting, additional factors and forces are manifested.

There is a body of knowledge about the dynamic factors that emerge when people work in groups, and the more a person understands these factors, the more effectively he can work with people in work groups. Rensis Likert has recently summarized much of the research in this area, and its implications for managers and organizations.[10] The research on morale and productivity indicates that people potentially meet their needs and accomplish work in the face to face work unit of the organization.

An organization using laboratory training could discover the following. The effects of status, influence, division of labour, and styles of managing conflicts are among organizational concepts that may be highlighted by analysing events in the organization. Learning experiences can be related to units within an organization. It is then possible to look at the relationships between groups, examining such factors as competitiveness, communications, stereotyping, and understanding.

One of the more important possibilities for an organization is that of examining the kinds of assumptions and values which underlie the behaviour of people as they attempt to manage the work of the organization. The opportunity to link up a philosophy of management with specific behaviours that are congruent with, or antithetical to, that philosophy makes laboratory learning particularly relevant to understanding the large organization.

Has This Approach to Learning Been Evaluated and Researched?

It is now possible to answer this question with a definite 'yes'. This does not mean that all the research is conclusive, or that more is not needed. While a number of pioneer summaries of research by Stock[11] and others can be cited as early evidence, let us look at some of the more recent reviews in the literature.

Robert House's review of the research on sensitivity training appeared in 1967. It focused mainly on participant characteristics and the change in the participant's behaviour back on the job. So far as participant characteristics were concerned, he concluded that trainees changed their opinions as to what constitutes good leadership, came to believe less in structure, and emphasized the need for consideration more strongly. As to the latter, House comments, after carefully reviewing six of the better studies:

> One of the most striking results of the above studies (at least to me) is the lack of contradiction among the findings. All six studies revealed what appear to be important positive effects of T-Group training. Two of the studies report negative effects as well. These findings take on special significance when one considers the rigor with which the studies were conducted. All of the studies employed control groups to discount the effects of factors other than the T-Group experience. All of the evidence is based on observations of the behavior of the participants in the actual job situations. No reliance is placed on participant response; rather, evidence is collected from those having frequent contact with the participant in his normal work activities. The source of the evidence is especially important because of the possibility of bias resulting from self descriptions of participants.[12]

In addition, House feels that human relations training also helps participants to listen better, to be more supportive of others, to be more considerate leaders, more sensitive, and to be less dependent on authority. Unfortunately, not many of the studies attempted to determine the precise cause of the changes.

Another review of research by John Campbell and Marvin Dunnette[13] is a comprehensive coverage with extensive references, and it is one of the few reviews that seriously examine in depth the methodology used in the various evaluation studies. While the general tone of the article is somewhat critical, the authors stress how tenuous any positive findings in the research are at this time. Yet they recognize the difficulties involved and are sympathetic to the efforts that have been made. As academic psychologists, not T-Group practitioners, they have little vested interest in positive conclusions. Their focus is on T-Groups in an organizational setting and they do not consider personal-growth-oriented groups. They indicate that the most positive findings relate to improved self-perception.

One of the more recent research reviews, published in 1971 by Jack Gibb,[14] is also the most comprehensive of the research on human relations training. Gibb covers the entire spectrum of groups, from the most conservative T-Group to the most radical encounter group. His specific interest is in whether or not change takes place, and what causes it. In examining the various training technologies, Gibb found that very little empirical evidence exists on the effectiveness of 'creativity growth groups', 'marathon groups', etc. In fact, 89 of the 106 studies reviewed were on what Gibb terms sensitivity training groups.

Some recent studies of encounter groups have been completed using control groups. The authors[15] measured effects immediately after the group learning and the six to eight months' delayed response in the person's life. This study was done with 206 students at Stanford University, and in seventeen groups. One of the outcomes of their study indicates the importance of the group leader/trainer in contributing to an effective learning experience.

The following generalizations can be made from the considerable research on sensitivity training:[16]

(a) people who attend sensitivity training programmes are more likely to improve their managerial skills than those who do not (as reported by their peers, superiors, and subordinates);

(b) everyone does not benefit equally. Roughly two-thirds of the participants are seen as increasing their skills after attendance at laboratories. This figure represents an average across a number of studies;

(c) many individuals report extremely significant changes and impact on their lives as workers, family members, and citizens. This kind of anecdotal report should be viewed cautiously in terms of direct application to job settings, but it is consistent enough for it to be clear that T-Group experiences can have a powerful and positive impact on individuals;

(d) the incidence of serious stress and mental disturbance during training is difficult to measure, but it is estimated to be less than one per cent of participants and, in almost all cases, occurs in persons with a history of prior disturbances.

Why Does this Training Seem Mysterious and Hard to Describe?

This problem is less true than in the past because of the excellent reporting in magazines, journals, and books. However, as indicated earlier, learnings about one's own behaviour are so highly personal that it is sometimes difficult to communicate them to another person in a meaningful way. It might be difficult to tell a superior, 'I learned that people mistake my seriousness for aggressiveness, and I'm going to try to do something about it?' Your boss could want to know 'how' you found this out. It is in this area that it is difficult to explain one's learning.

Perhaps it is a reflection of our culture and the need for this training that we find it difficult to share feelings, emotions, and behaviour. This is the nature of the laboratory learning experience.

There is less chance for misunderstanding about the content of the information sessions or the skill practice sessions in a laboratory programme. These you can listen to, talk about, read, and perform. These activities form an important part of the actual experience. Because the learnings of a personal nature are so vivid and meaningful, in comparison to the substantive learnings, it is understandable that the total training experience tends to be seen as that component of the learning activity in which trainees gained their most meaningful insights.

Perhaps one of the best ways to describe the learning is to provide the 'other' person(s) with a mini experience in which the reporter has the person or group to which he is reporting process their expectation of him, and their feelings about his going to a lab. The reporting participant can use this 'here and now' data to explain the meaning of the process learning methods in the laboratory. In addition, the literature in popular and scientific laboratories is now extensive. A participant may want to select one article, report, or book that may help to explain his experience to others.

What Conditions Seem to be Necessary to Make this Kind of Management Development Effective?

In using the laboratory training as a learning or change experience for an individual, group, or organization, it might be appropriate to ask certain key questions about the potential participant(s) or client system. Bennis[17] suggests a five-step model in diagnosing the readiness for laboratory training (see Fig. 17.1).

In a very real sense, a state of proper readiness and volunteerism is a key factor in programme effectiveness. This would not 'make' the programme a success, but it would ensure that the participants are not entering into the experience under any false concepts or perceptions.

How to Tell if a Laboratory Design is a Responsible One?

It is obvious to those utilizing the laboratory concept and the sensitivity training method that no two training groups or programmes are identical.

1. Are lab. training change goals appropriate to target system?	If *not*, *stop* and reconsider appropriateness of lab. training

If *yes*, then:

2. Is the 'cultural state' of target system prepared for lab. training?	If *not*, *stop* and examine areas where more preparation is needed or where value conflicts should be reduced.

Degree and type of value conflict?
Legitimacy of interpersonal phenomena?
Degree, range, intensity, and resolution of conflict?
Concepts of control and authority used?
Interdependence of target system?
Relationship of trust and confidence between change agent and target system?

If *yes*, then

3. Are key people involved and committed?	If *not*, *stop* and examine ways to develop more commitment to programme.

If *yes*, then:

4. Are members of the target system adequately prepared for, and oriented to, lab. training?	If *not*, *stop* and examine ways to develop more commitment to programme.

If *yes*, then:

5. Is volunteerism (regarding participation) ensured?	If *not*, *stop* and examine attitudes towards lab. training, or *why* people do, or do not, want to go to labs. After diagnosis, attempt to indicate the place of lab. training in career development accurately.

Fig. 17.1. Five-step model for diagnosing the state of the target system.

Part of this dissimilarity is accounted for by variations in the purpose, objectives, and nature of the overall programme of which the laboratory group learning experience is a part.

In addition, differences in group composition, size, sophistication, motivation, training facilities, group leaders, and numerous other similar factors combine, and interplay, to bring into sharp focus the awareness that each group has a unique learning experience.

Any laboratory training programme, with its specific learning opportunities and participant learnings, is the result of background events, trainer background, participants' backgrounds and needs, training location, and programme all impinging on a given session and moment to produce a training event. Whether this event (silence, leadership struggle, conflict between two members, apathy, hostility, subgrouping, etc.) will be utilized for appropriate learning will, in large part, be determined by the skill and sophistication of the trainer.

Figure 17.2, shows some of the major forces which impinge on a training programme designed to provide laboratory learning experiences and opportunities that are responsibly designed. Whether this rich and potent mix, culminating in a series of action learning events, will be the vehicle for meaningful learning is heavily dependent on the trainer and the sponsoring group.[18] This unique experience does not mean, however, that certain problems, group phenomena, sequential phases, and group behaviour patterns will not be predictable. Only when these factors are taken into

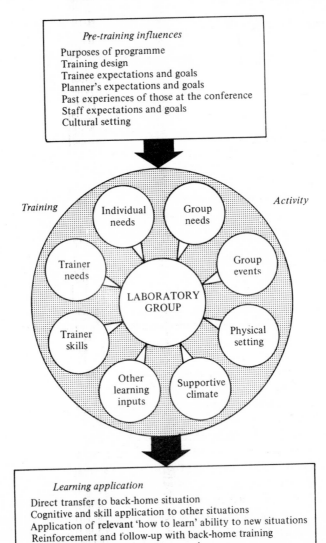

Fig. 17.2. Factors affecting laboratory group learning. (From Lippitt, Leaders for Laboratory Training, *ASTD Journal*, March 1967.)

account will the laboratory method evolve and be translated into a useful training technique. From twenty years of intensive use and study, a significant body of process knowledge and desired participant and trainer behaviour has emerged.

The success of the laboratory method as a training innovation usually occurs only if there is a qualified professional trainer in the training group itself, plus certain other conditions promoted by the educational sponsors. A responsible programme is one in which proper professional attention is directed to pre-planning, implementation, and follow-up of the learning experience. In addition, the promotion of the programme does not promise or allude to results that cannot be realistically achieved.

What is the Trainer's Role in Laboratory Learning?

The laboratory trainer has a number of roles to fulfil. There is no firm and fixed characterization for each of these roles. At least six are readily identifiable in a laboratory training programme. They are:

Initiator of Diagnostic Training Concepts

It is the responsibility of the trainer to help the learning group to see that its own processes and problems provide much of the 'curriculum' for the learning experience. In various ways, he initiates the concept of the diagnostic process in the learning of the group. Initiating diagnostic procedures can be done in a non-directive fashion or, at the other end of the continuum, a trainer may actually spell out his responsibility in a short training programme where interpersonal laboratory training groups are being used.

Diagnostic Observer at Appropriate Time and Level

One of the major functions of the trainer is to make appropriate diagnostic observations to the group at such times as seem most appropriate for the group's learning and ability to internalize. This does not mean that the trainer is responsible for all diagnostic observations. All laboratory trainers have, as their goal, that group members become their own diagnosticians.

Innovator of Learning Experience

The trainer, in varying degrees, will see his responsibility for initiating various techniques and methods to make possible the maximum learning experience as the group progresses. If the group does not know how to use a particular area of interest for its own learning, the trainer may set up a 'testing situation'. This might be in the area of procedural suggestions, such as role playing to test out different approaches to the situation, and that the group experiments with the role or situation being analysed.

Standards Protector

In the atmosphere of the training environment and the work of the laboratory group itself, a number of standards emerge, such standards as diagnosing the 'here and now' as against the 'there and then' life of individuals. There may be times when the group may depart from these standards, and the trainer needs to be sensitive to whether or not his function is to protect for the good of the learning experience.

Initiator of Selected Group Standards for Learning

This function of the trainer may be performed less often. Nevertheless, there are times when an individual or subgroup may be getting 'hurt' by the group, and the trainer may want to suggest standards to govern the level of diagnosis or personal attack. Of course, the vulnerability of an individual or subgroup to be affected by the group differs widely according to the personality structure of the individuals in the group. It behoves the trainer to be sensitive to these different strengths and weaknesses of individuals.

Group Member Function

In some of the literature about laboratory training, statements have been made that the trainer 'never becomes a group member'. The author believes that this is an unrealistic interpretation of the psychology and reality of group life. The fact that the training group is a cultural unit implies that it has all the potential aspects of group identification, cohesion, and growth. The group builds expectations for all persons in the training situation, and this includes the trainer.

The laboratory trainer frequently is faced with the question, 'Should I intervene in the group discussion or activity, or should I let the group find its own way?' There are several guidelines that will assist the trainer in making decisions about training interventions:

(a) intervention by the trainer has as its purpose, for the most part, the learning of the group about its processes;

(b) trainer interventions may be helpful to both the individual and the group in giving support to make possible the exposure of behaviour for analysis;

(c) intervention by the trainer is helpful in encouraging the use of feedback among members of the group, for both individual and group learning;

(d) trainer intervention may be necessary if, in the professional judgement of the trainer, a particular individual or subgroup is being 'overthreatened' by the analysis of the group. Individuals and groups vary widely in their ability to tolerate such feedback and perception;

(e) as the group takes over the observer function, the interventions of the trainer can become less frequent, and at a different level from the observations being made by the group;

(f) training interventions may be of a procedural nature to maximize learnings within a group experience;

(g) near the end of the laboratory experience, there is frequently an expectancy on the part of the group members not only to share their feelings about one another and the ways they have seen one another, but for the trainer to share with the group his feelings and observations about the group's growth, learning, and effectiveness. At this stage in the group's experience, such sharing is a legitimate aspect of the intervention and 'member-role' responsibility of the trainer.

These points about the role of trainer interventions are suggestive of their relationship to the laboratory learning process. Although interventions are basically conditioned by the goals of the training process, they are constantly affected by the situation, time, and member and trainer needs. It is also likely that trainer interventions will be affected by the group's concept of the trainer's role as experienced by the group and redefined at various points in its life.

What are the Professional Qualifications One Should Expect of a Laboratory Trainer?

While there is no clear-cut, agreed set of qualifications for the laboratory trainer, experience seems to indicate that a competent trainer would have most of the following characteristics:

Self-understanding

A laboratory trainer needs a great deal of self-understanding to enable him to operate effectively in his role. This is necessary to prevent his own needs from interfering with the training process and to enable him to have empathy with the interpersonal problems of others in the learning situation.

Personal Security

A laboratory trainer needs to have sufficient personal security to permit him to take a non-punitive role in the training and to have genuine respect for other people. Such personal security is a prerequisite for effective educational leadership. Coming from this personal security will be a willingness to share leadership roles with others and, appropriately, to relinquish authority in the learning transaction as training proceeds. Such personal security will also allow the trainer to participate adequately in the rather wide range of interpersonal situations inherent in a laboratory group, and to be able to deal with the many ambiguous and hostile situations faced by him.

Previous Group Experience

A trainer in a laboratory group should be sophisticated and knowledgeable about group life. He should have experienced the practical problems of working simultaneously as a group leader and a group member in a variety of settings. Such experiences, at both a theoretical and a practical level, are imperative for effective diagnostic trainer skill.

Professional Training

A background in the behavioural sciences is highly desirable for an effective laboratory trainer. A professional academic background in the field of education, sociology, psychology, social work, psychiatry, personnel, philosophy, organizational administrative theories, and similar areas will provide a theoretical base on which the laboratory trainer will build his educational sophistication, philosophy, and expertise. Although a professional academic background does not guarantee training competence, the concepts and constructs that come from such study in the social sciences are indispensable aspects of his qualifications, plus the ethics of his own discipline.

Ability in Verbal and Non-verbal Communication

A laboratory trainer must be able to communicate effectively with others. One of the prerequisites is to know how to communicate at the level, and in the words and imagery, appropriate for the particular group he is training.

Training Skills

With the proper personality and educational and experiential background, most training personnel can learn the design, diagnostic, instrumentation, and support skills needed to lead effective laboratory training programmes. It is advisable that any potential laboratory trainer have prior experience as a member of a T-Group. Specialized training skills can be acquired, after attendance at a sensitivity training laboratory, as a member of a training-for-trainers group, through an induction programme, serving as a training associate in an action learning laboratory, and finally, as a group trainer under the supervision of a senior staff person.

These criteria are suggestive of the factors that should be considered when selecting and developing persons to lead laboratory training programmes. Although too obvious to discuss in detail, the important areas of readiness, interest, and willingness to work with others in this kind of training are important basic dimensions. The philosophy of training that underlies the laboratory approach is a vital part of the commitment of any potential trainer. Such a trainer should have a penetrating concept of the laboratory approach, and thorough understanding of the conditions under which it operates. As an important innovation in the field of learning, the laboratory training philosophy, theory, and methods demand the highest calibre of professional competence and personal integrity.

What are Some of the Key Issues or Dilemmas About Laboratory Training?

This kind of training has developed a number of approaches in its application.

Issue 1—Length of Laboratory Training

Some training programmes last three weeks—others, for as short a period as two days. Some organizations have a series of two-day sessions at intervals over several months. There is some disagreement as to the desired length, or whether a continuous programme is better.

There can be little assurance as to how much more learning takes place in a week's programme v. a three week's programme, or a three-day programme v. a one-week programme. Probably commonsense is the best guide. One can expect that more can be learned in one week than in three days. Rarely has this kind of training been undertaken without having at least twelve hours of group learning time, plus the other aspects of the programme.

254

In the shorter programmes, the organization would need to identify what kind of skills, insights, and knowledges are most important, and to design the training programme for intensive concentration in these areas. Generally, most organizations seem to find a programme of at least one week's duration most desirable. This is particularly true if one is focusing on personal insight. It takes time to create a group atmosphere, and individual readiness, that will permit constructive and direct feedback of a hopeful nature to trainees.

Issue 2—Heterogeneous or Family Groups as Focus of Laboratory Training

Opinions differ as to whether it is better to train persons in programmes made up from different organizations, within one industry or business, within one department in an organization, along peer lines, or vertically from several levels. There are advantages and disadvantages to each. In general, the advantage of family training is that all members of a work group, or related work groups, get the same kind of training at one time and get to know each other quite well.[19] They can also use the learning process in their day by day work to solve operating problems. So-called team training is often used with a work unit in the organization development process.

One of the major disadvantages of family groupings is that participants can never completely forget the setting and the work relationships, and the interactions among participants may be less intense and direct.

It has proved valuable in heterogeneous training to send a team of persons from an organization, to increase impact back in the organization. Which pattern one chooses would depend on the length of the programme, the experience of the persons to be trained, the intensity of training desired, and the objectives of the programme for the organization.

Real impact for individual and organizational change is possible in either approach.

Issue 3—Use of Trainer or Instruments in the Unstructured Group Phase of the Learning

Some experiment has been performed with so-called instrument laboratory groups.[20] The instruments consist of both individual and group questionnaires in which reactions can be coded, analysed, then fed back to the participants. A trainer does not sit with the basic training group, but does assist in the design of the training activity, and provides materials to help the groups analyse their behaviour as they work together. The trainer may also lead data-summarizing sessions or presentations, as well as helping the group with practice exercises.

The results of these programmes do indicate that learning does take place under such circumstances. A group, through the use of well-developed data-collection instruments, can feed back data to itself for effective learning.

Many specialists in the laboratory field believe that the trainer should be present to help with interpersonal feedback and group analysis, as well as to prevent attempts at ill-advised therapy by trainees, for each other. It is also thought by some that such training needs a professional present at all times during the programme. The experience to date would indicate the value in using both the trainer and effective data-collection instruments to maximize the learning.

Issue 4—Use of Outside v. Inside Organization Trainers

Some organization leaders ask: 'Can't my training director do this kind of training?' Perhaps he can, if he has had extensive training.[21] Certainly, such a person can probably handle some of the elements, with proper knowledge and experience, e.g., of information presentations and skill exercises. However, the sensitivity training group experience, and the integration of all the elements of the programme into a meaningful experience, requires a great deal of specialized knowledge, skill, and experience.

These can be learnt by many training directors, but the expenditure in time, effort, and money is considerable. There is frequently the additional problem of the training director being handicapped by operating within the organization and not being seen as a resource in this kind of developmental process. Many organizations think that it is best to go outside for professional guidance in this field of training. The training director's job has so many responsibilities that, frequently, he cannot become an expert in this, or other, highly specialized areas of training if he is to serve primarily as a consultant to management on how training can help management solve its problems. However, as needs for laboratory training develop, more and more professional trainers are now on the full-time payroll of many organizations. The above four issues are just some of the key areas of debate in the laboratory learning field. So long as experimentation is encouraged and innovation needed, a healthy debate on a number of issues will help the field stay fluid and dynamic.

What Is Management's Role?

Management must see the training as compatible with organizational objectives, understand the training objectives, and help managers see that management 'buys' the philosophy of the participative way of working with staff. Management should publicly endorse the programme by its own way of behaving (men supervise as they are supervised—not as they are taught to supervise), be willing to finance the programme adequately, and provide conditions that will allow men to put their learnings into operational practice.

What Are The Risks?

There is always the risk that, here and there, an individual may be upset by the experience. A not too well integrated person may be threatened by self-knowledge. It is not demonstrated that the experience will really do more than precipitate a personal situation that existed previously.

There is the further risk that some managers exposed to this training may reach wrong conclusions about principles and ways of operating and be less effective than before. This is usually the result of the wrong application of a principle, or the misunderstanding of a learning. Specialists in laboratory training do not advocate that all decisions should be group decisions or that everyone in an organization needs to like each other, but a few participants in this type of training may draw inappropriate conclusions, which is a possible consequence of any form of educational endeavour.

There is always the risk of seeing the training as a panacea for too many organizational ills. It does not guarantee results. It promises only more knowledgeable personal performance. It cannot substitute for a better product or service; or for organizational imperfections in financing, advertising, production, etc.

Where Do I Start?

You begin by discussions with your top staff. Are the learnings that can be enhanced by sensitivity training seen as bearing on the problems of your organization? Enough to want you to do something about them? If not, you turn to some other approach.

If it all still makes sense to you and is seen as desirable, you find a reputable university or outside professional training organization that has knowledgeable resource persons to help you look specifically at your problems and the impact this kind of training can have on them.

Constantly, you keep testing the applicability of this kind of training in your organization for your kind of problems, the staff you possess, and with the other priorities facing you. Then, as with all decision making, if this course of action still seems to make good sense, you initiate the first action steps to implement it.

Thus, if an organization wants its managers to know organization structure and dynamics, to know themselves better so that they can conduct themselves more effectively as they work with other individuals, and to know the forces and factors at work when people work in groups, sensitivity training is probably a desirable part of its training programme. If these concerns, or objectives, are not seen as desirable, needed, or important, an organization should not consider sensitivity training.

Summary

There may be no one explanation to give the potential user of laboratory education in management development. In this chapter, I have tried to answer some of the most common questions.

In his doctoral thesis, Daniel Hogan states it well:

> The potential value of human relations laboratory training for our society cannot be underscored enough. Technological change, alienation, social mobility, bureaucratization, and the rigidity of traditional social institutions have brought about a situation where people in society have lost their sense of belongingness, their sense of stability, and their sense of intimacy. The small laboratory group represents a place where these needs can not only be met, but where new methods can be learned to deal constructively with the problems in our society today.
>
> Human relations training provides us with a tool to learn to adapt to change, and it has provided many techniques that have proven useful in psychotherapy.

257

The research evidence indicates that human relations training can be useful for personal, group, and organizational growth.

But as is true with any powerful phenomenon, human relations training has the capacity for bringing about harm as well as benefit. It is this dual potentiality that makes the question of regulation so vital.[22]

Hogan's recommendation for regulation is for professional standards and associations, not laws. This is now being implemented with the formation of the International Association of Social Scientists and the American Board of Professional Psychology. Such certifying groups provide a list of competent trainers. Regardless, the consumer still needs guidelines for deciding the kind, nature, and appropriate resource for laboratory training. It is hoped that the answers to the 'typical' questions cited in this chapter can serve this need. Laboratory education is a valid, tested and professionally developed method of learning used in management development by numerous companies and organizations in many countries around the world.

References

1. McGREGOR, D. *The Human Side of Enterprise*, McGraw-Hill, 1960, p. 221.
2. ODIORNE, G. S. Managerial Narcissism—The Great Self-Development Binge, *Management of Personnel Quarterly*, **1**, 3, 1962; Bureau of Industrial Relations, Graduate School of Business, University of Michigan.
3. SEASHORE, C. What is Sensitivity Training?, *NTL News and Reports*, **2**, 3, 1968.
4. Ibid.
5. KNOWLES, M. S. *The Leader Looks at Self Development*, Looking Into Leadership Monographs, Leadership Resources, Inc., 1961.
6. American Group Psychotherapy Association, Position Statement on Non-Therapy and Therapy Groups, January 1971.
7. FRANK, I. D. (Ed.), Human Relations Training Groups and Therapy Groups, in *T*-Group *Theory and Laboratory Methods* (Bradford *et al.*), John Wilcox, New York, 1964.
8. WESCHLER, I., MASSARIK, F., and TANNENBAUM, R. The Self in Process: A Sensitivity Training Emphasis, *Issues in Training*, Learning Resources Corp., 1962, chapter 14.
9. LIPPITT, G. L. Managerial Guidelines to Sensitivity Training, in *Training Director's Journal*, April 1963.
10. LIKERT, R. *New Patterns of Management*, McGraw-Hill, New York, 1962.
11. STOCK, D. A Survey of Research on T-Groups, in *T-Group Theory and Laboratory Method*, Wiley, New York, 1964.
12. HOUSE, R. T-Group Education and Leadership Effectiveness: A Review of the Empiric Literature and a Critical Evaluation, *Personnel Psychology*, spring 1967.
13. CAMPBELL, J. P. and DUNNETTE, M. D. Effectiveness of T-Group Experiences in Managerial Training and Development, *Psychological Bulletin*, **70**, 2, 1968.
14. GIBB, J. The Effects of Human Relations Training, in *Handbook of Psychotherapy and Behavior Change*, Wiley, New York, 1971.
15. LIEBERMAN, M., YALOM, I., and MILES, M. Encounters, The Leader Makes the Difference, *Psychology Today*, March 1973.
16. SEASHORE, C. *op. cit.*
17. BENNIS, W. *Beyond Bureaucracy*, McGraw-Hill, 1972, p. 147.
18. SCHEIN, E. H. and BENNIS, W. G. Personal and Organizational Change Through Group Method: The Laboratory Approach, in *An Overview of Our Learning Theory*, Wiley, London, 1965.
19. One example of the 'family' approach to training is reported in *Interpersonal Competence and Organizational Effectiveness*, by C. Argyris, Dorsey-Irwin Press, Homewood, Ill., 1962.
20. BLAKE, R. and MOUTON, J. S. The Instrumented Training Laboratory, *Issues in Human Relations Training*, National Training Laboratories, National Education Association, Washington, DC, 1962.

21. LIPPITT, G. L. and THIS, L. E. Is Training a Profession?, *ASTD Journal*, April 1960.
22. HOGAN, D. The Regulation of Human Relations Training: An Examination of Some Assumptions and Some Recommendations, unpublished manuscript, Harvard Law School, April 1972.

Suggested Reading

BRADFORD, L., BENNE, K., LIPPITT, R., and GIBB, J. *Laboratory Method of Changing and Learning*, Wiley, New York, 1974.

DYER, W. G. *Modern Theory and Method in Group Training*, Van Nostrand and Reinhold, New York, 1972.

GOLEMBIEWSKI, R. and BLUMBERG, A. *Sensitivity Training and the Laboratory Approach*, F. E. Peacock Publishers, Itasca, Ill., 1970.

LIPPITT, G. L., THIS, L. E., and BIDWELL, R. *Optimizing Human Resources*, Addison-Wesley, Reading, Mass., 1971.

MARROW, A. J. *Behind the Executive Mask*, American Management Association, New York, 1964.

SCHEIN, E. H. and BENNIS, W. G. *Personal and Organizational Change Through Group Methods: The Laboratory Approach*, Wiley, New York, 1965.

SHAW, M. *Group Dynamics: The Psychology of Small Group Behavior*, McGraw-Hill, New York, 1971.

18. The use of audio-visual aids in management training

Jørgen Roed

Constant innovation in technology and techniques, and gradual shifts of emphasis in basic principles and in structures, have placed enormous demands on management and on those responsible for management training programmes. There is always a new message to be put across, clearly and efficiently. The spoken and written word are alone no longer adequate.

Audio-visual aids represent technology's own answer to problems created by technology. But they must be accorded proper status; they must be evaluated, selected, and integrated, backed by expert skills to reach the stage where professional communication *becomes an accepted integral part of the concept of professional management. The result will be added impact, more precision and ultimately reduced costs.*

Innovations inevitably produce a variety of reactions : enthusiasm, scepticism, fear, and confusion. Audio-visual aids are no exception, and it is only recently that unprejudiced, realistic appraisal is replacing the tendency to invest wildly in sophisticated gadgetry, or, at the other extreme, overcoming an undue belief in the power of the spoken and written word, alone, to inform and to communicate.

The much abused terms, 'information' and 'communication', embody the essence of education, instruction, and teaching—whichever word is most acceptable—and, thus, have a direct bearing on management training. However much we resist it, all information is educational, and all education is essentially the conveying of information. The process of conveying or transmitting this information, in the form of knowledge, ideas, and experience, can be summed up in a single term 'communication'.

Of the host of definitions of management already coined, the most accurate, I believe, is 'getting things done through and with other people'. This means that one of the prerequisites of the leader is the ability to express himself in adequate terms, to deliver his message so as to achieve the required degree of understanding, while, simultaneously, motivating his personnel.

In an age of technical evolution and consequent changes in structures, it would be unreasonable to expect that the spoken and written word alone could convey the volume of relevant information, either in management training or in the execution of senior management functions. Audio-visual aids offer a solution, as a tool available to the leader or lecturer to produce a greater impact on the combined senses of the trainee or student. The lecturer ought to avail himself of the opportunity for a more varied interplay of the various responses whereby people pick things up, whether they be motor, visual or auditive, by offering the student a chance to see things, touch things, hear things, and so on. The result more than justifies the effort.

It is difficult to apply effectiveness criteria to a particular audio-visual aid, as it should always be part of an integrated communication process or system, but, in the context of education, there is gradual acceptance of the

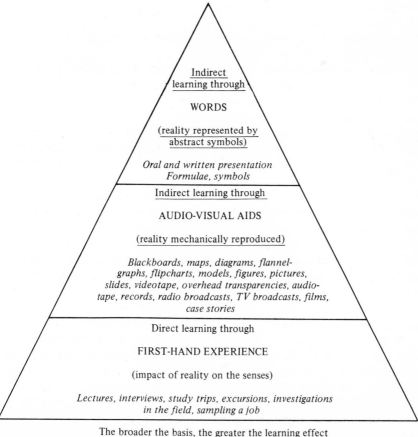

The broader the basis, the greater the learning effect

Fig. 18.1. The learning process pyramid.

'learning process pyramid', as depicted in Fig. 18.1. Although the classification therein is a matter for discussion, the main point to emerge is that the more abstract the study, the greater the demand placed on the student.

Nature of AV Aids

Audio-visual aids have also suffered by becoming fashionable, so that while many speak of them, fewer use them, and very few have gone to the trouble of considering the advantages and disadvantages of using them. The gushing praise or condemnation derive from attitude rather than experience. Anyway, what are these AV aids, when experts cannot even agree on the spelling! A short definition might suffice: *AV aids are educational aids used to convey information through the eye or ear, or through both senses simultaneously.*

Where teaching is merely a matter of passing on knowledge, the main aim is to convey the message in a form which enables the student to grasp it, understand it, and store it. AV aids can contribute enormously to a communication process of this nature, by making the matter more easily accessible and by increasing the retention factor. Individual study involving the acquisition of skills and knowledge is much more productive when AV aids are used.

The fact remains, however, that experience of AV aids is so far limited. Instruction is given in the use of these media, but often by the manufacturers, with the main emphasis on the technical aspects, and little or no attention to teaching problems. On the other hand, there is a corresponding reluctance by the teacher to consider these aids and their application in the learning situation. It is hardly surprising that there are wide gaps between the parties involved: the manufacturer, the user, and the ultimate consumer—the student. The real gap, and the unfortunate one, is between the need and the possibilities.

Is it because the teacher is afraid of getting involved with plugs and leads and technology? Another explanation is that he regards the aids as an attack on his own tested and successful methods. He may have to abandon them, and even risk being accused of eliminating the work factor from his job, by resorting to the infernal machine. A probable reason is that the teacher, and his financial backers, would like to have a guarantee of the effectiveness of these aids before buying them. There is a paradox here, because the same criterion is seldom applied to conventional methods, the talk-and-chalk field, where one could hardly issue a guarantee for effectiveness.

In a way, the executive in charge of a management training programme is well placed: before investing, he can consider the proper use of these tools. But whether to use them, or not, is a problem which management training will have to deal with very soon, as there is already tremendous competition for the attention of trainees, with a massive output of information by all the media—radio, TV, the cinema, advertising, etc. The management trainer will use, as a matter of course, the media which daily convey information to him, and, to an even greater extent, his students. He can no more afford to do without them than an airport can afford to do without visual display boards and a public address system.

The lecturer enjoys some valuable advantages over the mass media communicator. He can define his objectives so clearly as to allow him to evaluate and stucture his flow of information with greater precision and control. He, too, will have a deadline to meet, but it will not be so pressing. Applying the principles of good management, he can define his objectives for the programme in question before choosing the means—including AV aids—for carrying it out.

AV Aids and AV Know-How

Most management training in companies and public organizations is conducted by professionals in the relevant field; rarely is this background augmented by qualifications in teaching or in communicating. The brilliant economist or engineer may easily turn out to be a lacklustre platform performer. Despite the agony for the poor man, and the yawns from the audience, we still have a system where the expert, i.e., the economist, engineer, etc., must do the best he can in planning and devising the educational process. It seems to be widely accepted that if the man has taken on the role of lecturer, he is thereby capable of going through with it satisfactorily. This attitude is not surprising in a society which regards education as a matter of delivering a certain syllabus, a corpus of facts, accurate in terms of the relevant profession, without prior consideration as to whether conditions have been provided to enable the student to assimilate, and to learn. The focus is on the performer, not on the potential target.

This indicates that, in management training, we have not yet reached the stage where we automatically call in the professional. In several functions, we have no hesitation in drawing on the professional—the lawyer, the accountant, advertising agent, PR consultant, management expert, and so on—but when it comes to preparing a speech, a lecture, a lesson, or a course of instruction, we hesitate. Perhaps we refuse to acknowledge that this area—communicating, teaching—requires any specialist assistance. The communications specialist, as he might be termed, working on the basis of the professional data, can draw up a description of the aims of the programme in question, possibly subdivided into the company's aims, the lecturer's aims, and the student's aims, map out the various prerequisites, a choice of the educational principles, methods, and work patterns, and finally, the means, including AV aids.

Further specialist assistance is necessary for production of the AV software, the materials to be used with the various aids selected. It is a waste to have a slide projector without slides which illustrate what the lecturer intends to say, rather than slides which blur the issue, or even mislead. The do-it-yourself solution for the communication factor in management training must be abandoned. The professional management training lecturer must have professional communications assistance readily available.

Fig. 18.2. AV workshop—production of software.

When the executive or leader has understood the importance of using such consultancy and acquires adequate basic knowledge of the applications of the media, he begins to achieve the same level of performance in the lecturer role as in the leader role. He defines the aims of the course, submits certain plans to the communications specialist who must take over from that point, and proceeds to devise proposals for applications of methods and means, to be followed by production of the relevant materials.

The usual reaction to a suggestion of this nature is a sigh of despair; the moment you begin to use any of the media in your presentation you invite extra work. Yes, it does involve a lot of work, but the work involved is justified by the time saved which would normally be spent in writing what we intended to say.

The labour involved produces a bonus. The moment that we decide to use even a few simple AV aids, we force ourselves into more detailed consideration of the message, more careful selection, structuring, and editing of the

264

Fig. 18.3. Executives attending a management course.

material that we intend to present. The software will most probably form the nucleus of a library, a framework of reference to be drawn on later. If criteria are to be applied, the result will be at least an increase in quality, and most likely increased effectiveness, in terms of impact, retention, satisfaction, and motivation.

The aids can be revised, updated, and evaluated. Criteria will begin to present themselves which simply were not there when speech was the sole weapon in the lecturer's armoury. The media, ranging from blackboard to closed circuit television (CCTV), offer the opportunity to achieve:

(a) more involvement and greater variety in dissemination of ideas and knowledge;
(b) thorough details in research and structured programming in the communications process;
(c) and increased retention of information, usually accompanied by increased motivation to learn.

Most of us concerned with the training aspects of management may be new to this mode of thinking and acting, so the reaction will be: Let's call them all

Fig. 18.4. Closed circuit TV records and stores the performance for rerun later.

to a meeting or seminar and give them a talk'. The other favourite solution is the manual, with bar charts, graphs, and models—the carefully compiled and approved ringbinder. The result a few months later is an urgent call to the trouble-shooting team. Words have again failed.

Whether or not we are brilliant teachers—people who can produce the nucleus of all education: structuring and editing of material—the use of AV aids initially demands more work. The use of any new tool requires an initial effort, in planning and becoming familiar with the tool, how to operate it and, above all, how to apply it to achieve optimal effectiveness.

Some Useful AV Aids

While each of the wide range of aids has its own applications, there are some points that the user should bear in mind. The individual devices must be capable of fitting in with an integrated system, and not merely be isolated function aids. The lecturer must be fully aware of the relevant medium's range of applications. The auxiliary staff may be delegated the production of the software, printed matter, transparencies, slides, etc., technical preparation, and operation of the equipment.

To stimulate the potential user, here is a brief survey of some of the aids which I have seen used with success in management training courses.

The adult who has not seen a blackboard since his schooldays is in for a pleasant surprise; blackboard, dusters, and chalk have all undergone rapid development, incorporating the useful hand-and-slide units which allow ample space and flexibility. It may seem to be stressing the obvious but many practitioners of the talk-and-chalk method still forget the eyestrain imposed on the back row.

Special Boards

These include flannel-graphs, magnetic boards, and flipcharts.

Flannel-graphs. These provide a background for the display of cardboard figures, display sheets, etc., with burr strips which cling to the surface. They are ideal for step by step presentation, to illustrate organization and planning charts. They cling tightly enough to bear even fairly heavy objects and are an infinite improvement on the drawing pin.

Magnetic Boards. Such boards resemble flannel-graphs, except that magnets are used for attaching objects and sheets. The latter can be more easily moved about, and one can write on the surface with chalk, thus adding an extra dimension.

Flipcharts. These can be used to advantage for diagrams, drawings, headings, etc. prepared in advance with feltpens or markers in a wide range of colours. The charts can also be used 'live', especially by a lecturer who has no talent for drawing, as he can pencil in the outlines lightly beforehand, so that they are invisible to the participant. This procedure makes it possible to build up the diagram or drawing, step by step, in its correct proportions, to make things easier for the student.

To sum up, boards are useful for:

(a) attracting attention;
(b) retaining attention;
(c) conveying a message with the minimum of verbiage.

Slide Projector

The slide projector is another familiar aid, for showing slides individually or as composite units, like pictures in a magazine. Some automatic slide projectors can be linked to a timer or a tape recorder controlling the slide change by sound impulses; this is known as the *tape–slide system*.

It is essential to remember when using slides, that, as with any other visual medium, the fewer the items the lesser the strain. Do not require the viewer to absorb too much in one go and, again, don't forget the range of visibility of the back row. A rule of thumb: if an illustration can be read, i.e., easily assimilated by the naked eye, at a distance of six times the height of the illustration, it can be converted into a slide; otherwise it must undergo a reproduction process.

Individually mounted slides enable the lecturer to compile a sequence of slides before the lesson. If additional, reserve slides may be needed in dealing with questions—provoked or anticipated—it is advisable to use a rostrum projector, easily operated by the lecturer. The tiny sum needed to buy a 'lightbox', an illuminated slide holder, is well worth the trouble, as it helps to avoid slides being shown upside down.

To sum up, slides are useful for:

(a) colour reproduction;
(b) picture narration in sequence;
(c) involvement of the participant, both visually and with words.

The tape–slide system is useful for:

(a) combined use of sound and vision;
(b) concentrated presentation of a subject;
(c) the 'you are there' experience;
(d) step by step instruction.

Overhead Projector

The overhead projector is a daylight projector, whereas the slide projector and film projector need blacking-out. The projector consists of a horizontal plate of glass, on which the picture material, acetate foil, is placed, for projection via the projector head onto a tilted screen or even a light-coloured wall. The usual size of the transparencies is 25 cm^2.

The transparency is directly accessible to the lecturer, who can draw on it or point at features on it during his lecture. He can also operate the device while facing his audience, to evaluate the effect and modify his presentation accordingly. This aid can also be used in the same way as slides apparatus; finished transparencies can be projected onto the screen in any desired sequence. The real advantage is the freedom to choose a particular illustration to meet the needs of a spontaneous situation.

As in the case of all pre-produced material, the labour involved in selection and editing before entering the auditorium is rewarded by an even proportionately higher output in class time. The consumer, i.e., the student, should benefit, and the lecturer has added to his own skills and to his library of aids. The cost conscious will realize that production of transparencies is often less expensive, and usually faster, than production of corresponding slides, thus encouraging the lecturer to improve and update his material.

There are four main applications:

(a) the lecturer works 'live', drawing or writing on a blank transparency, using the overhead projector as a blackboard, while himself facing the students. Contact is thus improved, though a polished performance is achieved only through practice;

(b) a combination of finished material and 'live' pencil work, possibly by using a blank transparency superimposed on a finished one. This saves time, and activates the student;
(c) the overlay technique, several transparencies being laid on top of one another, to build up a total illustration in stages. It is advisable to mount the transparencies in a frame;
(d) the masking technique. Where a transparency has several illustrations, perhaps interrelated, the lecturer may wish to have the student focus his attention on the relevant section or sections. This can be achieved by masking part of the transparency with sliding cardboard masks, or a sheet of paper, easily manipulated by the lecturer. The technique is excellent for comparisons, a surprise element or structured sequences, and offers the lecturer an opportunity to control the medium with precision.

The overhead projector can augment, or even replace, the blackboard and is very valuable when used in conjunction with the slide projector.

To sum up, overhead transparencies are useful for:

(a) projection of multidetailed illustrations;
(b) step by step unmasking;
(c) gradual build-up of instruction sequences;
(d) modification of the illustration during the lecture;
(e) activation of the student.

Film Projector

The film projector's main contribution is that of conveying the sense of action to the audience, of achieving involvement. Like many other aids, it has undergone considerable evolution, one of the extremely interesting results being *cinevision*. This aid has a screen, the size of an ordinary TV screen. Short, 8 mm film loops are back-projected onto the screen, continuously, without rewinding, as the film is in a sealed cassette.

Cinevision has several advantages, being easy to operate and simple to install, and can be used for teach-yourself instruction or small groups. It produces the highest impact when used to illustrate a subject where it is essential to grasp a specific dynamic process.

Another sophisticated device, for back-projection of super 8 mm film, combining stills and moving pictures with sound, is also available. The film, in a sealed cassette, is run by sound impulses recorded on one track of an ordinary audio cassette which has two or more additional ordinary tracks, for narration, comment, film soundtracks, etc. Each impulse moves the film one frame forward: this makes it possible to operate at any speed, choosing stills, slow-motion sequences, real motion or fast motion at will, while each section can have synchronized sound. The audio tape can be coded, so that a picture or sequence of pictures may be skipped. The result of all this is that a single film can be used for a variety of programmes, requiring only taping of a new audio cassette. This is a useful point for those who wish to make versions of the same film in various languages, as the cost of producing the audio cassette is comparatively low.

To sum up, the film is useful for:

(a) simultaneous presentation of sound and picture, as in the cinema;
(b) demonstration of movement;
(c) making a point by using trick shots or effects;
(d) bringing the outside world into the classroom;
(e) storage and retrieval of complex processes.

Television

The simplest television unit for educational purposes consists of a TV camera, with zoom lens, a video tape recorder, a TV monitor, and a microphone. This basic unit is adequate for recording and showing uncomplicated series of instructional material without violent movement, and for presentation of smaller objects in large scale to a bigger group. It is thus ideal for direct-confrontation TV, e.g., salesman training, teacher training, public speaker training, etc., and for the lecturer who wishes to operate a rostrum camera himself, the latter system being referred to as *rostrum TV*.

Picture and sound are fed to the monitor, which can be easily placed quite a distance from the camera and microphone, but linked to them by a coaxial cable. The picture and sound may also be recorded on a video tape recorder for later presentation via the TV monitor.

Closed circuit television involves the use of several cameras, where a producer selects the images via a video switch, and controls several microphones via a sound mixer. CCTV also offers the possibility of feeding picture and sound to several monitors simultaneously.

It is essential to use two or more cameras for production of a programme intended either for direct transmission or for taping and storing for presentation later. The equipment can be extended by adding a telecine unit, which makes it possible to convert films, slides, or captions into TV signals for insertion in the programmes.

The more elaborate video tape recorders have an electronic editing device so that various recordings can be edited into a single, finished programme. Another device can be added to the unit to project the picture in enlarged form onto a screen.

TV has an extremely wide range of applications in education and training, from simple self-confrontation to the taping and storage of complex processes or cause-and-effect sequences which require constant revision by the student. The uses range from simple reportage, with one camera, to thoroughly edited instructional programmes.

The more widespread introduction of TV cassettes and cable TV in the next decade will eliminate many of today's distribution snags, and result in vastly cheaper dissemination of TV instruction on a more universal basis. Just as it accepted the typewriter or the adding machine, management training will certainly accept the challenge offered by this exciting and

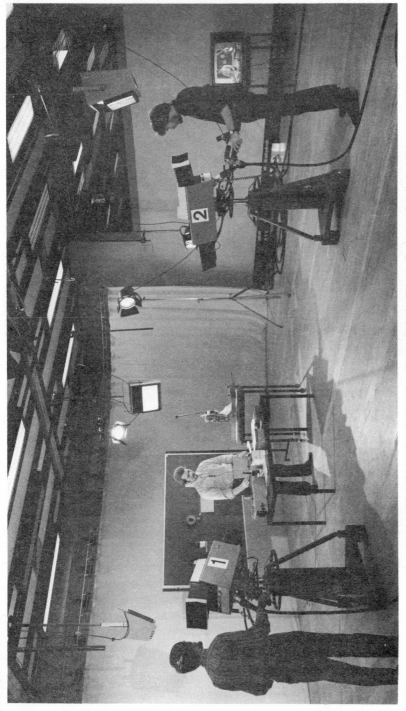

Figs. 18.5 and 18.6. Production, in the colour-TV studio, of a TV tape for instructional purposes. (Figures 18.1 to 18.6 reproduced with acknowledgement to Scanticon.)

271

valuable medium, either on its own, or in combination with other material, printed matter, instructional programmes, etc. Management responds to change and innovation and will base its decisions on these assessments:

(a) TV adds motivation, thereby improving the teaching situation and making management courses more effective;
(b) TV reduces the costs of courses and simplifies the arrangements;
(c) the demand for qualified lecturers exceeds the supply. TV is on the way to becoming a necessity.

One of the arguments most frequently raised against attending courses is the difficulty of implementing the newly acquired knowledge; notes and a fallible memory are all that remain as tools. The confident prediction is that the TV cassette will become an excellent aid. The individual participant in a management training course will have access to follow-up material which he can repeat as often as he pleases, and which can be updated to keep abreast of developments.

To sum up, TV in its various forms is useful for:

(a) capturing and storing complicated processes;
(b) storing TV programmes from ordinary TV channels;
(c) simultaneous screening of an action on the monitor;
(d) self-confrontation;
(e) teach-yourself systems;
(f) activation of the audience.

Management and the New Media

We must distinguish clearly between the two accepted concepts of management training: on-the-job training, with skills acquired as one goes along, and the organized training programme, conducted either internally or externally and consisting of courses, conferences, seminars, etc. The emphasis has so far been mainly on organized training, but it is very important to consider the role of the leader as communicator, and the significance that the new media have for him in this role.

There are very specific reasons, based on fundamental principles of management, for attaching importance to the ability of the leader to communicate:

(a) the leader *selects* the executives working most closely with him;
(b) he has the responsibility of *training* these executives to understand his ideas, aims, and plans for the relevant area of work;
(c) he has to *organize* these executives to form an effective team;
(d) he *communicates* all the information he possesses to his staff, not merely by informing them of his decisions, but by thinking aloud in their company.

Thus, it is of vital importance for the leader to be capable of communicating effectively with his staff and with people and organizations outside the company, on which the company may depend.

The leader can add precision and impact to his communication by aiming at influencing a broader spectrum of his audience's senses, instead of relying solely on the spoken and written word. Audio-visual aids are there to serve him as readily available tools.

The obvious reaction is, 'Does all this mean that the manager who doesn't know how to use the media, and perhaps can't even express himself adequately in speech or in writing, is in fact a bad manager?' Certainly not: the poor communicator may very well be a successful manager, but he will become an even more successful manager when he learns how to put his ideas across to others, by using the media to project his message. It simply means he will be the same—only more so.

To achieve this, the company must introduce some new functions to aid leaders in adapting their message to the appropriate media and to provide the necessary krow-how and production facilities. The idea ought to stimulate the keen innovator, because 'communications' and 'media' are overloaded with other associations. 'Link department', or 'editing department', will convey little until the executive, and later on, the layman, becomes familiar with the idea. Advertising, public relations, press and information are accepted function designations: innovation, product development, etc. have also spread rapidly. A 'communications' department might be established, and along with it, a range of audio-visual aids and equipment, in an AV workshop for production of the software. Executives would use its services quite naturally, internally and externally, for direct access to expertise and planning related to the process of communication, learning how to choose the right medium for the occasion. This would make *professional communication* an integrated part of professional management.

Suggested Reading

UNWIN, D. *Media and Methods*, McGraw-Hill, London, 1969.
CABLE, R. *Audio-Visual Handbook*, University of London Press, 1970.
HEINRICHS, H. *Audio-visuelle Praxis in Wort und Bild*, Kösel, 1972.
STROH, T. F. *The Uses of Video Tape in Training and Development*, American Management Association, New York, 1969.
DIAMOND, R. M., Jr. *A Guide to Instructional Television*, McGraw-Hill, London, 1964.
STORMES, J. and CRUMPLER, J. P. *Television Communications Systems for Business and Industry*, Wiley, 1970.
WRIGHT, A. *Designing for Visual Aids*, Studio Vista, London; Van Nostrand Reinhold, New York, 1970.
BROWN, JAMES W., LEWIS, RICHARD B., and HARCLEROAD, F. F. *Audio-Visual Instruction*, McGraw-Hill, New York, 1973.
WITTICH, W. A. and SCHULER, C. F. *Audiovisual Materials: Their Nature and Use*, Harper, New York, 1968.
QUICK, J. and WOLF, H. *Small-studio Video Tape Production*, Addison-Wesley, Reading, Mass., 1972.

19. Management training by teletuition

Georg Marais

In traditional correspondence training, there is a decentralization of learning activities, with the result that dialogue is limited. In the 'management training by teletuition' programme at the University of South Africa's School of Business Leadership, a strong element of dialogue is required, while maintaining the other advantages of independent learning—the individualized and autonomous elements.

The basis of independent learning is therefore not only maintained, but supplemented by interaction across the three interfaces that are so essential to a professional training programme; between the student and his business environment (the student must be a working executive), between student and student (compulsory study groups), and between student and lecturer (compulsory residential training periods and visits by lecturers to study groups). In the School's programme, independent learning is adjusted by building into the learning process a highly dialogic element.

This new teaching model of individualized, dialogic, distance learning requires a special system of activities or mechanisms. The main teaching activities used are small-group learning, seminar-tutorial methods, concentrated study, project or problem-centred study, independent study, self-paced study, sensitivity training, and the traditional activities of required reading, lecturing, written analysis of case studies, written assignments, or papers and business games reports.

To introduce the highly dialogic learning in the distance learning system, the main innovating development of these programmes is the use of semi-autonomous study groups—continuous interaction across the interface, between student and student in the different locations.

The School of Business Leadership offers tuition for Master and Doctorate degrees in business leadership (MBL and DBL), an advanced executive programme (AEP) and a middle-management programme (MMP).

In 1963, the need in the Republic of South Africa for the training of more people in management was considerable. At that stage, only one university—in Pretoria—offered a part-time evening-class Master's degree programme in business administration. In view of the need, four residential universities started to plan MBA degree programmes.

As in most countries outside the US, we have only a few organizations large enough to send their middle and top executives to attend residential training programmes for long periods. Traditionally, firms often shy away from appointing graduates from business schools in executive positions, because of their lack of practical business experience and because of problems of adaptation in their new surroundings. For this reason, a number of senior businessmen belonging to the South African Association of Business Leadership requested South Africa's 'Open University'—the University of South Africa, which was founded as an examining body in 1916 and began active teaching by correspondence in 1946—to offer a management degree programme in business administration for the experienced and working business executive. During the past ten years, the numbers of registered students at the University have risen from 13 158 in 1962, to 28 100 in 1972. In 1971, the University's academic staff totalled 520.

In 1972, the Faculty of Commerce and Administration had 8037 registered students. Like the rest of the University, the Faculty of Commerce and Administration, excluding the Business School, mainly uses correspondence instruction as its method of tuition where correspondence is the means of communication between student and teacher.

The problems confronting the University in introducing a management programme include its lack of knowledge of professional training, the problem of obtaining qualified staff, and that of gaining recognition.

The first problem arose because these South African businessmen clearly had in mind a professional programme with the emphasis on the teaching of theory and practice and outputs of qualified practitioners. The Senate of the University of South Africa, in common with such bodies at most universities, is traditionally opposed to the offering of a Master's degree programme which does not follow from a Bachelor's degree in the same field.

To a large number of Senate members, the professionalism required in a management training programme went against the grain. The biggest problem was that, although the University of South Africa has attained very great success with its academic programmes—teaching theory by the written word—experience in teaching theory and practice by correspondence was limited.

The traditional correspondence institution works with students who are in full-time employment; and the teaching process consists of imparting knowledge and techniques (to the student) by means of the written word. In this instance, individualized, limited dialogic, distance learning forms the core of the teaching process. But in the training of managers at post-graduate level, the chief requisite is that the knowledge and techniques transferred should be integrated into the working executive's learning process—observation, analysis, interpretation, planning, and acting. Some students

276

who acquire knowledge solely by correspondence study may well experience this integration process. But, generally, there seems to be a barrier between knowledge obtained from independent study, and its application. This barrier prevents interaction across the interface of the student and the business environment—knowledge, its discovery and acquirement, not its application, is the final result. In traditional correspondence training, teaching techniques such as programmed teaching, films, and video tapes are employed, but all merely for the discovery and acquirement of knowledge, and in many instances, only for passing the examinations.

A common feature of correspondence training is a high drop-out rate because of a lack of motivation, guidance, critical comment on individual progress, and self-discipline or self-control—this type of training requires an autonomous learner.

In full-time residential training or contiguous teaching, the planning, control, motivational, and operation (learning) functions are centralized in one location. In traditional correspondence institutions, the planning and control functions—administrative and teaching staff—are located in one centre, and the operating or learning function in another centre (the student), the motivational and dialogic function of the lecturer usually being absent. This decentralization of the learning function causes a lack of motivation, guidance, and critical comment on one's own individual progress—a lack of dialogue. Management training in general is one of the more expensive types of training for both university and student. The student is a working executive and, for him, time is a valuable factor. A high drop-out rate cannot be afforded.

A second important problem is the problem of recognition, by the business world, of a degree in business administration obtained by correspondence training. How is it possible to teach management or a professional course by correspondence? Although a few far-sighted businessmen requested our programme, most of the bigger firms had no faith in any management training programme offered in South Africa by South Africans. They preferred to send their people to the US or the UK or to invite lecturers from overseas to run their in-company training programmes.

A third problem was the availability of South African staff not only to teach management to middle and top management, but also to teach it by teaching media other than lecturing.

Most of these barriers seemed insurmountable, but, in March 1964, the Senate of the University of South Africa approved the proposed Master's degree in business administration (Business Leadership) programme, and the first 116 students were registered at the beginning of 1965. The School has since gone from strength to strength and, at present, some 800 students are enrolled for various programmes.

Objectives of the School

The School is designed with its main objective the establishment and development of programmes of training for executives at various stages in their careers; these programmes run parallel, and are complementary to, the continuous process of self-development and, over a period of time, will broaden the problem-solving and decision-making capacities of the executives, from the point of view of an organization as a system. To achieve the main objective the following requirements, among others, were considered essential.

Curricula had to be developed for the different programmes which would suit the requirements of the executives at different levels of development. Curricula had to be developed that included basic theory, applied theory, and practice in such an integrated fashion that it satisfied the Senate, as well as the business sector. Because of the constraints of distance teaching, a new system of mechanisms or teaching media had to be introduced, not only to discover and acquire knowledge, but to use this knowledge—integration of theory and practice into the cycle of the learning process. The written word had to play an important role in the system, but the new approach had to be management training by teletuition, utilization of all aspects of educational technology, and not management training by correspondence only. Programmes had to be of a standard acceptable to the academic, as well as the business world.

The School as an Open System

In the School as a task system, we have human and physical resources— lecturer's and university facilities, and a system of activities or mechanisms, or teaching media. The student is the input, and a system of activities is required to complete the process of transforming or changing the behaviour of the student to that of a graduate—the school's output.

We have stated that, in traditional correspondence training, there is decentralization of the learning function, with the result that dialogue is limited. In our management training by teletuition programme, a strong element of dialogue is required, while maintaining the other advantages of independent learning—the individualized and autonomous elements.

The basis of independent learning is therefore not only maintained, but supplemented by interaction across the three interfaces that are so essential to a professional training programme—between the student and his business environment (the student must be a working executive), between student and student (compulsory study groups), and between student and lecturer (compulsory residential training periods and visits by lecturers to study groups). In the School's programme, independent learning is adjusted by building into the learning process a highly dialogic element. Compared with the second and third years, the first year of study for the MBL has relatively low-individualization learning. In the final year, when students work on their theses, the learning is high individualized. During this last year, the student, to a large extent, is an autonomous learner—an ideal situation from a learning point of view.

This new teaching model of individualized, dialogic, distance learning requires a special system of activities or mechanisms. The main teaching

278

activities used by us are small-group learning, seminar-tutorial methods, concentrated study, project or problem-centred study, independent study, self-paced study, sensitivity training, and the traditional activities of required reading, lecturing, written analysis of case studies, written assignments, or papers and business games reports. Most of these mechanisms are used in different combinations but are discussed here, in three general groups, as in Fig. 19.1.

SELF-STUDY	STUDY GROUP	RESIDENTIAL TRAINING PERIODS
Reading	Mutual lecturing	Lecturing
Self-paced study	Case study discussions	Concentrated study
Written analysis of case studies	Tutorial methods	Case study discussion
Written assignments	Sensitivity training	Business games
Independent study	Project study	Sensitivity training
Project study	Business games	

Fig. 19.1. The new teaching model.

To introduce the highly dialogic learning in the distance learning system, the main innovating development of this programme is the use of semi-autonomous study groups—continuous interaction across the interface, between student and student in the different locations. A system of study groups consisting of between five and eleven individuals, at present totalling eighty, was established for all the programmes.

Student Population—The Input

The type of student, or input, selected is of the utmost importance to our system. An indispensable requisite for the student group is that they should have heterogeneous backgrounds. In constituting a group, the School brings together people of various ages, with varying academic backgrounds, business experience, and management positions in different concerns.

The acceptance of applicants depends on the experience, age, location, and academic backgrounds of the student. No applicant with less than three years' practical experience, or without an academic degree (excluding chartered accountants) is eligible. At present, most of the screening is done during selection and at the end of the first year. The School is doing active research in developing its own selection battery for screening applicants, with due regard to our special conditions.

For the AEP and MMP, screening and selection are done by the School in close cooperation with the personnel managers of the respective firms. The DBL candidates are screened according to their performance in their MBL or MBA studies, as well as their ability to undertake research.

Although students and graduates are analysed in detail in a later section, it is necessary to give some characteristics of the students in this section. The number of MBL students increased from 116 in 1965 to 661 in 1973.

Average age fluctuates around 32 years. The average age of our AEP programme is 42 years, and of the MMP, 34 years. An analysis of the academic background shows that 60 per cent of the 1973 MBL students have a technical or science degree, 19 per cent a commerce degree, the remainder consisting mainly of students with degrees in arts, law, pharmacy, and medicine.

Statistics show that in 1972, 50 per cent of the second-year students and 51 per cent of the third-year students were in line positions in their respective organizations. In 1972, first-year students earned an average of R7020, second-year students, R9285, and third-year students, R9000 per annum. In 1972, the top salary of a senior lecturer (associate professor) at the University was R8100, that of a professor, R9900. These salary comparisons indicate to some extent the seniority of the type of student registered.

At present, the students in the MBL programme come from 235 organizations; the AEP students from nine organizations, and the MMP students from the biggest South African mining house. A survey of the 1972 first-year students showed that 50 per cent of the students paid their own tuition fees. The tuition fees of the rest were paid by their employers. The indications are that the percentage of students paying for their own tuition is far smaller in the second and third years.

Software of the System

A very important resource is what we can call the software of the task system, the course material, case studies, business games, and library and computer services.

Curriculum and Course Material

One of the biggest problems confronting us in preparing our curriculum was to dovetail it to the requirements of the type of student we have, with due consideration to his business experience and the position attained in his firm. We found that our students require more emphasis on an integrated view, compared with those of typical residential business schools which allow more specialization in the second year. Our approach, therefore, is to teach basic courses in the first year, functional courses in the second, and integrated and policy courses in the third year. In the AEP, we concentrate more on top-management aspects, and in the MMP, on middle-management aspects.

Our system allows no exemption from subjects, and no optional subjects—our aim being to enhance the effectiveness of the group. A management accountant must take management accounting mainly because he has to assist the rest of the study group in this subject. Optional subjects would complicate the organizing of study groups.

Possibly, it is in the course material, especially in business policy in the world today, that our weakest link in general management training is situated. We must bear in mind that, in a graduate degree programme, the curriculum and course content must be of a high quality. The purpose of the written material is to give the student a frame of reference to be used in analysing business problems. We follow a systems approach, and limit the contents of our study guides to basic theory—the principles of management. We deliberately leave out most of the descriptive material, and force the student to discover for himself from various references—books and journals —the necessary additional reading to assist him with his problems.

Our students are already in management and thus have at their disposal considerable discretionary power in decision making. The theory must therefore provide a framework and a philosophy for diagnosing the problem, identifying alternatives, and making a choice.

When students with a number of years' business experience are trained, it is often said that it is necessary to emphasize increased awareness and the re-examination of previous experience as ends, rather than the acquisition for the first time of knowledge, analytical ability, techniques of management, or the orderly and systematic study of one or more business functions. One reason for this approach is that our working executive students have very limited time for study. The second reason is that management is an art, a skill, as well as a science, and that these need not be mutually exclusive. For many subjects, the turnover or obsolescence rate of knowledge is very high but, for all that, a body of fundamentals, even if it seems to be semi-permanent, has been developed in the last two decades. The fact that the executive has to study fundamentals, together with his self-development as an executive, may inculcate in him the habit of learning and keeping abreast of new approaches in management. Fortunately, we have four years in which to instil the knowledge. Our programmes are not high-pressure courses, so intensive that the student cannot digest more than 10 per cent of what is being taught.

Our system makes high demands on the staff. Only well-trained staff, doing constant research, can produce tutorial matter of a high standard. Our lecturers are in an excellent position to do research in business practices. Many of our students are in senior management positions and constantly feed back their practical experience and their evaluation of the knowledge transmitted to them by their lecturers.

Our lectures are submitted in printed form. This considerably facilitates vertical and horizontal integration between the different courses—something which residential universities find more difficult.

At present, an MBL student is supplied with 3600 pages of study guides for study and reference. Study guides are available in both official languages.

Case Studies

An important item of software of any business school is the case study material it uses. When this School was established, few South African case studies were available. Part of the study requirements is that, before graduating, each student must submit a case study based on his thesis. Already, more than 135 case studies are available. Consequently, the School is using a large number of South African case studies in its different programmes.

Business Games, Project Studies, and Planning Exercises

The School developed an elementary game for first-year accounting. A US business game is currently being used in the third year, and a project study and planning exercise based on this game, and developed by the School, is being used in the second year. Research is in progress to use more field studies.

The School has designed another planning exercise (Blue Skies Planning Exercise) to stimulate alertness for business opportunities. This exercise is conducted during the third MBL year and in the AEP. Each group is asked to identify two opportunities in the South African environment—they then have to motivate and defend their choice before their fellow students and a panel of judges.

Library and Computer Services

The staff of the School and its students make use of the central university library, which has 330 000 books, 30 000 bound journals, and 19 000 items of micro and audio-visual material, and there are university librarians who specially cater for the Business School. The School also has its own librarian to advise students. Librarians are on duty during the residential training periods, to supply reference material for theses. The University's computer is also used for all required computer work.

System of Activities

Self-Study

From the student's point of view, self-study, especially reading, is the most difficult. To assist the student, reading must be closely integrated with activities at study group meetings or residential training periods. We know, from experience, that a student who thinks that certain knowledge must be acquired for examination purposes only, does not study the material before the examination is on his doorstep. Unless this knowledge is applied at study group meetings, residential training periods, or in the business environment, its value is slight. One of the advantages of self-study for the working student, is that he can do it on his own, which lends some flexibility to his studying process. On average, the student seems to spend from six to eight hours a week on self-study. The time required for preparing for study group meetings is usually about three hours. If it is his turn to be secretary or chairman of the study group, an important activity is to write up the analysis of case studies. The rest of the time should be spent in working out individual assignments and reading study guides and textbooks. Many students take leave before examinations and use it to spend more hours a day on self-study.

The general problem attached to self-study is that the student cannot evaluate his own progress. Self-paced study, such as programmed instruction, is one method of solving this problem. In the first year of MBL, we use programmed instruction for management and financial accounting and are introducing it in economics, but still on a limited scale. This is one of the

282

reasons for requiring the regular submission of work assignments and written analysis of case studies by students, individually or in groups. In general, they receive about twenty-five different grades per annum in the first year, and forty-four different grades per annum in the second and third years, for work done at their home bases. To this, must be added the five grades obtained in the two residential training periods.

One of the most important activities of the students is the MBL theses and the report submitted by the AEP students. This activity is independent study and problem centred, and seems to be a very effective element of the MBL and AEP training programmes.

The thesis, to which the student has to devote about a year, is the analysis of an actual problem in the real world. Normally, the problem is one that has developed in the student's work environment. He has to do a detailed study of the theory applicable to this type of problem, before evaluating the way in which this problem was solved. On average, most theses run to about 150 typewritten pages. In addition, the student has to compile a case study from the information in the thesis.

The School has come up against a serious problem, i.e., that many students find it difficult to complete their theses. At present, we have 138 that have been submitted, and there are 195 students working on their theses—80 of whom passed their third-year examinations in January 1972.

In an attempt to stimulate more active work on theses, a scheme has been launched requiring students to submit research proposals as group assignments before the final examinations in the third year. After deciding on his topic, in consultation with his study adviser, the student prepares the first draft of his research proposal, with the aid of reference material from the library. He discusses it in his group and then submits it as a group assignment. After the third-year examination, he uses it as a basis for his thesis.

No problem is experienced with the reports (average length fifty pages) submitted by the AEP students.

Study Groups

Purpose of Study Groups. As stated, the study group system was the solution to the problem of introducing the element of dialogue in distance learning. The main purpose of study groups is to give the working student practice in integrating his practical experience and the knowledge he has acquired from self-study of his lectures with the experience and knowledge acquired by fellow students completing the learning process under quasilaboratory conditions—observation, analysis, interpretation, planning, and acting. Study group discussions can be compared with a pilot plant operating next to the actual plant. Tonight a problem solution is being tried out in the pilot plant (the study group); tomorrow it will be tried out in the actual situation— with a feedback or a learning loop back to the study group. The study group becomes the focal point of integration, of knowledge, techniques, and practice. The study group integrates the University into the practical business world.

An indispensable requisite for the student group is that it should consist of members with heterogeneous backgrounds. The motivating principle of this heterogeneous group composition is the maximizing of exchanged experience and academic knowledge. For the most efficient functioning of the group, a division of labour is also important, because the body of work is too comprehensive to be managed by self-study techniques.

In the study group system, more decentralization of the educational process is possible, resulting also in more effective functioning of correspondence education. A part of the control function is now also decentralized and the motivational function is brought back. The study group as an interacting system, controls and motivates its members.

To attain control and motivation the study group must, by means of group work, be impelled and motivated to work as an integrated system. The fact that a student is directly dependent on the other members of his group for examination entrance, and indirectly dependent on them for success in passing the examinations, motivates and impels him to contribute to group activities, to make a contribution to the dialogue.

Study groups are kept informed of the performance of other groups. In this way, a strong element of competition is introduced—something which plays an important role in motivating the group to function as an integrated system. A more positive motivation is the knowledge that the experience obtained in the group is extremely useful to the student in his work situation.

It is common to find strong leaders in a group keeping the group together by force of leadership. Only under leadership does a group become an integrated system (both formally and informally). The informal integration usually leads to the development of a 'study group personality' in the corporate student group with an individual 'group' approach to the assignments. The study group has to be seen as a learning and research cell. It functions virtually on its own and is an indirect means of training. Therefore, the effective functioning of groups requires leadership, in some form or other, from the students.

Activities of the Study Group. As stated, our aim is the group's integration of theory and practice into the cycle of the learning process. To develop the synthetic learning loop, the study group has the following activities: the case method, business games, project studies, individual students lecturing to other members of their particular group, group assignments, and research proposals. The students must learn to function not only in groups, but as groups. For this reason, the School gives them group goals in the form of group assignments. Our case studies are designed to train the student to use a theoretical framework with his practical experience, for diagnosing problems and indicating all the alternative solutions. This is conducive to observation, interpretation, and planning in the learning process. The groups submit (as a group assignment for evaluation and comment) written analyses of case studies. Copies of the two best answers submitted, as well as the marks of all groups, are sent to each group. Over three years of the

MBL, the groups submit forty-six case study answers—an important technique designed to give the students exercise in written communication. For the AEP, they submit sixteen case study answers.

In the business game, or, as it is sometimes called, the dynamic case study, the learning loop is completed with a continuous movement—by observing, analysing, interpreting, planning, and acting. Study groups in the MBL take part in business games in the first and third years, when this technique is, wherever possible, interrelated with the written lectures and workshops. The students are also required to consult reference books extensively in working out their assignments accompanying the business game reports. The business game also introduces a strong competitive element between groups.

Closely related to the business game is a project study and planning exercise done in the second year and consisting of a series of integrated exercises using modern management techniques. This is used to prepare the students for the business game, since all the information to be analysed comes from the game. Field studies are now replacing business games.

Lecturing within the study groups is a very successful technique, stimulating students to develop insight into the principles of management. A series of topics is sent to the different groups. A student selects a topic and lectures on it to his group. They evaluate him and send a mark to the University, and the student lecturer elaborates his lecture in written form and submits it as a work assignment. During the residential training period, the students complete a test consisting of questions selected from the topics on which they have received lectures from their fellow students. A new system was introduced in 1973, whereby students evaluate one another according to their contributions to the written analysis of case studies. This resulted in closer correlation between year and examination marks.

Group assignments are also used, e.g., to answer a list of questions on case studies to be discussed during residential training periods. This prepares the students for the case study discussions during residential training periods.

An interesting and important activity of the study group is the visits of the lecturers—in the MBL programme, two visits between the residential training periods and two between the last residential training period and the examinations. In the AEP and MMP programmes, the students are visited every third week, and when the lecturer spends a full day with the group. For these visits, we use the tutorial method, and it is not only important for the learning process but for the motivational aspect—interface between student and lecturer.

Organizational Structure of a Study Group. The deployment of resources to attain objectives and goals is possible only in a well-organized system embracing a number of subsystems. The study group is a system on its own and, at the same time, a subsystem of the total system.

At present, MBL students are arranged in sixty-six study groups. Membership of a study group is compulsory. Some students regularly drive more than 160 kilometres to attend study group meetings. A study group consists of five to eleven members. We try, as previously stated, to attract people with various academic backgrounds, working at different firms, and with varying ages and home languages. We use the two official languages in our training programmes and encourage the study groups to use both languages in their discussions.

The effective operation of the study groups is essential because of the large volume of group work to be completed. In the first year, we concentrate on self-study, and our students do only about five case studies and play eight rounds in a business game; they spend only between two and three hours a week at study group meetings, usually for no more than fifteen weeks per annum. Our estimate for the second and third years is about three to four hours a week on group work, for about thirty weeks per annum. Students so arrange their study group meetings that it is possible for all of them to attend. Sometimes these meetings are held in the evening, sometimes on Saturday mornings, the most important requirement being flexibility.

All members must be familiar with the policy and regulations for the operation of study groups. For each group assignment, be it a case study discussion or a business game, a group must have a chairman and a secretary, the former to preside and direct, the latter to record the group's responses. These appointments, together with the allocation of lectures, topics, and lecture dates assigned to group members, must be worked out in detail for a group at the beginning of the year. The programme is then submitted to the School. This method allows each group to work out its own programme within the scope of its possibilities.

The group members evaluate their chairman, in the case of each group task, and a student lecturer in respect of his lecture. From 1973, the group members also evaluate one another according to their respective contributions to case study analysis. The evaluating marks are then sent to the School. This method keeps students on their toes and makes it imperative for them to be well prepared. The School adds its own marks, both for the quality of the assignments and the manner of presentation.

To promote effective functioning of the study groups and to assist the student in self-development, we are conducting sensitivity training. In the second and third year of study, during residential training periods, each study group attends five two-hour periods of sensitivity training. A sensitivity training programme has been developed to accommodate our specific environment and demands.

Residential Training Periods

The third interface, known as the direct teaching method, is between student and lecturer. MBL students come to Pretoria for a week in the first year, for a week at the beginning of the second and third years, and for two weeks at the end of these years. In the first week of residential training, we introduce our teaching methods, answer queries, lecture to the students and, most important, try to motivate them. The second and third years are divided into two terms and we concentrate on two subjects in each. On the first two days of residential training, students complete tests on the subjects covered before the training period.

After the second residential training period, lecturers are required to assign marks to students, based on their participation in case studies. This is done for two reasons:

(a) to compel the lecturer to know the student;
(b) to motivate the student to take part in discussions.

During this second period, guest speakers are invited to lecture to the students. Because of the limited time, lecturers are required not to give lectures on subjects already covered in the study guides and textbooks but, to give lectures in which difficult and special topics are illuminated and discussed thoroughly. They must allow time for questions from students and time to put questions themselves.

In the second- and third-year residential training periods, forty-eight case studies are undertaken, in groups of twenty-five, with the lecturer taking an active part in the discussions, especially in introducing fundamental knowledge as a framework for defining the problem and looking for alternatives.

The AEP students meet for four days at the beginning of the course and for four one-week training periods spaced over the year.

In the residential training period, we use teaching activities or mechanisms such as lectures, case study discussions, business games, and for some subjects, concentrated study, especially in the special three-day programmes in business statistics and management and financial accounting in the first-year MBL.

DBL Programme

A Doctor's degree in business leadership (DBL) offers MBL and MBA graduates the opportunity to pursue their studies. The emphasis in the DBL programme is on in-depth academic study, where the candidate, through research, can contribute to the knowledge of management. DBL candidates are expected to complete advanced studies in business policy, and two other subjects chosen in conjunction with the School.

Tutorial sessions are held on Saturday mornings, when candidates have discussions with one another and with Faculty members. The candidates write research proposals and take examinations in each subject. After completing the formal part of the programme, they continue to write their theses.

Performance Assessment and Standards

One of the most difficult problems confronting the University of South Africa is to bring home to the general public the fact that it is able to maintain the standards of a residential university. The result is that the different departments, including the School of Business Leadership, tend to require too high a standard from their students. At present, the second- and third-year students take four tests during the year under examination conditions. At the end of the academic year, they take five papers in the first year, and eight in the second and third years. Four of the papers in the second and third years take the form of written analyses of case studies. In the second and third years, all examinations are open-book examinations. In the third and fourth years, inside and outside examiners are appointed for both examinations and theses. Outside examiners are, in most instances, professors from residential business schools.

In conclusion, we use different means for assessing the performance of our independent learner. Lecturers evaluate the individual student on class participation, written assignments, projects, and test papers; the groups, on written analyses of case studies, business game reports, and projects. The group evaluates its members on contribution to group work and teaching. Outside experts evaluate the students on final test papers and theses, and finally, the Faculty and Senate are responsible for maintaining high academic standards. This total system of evaluation of the independent learner is important for his own assessment of his growth and development and, at the time of graduating, the student's growth and competence is comparable to, if not higher than, that of students who graduate from more traditional institutions.

Evaluation of the Programmes of the School

Although it is not possible to provide a precise measure, in quantitative terms, of the effectiveness of the programmes, a study was made in 1972, as indication of the extent to which the School's activities contributed to the success of the students. The School's records were analysed, together with information obtained from a survey of both graduates and students working on their theses, and from their superiors. In December 1972, 290 questionnaires were sent out and, after six weeks, 83 had been returned by students and graduates, and 60 by their superiors. The response on the survey covers 66 organizations employing more than a million people.

Despite the small sample, a number of interesting characteristics are indicated. Most of the respondents are young and in the higher-income groups, and their financial positions improve according to the number of years that have elapsed since they obtained the MBL. Age shows little correlation to success. They are stable workers, but a large percentage change positions in the same organization.

Although the results are still meagre, the indications are that our students/graduates appear to be successful in the business world. There are indications that the students/graduates are highly rated by their superiors, that they are financially and professionally successful, and that they ascribe an important proportion of their success to the School's MBL course.

It is obvious from a paucity of figures that further research must be carried out, and this is being done.

Considering academic productivity, we have to compare the number of students who passed in 1972 with the number of academic staff actually used (excluding those on sabbatical and study leave). The School of Business Leadership has one lecturer for every 20 students who passed. This is a very economic use of staff, considering that at residential business schools the reported ratio is one lecturer for every eight students.

The Task for the Future

In striving to improve the presentation of our programmes, we are doing research so as to make more use of modern educational technology. At present, our MBL curriculum covers basic courses in the first year, functional courses in the second year, and integrated and policy courses in the third year, with specialization, in the form of a thesis, in the fourth year. We are changing in 1975 to basic courses in the first ten months, functional courses during the next eight months. During the following eight months, we hope to cover the middle-management courses, including logistics, MIS, formal organization and management planning and control. During the next ten months, we intend covering the integrative courses. These will include strategic planning and implementation, marketing and financial strategies, leadership and tasks of the manager, economic, social and legal environment, and international business. In the fourth year, we intend introducing an option to the thesis and written case study, namely a paper (essay), a written case study, and specialization in subjects such as hospital administration, real estate, finance, MIS, advanced human relations, etc.

Lecturers at present working on the behavioural objectives of their courses before updating the study guides. Behavioural objectives have already been worked out for most courses, and we hope to have this programme completed during the next three years.

Closely related to curricula and behavioural objectives are the systems activities or media. We have pointed out that we are aiming at introducing more dialogue in our system.

We started producing our own video tapes and have already completed three tapes on business statistics. Lecturers are experimenting now with tapes in evaluating group assignments. At present we are experimenting with telelectures between Cape Town and Pretoria, using conference telephones and telewriters. If this is a success, we hope to extend the systems to other centres.

Together with the development of new curricula, behavioural objectives, and improvement of system activities, we are introducing more flexible scheduling which includes the development of modular units.

References

1. See SCHEIN, E. H. *Professional Education—Some New Directions*, The Carnegie Commission on Higher Education, 1972, pp. 113, 135. Professor Schein included the School's programmes in 'some of the more innovative models'.

289

Suggested Reading

SCHEIN, E. H. *Professional Education—Some New Directions*,The Carnegie Commission on Higher Education, McGraw-Hill, 1972.

Ninth International Conference on Correspondence Education, 14–19 May 1972, theme: Between Evolution and Revolution in Education—Correspondence Study, Lost or Found? *Papers* edited by H. A. Bern, Indiana University, and F. Kulla, Xerox Corporation, vols. I and II.

GOULD, S. B. and CROSS, K. P. (Eds.) *Explorations in Nontransitional Study*, Jossey-Bass, San Francisco, 1972.

MACKENZIE, O., CHRISTENSEN, E., and RIGBY, P. H. (Eds.) *Correspondence Instruction in the United States*, The Carnegie Series in American Education, McGraw-Hill, New York, 1968.

LANGDON, D. *Interactive Instructional Designs for Individualized Learning*, Educational Technology Publications, Englewood Cliffs, New Jersey, 1973.

Part 3.   Management training programmes

---

20. Training for communicators

Thomas J. Attwood

Communication is a particularly vital part of management development. Managers spend 80 per cent of their time in communicating, and failures are costly. Better communication is better management. Yet few try to improve or realize their need for improvement.

Although deceptively simple, effective communication does not come naturally—contrary to some assumptions. Attitude surveys reveal that communication is one of management's poorest skills, and that management pay only lip-service to it. This chapter describes how to construct a training model and draft a plan to achieve balanced improvement programmes for all levels of management.

Communication is a major undeveloped resource for organizations.

Communication is the life line of every organization—no work force can be more effective than the communication skills which coordinate the various efforts. Indeed, communication is probably the greatest single factor contributing to success or failure. A manager's whole job depends on his ability to communicate (80 per cent of his time is spent in communicating). In short, he is a professional communicator. But unlike other professionals, he is likely to have had little or no training for his profession.

What do we Mean by Communication?

The word 'communication' can evoke a host of thoughts on what it is, and what is wrong with it. Is it telling people what to do? Is it posting a notice? Is it making an announcement? All too often, a manager may think that these actions are all there is to communication. He may confuse media and devices with the process itself, and, in doing so, overlook essential factors. The communication process is deceptively simple.

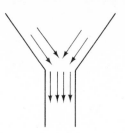

Fig. 20.1. Downward communication. A manager should not merely be a communication funnel.

A dictionary definition says that communication is 'an interchange of thoughts, opinions, or information'. The key word is *interchange*. Communication involves much more than just 'telling'. A manager must also listen and be sure that he is understood. He must get reactions from the people to whom he is communicating—up, down, and laterally.

Another misconception is that communication is a gimmick for use only on special occasions. Communication is a continuous process and an essential part of all management functions.

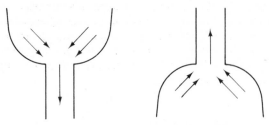

Fig. 20.2. The manager as a communication filter up and down.

Why is Communication so Important?

As organizations grow in size and complexity, departments tend to become more specialized; specialists have increasing difficulty in communicating with laymen or specialists in different fields. Management's main purpose is to get things done through people and to learn from others the progress of operations. This demands effective communication. Behavioural science evidence indicates that people work more effectively, and with greater job satisfaction, when they understand not only their own job but the objectives of their work group and the whole organization.

Yet attitude surveys disturbingly reveal that one of management's poorest skills is its ability to convey intentions and goals in a meaningful and acceptable way to the employees on whom it depends for success. While natural talent is a factor in the ability to communicate, specialized training plays a far greater part in developing it.

294

The Role of Communication

The problem of communication, although not new, is now receiving greater prominence in organizations. A combination of circumstances has brought this about. The apparent ineffectiveness of communication has lately become one of the most discussed problems in industrial relations, where communication failures have proved extremely costly. Employees are expressing dissatisfaction with the amount, or kind, of information given to them, and often, management's view of a situation is not in accord with theirs.

As management moves towards a less authoritarian leadership style, the need for effective communication becomes even more important. Successful communication is fundamental to good human relationships.

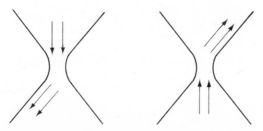

Fig. 20.3. The manager as a communication prism. He can redirect or deflect messages; magnify or diminish their importance; deliberately, or unintentionally, distort them.

Management Communication

Communication is a fashionable word. At least, most managers admit that it is one of their greatest problems; but that is about as far as agreement goes. It is also a subject about which managers tend to know rather less than they think they know—and less than they ought to know.

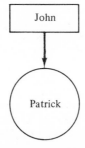

Fig. 20.4. One-way communication. However hard John tries to explain things clearly and simply, he does not know whether he is getting through to Patrick. The emphasis in one-way communication is always on the phrasing and appropriateness of the message.

295

The prime factor in good communication lies in a sincere interest on the part of management to communicate as much as is appropriate, and as well as is possible. Yet typical views expressed are:

Management's communication is unrealistic, erratic, synthetic and impersonal. There is far too much merely telling.

Management pays lip-service to communication and often leaves much of it to staff groups.

Management is unwilling to sacrifice the time and effort necessary to ensure understanding and acceptance.

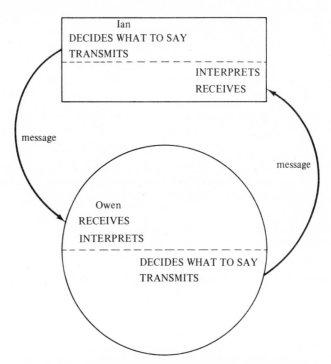

Fig. 20.5. Two-way communication. This is almost always the most effective way. There should be recognition that misunderstanding is inevitable so that Ian and Owen both test for understanding.

Let us define management communication as the capacity of an individual or group to convey ideas and feelings to another individual or group and (where necessary) to evoke a discriminating response.

Managing by Communication

Communication cannot be divorced from other aspects of management; except at the basic techniques level, 'communication' is simply one way of looking at everything a manager does. So, what does a manager mean when he says, 'We have a communication problem'? These are the main factors that affect management communication:

(a) the manager's personal 'style of management'; his assumptions about the nature of work and of human relationships at work;
(b) the way jobs are defined, and the way that the individual views his objectives;
(c) the structure of senior–subordinate relationships at each level;
(d) the flexibility of information flow systems;
(e) the organizational 'climate' built up over a long period.

Criteria for Effective Managerial Communication

While communication is a key part of every manager's job, no two people communicate alike. Individual differences make it undesirable to try to lay down rules for what must always be done or avoided. Nevertheless, there are certain principles which apply to all situations and people. Though these basic principles of good management communication are common-sense, the consistent application is by no means common. These principles are to:

(a) think before communicating. Management communication commonly fails because of inadequate planning;
(b) check the true purpose. Decide what *must* be achieved;
(c) consider the situation. Take into account the circumstances under which announcements are made;
(d) consult. Those who help plan a communication give it their active support;
(e) be aware of 'overtones'. The manager's tone of voice, his expression, his apparent receptiveness to the responses of others—all have tremendous impact on those whom he wishes to reach;
(f) convey something of value;
(g) follow-up. Feedback is important to ensure complete understanding;
(h) communicate for tomorrow. The message must be consistent with long-range interest;
(i) support the communication with actions. Persuasiveness is not what is said, but what is done;
(j) listen and see. Managers should be tuned in to reactions and attitudes.

Why Communication Fails

The greatest cause of misunderstanding in management communication is the assumption of understanding. Man has made enormous strides in the twentieth century. He has invented the computer, video tape, communication by satellite. Messages can now be sent with ease from country to country, continent to continent and from moon to earth. Many people assume that communication from man to man can be accomplished with equal ease. Yet man has not learnt how to overcome his greatest barrier—his limited ability to exchange ideas with his fellow man. He tends to be short-sighted,

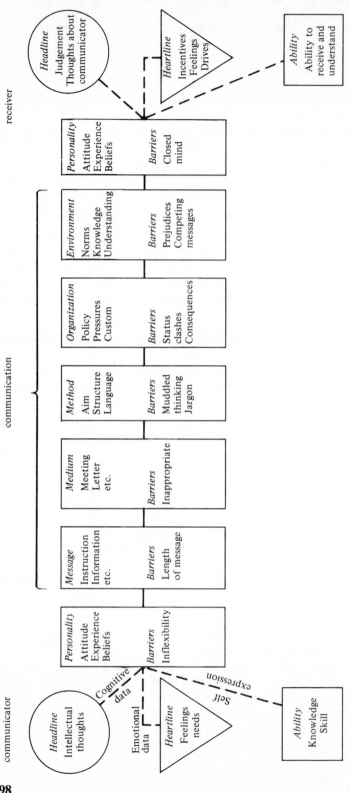

Fig. 20.6. The communication process. This model illustrates some of the problems and barriers to communication. In conveying meaning from one mind to another, one also has to consider the elements of meaning: the sense of the communication; the feelings that both the communicator and the receiver have about the facts, ideas, or state of affairs being communicated; the relationship between the communicator and the receiver; the purpose of the communication.

resistant to unfamiliar concepts, sceptical, and sometimes irrational. Some (false) assumptions about communication are that:

(a) managers are good (or at least adequate) communicators;
(b) the media and systems provide adequate and accurate information;
(c) developing technology will solve management's communication problems;
(d) communication is full, free, and useful for all who desire to engage in the process;
(e) communication is adequate in quality and quantity;
(f) the relationship between conceptualization and application is adequate.

Barriers to Communication

Many of the problems in managerial communication can be traced to a 'lack' of:

time;
knowledge about the subject, objectives or the recipient;
proper facilities (the 'mechanical' barriers);
training.

Other major barriers are caused by:

(a) abstract subjects: describing taste, colour, feelings, etc.;
(b) attitudes: towards communication itself—and prejudices;
(c) competition: the amount of messages competing for attention and interest;
(d) complexity: the complex nature of business, and of some subjects;
(e) differences: words mean different things to different people;
(f) location: geographical spread poses its own problems;
(g) structure: the organization may need re-forming;
(h) environment: external changes may demand appropriate adjustments.

How to Identify and Analyse Training Needs

Some preliminary steps are:

(a) to discuss with management the importance of passing information to promote greater understanding;
(b) to encourage management to review their own communication activities and be willing to improve them;
(c) to stimulate the interest of those who are doing well in communication, by using them as examples;
(d) to discuss simply, and practically, the psychological needs of people for improved communication;
(e) to review devices and techniques that have been found most useful in communicating with employees.

Note the *symptoms* of poor communication. To identify particular communication problems, examine comments such as:

If only they would tell us what it is for . . .

Managers tell you so many things . . .

Last week he told me quite a different story . . .

They said some time ago that we were going to . . .

Nobody ever tells me anything . . .

The trouble is that communications are so bad . . .

But my manager said . . .

If you want to know what is going on here, read the newspapers.

Note the *causes* of communication problems at different communication levels in:

(a) personal skills, e.g., communicating facts and thoughts clearly and concisely;
     rigid habits and assumptions;
     poor preparation;
     lack of confidence in presentation techniques, and fear of natural simplicity;
(b) motivational techniques, i.e., influencing people so that they behave in desired ways;
     failing to recognize opinions, attitudes, and motives of others;
     lack of empathy or ego drive;
     naïve views of human reactions, e.g., 'they should do as they are told';
(c) information handling, e.g., helping others to make the best use of information;
     giving too much/little information;
     bad decisions about who needs information;
     inappropriate choice of information level and poor timing;
(d) the management process, i.e., gaining knowledge for planning, directing and controlling activities;
     failure to define aims and priorities;
     under/overplanned delegation;
     management by crisis or activity rather than management by results;
(e) the organization's aims, i.e., coordinating efforts to achieve organizational objectives;
     narrow thinking;
     overrigid systems and lack of lateral communication;
     poor definition of objectives.

Diagnose Needs and Prescribe Training

There are numerous sources which can supply information about training needs. Many already supply information, others are waiting to be tapped.

Some, on the other hand, will require monitoring systems to be set up. Here are a few sources:

(a) annual performance appraisals;
(b) grievance, counselling, and exit interviews;
(c) the grapevine;
(d) briefing-groups feedback;
(e) complaints register;
(f) correspondence audits;
(g) written reports;
(h) telephone directories.

Before planning your communication improvement programme, it is essential to analyse the key areas of communication. Here are suggestions to help ensure that benefits justify the investment of time and money:

Communication and the Organization

The Need. Most serious controversies arise from misunderstandings—one manager not knowing facts which to another seem important, or failing to appreciate a point of view. In this technological age, departments have difficulty in communicating with each other.

The ability to put across ideas to staff means more productive work and better human relations. Effective communication is a way of life rather than a skill, but it takes a lot of skill to attain it.

Training. Training in organizational communication might well start with the techniques of conducting effective briefing groups. Briefing groups help to ensure that true meaning is conveyed to all concerned. (Normal length of groups is one to two days.)

Communication and Top Management

The Need. Good communication starts at the top. But often, the higher up the organization a manager gets, the less people tell him—and few top men will ever admit a failure to communicate!

The first task of top management is to form policy; the second is to communicate that policy both within and outside the organization. However good top management are in their first task, frequent failings are to be seen in their second task of communicating policy effectively.

Training. Training for key decision-making groups might well start with developing receiver skills—top management need a considerable amount of information to enable them to reach effective decisions. Training in receiver skills helps them to listen more perceptively, to read more quickly while getting the sense out of documents, and to observe critically. (Normal length of training, three days.) A second stage might be a study group on communicating policy.

Communication and Line Management

The Need. Communication is the essential ingredient in almost everything a manager does. In fact, no matter how varied his activities, or how special some of the skills involved, in the final analysis the job of every manager is communicating.

Middle management are mainly concerned with efficiency. Their problems are created by relationships with all other regions. Organizationally, they are divided into production, marketing, administration, etc.

Junior management are always under the strain of divided loyalties, to the enterprise, to organized labour and to their own functions and responsibilities.

Training. Communication training for management might well start with programmes on 'stating your case'—how to put ideas over effectively to seniors, subordinates, and in meetings. (Normal length of training, two to three days.) The second stage for middle management might be on chairmanship and, for supervisory management, the giving of on-the-job instructions. Other key areas include a 'communication workshop' to improve interpersonal or interdepartmental relationships. There can also be an 'external communication' seminar to help people communicate more effectively with those outside the organization, whether face to face, by letter, or by telephone.

Thinking

The Need. Clear thinking is the essential prelude to clear communication. It is impossible to communicate ideas effectively to others unless those ideas are clear in one's own mind and presented logically. Many people have valuable ideas, but few can express their thoughts clearly. Indeed, one of the hardest things in the world is to convey meaning accurately.

Training. Training in thinking would normally be incorporated into other programmes, e.g., it could be the starting point in helping people to prepare presentations and reports effectively. (Normal length of training, half to one day.)

This analysis should be continued to cover other communication aspects and media.

Planning an Improvement Programme

Communication appears in one form or another in all management development programmes. But, as a major subject, it is vital that it should be treated separately.

Constructing a Training Model

From performance appraisals related to the communication aspects of a manager's job description, one can devise an 'at a glance' chart or model of

302

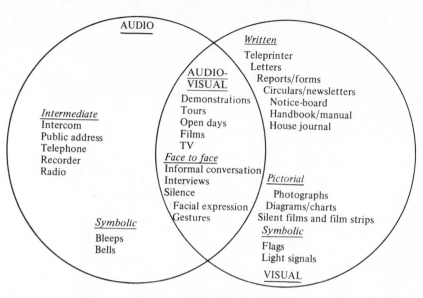

Fig. 20.7. Communication media.

Communication subject area (examples)	Training time (in days)	Executives by level and function (e.g., columns for)
Writing		
To give information	1	Sales managers
For action	1–2	Office supervisors
Financial reports	2	Production
Technical reports	3	superintendents
Marketing reports	3	Research scientists
Sales visit reports	2	etc.
Periodic reports	2	
Appraisal reports	1–3	
Project reports	1–2	
Business letters	2	
Sales letters	2	
Internal memoranda	1	
Dictating		
To secretaries	$\frac{1}{2}$–1	
To machines	$\frac{1}{2}$–1	
and so on		

Fig. 20.8. The start of a training model.

appropriate training activities for the organization (see Fig. 20.8). Every enterprise has its own unique pattern that must be studied if a model is to be set up which can be used for improving management education.

Implementing Communications Training

For any training to be effective, a person must identify and accept the need to change some aspect of his behaviour or an attitude. In communication

303

training, this process is particularly threatening to his self-concept. As learning often supplants comfortable and established ideas, opinions, beliefs, attitudes or ways of doing things, it tends to be resisted. Communications training is in the 'personal conceit' area. Few people would admit that their instructions or messages could be distorted, as this can reveal lifelong failings.

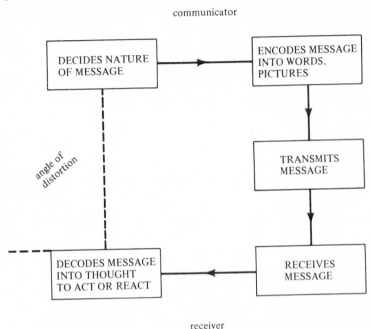

communicator

Fig. 20.9. The semantic parallelogram. Whenever management uses abstract or unfamiliar words, there can be a wide angle of distortion from the original meaning when the word is decoded by those receiving the message. A research team estimated that three-quarters of everyday English consisted of less than 1000 words, and that the average person has some knowledge of 5000 words. The fact that there are 600 000 words in the Shorter Oxford English Dictionary shows the magnitude of the problem that management face in achieving effective communication.

Draft a Training Plan

Start with a statement of the context and relevance of the proposed communication training. Each programme should then be clearly drafted to meet defined organizational and individual needs. Here is a skeleton to provide a working basis:

1. *The Training.* The title of the programme possibly with a subtitle defining the type of event, i.e., an instructional course, a study group, a workshop.

2. *For Whom.* To make the programme relevant, it must be pitched appropriately to the experience, seniority, and functional areas of potential

participants. The maximum, or desirable, number of participants needs also to be decided.

One example of a programme is for the manager who *believes* that knowledge of how to communicate to his staff, his seniors, and those outside the organization is important to him, and who wants to know more about it.

A further example is for the manager who *does not believe* that knowledge of how to communicate is important to him—and who wonders why his instructions are resented, his letters misunderstood, his talks fall on deaf ears, and why his reports go largely unread.

3. *Schedule.* Questions to consider are:

Should the programme be residential? (Not normally necessary for communications training.)

How long should it be, and what is the most suitable timing?

4. *Planned Continuity.* How should the programme be followed-up? If managers are allowed to practise their communication skills for a few weeks, then the refresher day will:

(a) ensure that points put over during the main programme are firmly underlined, and that lessons, once learnt, are not forgotten;
(b) check that the communication principles agreed are being put into practice;
(c) iron out any remaining communication problems.

5. *Objectives.* It is even more vital in communication than in any other areas of training to spell out clearly in behavioural terms, just what is to be achieved in your training programme.

It is all too easy to define objectives which are idealistic rather than practical. Here are some key objectives for a communications training programme framed in terms of knowledge increase, skill improvement, changes in attitude, and motivated behaviour:

Knowledge. What should the participants understand about communication concepts and methods, by the end of the programme? Examples:

(a) to define just what effectiveness means in terms of communication today, and how to achieve it;
(b) to give insight into the communication aspects of the manager's job description;
(c) to analyse the underlying principles of clear, objective thinking. As clear thinking precedes clear communication, participants will examine the most effective ways of communicating facts and their ideas, even attitudes of mind, to others.

Skill. At the end of the training programme, what should each participant be able to do? Examples:

(a) to diagnose, analyse, and solve practical communication problems;

(b) to develop skills in writing letters/memoranda/reports using a style designed to express thoughts rather than to impress the reader;

(c) to develop appropriate skills in leading meetings more purposefully.

Attitude. What overall or specific attitude changes towards communication need to be achieved? Examples:

(a) to develop a more flexible approach to communicating;

(b) to be convinced (for those who have to direct, persuade, and inform others) that many habits acquired by chance over the years are just not relevant today;

(c) to accept that by a simple, yet persuasive style of communication, one can obtain more cooperative attitudes and behaviour from others.

Behaviour. What behavioural changes do you want to achieve with this programme? Examples:

(a) to develop real understanding rather than merely improved knowledge of the communication process;

(b) to develop an effective remedial self-improvement programme;

(c) to produce workable solutions to current communication problems;

(d) to motivate the writing of letters, memoranda, and reports in such a way that true meaning and intention are conveyed to the reader, together with a clear implication of the action needed.

The driver of a car may *know* that seat belts save lives, he has the *skill* to do his belt up and he may have the right *attitude* to using seat belts in that he tells other people that they should always use them. But his *behaviour* might be wrong because he does not use his own seat belt. To get results in communication programmes, one needs to spell out the at-work behaviour which should result.

Communication objectives should be brief, specific, realistic, achievable, and (so far as is possible) measurable.

6. *Programme Synopsis (or Outline Content).* This must show clearly that it is based on effective practice and must emphasize workable guidelines in concentrating on day to day issues.

7. *Learning Process.* The training methods should be challenging, up to date, and effective. Certainly, in communication training, one should not rely on a single approach because no one way meets the needs of either all situations or all participants.

With communication it is particularly important to create a 'learning environment' rather than to try to 'teach' communication.

What is learnt cannot be separated from the way that it is taught— theory in communication programmes must be learnt through practice— practice interpreted and reinforced by theory.

8. *The Results.* Show how you anticipate that the enterprise and the individual will benefit from this training; in particular, stress that because the training is entirely job-based, there is no transference problem to work

situations. 'What a man finds out for himself he believes and will practice'; in communication training, participants must take a very active part in training themselves. Here are example benefits:

The manager gains: an improved ability to put his ideas across, which leads to better human relationships and more productive work; a more positive attitude to, and increased self-confidence in, his communication; and a better understanding of communication practices, which automatically influences all his interpersonal activities.

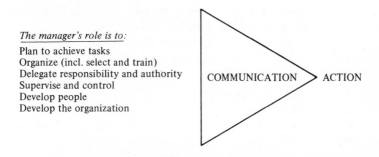

The manager's role is to:
Plan to achieve tasks
Organize (incl. select and train)
Delegate responsibility and authority
Supervise and control
Develop people
Develop the organization

COMMUNICATION > ACTION

Because communication is such a significant and crucial
part of management, it tends to become the centre
of all managerial frustrations.

Fig. 20.10. Management and communication.

His organization will find: projects going particularly well because everyone understands what is required; heightened standards of performance through increased job satisfaction; and its prestige and goodwill enhanced by improved external communications.

9. *Administration.* The dates, time, and place of the programme.

Choosing the Type of Event. After producing the training plan and establishing the objectives, management must decide whether to have *tailored* or *public programmes*. The training plan will prove the best pointer in theory, but theory and practice do not always provide a harmonious marriage. Are there enough managers with similar needs who can attend a training programme at the same time? What are the relative costs of both types of training?

Generally, a specially tailored programme conducted in-house is less expensive than sending the same number of managers out to any of the main all-comers' courses.

Another decision is whether to use the firm's *own staff* or *an external specialist*. This obviously applies only to in-house training. Training involving policy and procedures must be done by one's own staff. But, for most communications training, an outside specialist can operate more objectively (and acceptably) when challenging complacency in the 'personal conceit area'. Our company conducts, for example, a wide range of communication courses for such major corporations as Shell and Ford; this leaves their own training staff free to assess needs, administer programmes, and evaluate the training.

Evaluating Communications Training

This important aspect of training is often neglected because of the perceived difficulties attached to it. Difficult though it may be, it is nevertheless essential.

The starting point is the early involvement of the participant's boss. Unless his cooperation is sought, and gained, before the training starts, much of the resultant benefits can be lost or weakened.

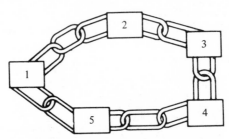

Fig. 20.11. Weak links in the management communication chain. The principal problems are failure to: (1) define aims correctly, (2) gain attention, (3) relate messages to the work of the recipient, (4) make messages understandable, (5) consider the human aspects.

If evaluation is to be successful, it should be kept as simple as possible and spread over a period—starting with post-course feedback and ending with the annual performance appraisal (in its turn, the beginning of the cycle).

Communication and Management—The Future

Communication can be regarded as one of the greatest undeveloped resources of an organization. In a technological world, the amount and complexity of information can rapidly overwhelm us. There is a possibility of information doubling every five years. Increasingly, therefore, formal and conventional communication will not be enough. A wider range of techniques must be used to build and maintain an effective organization.

Today, the importance of communication is greater than ever before, as we embark on a new industrial revolution. Success or failure to adapt to the new technological age depends largely on the effectiveness of our communication. The more the machine becomes a factor in our judgement and our decisions, the more there is a need for human communicators to transmit these decisions and explain them to those who implement them.

Managerial communication therefore receives new impetus, and the skills of men are at a higher premium than ever.

The manager who does not recognize his need to develop a broader spectrum of communication skills limits his ability to deal with the problems of today, let alone tomorrow.

Training for Communication—The Final Thought

Never before has the need for effective communication been so important. Yet, few managers take any real trouble to improve their techniques and skills—few even realize their own or their colleagues' need for improvement.

To achieve a balanced communications improvement programme, all levels of management from executive director to first-line supervisor should be trained appropriately in this vital subject.

Better communication means better management. Good communication pays dividends in the form of tightened operations, better morale, keener spirit, and the elimination of costly errors due to faulty communication.

Suggested Reading

ARCHER, R. M. and AMES, R. *Basic Business Communications*, Prentice-Hall, Englewood Cliffs, New Jersey, 1971.

BASSETT, G. A. *The New Face of Communication*, American Management Association, New York, 1968.

BRETH, R. D. *Dynamic Management Communications*, Addison-Wesley, Reading, Mass., 1969.

BORMANN, E. G. *Interpersonal Communication in The Modern Organization*, Prentice-Hall, Englewood Cliffs, New Jersey, 1969.

CHORAFAS, D. N. *The Communication Barrier in International Management*, American Management Association, New York, 1969.

DAWE, J. and LORD, W. J. *Functional Business Communication*, Prentice-Hall, Englewood Cliffs, New Jersey, 1968.

DEVLIN, F. J. *Business Communication*, Richard D. Irwin, Homewood, Ill., 1968.

GARNETT, J. *The Manager's Responsibility for Communication*, Industrial Society, 1968.

IVENS, M. *The Practice of Industrial Communication*, Business Publications, 1963.

LEYTON, A. C. *The Art of Communication*, Pitman, 1968.

MERRIHUE, W. V. *Managing by Communication*, McGraw-Hill, New York, 1960.

SPENCE, A. C. *Management Communication: Its Process and Practice*, Macmillan, 1969.

21. Creativity training comes of age

W. J. J. Gordon

Training people to be purposefully creative in problem-solving situations used to be limited to a select few. It was simply too expensive to train large numbers in creative skills because the training tools were not sufficiently operational.[1] This chapter demonstrates how the research effort of Synectics Education Systems has developed explicit tools for training in creativity, and how these tools have broadened the client base. First, we must understand something of the theory and practice that underlies Synectics investigations. Then, we shall follow a real-life, problem-solving process that led to a creative viewpoint. Finally, we shall examine the implications of all this for the future of creativity training.

The traditional view of creativity was completely élitist. It embraced words such as 'inspiration' and 'genius' and accepted as fact the belief that 'you had to be born with it'. In the face of such militant romanticism, I manifested an impious stubbornness, and I was prompted over twenty-five years ago to initiate research to find the process constants that underlie the creative condition. This research revealed irrefutable evidence of the metaphorical base of creativity. For example, from the time when he was a child, Einstein was plagued by the recurrent mental picture of a man closed in a falling elevator. This very image was the metaphorical connection that led to his general theory of relativity which defines the relationship of objects moving in the universe. When Sigmund Freud was reading *Punch* a cartoon sequence caught his eye. The first frame in the series showed a little girl herding geese. The next frame showed a governess herding her children. From the analogy inherent in the cartoon, Freud came to his idea of sublimation where reality is repressed in favour of a more acceptable fantasy alternative. Darwin observed that cattle were bred especially for certain characteristics that made their flesh more valuable in the market-place. He made the metaphorical connection (between this barnyard fact and a state of nature) which resulted in his theory of the survival of the fittest.

These, and a great many more, instances of creative acts being grounded in metaphor resulted in the hypothesis that the creative behaviour of people could be increased if they learned to apply metaphor in situations where new and innovative viewpoints were needed. Synectics research proceeded to make this hypothesis operational, and today, more than 200 organizations in the US and abroad have invested more than $100 000 000 in the Synectics technique; because it is the only approach to creative problem-solving that is tested and repeatable. Furthermore, metaphorically-based materials developed by Synectics Education Systems of Cambridge, Massachusetts, have influenced more than 10 000 classrooms around the world.[2] How did all this come about?

Synectics research revealed that the most important element in innovative problem-solving was *making the familiar strange*. 'Strange', because break-throughs depend on 'strange' new contexts by which to view a 'familiar' problem. For example, in the sixteenth century, people thought that blood flowed from the heart to the body, surging in and out like the tides of the sea. Harvey was familiar with this view and believed it till he observed that, after a fish had been opened up, the heart was still beating. He expected a tidal flow of blood, but was reminded of a pump he had seen. The idea of the heart acting like a pump was strange to him, and he had to break his ebb-and-flow connection to make room for his new pump connection. He made the familiar strange. Harvey's discovery has saved countless lives since it offered doctors an accurate account of the circulation of blood.

Interdependent with the innovation process is the learning process, by which an understanding of a new problem or idea is achieved by making the strange familiar. Understanding requires bringing a 'strange' concept into a 'familiar' context. For example, suppose that a student is observing a fish's heart. He knows nothing about physiology, and his professor has just explained how the heart acts like a pump. Since he is ignorant, this concept is strange to him, and he needs to digest this new fact into the rest of his familiar experience. Where Harvey had to break his ebb-and-flow connection and make his new pump connection, the student only has to make a learning connection. He is reminded of a swimming-pool where the dirty water is pumped through the filter, and back into the pool. The student, of course, makes the obvious connection between the heart and the water pump, but he develops other connections as well. He sees how lungs and the liver act as 'filters' when they cleanse the blood. Thus, through an example from his own experience the student creatively contributes to his own learn-ing. He makes the strange familiar to himself by means of a highly personal connection process.

Now, compare the learning process with the innovation process. Both Harvey and the student used creative comparisons. Harvey used his pump connection to make the familiar strange, to break the ebb-and-flow connec-tion. The student used his swimming-pool connection to make the strange familiar and learn about blood circulation. Harvey's creativity led to an innovative thought that was a benefit to all mankind. The student's creativity,

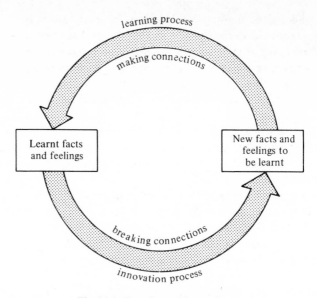

Fig. 21.1. Learning and innovations.

on the other hand, produced the discovery of a connection that only added to his knowledge. Both were creative. Furthermore, the creative connection making by each of them was highly personal and could have been made only by people with the particular character, knowledge, and experience of each of them. The learning process, however, led to a private result whereas the innovation process led to a public result. The student was always communicating with himself alone. Harvey communicated with himself during his connection-making process; but after he made his brilliant connection he communicated his discovery to the whole world.

Synectics has identified three operational mechanisms, each metaphorical in character, to evoke consistently both 'strange' and 'familiar' contexts. These metaphorical forms are used within the discipline of a simple flowchart. The freedom of Synectics use of metaphor necessitates a structure (flowchart) into which the generated freedom can be brought to bear on the problem being attacked. Figure 21.2 shows a sample Synectics problem-solving excursion which starts with a problem and ends with a practical viewpoint. On the left is the name and description of each step in the flowchart. On the right is an example of a new viewpoint being developed on a real-world problem.

The crash-landing fire problem of Fig. 21.2 was attacked with the weapons of direct analogy, personal analogy, and compressed conflict, which can be relied on to evoke creative responses with significantly more reliability than those which might be expected from probability alone. This operational approach has proved that it is not necessary to wait passively for the creative muse to strike, since there are concrete weapons with which to track and hunt the muse. This arsenal was described in 1961, but its application was

312

Excursion steps	Session transcript

1. *Problem as given* (PAG). The original statement of the problem is presented by the persons whose problem it is.

Airport fires due to crash landings of planes present a great problem. Fire-fighting apparatus cannot get there fast enough.

2. *Analysis of PAG.* This analysis should be concrete and tough-minded. No lengthy analysis is needed because the Synectics technique includes as a spin-off an analytical discipline that comes about very early in an Excursion. See step 3, below.

The first few seconds right after a crash are the critical ones. At present it is impossible to deliver fire-fighting equipment in time to do the most good. Foam on the runway is effective but requires time to prepare.

3. *Purge ideas and criticisms.* The Purge is an opportunity to present and criticize ideas that have come to mind by now. These ideas are likely to be superficial, but they will free you to concentrate on the process of making the familiar strange. Also, criticizing invalid solutions will more precisely define the PAG.

Purge idea 1. 'Install a flame-stifling foam-sprinkler system on all runways.'
Criticism: 'The installation cost would be astronomical.'
Purge idea 2. 'Place fire engines strategically over the airport.'
Criticism: 'So many fire engines might interfere with the landing procedures.'

4. *Problem as understood* (PAU). This is a simple statement of the *essence* of the PAG.

What is needed is apparatus that appears instantly whenever it is called for—like magic.

5. *Direct analogy.* This metaphorical form is a simple comparison between two things or concepts. Direct analogy is the primary mechanism for developing new contexts in which to view the PAU. You should try to make your direct analogies contain a lot of 'stretch' so that your comparisons make you see familiar things in strange ways.

An evocative question is a question that forces a metaphorical, rather than an analytical, response.
Evocative question for a direct analogy: 'What mechanical thing appears instantly whenever it is called for?'
Direct analogy *response*: 'An umbrella. Whenever you need it you just flip it open.'

6. *Personal analogy.* This operational mechanism is an emphatic identification with an object or thing. the goal of a personal analogy is for you to become the thing—to imagine how you would feel, and how your body and muscles would feel as the thing with which you are identifying.

Evocative question for a personal analogy: 'Imagine you are an umbrella that's just been opened in a driving rainstorm. How do you feel?'
Personal analogy *response*: 'My owner flips me open and I look around for rain to fight. That's my job, to strike back at the rain just as hard as it hits me. I've got to function like this because my skin is so thin that otherwise I'll get punctured. So I look out for each attacking raindrop, and smack it when it falls on me.'

7. *Compressed conflict.* This form of metaphor is a poetic, two-word description on a high level of generality. The two words should seem to contradict, and sometimes even fight each other. Make the words in your compressed conflicts 'fight' each other.

Evocative question for a compressed conflict: 'Now let's take two conflicting aspects of the personal analogy, and put them together into a short phrase to describe the umbrella.'
Compressed conflict *response*: 'The umbrella was both "thin-skinned" and an "attacker". A poetic way of using this conflict to describe the umbrella would be, "delicate aggressor".'

8. *Final direct analogy.* The purpose of a Synectics excursion is to help you get away from your problem. Therefore, it is crucial that your final direct analogy to be more remote, and apparently less relevant, to the problem than was your first direct analogy.

Evocative question for a final direct analogy: 'From the biological world, what is an example of "delicate aggressor"?'
Final direct analogy *response*: 'A frog's tongue. It is soft and delicate, but it shoots right out and grabs flying insects.'

9. *Analysis of the analogue.* You must unearth the underlying elements and functions of the final direct analogy. This description will be the framework for your new context. Do not limit your analysis to superficial descriptions.

A frog has a long tongue which is kept curled in his mouth. But it moves so quickly that you can't see it flip out and back without a special high-speed camera. The tip is broader than the rest of the tongue and is sticky.

[continued overleaf]

Excursion steps	Session transcript
10. *Fantasy force fit* (FFF). The descriptive framework of the final direct analogy is used to view the problem as understood in a new context. Don't worry if your FFF is really fantastic. If it isn't, there is little possibility of an innovative viewpoint. An FFF will probably emerge as a tentative, incomplete idea. However, it is better to explore the FFF material than to become too practical too soon.	*Evocative question* for a fantasy force fit: 'What if the airport fire-fighting apparatus were giant frogs? How would they use their tongues to put out fires?' Fantasy force fit *response*: 'I see only one huge frog. It's sitting on the control tower and whenever there's a fire, a crash, it shoots out its tongue, and slaps out the fire with its wet tip.'
11. *Practical viewpoint*. This is the final step in a Synectics problem-solving excursion. Now the metaphors, the fantasy, and all the apparently non-relevant material, are used to see the problem in a way that is completely different from earlier views. And constructive alternatives are developed.	*Evocative question* for a practical viewpoint: 'How can this "frog's tongue" idea be made practical? How can I use this huge frog to put out fires?' Practical viewpoint *response*: 'Well, I was envisioning the frog's tongue shooting out, and that made me think that we don't need fire engines or such apparatus. I just concentrated on the tip of the frog's tongue, and thought that we could have a gun, set on a tower, that would fire special cartridges containing foam. The whole airport could be divided into grids. When a crash occurs on a certain grid, this information is fed automatically into a computer which tells the gun where to fire.'

Fig. 21.2. A Synectics problem-solving excursion.

treated too implicitly.[3] Two major obstacles to clear, simple use were:

(a) the overemphasis on the group context where too much depended on the sensitivity and wit of the leader;
(b) the absence of a reference handbook that taught the process.

Therefore, in 1965, a further research step was initiated, and the implicit elements in Synectics were reduced to an explicit, written series of programmed workbooks.

It soon became apparent that making the Synectics process operationally explicit had sociological implications with ethical overtones that embraced an egalitarian as opposed to an elitist view. For instance, training on the basis of implicit elements to be learned was inefficient and therefore expensive; it required an enormous amount of time for study, travel, etc.; and the group context necessitated considerable planning. The explicit, programmed course for individuals, as well as groups, shattered the old elitism and opened opportunities for the many, not just the few. The result of the 'further research step', *The Basic Course in Synectics*,[4] is being used internationally as a fundamental creativity text. Whereas Synectics training used to be limited to a few chosen from management, this text is so explicit that it has opened up an entirely new and egalitarian client potential. And this is the inevitable direction that training in creativity will, and must, take in the future.

For instance, the text is currently being considered as a tool for solving the dangerous problem of low morale of people on automated production lines. Job monotony has become so critical that the workers in General Motors' new, 'show' plant at Lordstown, Ohio, actually went on strike because 'their jobs were too dull and the job pressure was too intensive'.[5]

Many attempts have been made to change workers' attitudes towards their jobs, and it is now agreed that the only hope lies in making jobs more interesting. Interest comes from within, however, and efforts to introduce 'better' working conditions (music, longer holidays, colourful plant interiors, etc.) have failed. What is being planned now is the use of the basic course to train thousands of workers in creative problem solving. Creativity is the highest form of human endeavour and this very epitome of human activity is lacking in job-monotony situations. To counteract this, workers will be trained in the skill of seeing old things in new ways, with the goal of inventing better ways to do what they are currently doing.

Thus, a worker will begin to view his job as a statement of a problem to be solved, i.e., *how to do this job better?* He will see a challenge, with rewards for him, rather than an inhuman monotony. He will feel that he is being trained to be creatively innovative. And he will gain a new dignity that derives from the process of creative thinking.

I have shown how Synectics research has removed the aura of sheerly accidental intuition from creative acts and replaced it with an increasingly explicit view of the creative process. The Lordstown example was selected since it contains the most powerful proof of the egalitarian effect of being explicit.

References

1. GORDON, W. J. J. 'Operational Approach to Creativity', *Harvard Business Review*, **xxxiv**, 6, 1956, pp. 41–51.
2. GORDON, W. J. J. *The Metaphorical Way of Learning and Knowing*, Porpoise, Cambridge, Mass., 1971.
3. GORDON, W. J. J. *Synectics*, Harper and Row, New York, 1961.
4. GORDON, W. J. J. and POZE, T. *The Basic Course in Synectics*, Porpoise, Cambridge, Mass., 1971.
5. *Business Week*, 9 September, 1972, p. 108.

Suggested Reading

GORDON, W. J. J. 'Creativity as a Process'. Paper delivered at the First Arden House Conference on Creative Process, October 10–12, 1956.
GORDON, W. J. J. and BRUNER, J. 'Motivating the Creative Process'. Paper delivered at the Second Arden House Conference on Creative Process, 7–10 May 1957.
GORDON, W. J. J. 'The Role of Irrelevance in Art and Invention'. Paper delivered at the Third Arden House Conference on Creative Process, 1–4 November, 1957.
GORDON, W. J. J. *Synectics*, Harper and Row, New York, 1961.
GORDON, W. J. J. 'Director of Research', *The New Yorker*, 4 November 1961.
GORDON, W. J. J. 'The Pures', *The Atlantic Monthly*, May 1962.
GORDON, W. J. J. 'The Nobel Prizewinners', *The Atlantic Monthly*, August, 1962.
GORDON, W. J. J. 'How to Get Your Imagination Off the Ground', *Think* (IBM Press), March 1963.
GORDON, W. J. J. 'Mrs. Schyler's Plot', *The Atlantic Monthly*, April 1963.
GORDON, W. J. J. 'The Metaphorical Way of Knowing', *Education of Vision*, Gyorgy Kepes (Ed.), Braziller, New York, 1965.
GORDON, W. J. J. and POZE, T. *Making It Strange—Book I and Book II*, Harper and Row, Evanston, Ill., 1968.

GORDON, W. J. J. and POZE, T. *Making It Strange—Book III and Book IV*, Harper and Row, Evanston, Ill., 1969.

GORDON, W. J. J. and POZE, T. *Making It Strange—Book V and Book VI*, Harper and Row, Evanston, Ill., 1970.

GORDON, W. J. J. and POZE, T. *The Metaphorical Way of Learning*, Porpoise, Cambridge, Mass., 1971.

GORDON, W. J. J. and POZE, T. *The Basic Course in Synectics*, Porpoise, Cambridge, Mass., 1971.

GORDON, W. J. J. and POZE T. *The Art of the Possible*, Porpoise, Cambridge, Mass., 1971.

GORDON, W. J. J. and POZE T. *Invent-O-Rama*, Porpoise, Cambridge, Mass., 1971.

GORDON, W. J. J. and POZE, T. *Facts and Guesses*, Porpoise, Cambridge, Mass., 1971.

GORDON, W. J. J. and POZE, T. *Making It Whole*, Porpoise, Cambridge, Mass., 1971.

GORDON, W. J. J. and POZE, T. *Strange and Familiar*, Porpoise, Cambridge, Mass., 1972.

22. Training in decision making

Jerome Rhodes

Decision making is largely unconscious and inconsistent. Yet it is the way in which we try to influence both the future and other people. Analysis both increases our control and reduces the consequences of error which apply to major single-shot decisions.

We need a discipline to help focus our thinking energies most effectively. Whether this means separating where we want to be from how to get there, or refining the many different kinds of objectives, it helps if we have an approach in common with other people involved.

The very uncertainty of the future makes it critical to evaluate whatever information actually is available.

Because of its central nature, the effects of improving decision making throughout an organization are extremely varied and far-reaching.

Making decisions is perhaps the most central and universal of man's activities: it epitomizes two aspects of his nature—dissatisfaction and freedom of choice.

Unless a man perceives a gap between what *is* and what *should* be, he has no reason for making any decision at all. Only when he can choose between more than one way to close that gap, is there a decision to make. Yet, as soon as he achieves this closure, he opens up new horizons. Equally, it is his nature to be warring within himself over the values which govern his choice between competing ways of reaching those horizons.

Decision making is, therefore, a matter of conflict. And in this mutually conflicting 'system', hardly any of the elements remain constant in a man's mind until he can somehow identify what they are, and invest each of them with some tangible value and some relationship one with another. If he hopes to control the future, rather than react to unconscious pressures and changes in his own thinking, some discipline is needed.

Discipline in thinking clearly does not mean rigidity. It means the deployment of experience and imagination and logic where each is most appropriate.

Everyone has his own way of making decisions. They may not be consistent with one another, and this is particularly awkward when an individual makes decisions with others who have different inconsistencies.

The future is innately uncertain. Men do not argue about facts, which can easily be verified or otherwise, only about opinions or values, which cannot. A process or system of thought which is intrinsically sound provides a framework and structure which is more akin to fact than opinion. It is so easy to disagree endlessly on any subject, that most of the energy spent in an organization is directed towards other managers in the company rather than the interests of the customer. Managers need to persuade others, whether above or below or sideways in the hierarchy. They need to avoid pointless friction between departments, while utilizing the spirit of competition. Always, they need the commitment of others to make their decisions work.

Definitions and Misconceptions

Many people think of decisions as rare and major events in their lives, rather than the evaluation which goes with everything we ever do. Others restrict themselves to balancing the pros and cons between just two courses of possible action. Decision making can also be confused with one of its critical elements, decisiveness, or even with the system of communication and authority which may either spread or concentrate the power to make decisions. Finally, there is the frequent retreat into some concept of mystical exclusiveness, which is explained by words like intuition, quality, flair, creativity, and even genius.

'Decision analysis' is used here to describe all of the following activities: evaluation, selection, negotiation, purchasing, design, persuasion, and resource allocation. In the hundreds of day to day decisions, the process is carried out in one's head, but should follow the pattern of analysis needed for more complex decisions.

Analysis merely splits the decision-making process into a number of stages or subcomponents, so that information can be better directed and used. Where the variables are too complex to hold in one's head, they are made visible. Identifying these variables enables the decision maker to recognize what further ideas or information will be needed. It enables him to simulate the effects of altering either the variables or their relationships with one another. He can test, and therefore control, his decision process. And he will often help himself evolve new ideas by doing so.

Process and Example: Focus on Key Difficulties

Every executive who wishes to decide on a programme of management development is faced with a complex decision. There are innumerable ways of going about it (*alternatives*). His criteria for choosing between them are in conflict with one another (*objectives*). The *consequences* of choosing wrongly could have a severe effect on the achievement of his main purpose for investing such time and money. At this level of abstraction, the decision model developed by Kepner–Tregoe[1] seems too obvious. However, the concept of 'levels of abstraction', which appears to exist in three dimensions for any complex decision, is one of the key difficulties for decision makers.

The executive has already made several decisions. He has chosen a management development programme as the best way to achieve some higher-level goal such as increased profitability, faster growth rate, continuity later on, etc. He has also chosen to focus on the development of management, not his sales force or his production workers.

His management development programme idea was, in fact, one possible alternative of many, including a surge in recruitment, more capital investment, greater incentives or a reorganization. If the higher *purpose* was, say, a faster growth rate, could we not equally say that this, too, was an alternative strategy, chosen against the competition of several others as the best way of achieving a higher-level purpose still?

Likewise, once a management development programme has been chosen or designed, there are lower-level decisions to be made as to the best ways of carrying out its different parts, who should be involved, in what sequence and mix, and so on.

There is an endless vertical chain or hierarchy of the 'levels of purpose' which limit the scope and range of each decision. Some general classification of the nature and level of alternatives is intrinsic to any such statement of

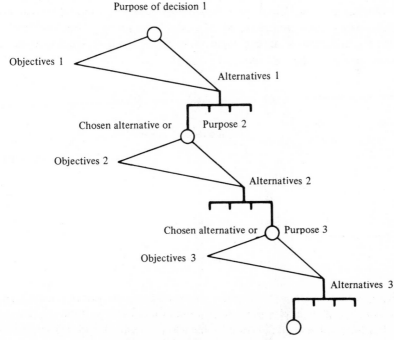

Fig. 22.1. The hierarchy of purpose.

purpose. The difficulty is determining the most appropriate level at which to intervene on this vertical chain. No one stays on the same level constantly, wherever he is in the authority structure.

It is equally important that those concerned should not feel that all the possible alternatives have been identified at this stage. Otherwise, the company could opt for an obvious solution which may not prove to be the best. But what does 'best' mean? Maximum gain/cost. Yet only simple decisions can be made on these two criteria alone, unless the decision process is split into a long series of binary decisions which only a computer can handle.

Kepner–Tregoe use objectives to identify the reasons why one should choose one alternative rather than the others. Objectives should therefore be the main source for alternatives. They are, literally, the ends being aimed at and, also, the constraints which are judged relevant to their achievement. 'Alternatives' means not just one of two alternatives, but all possible means of achieving those ends.

In our example, the alternatives could include management development programmes for improving skills of communication, motivation, quantitative techniques, management style or sensitivity, sharing information, and so on. On what basis, then, could the executive choose between these, or, say, between in-house and external, between MBO, Blake, Coverdale, and Kepner–Tregoe?

The latter group could all be regarded as alternative ways of achieving any of the first group. All could, in varying degrees, be internal or external, or a mixture of both. The Kepner–Tregoe programme could be seen as one possible way of causing improved information handling or communication skills or more effective management style. So, in a different plane from the concept levels of purpose, there is the cause–effect chain.

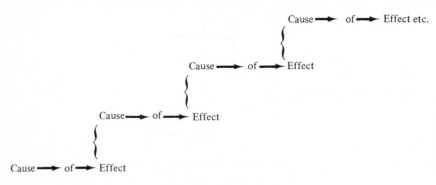

Fig. 22.2. The cause–effect chain.

We live in a cause–effect world. Yet nothing in this world is exclusively a cause or an effect, except in terms of a man's focus in a particular situation. An alternative such as Blake is a possible way of causing improved sensitivity, which could be a desired effect. But, given a different focus, improved sensitivity is a possible cause of reduced friction in a management team, which could be the real desired effect. If so, there are possible causes other than a sensitivity programme for reducing friction, and they could meet a company's other objectives more effectively. Only his statement of purpose enables a manager to avoid the unconscious adoption of an alternative as if it were an objective, which is one of the main reasons for a poor decision process.

So how is the executive to make his choice? What factors will he take into account? What limitations are there in his resources or in what he is prepared to invest? What does he want to achieve which can spell out, or reflect in more detail, his general purpose or his gain:cost ratio? What values does he judge to be relevant? What are his motives? What criteria will he use to discriminate between one form of management development and another?

Now the third dimension is relevant—a frequent reason for poor evaluation of alternatives. How general or how specific should one's focus be when attempting to reflect the purpose of the decision? If alternatives are possible ways of causing the objectives we seek, with what precision should we describe those objectives? Should we draw on the accuracy of *problem analysis*, described by Kepner and Tregoe? How should future actions be informed by the cause of the present situation, or the disciplines used in searching for change only in its *distinctive* aspects?

All decisions reflect some strategic attitudes, e.g., the pairs shown in Fig. 22.3. By placing his attitude to each decision on the continua, the decision maker can identify a strategic profile which should be reflected in the balance of his objectives. Let us take the last of the pairs. Every decision maker looks both inwards and outwards. He may first identify his own internal forces/values/motives, which he hopes to find fulfilled in the best alternative. He will also recognize externally imposed constraints which he may accept in the interests of realism, to gain the support of others, or to avoid potential consequences.

There will, in fact, be tension or competition in any set of well-defined objectives. If not, the same objective may have been inadvertently expressed

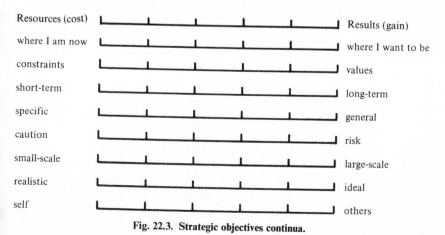

Fig. 22.3. **Strategic objectives continua.**

twice. Indeed, objectives with little internal conflict reflect either an arbitrary decision or a highly specialist alternative. Difficult or complex decisions require the optimization or trading-off of objectives that cannot all be met perfectly. Here are some typical management development objectives:

(a) to enable managers to use more effectively the increasing volume of information needed to run the business;
(b) to encourage the anticipation of potential problems, the calculation of risk, and provision against it;
(c) to improve the presentation of proposals making visible the key judgements used;
(d) to reduce time wasted in meetings;
(e) to improve the ability and opportunity for each member of a management team to make his optimum contribution;
(f) to improve the consciousness and communication of objectives throughout the company;
(g) to facilitate the design and review of systems and procedures which will encourage and support effective management;
(h) to enable the organization to operate with a smaller work force;
(i) to have no more than x man weeks of managers' time spent away from the job in the next three years.
(j) for the maximum outlay not to exceed £y in any budget year;
(k) that nothing should be begun in any division without the prior involvement of its functional heads;
(l) for no department to be involved unless 60 per cent of its management can be released within two years.

The statement of purpose has already indicated the kind of alternatives that the decision will cover. These will be further restricted if the decision maker can realistically identify the absolute requirements for success of the decision, and the absolute boundaries of time, place, and extent which will separate success or failure. These *musts* will later reject out of hand useless alternatives and thus save time. If accurately identified they will, by definition, guarantee the success of the decision. Yet, if these standards are too tightly set, the programme that would have met all the other objectives best may be excluded. Which of the above objectives seem to be musts?

Objectives which we only *want* to achieve vary in importance or weight. The executive will later need to take this difference into account when comparing those programmes that survive the *must* screen. It is of little use to regard objectives as values, without putting relative values on them. Immediately one tries, the competition between them is obvious. Indeed, the discipline of having to distribute weight among them, so as truly to reflect the purpose, confronts any vagueness of description. Yet, several companies, all with the same objectives, could weight them so differently as to choose completely different programmes.

The executive who has thought through his objectives can identify, or even design, alternative programmes which are more likely to reflect his

Fig. 22.4. Decision analysis matrix.

Objectives	Alternatives							
	A	B		C		D		
Must	Info.	Info.	Go/No	Info.	Go/No	Info.	Go/No	
Want	Wt. Info.	Sc. Wt. Info.		Sc. Wt. Info.		Sc. Wt. Info.		Sc. Wt. Sc.
		Sc.		Sc.		Sc.		Sc.
	Total	Total		Total		Total		Total

objectives precisely than would his rough and ready reaction to the first programmes that came to mind. It is so easy to choose a programme and then find reasons for having done so, when actually the most suitable one was never considered.

Some programmes could be eliminated when compared against the musts. The survivors need to be evaluated against one another. A matrix identifies the facts as to how the management programmes fulfil each objective. These facts can be scored, and multiplied by the weights of each objective. The comparative strengths and weaknesses of all the programmes are thus clarified, and the tentative choice is literally the result of optimization.

Of course, objectives have reflected the *positive* advantages sought. What of the adverse consequences that might discriminate still further between the tentative choice and one or two close rivals? What of the missed objectives, things to avoid, the niggling doubts which appear only when the moment of decision is nigh because the focus is now on just a few of the alternative programmes? What of the data used to evaluate, which is hard to quantify or rely on? Where are the features on which the close rivals were critically dependent for their high scores? Which alternatives only just scrape through the *must* boundaries?

It has to be remembered that decision making is about the future. The future is uncertain. One can only use best judgement in interpreting whatever information is available. Clearly, the risks must be foreseen and evaluated. Considering the leading contenders in turn, what could go wrong? If this happened (*probability*) what would be the consequences (*seriousness*)? What unwanted threats can we anticipate for our decision; what unwanted effects on other things would our decision cause? If horizons were widened too much from a major exposure to business schools, what effects would this have on resignations? Would our competitors make the gain?

When all these facts and assumptions have been taken into account and weighed against one another, there is a point when the final decision has to be made. Many who lack decisiveness have found this point easier to reach when they have taken it in stages as described. Others summon enough confidence by applying the analytical approach known as 'potential problem analysis'. This begins only when the decision is made, and an implementation plan needs to be generated, improved, and monitored. Such thinking should be almost an integral part of any decision-making process, while remaining separated from it in time. The disciplines used for anticipating potential problems, examining their likely causes and investing resources wisely in preventive, as well as contingent, action have many links with both problem analysis and decision analysis.

Areas of Application in an Organization

The process of decision analysis is clearly useful for making better decisions. Yet, there never will be a process which guarantees right decisions. Most information available to a decision maker at any point of time relies heavily on assumptions. Much of the data is missing—or missed. No evaluation can be exhaustive, and short cuts are essential. Analysis helps the decision maker to identify the missing, test the assumptions, and to have his judgement judged, either by himself later, or by others.

When a company systematically trains its management in this process, the effects of the organization can be of a different order altogether. Just as a single decision analysis can be used as a simulation model, enabling the decision maker to see the potential effect of altering the variables, so the decision processes of an organization can be monitored over a period of time, with a view to some organic improvement.

Companies are already observing the effect of a common language and approach to decision making. This is not just for multinationals, companies that have merged, or the communication problems between functions and levels. Obviously, knowledge and experience will be drawn upon more efficiently through the directed search of decision analysis. Reports contain only information that is relevant, i.e., related to objectives, alternatives, and consequences so simply and clearly that evaluation of proposals is improved when information is well handled in concert. Meetings produce more results than frustration. Decisions can be delegated further down, and nearer the source of information, with more confidence in the method of processing it. Systems and procedures are modified and thus contribute almost invisibly to the more efficient operation of the company and the training of those who operate them.

All these effects, and many others, are what would be expected. Yet people do not merely operate faster and more efficiently when handling information together. Their improved awareness of *why* they are likely to disagree makes it easier for them to see the reasons for the pressures from another department, or another level of the organization, and thus to resolve the conflict more rationally than otherwise.

By recognizing that the Kepner–Tregoe concept of objectives embraces not only values but motives, a significant implication for organization development becomes clear. Even an individual on a desert island who is making a decision has to accept certain practical constraints from outside himself. In an organization, all decision makers, including the chairman, are in a similar position. If such constraints are used as musts, their power to eliminate an alternative from any further consideration needs recognizing. Is a head count of seventeen really an absolute, or would eighteen be all right if the results produced were significantly better?

Other objectives, whether from outside or within the decision maker, are bound to reflect or affect the motivation of those concerned. Whose motivation apart from the decision maker and his boss should be accounted for in identifying objectives for a decision? How will the involvement of others, or the anticipation of their motives, help to improve the chances of getting their commitment to implementation? It is hard to move someone from his entrenched position in favour of a particular alternative: much easier to modify the objectives that are really relevant or to raise or lower the level of the decision statement; easiest of all, perhaps, to come up with different adverse consequences or change the assumptions about probability and seriousness.

Yet a different effect can be seen when the practice of making a decision analysis visible is adopted. Often, decisions are made with all the facts and assumptions held close to the man's chest. Making visible the elements used in reaching a conclusion, going out on a limb and identifying one's values even to the extent of putting numbers on them, introduces an element of openness in a management culture, which may be just what is needed.

There are other implications of this form of decision analysis in the area of team building, management style, and organizational climate. To understand them fully, requires more than the printed word. Even the ideal training course, full of practical application and feedback, is not enough. It needs involvement in a concerted and sustained effort to bring about changes in operating behaviour wherever they may be desirable.

Future Trends

Many specialized techniques have been developed for decision making. All aim to reduce the burden of qualitative judgement that rests on the decision maker. Qualitative data is made more tangible, whether by quantification, by building sequences of decisions, or by the use of models which show variable relationships spatially. Statistical and probability techniques increasingly require computers. Each method tends to be rather specialist. DCF is found to have flaws, mathematical models never seem quite to reach maturity, OR techniques fill the ordinary manager with a fear of mystique or a feeling of inadequacy. Even where computers are believed to give the right answers, it is hard to ask the computer the right questions.

Perhaps the working manager under pressure is looking for two things. He also wants a simple tool, or, at least, one which he can use with varying precision according to the importance and complexity of the decision to be made. Increasingly, he will look for one which can encompass the humanness of decision makers, one which bridges the interface between man and computer, between values and effects, between ideas and things, between quality and quantity.

The central role of evaluating information in a world of accelerating complexity, and one of larger and larger organizations, is becoming more apparent. Decision-making processes are more and more likely to be used to help bring about improvements in communication, in the attitudes of people to one another, in the climate or nature of a social organism.

This trend, and the basic soundness of efforts at quantification, suggest that decision making will develop along two separate streams, each drawing on and feeding on the other. There will be the specialist techniques which will quantify more of the information hitherto regarded as sublimely qualitative. These would include probability and statistical devices and would focus on the simulation and the prediction of the output of decisions. Then there will be the stream which will explore further the subjective and qualitative inputs of man. The latter will impinge more on the motivation of decision makers and will add to understanding of creativity and intuition.

References

1. KEPNER, C. H. and TREGOE, B. B. *The Rational Manager*, McGraw-Hill, New York, 1965.

Suggested Reading

GRAYSON, C. J. *Decision Under Uncertainty*, Harvard Business School, 1960.
MORONEY, M. J. *Facts from Figures*, Pelican, 1969.
RAIFFA, H. *Decision Analysis*, Addison Wesley, Reading, Mass., 1968.
SIMON, H. A. *The New Science of Management Decision*, Harper and Row, New York, 1960.
WINKLER, R. L. The Consensus of Subjective Probability Estimates, *Management Science*, **15**.

23. Developing planning skills in managers

Edward J. Green

In a complex, rapidly changing, unpredictable environment, planning is more important, more difficult, requires a different technique, serves a different purpose, and takes greater effort to develop planning skills in managers. This chapter identifies the major factors that have created the current situation and describes their impact on management and planning. It outlines the benefits that should be derived from planning and the specifications required to produce them, and reviews the categories of information that should be maintained in focus for coordinated planning. The various planning responsibilities are also specified as well as steps to develop planning skills. Finally, a summary reviews the four basic factors which govern the success that an organization will achieve as it strives to increase planning effectiveness.

There has been more change in management during the past ten years than in any other area of organizational activity, and there has been more change in planning than in any other element of management. Before attempting to develop planning skills, we must identify the changes in purpose, responsibilities, techniques, and requirements. To direct our effort intelligently, we need answers to these basic questions:

What are the major factors that caused these significant changes in planning?
What response is management making to these major developments?
What is the fundamental purpose of planning, and what benefits should be derived from the planning process?
What specifications must be built into the planning process to provide those benefits?
What are the categories of information that should be maintained in sharp focus at the times and places where plans are formulated, reviewed, and authorized?
Who is responsible for the various elements of planning, and what can be done to develop their planning skills?

Major Change Factors

Discontinuity

The most serious planning problem has been the tremendous increase in the rate and volume of change. And the changes which take place before the year 2000 are likely to be even greater in volume than those experienced since the beginning of the century. This increase in the rate of change will be devastating unless we plan more effectively. Many years ago, planning was based on the premise that the future would be like the past; ten years ago, it was based on the erroneous assumption that forecasts would be accurate. We now recognize that many important developments will turn out differently than expected. To cope with discontinuity, we must develop planning skills that will make it easier to revise our plans in response to new developments.

Information Explosion

In the past, managers operated on the premise that the more information they had, the better planning would be, but we now realize that the more data we have, the more difficult planning becomes. A surfeit of incidental information causes planning to deteriorate. Managers must identify the decisions that they are trying to make, and determine the minimum amount of reliable information for planning at an acceptable risk. To be effective, planning must be based on processed *intelligence* rather than raw data, prejudiced information, or uninformed opinions.

Managerial Lag

It is now more difficult to manage organizations than it was ten years ago. Although we have improved our management effectiveness during the intervening period, it has not always been enough to offset the increase in speed and complexity. Many executives recognize that:

(a) the problems with which they are confronted may seem to be the same old problems, but there is a vast difference in size and impact, and the situation will get worse before it gets better;
(b) they are relatively less able to cope with the current situation than they were ten years ago, and this managerial lag cannot be corrected until they improve their planning skills.

Attitudes

Since most problems are *people* problems, attitudes—especially shifts in attitudes—have a major impact on both the need and ability of managers to plan.

Authority. The deterioration of command authority in Church, school, business, and military has caused major repercussions, because it is impossible to manage an organization without authority. With the decline in command authority, managers must find other ways to establish and maintain authority —and this will require better planning.

Participation. With their physical requirements increasingly well satisfied, people are now demanding fulfilment of higher psychological needs— acceptance, recognition, participation, involvement, self-realization. After managerial people are reasonably well compensated, the strongest motivating factor is a real opportunity to plan for their own future.

Public Support. Enlightened business leaders are seriously concerned with the attitude of the public towards business and the economic system. In recent years, public apathy has assumed more dangerous proportions. Seven years ago, 60 per cent of the US population supported business; 40 per cent were indifferent or antagonistic. The latest analysis reveals that these figures are now reversed. To cope with this problem, we must have better planning.

Managerial Response—MBO

Alarmed by these trends, beset with mounting pressures, and with the commendable desire to find a simple solution, managers of business, educational, government and health-care organizations have been moving towards decentralized, participative Management by Objectives. Although headed in the right direction, the results have frequently been disappointing because of a failure to understand underlying problems, and unwillingness or inability to plan effectively.

Participative management is based on the premise that every manager will use his resources to get the best possible results. To accomplish this, he must plan for his own area of responsibility in a way that can be *co-ordinated* with his associates, *consolidated* to support the objectives of the organization, and *changed* when important developments turn out to be different from those expected.

In participative management, many types of planning are in progress all the time—strategic, operational, budgetary, long- and short-range— for every division, department, programme, and function. Everything tends to affect everything else, and everything is changing. Since the quality of planning cannot consistently rise above the quality of the information on which it is based, adequate information must be kept in focus at the various times and places where the plans are formulated, reviewed, and authorized. This requires a dynamic planning system that is more comprehensive and responsive.

Purpose and Benefits of Planning

In the past, most managers believed that the purpose of planning was to produce a plan—and the process was designed accordingly. But in our complex, rapidly changing, unpredictable environment, we are beginning to

330

	Static planning (old way)	*v.*	*Dynamic* planning (new approach)
Purpose	Get a 'plan'		Achieve optimum results
Basic premise	Forecasts are accurate		Future is unpredictable
Technique	Static, periodic		Dynamic, continuous
Process	Rigid, formal, prescribed		Flexible, selective adoption
Management style	Traditional, authoritative		Decentralized, participative
Responsibility	Top management VP, Planning Centralized planning staff		Every manager Director, planning services Decentralized planning coordinators
Types of planning Strategic Operational Logistic	Separate plans		Integrated planning
Functional planning Marketing Financial Personnel etc.	Separate plans		Integrated planning
Time spans Short Medium Long-range	Separate plans		Integrated planning
Support	Resistance and resentment		Enthusiastic participation
Durability	Tapers off to discouragement		Growing value and enthusiasm
Cost benefits	Too much time, effort, paper Higher cost Limited benefits		Better decisions and programmes Less time and effort Better results

Fig. 23.1. Planning characteristics.

realize that a 'plan' is an important benefit, but not the purpose. The purpose of planning is to get the best possible results, regardless of what happens. Whenever you have a deviation in anticipated results, you have a problem or an opportunity. At such times, a 'plan' may be detrimental unless it is conveniently possible to change. The comparative analysis chart of Fig. 23.1 identifies the distinctive characteristics of static and dynamic planning. A manager needs dynamic planning to get the best possible results when an important development turns out differently than expected because he will *always* have to change the programme of action, the resource allocation, or the objective. Expressed in a different way, the purpose of planning is to enable managers to achieve effective management. Management is effective when an organization is able to use its resources to accomplish the things

Planning is more than a mere *function* of management, it is the *way* you manage.

1. Identify and evaluate problems and opportunities.

2. Clarify and evaluate goals and objectives.

3. Determine which are the most important.

4. Develop and execute programmes of action . . . to achieve.

5. Allocate essential resources . . . to support.

6. Cope with continuous change.

7. Gain and maintain acceptance and support of key people who are involved or affected.

Fig. 23.2. Optimum results.

that are most important. To achieve optimum results, adequate action must be taken in the essential areas outlined in Fig. 23.2. This cannot be accomplished without planning—therefore planning is more than a mere *function* of management, it is the *way* you manage.

If you do not know what benefits you want from planning, you will not know how to design your planning process to get the benefits you need. A good planning programme is designed to meet the particular needs at the present time, with sufficient flexibility to respond to future requirements. If the organization is committed to Management by Objectives, the managers need a planning process that will help them:

(a) accomplish 'optimum' results—the best that can reasonably be expected in the light of the circumstances that prevail;

(b) minimize surprise—while it is impossible to eliminate surprise in an unpredictable environment it is desirable to detect deviations as soon as possible in order to optimize results;

(c) plan for their own areas of responsibility in a way that can reflect the consolidation of subordinate planning, be coordinated with the planning of associates, and be consolidated to achieve organizational objectives;

(d) coordinate their planning:
   horizontally, among the functions (personnel, finance);
   vertically, among the echelons (departments, divisions);
   among the time spans (short- and long-range);
   among the types (strategic, operational, logistic);

(e) provide reliable information in focus at the times and places where it is needed—when recommendations are formulated, reviewed, and authorized;

(f) communicate more effectively—with less time, effort, and paperwork;

(g) gain and maintain the acceptance and support of the key people who are involved or affected.

332

Specifications for Planning Process

Having identified the benefits wanted, it is possible to determine the specifications required to provide them. Unless the planning process incorporates the following features, it is difficult to develop adequate planning skills.

Simplicity

The process must be sufficiently simple for an average manager to use despite the pressures of his job, the lack of intensive training, and the fact that he really does not like to plan because it requires him to think and involves risk. This degree of simplicity can be accomplished through selective adaptation and by applying the principle of commonsense and value. No manager should be required to use any more of the planning process than he needs to plan for his own area in a way that can be coordinated and consolidated.

Flexibility

The minimum standard of flexibility should make it possible to change any part of the planning when anything happens that is so urgent or important that it must be changed to optimize results—but planning should not be changed more often than necessary. This standard dictates methodology since there are only two ways to achieve that degree of flexibility in a complex organization: by using a looseleaf manual system with controlled distribution, or by using a computer. The ideal is a proper combination of the two.

Delegation/Communication

Provide clear delegation with adequate communications. To plan effectively, a manager needs an adequate way to reach and revise agreement regarding:

(a) the areas in which he is expected to produce results;
(b) the results he is expected to produce;
(c) the programmes he must carry out to achieve objectives;
(d) the resources necessary to support the programmes;
(e) the recommendations and decisions he is expected to make;
(f) the information he needs to make those recommendations with acceptable risk.

Information

Establish an appropriate method to provide and maintain two types of reliable information in focus when, and where, needed:

(a) administrative information (policies, procedures) which tell the managers what they are permitted or expected to do;
(b) operational intelligence that enables them to formulate plans within a common frame of reference.

Basic information should be provided from a common source to prevent needless duplication and unnecessary paperwork.

Planning Process

As already noted, in the typical organization, many types of planning are proceeding all the time: strategic, operational, logistic, long- and short-range, facility, technological, financial—for every division, department, function, and programme. Everything tends to affect everything else, and everything is changing. Under these circumstances, it is impossible for a manager to plan for his own area in a way that can be coordinated and consolidated unless he has a process that enables him to do it. To gain the enthusiastic and effective participation of the key people, it is necessary to provide the process before you apply the pressure.

In-house Specialist. To obtain best results in the shortest time, at the lowest cost, on a sustained basis, there must be a well-qualified, in-house planning specialist. He does not do the planning, but sees that you have a proper planning process, and that it works; and he provides common services to make it work. A competent planning specialist may be more important to successful planning than a professional accountant is to proper accounting —because the job is more difficult and less well understood. The planning specialist needs the qualifications outlined in Fig. 23.3. It is an expensive delusion to assume that an effective planning programme can be designed and operated without a well-qualified planning specialist. In a large organiza-tion, this is a full-time job. In a small organization or subunit, this could be a part-time assignment. In either case, the specialist should be inherently qualified and well trained.

Combination of intelligence, creativity and sound judgement.
Excellent communications skills—both oral and written.
The type of personality conducive to non-direct counselling.
Broad training and experience in the practice of management.
Intensive indoctrination in modern concepts, principles, and practices of MBO.
Extensive training in the special techniques, processes, and procedures of dynamic planning and control.
Uncommitted time, free from distracting pressures and other responsibilities.

Fig. 23.3. Qualifications of planning specialist.

Standard Categories of Information

The quality of planning cannot consistently rise above the quality of the information on which it is based. But you can give a manager good information and still get bad planning unless it is properly coordinated and consolidated. It is much easier to coordinate and consolidate when there is a common frame of reference and the information is organized in similar categories. There are various ways to accomplish this, but we shall take, as an example, one in which the planning data is organized in a looseleaf planning book with nine standard sections. This approach provides for the controlled distribution and revision of common data from a common source. Each manager organizes in his planning book the *minimum* amount of additional information that he is continuously using for his planning and decision making. To minimize paperwork, he uses outlines wherever possible and supplements the written work with improved individual communications, group discussions, and organized presentations.

The nine sections in the planning book are used selectively, like the pigeon-holes in a post office. The managers do not necessarily start with the first section and proceed in sequential order. They use each section only as it is needed. No one is encouraged to use more of the planning book than he needs to do what he is expected to do; i.e., plan for his own area in a way that can be coordinated and consolidated. The nine standard categories are described below.

Scope/Purpose

This section defines the nature of the business—or the scope and purpose of the programme, function, or activity. No one can plan effectively for his business or activity until he understands what it is. Managers in the same organizational unit need common guidelines to plan together.

Environment

Pertinent data regarding those important environmental and competitive factors are organized in this section, which includes relevant information about climate, economy, government, regulatory agencies, markets, industries, consumer attitudes, public relations, and competition.

Capabilities/Opportunities

This section should contain a critical, objective analysis of a manager's relative ability to conduct his particular programme or activity, within his environment, in the face of his competition.

Assumptions

These are temporary estimates of important, probable developments that cannot be predicted with accuracy—and over which the managers have no significant control—that will have a major impact on performance or results. An assumption is *not* a prediction; it is a temporary estimate regarding an important anticipated development. Whenever there is a significant deviation in an assumption, you have a problem or an opportunity. To accomplish optimum results, you must change the assumption, review all plans that were based on that premise, and make appropriate revisions.

Goals/Objectives

Goals provide a general sense of direction or accomplishment. Objectives are estimates of desirable future results, that the manager believes can, and will, be achieved through his efforts, for which he is willing and able to provide resources. Assumptions and objectives are similar in that both pertain to the future, and neither can be predicted with accuracy. Assumptions are important developments beyond your control, and objectives are desirable results achieved through your effort. More attention should be given to assumptions, because without quantified assumptions, objectives tend to become vague and imprecise. Objectives should also be quantified so that progress can be measured more accurately.

Policies/Strategies

Policies are broad statements of general intent that tell what is permitted or expected. It is difficult to achieve good planning for any area of responsibility without clear and consistent policy guidelines. A good strategy is that combination of consistent policies, objectives, programmes, and resources that will enable management to get the best possible results by optimizing their capabilities and opportunities.

Programmes/Schedules

Programmes are the courses of action that enable a manager to achieve his objectives within the frame of policy guidelines and thus convert strategic concepts into profitable results. Managers are beginning to realize that programmes and projects are the most difficult and important part of planning. Schedules help determine and control who does what, and what comes first. It is essential to have a good system of priorities and schedules to accomplish optimum results.

Organization

This section deals with the effective use of people. Just as programmes and projects are considered the most important and difficult part of the planning process, people are generally recognized as the most critical resource. Not only does the organization structure have a great influence on the effectiveness of planning, but improved planning will create a need and opportunity to streamline the organization structure.

Budgets/Resources

This section should help managers get the right resources, in the right quality and quantity, at the right time and place, and at the right cost. A properly developed budget should reflect approved programmes of action with price tags.

Responsibilities and Opportunities of Management

Having reviewed the major factors that have changed the purpose and requirements of planning, it is desirable to identify the responsibilities and to recommend specific steps to develop planning skills.

Board of Directors

The constitution of many organizations prescribe that the directors are responsible for planning, and this is as it should be—in a broad, strategic sense. They are certainly responsible for seeing that the organization develops and executes programmes of action to achieve profitable survival;

has an adequate plan for the succession of top management; has adequate budgetary planning and control; and gives appropriate consideration to strategic programmes that involve unusual risk, heavy commitment, or tend to change the nature of the business. It is a mistake, however, to expect the directors to do the planning; they should, rather, see that it is done adequately and review and approve major elements. The following steps should be taken to develop planning skills in these areas:

(a) arrange an executive briefing session for directors, to achieve understanding and working consensus regarding the managerial style and its implications. Particular attention should be directed to the major changes in planning requirements if the organization is moving towards participative management;
(b) provide the directors with summaries of corporate, divisional, and strategic programme planning. It will be helpful if these are organized in standard format, with appropriate supplements;
(c) arrange organized presentations to the board several times a year. In the first half of the fiscal year, concentrate on longer-range implications, and in the last half, present the operational budget for the next year. Supplement with special presentations of major divisions and strategic programmes.

Chief Executive Officer

The CEO is responsible for determining the managerial style, gaining understanding, seeing that appropriate planning and control processes are developed to support the managerial philosophy, and doing whatever may be necessary to gain and maintain the acceptance and support of the line and staff managers who are involved or affected. He is also responsible for seeing that policy guidelines are formulated, distributed, and understood in the following areas:

managerial philosophy;
policies and procedures;
planning;
growth;
profitability;
corporate identity;
organizational relationships and development.

These steps should be taken to improve planning at the top executive level:

(a) under ideal circumstances, the CEO should accept personal responsibility for general direction and supervision of the corporate planning programme. If this is impractical or undesirable, he should see that this important responsibility is assigned to a well-qualified senior executive;
(b) arrange an executive briefing for the top management team to achieve understanding of the managerial style and its implications, and a working consensus as to the seven strategic policies outlined above;

337

(c) appoint an in-house planning specialist who is fully qualified to help develop and implement a planning process responsive to the organization's unique requirements;

(d) make sure that the planning responsibility for every important area of organizational activity is specifically assigned to a well-qualified responsible person;

(e) see that periodic business, budget, and strategic programme reviews are conducted for the top management team;

(f) it may be desirable to establish a planning council or task force of executives to facilitate the design, development, implementation, and operation of the planning programme, but usually this can be handled by the executive committee or some other established group. In any event, the responsibility of this group should be limited to communications, coordination, and review—plans should be formulated by the person responsible for the activity.

Staff Officers

Staff officers should not only plan for their respective areas, but serve as substantive planning specialists in their areas of expertise. The following steps should be taken to develop their planning skills:

(a) make sure they understand the managerial concepts, the implementing processes, and their planning responsibilities;

(b) provide planning counsel and technical assistance in helping them selectively adapt the planning process to meet their requirements so that they can plan more effectively with less time and effort;

(c) if their area is large or complex, give them a full or part-time planning specialist to provide the services outlined later;

(d) provide them with orientation and general training in the management concepts and implementing processes of your organization—but do not try to make them planning specialists;

(e) encourage them to apply the principles of commonsense and value. Help them to realize their responsibility for decentralized planning, but do not require them to use more of the planning process than they need to plan for their own areas in a way that reflects subordinate planning, can be coordinated with their associates, and consolidated to support organizational objectives.

Line Managers

Line managers are responsible for planning for their own areas of responsibility (and for seeing that their subordinates plan for theirs) in a way that can be coordinated and consolidated. The steps to improve their planning skills are the same as those recommended for staff officers.

In-house Planning Specialist

The qualifications for the planning specialist were outlined in Fig. 23.3. The following steps should be taken to increase his effectiveness:

(a) he must recognize that he does not *do* the planning, but help to design a planning process responsive to the requirements of the organization and help in the selective adaptation by all those who need to plan, for all types of planning that need to be done;
(b) in selecting the planning specialist, avoid the brilliant, brittle person with an inferiority complex who is under constant pressure to impress others with his knowledge. Also avoid the person who claims to be a 'planner' and wants to tell everyone how to run his business;
(c) an MBA or equivalent would be desirable, but more important are a high degree of intelligence, intellectual curiosity, and special interest in management concepts and practices. This can be supplemented by courses in management, systems and procedures, budget and control, all types of planning, economics, market research, and behavioural science;
(d) he should be thoroughly grounded in the managerial concepts and administrative processes of your organization and given as much special training as possible in planning techniques and non-directive counselling.

Education and Training

A good planning process is one designed to meet the current needs of an organization, with sufficient flexibility to respond to future requirements. The education and training responsibilities will vary widely, depending on the style of management, the rate of change, and the degree of commitment to the new managerial concepts and implementing processes. The following steps should be taken to develop planning skills in managers:

(a) start at the top with executive briefing sessions that will help the directors and top management understand the philosophy of management, its implications, and what sort of administrative and planning processes will be required to make it work;
(b) follow this up with a series of management seminars to achieve similar understanding among all members of management. Do not attempt to go further or faster than will gain acceptance and support from the key people involved or affected;
(c) if the organization is committed to a concept of decentralized, participative management in which every manager is expected to plan for his own area in a way that can be coordinated, consolidated, and changed— make sure that the planning process is responsive to the requirements— then provide adequate education and training in that concept and process;
(d) the education and training programme should be designed to help every manager to discharge his responsibilities more effectively at his own level. The managers are responsible for doing the planning, but, in most instances, it is no more necessary or practical to teach them to become planning specialists so that they can participate effectively in the planning

339

programme than it would be to teach them book-keeping or programming so that they can use the accounting system or computer;

(e) the training programme for the in-house planning specialist should be designed to help him to perform the functions outlined earlier and in Fig. 23.3. He should have broad knowledge in the field of modern management, with particular emphasis on economic research, systems and procedures, statistics, marketing, finance, and personnel administration. This should be supplemented by as much special training as possible in Management by Objectives, behavioural science, non-directive counselling, and all aspects of management planning. He will need to be thoroughly familiar with the management concepts, practices, and processes of his own organization.

Summary

There are four basic factors that control the success that any organization can achieve as it attempts to increase planning effectiveness. These have a direct bearing on the effort to develop planning skills in managers.

a. Management Concepts. Until there is clear understanding of the management philosophy, its implications, requirements, and commitments, it is impossible to develop planning skills that are responsive to needs.

b. Planning Process. If the management concept is based on the premise that every manager will plan for his own area in a way that can be coordinated, consolidated, and changed, and if there are many types of planning going on in a complex, rapidly changing environment it is impossible to develop adequate planning skills until there is a planning process that will enable managers to do what is expected.

c. Operational Intelligence. Since the quality of planning cannot consistently rise above the quality of the information on which it is based, it is essential to see that adequate information is maintained in focus at the times and places where plans are formulated, reviewed, and authorized.

d. Motivation. The most important single factor governing the success of a planning programme (particularly with participative management) is the degree to which you gain the acceptance and support of the key people involved or affected. To accomplish this, it is not only necessary to create an environment and provide a process responsive to requirements, but to provide adequate training and technical assistance so that managers can plan more effectively, with less time, effort and paperwork.

Suggested Reading

ACKOFF, R. L. *A Concept of Corporate Planning*, Wiley, New York, 1970.
ANSOFF, H. I. *Corporate Strategy*, McGraw-Hill, New York, 1965.
BUNGE, W. R. *Managerial Budgeting for Profit Improvement*, McGraw-Hill, New York, 1968.
BOWER, M. *The Will to Manage*, McGraw-Hill, New York, 1966.

CANNON, J. T. *Business Strategy and Policy*, Harcourt, Brace, New York, 1968.
DRUCKER, P. F. *The Practice of Management*, Harper and Row, New York, 1954.
DRUCKER, P. F. *Managing for Results*, Harper and Row, New York, 1964.
DRUCKER, P. F. *The Effective Executive*, Harper and Row, New York, 1966.
DRUCKER, P. F. *Age of Discontinuity*, Harper and Row, New York, 1969.
EWING, D. W. *The Practice of Planning*, Harper and Row, New York, 1968.
EWING, D. W. *The Human Side of Planning*, Macmillan, New York, 1969.
FOMULARO, J. H. *Organization Planning Manual*, American Management Association, New York, 1971.
GREEN, E. J. *Workbook for Corporate Planning*, American Management Association, New York, 1970.
Harvard Business Review, Planning Reprints, I–III, 1970–72.
JUDSON, A. S. *A Manager's Guide to Making Changes*, Wiley, New York, 1966.
KAHN, H. and BRUCE-BRIGGS, B. *Things to Come*, Briggs, Macmillan, New York, 1972.
KEPNER, C. H. and TREGOE, B. B. *The Rational Manager*, McGraw-Hill, New York, 1965.
KOONTZ, H. and O'DONNELL, C. *The Principles of Management*, McGraw-Hill, New York, 1968.
MCCONKEY, D. D. *Planning Next Year's Profits*, American Management Association, New York, 1972.
MCGREGOR, D. *The Human Side of Enterprise*, McGraw-Hill, New York, 1960.
NEWMAN, W. and SUMMER, C. *The Process of Management*, Prentice-Hall, Englewood Cliffs, New Jersey, 1961.
STEINER, G. *Top Management Planning*, Macmillan, Toronto, 1969.
TOFFLER, A. *Future Shock*, Random House, New York, 1970.
WARREN, E. K. *Long-Range Planning*, Prentice-Hall, Englewood Cliffs, New Jersey, 1966.

24. Life Goals Planning for managers

Donald H. Swartz

Life Goals Planning can increase individual and organizational effectiveness. It is essential for a manager, the leader of others, to be self-motivated. Self-motivation derives from knowing and caring for oneself; taking charge of one's own life; planning for personal and professional growth; and, ultimately, finding that satisfying point where personal needs and organization requirements are being met simultaneously. This chapter answers six questions:

What is Life Goals Planning?
What is its origin and evolution?
Why is it important for managers to experience Life Goals Planning?
What are some specific results for managers?
What does the process design look like?
What has been learnt from application experience to date?

What is Life Goals Planning?

Life Goals Planning is a practical process that enables a person to identify and visualize his wants and needs, and to develop flexible plans to achieve them within the reality of changing organizational requirements and conditions. The process blends interpersonal and intragroup learning methods from the behavioural sciences with dynamic planning methods from the management sciences. Each participant can achieve the following:

(a) develop practical plans to achieve priority behaviour change and material goals in career, social, family, and personal life settings;
(b) learn and be able to apply a Life Goals Planning process when desired—for self, for others, with others;
(c) learn how to utilize more effectively the resources of self and others in achieving life goals;
(d) learn and practise effective communication skills—particularly as they apply to improving relationship with others.

How did Life Goals Planning Emerge?

Life Goals Planning was introduced to the training and education profession in the summer of 1969 by Herbert Shephard of Yale University, in a programme for specialists in organizational training and development (sponsored by the NTL Institute for Applied Behavioural Science), at Bethel, Maine, and at Vail, Colorado. I participated with the Vail group, and there met Weldon Moffitt of Brigham Young University, and Barbara Fisher, a post-graduate student and community relations consultant, both of whom had done some life planning work with volunteer groups and added some valuable dimensions to Shephard's experiences.

In November 1969, a 'Couples' Life Planning weekend laboratory was organized, based on the combined experiences of Shephard, Moffitt, and Fisher. The prime objective was to structure the lab sufficiently for participants to emerge with practical, written plans. This first volunteer group was successful. Businessmen and housewives, alike, understood the process and worked together to produce actual plans. This experience encouraged me to try Life Goals Planning with managers in a business organization.

In early 1970, Bill Owen (then director of management and organization development for the Weyerhaeuser Company) collaborated with me to develop a strategy for introducing Life Goals Planning to managers. We chose the Weyerhaeuser Management School as the entry point and tried our semistructured design with one class in April 1970; we then asked Dr Shephard to apply his less structured approach with another class in May 1970. The detailed feedback collected from each group led us to use the semistructured design in future schools.

Since April 1970, Bill Owen and I have conducted seventeen Life Goals Planning sessions for 340 people. Twelve of these sessions were conducted for 'captive' groups of managers, as part of the Weyerhaeuser Management School. The other sessions were conducted for volunteer, fee-paying groups representing a variety of organizations and interests.

Why Life Goals Planning for Managers?

I have encountered both scepticism and resistance to Life Goals Planning from individual managers and from the organization power structure. The individual says 'What I do with my life is my business.' The organization wants to know: 'What relevance is there to achieving business goals? What's the advantage?'

Both these resistances are based on the archaic assumption that personal life and organization life are two different things. At one time, this assumption and the resulting organization behaviour towards individuals was valid and successful. It is not valid in today's changing organizational climate.

Fortunately, there have been enough individuals and organization power-structure supporters to sponsor attempts at Life Goals Planning. These supporters subscribe to modern assumptions about the organizational–individual relationship. The rationale behind this new position is well stated by Harry Levinson, visiting professor, Harvard Business School, and president of the Levinson Institute.[1]

> If a man's most powerful driving force is comprised of his needs, wishes, and personal aspirations, combined with the compelling wish to look good in his own eyes for meeting those deeply held personal goals, then Management by Objectives should begin with *his* objectives. What does he want to do with his life? Where does he want to go? What will make him feel good about himself? What does he want to be able to look back on when he has expended his unrecoverable years?
>
> At this point, some may say that those are his business. The organization has other business, and it must assume that the man is interested in working in the organization's business rather than his own. That kind of differentiation is impossible. Everyone is always working towards meeting his psychological needs. Anyone who thinks otherwise, and who believes such powerful internal forces can be successfully disregarded or bought off for long, is deluding himself.

The Mutual Task

> The organizational task becomes one of first understanding the man's needs, and then, with him, assessing how well they can be met in this organization, doing what the organization needs to have done. Thus the highest point of self-motivation arises when there is a complementary conjunction of the man's needs and the organization's requirements. The requirements of both mesh, interrelate, and become synergistic. The energies of man and organization are pooled for mutual advantage.

What's in it for the Individual?

The following is a summary of what individual managers say they have derived from participating in a Life Goals Planning session:

> Identified and made visible my strengths, likes, desires, weaknesses.
> Learnt how I come across to others, and what behaviour changes I can make to strengthen my relationships with others—at work and at home.
> Learnt the importance of integrating organization and personal life—in order to strengthen both.
> Learnt that I have the responsibility, power, and ability to initiate career and personal growth actions. Don't have to wait for the organization to 'select' me.
> Learnt that business planning principles can be applied to my life goals just as effectively as they are applied to organization goals.
> Identified and learnt how to utilize many untapped resources to achieve my career and personal goals.
> Improved relationships within my family.
> Helped me improve my effectiveness as a consultant to my subordinates.
> Impressed on me the value of dealing with the 'whole person' in order to manage my work group effectively.
> Helped me identify and decide what I really want to do with my life.
> Gave me a needed discipline to develop dynamic plans to achieve my important goals.

What's in it for the Organization?

If a business organization invests time and money to sponsor Life Goals Planning for its people, it wants to know what the return on its investment will be. It is difficult to place such a value on training and education. Later, I shall present a realistic, though not totally satisfactory, response to the question. At this point, I shall generalize by quoting from a paper written by Gordon Lippitt in 1970:[2]

> There are several reasons why a company, agency, or organization should assume such a responsibility for its employees:
>
> 1. To demonstrate the larger *social responsibility* of a mature organization.
> 2. To indicate to adult employees that the organization *cares* about them as individuals.
> 3. To more effectively *release the potential* of the individual on behalf of the organization.
> 4. To help the individual prepare for *change* in society, the organization, and himself.
> 5. To strengthen the *psychological contract* between the individual and the organization.
> 6. To *plan* more effectively the *learning experiences* the individual will require to achieve his life goals. [My note: the basis for a meaningful manpower development plan.]
>
> and I can add, from my own experience:
>
> 7. To obtain data about the *real career desires* of employees in order to maximize the results of manpower and organization planning efforts.
> 8. To *reduce* the incidence of the '*Peter Principle*' by giving employees the opportunity and freedom to continually assess and change (if desired) their career goals.
> 9. To *reduce* the number of *losses of 'good employees'* who feel 'stuck in dead-ended jobs with little challenge or opportunity for growth'.

Where has it Been Used in Organizations, and what are the Results?

This section moves from theory and generalization to specifics about the application and results of Life Goals Planning in a business organization setting.

The Weyerhaeuser Company Case

Weyerhaeuser Company is an international forest products organization with its headquarters in Tacoma, Washington, USA. The company has an illustrious history of effectively managing its vast renewable timber resources. In the past ten years it has learnt to manage its powerful financial resources to achieve an even greater profit for its shareholders.

During the last seven years there has been an increasing emphasis on more effective use of the company's human resources. This emphasis was heralded in the mid-sixties by the establishment of Weyerhaeuser's Management School. Each WMS class is comprised of 20–22 managers, carefully selected from a wide variety of the company's businesses and locations. Since 1966, 31 classes of Weyerhaeuser middle and upper managers, numbering 620, have graduated from the school. Nearly 90 per cent of the company's key managerial posts are occupied by WMS graduates.

Weyerhaeuser Management School—General Design

Currently, WMS is conducted in-house in four one-week sessions per class. Although class agendas vary slightly, a typical design is as follows:

Week 1   The Individual and the Work Group

Day 1	Building a learning team	Internal consultant
Day 2	Motivation in self and others	External consultant
Day 3	Life Goals Planning	Internal consultant
Days 4–5	Releasing human potential for creative action	External consultant

One month back on the job

Week 2   The Organization and its Systems

Days 1–2	Weyerhaeuser strategic and tactical planning	Internal resources
Day 3	Organization concepts and the Weyerhaeuser organization	External consultant and internal resources
Days 4–5	Planning for, and managing, management time	External consultant

One month back on the job

Week 3   Leadership Skills

Days 1–5	Group leadership techniques to: build effective teams; utilize group resources; problem solve; develop alternative solutions for decision making; provide growth opportunity for subordinates;	Internal consultants

Six months back on the job.

Week 4   Action Reporting and Clean-Up

Days 1–2	Participant reports to top management on projects undertaken to apply learnings from WMS	Internal resources
Days 3–5	Designed by participants to cover priority issues and subject matter	Internal or external resources

Life Goals Planning and Weyerhaeuser Management School

When Life Goals Planning was introduced in WMS, in April 1970, the school design was somewhat different. What is now week 1 was then the third week in the sequence. In addition, no team building was done because class members had already worked together for two previous one-week sessions. The present WMS design was incorporated in 1972. Thus, to date, nine classes have experienced Life Goals Planning in their third week, and three classes have been exposed to it in the third day of week 1. This earlier exposure required a day of trust building ('Building a learning team') in order to enhance the value of Life Goals Planning.

Based on the feedback from all twelve classes, there is no significant difference in results as related to the placement of Life Goals Planning in the agenda. The essential element for the success of a Life Goals Planning group session is a better than average, and growing, trust level in the group. This climate of trust and openness can be developed through normal classroom methodology and small-group tasks (as with the first nine classes), or through a concentrated set of task and process exercises (as used in day 1 for the last three classes).

Participant Survey

In December 1972, I surveyed 238 managers who had participated in Life Goals Planning in WMS since April 1970 (see Appendix 24.1). I wanted to learn:

(a) to what extent participants thought that Life Goals Planning was *potentially* useful in their business career.

   (This question was important because participants in the 1972 classes have not had sufficient time to see the results of their planning as it relates to business.)

(b) to what extent participants found Life Goals Planning useful to them in achieving success in their business careers;

(c) how many participants would report actual examples of how Life Goals Planning had been useful to them in their business careers;

(d) to what extent participants thought that Life Goals Planning was potentially useful in achieving goals and harmony in their personal/family/social life;

(e) to what extent participants thought that Life Goals Planning *had* been useful to them in achieving goals and harmony in their personal/family/social life. (Even though we emphasize the interdependence of personal and business life, I wanted to learn if participants applied Life Goals Planning at home, even if not specifically at work.)

(f) how many participants would report examples of how Life Goals Planning had been useful to them in achieving goals and harmony in their personal/family/social life.

Survey Results

Number of graduates surveyed	238
Number of graduates responding	87
Number of respondents giving examples of actual use of Life Goals Planning in business setting	62
Number of respondent giving examples of actual use of Life Goals Planning in personal/social/family life setting	63

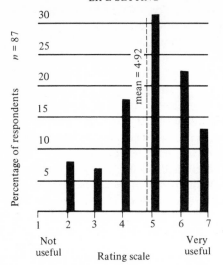

POTENTIAL VALUE TO BUSINESS
LIFE SETTING

To what extent is Life Goals Planning
potentially useful in achieving success
in your business career?

**Fig. 24.1. Potential value to business life
setting.**

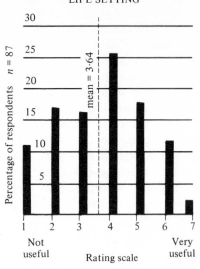

ACTUAL VALUE TO BUSINESS
LIFE SETTING

To what extent has Life Goals Planning
actually been useful in achieving success
in your business career?

**Fig. 24.2. Actual value of business life
setting.**

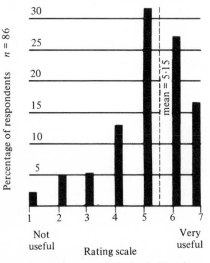

POTENTIAL VALUE TO PERSONAL
/SOCIAL/FAMILY LIFE SETTING

To what extent is Life Goals Planning
potentially useful in achieving goals and
harmony in your personal/family/
social life?

**Fig. 24.3. Potential value to personal/
social/family life setting.**

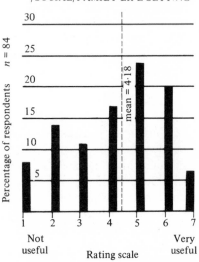

ACTUAL VALUE TO PERSONAL
/SOCIAL/FAMILY LIFE SETTING

To what extent has Life Goals Planning
actually been useful to you in achieving
goals and harmony in your personal/
family/social life?

**Fig. 24.4. Actual value to personal/social/
family life setting.**

348

Figures 24.1 to 24.4 plot the responses to four rating-scale questions. I find the following of significance in the survey results.

The respondents see the potential value of Life Goals Planning for the business setting (mean = 4.92), and for the personal/social/family setting (mean = 5.15), as being nearly equal. This substantiates the underlying assumption that business and personal life are not separable in today's business environment.

The actual usefulness of Life Goals Planning is higher for the personal/social/family life setting (mean = 4.18) than for the business setting (mean = 3.64). This indicates that managers find the process easier to apply at home than at work; that beneficial results are more quickly evident at home; and that many are eager to share the process with their families and close friends—important resource people.

Much of the verbatim feedback regarding the actual use of the process as related to achieving career goals indicated that the participant had not yet seen results and, thus, had to rate the process low. As the rating data indicates, however, many of these managers see a high potential value for Life Goals Planning in the business setting.

Some 72 per cent of the respondents gave at least one specific example of the usefulness of Life Goals Planning in their business career setting; 71 per cent shared specific examples related to their personal/social/family life setting. These percentages correlate with the percentage of respondents rating 3 or more in Fig. 24.2 (72 per cent), and Fig. 24.4 (78 per cent). I therefore conclude that a rating of 3, or higher, indicates 'some' benefit realized from the Life Goals Planning experience.

Assumptions about non-respondents' (151) rating responses	Percentage of all (238) participants who found some actual usefulness for Life Goals Planning	
	In business-career setting	In personal/social/family setting
Assumption A All 151 rated the actual value of the process as 1 or 2	26	27
Assumption B The responses of the 151 are distributed evenly from 1 to 7	71	72
Assumption C The responses of the 151 are distributed in the same percentage as among the 87 respondents	72	78

Fig. 24.5. Extrapolation of Life Goals Planning survey data.

With a rating of 3, or higher, indicating at least 'some' benefit from the process, I was able to extrapolate the data to the entire 238 manager population. Based on three assumptions about the 151 managers who did not respond to the survey, Fig. 24.5 indicates this extrapolation.

I believe, that, from this extrapolation, it would be safe to assume that at least 30 per cent of any 'captive' group will find some useful benefit from Life Goals Planning in their business and personal settings.

Life Goals Planning—What Does the Design Look Like?

It is not my intention to present a complete, detailed design here. Semi-structured processes allow for many alternative design options. I shall therefore present only the key elements and rationale for each. Leader certification training and leader's guides are available commercially[3] for those who are interested in learning how to conduct Life Goals Planning sessions.

So far as the *time frame* is concerned, Life Goals Planning can be conducted in as little as a one-day and one-evening session for groups who have already developed a strong trust relationship. For new groups, the recommended time is 2 to $2\frac{1}{2}$ days, including evening sessions.

The following elements should be included in the *design*:

(a) ice breaking—building trust within the group;
(b) rationale—an introduction to the Life Goals Planning process;
(c) implementation—putting the process to work;
(d) evaluation—session evaluation and critique.

I shall now discuss the purpose and general content of each element.

Ice Breaking
This element is used with newly formed groups. The purpose is solely to build intragroup trust in preparation for the Life Goals Planning process work. This design element includes these subparts:
(a) recognition of the 'foreigner phenomenon':
    the leader and the group are 'foreigners';
    individuals in the group are 'foreigners';
    subgroups within the group are 'foreigners';
(b) because we are 'foreigners', we tend to have little trust in each other. Discussion of behaviour relationships: 'sceptical' to 'quizzical' to 'confidence' to 'trust';
(c) actions to offset the 'foreigner phenomenon':
    leader asks group for their concerns or questions about Life Goals Planning, in order to get data about group. He shares *his* concerns. *Purpose:* to increase data flow between leader and group, and increase trust;
    leader asks individuals to complete a self-analysis form, 'Analysis of behaviour in groups'. Triads are then formed, and individuals take turns sharing one behaviour in groups they would most like to improve. Triads then share their general feelings with total group. *Purpose:* to share data with each other, to build trust among individuals and subgroups;

(d) building skills in interpersonal communication:
study and discussion of the helping relationship;
study and discussion of ways to give and receive effective perceptive feedback. *Purpose:* to give participants some basic skills that will encourage and support attempts at sharing and constructive openness.

Rationale

This element introduces the Life Goals Planning process with the specific purposes of:

(a) removing any mystery about the process steps; dealing with concerns; confronting antiquated assumptions;
(b) establishing mutual expectations (leader and participants);
(c) presenting a visual model of what will happen during the process;
(d) reviewing each process step.

The heart of this rationale element is the presentation of the Life Goals Planning model of Fig. 24.6. This model is built, step by step, through group

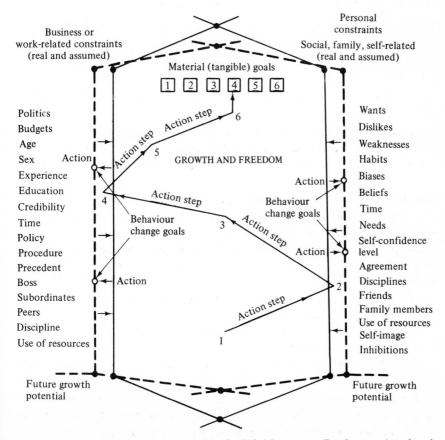

Fig. 24.6. Life Goals Planning process model. (© 1972, Management Development Associates.)

351

participation. When it is completed, several strong messages will have been transmitted:

(a) behaviour change actions in one's personal life can have an effect on one's business life, and vice versa. The net result of behaviour change action is an increased area for growth and freedom, within which we can pursue material goals more effectively.
(b) the process can help each individual determine:
> his real constraints—business related and social/family/self-related;
> how do these constraints hinder material goal achievement;
> the possible consequences when real constraints are violated;
> what real constraints should be reduced, removed or modified;
> what specific behaviour change actions will reduce, remove, or modify targeted constraints;
> what specific actions must be taken to achieve priority material goals —business or social/family/self-related.

Implementation

The implementation element includes four subparts:

(a) mind stimulation;
(b) inventory;
(c) analysis;
(d) action steps.

Mind Stimulation.   This subpart consists of a series of individual and group exercises designed to:

> stimulate greater freedom of thought and creative action;
> aid learning to use others as resources through group interaction;
> help individuals visualize the future as if it were real. To relearn the art of dreaming.

The number and type of exercises used varies depending on group size, trust level, and membership background. A typical starter exercise used with all our groups is described below.

The group is seated in a semicircle, or around a U-shaped table. Individuals are instructed to 'Close your eyes (when I signal) and picture yourself five or ten years from now':

> picture places around you—home, office, geography;
> picture the people around you;
> visualize these places and people in motion pictures;
> try to see them in colour;
> experience your feelings about what you can see—comfort, happiness, surprise.

At the end of three minutes, group members are asked to share their excursion into the future. Our experience has been that more than 95 per cent will share with the total group. The visions are accepted as presented. No analysis is permitted by leader or group members.

All exercises used are relevant to the group members. There is no good reason for games playing or simulation.

Inventory. This is the data-gathering part of the process. Its purpose is to help each participant develop a data base about himself in the general areas of:

(a) successes;
(b) capabilities;
(c) desires;
(d) goals;
(e) personal constraints;
(f) resources and their uses.

Working in foursomes, participants answer a series of eight questions. Each question is presented by the leader, after which the foursomes follow a procedure similar to the following:

the leader presents a question and gives personal examples to explain it;
foursomes discuss question for clarity, understanding;
each individual *writes* his responses to the question (5 minutes);
individuals share responses within the foursomes (15 minutes). (This stimulates more written responses for each individual—increases trust level.)

Specific questions are worded around these topical headings:

(a) peak experiences—past;
(b) things I do well;
(c) things I should improve;
(d) peak experiences—desired;
(e) material goals—first step;
(f) things I'd like to stop doing;
(g) things I'd like to start doing;
(h) resources—underutilized or underdeveloped.

At the end of this inventory phase, each participant has eight written segments of data about himself. He is now ready to do some analysis work—with the help of others.

Analysis. This is the most crucial step in the Life Goals Planning process. The first purpose is to review the inventory data and look for clues, trends, and recurring themes that seem to be pointing out a current direction for one's life. These clues, trends, and themes are written by each individual, with the help of one or more partners. Once written, they become a set of criteria that can be used to rank the goals in order of priority.

The second purpose is to list goals suggested by the data. The goals are of two general types:

(a) specific changes in behaviour that will increase the individual's freedom for action and growth;

Name _____

Plan date _____

Specific goal statement	Specific action steps to achieve goal	resources I will use	Persons or groups affected by this action step	Person(s) or group who will do this action step	Action step schedule			At what investment
					Started (date range)	Finished (date range)	Progress checkpoints date(s)	
							Time	$

Fig. 24.7. Life Goals Planning form. (© 1972, Management Development Associates.)

(b) specific material (tangible) goals that the individual wants to achieve—short- or long-term.

These goals are written in rough form. This work is usually done without the help of others.

The third purpose is to 'priorize' the goal list. Each individual compares his goals with his criteria list (purpose one), and makes these decisions about each goal:

Is it a must or a want?
If it's a want, where is it on a scale of 1 to 10? (1 being low, 10 high)
Is it a short-term or a long-term goal?

The leader provides guidelines and consulting help during this phase of the process.

Action Steps. Participants enter this phase with goals 'priorized'. The purpose of this phase is to help each participant prepare an action plan for at least one high-priority behaviour change goal, and at least one high-priority material goal. As aids to accomplishing this, the participants are provided with:

(a) guidelines for writing specific goals;
(b) Life Goals Planning form (see Fig. 24.7).

Evaluation

This is an important step both for the leader and group members. The leader gets immediate feedback regarding programme content, relevance, and his performance. (Our participant feedback form is reproduced in Fig. 24.8). Group members have an opportunity to reflect individually; share in threes, and finally, discuss in the total group their feelings about the Life Goals Planning experience.

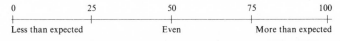

PARTICIPANT FEEDBACK

Let's give some feedback about the programme so that:

(a) it can be strengthened;
(b) it can be appreciated;
(c) we, and others, can learn from it.

1. What parts of the programme were most meaningul/helpful to you? Why were they helpful?

2. What parts of the programme should have had more motion, or be strengthened? (Can you say why?)

3. If the programme were to be shortened, what parts could be taken out?

4. As you see it, what could be added to the programme in the way of better presentation or more information?

5. As related to your expectations, check what you think that the programme achieved.

0	25	50	75	100
Less than expected		Even		More than expected

Fig. 24.8. Participant feedback.

What Has Been Learnt From Past Experience?

The present design for Life Goals Planning is the product of a failure–analysis–revision–risk process which never ends. To conclude this chapter, I shall list some important recommendations which have helped to change the process, in the past, and which will, I am sure, guide us in developing future designs.

(a) Maintain a balance between structure and free-flow. Avoid imposing forms on participants. Suggest their use, but allow participants to develop their own system.

(b) If possible, opt for voluntary participation in group sessions. The percentage return on the investment will be higher than for 'captive' groups.

(c) The results from groups that 'live-in' and concentrate on the process for $1\frac{1}{2}$ to $2\frac{1}{2}$ days is better than from groups who go through the process piecemeal.

(d) Where possible, spouses or close personal friends should participate in the process together. Our experience with 'couples' groups indicate a very high immediate return for participating couples. Where these groups comprised people who work together in an organization, the return transfers to more effective work relationships.

(e) Allow ample relaxation-integration time periods during the process. Life Goals Planning is tiring for participants. A good schedule includes a solid morning of work, several hours off for lunch; $2\frac{1}{2}$ hours' work before supper, several hours off for supper, two hours' work in the evening, and a similar schedule the next day, until adjournment at suppertime.

(f) The process is not effective if conducted mechanically by untrained leaders. The leader must develop personal belief and commitment to the process through personal involvement in, and use of Life Goals Planning. In addition, the leader must have the skills to develop group trust. Only then can the process be administered effectively.

Conclusion

Life Goals Planning is a successful training intervention—'successful' as defined by participants. It is of value to a significant percentage of participants in both their personal and business settings. I am convinced that Life Goals Planning offers a high return on investment for individual participants and for the sponsoring organization.

Appendix 24.1. Confidential Survey of WMS Graduates Regarding Career and Personal-growth Planning

Circle one of the whole numbers on each of the following scales.

1. In your opinion, to what extent is career and personal growth planning (Life Goals Planning) potentially useful in:

(a) Achieving success in your business career?

| Not useful | 1 | 2 | 3 | 4 | 5 | 6 | 7 | Very useful |

(b) Achieving goals and harmony in your personal/family/social life?

| Not useful | 1 | 2 | 3 | 4 | 5 | 6 | 7 | Very useful |

2. To what extent has Life Goals Planning actually been useful to you in achieving success in your *business career*?

(a)

| Not useful | 1 | 2 | 3 | 4 | 5 | 6 | 7. | Very useful |

(b) Please give one concrete example of how Life Goals Planning helped you achieve increased success in your business career. (A significant behaviour change, a tangible plan to achieve a goal, etc.)

3. To what extent has Life Goals Planning actually been useful to you in achieving goals and harmony in your personal/family/social life?

(a)

| Not useful | 1 | 2 | 3 | 4 | 5 | 6 | 7 | Very useful |

(b) Please give one concrete example of how Life Goals Planning helped you achieve specific personal goals in relation to your personal/family/social life. (A significant behaviour change, a tangible plan to achieve a goal, etc.)

4. Participant data
(a) Participated in Life Goals Planning.

yes   no

(b) Participated as a member of WMS Class
(c) Name (optional)
(d) You have my 'OK' to quote the example(s) I've given in this survey, providing you in no way identify me.

yes   no

References

1. LEVINSON, H. 'Management by Whose Objectives', *Harvard Business Review*, July–August 1970. (Reproduced by permission.)
2. LIPPITT, G. L. 'Developing Life Plans', *Training and Development Journal*, American Society for Training and Development, May 1970. (Reproduced by special permission.)
3. For more detailed information about Life Goals Planning (Career and Personal Growth Planning) Leader Training:
   Effectiveness Resource Group Inc.
   6709 Topaz Drive SW
   Tacoma, Washington 98498 USA

Suggested Reading

'What do You Want Out of Life?', *The Royal Bank of Canada Monthly Letter*, **52,** 12, Montreal, Canada, December 1971.
REPUCCI, L. C. 'What is Creativity', *The Creativity Review*, **XIII,** 4, November 1971, pp. 11–22. Creativity Publications, Inc., P.O. Box 306, Midland, Michigan, 48640, USA.
SWARTZ, D. H. 'Everyone Wants to Succeed—AT WHAT HE WANTS TO DO', September 1969 Editorial Contribution.
JENNINGS, E. E. 'Two Worlds of the Executive', *TWA Ambassador*, **4,** 3, March 1971. TWA Ambassador, 1999 Shepard Road, St. Paul, Minnesota, 55116, USA.

25. Training managers in industrial relations negotiations

Arthur Marsh

In the way that industrial relations are conducted in Britain, line managers are likely to become involved in negotiation. This chapter argues that negotiating skills can be developed by practical training, and companies ought to develop appropriate documentation for this purpose—including exercises in which managers can act out negotiating roles.

Training: Why and for Whom?

Negotiation is the process whereby terms and conditions of work are resolved between employers, on the one hand and trade unions on the other. Officials of trade unions and employers' associations and professional industrial relations staff involved in negotiation are clearly using an expertise for which, by experience or otherwise, they have been trained. This chapter is concerned with managers who are not full-time 'professional' negotiators in this sense. Why should they be trained in negotiation? Ought they all to receive training, or should this be reserved for the chosen few?

This depends what you mean by 'negotiation'; it also depends on the attitude of companies on the involvement of line managers in the negotiating process. These two points are related: if 'negotiation' is narrowly and formally defined, companies may not think it appropriate that a wide band of management should be trained in negotiation; if the term is broadly and informally defined, the opposite tends to be true.

The argument runs like this. Those companies which define negotiation narrowly tend to see it as a job for experts. The experts make agreements with trade union officials at industry or plant level, and this is all too delicate to be tampered with by managers. When agreements are made, their application in the works may be assigned to other experts, such as personnel or industrial relations officers, or the situation may have been so well contrived that no such follow-up is necessary. In either event, the line manager need not be concerned and can be left free to pursue the usual processes of human relations or man management.

By contrast, other companies take a different view. Formal agreements between experts seem to them to have little relevance to the situation in question. National or industry wide agreements form only frameworks, or constitute only points of reference, for what goes on in their plants, and they see no reason to make formal company or plant agreements or, indeed, to make much use of negotiating specialists. Works managers are expected to carry on their own negotiations with trade union officials and shop stewards, and managers at lower levels to do their turn as the occasion arises. Everybody is expected to negotiate, sometimes with professional advice, but often without it. Do-it-yourself kits are the order of the day.

Undoubtedly, the latter situation is the most common in Britain, though, under pressure from governments for industrial relations reform, formality in handling industrial relations is increasing. And where the do-it-yourself kit prevails, training is obviously a sensible development. It is true that managers can discover by practice how to negotiate; it is also true that the lead time on this discovery can be shortened by training. But should one attempt to train in companies where a professionalized formality is the rule? I believe that the answer is at least a modified 'yes', and for several reasons. First, I do not think that there are *any* situations from which negotiation in some significant sense is wholly absent; second, I do not believe that any collection of formal agreements will eliminate negotiation at lower levels; third, it is my experience that, however formal a view companies have of negotiation, they will sooner or later wish their line managers to be involved. The thoughts and experience behind these views are too complex to be elaborated here, but the upshot is clear. There are few companies in which some training in negotiation would be a disadvantage, many in which it would be an advantage, and many in which it would seem to be essential.

What Kind of Training?

'Negotiators', they say, 'are born, not made'. The same is said of many activities which depend, in the last resort, on personal aptitudes and qualities possessed by some individuals but not by others. Individuals certainly exist who have so little aptitude for negotiation that training is useless, but this is rare. Most people have some aptitude, and this flourishes with attention to negotiating skills. Nor does it seem to matter much if people are 'overtrained', i.e., if they are taught to apply higher standards or more formal routines than they will ever be expected to apply. It is better, of course, if managers can be taught within the framework of company policy; but, of this, more later.

What are the 'negotiating skills' which need to be taught? In broad terms, there are three: those of preparing material for negotiating purposes, those of conducting, or taking part in, meetings for negotiating purposes, and those of developing a sense of negotiating strategy and tactics. The final skill is the most difficult and sets the ultimate constraint on the first two. Instruction on the preparation of material can be done in the classroom; advice on the handling of meetings begins to demand not only precept, but practice. It is, however, the need to inculcate in negotiators a strategic and tactical view of situations which demands that those being trained shall actually be given the *opportunity to negotiate*. This demands role playing. It is impossible to get far in training in negotiation without something to replace the experience through which most existing negotiators have developed their negotiating skills. Surrogate experience is no substitute for the real thing. Good negotiators cannot be made by training; that takes time. Those with no experience can be given a start, and those with some experience can be improved. How much more could one reasonably expect?

Preparing Material for Negotiation

It is astonishing how often managers are poorly prepared for negotiating. The great set pieces at company level—like those at Ford and Massey-Ferguson—are, almost by definition, immaculately prepared. The same is true in those companies which have developed plant-based productivity bargains, or developments from such bargains. But, in most companies, negotiation is relatively discontinuous; matters are dealt with as they arise, and the information available—incident by incident—is difficult to collect quickly; sometimes it is not available. Management may well be caught out by apparently knowing less than their shop stewards. This is seldom fatal but always embarrassing.

It matters little, in principle, whether the issue for negotiation is a minor matter raised from the shopfloor, or a major issue relating to a plant as a whole. It is essential to collect all the relevant information: what agreements, if any, apply; what is being asked for, or what has happened; the circumstances; the facts; the difficulties of taking this course or that; what workers are being paid; how much a concession would cost; how far it would affect other parts of the plant. A magpie mind and a research worker's curiosity are a great help. So is a sense of relevance, which can only be developed by practice. The object of training is to see that no manager goes into negotiation, however small, unprepared.

Conduct of Meetings

Standards of conduct for management meetings are often poor. Rules for procedure can be derived from Lord Citrine's *ABC of Chairmanship*. Some are helpful in negotiation, and some are not. Negotiation does not demand meeting procedure in the ordinary sense, though a knowledge of this is helpful. As in any committee, the object is to come to a conclusion, an agreed conclusion, but in negotiation there are two sides. A number of things therefore become important. How many representatives on each side? How do they sit in relation to each other? Who does the talking?

These may be technical points, but they are of the utmost importance. It is wise to insist that, on the management side (and the same applies to the union), only one spokesman is used, or, if the argument is to be passed round, others do not intervene without the main spokesman's permission. Procedural devices, such as adjournments, can be used, if sparingly. The atmosphere has to be right; excessive formality is generally to be avoided if progress is to be made. But negotiating meetings must be kept under control. If they are not, issues will never be clarified and solutions will fail to emerge. There is a good deal that most managers can be taught about the techniques of getting the best out of the meeting situation.

Negotiating Strategy and Tactics

Strategy in negotiation constitutes an advance view of what management would like to achieve in a negotiating situation; tactics are the means of reaching the given objective with such compromise as may prove necessary or expedient. The former emerges from case preparation; the latter develops from practical negotiation. Strategy can be short- or long-term. Is the object simply to keep workers from striking on an issue about which they feel strongly, or is the aim to develop the negotiation as part of a longer-run policy on wage or salary structure? How much compromise would the management be willing to accept? How much room for manoeuvre does there seem to be on the union side? These things can be thought out in advance—but only up to a point. During negotiation, new information may emerge, new slants on the union attitude may be revealed. It is here that tactics become important. Is it a good idea to ask for an adjournment so that management or union can think out their position afresh? Is it a good idea to make a new proposal to change the course of a negotiation, or is it better to stick to one's guns? At what point ought one to agree or fail to agree? Would it be useful to suggest conciliation or arbitration by a third party?

All these are questions which ought constantly to be in the minds of negotiators. With experience, the negotiator becomes like a skilled driver: he makes his choice of gear, the corrections to his route, and copes with traffic almost automatically; crisis points occur and are circumvented without undue fuss, and a destination is reached, perhaps not entirely satisfactory to the passengers, but involving a situation with which they can live until the next time. Negotiation is not debate in which verbal cleverness and persuasion produce a majority in favour; nor is it a war to be won. The object is to settle issues with the least possible disturbance. There is no gallantry, only a systematic erosion of problems and a bridging of gaps until agreement is reached.

Setting about Training

Managements unfamiliar with the techniques of negotiating training should consult someone who is. Such people are often to be found in universities and among adult educationists, in national institutions concerned with training, in local polytechnics or technical colleges, and more rarely, among consultants. Avoid the package. Be frank about your problems, and let your adviser have material to devise training sessions suited to your needs.

In practice, this will involve discussing the objectives of your course, your agreements and procedures, your industrial relations policies, whether these are explicit or implicit, and giving some idea of your future intentions. It will involve specifying your objects in starting the training, the managers it is intended for, and its part in your training programme generally. If you have your own specialist, encourage him to ask the same questions, and give him the same answers.

Negotiating training requires adequate documentation—not too little, and not too much. In discussing preparation and initial strategies, checklists are useful. Figure 25.1 shows a list adapted from one in use at Oxford University's Department for External Studies.

Aims	Analysis	Tactics
What would the company ideally like to achieve? What might it realistically hope for in practice? What must we have, or 'fail to agree'? (It could be that *nothing* vital is at stake.)	The facts of the incident (or claim, etc.) Relevant rules, agreements, or 'custom and practice' (management policy?) Relevant precedents or comparisons Attitudes of unions and workers on the issue Significance of the issue for management (and the attitude of management)	Who is to speak, in what order and *on what subjects?* (Some signal system needed? Determination of who is to lead?) Anticipation of most likely of the other side's arguments; and counter to them Use of adjournment and other devices to avoid being put in false position. (Someone to be on watch for such need? Value of non-participant observer)

Fig. 25.1.

Most of all, however, negotiating exercises need a case, or cases, involving issues to be negotiated by groups representing management and union. Is this artificial? Some begin by thinking so but, by the time that a negotiation is completed, become so absorbed in the process that they continue to argue the pros and cons long after the session is over. Some hate role playing; the vast majority enjoy it. But participants must be properly briefed, and cases properly documented. It is better to adapt from events which have actually happened than to make them up from scratch. Participants like to feel that the situation which they are negotiating is a real one. Books of case studies can be a help, and several are available, but it is better to write your own, and to take these from your own files.

Experience shows that the subject of cases for role playing should be carefully picked. Initially, a case should not be too complicated; both sides should be given the same general notes about the case itself, its background, previous history, and any relevant agreements; each side should also be given the main points for its own side of the case. Two examples, the first relating to manual, and the second to non-manual workers,* are given in the appendix to this chapter.

Negotiating Exercises, their Uses and Limitations

With all the negotiating documents prepared, it remains to stage the exercise. Do not try to do it too quickly—each case is likely to take at least a half-day. First, there is the need to see that, with students divided into management and union teams, both have grasped the same basic information about the situation in which they are negotiating. The teams need then to be encouraged separately to nominate their spokesman, reminded of the main points of their case, and have some initial discussion on the tactics of presentation. Is the union side proposing to present all the case at one time, or is it wise to keep back some information? Is the management side proposing to adjourn as soon as the union has made its initial statement?

Experience shows that it is of enormous help if experienced negotiators, full-time employees of the company or the union, or employer association officials, can be persuaded to lead the teams on a demonstration run before the managers embark on role playing. Such a demonstration brings out the atmosphere in which negotiations are conducted, and the style required. Failing this, some companies have demonstration sessions available on video tape.

Negotiating sessions, proper, should not be allowed to continue too long, and should always be followed by appraisal. It is not necessarily wise to run a series of case studies, one after the other. Years of experience suggest that managers improve their appreciation of negotiating very rapidly for the first few cases, and that diminishing returns then set in—evidently because the novelty has worn off, and because most of them know, by that time, all that they think they need to know for their purpose. Sessions ought to be terse and well controlled. If they can be recorded on video tape, so much the better. Preparation, the conduct of the negotiation, and the strategies and tactics employed need to be discussed after each session. For managers to see and hear what they have done is most helpful. They seldom appear to find the camera inhibiting, and are frequently astonished at what they said and did.

Finally, training in negotiation makes better sense if the company has developed, or is developing, industrial relations policies, and if it has views on procedures, pay, and the handling of day to day problems which can also be fitted into case study work. All training should have an obvious purpose. It may even give management a cue to develop industrial relations policies if none exist already.

* I am indebted to the Oxford University Department for External Studies, and to Mr E. O. Evans, for the first example; to the National and Local Government Officers' Association, for the second.

Appendix 25.1.   Case Studies

The Modern Manufacturing Co. operates a factory which employs about 1500 hourly paid workers, of whom, some 275 are employed in the engineering department. The firm's operations make it necessary for a large range of components and materials to be stocked, and the stores have, at any given time stock valued at about £1 million, with more than 30 000 items and a stores staff of 23 people. Checking the stock is a matter of serious concern to the company, and an auditor (who reports to the accounts department) is employed full-time in stock-taking.

The company has a works agreement with the Associated Engineering Federation, and this agreement regulates wages and working conditions for all manual workers in the factory. The agreement also contains a section setting out the procedure to be followed in case of disputes which may arise between union members and the management.

The case concerns Mr Redford, who is employed as a machinist in the engineering department. He has been with the company for twelve years, and is a skilled worker. There have been no complaints about the quality of his work, and he has been an AUEW shop steward for several years.

Recently, Mr Redford was suspended by the management for two days, following an incident in which he refused to obey an instruction from his supervisor. The incident arose in connection with the procedure for the issue of materials from the factory stores. Since November 1965, the company has made it a rule that materials may only be issued from the stores on the presentation of a requisition card (known as form AW 234) signed by an authorized person, and bearing the signature and clock number of the person drawing the stores.

The company instruction setting out this procedure took the form of a circular to all department heads and supervisors, who were instructed to notify all workers. The procedure was confirmed in a circular issued two months later.

The Incident which Led to the Case

On 4 October last, Mr Redford took a requisition card to the stores to draw some mild-steel bar. After drawing the material, he was asked by the storeman on duty if he would add his clock number to the requisition, in addition to his signature. Mr Redford refused to do this saying: 'Redford is my name: I don't go by number.'

The storeman reported the matter to the supervisor, who approached Mr Redford and asked him to put his clock number on the requisition. Mr Redford again refused, on the grounds that he had a name and not a number. The supervisor (in the presence of the assistant supervisor) gave Mr Redford one minute in which to obey the instruction, and when he refused to comply, the supervisor sent him home, suspending him for the rest of the shift.

The following day, when Mr Redford came in to the shop, he was refused permission to start work and was sent, instead, to see the shop superintendent.

Mr Redford was asked why he had refused to obey the instruction of his supervisor the previous day, and he replied that the instruction from the company that clock numbers be added to requisition cards, as well as signatures, was one which was not generally followed, and that he, Redford, was being 'singled out'. He said that he would follow the rule when it was applied to everyone, and not before. The superintendent then suspended Mr. Redford for a further day.

This whole matter has been taken up by the union in accordance with the factory disputes procedure.

Terms of Reference

Claim by the AUEW that the action of the company in disciplining Mr Redford is unfair and unjustifiable, and that, this being the case, he be paid two days' wages in respect of the period for which he was suspended.

Points for the Management Case

(a) It is of great importance to the company's business that a proper check should be kept on the issue of items from the factory stores, and that, therefore, the rules laid down for the issue of such items are essential, and well within the area of management authority.

(b) Mr Redford was well acquainted with the proper procedure for completing stores requisitions.

(c) Mr Redford, in refusing to add his clock number to the requisition, was guilty of a breach of a known procedure and, in refusing to obey the instruction of his supervisor, was guilty of refusing to obey a perfectly proper instruction from management.

(d) There is no question of Mr Redford being 'singled out' or in any way victimized.

(e) The rule in question is generally complied with, and the company has no knowledge of any other case of an employee refusing to add his clock number to a stores requisition.

(f) This is not the first time that Mr Redford has acted in this way. Earlier this year, Mr Redford refused to add his clock number to a similar requisition. On that occasion, however, Mr Redford did obey the instruction of his supervisor when he was approached on the matter.

(g) In connection with the case, the company has reviewed the stores records for the shift in question, and these records show that, of 245 requisition cards dealt with, 197 carried both signature and clock numbers, 17 carried signatures and no clock numbers, and the remaining 31 carried neither signature nor clock number.

Points for the Union Case

(a) The union submits that Mr Redford was suspended not for breach of discipline but, in fact, because he was a shop steward.

(b) In support of the point stated above, it has been established that, during the same shift in respect of which Mr Redford was suspended, a number of stores requisition cards, apart from the one presented by Mr Redford, were found not to carry clock numbers; however, no action was taken by the company in respect of these other persons.

(c) The stores-issuing procedure is not properly and clearly laid down. No rules on this topic appear in the works rulebook, and no written statement of the procedure has ever been posted on shop notice boards. In addition, while the requisition cards carry a space for the signature of the person drawing stores, no space is provided for a clock number.

(d) Mr Redford has been with the company for twelve years. He is recognized as a highly skilled worker, and tribute has been paid to his skill and diligence.

(e) The union has been told by a 'friendly' office clerk that the management has carried out an analysis of the requisition cards for the relevant shift.

'THE REDUNDANT TEA BREAK'

The administrative headquarters of the Wandle Harbour Authority is a three-storey building which houses a staff of approximately 200; there is a staff canteen which has a 30 per cent subsidy, in the basement.

Traditionally, all the staff are allowed a fifteen-minute break in the morning and afternoon; coffee, tea, and a wide range of other light refreshments are on sale in the canteen, which is very popular, from 10.00–11.15 a.m. and from 3.00–4.15 p.m. each day.

Management have decided that they want to do away with the traditional tea break, and install vending machines on each floor. The personnel manager has invited the union representative to 'talk it over'.

Points for the Management Case

(a) Canteen has manageress, four kitchen staff, and two counter assistants. It is becoming increasingly difficult to keep these staff, or replace them when they leave. With vending machines, the canteen would be able to cope, at lunchtime, with only two kitchen staff and two part-time counter assistants; would need one person to help service machines.

(b) The 30 per cent subsidy at present costs the Authority approximately £5000 per annum. Vending machines should be self-supporting and the reduction in canteen staff should effect a saving of approximately £3000 per annum. This will enable the manageress to keep prices down to existing level. Otherwise, prices will have to go up substantially to meet rising costs.

(c) The fifteen-minute break is regularly abused, particularly by the junior staff.

(d) Vending machines are now very good and can supply modest, but reasonably interesting range of goods.

(e) Will give flexible service, i.e., staff will be able to get their beverage anytime, and not just between the set hours as at present.

(f) Tea breaks are old-fashioned, or unnecessary.

Points for the Union Case

(a) Social meeting of staff from different departments is very valuable to 'team spirit'.
(b) The canteen is frequently used to discuss interdepartmental business. Therefore not abused as much as may seem.
(c) The tea break is a valuable aid to relaxation; research shows that work rate declines if break is removed.
(d) There will be a reduction in facilities, i.e., a much smaller range of goods available from vending machines.
(e) Loss of the break will merely encourage unofficial tea clubs.
(f) Machines serve 'rotten' tea or coffee.
(g) Loss of the break is a removal of a privilege.
(h) It is an attempt to get thirty minutes' more work from everybody.

Suggested Reading

PE Consultants, *Managing Industrial Relations*, 1972.
POOLE, T. G. *The Industrial Relations Exercise*, BL Industrial Training Aids, Wokingham, Berkshire, 1970.
SHAW, M. *Role Playing—A Procedural Approach*, Cornell University, New York State School of Industrial Relations, 1967.

Part 4. Organization development

26. The contribution of behavioural sciences to organization development

Meyer Feldberg and John D. Simpson

This chapter illustrates the value of behavioural science research studies to the organization development specialist. It traces the evolution of certain behavioural science concepts in the areas of group dynamics, individual behaviour, conflict arousal and abatement, and learning theory, and shows how organizations' development specialists have been able to adapt these concepts into meaningful and useful techniques and systems. Organizational designs, training methods, Managerial Grid and laboratory training techniques are considered in some detail. The authors evaluate these techniques, showing their strengths and weaknesses in modern-day organizations.

Throughout this century, businessmen and academics have continually stressed the importance of the human resource to industry. Phrases and concepts such as the 'dignity of man', 'human relations', 'organizational development', 'job enrichment', etc. have been with us for decades. For a variety of reasons, much of the interest in people has been theoretical and philosophical. It has been far easier to get to grips with the more tangible and measurable aspects of business, such as production, finance, and marketing, than with the enormously complex and variable aspects of human needs and development.

During the first few decades of the century, interest centred on the production process and the engineering function. Two world wars stimulated management interest in this process. The period 1900 to 1950 also marked the growth of interest in the financial functions of corporate business. Some time during the 'fifties, increased production capacity and consumer sophistication combined to favour the start of the marketing era. The 'sixties saw enormous stress on consumer wants and desires. Consumer orientation became the catchword of most dynamic firms. Product orientation was considered myopic, and business objectives were redefined in terms of satisfying consumers at a profit.

Business in much of the Western World is currently facing the issue of human development in a positive and practical manner. The growth of sophisticated personnel and manpower departments reporting to the managing director, the upsurge in management training and development, the growth and use of practical tools for the motivation of people are all part of the manpower and organizational development phase of Western business. The manpower and personnel functions are no longer being fobbed off to those managers who cannot succeed in other areas of business.

Within the manpower function of business, few areas have excited as much interest as organizational development. This term has broad ramifications and can be considered to be the process of continually reviewing and evaluating the effectiveness of an enterprise and initiating action to improve the overall performance of the organization. This definition is possibly too broad to be meaningful for the practitioner concerned with organizational development. It is suggested, therefore, that the definition of organizational development be constrained to include the analysis, review, and evaluation of the essentially human factors contributing to an organization's health and effeciveness and the actions necessary to correct and improve the human element in business.

In this sense, then, organizational development is concerned primarily with the development of the human resources of the organization at both the micro and the macro levels. It is concerned with the recruitment, placement, and development of people; with manpower planning, career development, training, interactions, communications, motivation, etc.

Much of the thinking and impetus behind organizational development is derived from the work of behavioural scientists. Organizational development practitioners, be they consultants or in-company specialists, tend to have a strong background in the prime disciplines of the behavioural sciences, including sociology, psychology, anthropology, and industrial relations. In addition, the field has also attracted manpower and personnel specialists, group dynamics and systems experts.

This chapter evaluates the contributions made by the behavioural sciences and their proponents to the development of organizational development and, specifically, to management development and training.

The student of organization development should not find it surprising that behavioural scientists have directly, and indirectly made major contributions to the subject. Behavioural scientists—whether psychologists, sociologists, or anthropologists—are deeply concerned with the analysis of people as individuals, in groups and in organizations. Their studies therefore encompass a wide variety of situations in which people occupy the major role. Consequently, the behavioural scientists' work which has been most attractive to students of organization development is that which centres around analyses of individual and group motivations, organizational structures, interpersonal, intra- and intergroup relationships, and individual and group response to changes. Thus, an organization development scientist like Beckhard emphasizes the behavioural role when he defines the subject as 'an effort, planned organization-wide and managed from the top, to increase organization effectiveness and health through planned interventions in the organization's process, using behavioural science knowledge'.[1]

Although organization development is still relatively new as a topic for study, many of the major behavioural concepts on which its development is based have been adopted from work done some years ago. Organization development's role in this regard has been basically to accumulate these studies and integrate them within a defined framework. Many of these studies were originally undertaken in isolation, the terms of reference being their authors' particular disciplines. Thus, we encounter Harvard-based sociologist George Homans' model of emergent behaviour in the work group, which was initially devised to explain group development on a purely sociological context.[2] And Abraham Maslow's much-quoted 'need hierarchy' was developed by its founder, a pure psychologist, to explain human motivations. This dynamic model is today used extensively in modified form by management trainers.[3]

Our purpose here is twofold. Firstly, to present readers with a summary of what the authors consider are the major contributions to organization development by behavioural scientists. In this regard, some aspects have been tackled more enthusiastically than others by behavioural scientists, and, naturally, contributions arising from these areas will receive a greater amount of attention; we shall find certain names, e.g., Maslow, Homans, Likert, and Blake and Mouton, appearing fairly often.

Secondly, in the light of recent conceptual and empirical research, we shall attempt to evaluate these contributions in terms of some sort of perspective. These will necessarily smack of subjectivity because most behavioural scientists would be the first to admit that universal acceptance of many of even the most basic concepts is lacking. Indeed, there are a number of students of organization development who would suggest that behavioural science's contributions to the business world are often, at best, speculative; it is not, therefore, surprising that some business executives regard behavioural scientists' proposals caustically.[4]

The areas of behavioural science's contribution to organization development on which we shall concentrate can be categorized conveniently into five sections:

(a) organization structure, characteristics, and dynamics;
(b) individual behaviour;
(c) organizations and change;
(d) conflict and conflict resolution;
(e) techniques used in organization development.

Organizational Structure, Characteristics, and Dynamics

Organizations are generally made up of individuals who, for social and structural reasons, gravitate into a number of groups. The size, shape, and characteristics of these groups have been the subject of considerable study over the years; so as far as organizational development is concerned, the most important originating with those undertaken by Whitehead, and Roethlisberger and others in the now well-known Hawthorne experiments.[5,6] Between 1927 and 1932, the initial objectives of these experiments were to see what sort of influence on productivity in the work situation could be achieved through adjustments in the physical restraints of the work. Thus, a group of average workers was selected, isolated, and observed while changes in illumination, payment, and working hours, etc. were made. The findings were of interest to the student of organizational development in so far as most changes which were observed could be put down to attitude changes as a result of restructuring of the work groups, rather than to the effects of the physical changes. The group developed norms and attitudes which seemed to reflect the status with which they perceived that management had honoured them. Furthermore, the group, in a desire to reinforce this newly acquired status, set norms of quality and quantity in the work place, even to the extent that they set up systems which were aimed at helping low-producing workers in an attempt to maintain this high standard. They also devised a group structure or hierarchy which aimed at assisting the group in its new goal achievement.

Another study which tends to reinforce the Hawthorne findings is that of George Homans.[7] His model of emergent group behaviour is applicable to social systems at the level of the small group or the large organization. Homans' approach, although first published more than twenty years ago, has withstood the test of time remarkably well, and its value lies mainly in its obvious success in explaining the emergence of particular behaviour and group structures in developing groups and organizations, and the importance of mutual dependencies between various states in the group development.

According to the model, a social system operates in a tripartite environment—a physical environment (i.e., the climate, the layout, etc.), a cultural environment (i.e., the norms, values, and goals of the particular society), and a technological environment (i.e., the level of knowledge, and the equipment which can assist in completion of the task.) The environment requires that members of the systems carry out certain activities and interactions, and these in turn arouse certain attitudes and sentiments among the participants, towards each other and the environment.[8] This collection of sentiments, activities, and interactions is termed the 'external system', and Homans suggests that they are mutually dependent, such that a change in one of the variables will cause a usually predictable reaction in the other two. In Homans' view, increased interactions in the work place can create new sentiments, and new norms; these in turn generate new activities. This new pattern, which has its origin in the external system, is called the 'internal system', which encompasses the emergent behaviour.

Homans proposes that the internal and external systems are mutually dependent. Thus, a change in one will result in a change in the other. As an example, it is plausible to perceive that a change in the work technology (part of the external system) will cause a change in the internal system. He also suggests that the two systems and the environment are mutually dependent. Changes in the environment can produce changes in both the formal work organization (i.e., that required by management in its work design) and the informal work organization (i.e., that which develops on its own and which may, or may not, be identical to the formal structure, depending on management's perception of workers' norms and values and the actual internal system).

The most important contribution which Homans' model makes, so far as organization development is concerned, is that it recognizes these various dynamic mutual dependencies. It shows how—and this has received adequate empirical proof—events emanating from one group of the organization can cause reactions in another.

It follows, therefore, that while group behaviour should be viewed in an overall context, observation of individual group behaviour is also of extreme importance to the management of an organization. Thus, we believe that it is important to discuss the role of group dynamics within an organization in somewhat greater detail.

Groups tend to develop a form of hierarchy, with some members being given more prestige than others. This prestige or status is generally carried by the individual, and the greater the prestige, generally the greater is his conformity to the group's emergent norms. Just as the group develops a hierarchy internally, so, within the organization, constituent groups are often arranged in a hierarchy, some achieving higher status than others. The vying for, and achievement of status by a group to a large extent determines the group's cohesiveness. Seashore reports that group cohesiveness is a function of its prestige, its temporal existence, and its size.[9] Cohesiveness, which management should encourage provided the group's norms are congruent with those which management sets, is likely to decrease as the group's size increases. A smaller group, for instance, allows for less ambiguities in interaction and in interpretation of norms. Thus, the organizational development specialist would be wise to discourage the formation of large groups. Obviously, in a large organization, the development of a vast number of small groups becomes unmanageable and extremely difficult to direct as far as management is concerned, so within technological constraints, there is a happy medium.

Research by Heinicke and Bales suggests that where the status hierarchy within a work group is stable, well defined and agreed on by its members, the group's functioning will be more efficient; it becomes more cohesive and, thus, is seen to be more attractive to potential members who can readily perceive its efficiency. The degree of success in satisfying the needs of the group members is a further reinforcement to members to maintain this highly successful hierarchical structure.[10]

As Asch, among many others, has shown, the successful or cohesive group's power over its members to conform to its emergent norms is so great that individuals can markedly adjust their behaviour—even value judgements—to be accepted. Asch's well-known experiment required subjects to match the size of a line on a card to three lines on another card. Where individuals judged the lines independently, little error was reported, but when confederates were introduced who were primed to announce incorrect answers, naïve subjects often conformed to these group pressures and gave obviously incorrect judgements.[11]

Characteristics such as quality and quantity of output, types of inter-action, etc. have also been shown by a number of researchers to be dependent, among other things—some of which were mentioned above—on the technology of the work. In fact, it is suggested by some writers on organizational development that organizational structures should be designed with this in mind. Considerable work on this aspect has been undertaken by behavioural scientists, and although many of the findings may not always seem to agree, there are conclusions which seem to have general support. For instance, for work which is basic and uncomplicated, the most efficient performance seems to be achieved with a wheel structure (i.e., where the formal leader, no matter how unpopular, occupies the control spot) even though morale may be low. Where workers are required to undertake more complex tasks, linked-chain or each-to-all structures have been shown to produce the most satisfactory results, both in terms of output and job satisfaction. Where organizations are subjected to changes in technology, those comprising less-structured group patterns seem more able to adapt to these upheavals.[12,13]

Individual Behaviour

Behavioural scientists have produced vast documentation on individual behaviour in organizations. This is to be expected, since it is probably far easier for the observer to study, note, and analyse the behaviour of an individual than it is to study (as thoroughly) the interactions, norms, and goals of a group.

From time immemorial, philosophers and, later, psychologists have shown an almost insatiable interest in what motivates an individual. This attention has not been limited to the laboratory or the clinical environment. Businessmen—who are aware of their investment in labour—realize that if an employee is well motivated to produce efficiently, his value to the organization is considerably enhanced. A number of researchers are reported in the literature. The first to make a noticeable impact was probably Maslow who, in terms of his need hierarchy, suggested that efforts to motivate workers should be consistent with the theory that a level of needs must be satisfied before a higher level of needs becomes activated. This hierarchy ranges from basic physiological needs which are at the base of the hierarchy, and progresses through safety needs, social needs, and ego needs, peaking with self-fulfilment needs. The converse to Maslow's belief that a level of needs must be totally satisfied before the next level can be tackled is the theory that a satisfied need does not offer opportunities for motivation. Therefore, higher-order needs must be recognized as occupying the role of motivation once lower-needs are fulfilled.[14] Although developed at a theoretical level, Maslow attempted—through observation in a factory—to satisfy himself that his theory adequately described human motivation in the work situation.[15]

Following the publication of Maslow's theory, a number of researchers criticized the approach, many pointing to the fact that it is highly unlikely that any level of needs can ever be totally satisfied. Among these critics was Douglas McGregor, who suggested that management often assumes that man is basically lazy and needs continual watching and prodding (theory 'X') whereas, in fact, the worker is a self-motivator, seeking responsibility, the opportunity to achieve, etc. (theory 'Y').[16] Likert's well-known 'systems 1 and 4' approach is similar to McGregor's.[17]

There are some organizational development students, such as Bennis, who express doubt at the conceptual value of Likert's and McGregor's theories. They believe that their main attribute lies in the authors' 'rare empathy for a vast audience of managers who are wishful for an alternative to the mechanistic concept of authority'.[18]

Another behavioural scientist, Frederick Herzberg, also tackled the problem of explaining human motivation in the work place, in a somewhat different way. He proposed that the 'hygiene' factors (i.e., working conditions, fringe benefits, etc.) are essential, but are not motivators. (This contrasts markedly with Maslow's approach). Herzberg believed—not unlike McGregor—that the real motivators, such as responsibility, achievement, etc., are the key to improving worker performance.[19]

The major contribution which these researchers have made to organizational development is probably reflected in Blake and Mouton's integrated Managerial Grid.[20] Their 9,9 manager (who shows 'people and output' orientation) is not unlike McGregor's theory 'Y' manager, or Likert's system 4 manager. The Managerial Grid, as a system in organizational development, will receive more attention later.

Organizations and Change

Interest in almost any business organization today centres on the likelihood of change. Some organizations, because of the particular industry in which they operate, are geared to change and, thus, are more adaptive to it. In fact, in industries such as chemical engineering, aerospace, and electronics, the ability of a firm to encourage change is to a large extent a determinant of its survival. Other organizations, however, operate in industries where major technological advances are infrequent, and the adaptation to change in the work tends to be slow and tolerable.

However, irrespective of the industry in which a firm participates, a number of external forces encourage—admittedly, indirectly—the need to change in the work place. Social, political, economic, and cultural evolutions are external influences (in Homans' terms) which can have a marked effect on the internal system. Indeed, the effects of accelerations in change—either at the technological or social level—are considered by many students of organizational development to be the real cause for the recent intensive study into the subject.[21] In today's constantly changing world, then, those organizations which can readily adjust to, and accommodate the organizational upheaval, are those which must be more successful.

Despite the fact that we live in a world which is constantly subjected to change, many behavioural scientists have shown that there are limits to human endurance of change, both in our social systems and the work place.[22,23] This resistance may be manifested in one, or more, ways. It may show itself in the form of absenteeism, resignations, requests for transfer, or as the 'expression of a lot of pseudo-psychological reasons why the change will not work'.[24]

Change is resisted for a number of reasons, as behavioural scientists like Stewart have demonstrated. Well-established habits and patterns may have to be changed—the accomplishment of which may well be the reason for an individual's status in his organization. This is particularly evident among craftsmen when automation is introduced. They see the skills which have taken years to develop suddenly becoming of little relevance as a measure of their status in both the formal and informal organizational structure. Indeed, Stewart suggests that it is often not change *per se* which can be attributed to the resistance; rather, it is the meaning of change to the individual or to group.[25]

Resistance to change is not only experienced in technologically oriented organizations. Indeed, white-collar workers exhibit it as much as their blue-collared colleagues do. With today's emphasis on youth, who, supposedly, can bring fresh and dynamic ideas into an organization, older and more experienced staff members will point to the value of experience and loyalty, and many will develop complex and tedious systems within the organization, which are understood only by themselves. In this way, staff who are relatively new in the organization, and who may be regarded as change agents, can be thwarted since, without a thorough understanding of the systems, they will be incapable of introducing their new ideas.

Where resistance to change is likely to be experienced in an organization, most often this change has been initiated by management, and it is therefore their obligation to see that this is satisfactorily accepted by the organization. This demands far-sighted planning and development to assist technological and organizational changes. This is not always as easy as it sounds since, as Whyte points out, any organizational activity is perceived as being carried out in terms of organizational models which are at least implicit in the thoughts and actions of those making the critical organizational decisions.[26] So, a look into the future, in order to design an organization to accommodate the predicted changes, must be undertaken with this in mind. To quote an example, the organizations prevalent in Taylor's mechanistic environment would have little place in today's somewhat more democratic and less authoritarian culture.

Another technique of planning for tolerable change is to see that members of the organization are developed to accommodate change. Possibly, the organization development specialist would argue, the experienced white-collar worker would find the young, newly introduced trainee manager less of a threat if the company had taken the trouble to update knowledge and management ability continually through training courses. Further, they would suggest that continual communication of plans and anticipated changes to staff members will assist in improving support for the change. For instance, even if a change will affect only one or two in a work group, studies into group dynamics point to the necessity of all of them needing to know about the change in order to feel secure and maintain group co-ordination.

Conflict and Conflict Resolution

The growing complexities of organizational life, and the demands made on groups and individuals, can result in conflict, which is most often seen in the form of a clash of opposite demands. For example, a manager of a research and development department may wish his department to concentrate on a certain area, since he sees promise for product development there. On the other hand, the production department manager may want the research development to concentrate on improving an existing product, since he perceives that this is more important for his department and his company. Inevitably, conflict—both at interpersonal and at intergroup levels—will occur.

Behavioural scientists like Boulding[27], Lewin,[28] and Schelling[29] have recognized for some time that conflict is a general social phenomenon which has implications for organizational development. Empirical studies undertaken within organizations tend to reinforce this belief,[30,31] and, though writers such as Margulies and Raia suggest that the existence of conflict (at intergroup, interorganizational, or interpersonal level) can be healthy—indeed, a necessary characteristic of organizational life—management should be aware of the conflict in order to manipulate it towards the goals of the organization.

In order to be cognisant of the conflict, management must be able to diagnose it as soon as possible, preferably before it even starts. Where conflict is judged to be dysfunctional to the organization, then hopefully, management will apply conflict resolution techniques, the effectiveness of which seems largely dependent on the nature of the conflict and on the administrator's philosophy of management.[32]

Conflict in organizations is shown by behavioural scientists as manifesting itself in one of two ways. The first group are those evolving out of personal needs and values attached to scarce resources, e.g., status, authority, responsibility, control. In this category, conflict is related to similarities in needs among participants. By contrast, the second group of conflict areas is based on differences in needs and values—different backgrounds, and general perceptions, ways of doing things, etc. Of the two, this group of conflict areas tends to be the most virulent and generally aims at a win-or-lose state. Under these circumstances, according to Kuriloff, members play it 'close to the chest', communication lacks authenticity, and innovations are stillborn.[33] Energies of individuals are survival oriented, and goals of the organization tend to be ignored or, at best, lip-service is paid to them; organizational effectiveness is, in fact, the main sufferer.

The resolution of conflict is also an area which has received behavioural scientists' attention and is of value to organizational development personnel. Where resources may be scarce, it may be a solution to enlarge the supply. For instance, if conflict arises over status or control, it could prove possible to redesign the organization. Or team building, in which cooperation is the aim, may be a successful method of enlarging the supply of values.

Where conflict has its base in individual or personal differences, solutions are often more intolerable to one or more of the parties, and, as Seiler points out, the old wives' adage, that no remedy is without pain, is generally applicable.[34] In this case, it may be necessary to remove one of the person-alities involved, from the conflict area, or at least to show the individual up: hence, the pain.

Techniques Used in Organization Development

Up to this point, we have shown how behavioural scientists have contributed to concepts in organizational development. We now introduce some of the better-known techniques used in organizational development which originate from the behavioural sciences. Those mentioned, although not all-inclusive, are designed to give the reader some indication of the value of these techniques. Here, we think of the group of development techniques, for individual, interpersonal, and intergroup development, which can be classed as of 'laboratory methods', and which include the often controversial T-Group or sensitivity training technique.

The laboratory method is attracting more and more adherents, despite the fact that it is still relatively new. Its use continues to grow, along with the belief 'that the technology of the Behavioural Sciences can be applied to help cope with a society in which change and the maximum utilization of human resources are desirable'.[35] However, the technology is growing and adjusting all the time; many scientists believe that the concept of laboratory is still embryonic, and, thus, techniques can be expected to be in a constant state of flux.

Laboratory research is basically the process of learning and of action research. How it is applied depends on the task it must tackle. At an individual and interpersonal level, T-Groups are often used, but where a whole system needs attention, a variation can be used, in which exploration of the sub-systems is made by a work team in a work development exercise. The core of most laboratories is the T-Group. In simplest terms, this is a group experience designed to give each participant the maximum opportunity to lay bare his behaviour, give and receive feedback, experiment with new behaviour patterns, and achieve awareness of his impression on others. It can also be successful in showing the participants how effective groups can be, and how to direct this group behaviour towards goal achievement at minimum cost. As Argyris sums up,

> The T-Group becomes a learning experience that most closely approximates the values of the laboratory regarding the use of leadership, rewards, penalties, and information in the development of effective groups. It is in the T-Group that one learns how to diagnose his own behaviour, to develop effective leadership behaviour and norms for decision making that truly protect the 'wild duck'.[36]

However, while a number of research and business-oriented students of organizational development place great value in the use of T-Groups, there is, and always will be, controversy surrounding the subject. It raises questions about the very nature of man, concentrating on his feelings, his attitudes, and his sense of well-being. T-Groups take man's emotional life as its central issue and seek to ascertain how these emotions affect the individual's relationships with others. In other words, besides being possibly traumatic for some individuals, it runs the risk of setting up defence mechanisms—even reinforcing them—and its value could be seen, in some cases, to be questionable. Further, we should be aware that there are marked differences in learning patterns used by individuals. Whereas some thrive on an unstructured learning situation (which is exemplified by the T-Group), others prefer a more rigid and directed approach.

The Blake–Mouton Managerial Grid concept is another approach used effectively in organizational development and based on behavioural science. Stemming basically from concepts of team learning, to form a link between individual learning and total organization development, the Managerial Grid identifies five theories of management behaviour, based on two key variables—concern for people, and concern for production. 'Concern for' refers to the degree of concern rather than the actual results.[37]

The combinations of these two variables are seen in Fig. 26.1, the Managerial Grid, and depending on these combinations, the five management theories are readily identifiable. The grid revolves about two axes, which are scaled from 1 to 9; thus, the x-axis indicates concern for production, and an individual manager can be scaled anywhere along the 9-point axis. On the y-axis, concern for people is measurable.

The combinations then, are as follows:

1,9   *country club* management, where production is incidental to lack of conflict and good fellowship;

9,1   *task* management, where men are regarded as a commodity, not unlike machines. A manager's task is seen as one where he must plan, direct, and control the work of those subordinate to him;

1,1   *impoverished* management, effective production apparently not possible because the people are lazy, apathetic, and indifferent. Sound and

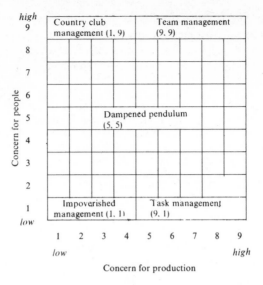

Concern for people

9	Country club management (1, 9)				Team management (9, 9)				
8									
7									
6									
5				Dampened pendulum (5, 5)					
4									
3									
2									
1	Impoverished management (1, 1)				Task management (9, 1)				

low

1   2   3   4   5   6   7   8   9

low   high

Concern for production

Fig. 26.1. The Managerial Grid. (From Blake et al.[37])

mature relationships are not easy to achieve, with conflict always possible;

5,5 *dampened pendulum* management, middle-of-the-road approach, where there is a drive for production, but something of a brake is imposed. The same applies to the concern for staff;

9,9 *team* management, the ideal state, where production is attained from an integration of task and human requirements.

The authors admit that much of their thinking which led to the Managerial Grid approach is consistent with work by Likert,[38] Fleischman et al.,[39] Argyris,[40] and McGregor.[41] Certainly, we see many of these writers' concepts employed by Blake and Mouton.

The advantages of the Managerial Grid are not limited to the reflective model of managerial approaches. It is true that it permits an appreciation of organizational structures and the relationship between organizational and human needs. But, in our opinion, it is of greater value in setting up programmes for future organizational effectiveness. In other words, an analysis of the organization can then be set in terms of the Grid, and programmes can be designed to lead management to the stated position. In fact, this aspect of Managerial Grid is receiving attention from its authors, as in their excellent article 'Breakthrough in Organizational Development'.[42]

An area which is of great concern to management is measurement of their organization's performance. As Likert suggests, progress in the behavioural sciences has enabled management to gauge the results of different types of supervision in terms of production and human assets.[43] He points out that there are measures to test the structure, its goals, levels of loyalty, motivation, interaction, skills, and competence. A Managerial Grid base is a case in point. Management's attitudes can certainly be measured on the matrix basis. When it comes to group participation in goal achievement, carefully controlled contrast techniques have also been successfully adapted. Use of appraisals can also point to loyalty measures, motivation, and perceived competence, thus providing management with feedback for future development and trouble identification.

Management and staff training, a critical aspect of organizational development, relies very heavily on the behavioural sciences. So much of training programmes' effectiveness is taken for granted, but, hopefully, the programme designer will be aware of the variety of teaching methods available to him, the advantages and disadvantages of each under differing circumstances, and their suitability (or lack of it) for different types of situations. He should also be cognisant with the criteria for optimal learning, when he evaluates or modifies a training method, e.g.,

The learner has goals; he wants something.
The learner makes a response; he does something to achieve what he wants.
The responses which he makes initially and continues to make in trying to achieve what he wants, are limited by:
The sum total of his past responses and his abilities.
His interpretation of the goal situation.
The feedback from his responses, i.e., the consequences of his response.[44]

It will be noted, then, that the learner, having achieved his goal or something in its place, can make responses which he was unable to make before the goal seeking. In other words, he has learnt.

References

1. BECKHARD, R. *Organization Development: Strategies and Models*, Addison-Wesley, Reading, Mass., 1969, p. 9.
2. HOMANS, G. C. *The Human Group*, Harcourt, Brace, New York, 1950.
3. MASLOW, A. H. A Theory of Human Motivation, *Psychological Review*, **50**, 1943, pp. 370–96.
4. See, particularly, J. A. LEE, Behavioural Theory *vs* Reality, *Harvard Business Review*, **49**, 2, 1971, pp. 20–8.
5. WHITEHEAD, T. N. *The Industrial Worker*, Harvard University Press, Cambridge, Mass., 1938.
6. ROETHLISBERGER, F. J. and DICKSON, W. J. *Management and the Worker*, Harvard University Press, Cambridge, Mass., 1939.
7. HOMANS, G. C. op. cit.
8. SCHEIN, E. H. *Organizational Psychology*, Prentice-Hall, Englewood Cliffs, New Jersey, 1965, pp. 91–2.
9. SEASHORE, S. F. *Group Cohesiveness in the Industrial Work Group*, University of Michigan, Survey Research Centre, 1954.
10. HEINICKE, C. J. and BALES, R. F. Development Trends in Structure of Small Groups, *Sociometry*, **1**, 1953, pp. 7–38.
11. ASCH, S. E. *Social Psychology*, Prentice-Hall, Englewood Cliffs, New Jersey, 1952, pp. 451–4.
12. CARZO, R. Some Effects of Organization Structure and Group Effectiveness, *Administrative Science Quarterly*, **7**, 4, 1963, pp. 393–424.
13. GLANZER, M. and GLASER, R. Techniques for the Study of Group Structure and Behaviour: Empirical Studies of the Effects of Structure in Small Groups, *Psychology Bulletin*, **58**, 1961, pp. 1–27.
14. MASLOW, A. H. *Motivation and Personality*, Harper, New York, 1954.
15. MASLOW, A. H. *Eupsychian Management*, Richard D. Irwin, Homewood, Ill., 1965.

16. McGregor, D. *The Human Side of Enterprise*, McGraw-Hill, New York, 1960, pp. 36–40.
17. Likert, R. *The Human Organization*, McGraw-Hill, New York, 1967.
18. Bennis, W. G. *Organization Development: The Nature, Origins and Prospects*, Addison-Wesley, Reading, Mass., 1969, p. 22.
19. Herzberg, F. *Work and Nature of Man*, World Publishing, Cleveland, Ohio, 1966.
20. Blake, R. R., Mouton, J. S., Barnes, L. B., and Greiner, L. E. Breakthrough in Organizational Development, *Harvard Business Review*, **42**, Nov.–Dec. 1964, p. 133.
21. Bennis, W. G. and Slater, P. E. *The Temporary Society*, Harper, New York, 1968, chapter 3.
22. Schon, D. A. Champions for Radical New Inventions, *Harvard Business Review*, **41**, Mar.–Apr. 1963.
23. Davis, K. *Human Relations at Work: The Dynamics of Organizational Behaviour*, third edition, McGraw-Hill, New York, 1967, pp. 387–404.
24. Lawrence, P. How to Deal with Resistance to Change, *Harvard Business Review*, **32**, 3, 1954, p. 49.
25. Stewart, M. Resistance to Change in Industry, *Human Organizations*, **16**, 3, 1957, pp. 36–9.
26. Whyte, W. F. Models for Building and Changing Organizations, *Human Organizations*, **26**, 1, 2, 1967, pp. 22–31.
27. Boulding, K. *Conflict and Defence*, Harper and Row, New York, 1962.
28. Lewin, K. *Resolving Social Conflict*, Harper and Row, New York, 1948.
29. Schelling, T. C. *The Strategy of Conflict*, Harvard University Press, Cambridge, Mass., 1961.
30. Dalton, M. *Men Who Manage*, Wiley, New York, 1959.
31. Kalin, R. L. *et al. Studies in Organizational Stress*, Wiley, New York, 1964.
32. Pondy, L. R. Organizational Conflict: Concepts and Models, *Administrative Science Quarterly*, **12**, 2, 1967, pp. 296–320.
33. Kuriloff, A. *Organizational Development for Survival*, American Management Association, New York, 1972, pp. 106–20.
34. Seiler, J. A. Diagnosing Interdepartmental Conflict, *Harvard Business Review*, **41**, 5, 1963, pp. 121–32.
35. Margulies, N. and Raia, A. P. *Organizational Development: Values, Process and Technology*, McGraw-Hill, New York, 1972, p. 288.
36. Argyris, C. T-Groups for Organizational Effectiveness, *Harvard Business Review*, **42**, 2, 1964, p. 64.
37. Blake, R. R., Mouton, J. S., and Bidwell, A. C. Managerial Grid, *Advanced Management—Office Executive*, **1**, 9, 1962, pp. 12–15, 36.
38. Likert, R. *Developing Patterns of Management*, General Management Series no. 178, American Management Association, New York, 1955, pp. 32–51.
39. Fleichman, E. A., Harris, E. F., and Burtt, H. E. *Leadership and Supervision in Industry*, Ohio State University, Bureau of Educational Research, 1955.
40. Argyris, C. *Personality and Organization*, Harper, New York, 1957.
41. McGregor, D. *The Human Side of Enterprise*, McGraw-Hill, New York, 1960.
42. Blake, R. R., Mouton, J. S., Barnes, L. R., and Greiner, L. E. Breakthrough in Organizational Development, *Harvard Business Review*, **42**, 6, 1964, pp. 37–59.
43. Likert, R. Measuring Organizational Performance, *Harvard Business Review*, **36**, 2, 1958, pp. 41–50.
44. McGehee, W. Are We Using What We Know About Training? Learning Theory and Training, *Personnel Psychology*, **11**, 1958, pp. 1–12.

Suggested Reading

Kuriloff, A. H. *Organizational Development for Survival*, American Management Association, New York, 1972.

Margulies, N. and Raia, A. P. *Organizational Development: Values, Process and Technology*, McGraw-Hill, New York, 1972.

Newry, P. and Blanchard, K. H. *Management of Organizational Behaviour: Utilizing Human Resources*, second edition, Prentice-Hall, Englewood Cliffs, New Jersey, 1972.

Hunt, J. W. *The Restless Organization*, Wiley, Sydney, Australia, 1972.

Bennis, W. G. *Organizations Development: Its Nature, Origins and Prospects*, Addison-Wesley, Reading, Mass., 1969.

Hampton, D. R. *Behavioural Concepts in Management*, Dickenson, Belmont, Calif., 1968.

27. Managerial Grid in practice

Robert R. Blake and Jane S. Mouton

*The many industrial applications of Grid organization develop-
ment provide the basis for this chapter. After reviewing a
number of independent studies of Grid OD's impact on profit,
productivity, and people, the authors describe the Grid and the
six phases of Grid OD.*

*The last part of the chapter summarizes fundamental prop-
ositions that are thought to account for the organizational
change effects attributed to Grid OD.*

Fifty-two evaluations and clinical studies of Grid organization development
have been published since 1964. Most of them written by corporate users
of the system, these studies provide the basis for the following generalizations:

(a) the further an organization moves into the phases of Grid OD, the
greater the likelihood that more substantial benefits will accrue to
individuals and the corporation. However, participation as an individual
development activity in Managerial Grid seminars is reported as having
beneficial personal effects;

(b) greater personal satisfaction stemming from individuals' fuller participation, involvement, and commitment to reaching corporate objectives
is also widely reported; there are no studies that point to reduced
satisfaction;

(c) increased profit or productivity, or both, is reported as a widespread
conclusion; none of the studies indicate a contrary conclusion.

Many more detailed generalizations are reported, but they are of more
restricted interest and can be investigated from the bibliography at the end
of the chapter.

How Grid OD Works

The Managerial Grid identifies theories of managerial behaviour based on
two key variables occurring in organizations. One variable reflects concern
for people. In this instance, the term 'concern for' refers to the degree of

concern, not the actual results, i.e., it does *not* represent real production or the extent to which human relationship needs are actually met. It *does* indicate managerial concern for production and/or people, and for how particular degrees of each of these join together to form identifiable managerial orientations that are expressed in associated qualities of feeling, thinking, and actions.

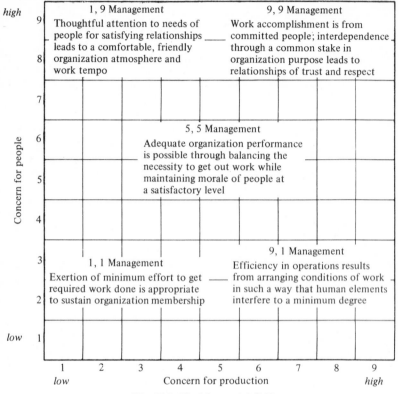

Fig. 27.1. The Managerial Grid.

These two variables and some of their possible combinations are shown in Fig. 27.1. The horizontal axis indicates concern for production, and the vertical axis indicates concern for people. Each is expressed on a scale ranging from 1, which represents minimal concern, to 9, which represents maximal concern.

The 1,1 style is located in the lower left corner of the Grid diagram. This represents minimal concern for production, and minimal concern for people. The 1,9 style in the upper left corner depicts maximal concern for people, but minimal concern for production. The 9,1 style in the lower right corner portrays maximal concern for production, and minimal concern for human relationships. The 9,9 style in the upper right corner represents maximal concern for both human relationships and production. The 5,5 style in the centre is 'middle of the road' in both areas of concern.

Once managers have studied the educational materials associated with the Grid, and have, preferably, participated in one or more instrumented behaviour laboratory experiments, such as provided in Grid seminars, it becomes possible for them, first, to identify, then, to revise inadequate practices and procedures so as to work towards a 9,9 organizational climate. These efforts use an educational programme as the core. This is in contrast to more conventional ways of getting better organizational results, such as changing organizational structure, leadership replacement, tightened accounting controls, or simple pressuring for more output.

Educational Steps

The educational steps are simple in concept, though complex in execution. They include the following:

(a) An investigation by each man of his own managerial style, using Managerial Grid methods of analysis through:
    self-evaluation instruments;
    self-administered learning quizzes;
    in-basket exercises;
    organizational simulations.
(b) Detailed evaluations and comparisons of intrateam effectiveness, as well as interteam resolution of collaborative problems. These are repeated in a sequence which facilitates learning from successive critiques; these are learnings frequently applied by experiment with new behaviours or problem-solving approaches.
(c) Diagnosis of major organization problem areas, e.g., long-range planning, marketing, profitability of operations, union–management relations, promotion policies, incentive awards, new-product development, absenteeism, preventive maintenance, and safety.

The entire approach to organization development is administered by an organization's own management except for occasional consultation regarding major issues. The Grid OD approach has been used in both industry and government.

Six-phase Programme

Grid organization development comprises six overlapping phases. Taken sequentially, these phases can occupy between three and five years, but they can be compressed into a shorter period of time.

Individual Manager Development

The six phases realistically and conveniently divide into two major parts. The first two phases involve *management* development so that the other four phases can help managers work towards 9,9 goals of *organization* development. Here are the two management development phases:

Grid Seminar Individual Training. This is a one-week conference designed to introduce the manager to Grid concepts and material, and to stimulate self-review. From 12 to 48 individuals are assigned as members of (usually) six-man problem-solving teams during each Grid seminar. When scheduled for in-company application, these seminars are conducted by line managers who have participated in one seminar and undergone instructor training in another, and thus know its material and schedules.

The seminar begins with the study and review of one's own Managerial Grid style of behaviour, as outlined in a series of questionnaire booklets completed by each manager. It continues with fifty hours intensive problem solving, evaluation of individual and team results, and critiques of team performance. The problems typically simulate organizational situations in which interpersonal behaviour affects task performance. Each team regularly evaluates its own on-going behaviours and problem-solving capabilities, compares them with previous experiences, and plans the next steps of improvement. In this way, a team which has performed poorly on one problem exercise is able to assess and adjust its problem-solving style in time for the next exercise. Towards the end of the seminar, another exercise involves feedback from team members to each individual in regard to observations of his managerial styles during team interaction.

Though Grid seminars are sometimes compared with T-Group or sensitivity training, the two types of training experiences are quite different. The strongest similarity comes in the face to face feedback experience of phase 1. Even here, however, the Managerial Grid seminars take a more structured approach by focusing on currently employed managerial styles that affect the quality of results, rather than on personal behaviour characteristics and psychic history which might not be related to management.

Phase 1 is not intended to produce immediate organizational improvement. It serves more as the trigger which creates a readiness to work on human problems of production. Participation in a Grid seminar is set up so as to include a 'diagonal slice' of the organization's formal hierarchy. No man is in the same group as his boss or immediate work colleagues. At the same time, this arrangement permits many organizational levels and departments, with their particular points of view, to be represented in each session.

Team Development. This represents an on-the-job extension of phase 1. The concepts and personal learning of the Grid seminars are transferred to the job situation, through each work group or department analysing and improving its own ground-rules and relationships. Team development usually starts with the boss and his immediate subordinates exploring their managerial styles and operating practices as a work team. The norms of openness and candour which were established in phase 1 can now become the phase 2 daily operating style. When, as we recommend, they are undertaken in closely connected sequence, phases 1 and 2 provide management development conditions which are designed to:

(a) enable managers to learn Managerial Grid concepts as an organizing framework for thinking about management practices;

(b) increase self-examination and constructive discussion of personal performance characteristics;

(c) increase a manager's willingness to listen, to face and creatively resolve work-related conflict, to reduce and work out interpersonal frictions, and to reject 'half-effective' compromise as a basis for organizational decision making;

(d) increase colleagues' and subordinates' willingness to 'level' with a manager on work-related problems at a time when there are opportunities for remedying them, rather than, under personal safety considerations, by keeping quiet while such problems worsen;

(e) build improved relationships between groups, among colleagues at the same level, and between superiors and subordinates;

(f) make managers more critical of outdated practices and precedents while extending their problem-solving capacities to coordinate interdependent situations and achieve intended results. Words like 'involvement' and 'commitment' become real in terms of day to day tasks.

Organization Development

The last four phases build on this management development base, and help managers work towards the more far-reaching and complex goals of organization development.

Intergroup Development. This involves group to group working relationships and focuses on building problem-solving ground-rules and norms between organized groups. Situations are established whereby operating tensions that may currently exist between groups are identified and explored by group members and/or their representatives.

The goal is to move from the appallingly common win–lose pattern of 'warring kingdoms' in an organization, towards an overall problem-solving activity on behalf of corporate goals. This becomes possible when two or more groups—each of which, previously, has concentrated on its local goals—begin working their problems through to resolution, using intergroup procedures developed from behavioural science studies. A second type of intergroup development helps to induce mutually beneficial problem solving between the organization and semiautonomous groups such as employee unions, or between the organization and other independent units with which it has problems that are impeding attainment of otherwise realizable collaborative possibilities.

Ideal Strategic Modelling. In phase 4, an ideal strategic model can be constructed around six key corporate elements. These are:

(a) Definitions of minimum and optimum corporate financial objectives. In the case of non-profit-making organizations, these may be agency service objectives as related to cost.

(b) Descriptions in explicit terms of the nature and character of business activities.

(c) Definitions in operational terms of the scope and character of customers and markets.

(d) Structure for organizing and integrating business operations for synergistic results.

(e) Basic policies to guide business decision making.

(f) Development requirements for avoiding obsolescence and exploiting growth capacity.

Designing an ideal strategic model is an exercise in the rigorous application of business logic. Taking nothing about the operation of the business for granted, key executives apply 'pure reasoning' to business actualities. Through this approach, corporate leaders can identify and evaluate the assumptions on which the corporation has been built and is operated. These assumptions are tested for validity. Those which are unacceptable are rejected and replaced with others that are sound. In this way, executive leadership can study the corporation, free itself from past and present thinking, and gear the organization for the strongest possible business action.

Implementing the Plan. Some of the same instrumented individual and team learning procedures of phase 1 are utilized, but, here, the issues are major organizational concerns. The stakes are real.

The objective of phase 5 is to utilize the intellectual and emotional energies of the entire corporation to shift from historically based practices to ones that have been deliberately tested for soundness in the perspective of present and future conditions. The importance of the ideal strategic model is difficult to overestimate. Not only is it a framework for planning change; it also provides the most challenging statement of corporate objectives that managers can confront. When members of an organization review and evaluate the properties of the ideal strategic model in comparison with what they are accustomed to, they often see a vivid contradiction between what *is* and what *should* be. When managers see this, not only are they pulled towards changing things to what they should be, but they experience a heightened repulsion with things as they are. This general situation is shown in Fig. 27.2.

The wider the gap between the ideal strategic model and the properties of the existing corporation, the greater the motivation to change, providing that all managers see the contradiction between the actual and the possible; see how the transition might be made; and are encouraged and challenged to bring about change.

Spontaneous implementation can no more be expected in phase 5 than in other Grid OD phases. A sound strategy is essential, but without specific tactics for bringing it into daily operations, few results are likely to accrue. Tactical considerations are important in ensuring that the planned transition is made. There are two crucial dilemmas associated with the transition. One centres on keeping the corporation running while the changes needed for shifting towards the ideal model are being planned and implemented.

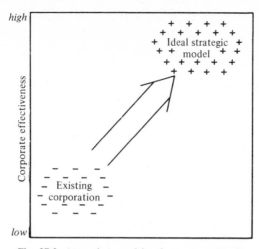

Fig. 27.2. Attraction–repulsion forces compel action towards excellence in phase 5. (From Blake and Mouton, *Corporate Excellence through Grid Organization Development*. Gulf, Houston, 1968, p. 243.)

Another concerns the choice of tactical approach, i.e., how to plan and implement in a way that maintains and strengthens enthusiasm for change.

Accordingly, phase 5 relies on one selected manager serving as a part- or full-time coordinator during phases 4 and 5. His primary goal is to help achieve the goals set during phase 4. His secondary aim is to help identify previously unrecognized problems. He should have neither line nor staff responsibility in the conventional sense, but should hold a position similar to that of an industrial medical officer. It is preferable for him to be—or become, by means of a Grid OD induction programme designed with his organization's particular conditions in mind—a specialist in organization development, intervening at those times when proposed steps are demonstrably inconsistent with 9,9 theory. He would propose and seek action primarily based on understanding and agreement, not because of any formal authority he may hold. This approach, though it may, at first, seem more difficult than 'getting things squared away' by imposition of authority, avoids generating resistance. Instead, it encourages and facilitates the progress of individuals and teams, and so improves the quality of joint effort.

Systematic Diagnosis, Critique, and Stabilization. This final phase is designed to support the changes brought about in the earlier phases. These changes are assessed and reinforced so as to withstand and dissolve any regressive tendencies to slip back into former habits. Phase 6 also gives management an opportunity to evaluate its earlier gains and mistakes during the organization development programme. It is stabilization, not in the sense of making recently adopted practices inflexible, but of providing a stable higher-level 'foundation' on which further improvements can be built in the future.

Thus far, we have briefly outlined the concepts and phases that go into an OD programme using Grid concepts and instruments. In some respects, the programme seems simple and straightforward; yet any manager will recognize the difficulties involved in influencing a large organizational unit towards positive changes in its values and performance.

Underlying Dynamics

The Grid approach to organization development has demonstrated impact in terms of heightening the effectiveness with which individuals and organizations achieve their legitimate goals. It remains for us to deal with underlying dynamics that may be accountable for the results that are obtained. Some of the more important of these are briefly discussed below.

Grid OD Values

There are three different sets of values that can be identified among OD practitioners today. These are not mutually exclusive, and yet the kinds of results likely to accrue as a consequence of an organization development effort are very much affected by the basic values held by the OD practitioner.

One of these sets of values can be termed the 'love/trust' set. Here, the underlying assumption is that if people accept one another for what they are—foibles, irrational reactions, and all—trust will increase. With increased trust, greater mutual understanding is expected with beneficial results for individuals, as well as for their operational contributions. Superficially, the love/trust model is quite attractive; it leads to approaches to organization development that are primarily based on trying to improve the flavour of the *status quo* through cathartic and catalytic types of interventions. These concentrate on people's feelings and, by facilitating the reduction of internal and interpersonal tensions, enable people to relate better with one another. In Grid terms, the love/trust model is likely to be located in the 1,9 corner of the Grid. Its programme may cause people to become so concerned with appreciating one another and achieving harmonious relationships that they tend to lose sight of the production rationale for their being together.

A second model is termed 'power/coercion'. Here the underlying assumption is that misuses of power have caused tensions in the system. Therefore, if the nature of power that managers have over subordinates can be modified —often by increasing the influencing power of subordinates relative to their bosses—better problem solving will result. The effort to do so involves OD practitioners in various power redistribution activities, such as confronting bosses with the proposition that they need to understand what subordinates are saying; and with the associated suggestion that bosses could respond in more tentative and accepting fashion. In effect, what this does is to shepherd managers out of the 9,1 corner and towards the 5,5 middle. It is likely to produce an environment of compromise, accommodation, and mutual adjustment, rather than one of problem solving.

The third basic value orientation to be found in organization development work is one that underlies Grid OD. This is the 'insight/consensus' model. The underlying assumption is that people already have—or can learn—theories, principles, and models against which to evaluate how they are working together in problem-solving endeavours. Because they know and aim to apply these theories, they will be apt to notice faulty or limiting characteristics of their interactions, and, having done so, will prefer to phase out power-oriented techniques of gaining control, or the love/trust model of trying to achieve harmonious interaction—replacing these with systematic ways of problem solving through teamwork. The consensus/insight model is based on the idea that once people who work together gain insight into the fundamental dynamics of human relationships in a context of purposive joint effort, they are ready to implement problem-solving approaches of the 9,9 sort, with guidance based on understanding and agreement.

Organization Culture

While it is often tempting to see the fundamental problems of organizations as inherent in the individuals employed, or in the structure of the organizational system, it is becoming more apparent that the way individuals behave—and the way the structure is arranged—reflects the culture of traditions, precedents, and past practices that has grown, like a mound of consequences, from the past. It is easy to place reliance on a culture of traditional expectations that people have learnt from yesterday. What 'outsiders' see as snug, smug, and quaint may indeed be giving 'insiders' comfort and security, but such cultural arrangements are often out of line with the needs of organizations for contemporary survival. A viable organization is 'culture free' in the sense of being able to design human and structural arrangements for productive collaboration consistent with the requirements of the external environment, rather than being controlled by the requirements of history. Phases 1 to 3 of Grid OD are designed primarily to remove such cultural obstacles to corporate effectiveness, together with the communication difficulties associated with them.

Conflict

One of the main reasons why cultures remain as stable as they seem to is that any single individual's efforts to change them tends to be openly or covertly resisted by all who, for various reasons, have personal stakes in the *status quo*. In all other respects they may be fine hard-working people. Yet they resist changes in present values, procedures, and power arrangements because most of the changes they have seen were for the worse; i.e., they have seen earlier examples of piecemeal change that, in aggregate, have not done much good. 'Therefore,' belief has it, 'all change is fraught with danger, and most cures seem worse than the disease.' Frequently, *status quo* conservatives so overwhelmingly outnumber those seeking change that their reluctance usually defeats initiatives to bring about change.

People in organizations have traditionally learnt to 'go along to get along', 'don't upset the apple cart', and that 'half a loaf is better than none'. Thus indoctrinated, they fear the frictions and antagonisms that trying to change the culture might create. But the Grid contains in one of its aspects a theory of conflict management. It enables people, from the initial seminar onwards, to learn the difference between 1,9 smoothing; 5,5 compromising; 1,1 neutrality; 9,1 suppression; and 9,9 expression, comparison examination, and resolution of divergent views into a creative 'what is best' focus for synthesis. In a 9,9 context, change is not fear provoking, so that those engaged in organization development, particularly doing phases 2 to 5, are able to face up to organization circumstances that must be changed if progress for the organization itself, and its individual members, is to be achieved.

Critical Mass

As has been mentioned, one person, or a group of people, trying to change an institution is up against such terrific odds from the sheer inertia present in the rest of the organization, that those seeking change are likely to be frustrated, with little constructive as a result. This phenomenon suggests that critical mass is a highly significant dynamic in organization change. It is only when an organization has reached a point of critical mass, in the sense that a significant proportion of its members are now ready to be more open and constructive in their attitudes towards the need for change, that it becomes practically possible for people to see, and approach with enthusiasm, the large-scale constrictive opportunities of change. In Grid OD, the point of critical mass—at least, in US organizations—seems to be reached when about 60 per cent of the organization's membership has participated in at least one Grid learning experience and its linked activities.

Instrumented Team Learning

The massiveness of an organization development effort, that realistically must take into account critical mass questions, is such that the use of consultants would be prohibitive, not only in terms of the scarcity of skilled consultants to work with individuals and teams, but also from the standpoint of the expense that would be entailed.

Under an innovative approach to education—called 'instrumented team learning'—such extensive use of consultants is unnecessary. Instead, Grid concepts and educational strategies are embodied in booklets and other materials, and these instruments structure active individual learnings, often in a team context. A 'manager of learning' is trained to use sets of instruments so that he can run effective Grid seminars, conduct team-building sessions, make the administrative arrangements for intergroup development sessions of the phase 3 sort, and so on. It is for this reason that all the phases of Grid OD—starting with individual learning and ending with stabilization—are of the instrumented character.

A currently popular conception is that 'the clear statement of objectives' serves to bring about organization development without other preparatory activities. But the results of 'stating and waiting' have been rather disappointing. The reason for this, we think, is not that clear objectives are unimportant. Indeed, they are most important. The issue is that organization development practitioners who are oriented towards management by objectives are more than likely to try to implement this system in a somewhat mechanical way, while bypassing all the fundamental issues discussed above, i.e., the requirement of gaining clarity as to what values organization members intend to embrace as they seek problem solving—whether love/trust, power/control, or insight/consensus; the requirement of *not* leaving the historically defined culture unperturbed and still pervasive in its impact; the requirement of dealing with the issues of aiding managers to handle conflict of the sort that is most likely to arise when goals are set, and to transmute initial conflict into solution-seeking team creativity; the requirement of comprehending the concept of critical mass; and so on.

Management by Objectives is provided for in phase 4 of Grid OD, after the top leadership of the firm has had an opportunity to approach the above-mentioned fundamental issues and resolve their own attitudes and convictions relating to the exercise of vigorous and enthusiastic leadership.

Top Leadership

A final point needs to be made about Grid OD. The kind of change being described here cannot be brought about by appealing to people at lower levels to work harder, by asking middle managers to be more responsible, or even by the top man asking his immediate subordinates to be more autonomous and independent controllers of the organizations for which they are responsible. All these methods have been attempted; none really work, except under unique circumstances such as a severe survival crisis. More usually, they do not work because there has been no fundamental change in the capacity of people to think about their own behaviour and about the culture of the organization, and about what needs to happen in themselves and in the organization if significant progress is to be made. Furthermore, if they do not see top-level leadership practising the high performance and relationship ideals it professes, lower echelons respond with the fundamental attitude of doing as they see others doing, rather than doing as they are told to do. If the top is not really leading, lower levels are much less likely to exercise leadership over that part of the activity of the firm for which they are responsible. Under 9,9 circumstances, while hierarchy remains, each member can exert leadership in aligning practical activities in the direction of clarified objectives, so as to close the gap between actual and ideal.

Summary and Conclusions

Results of the Grid approach to organization development described here have been described in a number of evaluation studies. It has been found that Grid OD has significant positive impacts on the capacity of organizations to increase their productivity and profit. Equally important, it has been demonstrated to be a way of increasing individual involvement, participation, and commitment, and, therefore, the resultant satisfaction that individuals gain as a result of being engaged in productive employment.

The six-phase Grid approach to organization development, starting with individuals and proceeding into a series of ever-wider applications, such as team building, intergroup development, ideal strategic modelling, and systematic implementation and stabilization, was then described.

Some of the key human dynamics that underlie change through Grid OD were identified, including such vital aspects of human activity as the values that people adopt as they seek to work together, the management of culture rather than being managed by it, the significance of learning how to deal constructively with conflict, the significance of critical mass in the induction of change, the role of instrumented learning in aiding an organization to change itself, and, finally, the importance of Management by Objectives in the context of culture change.

We see the future as offering opportunities for a broad shift in societies towards 9,9 culture. There are already some 'natural' tendencies in this direction. For example, there is an increasing rejection of 9,1 as a way of control. 1,9 as a love/trust model is daily demonstrating its shortcomings in terms of getting things accomplished. 5,5, as a way of getting along by simply going along, and as a simple-minded eclectic way of maintaining the *status quo*, is becoming more unacceptable in the light of some vast human survival problems that face mankind in the closing decades of this century. Reliance on 9,1 by 'tightening up' is no solution either, because a typical reaction to 9,1 is for an individual, or a mass movement, to generate the capabilities that will enable him, or them, to take super-9,1 counteraction.

9,9 is by no means an inevitable reaction to present disillusionment with approaches that originate from other points on the Grid. Rather, it constitutes a viable possibility for getting to, and correcting, the roots of present-day maladies in individual and organizational competence. It is not based on the notion that man is rational and should, therefore, be expected to respond to problems in solution-seeking ways. It is built on the concept that when men are provided access to strong principles, theories, and models and are afforded opportunities for experiencing how to use them in concrete situations, their capacity for using rational approaches to problem solving can be significantly increased. Such hoped-for outcomes constitute a significant promise for the future.

Suggested Reading

RUSH, H. M. F. *Behavioral Science Concepts and Management Application*, The Conference Board, Studies in personnel policy no. 216, 1969.

BLAKE, R. R. and MOUTON, J. S. *Corporate Excellence Through Grid Organization Development: A Systems Approach*, Gulf Publishing, Houston, 1968.

BLAKE, R. R. and MOUTON, J. S. *The Managerial Grid: Key Orientations for Achieving Production Through People*, Gulf Publishing, Houston, 1964.

BLAKE, R. R., SHEPARD, H. A., and MOUTON, J. S. *Managing Intergroup Conflict in Industry*, Gulf Publishing, Houston, 1964.

PRINDLE, J. The Quest for 9,9, *The Credit Union Executive*, **2**, 2, 1972.

KREINIK, P. S. and COLARELLI, N. J. Managerial Grid Human Relations Training for Mental Hospital Personnel, *Human Relations*, **24**, 1, 1971.

HART, H. A. The Grid on a Grand Scale, *Industrial Training International*, **6**, 12, 1971.

BLAKE, R. R. and MOUTON, J. S. 9,9 Sales Grid Style Produces Results, *Training and Development Journal*, **24**, 10, 1970.

BLAKE, R. R. and MOUTON, J. S. International Research on Managerial Behavior: Understanding and Application of Behavioral Science Concepts and Value Preferences by Managers in 4 English-Speaking Cultures, *Interpersonal Development*, **1**, 1, 1970.

DAVIES, R. The Grid—A Personal Experience, *Industrial Training International*, **5**, 4, 1970.

Encouraging Profit-directed Momentum in World-wide Operations, *World Tobacco*, **3**, 29, 1970.

Naval Electronics Laboratory Center, US Navy. OD Continues at NELC, San Diego, *Trade Talk*, **4**, 2, 1970.

Stretched on the Grid, *Shell Magazine*, **50**, 733, 1970.

MOUTON, J. S. and BLAKE, R. R. Organization development in the Free World, *Personnel Administration*, **32**, 4, 1969.

SMITH, P. B. and HONOUR, T. F. The Impact of Phase 1 Managerial Grid Training, *The Journal of Management Studies*, **6**, 3, 1969.

Naval Electronics Laboratory Center, US Navy. Organization Development at NELC, *Trade Talk*, **3**, 7, 1969.

BLAKE, R. R. and MOUTON, J. S. Managerial Grid Develops Team Action, *Industrial World*, **182**, 6, 1968.

BLAKE, R. R., MOUTON, J. S., SLOMA, R. L., and LOFTIN, B. P. A Second Breakthrough in Organization Development, *California Management Review*, **11**, 2, 1968.

MORRISON, H. R. W. Object: Managerial Perfection, *Board of Trade Journal*, Apr. 1968.

Naval Electronics Laboratory Center, US Navy. Grid Method Stresses Pattern for Excellence, *The Calendar*, **9**, 3, 1968.

RUSH, H. M. F. A Case for Behavioral Science, *The National Industrial Conference Board Record*, **5**, 9, 1968.

Texas Instruments Corporation. Grid Objectives Support Achievement of TI Goals, *TI World*, **2**, 25, 1968.

BIRD, J. Management and the Managerial Grid, *Business Review*, **10**, 7, 1967.

BROLLY, M. The Managerial Grid, *Occupational Psychology*, **41**, 1967.

MCCORMICK, A. D. Management Development at British–American Tobacco, *Management Today*, June 1967.

McGill Industrial Relations Center, 'Dialog': A Steinberg Experiment, *McGill Industrial Relations Center Review*, autumn 1967.

Merck and Company. The Managerial Grid, *Merck Review*, **28**, 1, 1967.

National Foremen's Institute. The Managerial Grid Goes Into Action, *Employee Relations Bulletin 1034*, 25 Jan. 1967.

National Foremen's Institute. The Managerial Grid, *Executives' Bulletin 269*, 15 Jan. 1967.

PARKER, A. Dr Blake's Prescription for BAT, *The Director*, **20**, 11, 1967.

SIMMONDS, G. R. Organization Development: A Key to Future Growth, *Personnel Administration*, **30**, 1, 1967.

Steinberg's: People Are the Pulse, *Food Topics*, **22**, 7, 1967.

BLAKE, R. R. and MOUTON, J. S. The Rich Grow Richer, *Training and Development Journal*, **20**, 8, 1966.

BLAKE, R. R. and MOUTON, J. S. Some Effects of Managerial Grid Seminar Training on Union and Management Attitudes Toward Supervision, *Journal of Applied Behavioral Science*, **2**, 4, 1966.

BLAKE, R. R., MOUTON, J. S., and WALLACE, E. Use of the Managerial Grid to Increase Bank Management Effectiveness, *Bankers' Magazine*, **149**, 3, 1966.

CLASEN, E. A. Blake in the Corporate Bloodstream, *Proceedings: National American Wholesale Grocers' Association, Executive Conference*, Sept. 1966.

COOPER, B. Management Training—How to Make it Pay, *Statist*, Oct. 1966.

FOSTER, G. Making Managers—Executives on the Grid, *Management Today*, Apr. 1966.

FOSTER, G. The Managerial Grid in Action at Ward's, *Stores*, **48**, 12, 1966.

MCALLISTER, J. The Pursuit of Excellence, *Sales Management*, Mar. 1966.

397

MALOUF, L. G. Managerial Grid Evaluated, *Training and Development Journal*, **20**, 3, 1966.
OWEN, G. Bringing Personal Conflict into the Open, *Financial Times*, Apr. 28, 1966.
The Principles of Successful Man Management, *Rydge's Management Service*, **1**, 2, 1966.
BLAKE, R. R. and MOUTON, J. S. International Managerial Grids, *Training Directors' Journal*, **19**, 5, 1965.
BLAKE, R. R., MOUTON, J. S., and SLOMA, R. L. The Union–Management Intergroup Laboratory: Strategy for Resolving Intergroup Conflict, *Journal of Applied Behavioral Science*, **1**, 1, 1965.
MARSH, A. An Introduction to the Managerial Grid, *Industrial Welfare*, Oct. 1965.
MORRISON, H. Towards 9,9, *Keeping Track*, **8**, 4, 1965.
PORTIS, B. Management Training for Organization Development, *Business Quarterly*, **30**, 2, 1965.
ROBERTSON, W. The Managerial Grid, *Monetary Times*, **5**, 8 and 9, 1965.
ROBERTSON, W. A New Way to Develop Management Resources, *Canadian Transportation*, Aug. 1965.
CLARK, G. Managerial Grid Training: An Application in ICI Pharmaceuticals Division, *Group Training Techniques*, Gower Press, 1972.

28. Management by Objectives in practice

Peter Hives

Management by Objectives defies simple definition. It has many variants which emphasize different needs. However, one common characteristic is that it is a system and, as with any system, it can be considered from two standpoints—its design or its operation. This chapter first considers the rationale of MBO, and should be of interest to those charged with the job of evolving such a system. A typical system designed for a manufacturing company is then explained.

The Rationale of MBO

During the 'sixties, the term 'Management by Objectives' became something of a managerial talisman. It has undoubtedly struck a chord with numerous managers throughout the world in all manner of enterprises—small, large, public and private—and at all levels of management. Clearly, it has been seen as providing a well-ordered and much-needed response to the problem of coordinating action to achieve results in conditions of increasing competitiveness, complexity, and self-assertiveness among the members of the organization. The growth of its application has been little short of astonishing. For example, in a survey of UK companies in 1968, some 40 per cent claimed to be applying some sort of MBO whereas, a few years previously, the corresponding figure was in the order of 3 per cent. Now, in 1974, there is continuing evidence not only of new applications—and reapplications—but of interesting new variants, as well as applications in new fields in the public sector, in the armed services, the professional services, and the academic world.

The numerous interpretations of MBO, in terms of systems and sets of procedures, have varied widely, and inevitably, some applications have been inept, inappropriate, or ill-digested, causing something of a backlash to develop in the early 'seventies and a hardening of opinion both for, and against, a range of MBO stereotypes. Some critics have been vociferous in their disapproval of the complex procedures and the proliferation of paper which characterized a number of applications. Others have challenged some of the concepts which the procedures seemed to imply, particularly those which appeared to lean towards a reward/punishment view of motivation.

The obvious danger that a widely acclaimed movement such as MBO faces is that it can degenerate into a caricature of its original commonsense view of management if it becomes regarded as a package of specific routines to be employed with little modification in any management situation. An understanding of what MBO is, and what it can do, demands some knowledge of its history of development, and a thorough appreciation of the concepts on which it is based. Against this background of understanding, it should be possible to devise a coherent approach to the management of any type of situation.

Historical Background

The development of MBO goes back a number of years before it acquired its name. Its beginnings are discernible in the responses made to doubts about the effectiveness of the management development programmes and appraisal systems fashionable in many organizations in the 'fifties. The disenchantment with the then current practice caused a number of people to begin experimenting with new approaches. Among them was John Humble—the pioneer of MBO in the UK. He became involved in assisting companies to reorientate their management development programmes against a more perceptive assessment of needs. Parallel developments were taking place in the US where, among others, Douglas McGregor was voicing misgivings about appraisals.

The initial work took as its starting point an analysis of some basic needs of a manager which were assumed to be the prerequisites of individual effectiveness. These basic needs have been expressed in many ways but, in essence, they were:

(a) The manager must know what is expected of him in terms of results. Meeting this need gave rise to a revolution in the form and content of management job descriptions. Instead of being task oriented, they became result oriented. They changed from being a long, tedious list of inputs to being a short, crisp list of outputs.

(b) He must be given the opportunity to achieve his results through the provision of the appropriate facilities, resources, and job environment. This precondition highlighted the need to identify each of the workflow systems of which the job formed part, and to structure it in relation to the other jobs involved in the systems. It had a profound effect on the detailed aspects of organization structure.

(c) He must have a proper feedback of information relevant to the results he is aiming to achieve. This need focused attention on the inadequacies of those control systems designed by the providers of the information without due regard to what the user of the information really required. In many instances, it prompted major revisions in information systems.

(d) He must be assured of the right sort of back-up particularly from his superior, in terms of support, guidance and training. This need struck at the heart of the relationship between superior and subordinate. It aimed to replace the master/servant idea with one which was essentially more supportive and collaborative. Against this background, so-called appraisals started to develop into means of facilitating future performance, rather than merely passing judgement on past performance. The emphasis was on problem solving and planning. The term 'appraisal', which, in the strict sense, means putting a price on something, tended to be replaced by the expression *performance review.*

(e) His efforts must be recognized in a manner which ministers to his self-esteem. While recognizing that reward in terms of salary is one factor in achieving the level of self-esteem necessary for high commitment to the job, the process aimed at providing some of the other ingredients of self-esteem. In particular, it provided the means of continuously matching job responsibility, on the one hand, to the changing level of competence and ambition of the individual, on the other, i.e., it provided the basis for dynamic, rather than static jobs frozen by an unchanging job specification.

Almost coincidentally with the introduction of these ideas for improving management development came the formalization of a process for encouraging suggestions for performance improvement from every manager. The effect of this was sometimes unexpected, and not always welcomed. It opened a floodgate of ideas and proposals for dealing with unresolved problems and unnecessary frustrations. It emphasized that there was an emerging and, as yet, pent-up need—that of individuals participating in the decision-forming process of the organization to which they belonged. Most managements were reasonably happy while the communication-upwards process generated ideas for improving detailed aspects of efficiency but many of the proposals were found to be outside the authority or capacity of the immediate man–boss pair. Inadequacies and the shallowness of thought of senior management tended to be identified in this view of problems. In some cases, top management found it irksome and embarrassing to be pressured from below, especially through the medium of a management development programme—not normally considered as something that made life uncomfortable for top management.

The process had become bigger than the conventional view of a management development exercise carried through by the personnel function. Those who were involved in developing the practices saw the need to break out from these confines and to encourage line management to learn how to 'ride the tiger' that a widening of the influence of subordinate managers had created. The step they took was to compound the suggestions for performance improvement into a development plan which consolidated the ideas for change into a coordinated programme for the department or division of the company. Inevitably, this process had to be harmonized with the normal operational planning systems, if only because the activities generated in the development plans competed for the scarce managerial resources which were otherwise devoted to the day to day running of the business.

It is arguable whether Peter Drucker, in the *Practice of Management*, prompted this trend towards a more collaborative style of management. Certainly he interpreted it, widened its perspective, and gave it a rationale. He also gave it its name—'Management by Objectives and Self-Control'—and a considerable impetus. Some of his insights have been given a false construction in some MBO applications, while others of his concepts were, for a long time, ignored—possibly because they demanded too great a discontinuity in thinking and practice.

In methodological terms, the impact that Drucker's thinking had on the evolving process was to provide a framework of success determinants—he called them 'key areas'—aimed at giving a common direction of thought and effort to all involved in the enterprise. The development of this concept ensured that the output of all jobs could be defined in terms of contributions to a carefully predetermined set of vital decision areas. It provided the basis for the rigorous application of the principle of concentration of effort which Drucker re-emphasizes in almost every book he writes. It gave a new dimension to the idea of teamwork—something that was lacking in the earlier MBO type of procedures, with their concentration on the individual job. It paved the way for the subsequent introduction into MBO of an ordered system of task force management, replacing in some measure the *ad hoc* use of committees and study groups to deal with managerial pressure points.

While this largely 'bottom-up' evolution of new practices was going on—closely associated with the husbanding of human resources—a 'top-down' process was gathering momentum almost independently. The increasing competitive pressures which built up in the 'sixties, allied to the advancing rate of technology and the increase in size and complexity of industrial enterprises, was causing the emergence of corporate planning as a more widely practised management process. But the two streams of development were taking their inspiration from the same books. Certainly, Drucker had as much influence on the business results school as he did on the human resources school. It was as if the protagonists of the two approaches were tuned in to a narrower bandwidth of thinking than those who were leading the movement. Humble's book *Improving Business Results*—which followed his previous book *Improving Management Performance*—was the first comprehensive statement of an all-embracing methodology.

This history of separate development has had a profound effect on the evolution of a unified process encompassing the management of all resources —human, physical, and financial. Even now, there is evidence, particularly in large organizations, of disjointed application and an uneasy marriage of corporate planning, policy formulation, management development, operational planning, budgetary control, information systems, methods of remuneration, and succession planning. The challenge of the 'seventies is to evolve more effective relationships between these subsystems.

A third line of separate development which excited widening interest in the 'sixties was led by behavioural scientists and has now largely formed itself into a body of knowledge under the title 'organization development'. The need to build a bridge between this body of thought and MBO has been answered by W. J. Reddin, in his book *Effective MBO*.

The Concepts Underlying MBO Practice

The history of the development of MBO illustrates that it is essentially eclectic in nature. During its evolution, it has successively imported concepts, principles, and models from a variety of disciplines and has compounded them into a general pattern of management. The conversion of its general format to a specific pattern appropriate to a unique situation—a company, a public undertaking, a project, etc.—is not, therefore, a matter of applying a set of prefabricated procedures but of assessing the relevance of each of the underlying concepts and modifying existing systems as necessary to conform to them. The application of MBO is largely concerned with changing existing systems and procedures in the light of new perceptions rather than adding to the mass routines that managers already have to perform. Inevitably, the embracing of the concepts underlying MBO implies discarding some earlier concepts which prompted the existing management practices.

The unfreezing of attitudes is therefore essentially a process of displacing inappropriate concepts, false ideologies, and outdated customs with ones which accord more nearly with the current state of the management art. The concepts and principles which should underly an MBO process can be listed as follows.

The Definition of Purposes and Obligations

This assumes that an important requisite of organized life is that there should be a clear understanding of the services being rendered—and to whom they are being aimed—whether it is by a company, a department, or an individual. It also assumes that it is necessary to comprehend any disservices to other parties which may be incurred in providing the main services, so that value judgements can be made as to the overall balance of advantage—thereby recognizing the obligations surrounding the activity. It underlines the fact that it is not only irresponsible to determine economic purpose without due consideration of social obligation but that, in the long run, it is almost certain to give rise to the imposition of restrictions. Since legislation can never hope to keep up with innovation, the innovators have to write their own licence to operate. The thought implicit in this concept is that the success and survival of any activity is dependent on there being a sound set of beliefs on which to base all objectives, policies, and plans. Rarely are these premises thought through, still less often are they communicated.

The Concept of Objectives and Policies

The underlying concept, here, is that an organization can best be regulated by defining a set of action-provoking and action-guiding constraints, preferably (where possible) of a self-imposed nature, but often of a superordinate form. This assumes that if a degree of freedom and initiative is to be achieved by managers in a complex undertaking, then, inevitably, it must be of the 'snake in the tunnel' variety, i.e., with freedom within clearly defined limits.

H. A. Simon in his paper, 'On the Concept of Organizational Goals' puts it thus:

> It is easier, and clearer, to view decisions as being concerned with discovering courses of action that satisfy a whole set of constraints.
>
> Those constraints that motivate the decision maker and those that guide his search for actions are sometimes regarded as more 'goal-like' than those that limit the actions he may consider or those that are used to test whether a potential course of action he has designed is satisfactory. Whether we treat all the constraints symmetrically or refer to some asymmetrically as goals is largely a matter of linguistic and analytic convenience.

Drucker gave form to the concept of a range of constraints and suggested eight key areas in which a business must be clear about the *minimum* level of results necessary for survival: market standing, innovation, productivity, physical and financial resources, profitability, manager performance and development, worker performance and attitude, and public responsibility. He refers to a 'minimum concept—the minimum of profit needed for survival and prosperity of the enterprise'. This aligns closely with the idea of constraints and avoids the inefficient deployment of resources inherent in trying to maximize all results and opportunities. The force, urgency, and cost-reduction potential of minimum essential standards is insufficiently exploited in MBO applications. Paradoxically, maximum possible standards are easier to live with, particularly when they are not achieved—as is frequent. They also tend to legitimize any profligate use of resources.

The Principle of Concentration

In *Managing for Results*, Drucker makes the point that: 'Concentration is the key to real economic results ... human resources must be concentrated on a few major opportunities ... no principle of effectiveness is violated as constantly today as the basic principle of concentration.' Nevertheless, this violation occurs, even in so-called MBO systems, when managers dissipate their managerial resources on too wide a range of opportunities and problems. The real skill to be learned in MBO is that of choosing a balanced set of objectives from the invariably wide range of options.

The Concept of Job Review

There is considerable evidence to support the contention that a deeply felt want of individuals in large organizations is for less detailed interference from above on day to day matters, but for more effective support and guidance when needed. Managers respond to a superior who conceives his role as an 'enabling' one rather than to one who acts as a work pusher, cajoler, and pressurizer. Paradoxically, some misconceived versions of MBO actually reduce the freedom of action of the individual by providing a means whereby the superior can get more involved in things which could well be left to the good sense of the subordinate. This has led H. Levinson to the conclusion that 'a typical MBO effort perpetuates and intensifies hostility, resentment and distrust between a manager and his subordinates'.

The necessity to differentiate between job review as an enabling process, the control of results, and the appraisal of future potential would seem to be the least well-understood feature of MBO.

Job review sessions between superior and subordinate should not be for the purpose of control—this must be exercised, on a feedback principle, when situations get out of control. It is unrealistic to hold back such action until a formal review session, which may be held at six-monthly intervals. It is equally inappropriate for a subordinate to conceive a review session as being both a means of helping him overcome impediments to performance and a basis for decisions which may fundamentally effect his future career development.

Review sessions are essentially developmental in nature and are concerned with the examination of trends, opportunities, needs, and levels at which standards should be set. The success of such a review process depends on two factors: the degree of trust and respect that exists between the different levels in the hierarchy, and the objectivity of the discussions. Figure 28.1 illustrates the related importance of these two factors. If all an MBO system did were to move the locus of subordinate viewpoint horizontally on this grid, from a position of low respect for his boss as a mentor, then all that is likely to happen is a substitution of hope for despair—but without much faith. This is, clearly, a state from which cynicism and disillusionment can quickly develop.

Discussing formal reviews, Harold Koontz puts it this way:

> There appears to be strong evidence that such reviews strongly motivate people to performance. This motivation seems to arise partly from the desire for peer approval, partly from desire to participate in solving enterprise problems, partly from the satisfaction of obtaining approval of courses action (and thereby more meaningful delegation of authority), and partly from the opportunity to take advantage of the presence of superiors to get impediments to performance removed.

high Degree of trust and respect	He is likely to have *faith* that it could be useful	He will be *confident* that it will be useful
low	He knows that it is a *waste of time*	He may *hope* that it could be useful
	low Objectivity of their discussions	*high*

Fig. 28.1. The different views likely to be taken by a subordinate, of his superior's supportive actions.

The Concept of Control

The underlying proposition, here, is that all objectives and standards recognized by the system are, in the final analysis, company objectives and standards, and that their allocation to specific individuals for the purposes of control and action has a dual basis, so:

(a) that the individual can be trusted to do the job but, more important, can be relied on to make it known when any of the standards are at risk;
(b) that there is an appropriate delegation of authority, albeit conditional.

The condition is that control remains entirely with the individual (i.e., self-control) until it becomes apparent that he cannot, unaided, attain or maintain the required conditions.

It follows that a superior must recognize that he is accountable for the non-attainment of the performance criteria of his subordinates. This does not mean that the subordinate avoids redress for the inability to cope, but it does establish the superior–subordinate relationship as one of back-up, and sharing the load when needed. It underlines that effective delegation means taking risks, and, therefore, that some performance shortfall is to be expected—but the biggest danger is its concealment. It infers that the least helpful attitude of a superior when a situation goes out of control is to go into a blame-laying routine. What is needed is to get the situation under control as quickly as possible, and this usually means teamwork.

The control process is therefore based on the principle of self-control allied to the exception principle, i.e., senior management must be implicated in the control of all exceptional and threatening situations. Subordinate management's prime responsibility is to identify and make known the exceptions.

The Concept of Appraisal

Most formal appraisal systems are based on assumptions that future potential can be predicted from assessments against criteria related to either results, competence, intelligence, experience, or personality traits. Speculation as to the validity of these criteria is considerable, but an MBO system can improve the objectivity of assessments based on both results- and competence-oriented criteria. It also provides—by virtue of its use of teams and task-forces—an opportunity to appraise by observation, rather than inference, an individual's capacity to cope with wider problems than he usually meets in his present job.

The Concept of Teamwork

The coordinating of effort in work is inherently a feature of any organization, and work teams are a feature of most organizations. This, however, is the narrow concept of teamwork. Chester Barnard's much quoted definition of a formal organization states that it is 'a system of consciously coordinated activities or forces of two or more persons'.

406

The coordination of 'activities' represents the more straightforward work-centred aspect of teamwork. The reconciling of the 'forces' generated by a number of people with different viewpoints, values, aspirations, and skills gives rise to the need for a wider concept of teamwork, concerned with how decisions are arrived at, and not merely how they are implemented. Relatively few organizations have fully come to terms with the need to widen the collaborative basis of their decision-making processes.

The Concept of Enlightened Self-interest

The desire to collaborate in the decision-making process should not be confused with the desire to share in the benefits and advantages that membership of an organization can potentially bestow. The increasing clamour to take part in decision making most likely represents a need for only a small proportion of employees; meeting it may not, of itself, ensure greater job satisfaction.

More important is the need for an accepted basis on which to achieve changes—a form of 'expectations bargain' between the enterprise, which is often forced to change to survive, and the bulk of its members, who may fear the consequences of change.

Changes will obviously be more acceptable if they can be seen to offer a personal advantage, as well as a corporate benefit. A process such as MBO, which aims to provoke change, is therefore more likely to succeed if it contains within it the means of enlightenment on the balance of advantage.

Bargains of this form can never be represented in the simplistic manner which characterizes some productivity bargains. The gains to the individual and the enterprise may be different in nature, and in the time scale in which they are realized. There is, therefore, all the more need for face to face communication, explanation, and discussion on an individual basis, such as provided in MBO-style review sessions.

The Application of MBO

The following descriptive notes represent a manual used by a company to assist in developing an MBO system.

What MBO is Aiming to Achieve

Stated in simple terms, Management by Objectives is an interrelated set of means of improving the management practices associated with decision making, planning, controlling, and motivating. It does this by:

(a) clarifying the results required at unit and individual level;
(b) focusing the efforts of managers on the achievement of those results through systems of review and control;
(c) developing teamwork, particularly in the search for opportunities to improve results;

(d) improving each manager's competence, by creating an atmosphere between himself and his superior such that management development can take place on the job.

The assumption is that, in doing these things, the basic needs of the organization for profit and growth are met, together with the personal needs of managers to contribute and develop themselves.

The routines associated with MBO are straightforward and have been codified to make them easily learnable. They do, however, recognize that the process of management is complex, and that it is as unrealistic to oversimplify as it is unhelpful to overcomplicate. Therefore, while the main emphasis of the approach is on making all aims and intentions specific, there are some indeterminate situations with which managers have to deal, for which it is impractical to lay down specific result targets.

In such cases, the approach is to formulate objectives to improve competence for coping with a range of probabilities. This applies particularly, for example, in respect of centres of expertise or advisory functions, where it is not always possible to be specific about the particular situations to which they may have to contribute.

MBO is, therefore, concerned both with achieving specified improved results where it is possible to determine what is required, and with improving competence to deal with situations which are not wholly predictable.

The Essential Features of MBO

The popular stereotype of MBO is that it is a system of spelling out objectives in quantitative terms, and holding managers accountable for achieving them. While formal goal setting and review routines are important elements, they represent only the procedural components of the MBO approach. The essential features of MBO are as much concerned with the inculcation of new attitudes as with the application of new procedures. Changes in procedures are fairly easy to introduce. What is more difficult is to bring about the change in attitude at all levels, without which new procedures amount to little more than superficial behaviour changes liable to disappear when those with a vested interest in their introduction have moved on.

The Attitude to Business Results

The emphasis on results-oriented thinking is both the most demanding and the most fruitful aspect of MBO. The assumption is that, due to the pressures on them, there is a tendency for managers to concentrate on the immediate tasks required within their own specialization. They tend to a preoccupation with means, without fully understanding their effect on end-results in corporate terms. At the same time, at the higher-management levels, there is a tendency to determine the end-results required without full appreciation of the availability of means to improve them. The interdependence of means and ends is insufficiently recognized if it is dealt with at different levels in the hierarchy. The MBO system aims to bring consideration of these closer together. The procedures that make up the system have therefore been designed to cause managers to stand back at intervals from day to day pressures, and question their efforts in the context of their received understanding of the wider aims of the business.

Without such a discipline the process of challenging the *status quo* is frequently left to specialist groups, e.g., O and M studies, systems analysts, consultants, or internal study groups. The impetus for such investigations is usually a response to a recognized unsatisfactory state of affairs rather than a means of preventing it happen. The systematic encouragement of result-oriented thinking induces managers at every level to collaborate in the examination of questions such as:

> How should we measure the success of our function or department, and how does each job contribute to it?
> In the light of our understanding of present and future conditions, which activities are likely to have the greatest effect on improving our overall success?
> What areas for improvement in efficiency should we select if we are to use our limited resources to best effect?
> What new areas of competence should we develop in order to respond to changing requirements?

Discussion of these questions leads to the identification of required levels of performance which then have to be translated into individual standards and objectives. In doing this, it is recognized that, in a large organization, decisions having a vital bearing on ultimate end-results, e.g., in terms of group profitability, are made by those responsible for detailed aspects of operational performance but not for profitability. Managers in the middle of the organization can only be held accountable for 'intervening variables' and, in such circumstances, must be provided with criteria for these variables in accordance with ultimate success criteria. In other words, individual objectives and standards need to be defined in such a way as to cause managers to act in a manner consistent with overall objectives, and are intended to prompt better-directed joint effort rather than greater individual effort. The spirit of MBO is contained in the methods used to arrive at a pattern of congruent objectives and standards. The belief implicit in the process is that a positive attitude to business results is only possible when managers know clearly what is expected of them, and, also, *why* it is important.

The Attitude to Change

Resistance to change frequently arises from a lack of appreciation of its causes and possible effects. The MBO approach aims to minimize these fears by a more explicit and open examination of the need for change in all aspects of the internal environment of each organizational unit, i.e., in its structure, its relationships with other units, its systems, training needs, performance criteria, budgets, etc. The system further recognizes that changes made in one sector of a business are liable to have an effect on other sectors, and, therefore, it provides a mechanism for harmonizing changes within all the units and functions affected.

The Attitude to Participation

The participative element of MBO is an explicit recognition of the view that a person is more likely to subscribe to a programme of performance improvement if he is thoroughly involved in appreciating and interpreting the situations *which bear directly on his work*. Only in this way can he be expected to take an enlightened view of the ultimate benefit to himself of action which, in the short term, may make unwelcome demands on him.

The participation of managers in determining their own objectives is invariably time consuming, particularly in complex centralized organizations. It is often dismissed on this score, but it is a basic tenet of MBO that influential participation is an important factor in achieving sustained acceptance of the need for change and improvement.

The Procedural Features of MBO

The MBO procedures are designed to bring about two conditions:

(a) a better-directed effort of individuals to the aims of the company;
(b) a better response by the company to the personal expectations of individuals for self-fulfilment in their jobs.

A set of procedures which concentrates on the former would give rise to a manipulative management process, while undue emphasis on the latter would be little more than indulgence.

The achievement of an acceptable balance in this two-way 'expectations bargain' requires careful thought since failure of MBO-type systems can sometimes arise from a wrong placing of emphasis (e.g., if the procedures impinge on subordinate managers without any observable change in the way that senior managers perform). A change in the style of the boss is often the most important element in the successful changing of attitudes of all members of his team.

Style can be defined as 'the way in which a unit is led'. MBO procedures aim to provide a vehicle for managing in a style which is responsive to the needs of all parties and which has been proved by experience to be conducive to high economic performance. They provide a set of guidelines by which to convert a philosophy into a learnable and coherent practice of management.

Inevitably, learning to use the MBO routines demands effort but the time required is largely taken up in thinking about jobs, and their purpose, in a more organized and penetrating fashion. The time necessary to commit the ideas to documents is marginal by comparison. Broadly, the procedures consist of:

(a) the initial stating, and subsequent periodic review, of the purpose of every organizational unit in terms of the services it has been set up to provide and the intended nature of its impact on corporate aims;
(b) identification of the key activities on which attention must be focused if MBO is to achieve its stated purpose;

410

(c) identification of the nature of the contribution expected of every member of the unit in respect of these activities, and an agreement as to the currently accepted performance standards, so that members can exercise a high degree of initiative in the control of activities;

(d) regular review of the need that each member of the unit has for guidance, support, enlargement of authority, additional resources, training, etc., so as to ensure that agreed standards are maintained;

(e) periodic in-depth examinations of internal and external factors influencing performance in relation to the purpose of the unit so as to identify opportunities for improvement;

(f) formulation and communication of objectives and plans aimed at converting identified opportunities into actual achievements within a specified period.

This list represents a broadly based strategy for widening the perceptions of managers and improving the environment in which they operate. Inevitably, in any particular unit, some of these routines will already exist while others may require careful and sustained effort over an extended period in order to achieve the desired change in management style. The tactics for the application of MBO in any unit are, therefore, likely to be different. The installation is not something that can be achieved by the mere issue of a directive accompanied by a procedures manual and a set of forms. It requires either an individual (or a small team working full-time within the unit) who has both the time and the expertise to guide managers through the processes. In this chapter, he is referred to as an MBO adviser.

The Factors Which Determine a Successful Application

The success of the installation of MBO, and the subsequent survival of the system as a continuing and effective feature of management, depends on a number of factors, of which the following are possibly the most important:

(a) Everybody involved in the exercise must be in no doubt as to why MBO is being applied, and they must support its broad aims. Briefing as to purpose is more important than briefing as to procedure.

(b) The head of the unit must be prepared to set aside a significant portion of time and be directly involved in setting objectives. He must be prepared to support and push through ideas for performance improvement generated by his subordinates, and accepted by him as valid. If this does not happen, the concept of participation will be sterile.

(c) The purpose, objectives, and performance standards of the unit should be stated in a simple document given wide circulation within and outside the unit. The restating of these intentions should be seen to be an important annual routine from which budgets and other plans are derived.

(d) The application should not be rushed, and should be allowed to evolve over a period of years. The advisory team have not completed their work until the system has evolved to the stage at which it is accepted as a necessary and beneficial process.

(e) Any organizational problems must be ironed out during the initial stages. A failure to resolve such conflict is liable to reduce the confidence of the managers affected.

(f) Another important success factor, particularly in the long term, is the contribution of management development. The spirit of MBO will only be kept alive by constantly extending managers' horizons, as their awareness of, and competence in tackling current problems is enhanced.

(g) Finally, while the decision to apply MBO starts as an act of faith, it is important to be able to reinforce this faith at an early stage by positive evidence of benefits. The tempo of application must be such as to retain the interest and commitment of those involved.

Establishing Where to Start

For the purposes of installing MBO, it is best to regard it as a number of separate routines which can be introduced either simultaneously or sequentially, in any order—depending on circumstances—over a period of time. The perception of the need for changes in management processes should determine the order in which the various elements of MBO are applied. The disciplines are unlikely to thrive if an attempt is made to persuade a management team to adopt an MBO procedure which does not, in their view, respond to some important need. For instance, one unit may see its prior need in terms of a method of facilitating greater participation in the examination of ideas for improving cost effectiveness, while another may decide that it needs to clarify detailed aspects of its organization, or to set more explicit performance standards for its managers.

Logically, therefore, the starting point in considering the application of MBO is to decide—with the management of the unit—the areas most in need of improvement.

Appendix 28.1 contains a series of questions which can be used as an aid to this initial diagnosis. At appropriate intervals after the introduction of MBO routines, the list can be used as the basis for an opinion survey of the effect that the system is having.

Establishing the MBO Framework

The initial diagnosis of needs will determine the pattern of application best suited to the particular unit. Whatever application strategy is decided, the first step must be to establish a framework for correlating all procedures as they are subsequently applied. The framework consists of two elements, as follows.

Identification of the Purpose of the Unit

This is an explicit statement of the services and benefits which the unit is there to provide. It should identify to whom these services are provided, and should give an indication of the ultimate effect they have on overall corporate aims. No step by step or formal routine is laid down for arriving at an agreed statement of the purpose. Sometimes, the role of a unit may appear so self-evident as to make defining it in writing unnecessary. Deeper examination usually shows that the full implications of purpose are not so clearly apparent as they should be.

The process of defining unit purpose usually requires a series of discussions guided by the MBO adviser and involving at most, four or five senior managers of the unit. When the services provided by the unit are identified, they should be confirmed with the identified recipients. Involvement of representatives of the unit's 'clients' is an important part of the process of establishing the *accepted* purpose of the unit. It can reveal interdepartmental misunderstandings which would make subsequent harmonizing of objectives difficult to achieve.

The Identification of the Key Issues of the Unit

The effective pursuit of the purpose of the unit invariably depends on a relatively small number of factors or key issues on which a concentration of effort and expertise is required. The derivation of a list of major issues for a unit provides a coordinating framework within which to define the jobs of all managers.

The process of identifying the vital success factors requires a thorough investigation, usually involving a series of sessions in which the MBO adviser and senior managers of the unit examine all aspects of the work currently being performed. A list of key issues of a production unit might be as follows:

(a) achievement of production programmes;
(b) raw material yield;
(c) labour productivity;
(d) level of inventories;
(e) plant utilization and efficiency;
(f) customer satisfaction;
(g) employee job satisfaction;
(h) management development;
(i) competitiveness of technology and processes;
(j) cost effectiveness of overheads;
(k) accident prevention;
(l) pollution prevention.

A comprehensive list of key issues should embrace the important aspects of economic performance in the short and long term, and, also, matters of management concern relating to the legitimate expectations of customers, employees, and the community. In effect, a list of key issues forms the headings for a survival strategy or, at least, for a plan for remaining economically viable.

The Improvement Planning Procedures

These procedures are a means of systematizing three essential functions of management:

(a) the search for, and analysis of, opportunities for improving the effectiveness and efficiency of the activities performed by a unit;
(b) planning the action to cash in on these opportunities;
(c) progressing and controlling the action.

The routinization of these functions is achieved, as follows.

The Search and Analysis Routine

This calls for an annual survey and investigation of results and capabilities in respect of each of the unit's key issues. The form and depth of the investigation will vary but, for those key issues chosen as priority areas, will normally involve a number of managers organized into an investigation team or task force. The team carries out a problem analysis routine in order to arrive at a thorough appreciation of the situation. The sort of questions that they will attempt to answer are:

Is there room for improvement in results, and what would be the pay off?
Do we have any weaknesses in organization, competence, procedures, which we ought to tackle?
What demands for service are being made, to which we are not responding effectively?
Are we aiming high enough in terms of results?
Is our level of performance comparable with other standards in the industry?
Are there likely to be new pressures affecting this area and are we going to be competent to deal with them?
Are we vulnerable because of lack of trained staff?
Are there any recommendations stemming from previous studies which need to be put in action?
Are there any studies in progress which need to be considered in arriving at objectives?
Are there any likely changes in the external environment which we should exploit?
Are all the activities and resources devoted to this issue necessary, and are they cost effective?
Are there any organizational impediments to effectiveness?
Do we have an information system which meets the need of the situation?
How do the departments, or managers, for whom we are providing a service view our contribution?
Are there any objectives that we set out to achieve last year which are still unattained?

The team is guided by the MBO adviser in the first instance, and will normally record the often large amount of data and ideas on an analysis document which highlights *strengths*, *weaknesses*, *opportunities*, and *threats*.

Setting Objectives

The above investigations provide a series of pointers to improving results from which a choice of objectives can be made. The choice involves:

414

(a) inferring from the data the root cause of adverse situations;
(b) evaluating the resources required, and establishing their availability;
(c) deciding on the extent of change and improvement feasible within the next year;
(d) establishing the extent of outside or specialized assistance required to achieve the objective;
(e) assessing the balance between the effort required and the likely economic benefits;
(f) assessing the risks and side effects of the proposed changes, e.g., redundancies, transfer of staff, resistance to changing long-established practices and procedures, etc;
(g) deciding who will be affected by, or involved in, the action and ensuring their support;
(h) selecting a course of action from a number of possible alternatives, and assessing its viability.

The head of the unit and his superior must be deeply involved in the final choice of objectives, since the diverting of significant resources to achieve future benefits is a major risk-taking act. If he delegates this responsibility, his subordinates will inevitably limit the degree of risk and, therefore, the degree of benefit. Under such conditions, MBO amounts to little more than an incidental efficiency drive.

Peter Drucker has an apt definition of the process.

> It is a continuous process of making risk taking decisions systematically and with the best knowledge of their futurity, organizing systematically the efforts needed to carry out these decisions, and measuring the results of these decisions against the expectations through organised, systematic feedback.

Progressing the Action

If the objectives which have been set have any 'stretch' in them, they will need to be carefully watched. Each objective can be regarded as a performance improvement project requiring action from a number of individuals throughout the course of the year, and, therefore, the normal features of project management can be applied, i.e., there should be a project leader, a project plan, a project team, and a system of project control and evaluation.

The frequency and form of project control is liable to be different for each objective but, in all cases, the procedure for control needs to be agreed in advance.

The failure of some MBO systems can be attributed to the lack of follow-through. The discipline of regularly reviewing the status of improvement objectives is often the most difficult new habit that managers have to acquire. Strong discipline in insisting on the review process at the outset is required in order to institutionalize the process.

A process chart of the improvement planning cycle is shown in Fig. 28.2, and a typical form of presentation for the unit improvement plan is given in Appendix 28.2.

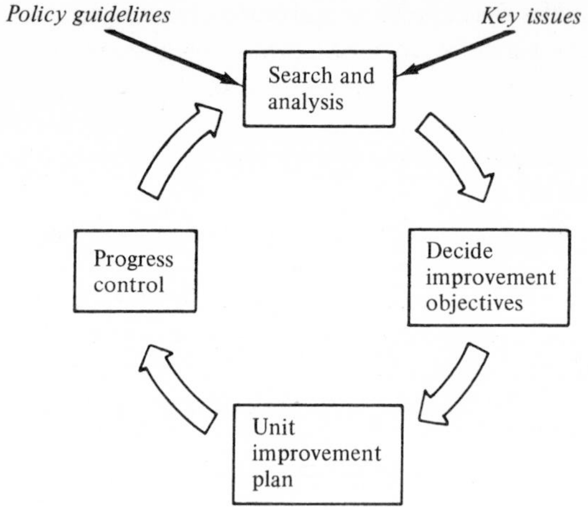
Policy guidelines
Key issues
Search and analysis
Decide improvement objectives
Unit improvement plan
Progress control

Fig. 28.2. The improvement planning cycle.

The Individual Control of Results

However successful the improvement planning process is in causing major changes, little will be achieved if the many other results which, in combination, constitute stable performance, are allowed to get out of control. The need is, therefore, for a sound system for allocating responsibility for monitoring all aspects of performance. The questions that need to be answered are:

What needs to be monitored?
Who should be monitoring what?
What power to act should each individual have to control what he asked to monitor?

The situation which typically exists in a sizable department, or associated company, is that between 100 to 300 aspects of performance need to be monitored and controlled at various levels throughout the organization, but in many instances it is not clear where true responsibility lies. Due to this lack of clarity, there is a tendency to resist the delegating of authority.

The MBO process, at individual level, aims to widen participation in the making of day to day control decisions. To establish a sound basis for this, it is necessary to undertake a preliminary survey of where responsibility for action lies. Invariably, this validation of the existing terms of reference brings to light misunderstandings, misconceptions, and overlapping and underlapping responsibilities. It provides the basis for a detailed sorting out of organizational relationships, and the clarifying of the relative contribution of all members of the organization to its key issues. Only when this micro-reorganization has been settled, is it practical to proceed with the defining of individual accountabilities.

Conventional terms of reference define the place of a particular job in the organization, they delineate duties and responsibilities, authority and relationships in general terms.

An individual *management guide* complements this document by enumerat-ing specific points related to required outputs, in terms of results, and per-mitted inputs in terms of resources to achieve these results. Every point is defined so that it is possible to get a 'yes' or 'no' answer to the question, 'Is this aspect of performance within agreed limits?' The purpose of the management guide is:

(a) to assign accountability to individuals in as specific a way as possible;
(b) to provide every job holder with a means of assessing his own performance;
(c) to provide a basis for periodic, constructive job progress reviews be-tween a job holder and his superior so that they can assess how the job is going and discuss any action that needs to be taken;
(d) to identify organizational dilemmas, inadequate control information, lack of service, etc.

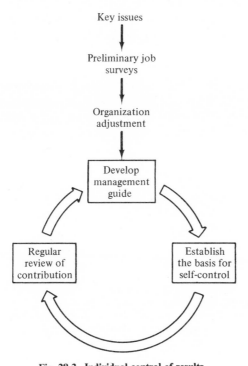

Fig. 28.3. Individual control of results.

Appendix 28.3 shows an example of a management guide form; Figure 28.3 is a process chart showing the cycle of events in the individual control of results.

The management guide provides a list of results required for which the job holder is either individually or jointly accountable. Since this document is central to the MBO system, some points about how performance standards are reached are appropriate.

Types of Performance Standards

The important characteristic of all performance standards is that they should define either:

(a) desired outputs or outcomes;
(b) the desired relationship between outputs and inputs;
(c) limitation of inputs in terms of resources.

The desired level may be described in terms of either an upper or lower limit, or, in some cases, in terms of a range where both the upper and lower limits are defined.

Performance standards are not necessarily expressed in terms of numbers, and there are two main categories: 'measured' or quantitative, where the results to be maintained are expressed in measurable/quantitative terms; 'judged' or qualitative, where results are assessed by comparison with a word picture of the condition to be maintained. Measurable results are, of course, preferred and—given time and thought—many aspects of performance which, at first sight, appear to require subjective judgement can be quantified.

However, since the defining of a standard is intended to provide a talking point at the job progress review session, no important part of the job should be omitted because it cannot be measured in an elegant and satisfying way. Crude criteria or surrogate measures ensure that all aspects of the job will be assessed.

The Determination of Standards

A standard must refer to conditions which have been agreed as feasible, and necessary, to achieve and maintain. All standards are defined within the framework of the agreed key issues, and need to be related to agreed tasks or responsibilities. The precise nature of a performance standard usually becomes apparent if the following questions are posed:

> Is the difference between the task being well done and not well done related to the *time* when things happen? (i.e., a *time* standard)
> Is it related to the degree of achievement? (i.e., a *how well* or *how much* standard)
> Is it related to the cost incurred in performing the task? (i.e., an *at what cost* standard)
> Is it related to the manner in which the task is performed? (i.e., a *how* standard)

A 'how' standard is usually only appropriate if the method of doing the task is prescribed.

Difficulty is often experienced in setting standards in advisory or 'enabling' departments, as distinct from operational or direct result-achieving departments. It is of limited value to assume that a person is accountable only for the excellence of his advice, or merely when or how often it is given. The real criteria is whether or not results are improved as a consequence. Standards have, therefore, to be regarded as either joint or individual. To assume that all results can be allocated on an individual basis is to assume that teamwork has no meaning in management.

418

The Policy Clarification Process

The reason why the determination and clarification of policy has been separated as a distinct MBO routine is that, by its very nature, it is largely the prerogative of top management and, therefore, cannot usually be arrived at in the same participative manner which characterizes the improvement planning and individual control processes. The assumption on which this routine is based is that any action taken by an individual, or department, is bounded by externally imposed constraints and requirements, or is regulated by internally imposed limitations. Many of these are understood as 'the way we do things', and do not need further spelling-out. However, since the effect of MBO is to spread the delegation of decision making more widely through the organization, it inevitably gives rise to people calling for more explicit rulings on how they should deal with situations.

The tendency—which MBO aims to correct—is for this to be done only as the occasion arises, when the person is asked to provide the facts of the situation and is then given a unique ruling rather than a policy ruling. This practice negates delegation.

The MBO routines in respect of policy clarification set out to cause the senior management of the unit to do three things:

(a) annually, to examine the aims and function of the unit in the light of corporate strategies, etc. and to restate these if necessary;

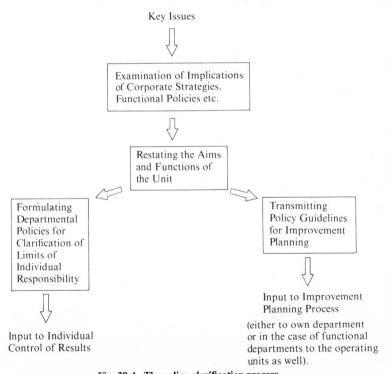

Key Issues

Examination of Implications of Corporate Strategies, Functional Policies etc.

Restating the Aims and Functions of the Unit

Formulating Departmental Policies for Clarification of Limits of Individual Responsibility

Transmitting Policy Guidelines for Improvement Planning

Input to Individual Control of Results

Input to Improvement Planning Process

(either to own department or in the case of functional departments to the operating units as well).

Fig. 28.4. The policy clarification process.

(b) annually, as a prelude to the resetting of improvement objectives, to produce a 'trigger' document which takes each key issue in turn and points the way in which the best interests of the company will be served. In effect, they are providing the terms of reference for the investigations which will take place in the improvement planning process;

(c) as required, to lay down departmental policies which define limits of authority, etc. (e.g., authority to authorize expenditure, to change procedures, etc.)

The following is a checklist for policy formulation:

What implications of the group plan and company policies need to be communicated?
What priorities need to be stressed?
What planning assumptions need to be communicated?
Are there any implications of the aims and functions of the unit which need to be spelt out?
Is there a need to give rulings on how to deal with possible situations that might arise?
Are there any aspects of recurrent poor performance of the unit as a whole, for which some general guidance is needed?

Figure 28.4 shows a process chart of the cycle of events related to policy clarification.

How Much Time do the MBO Disciplines Require?

The question that is invariably asked about MBO is 'Can we find the time to do it?' This could be put another way: 'Can we afford not to be systematic about managing our affairs?' Whichever way the question is posed, it has to be faced that a deal of time must be spent on the routines if they are to produce any worthwhile effect. In accordance with this, Appendix 28.4 shows a typical MBO calendar of events. The time required to be spent by each manager is roughly as follows (during the introduction, more time may be required):

Senior manager of the unit	5–15 days per year
Managers involved in the investigation stages of objective setting	5–15 days per year
All other managers	2 days plus 2 or 3 days per subordinate per year

The Role of the MBO Adviser

The purpose of an MBO adviser's job must be put into the context of the criteria for judging whether MBO is successfully operating. These criteria are:

(a) that every manager in a unit, from first-line supervision upwards, has a clear knowledge of the results he is required to achieve (i.e., he is working to a comprehensive set of performance standards);

(b) that a regular system for comparing the results required with the results being achieved has become the accepted practice in the unit;

(c) that every manager is committed in an organized manner to seeking out opportunities to improve results in those areas of business activity with which he is involved;

(d) that the unit's objectives are regularly and realistically defined and are seen to be compatible with the higher objectives or policies of the company;

(e) that a pattern of challenging improvement plans is the adopted method for generating action to achieve these objectives.

With the above as a background, the purpose of the MBO adviser can be summarized thus: *to guide the installation of a system which is accepted and perpetuated by the unit itself, and which corresponds to the above set of criteria.*

It is not the function of an MBO adviser to effect greater efficiency by virtue of any superior knowledge or experience which enables him to tell managers how to do their job better. His stock-in-trade are the procedures and methods described in this chapter, and his ability to get them accepted.

The training of MBO advisers is crucial to the success of the installation. The detailed problems occurring in the introductory stages are at least as involved as, say, the introduction of standard costing, or job evaluation; few people nowadays would entrust the application of these techniques to untutored individuals, however bright they may be. Experience suggests that the minimum time for a course to train an MBO adviser is two weeks, this being followed by guidance and support from an experienced practitioner for a further period afterwards.

Appendix 28.1.

	There is a pressing need to take concerted and systematic action to change the way that these aspects are managed				Action is necessary but would best be dealt with on an *ad hoc* basis			Present methods stand comparison with the best management practice		
	0	1	2	3	4	5	6	7	8	9
1. Is the purpose of the unit clear to both those within and outside it?										
2. Is each manager sufficiently aware of the results expected of him, and are others who link with his activities also aware of his role?										
3. Are the standards of performance required sufficiently demanding to bring the best out of each individual?										
4. Do existing controls give adequate feedback to enable all important activities to be monitored?										

	There is a pressing need to take concerted and systematic action to change the way that these aspects are managed			Action is necessary but would best be dealt with on an *ad hoc* basis			Present methods stand comparison with the best management practice		
5. Is there evidence of unnecessary or uneconomic duplication of performance monitoring?									
6. Are all managers positively motivated in the search for opportunities to reduce inputs in terms of resources and/or to increase outputs in terms of results?									
7. Is interdepartmental collaboration in the process of improving results effective?									
8. Is the process of a superior guiding and assisting the development of his subordinates effectively carried out?									
9. Are all the activities being performed by the unit being regularly challenged for cost effectiveness?									
10. Are corporate, functional, and technical policies sufficiently communicated and understood in the unit?									
11. Are the ideas, views, and problems of middle- and lower-level managers sufficiently understood at the more senior levels?									
12. Are decisions usually taken with a thorough appreciation of all the factors influencing the situation?									
13. Is the way that decisions are normally arrived at conducive to high commitment of all the persons who subsequently have to implement them?									
14. Are decisions arrived at in a conclusive manner and is the subsequent action then regarded as beyond debate?									
15. Is there a tendency for the recommendations of investigations, or special studies, to 'hang fire' or remain unimplemented?									
16. Is management training specifically geared to provide managers with the necessary capabilities to do their job?									
17. Does senior management time tend to be concerned with detail that could be delegated?									
18. Do managers believe that their worth to the company is appraised on the basis of objective criteria?									

Fig. 28.5. Diagnosis of the need for improvement.

Appendix 28.2.

Appreciation of situation	Objectives	Action required	Benefits
Summary of assumptions regarding factors which make it important to take priority action	Statements of intention to change or improve conditions by a specified amount in a specified time	By managers involved in achieving the objective	Estimate of economic benefits, if assessable

Fig. 28.6. Statement of improvement objectives.

423

424

Appendix 28.3.

MANAGEMENT GUIDE

Position ___Area sales manager___

Name ___J. Green___

The purpose of this document is to list the agreed performance criteria relative to the job so as to form the basis for continuous self-control and for periodic formal review meetings with ___R. Brown—Regional sales manager___
(name of superior)

Tasks/Key issues/Limits of discretion	Performance standards	Comments e.g., means of monitoring or degree of accountability
1. *Profit contribution of sales* Responsible for directing activities of reps, developing new outlets, ensuring continued share of market *Limitations* No authority to alter discounts, terms, etc.	(a) Is sales volume of each product code at least 75% of budget?	Full accountability depending on deliveries from production
	(b) Is seasonally adjusted rate of growth of sales in area not less than 10% per annum?	Full accountability depending on deliveries from production Moving annual totals date supplied by regional office
	(c) Is the proportion of sales at given gross margins being maintained not less favourably than 20% of sales, gross margin above 40% 70% of sales, gross margin between 20–40% 10% of sales, gross margin below 20%	Full accountability depending on deliveries from production
2. *Sales force effectiveness* Responsible for journey planning, elimination of non-economic outlets, reclassification of outlets *Limitations* No authority to increase the number of reps in area	(a) Are call frequencies of reps being maintained at the following level A class outlets not less than 2 per month B class outlets not less than 2 per month C class outlets not less than 1 per month	Full accountability Records to be kept in sales rep statistics
	(b) Is sales turnover per call being maintained within the range £75–300?	Full accountability

3. *Training and motivation of staff* Responsible for ensuring that all staff are put through agreed training programmes; selecting new staff	(a) Is at least one member of your staff competent to take over your function for a period of up to a month?	Full accountability Evidence of this will come from performance during your leave periods
	(b) Do all new staff achieve their order points targets within six months?	Joint accountability with regional sales training officer
	(c) Are all reps being accompanied on at least ten of their routine calls per year, as a check on their approach to the customer?	Joint accountability with regional sales training officer Records to be kept in personnel files
	(d) Is every member of your staff being reviewed against the accountabilities in his result guide at least three times per year?	Full accountability Records of reviews should be kept in MBO file
Limitations No authority to advertise for staff, set levels of remuneration or to dismiss staff who have been with the company for more than six months		
4. *Launching of new products* Responsible for carrying through all new-product launches	(a) Is every rep thoroughly acquainted with selling features of new products before launch dates?	Joint accountability with product manager and sales training officer
	etc.	etc.
Limitations No authority to alter launch dates		

Note: This is a fictitious example of a typical management guide designed to illustrate a number of important points about defining performance standards.

Fig. 28.7. Management guide.

Appendix 28.4.

	Months											
	Sept.	Oct.	Nov.	Dec.	Jan.	Feb.	Mar.	Apr.	May	June	July	Aug.
Review and restatement of aims	*(see note 1)											
Review of policies	▒ (see note 2)											
Resetting of improvement objectives			▒▒ (see note 3)									
Progress review of improvement plan					(see note 4)							
Updating of result guides and communication of improvement plan				▒▒ (see note 5)								
Intermediate man/boss job progress-review sessions							▒	(see note 6)			▒	

Beginning of financial year ←

Notes

1. Usually a one-day session.
2. A series of meetings of the top management of unit, spread over a month.
3. A series of investigations with participation of about 10 to 20 managers at various levels, working in different teams.
4. Half-day progress-report sessions involving everyone named in the improvement plan.
5. Each man/boss pair throughout the organization takes a half-day to update individual result guide in the light of the improvement plan.
6. Each man/boss pair takes a half-day to monitor progress at individual level.

Fig. 28.8. The typical MBO calendar.

Suggested Reading

BARNARD, C. I. *The Functions of the Executive*, Harvard University Press, 1968.

DRUCKER, P. F. *The Practice of Management*, Heinemann, 1955.

HUMBLE, J. W. *Improving Business Results*, McGraw-Hill, 1968.

HUMBLE, J. W. *Management by Objectives in Action*, McGraw-Hill, 1970.

KOONTZ, H. *The Board of Directors and Effective Management*, McGraw-Hill, 1967.

LEVINSON, H. Management by Whose Objectives? *Harvard Business Review*, Jul.–Aug. 1970.

MCGREGOR, D. An Uneasy Look at Performance Appraisal, *Harvard Business Review*, pp. 89–95, May–June 1957.

MCGREGOR, D. *The Human Side of Enterprise*, McGraw-Hill, New York, 1960.

MORRISEY, L. *Management by Objectives and Results*, Addison-Wesley, 1970.

The National Industrial Conference Board, *Managing by—and with—Objectives*, New York, 1968.

ODIORNE, G. S. *Management by Objectives—A System of Managerial Leadership*, Macmillan, New York, 1965.

REDDIN, W. J. *Effective MbO*, Management Publications, 1971.

SIMON, H. A. On the Concept of Organisational Goal, *Administrative Science Quarterly*, **9**, 1, June 1964.

29. Job enrichment in practice

W. J. Paul

Management in most developed countries seem to be confronted with similar dilemmas. They are faced with compelling pressures to become more efficient and at the same time, are being asked to 'humanize' work. Traditional approaches to achieving these objectives have often been divergent and frequently required the manager to choose between them. Contemporary research and theory in the behavioural sciences suggests that the dilemma may be more apparent than real. The work of Frederick Herzberg in particular has demonstrated that traditional approaches to improving human relations based on better social and physical environments has, at best, only provided a partial answer to the problem. An equally important consideration is the degree to which what the man actually does gives him a sense of achievement and purpose and what it makes of his 'human' talents. The process of building these elements into a man's job has been called 'job enrichment' and the results of applying these concepts suggests that it may provide the link between achieving efficiency and humanizing work.

The UK has suffered from the highest level of unemployment that it has known since the depression and, yet, for the first time, the increasing rate of unemployment did not result in a decline in the level of wage claims or a reduction in the demand for additional fringe benefits. It seems that unemployment, or the threat of it, is no longer as punishing as it used to be. What is particularly galling in this situation, for those who have long recommended a dose of depression as a means of curing the nations industrial malaise, is the knowledge that even when the wage claims were met and the benefits increased, it provided no assurance that productivity would increase, or cooperation improve, or even that the same workers would not make similar demands in the future.

In France, Sweden, and other European countries, jobs for unskilled and semiskilled workers, and particularly those on the assembly line, can only be filled by relying on an immigrant population—with all the additional costs and cultural problems that are inevitably generated. The US has already learnt that the sons and daughters of immigrants are no more inclined to accept this type of work than are the children of nationals.

In most industrial nations, the problems of absenteeism and lateness have become serious obstacles to the efficient organization of work. Coping with it has not only meant carrying extra staff, but diverted a great deal of management time and effort from other problems.

Many people have commented on the implications for industry of the substantially improved level of education that has been achieved in the last 10 to 20 years. What few seem to have recognized is that we are not only educating more children to a higher standard than in the past, but we are educating them differently. If you accept the argument that, while at school, children are not only taught but for the first time managed, by someone without a blood right, then it is perhaps reasonable to suggest that the basic attitudes that they have to being managed are formed while still at school. The modern school tends to have open-planned classrooms, greater freedom of choice of study groups for the individual, and self-paced learning. It concentrates on learning how to learn instead of accumulating facts, and is prepared to let the students participate in the establishment of rules and their adjudication. If you compare it with the more traditional kind of school, in terms of the concept of being managed that is bred, you begin to get a glimpse of the expectations that students from these kinds of schools will bring into industry. Their ideas will, at the very least, be different and in their own right bring a requirement for change in the processes by which we manage people.

It is becoming increasingly difficult to recruit, deploy, and utilize our human resources effectively. The truth is that labour is no longer a cheap or pliant commodity, and all the available evidence suggests that it never again will be.

For all these reasons, management is being confronted with the necessity to reconsider the way that it treats and uses its human resources. We are confronted with an apparent dilemma. How can we on the one hand increase efficiency and on the other meet the demand to 'humanize' work. The dilemma is, in fact, more apparent than real but the solution requires us to re-examine in fundamental terms our understanding of what motivates people to work.

It is worth considering, in this respect, the concept of employment itself. Managers, who are in a sense both employer and employed, if asked to define the concept, often have considerable difficulty in formulating an answer. What usually emerges is a definition which, in essence states that employment is an arrangement by which both employer and employee agree to exchange some of their resources in order to fulfil certain needs which neither can fulfil by other means. The medium for this exchange is a job, and the amount and kind of contribution that either is prepared to make

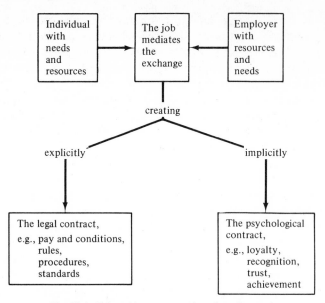

Fig. 29.1. Schematic representation of employment.

at the outset, or indeed thereafter, is dependent on the degree to which either believes that the exchange remains equitable.

In most organizations, there exist contracts of employment which ostensibly define the terms and conditions of the exchange. Most managers would readily agree that contracts at best describe only a small percentage of what is actually given and taken in the relationship. The bulk of what is actually given or taken occurs on the basis of an implicit understanding of what each requires and is most likely to respond to. In a sense, there is a psychological contract which supersedes the legal one. The point seems obvious, and yet, the majority of formal machinery for dealing with disputes and grievances in industry is ultimately confined to an examination of the terms which appear in the contract of employment. Which, if managers are right about the poverty of the document, is the least likely place for the causes or solutions to be found.

It is these non-contractual or psychological elements which need a great deal more understanding. In their attempts to come to terms with these undefined and consequently somewhat unpredictable elements, managers are being increasingly influenced by the behavioural scientists, who, if they cannot provide a simple or complete answer to managements' questions, can at least begin to lend some definition to the terms.

One of the most influential of these behavioural scientists is Frederick Herzberg. In the late 'fifties, Herzberg and his colleagues, puzzled by the apparent contradiction of many of the findings of industrial psychologists, embarked on a new approach to the investigation of human motivation in work situations. They asked people to describe in detail what was happening in their jobs at times when they felt unusually satisfied, interested, or

430

enthusiastic about their work, and again when they had felt unusually dissatisfied, frustrated, or unhappy. Analysis of these events has shown a remarkably consistent and surprising result. Satisfaction and dissatisfaction appear to arise from two quite different roots. It had always been assumed that satisfaction and dissatisfaction were opposites—that the presence or absence of any factor was capable of producing the whole range of feelings. It was apparently true that if you paid a man more money he would be happy, and even more apparently true that if you did not he would be dissatisfied. Herzberg's research suggests that this is not necessarily the case.

There tend to be two clusters of factors, one contributing primarily to the satisfying sequences of events, and the other to the dissatisfying events. Those which were of greatest use when coding positive events all tended to be things which were concerned with what a man actually did—his *job content*. These same factors, even when expressed negatively (for achievement, read failure; for a 'pat on the back', read a kick in the pants), did not have a similar utility when negative events were coded. Here, quite different factors had greater utility, and they, as a group served to describe the environment in which a task was carried out—the *job context*.

If this data is analysed on the basis of a content–context split, as has been done at the bottom of Fig. 29.2, it can be seen that 81 per cent of the factors

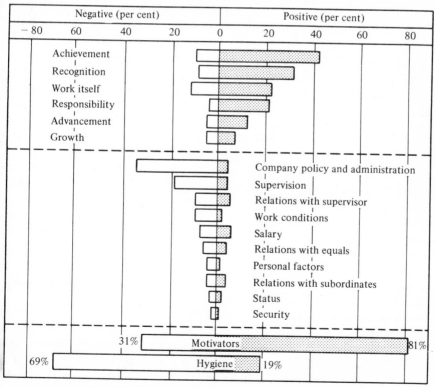

Fig. 29.2. **Herzberg's satisfying and dissatisfying factors.**

used to summarize satisfying sequences described the job content, and only 19 per cent the job context. For dissatisfying sequences, there was a similar, but inverse split, with 69 per cent of the factors describing the job context, and 31 per cent describing the job content!

These results suggest that improvement in the job context serves primarily to alleviate continued dissatisfaction, and contributes only minimally to people's experience of job satisfaction. Because the context factors are environmental and, in this sense, essentially preventative, they have been called 'hygiene factors'. Just as inoculation is not concerned with making people healthy, but with preventing illness, these factors are not concerned with satisfying people, but with keeping them from being dissatisfied. Further research, and indeed the whole history of industrial relations, suggests another interesting characteristic: people's dissatisfaction with the hygiene factors can at best be allayed temporarily. Increased wages, more fringe benefits, and better working conditions have never more than temporarily abated the demand for further increases and better conditions. The feeling of dissatisfaction that inevitably sets in is both very real and natural. Having had a meal, it will soon become essential to eat again. The quality and quantity of the meal will only affect how long it will be before the need arises again. Hygiene factors are the industrial expression of man's primary needs and people's response to them is equally cyclical.

The content factors, however, seem to have their roots in a different source. These factors, in their absence, do not seem to create dissatisfactions equivalent to hygiene factors, but they do seem essential in any situation which individuals find satisfying. Additional research by Herzberg and others also suggests that the content factors are characteristic of situations in which people are more productive or creative, and, for this reason, have been called 'motivators'. Their impact on people's attitudes seems to be of much longer duration, and the individual's appetite for them more limited. They are the industrial expression of a more peculiarly human psychological need which characterizes man. This is the need for psychological growth, the need to express one's capabilities. The need is not new; it has been commented on by Aristotle and Mao Tse-Tung, written about eloquently by Jung and Freud, and forms an intrinsic part of any major theory of human behaviour. What Herzberg's research and theory provides is an understanding of how this need forms an integral part of man's more prosaic and day to day existence. More important, the research provides insight into the mechanism for the satisfaction of this need.

Psychological growth is apparently the product of a very personal encounter that each of us has with a task, wherever we find it, in which we find some meaning, some challenge, and some worth. How we are treated will determine how comfortable we are in the process of growing, but the growth itself can only come when we are confronted with a task or problem which stretches our abilities and talents. 'Psychological tissue', like muscle tissue, seems to require exercise if it is to be added to or maintained. Herzberg postulates from his data that man has a dual need structure. One set of needs deriving from man's primary drives requires continual replenishment if he is not to become dissatisfied, or feel inequitably treated; the other, which is independent of the first, derives from man's need to maintain pscyhological growth and is limited by the ability and capacity with which he was endowed. In essence, the theory maintains that, in exchange for treating people well by prividing good working conditions, reasonable pay, competent supervision, and effective interpersonal relationships, an employer can reasonably expect a fair day's work and a minimum amount of conflict and complaint. However, if he also wants initiative, commitment, enthusiasm, and creativity from his employees, he must look to the way that he uses people, and structure work in a manner which provides them an opportunity to derive 'psychological income' from what they do. The process by which this is done has come to be known as *job enrichment.*

Contrary to popular view, this has not meant taking a given task and enlarging it, or simplifying it, or varying it, or setting a target for its achievement. These have been traditional concerns of industrial engineering, which might be said to be seeking to make up in efficiency what has to be given away for employee satisfaction. Nor has job enrichment meant being 'nice' to people, to improve the environment in which the task is done, or to be democratic in managerial style. These have been traditional concerns of the personnel departments, which might be said to be seeking to make up in employee satisfaction what had to be sacrificed for efficiency.

Job enrichment crosses the old frontiers between work study and welfare-style personnel work. It rejects the inevitability of a win–lose conflict between task efficiency and human satisfaction, and postulates instead an interplay between the two. Neither task boundaries nor people's attitudes are accepted as a given constraint: both are held to be open to change in a related way.

The link between them is found in the motivation–hygiene theory, and the process of job enrichment is one which seeks to improve both task efficiency and human satisfaction by building into people's jobs, quite specifically, greater scope for personal achievement and recognition, more challenging and responsible work, and more opportunity for individual advancement and growth.

It is not a panacea. It cannot, and will not, solve all the problems that management may have with people. It will not, for example, eliminate industrial relations problems although it may reduce the amount of frustration and emotion which is vested in many negotiations and could reduce the number of small, niggling problems which are only symptomatic of problems for which there is no other recourse.

Job enrichment will not solve the problem of incompetence. Motivating the incompetent only provides failure on a grander scale. Training is frequently a necessary prerequisite of job enrichment though, typically, our judgements of what people are capable of underestimates them, and the problem is often not as great as it may seem.

It is not welfare. Unless seen as a business strategy, and its effectiveness judged by normal business standards, it will merely be a gesture of goodwill and is not likely to achieve the depth required for the full benefit of all concerned. It is also likely to be abandoned when times are difficult and it is most needed.

In practice, it is essential—if a programme of job enrichment is to be implemented—to proceed on an evolutionary basis rather than a revolutionary one. Although the theory is intellectually acceptable to most management, its practice forces a confrontation with longstanding assumptions and well-conditioned reactions. A lengthy list could be assembled of good management ideas which have been discarded because an attempt had been made to introduce them immediately, and throughout the organization. In most cases, the process has led to a severe case of indigestion.

Most managers are, by definition, successful, with success achieved by operating on the basis of premises developed through years of experience and by using approaches which have solved problems for them in the past. Any new approach will have a difficult time in being accepted, particularly if it contradicts what has been successful in the past. If, in addition, it requires the manager to put the performance of his unit at risk, alters the basis of his authority and changes his own accountability, it is not difficult to appreciate any reluctance on his part to commit himself whole-heartedly to the exercise. It is of little value, in the face of his reluctance, to explain what a good idea it is—no matter how obvious—and to assure him that it has worked in other companies. Any strategy for implementation must accept that the attitude is a realistic one, and permit a manager to approach the objective by stages, each of which provides its own argument, in his terms, for proceeding to the next.

Experience of job enrichment programmes in several countries suggests that this can best be done by adopting an experimental or pilot study approach. Essentially, this involves building up a foundation of data and experience by carrying out trials within representative areas of the business. These need to be carried out under controlled conditions and in a manner which permits the measurement of their effect and assessment of their implications before the company is committed at a policy level. There are numerous advantages to this approach:

(a) it does not require a manager to accept the concept without question; it merely asks him to give it a fair trial under controlled conditions;
(b) it provides an opportunity to determine what problems will be caused by implementation, and for solutions to be found while problems are still on a manageable scale and unlikely to be overwhelming by sheer weight of numbers;
(c) providing a situation in which it is possible to measure the consequences in real terms, it frees the managers of arguing the merits of this approach on ideological grounds or having to rely on the incongruence of other people's experience;

(d) if a number of pilot studies have been carried out in different parts of the business, it provides a basis for establishing which features are common, and likely to be of use elsewhere, and which are specific to particular situations;

(e) the accumulation of experience and data permits an assessment of whether the programme needs the support of a policy, and provides a basis for determining what that policy should be;

(f) a sufficient number of successful pilot studies achieves a kind of critical mass and creates among management an interest which gives the programme the necessary impetus, and ensures that the implications of this approach will not be ignored when decisions are being made in other areas.

If the pilot study approach is adopted, it is essential that the first trial be conducted in an area in which there is at least a reasonable chance of applying the concept more than superficially. To provide a convincing demonstration of the general efficacy of this approach, such a trial would need to satisfy the following conditions:

(a) it must be demonstrably successful, i.e., it must solve problems which are inherent in the situation, and the degree of its success in doing so should be measurable in concrete terms;

(b) the solution of the problems must be clearly identifiable with the application, and not significantly influenced by chance or other independent factors. (This usually implies a situation in which the selected area can be compared in equivalent terms with a similar unit elsewhere—on the assumption that extraneous events are likely to affect both equally, i.e., experimental and control groups);

(c) the solution of problems in a particular area should not create other problems of equal or greater size in the long term; nor in other areas;

(d) the lessons learnt should be translatable into other situations in the company.

In order to be certain that these conditions can reasonably prevail it is usually prudent to carry out a feasibility study beforehand. The feasibility study is designed to provide necessary information along two dimensions.

The first dimension is the technical/organizational make-up of the unit. It analyses its purpose, and how this is achieved—paying particular attention to the way in which the activities and decisions related to key tasks are distributed. It determines whether there is a gap between the people who carry out the actions and those who take the decisions. It also examines the limits of people's authority at different levels and the degree to which there is consensus about its distribution within, and between, levels. Both kinds of information are less obvious than most job descriptions would have one believe, and of great value in considering the possibilities for reallocating responsibilities.

The second dimension of the analysis needs to assess the attitudes and reactions which the people employed in the unit have to their jobs, in terms of the degree to which they believe that the motivators currently exist in their jobs. This can most usefully be done by means of an attitude survey, which permits some assessment of how welcome job enrichment would be to the job encumbent and can also provide useful guidelines for the direction that change is likely to have to take. It is often useful to supplement this with a preliminary brainstorming session with the managers, to elicit their ideas on how the jobs might be changed. When these ideas are checked for practicality and motivational content, and related to the results of the attitude survey, an assessment can be made of the kind of change that the exercise will entail. Finally, the feasibility study should determine the bases on which the effectiveness of the exercise can be measured. If it is decided to go ahead with the trial, detailed plans for the implementation can be made, with the provision of any necessary training for managers and employees, alterations in control and information systems made, and systems of measurement finally agreed.

The feasibility study is often difficult, and sometimes laborious, but it at least ensures that, if a trial takes place, it does so with a reasonable chance of success and the likelihood of providing sufficient information for effective evaluation.

A brief description of three examples of job enrichment illustrates the type of situation in which job enrichment has proved effective, the type of changes which may be involved, and their effect.

The first example concerns sales representatives in a major UK chemical company. The company, which had suffered from a decline in market share in a range of products considered to be competitive both in price and quality, was concerned about the efforts of its sales force, who were paid well—though not on commission—and judged to be very able. It seemed essential to the company to regain the initiative in this market; to do so would require a sustained extra effort from its sales force. It was thought that job enrichment might be the means for achieving the extra effort, and a specific programme of action was devised which embraced the following changes in the sales representatives' jobs:

(a) sales representatives were no longer obliged to write reports on every customer call. They were asked merely to pass on information when they thought it was appropriate, or request action as they thought it was required (*responsibility, recognition*);
(b) responsibility for determining calling frequencies was put wholly with the representatives themselves, who kept the only records for purposes such as staff reviews or research (*responsibility, growth*);
(c) the technical service department agreed to provide service 'on demand' from the representatives. Nominated technicians regarded such calls as their first priority. Communication was by direct contact, paperwork being cleared after the event (*achievement*);

(d) in cases of customer complaint about product performance, representatives were authorized to make immediate settlement of up to £100 if they were satisfied that consequential liability would not be prejudiced (*responsibility, achievement*);

(e) if faulty material had been delivered, or if the customer was holding material for which he had no further use, the representative now had complete authority, with no upper limit in sales value, to decide how best to deal with the matter. He could buy back unwanted stock, even if it were no longer on the company's selling range (*responsibility, achievement*);

(f) representatives were given a discretionary range of about 10 per cent on the prices of most products, especially those considered to be critical from the standpoint of market potential. The lower limit given was often below any price previously quoted by the company (*achievement, responsibility*).

The changes were introduced for a representative sample of the salesmen selling into three trade areas, rather than for the entire sales force, in order that the effect of the changes could be assessed before standard procedures were altered at policy level. The balance of the sales force would serve as a control group in these trade areas so that performance could be compared. During the trial period, the experimental group increased its performance by almost 19 per cent against the same period in the previous year, a gain of more than £140 000 in sales value. The control group's sales, in the meantime,

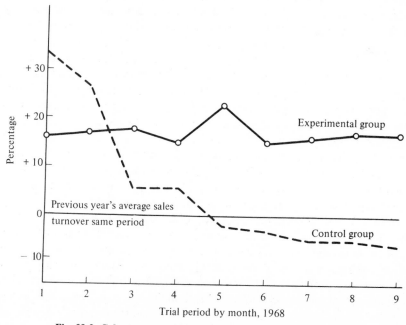

Fig. 29.3. **Sales turnover within nominated trades during trial period.**

showed a decline of 5 per cent. The equivalent change for both groups in the previous year had been a decline of 3 per cent. All sales at other than standard prices were checked for gross margin, and those for the experimental group were proportionally as high—if not higher—than those of the control group. The experimental group had not taken the easy route, and sold at lower limit prices, unless the volume justified it.

Indeed, managers had the impression that representatives actually used their price discretion less often than they had previously asked for special prices to be quoted by the sales office. It was also thought that, now that the sales representatives have been given broad negotiating authority, they were better able to judge what the real obstacles to sales were in each individual case, and adjust their approach accordingly.

A second example concerned assembly-line personnel in an electronics and electrical appliance manufacturing firm in Holland. The company wanted to reduce the incidence of product faults in manufacture, and the overall cost of quality control and inspection procedures. Traditionally, the products had been assembled by using flow-line techniques, with each girl doing only a small part of the total assembly. Although this had permitted the rate of production that the company required, it made it extremely difficult to give the girl a sense of responsibility for the quality of the product.

In an attempt to focus the responsibility for quality on the individual who actually produced the article, they decided to scrap the line-assembly method and gave each girl her own workbench, with a carousel containing all the necessary parts to assemble a complete appliance. She would be permitted to work at her own pace and carry the complete responsibility for the appliances that she assembled. Though this would make the rate of production more difficult to control, it was thought that this would be worthwhile if the desired quality could be achieved. At the end of the trial period, it appeared that the changes not only provided the improvement in quality that the company sought but, in some instances, yielded an increase in production of more than 10 per cent. As an additional bonus, they provided substantially greater flexibility in manning, during both normal shift working and overtime, as well as an opportunity to reduce the amount of direct supervision.

The third example involved laboratory technicians in an industrial research department. In this instance, the problem was essentially one of frustration and declining morale. The average age of the technician or 'experimental officer' was increasing, and many had reached their salary maximum. Their normal promotional route into plant management had been blocked, as the qualifications for these jobs had altered, and other people were brought in to fill them. The EOs were employed to do the more routine work associated with the experiments devised by the scientists and to look after the laboratory assistants who carried out the simpler operations. Many of them thought that their technical ability and experience were being wasted. Management wanted to relieve the frustration and, if possible to develop the EOs into 'better scientists'.

After an assessment of the situation and a management brainstorming session, the following actions were agreed:

(a) EOs would be encouraged to write the final report, or 'minute', on any aspect of a project for which they had had major responsibility. The report would carry their name and only be checked by a scientist if the EO requested it; further, it would be issued in the normal manner, with those of the scientists (*recognition, responsibility, achievement, growth*);
(b) they would be involved in planning projects and setting targets for their completion (*responsibility, growth*);
(c) they would be given time—if they asked for it—to pursue their own research ideas, so long as they reported fully on the consequences (*achievement, growth*);
(d) they would be permitted to authorize the requisition of stores materials, and analytic and maintenance services (*responsibility*);
(e) senior EOs would be involved in recruiting laboratory assistants and devising and implementing their training programme and schedules, and would carry out staff assessments on their own assistants (*responsibility, achievement, growth, advancement, recognition*).

The changes were made for the EOs in two sections of the research department; those in two other sections acted as a control group. After six months, the same changes were implemented for the EOs in one of the two sections making up the control group, to see whether the pattern of performance would hold, and that it had not merely been the result of the original choice of a particular experimental group.

In order to assess the effect of the changes, all EOs were asked to write monthly reports on the work that they had been doing, and these were scored against criteria designed to reflect their ability as scientists. The score itself was merely the sum of the number of times that the assessor believed there to be evidence of one of these criteria in an EO's report. These measures were taken for three months prior to the introduction of any change, then for a further twelve after the changes were introduced. As can be seen from Fig. 29.4, both groups showed improvement but after the introduction of the changes for the experimental group, their performance increased at a faster rate, and to a higher level. Similar improvements were made following the introduction of the changes in one of the control group sections.

In addition to scoring the monthly reports, scores were made on the minutes written by EOs; these were then compared with a sample of those written by scientists. Thirty-four minutes were written by EOs during the experimental period, compared with two in the previous twelve months, and the average score was not significantly different from those of the scientists. All but three fell within the range of scores achieved by scientists, and three were as good as the best of the scientists' minutes. In addition, management felt that the morale of the EOs had improved considerably.

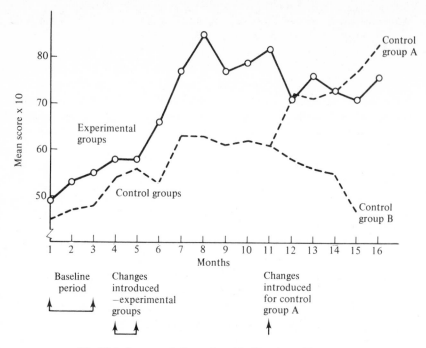

Fig. 29.4. Assessment of experimental officers' monthly reports.

In all three examples, the theme of the changes was to build a job that was more complete in its own right, which would give the individual greater responsibility and more opportunity to use his skills and talents. The problem, the people, and the specific changes were in each case very different. The only common denominators in the three examples were that the changes made were predicted from Herzberg's motivators, and that, in each case, they made a substantial and positive impact on people's performance and job attitudes. What emerges is a strategy with apparently wide possibilities for application which has, at least, the potential for resolving the dilemma which now confronts management. It suggests a means by which the need to become more efficient and human in the design and conduct of work can be achieved. The need to resolve this dilemma is already important. In the future it may be essential.

Suggested Reading

HERZBERG, F. *The Motivation to Work*, Wiley, New York, 1959.
HERZBERG, F. *Work and the Nature of Man*, Staples Press, 1968.
GELLERMAN, S. W. *Motivation and Productivity*, American Management Association, New York, 1963.
LIKERT, R. *The Human Organization: Its Management and Value*, McGraw-Hill, New York, 1967.
MYERS, S. M. *Every Employee a Manager*, McGraw-Hill, New York, 1970.
PAUL, W. J. and ROBERTSON, K. B. *Job Enrichment and Employee Motivation*, Gower Press, 1970.

FORD, R. *Motivation through the Work Itself*, American Management Association, New York, 1969.

MAHER, J. *New Perspective in Job Enrichment*, Van Nostrand Reinhold, 1971.

FOULKES, F. K. *Creating More Meaningful Work*, American Management Association, New York, 1969.

GOODING, J. *Blue Collar Blues and the Assembly Line*, Fortune, **xxii**, 1, 1970.

WILSON, N. A. B. *The Quality of Working Life*, Committee on the Challenges of Modern Society, 1972.

HILL, P. *The Motivation Problem in Industry*, Gower Press, 1971, chapter 1.

30. Action-Centred Leadership

Edwin P. Smith

The success of an organization primarily depends on the ability of its management to obtain the highest commitment and enthusiasm from those responsible to them. Managers, therefore, need to have a clear understanding of the role and responsibilities of leadership and of the practical actions necessary to be effective leaders.

The functions performed by a successful leader fall into three groups which continuously overlap. He ensures that the required tasks are continually achieved, that group cohesion is built and maintained, and that each individual in his care is developed to the best of his/her ability.

The objective of Action-Centred Leadership training is to increase the effectiveness of the individual manager by helping him develop and improve his ability as a leader.

The Need for Leadership

It would seem that heads of governments, of church, of national services, and captains of business in the city and industry—private and national—never tire of telling us that what the country, the department, the group, the company needs most is better leadership. Ask a chief executive in industry or business what is currently his greatest need, and it is more than likely that his reply will be not finance, nor government legislation, not new ideas, not specialists but an improved standard within his organization of general management ability: for men who are clear as to their objectives and who can define and provide the resources necessary, and through them, achieve the required results. Now, ask such a general manager what are *his* needs if he is to fulfil this purpose, and it is equally likely that his reply will boil down to the need for subordinates, managers, and supervisors who can produce the required results consistently, by obtaining devoted service from the team or group for whose work they are responsible. In both cases, it is the need for leadership and leaders which is being identified.

The last decade, especially, has produced a formidable array of management aids, systems, processes and drills, all designed to improve management efficiency: the success of applying such methods as statistics, linear programming, cost effectiveness, Managing by Objectives, etc. is beyond question. However, those with even the deepest knowledge of any, or all, these skills do not necessarily make effective managers. There is another element to the formula, and that is leadership.

A manager's job is to produce the required results through the optimum use of the resources available to him. Of all his resources, potentially the most difficult and refractory—yet the one with probably the most unused, untapped potential—is the human resource within his group. The maximization of this resource amounts to effective leadership. There is a universal need in business, in government, in social services, and in voluntary organizations for managers who are effective leaders.

The Need for Leadership Training

Too often, a man is made a foreman because he is a good craftsman, or he is made a manager because he is a good chemist, engineer, accountant, or salesman, but he receives no training in management skills. Little wonder that he sometimes fails, or manages without distinction. A manager must, of course, have the technical competence necessary to achieve the results required, but he must also have the requisite understanding and skill needed in his unique position of having to get work done by others, i.e., to lead others.

As some of the older methods of motivation become less effective, the importance of the leader increases. In an era of high employment, fear of the sack is fortunately no longer the driving force that it once was. Bonuses and similar financial incentives are limited in what they can achieve; as the amounts rise, men can afford to take value judgements as to whether to work less hard for less money. Good fringe benefits and welfare provisions may attract people to an organization, but they will not, in the long term, affect performance on the job. Moreover, in many fields, the satisfaction provided by the job itself is no longer an incentive, because the skills which gave the job its interest are superseded by new machinery or automatic control mechanisms.

More and more, the manager has to stand or fall by his own performance as a leader. The responsibility for ensuring that each person gives of his best rests squarely with him, whether he be called department head, chief accountant, office manager, superintendent, or foreman. He is responsible and accountable for the work of his subordinates. He has to get work done through them, and his aim must be to make full use of their strengths, abilities, and qualities, to minimize the effects of their deficiencies and, where possible, constantly to try to improve their performance.

This is the object of effective leadership. It makes sense both psychologically and economically. For most individuals, it is important that their abilities should be fully used. For the enterprise and for the country, it is essential that manpower is not wasted.

Those factors which differentiate a leader from those whom he manages can be defined, and indeed, taught and developed. Further, it seems probable that those people capable of being thus developed are more widely distributed in the population than was at one time thought. Potential leaders in industry, business, and government are by no means scarce. What is scarce is training of the kind which will realize their potential.

Leadership Training

The Industrial Society's Action-Centred Leadership (ACL) course arises directly from the urgent need to develop in those capable of benefiting— potential leaders and the many existing managers untrained in leadership— their latent abilities to lead. Concentration on the *functions* of the leader (rather than his qualities)—on what a manager actually does in response to the needs of his situation—ensures that delegates are trained in the skills necessary to bring those for whom they are responsible to their full potential, thereby increasing the efficiency and effectiveness of the organization. The training emphasizes the interrelation between achieving the task, building and maintaining the team or group, and developing the individual and is based essentially on learning through doing.

The concept of functional leadership, which forms the basis of this course, was developed and tested by Dr John Adair.

The Place of ACL in Organization Development

One of the chief characteristics of modern business and government is that never before has it operated in such an atmosphere of change—even the rate of change is unique. There is change in the external environment; in the general economic climate; through Europeanization; metrication; increased fierceness of competition; greater demand for higher standards of living; greater emphasis on legislation to regularize industrial relations, with consequent growth in union activity; change in market and employee expectations for more participation in the affairs of the organization; the decay of authoritarianism and the power to command.

Managers are realizing that it is their responsibility—so far as it lies within their power to control change, or at least to attempt to organize it— to plan, across the total organization, an increase in health and effectiveness, through a controlled intervention in the organization's structure, systems, and processes. Much of this change has been attempted via drastic reorganizations, exercises in divisionalization, definition of profit centres, merging, rationalizing, Managing by Objectives, etc.

But ideas, alone, do not change things, and many an exciting voyage planned in the boardroom has ended on the rocks because insufficient account has been taken of the human factor in the situation. Such exercises

444

have foundered, or, at best, been ineffective, because the 'health' of the organization could not sustain the extra effort needed: there was insufficient creativity and flexibility, inadequate commitment to the goals, the absence of a climate of support and security—in short, the lack of any history of effective leadership throughout.

Action-Centred Leadership training is being increasingly used catalytically as an agent of change in organizational development, to provide motivation and add life and action to an otherwise sterile intellectual idea or plan.

In a recent example of a merger between chemical companies, ACL was the instrument used to develop a new management style needed 'to meet the new opportunities opened to use in an ever-increasingly competitive market'. The training programme resulted in easier organizational changes; more effective communication within and between groups; greater identity with company objectives throughout; sharpened sensitivity, individually and between groups; and increased confidence among management—all of which added up to a comparatively smooth and efficient union of the two companies concerned.

The Place of ACL in Manager Development

In times of total company development, mergers, backs-to-the-wall crises, when changing a company's management style or ethos, or even during the introduction of an across-the-board exercise in Managing by Objectives, a successful outcome relies invariably on the generation of a new spirit in all concerned, an unleashing of dormant 'drives', an unlocking of enthusiasm resulting in new attitudes, and a kindled desire to achieve new results. In these circumstances, the need for training in leadership is self-evident.

Not all companies, however, are in a situation of such urgent needs. But without the impetus of crisis or major drives, many companies are often unaware of the dangers inherent in their own steady(?) state of progress. Too many managers, it seems, go along placidly in the old way while all around them is change.

To keep up with technological change in materials, methods, or machines is an intellectual exercise. To be aware of, and accommodate to the changing attitudes, aspirations, and needs of people is an exercise of an entirely different nature. It implies a development in empathy, in an understanding of human needs both of individual people and of people in groups, and an increase in sensitivity to human interactions. All this is additional to the need for an increased knowledge of proved, modern management methods. It implies, further, that this increased sensitivity and knowledge is then translated into practice—into skills which produce improved results. It is no longer acceptable that the purpose of training is to produce a change in attitudes. It must also show in improved performance.

By concentrating on the functions of the leader, ACL is designed to improve the performance of a manager in the use he makes of his resources, including human resources. It provides him with a simple model, covering three broad, basic functions, which reflects the ways in which a manager must operate to meet, or react to, the needs of his situation at any given moment: the need to achieve the task, the needs of the group for whose work he is responsible, and the needs of each individual within his group.

Wherever a person is responsible for the work of others, whether in industry, business, government, education, voluntary agencies, or church, this 'functional' approach to leadership or managing human resources is relevant and is currently proving its value. It has now been adequately shown that a manager's effectiveness can be materially improved through functional leadership training, whatever his particular discipline, and whatever his level in the hierarchy. Directors and chief executives have acknowledged the value of the ACL course, as have supervisors, section heads, foremen, nursing sisters, senior clerks, etc. in improving their ability to obtain, and maintain, a high level of commitment from their group.

On the occasion of mergers, take-overs or changes of top management, requiring a different companywide management style, the ACL course is particularly effective as an agent of change in getting managers hitherto operating without real responsibility to accept greater initiative and delegation, to take up proffered authority, and to develop their decision-making and problem-solving powers (perhaps hitherto the prerogative of directors only) in order to match the new challenge and opportunity. One suspects that, too often, the attempt to improve the fortunes of an enterprise has aborted not for lack of leadership at the top, but for the want of a means whereby other managers (one has heard them referred to by managing directors as their 'soggy middles') could be persuaded, and materially helped, to update and make more effective their use of resources, and human resources especially. Not least in the list of improved skills resulting from leadership training are those involving a manager's personal skills in setting priorities, objectives and targets, planning and monitoring the work of himself and his group, and the vital skills of communicating, listening and motivating. He sees at once how all these arise immediately out of the three basic functions of the ACL model, which he is able to use as a constant reminder and guide. In short, it is found that a manager's day to day performance is affected so as to produce more effective results more efficiently—he actually *seeks* changes in order to make improvements; acquires better powers of analysis; questions previous assumptions; improves his interpersonal relationships through a better understanding of people's potential and needs; and gains more effective communications with colleagues in all directions.

Leadership Redefined

Before describing the ACL development programme, it is necessary, briefly, to outline the thinking leading up to it.

The Qualities Approach

The traditional approach to defining leadership has been through the analysis of the lives of outstanding leaders, to try to determine what qualities they possessed and to arrive at the essential elements of leadership.

Charles Bird quotes 79 traits of leadership, abstracted from a number of lists. More recently, the qualities of managers who have been outstanding leaders have been analysed. In a recent survey of the qualities of 75 top executives, a list of 15 qualities was derived—judgement, initiative, integrity, foresight, energy, drive, human relations skills, decisiveness, dependability, emotional stability, fairness, ambition, dedication, objectivity, and co-operation. A third of these executives said that all 15 qualities were indispensable. However, the very definition of the qualities proved a stumbling block, there being 147 different concepts of the quality 'dependability' alone. In a recent paper, two economists derived a list of six qualities essential to the leader who was also a manager—strength; willingness to work very, very hard, perseverance, and determination (fanatical single-mindedness); taste and flair for commerce (understanding the market-place); audacity (willingness to risk, gamble); ability to inspire enthusiasm; toughness (ruthlessness).

However, analysis of leadership into such qualities does not define leadership. We all know people who have many of these qualities, but are, in no sense, leaders. Attempts to synthesize an outstanding leader by piecing together the relevant qualities obtained from analysis are also doomed to failure.

Furthermore, the concept that leaders are born, not made, implied that only a few people had the qualities of courage, integrity, single-mindedness, etc. in sufficient quantities to be able to become leaders. It placed the emphasis on natural selection of leaders, but, entirely precluded training. (Is a sense of humour developed by regularly reading *Punch* after dinner?) That this was an exercise without profit soon became apparent to the military cadet who tried to practise five leadership traits a day on a rota basis. That leaders are born, not made, is therefore only partly true.

The qualities approach, however, is relevant in the sense that the leader should possess those qualities needed by the group to accomplish their task. For example, if one of the main qualities which the group regard as vital to their existence is absolute honesty, the leader who is himself not entirely honest will have little chance of remaining the leader of that particular group.

The Situational Approach

Research into the behaviour of small groups has shown that other factors enter into leadership, in addition to the qualities inherent in the leader himself. The situational approach suggests that, in any group, the leader will be the person who at that time possesses the best skill or knowledge to deal with the situations and problems facing the group. It can be summed up in the phrase 'authority flows from the one who knows'. For example, in a serious road accident, the person who takes charge until the ambulance arrives is the one with medical knowledge or nursing experience.

In his play, *The Admirable Crichton*, J. M. Barrie wrote about the butler who went, with an aristocratic family, at the turn of the century, on a cruise in the Pacific where they were wrecked on an uninhabited island. It was the butler who knew how to rub two sticks together to make a fire and how to trap animals and make soup, and he very quickly became the acknowledged leader. When they were rescued some years later, they all reverted to their previous positions. This approach is all very well in an unstructured group, i.e., one where the group throws up a leader to suit the situation. But, in business, we cannot have the leadership passing round from person to person as circumstances change. On the contrary, someone has to be made responsible for achieving the results, someone has to be held accountable for the running of the group, whatever the situation. Thus, the group must be structured and the leader appointed, and the situational approach is of little help.

The Functional Approach

The ACL course is based not on what a leader is but on what he must do to be successful—the 'functions of a leader'. Research into the behaviour of small groups has shown that groups have three basic needs. It is the leader's task to ensure that these three basic needs of the group are met.

The Need to Achieve the Task

The difference between a team or group and a random crowd is that the team has some common purpose, goal, or objective; this is applicable to groups whether business, political, religious, military, or social.

The members of the group feel a strong need to accomplish the task, and they need to feel that their leader will enable them to do this. They want to feel that he can plan, organize, and control effectively, that he knows where he is going, and that their work is efficiently directed towards relevant goals. If they do not feel this, and if it becomes evident that they are not achieving their task, they will become demoralized and frustrated. This will happen however well and humanely they are treated by their leader, or however much they like him.

The Need to Build the Group

Any group develops its own personality which is distinct from that of its members. This can become apparent when the views expressed privately, and sincerely, by individual members are compared with those which emerge later from those same members meeting as a group. A group has the power to set its own standards of behaviour and performance and to impose them, even when they are contrary to the interests of the individual and the organization.

It is the leader's responsibility to gain the commitment of the group so that this power is directed towards, rather than against, the achievement of the organization's goals. The leader must consciously set about developing the loyalty of members to the group, their pride in belonging, their desire to work together as a team, and the group standards that they accept—in short, their morale. He must also make effective use of the conflict which will arise in the group—neither allowing it to become disruptive nor stifling it—and with it, the creativity and ideas which such conflict can generate.

The Individual's Need for Satisfaction

Each member of the group has his own individual needs. He needs to know what is expected of him, to feel that he is making a significant and worthwhile contribution to the task, and that he is receiving adequate recognition for this. He needs to feel that the job is demanding the best of him, that his abilities are not being underused, that he has responsibility to match his capability, and that he is being stretched, challenged, helped to grow in stature psychologically, so that he can look back and think: 'A year ago, I would have been really worried about doing this job and now I'm taking it all in my stride.'

He needs to feel that he belongs to the group, that he is an accepted and valued member, that he counts. Occasionally, he may need help or counselling over some problem which is new, unfamiliar, and perhaps frightening to him. If these needs are not met—and it is the task of the leader to see that, somehow or other, they are—then he may withdraw from the group. He may be at work, but not working.

Drawing on this research, Dr Adair developed the concept of functional leadership and evolved a simple model to express it (Fig. 30.1). Through the expression of leadership in terms which are definable, and capable of being

Fig. 30.1. The functional leadership model.

taught and developed, much of the mystique surrounding leadership for so many centuries has thus been dispelled. In Fig. 30.1, it will be seen that the circles overlap. They are not, in fact, isolated; actions by the leader in one area often have effects in one, or both, of the other areas. For instance, effort directed at meeting the needs of the group, or the individual, derive directly from the need of the leader to achieve the task. Conversely, successful achievement of objectives is essential if the group is going to be held together as a cohesive force or if the individual is to be motivated to give his best effort to the job. Again, if the leader takes action to strengthen the team, e.g., by training, it will make each individual more confident, and the team more likely to succeed in its task.

Removal of, say, the team-building circle from the model will create gaps in the other two. Unless the leader actively sees that the needs of the group are satisfied, his chances of achieving the required results in the long term are in jeopardy. The group and individual circles may be regarded also as batteries which may, from time to time, become exhausted, e.g., after a period of hard pressure. In this case, the leader must take action to recharge them, and pay specific attention to these areas.

It would be wrong, of course, to imply that these motions or activities will automatically make a leader out of anyone or everyone. The 'persona' of the leader, his 'humanity'—as well as what he actually does, and how he does it—is a basic factor in the formula which makes a man an effective leader. The functions, the 'work' that a manager has to perform if he is to lead successfully, are not inborn traits. They are skills which can be recognized, practised, and developed. A manager becomes a better leader when he improves these skills.

The ACL Development Programme

Background to the Course

The course concentrates attention on the functions of a leader, i.e., what he actually does in response to the needs of his group. It provides a practical framework which the course member can apply to get the best out of his own team when he returns to his job.

In the ACL course, formal lectures are kept to a minimum while great emphasis is placed on obtaining the involvement and participation of course members. To achieve this, every member takes part in group discussions, case studies, and practical leadership exercises. The latter serve an additional purpose. Inevitably, each course member brings to the course his own experience of leadership and his own analysis and conclusions about it. Discussion based solely on this tends to be abstract, theoretical, and unrelated to other members' experience. The purpose of the leadership exercise is to provide a common shared experience which can be observed and analysed by the whole course.

Objectives of the Course

The objectives of the course are to assist course members:

(a) to appreciate the essential *functions* of a leader, i.e., to see what a leader *does*;
(b) to develop the ability to *recognize* these functions when they are happening—and to recognize when the situation demands them;
(c) to apply them back at work.

In short, the aim is to improve leadership performance back on the job by getting members themselves to think out the role of the leader in their own working situations; by making available to them a useful practical concept—a model which they can constantly use; and by translating the recognizable needs of the leader into practical action.

The Role of the Tutor

There are two main roles. As tutor, to promote understanding of the concept of functional leadership and its practical implications to the course members' own jobs. As coordinator, to ensure that everyone participates in the course and exercises, that tasks are fairly distributed, and that matters learnt at each session are relevant to the stated purpose of the session, and vital lessons are not omitted or overlooked.

The Leadership Exercises

These are basic to the success of the course. They not only give an individual member practice in leading, but give the rest of the team participating roles in a leadership situation, the opportunity to observe the leader's actions or omissions, and the chance to learn from successes and failures.

Since a manager is invariably appointed by higher management, and not elected by his subordinates, the course exercises are not designed for leaderless groups, where the leader naturally emerges from the group. For each exercise, therefore, the leader should be chosen by the course tutor, who, either explicitly or implicitly, thereby invests him with sufficient authority to achieve the given task.

Leadership Assessment

The importance of the immediate assessment of the exercises and the recognition of lessons arising from it cannot be overstated. Not only are the team and leader under scrutiny but the tutor must also ensure that those observing have recognized the leadership functions (or their absence), that they have drawn the lessons that are there to be drawn, and that these skills of recognition and analysis improve as the course proceeds.

The ACL Course

The essential involvement of each course member limits their numbers to a maximum of 24, while for practical purposes, there should be a minimum of 12. The basic course is of two days' duration, but three days may be needed should extra attention to motivational aspects be required—perhaps for more senior managers. Tutorial time is confined to course introduction, brief leadership analysis, and definition of the practical implications of functional leadership back in the business situation. The rest of the time is spent in exercises involving discussion leading, role playing, case study, films and practical exercises, of increasing sophistication.

The course ends with an action session in which members are expected to apply the lessons learnt on the course, by deciding the action they will take on return to work.

Results of Using ACL Training

An example has been given of the results claimed by a company in a merger situation in which ACL was used as an instrument of organizational change. An increasing number of companies are linking ACL training with on-the-job projects on return from the course, not only to show the results of improved management performance, preferably in measureable terms, but, thereby, to evaluate the relevance of this leadership training to the individual's job situation.

Such an evaluation has been conducted by a prestige car manufacturer of global repute, which has taken ACL training throughout one plant; the assessment was made through interviews—conducted without previous warning—of a random sample of course members three months after finishing the course. Their bosses were also interviewed and asked to give examples of and, if possible, to specify the degree of improvement in performance of their subordinate since the training. Assessments varied between 5 and 40 per cent, averaging about 10 per cent, with estimates averaging 25 per cent (5 to 50 per cent) of increased effectiveness in the performance of the subordinates of course members.

A nationally known brewing company quantified the savings or increase in profitability resulting in the departments in the charge of those managers who had been through ACL training, and concluded that their investment in these courses—some £30 000—had shown a return of around 500 per cent in tangible benefits alone.

Other companies are finding that ACL training so widens the thinking, opens the mind to change, and reveals potential hitherto dormant that many managers who have undergone this form of training are seeing the need and asking for further training in order to continue the opportunities of improving their management and leadership performance. As a direct consequence of this pressure, a major bank now links ACL training with decision-making and creative-thinking exercises: a major fibre company links it with target setting and Management by Objectives—using the enthusiasm generated by the ACL course to ensure success in the exercise to bring all effort effectively behind company objectives.

ACL Programmes

To date, some 10 000 managers from nearly 2000 companies have been trained by The Industrial Society through their two- and three-day courses held regularly in London and at regional centres, and through courses run for members on their own company premises.

In addition, some 50 000 managers have now been trained by organizations running their own training schemes through their own company tutors themselves trained by The Industrial Society. For this purpose, there is a structured programme specially designed to enable an experienced tutor, by stages, to assume full control of his own company's ACL training.

From time to time, a two-day workshop is also held for qualified ACL tutors to exchange experiences, develop new material and exercises, and discuss means of evaluation. The annual Progress Conference enables companies to share their experience and exchange ideas and views on ACL training. Short (half-day) 'Appreciation' courses are also held to enable directors and senior managers to appraise the value of ACL and to study its objectives, methods, and relevance to the situation of their own company.

Further details of leadership training, and its effectiveness, are available from the author, c/o The Industrial Society, 3 Carlton House Terrace, London, SW1Y 5DG.

Suggested Reading

ADAIR, J. *Action-Centred Leadership*, McGraw-Hill, London, 1973.
SMITH, E. P. *The Manager as a Leader*, The Industrial Society, 1969.
ADAIR, J. *Training for Leadership*, Macdonald, 1968.
BROWN, M. *The Manager's Guide to the Behavioural Sciences*, The Industrial Society, 1969.
MCGREGOR, D. *The Human Side of Enterprise*, McGraw-Hill, New York, 1960.
MASLOW, A. H. *Motivation and Personality*, Harper and Row, New York, 1954.
PAUL, ROBERTSON, and HERZBERG. *Harvard Business Review*, 1968.

31. The Organization Renewal process in practice

Frank T. Laverty

This chapter is based on the author's experiences with more than 1000 Canadian managers in continuing Renewal activities.

The 'Organization Renewal in Practice' model is a systems approach of inputs, activities, measurable outputs, value added, and positive feedback which is applicable to any form of organization development intervention. The process is traced from the concern of management for the effectiveness of the organization, through training and continual projects, to organizational improvements and to closing the loop back to management via positive feedback.

The author describes the process and cites practical examples of management concern, reasons for selecting Organization Renewal, the steps in the process, and continuing renewal projects which expand the process into a comprehensive organization development intervention.

The participating organizations are challenged to clarify their objectives, to re-examine their structure and organizational functioning, to improve their individual and group relationships, and to redefine their responsibilities. Participants are stimulated to learn from their experiences, to operate effectively, and to prepare for the external and internal pressures which all organizations must eventually face.

Organizational Renewal is an effective process for coping with the new dimensions of internal people power. It combines the needs of the individuals with the needs of the organization so that a more viable balance is created. The cold issues of production and the warm issues of people are integrated. The need for power is replaced by a need for achievement and affiliation so that an organization can progress to the highest state of organizational maturity.

'Organization Renewal is the process of initiating, creating, and confronting needed changes so as to make it possible for organizations to become or remain viable, to adapt to new conditions, to solve problems, to learn from experiences and to move toward greater organization maturity.'[1]

The past fifteen years have been a difficult time for most organizations. Rapid and complex technological changes gave rise to new products, approaches, and industries. Companies moved from a stable situation to a survival posture in a very short span of time. Effective managers learnt how to cope with this technological revolution, but, now, the economic and social revolutions are penetrating organizational life. In addition to external forces, managers are faced with a new dimension—people power.

An effective reaction to organizational people power is organization development. Organizational development recognizes the requirement for effective utilization of the organization's human resources. The organization's climate and work is arranged so that organizational objectives are not met at the expense of the workers' needs. Organization Renewal is an OD process which assists organizations in reaching this necessary balance of needs.

Organization Renewal challenges organizations to clarify their objectives, re-examine their structure and organizational functioning, improve their individual and group relationships and to redefine their responsibilities. Renewal is a process which stimulates organization members to learn from their experiences, to operate effectively, and to prepare for the pressures which all organizations must eventually face.

The practices described in this chapter developed during Organization Renewal activities with more than 1000 Canadian managers in several organizations. Throughout the discussion, the reader may find it useful to refer to the diagrammatic representation of our approach, in Fig. 31.1.

Organization Renewal begins with managerial concern for the organization's effectiveness and relevance. Examples of issues of concern are: unsolved problems, unsatisfactory teamwork, inability to cope with major changes, past rather than future orientations, bypassed opportunities, and activity confusion.

Managerial concern which leads to Organization Renewal is explained more clearly in the following accounts of our experiences with three clients.

Client 1

A large, public-accommodation and construction organization had operated for more than 100 years in a service posture. A newly appointed top executive, who is future rather than past oriented, visualized a dynamic change to a revenue-dependency operation in which managers and subunits would be measured and survive on the revenue they could generate. The executive appreciated that this change would mean new managerial dimensions, for which some managers were not equipped. However, he was cognisant of his obligation to those members who had served the organization faithfully and well. Organization Renewal was implemented to prepare for major

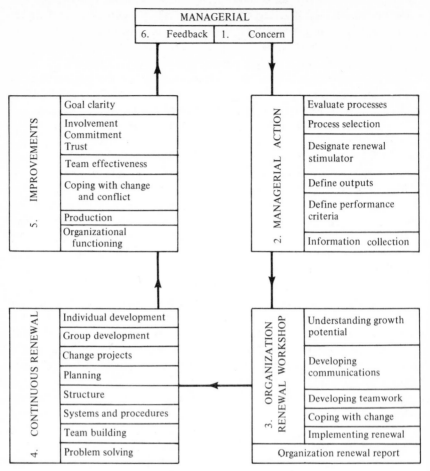

Fig. 31.1. Organization renewal in practice.

operational and structural changes and to assist managers develop for their emerging responsibilities.

Client 2

A public-service organization had made a number of exciting advances in the last few years but the senior executive was concerned that the input was coming from a relatively few innovative managers at senior levels. Renewal was selected to involve all managers down to the supervisory level. The senior executive wanted increased involvement, commitment, and teamwork to assist the organization to continue its established progress pattern.

Client 3

A line manager was appointed director of personnel, a position which, up to that time, had been filled by personnel specialists. The new director observed the branch operations for a few months and considered that a number of improvements were needed. He realized that it would be unwise for him to initiate changes, as there was still some resentment over his appointment. Renewal was selected as a means of clarifying his position and confronting many of the issues which were decreasing the quality of personnel services.

Organization Performance. Each organization in which we have implemented Renewal was already performing satisfactorily or better. Each organization had a dynamic, progressive, senior executive who had a good appreciation of the internal and external pressures affecting the organization. Each executive was cognisant of his obligation to the members of the organization and was aware that continual progress and growth had to be nurtured by effective leadership, involvement, and commitment. One would expect organizations in difficulty to implement Renewal but this has not been the case. We have implemented Renewal with effective organizations which wanted to become more effective.

Managerial Action

The second Renewal step is managerial action. Information is collected on the available OD processes, and the advantages and disadvantages of each are considered. A process is selected which meets the needs of the organization and its members. In addition, the task force responsible for final selection must consider the very real issues of available resources such as time, cost, and personnel.

The selection task force must decide whether the process should be introduced by external consultants, internal consultants, or a mixture of both. We had one very successful experience with an internal–external mix. Fortunately, the internal consultants had broad knowledge and experience in different forms of OD. It is unusual to find an organization with all the necessary skills in-house. It is not a difficult task for an efficient trainer to present the Renewal concept but he must be prepared to deal with issues which arise during the sessions. In most sessions, a resource person is required to use other interventions and, at times, he must design and implement interventions on the spot. These skills come from broad experience and continual OD practice. It is unrealistic to expect an internal resource person to have acquired these capabilities.

Maximum Renewal benefits are derived from the use of external consultants although a mix of internal–external consultants can do a creditable job. An organization which is implementing Renewal, or any other OD process, is taking a major risk when it attempts to do the task with internal resource persons only. Renewal is introduced most effectively by outsiders with management support. Disregarding this suggestion is comparable to jumping out of an aeroplane with a parachute which was packed by your mother-in-law.

The decision to implement the Organization Renewal process is followed closely by the designation of a Renewal stimulator. The Renewal stimulator must be a manager who has access to senior management, supports Organization Renewal, and is credible in the eyes of the participants. He can continue his normal duties, since the Renewal stimulator role takes about one day a week at the start, gradually decreasing to a half-day per week once Renewal is on a continuing basis. His role is of a helping, advisory, and stimulating nature. It is not a power or authority role in any sense. He keeps records of the Renewal projects, telephones group leaders weekly to gather information on projects and has a meeting with each group three times yearly. One of his major tasks is to provide internal or external resources to groups on request. The Renewal stimulator keeps top management advised on the state of Renewal in the Organization and makes recommendations which will further continual Renewal.

The Renewal stimulator does not have to be an OD practitioner, nor does he have to be an Organization Renewal resource person. In one organization, the head of manpower development participated as an Organization Renewal consultant and carried out the renewal stimulator role. In a second organization, a special projects manager with minimum experience in OD performed the Renewal stimulator role. Their approaches to Renewal stimulation are different in that one combines the function with an internal consultant approach while the other keeps detailed records and provides resources as necessary. Both have been effective. It is apparent that the Renewal stimulator role can be adequately performed by any manager of quality who has sufficient interest and energy. My one concern about selection is that managers who meet the requirements for an effective Renewal stimulator are candidates for promotion either internally or externally. In the last year, we have worked with three Renewal stimulators. One was promoted internally, one accepted an external promotion, and the other has received external offers. The Renewal stimulator should be a manager who can be expected, under normal circumstances, to be available for at least two years. Continuity in Renewal is important, and the stimulator provides that continuity.

It is imperative that management define the outputs and performance criteria for Organization Renewal. Positive feedback can be accomplished only if there are predetermined measurable goals. Some typical Renewal goals are described as improvements in step 5 of Fig. 31.1. They include improved goal clarity, improved involvement, commitment and trust, improved team effectiveness, improved ability to cope with change and conflict, improved quantity and/or quality of production, and improved organizational functioning. Once the outputs are determined, performance indicators are developed so that the benefits can be evaluated against a predetermined standard.

Information collection and feedback is an integral part of Organization Renewal. Management reviews both qualitative and quantitative information during the managerial concern and action steps. They may consider items such as turnover, absentees, grievances, types and numbers of errors, profitability, wastage, suggestions, customer complaints, and efficiency and effectiveness indicators, in terms of goal attainment and disaffection statistics.

Prior to Organization Renewal, information is collected on the participants' perceptions of their organization. We use an instrument which combines elements of climate and attitude surveys. This provides a picture of individual and group perceptions. The results are shared with each group. Combining the results from all groups provides an organizational picture.

A year after the final Organization Renewal workshop, the groups are resurveyed to measure changes in perception. The information is keyed to the six improvement outputs shown as step 5 in Fig. 31.1. Figure 31.2 is a

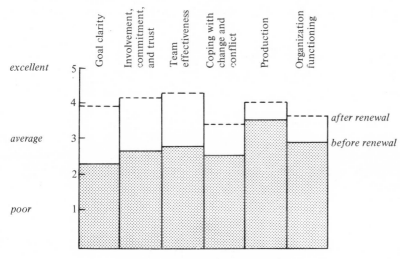

Fig. 31.2. Organizational perceptions.

'before and after' picture of one work group. In each area, the participants perceived an improvement. The improvements perceived by this group are similar to results from other groups. Feedback of this perceived improvement has a significant impact on group morale and expectations. The encouraging feedback gives further impetus to renewal projects.

Organization Renewal Workshop

The third Renewal step is participation in an Organization Renewal workshop which introduces members to the concept and techniques. The focus is on developing the organization to achieve increased effectiveness. The workshop allows managers to interact in work groups, investigate problems in group and interpersonal relationships, and develop team effectiveness. The major emphasis is on dealing with issues related to the real business of the organization. Organization Renewal was not designed to be a complete OD process. It identifies issues of concern to the organization members, and sets the stage for solutions. The continual follow-up is based on specific interventions designed to solve the issues which surface during the workshop and afterwards. The continual Renewal phase expands into a complete OD effort.

There are five interdependent sessions in the Organization Renewal workshop. Initially, the participants evaluate the elements of management in relation to the organizational stages of growth. The second part of the evaluation is to investigate the dimensions of Renewal and to formulate an inventory of issues which require investigation. This is an important element of Renewal. It provides the manager with a frame of reference as to where the organization is at the present time, and stimulates thought as to where it should be—and how to get there.

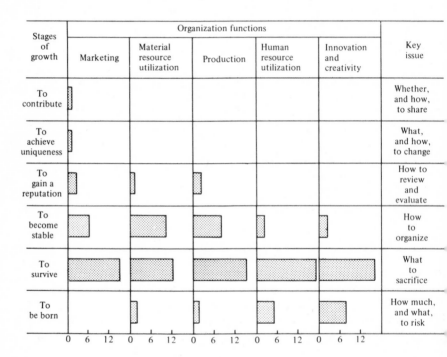

Fig. 31.3. Evaluation of the organization.

An example of one group's initial evaluation is shown in Fig. 31.3. The participants considered their organization to be at a survival stage and followed this self-critical trend, through the inventory shown in Fig. 31.4. These perceptions were tested against a random sample of customers and support staff, whose ratings supported the overall pattern of the evaluation; however, for most elements, they rated the organization a step higher on the scale.

460

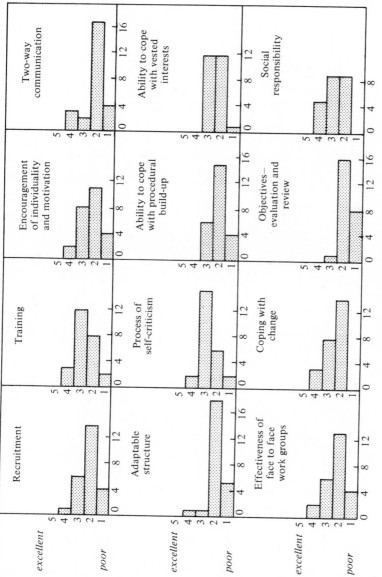

Fig. 31.4. Organizational inventory.

461

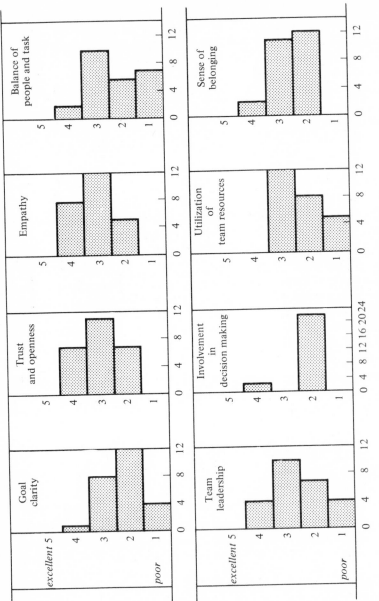

Fig. 31.5. Analysis of team effectiveness.

The second session of the Organization Renewal workshop deals with improved organizational communications. Communication in the Organization Renewal concept goes much farther than the usual definition. It means the process of interfacing and includes definition and confrontation of issues, searching for alternative solutions and mutually coping with the outcome. The interfacing process leads into a logical analysis of organizational roles. Managers have some idea of their individual and work group roles, but lack an understanding of their organizational role. This session enables the participants to investigate, in specific terms, the multiple roles which affect organizational output.

Session three of the Organization Renewal workshop provides members with an opportunity to analyse team effectiveness. The understanding created through the analysis tends to initiate a trend of continuous team building. Renewal stimulates managers to link operational teams into the higher order of institutional teams. Figure 31.5 is an example of one group's analysis of their team effectiveness. This team has continued their team-building activities. They use every group meeting as a team-building exercise and have made major improvements in the decision-making process and the utilization of team resources. The next project, decided upon by the group, is an intensive weekend of team building and positive encounter.

Session four of the Organization Renewal workshop deals with an understanding and an analysis of change. Real work-change projects are started, and completed following the workshop. Some examples of change projects originated in the workshops are: to regularize workload, to develop an image of effectiveness, to bring about a more meaningful relationship between a service unit and the pensioners they service, to introduce a new reporting manual, to change from a service to a marketing posture, to introduce a standard 'system documentation' package requiring client/user participation, to reorganize an operating section, to introduce the four-day week, to develop an effective two-way communication system, to introduce open-plan offices, to decentralize operations, and to establish effective standard documentation.

The final session of the Organization Renewal workshop is to plan the follow-up and continual implementation of Renewal. It is at this time that participants plan future mutual action with the other members of their team. It is useful to introduce the Renewal stimulator at this session and allow the participants to discuss his role. His helping relationship is established, and members feel more comfortable in the on-going relationship which follows the workshop.

The information from the workshop is collected and put into a report, with a copy to the Renewal stimulator and a copy to each workshop participant. This report contains diagrams such as those of Figs. 31.3 to 31.5. It includes details on change projects, and issues which must be solved. After the last Organization Renewal session, a final report—with recommendations and comments—is provided to senior management. This is part of the continual feedback loop which is an important element of Organization Renewal.

During the Organization Renewal workshop, we use an issue commitment approach. Each issue is entered on a piece of newsprint, and an appropriate participant volunteers to investigate the problem. The group suggests some approaches for investigation and determines who, within or outside the group, can provide assistance. They also decide when, and to whom, findings and/or recommendations will be reported. This information is included in the session report. Members leave the workshop with issues and change projects which require action. The issue commitment approach is successful because the requirements and responsibility for results are specific to individuals. Successful Renewal requires action and involvement. The issue commitment approach is one method of establishing this principle. An example of a commitment sheet from one session is shown in Fig. 31.6.

```
WHAT   More effective utilization of team resources
HOW    Inventory of skills
       Analysis of existing work
       Priorities
       Equitable work distribution
       Develop a mechanism to match skills and tasks
       Constant evaluation of needs, priorities, etc.
WHO    Task force
       Leader:   Peter Gray—staffing
       Members: Jack Smith   training
                John Graham—manpower planning
WHEN   Report to management committee
       Interim report: 1 October 1972
       Final report: 7 January 1973
```

Fig. 31.6. Renewal issue commitment sheet.

Implementing OD

Organization Development is a long-range process to develop the members of an organization so that:

(a) channels of communication are open;
(b) conflict is coped with, not suppressed;
(c) organizational climate is based on trust, not power;
(d) feedback is by design, not chance;
(e) structure is flexible, not rigid.

Unfortunately, some senior managers preach the OD philosophy but their behaviour has not changed. OD requires senior management to give a little of itself to meet the needs of individuals and the organization. When the need for power overcomes the need for OD, members who have tasted the seeds of trust, commitment, involvement, and teamwork are left in an untenable position. The usual result is disaffection which can take two forms—leaving the organization or looking outside for the psychic rewards that one should get on the job. Both types of disaffection are a serious loss to an organization.

Continual Organization Renewal provides the opportunity for senior management to utilize positively the growth of the organization members.

Renewal projects are originated from any position in the organization. Some are minor, involving work teams, while others encompass the complete organization. The major requirements are that renewal projects will contribute to the organization and its people, and allow maximum input from those members who must react to the outputs.

Examples of Renewal Projects

The range of minor and major continual Renewal projects is best illustrated by examples from two organizations which have introduced the process effectively.

Case 1

Some 450 managers of Public Works, Canada, are participating in the Organization Renewal process. The senior management has shown by action and behaviour that it welcomes input from all levels of the organization. As projects are identified and agreed upon, material resources and man days are provided. The outcome is an organization with highly motivated members who accept ownership and responsibility for the effectiveness of their organization and its contribution to society.

'Project renewal' is the term that Public Works, Canada uses to describe a wide range of activities, related to clarifying its mission, reviewing its structure, and attaining its objectives. This major project has been under way for more than twenty-four months. The project is managed by a steering committee established at the head office. A network for gathering input from the field, communicating output, and soliciting feedback is in effect. This elaborate communication system has been instrumental in developing the commitment required for a change of major significance.

The business of the organization had become clouded by history and vested interests. When the mission was clarified to meet the modern demands on the Department, it was found that the organizational structure was not suitable. Public Works, Canada, has six Regions spread out across the country. The geographic line organizations could adequately cope with the day to day operational requirements but the complexities and rapid changes in the design and construction and realty functions indicated a need for specialist advisers at the head office. After a detailed study of organizational designs, a system of functional advisers was matrixed from headquarters through the Regions. These functional directors are a specialist resource for field managers and ensure that the mandate and objectives of their functions are consistent with the corporate and strategic plans.

The complications from a functional matrix system superimposed on a geographic line organization has caused some concern. Geographic line managers must put up with functional directors communicating directly with regional managers. Functional directors must thread the thin line between effective specialist involvement and encroachment on line responsibility. The participants are facing up to the concerns with tolerance and flexibility.

465

The common thread which permeates exchanges is that a matrix organization was selected by design and choice. Managers realize that it gives them the balance which was missing from the previous hierarchical organization. The members are adapting to the realization that authority, responsibility, and obligation cannot be neatly packaged any longer. The key to effectiveness in these days of change and complexity is teamwork and sharing. Team spirit is an important requirement of matrix management.

The outcome of project renewal and the resulting matrix organization is a significant experiment in organizational functioning. It is possibly the most ambitious matrix operation in the world, covering thousands of employees throughout Canada. The organizational lessons learned at Public Works, Canada, will have an impact on much of our untested views on organizational theory.

The following are examples of minor projects originated by Public Works, Canada, managers:

(a) Now that Departmental mission and structure has been established, geographic line managers are meeting in three-day conferences to clarify their mandate and establish work planning objectives. The conferences are structured to further team building and improve communications: the major needs of matrix organizations. The practicality of the matrix organization becomes more and more evident as participants become aware of the increasing number of 'superordinate' or joint objectives. The impact of two separate functional teams establishing identical objectives emphasizes role interdependence.

(b) The senior managers of the department were concerned about their development as group problem solvers. They agreed to participate in a twelve-hour series of problem-solving exercises, which were recorded on television. The participants used evaluative instruments to discover their problem-solving style from the video playback and shared, openly, their comments with their colleagues. I provided process analysis of the group functioning at the end of each session. A key to the success of this experience was the use of a group dynamics specialist as the television operator. His knowledge allowed him to record activities which were significant for the group's development. The cost of using an operator of this calibre is considerable but the benefits in experiential discovery by the participants make it worthwhile.

(c) The architects and designers were concerned about the rate of change in their professions and decided to investigate means of coping with the obsolescence factor. A task force studied the issue within and outside the organization and agreed to run a series of developmental conferences. The conferences—of ten days' duration—have a future orientation and are directed at creative problem solving. Senior management not only support the project with the necessary resources but take an active part in confronting the issues facing these professionals. The plan is to allow all the architects and designers to participate. The conferences have stimulated an increased involvement with professional societies, and increased attendance at seminars and workshops. In addition, the Department has increased its support of long-range development opportunities for its professionals.

For a long time, professional obsolescence has been a major concern in organizations with a large number of professional employees. The senior management of Public Works, Canada, were cognisant of this situation. They vigorously support professional growth, with time and resources, but have taken an enlightened approach. They have placed the decision for, and ownership of, development in the hands of the involved professionals. The commitment and personal involvement of the participants at the first two conferences indicates the viability of this approach.

Case 2

Three-hundred managers of Services, Canada, participate in the Organization Renewal process. The process has been operating for eighteen months and is gaining momentum. This is due mainly to the willingness of senior managers to listen attentively to feedback and react appropriately. Examples of their continued Renewal are as follows:

(a) There was general agreement among the participants that the available human resources were not utilized to the maximum extent possible. Several participants thought that the appraisal system did not adequately indicate their skills and potential, and that there was insufficient reaction to development recommendations on the appraisal reports.

The top managers accepted the human resource utilization observation as constructive criticism. They were cognisant that, a few years ago, their sector had absorbed a number of like functions from other agencies. The services were being performed in an acceptable manner, and it was appropriate now to consider long-range personnel needs.

A flexible, manpower plan was prepared, based on a systems approach, with allowance for annual updating and monitoring of progress. The plan contains demographic data on age, education, sex, bilingualism, performance, promotability, potential, strength, and attrition rates. The manpower planners compared the demographic results with the personnel situation a year earlier and analysed the reasons for major changes. They also compared the results with public-service averages. They estimated personnel needs for the next five years and made recommendations dealing with the issue of effective human resource utilization.

The plan was developed with input from individuals and branches. It is in the review and feedback phase. Some amendments are required but, in general, it is a valid picture of the personnel state of the organization and the steps needed to move it to the higher order of human resource utilization.

(b) The age-old question of 'When does a service agency become a marketing agency' came up time and time again during the Organization Renewal workshops. The members consider that their functions are of such a socially responsible nature that it is necessary for them to adopt a marketing posture. A task force conducted a marketing survey. Plans are being developed to suit the emerging marketing philosophy.

(c) Each year, there is an intake of management trainees who participate in a rotating, experience programme for two years. There was a general dissatisfaction with the mechanics of the programme. Interviews with trainees and managers indicated that the expectations of the trainees and the needs of the organization were not coordinated. The expected mix of skills and experience for each function had not been communicated to supervisors and trainees. This resulted in an image of *ad hoc* placement; work which did not appear meaningful; non-communication of development goals and measures; and general frustration for the trainees.

The top executive, involved managers, and trainees met for a problem-solving day. Teams composed of managers and trainees considered programme planning, programme coordination, assignments, meaningful work, supervision, and performance review. The teams reported their deliberations and recommendations at a plenary session. The trainees assumed responsibility for a portion of their training and formed task groups to investigate issues and recommend solutions. All trainees agreed to provide the personnel officer with a description of each training appointment so that appropriate training goals can be established and unacceptable assignments deleted from the rotation.

The frustrations of trainees in a rotational plan is a usual occurrence. They arrive in an organization with great expectations, to find that supervisors are too busy for them—a trainee available for six months is not considered a productive source; that much of the work is repetitive and clerical; succeeding appointments do not contain opportunities for increased responsibility; and changing appointments every six months does not provide the sense of belonging necessary for personal development. Organization renewal provided the vehicle for bringing these issues out in the open at Services, Canada, and the participants were ready and willing to cope with the outcome in a positive manner.

Conclusion

Organization Renewal is an effective process for coping with the new dimensions of internal people power. It combines the needs of the individual with the needs of the organization so that a more viable balance is created. During Renewal, the cold issues of production and the warm issues of people are integrated. Renewal requires senior executives with the 'guts' to release power, and trust subordinates. As the need for power is replaced with a need for affiliation and achievement, Organization Renewal is truly in practice.

Reference

1. LIPPITT, G. L. *Organization Renewal*, Appleton-Century-Crofts, New York, 1969, p. 1.

468

Suggested Reading

ARGYRIS, C. *Integrating the Individual and the Organization*, Wiley, New York, 1964.

BECKHARD, R. *Organization Development: Strategies and Models*, Addison-Wesley, Reading, Mass., 1969.

BENNIS, W. G. *Changing Organizations*, McGraw-Hill, New York, 1966.

BENNIS, W. G. *Organization Development: Its Nature, Origins, and Prospects*, Addison-Wesley, Reading, Mass., 1969.

FORDYCE, J. K. and WEIL, R. *Managing with People*, Addison-Wesley, Reading, Mass., 1971.

GABORA, H. N. and LAVERTY, F. T. 'Organization Renewal—Why and How', *Canadian Training Methods*, January–February 1972.

GARDNER, J. W. *Self-renewal: The Individual and the Innovative Society*, Harper and Row, New York, 1963.

GOLEMBIEWSKI, R. T. and GIBSON, F. *Managerial Behavior and Organization Demands: Management as a Linking of Levels of Interaction*, Rand-McNally, Chicago, 1967.

HOFFER, E. *The Ordeal of Change*, Harper and Row, New York, 1963.

KATZ, D. and KAHN, R. L. *The Social Psychology of Organizations*, Wiley, New York, 1966.

LAVERTY, F. T. 'Renewal with Objectives', *Canadian Training Methods*, October 1973.

LAWRENCE, P. R. and LORSCH, J. W. *Developing Organizations: Diagnosis and Action*, Addison-Wesley, Reading, Mass., 1969.

LIKERT, R. *The Human Organization: Its Management and Value*, McGraw-Hill, New York, 1969.

LIPPITT, G. L. *Organization Renewal*, Appleton-Century-Crofts, New York, 1969.

LIPPITT, R., WATSON, J., and WESTLEY, B. *The Dynamics of Planned Change*, Harcourt, Brace and World, New York, 1958.

LITTERER, J. A. *The Analysis of Organizations*, Wiley, New York, 1965.

SCHEIN, E. H. *Organization Psychology*, Prentice-Hall, Englewood Cliffs, New Jersey, 1965.

SCHEIN, E. H. *Process Consultation: Its Role in Organization Development*, Addison-Wesley, Reading, Mass., 1969.

THOMPSON, J. D. *Organization in Action*, McGraw-Hill, New York, 1967.

WALTON, R. E. *Interpersonal Peacemaking: Confrontations and Third-Party Consultation*, Addison-Wesley, Reading, Mass., 1969.

ZALEZNIK, A. and MOMENT, D. *The Dynamics of Interpersonal Behavior*, Wiley, New York, 1964.

32. Organization development in the small business

Philip J. Sadler

This chapter discusses some of the special problems encountered in smaller enterprises seeking to introduce planned programmes of organizational change. Two basic types of small business— the family firm and the entrepreneurial company—are singled out and considered separately. Finally, some of the problems are exemplified in a case history of organization development in a family firm in the printing industry. This work involved systematic evaluation of the effectiveness of the organization development programme; results of this evaluation are presented at the end of the chapter.

Business enterprises employing between 100 and 1000 people are large enough to have problems of organization, yet not so large that they can command sophisticated resources of expertise. Moreover, as social systems, they differ in important respects from the larger more formal organizations which have been the principal focus of organizational research, and around which contemporary organization theory has been built up.

Types of Small Enterprises

Smaller enterprises can be divided into two broad categories, each of which has special problems of organization development. One category consists of the traditional family business, an enterprise which is controlled by second, third, or subsequent generations of family members. This group embraces all such enterprises falling within the size range suggested above, and which are controlled *in practice* by members of a single family or small group of families. This definition includes not only the private company in which share ownership is for the most part confined to family members, but the public company in which the nature of the shareholding enables the family or families to wield effective control. (It may not be necessary for them to have a majority shareholding for this to be so; much depends on who the other shareholders are, and the extent to which shareholding is concentrated or dispersed.)

The second category consists of those businesses still controlled by their entrepreneurial founders. It is more difficult to generalize about such firms since their characteristics tend to reflect the individual personalities of the entrepreneurs who have built them up.

The Family Firm

In enterprises of this type, two social systems—the family and the business organization—are closely interwoven.[1] If the business organization is to change and develop in response to a changing environment, related adjustments within the family circle will be necessary. In some circumstances, changes which favour the growth and development of the business may be destructive to family ties and relationships, and there is a real possibility that the interests of the two institutions may be conflicting. The owners of family businesses will feel strong pressures on them to balance these conflicting claims, with the result that their decisions will not always appear wholly rational from the perspective of business management alone.

It need hardly be said that a programme of organization development should be related to the overall objectives of the enterprise concerned. Yet one of the perennial problems facing the family firm is the complexity and elusiveness of its objectives. Although lip-service may be paid to the usual criteria of profit and growth, the actual behaviour of enterprises of this kind indicates that straightforward economic motives are often relegated to a lower order of priority.

One reason is that the family business is seen not only as an investment which should provide its owners with an adequate return, but as a calling or field of service within which are to be found opportunities for various forms of non-economic satisfaction. Indeed, in many industries, it is more customary to think in terms of carrying on an honourable trade or profession rather than in terms of managing a business. This view of the purpose of the enterprise is reflected in terms such as 'Master Builder' or 'Master Printer' and in the fierce pride with which people point to family connections with an industry over several generations. Such people will be unlikely to consider diversification as an acceptable way out of a firm's economic difficulties.

It is not uncommon for family members to serve the business as managers with considerable reluctance. Many would have preferred a free choice of career. They enter the firm because of a sense of duty to the family and not because they wish to excel as businessmen.

In the process of discussing and agreeing objectives—a process which is seldom free of conflict in any kind of organization—differences of opinion may constitute a threat to family unity. A manager who disagrees strongly

471

with company policy can always resign and go elsewhere, but it is not possible to resign from a family. So the conflict has to be contained, and at least some semblance of unity achieved. Often, this will be done by avoiding the conflict, delaying decisions, or trying to build compromises. Such an approach may save the family but destroy the business.

A highly sensitive topic in the typical family business is the question of managerial competence. In the past, the right of family members to participate in the management of the family owned concern was unchallenged. This is not so today. Competence is demanded from all and is regarded as more important than ties of blood or marriage. Family members who occupy senior management positions are likely to be highly sensitive to any implication that they hold their jobs only because of the family connection, and often try to convince themselves—and others—that career success is unrelated to family influence (whereas, in fact, the two are quite inseparable in any family firm). In general, the non-family members of the firm will accept the superior career opportunities of family members, provided that they are reasonably competent and provided that the differences in opportunity are not out of all proportion.

At the same time, if able outsiders are to be attracted to management jobs, then at least some of the top positions must be open to them. Even where this is so, however, problems remain since the outsider who is in this way admitted to the inner circle of the family firm must not only be acceptable as a businessman—he must also be capable of being accepted as a 'friend of the family'. He must be worthy of the family's trust, socially acceptable and, in some cases, even marriageable.

Programmes for management development and succession in family firms, not surprisingly, are subject to special considerations.[2] One stream of recruits to management comes from the family and is subject to natural constraints of one kind or another. Sometimes, a generation fails to produce sons (or marriageable daughters) or produces them at the wrong time, or they turn out to have no talent or liking for business. Such problems give rise to an observable tendency for the fortunes of family firms to fluctuate in relation to the cycle of family life. The enterprise may be at a low ebb when steered by a chairman or managing director who is hanging on, past retiring age, waiting for his grandsons to finish their education and take over. Equally disastrous can be the early death of the head of the family before the next generation is ready to assume control. The vulnerability of the family firm to the forces of birth, maturity, decline, and death makes it difficult to sustain the development of the organization.

Managers can also be recruited from two other sources—from outside the firm or from the rank and file. Where outsiders are concerned, it is frequently difficult to persuade family firms to use systematic recruiting and selection procedures (although they may go through the motions). The preferred course of action is to choose people already known and trusted, or to go on personal recommendation. Often, such appointments are disastrous.

Where managers are promoted from within, much depends on the validity of the firm's approach to training and development. The practice can be successful, but it has a built-in weakness. People promoted in this way usually feel that they owe their advancement in life to the generosity and benevolence of the family. The result is that they give their loyalty to the family rather than to the business.

With regard to management development, there are some further problems. First, family firms are usually slow to recognize the need to do anything about it. Second, where the need is recognized, it is not always easy to avoid an approach which savours of nepotism, 'Crown princes', and family intrigue. This reflects the fact that it is so difficult to separate the two processes of developing managerial ability and sharing the family inheritance. It is the most natural thing in the world for a senior member of a family firm to single out a promising young employee and to treat him like a son. Equally naturally, this creates resentment among those not so favoured, and scarcely constitutes systematic management development.

One of the most well-documented characteristics of the family firm is the tendency to use a paternalistic style of management. This involves extending the concept of family to the whole of the work force and combining feelings of concern for employees' welfare with the conviction that management knows best what workers want. This approach to management was highly successful and widely praised in the social climate of the 'thirties, and was typified in the great family businesses such as Cadbury's, Wills, and Pilkingtons. Today, it finds less favour and, indeed, may give rise to active resentment. No sensible programme for organization development can skirt this issue, but the difficulties involved in bringing about change in this highly sensitive area do not need to be emphasized.

The First-Generation Entrepreneurial Firm

Firms of this type have not had time to develop strong traditions, nor are the proprietors the trustees of the family's inheritance in the same way as in the case of the old established family business. It is also true that, for obvious reasons, the competence of the entrepreneur who has built up a business from scratch is less likely to be challenged.

At the same time, there are some special problems which inhibit the further development of enterprises of this type, and which arise out of the special position of the entrepreneur in relation to the organization he has created. He tends to regard the firm as 'his' and, as such, subject to his complete control. In many cases, this leads to the adoption of a highly autocratic management style. Entrepreneurs frequently find it difficult to delegate real authority and responsibility, and once the organization has grown to a size which makes a measure of delegation essential, this can be an important source of inefficiency and inflexibility.

The entrepreneur's approach to the management of the organization will tend to reflect the qualities and drives which made him successful in the first place. He tends to regard flair and hunch as indispensable to success and to eschew formal, systematic, or scientific procedures. He cherishes his independence and may be reluctant to see his firm grow beyond a certain size lest that independence should be threatened. He often finds difficulty in effecting the transition from entrepreneurial vitality to administrative vitality—he is more effective in starting things and building them up than he is in managing a larger, on-going organization.

Finally, he is not uncommonly a man of sudden enthusiasms which, equally suddenly, die away to be replaced by others. Organization development may be his latest enthusiasm but this may not guarantee a sure basis for a sustained programme of organization change.

The Objectives of Organization Development in Smaller Enterprises

In a general sense, organization development is a programme of planned organizational change concerned with altering the beliefs, attitudes, values, and structure of an organization in order to facilitate adjustment to new environmental conditions, new technologies, and to the stresses of growth. In practice, the specific objectives of organization development tend to differ from one type of small enterprise to another. In the typical family firm, the most common set of problems which give rise to the need for planned change include:

(a) lack of commercial competitiveness, often to the extent that the firm's survival is threatened;
(b) lack of capacity for innovation; adherence to traditional practices;
(c) problems arising from a lessening acceptance of a paternalistic approach in personnel matters;
(d) problems of managerial competence, managerial succession, and development;
(e) problems of conflict between family objectives and business goals.

In the first-generation entrepreneurial firm on the other hand, the following issues are more likely to be the ones of urgent concern.

(a) problems arising from rapid growth in previous years—poor communications, overdependence on the knowledge and competence of a small number of individuals, shortage of capable managers;
(b) problems of relationships with the chief executive (entrepreneur), including problems of management style;
(c) problems of provision for succession to the leadership role.

The Directions of Organizational Change

No matter whether the starting point is a traditional family firm in decline or an entrepreneurial business in which initial, dynamic growth has levelled off, the process of organization development in the small enterprise will normally involve radical change in the whole character of the social system.

It involves moving away from forms of social organization which, in an important sense, are mere extensions of the family or of the entrepreneur's personality towards that much more highly formalized, more impersonal social system which characterizes the modern business enterprise. This is not the sort of change that can be effected overnight. It involves, of necessity, movement into transitional forms of organization such that the radical nature of the transformation can be cushioned and made tolerable for those involved.

Social science research into business organizations has involved many attempts to classify organizations into types. Whether or not, pure types as such exist is perhaps less important than the fact that people certainly have different ideas about the form that an ideal work organization should assume. For some, the ideal involves a cluster of characteristics which, taken together, has come to be termed the industrial bureaucracy. The principal features of this form of organization include:

(a) a well-defined chain of command;
(b) a formal system of rules and procedures;
(c) a division of labour based on functional specialization;
(d) promotion and selection based on objective assessments of competence;
(e) impersonality in relationships, with emphasis on role or office rather than individuality.

For others, the ideal organization exhibits other characteristics:

(a) a flexible organization structure emphasizing lateral relationships;
(b) participation and involvement in decision making, coupled with openness in personal relationships;
(c) authority derived from the task rather than personal authority or authority derived from hierarchical status;
(d) emphasis on teamwork in relation to whole task as against specialization.

Organizations with the above characteristics have been termed 'organic' or 'organismic', stressing the biological rather than the mechanical analogy.[3]

It would be wrong to regard these two types of organizations as stark alternatives, with nothing in between. It is more helpful to regard them as opposite ends of a continuum, in which case the question is not which type of organization should be developed—the bureaucratic or the organic—but, rather, that in developing the organization, consideration should be given to the extent to which it should be relatively bureaucratic or relatively organic in orientation in the short run and to the direction in which it should develop in the long run.

The answers to these questions will depend not only on the type of enterprise (i.e., family business or entrepreneurial) but on factors such as the task, and the technology with which it is pursued. For example, a long-established family firm will normally find it easier, at least in the short run, to develop along relatively bureaucratic lines than to attempt to develop an organic management system. This is because the fluid, and relatively less well-defined relationships of the organic mode may represent too great a threat to those accustomed to the strongly traditional nature of the family business and its emphasis on status and ritual.

On the other hand, a much younger business—run on entrepreneurial lines with a minimum of formality, and great flexibility—can more easily develop organically, provided that the chief executive is willing to share the decision making with others.

Other things being equal, firms with tasks most capable of being routinized and using mass production technology are more likely to meet with success by moving towards the bureaucratic type in the long run, whereas firms with more creative tasks, or one which employ craft technologies or continuous flow, are more likely to encounter success by moving, long term, towards the organic end of the continuum.

A Case History

The issues involved in determining directions for organizational change in the smaller enterprise, and the processes involved in the programme of organization development, can best be illustrated by an example from practice. A full account of this case has been published elsewhere.[4]

In 1964, Williams Lea—a firm of general printers in the City of London—embarked, with outside help, on a programme of organization development which has been sustained to the present time (1973) and is still continuing. The firm is an old-established family business, in 1964 employing about 350 people.

Like many companies in the printing industry, this firm faced a number of problems which, taken together, were creating immense pressure for change and were threatening profitability and survival prospects. These included new developments in the technology of printing, changes in the market for print, rising manpower costs, and the general social changes which make paternalism increasingly less acceptable.

Before the programme began, top management had accepted the need for change, and a start had been made—using management consultants—to develop the organization along bureaucratic lines. An organization structure had been developed and published in the form of a chart, work study had been introduced, and a handful of outsiders had been recruited at senior management level. These changes had, however, been introduced piecemeal, and, prior to 1964, there had been no attempt to plan the future development of the organization as a whole.

The Diagnostic Stage

The first step in the organization development programme was to carry out a diagnostic study. The main elements in this were, first, a review of company performance, using interfirm comparisons as a basis; second, a series of semistructured interviews with members of the organization, including all managerial and supervisory personnel. The main conclusions to emerge from this study were:

(a) Relative to other companies of similar size in the same industry, Williams Lea was reasonably successful commerically. Its growth and profit record in the recent past were slightly above average. The one danger area appeared to be a high (and rising) wage cost per unit of output.
(b) Productivity, as measured by value of output per employee, was above average for the industry. This reflected investment in modern plant and equipment in previous years, coupled with a locally favourable industrial relations climate. However, the figures suggested a relationship between high wages, high productivity, and good industrial relations which could render the firm highly vulnerable if, for any reason, wages were to rise faster than productivity over a sustained period.
(c) The organization was working reasonably effectively. This, however, reflected more the successful establishment of a network of informal relationships than it did the adequacy of the formal organization structure. The smooth working of the system relied greatly on personalities and on feelings of loyalty and teamwork among long-serving, ex-shopfloor managers and supervisors. Where such relationships did not exist the structure did not work well. Some managers were overloaded, while others appeared to have little to do. There was evidence of a not uncommon conflict of interest between production and sales personnel and of a lack of coordination between day and night shifts.
(d) Certain important functions which would be needed as a foundation for future growth and development were lacking completely, or existed in rudimentary form only. These included management accounting (as distinct from historical accounting), market research and development, personnel management and training, and technical development.
(e) While relations with the shopfloor were good, and there were no really serious morale problems, there was a general feeling that communications had to some extent broken down. There was a widespread need for a stronger feeling of direction and purpose, for a clear statement of company policy and objectives—'Where are we going?'
(f) Top management appeared to be tied down by immediate problems with the result that long-term planning had never really developed.
(g) In terms of the organic–bureaucratic dimension referred to previously, Williams Lea appeared to combine some of the features of each type of managing system. A conscious effort had been made to develop along bureaucratic lines—organization charts and job descriptions had been produced, the hierarchy was steep relative to the size of the firm, the main emphasis in the structure was on functionally specialized departments, and attempts to rationalize work were under way. At the same time, there was in practice a great deal that was organic. A high proportion of the communication and interaction that took place was lateral rather than vertical, and the level of teamwork was high. Formal

systems were used minimally, and people were prepared to ignore standard procedures in the interests of getting the work done.

The essential characteristic of this diagnosis is not its uniqueness but the fact that it could be replicated a thousand times in family firms facing the pressures of environmental change.

Prescription for Change

Following the diagnostic study, the findings were discussed with the company's top management, and an agreed plan for organizational development was worked out. The first and essential stage in this process involved the redefining of company objectives. Prior to this, no formal statement of objectives existed—there is a natural tendency in small companies to feel that the objectives are obvious and can be taken for granted. In practice, the formulation of a company strategy, involving a set of longer-term objectives and a related set of more immediate goals, took many meetings—over a period of months. This was the beginning of systematic corporate planning for the company, and from this time forwards, all questions of organization development reflected the overall strategies set out in the corporate plan.

The second stage was concerned mainly with the redesigning of the organization structure. The chief concern was to assist in the development of a healthy organization in human terms, with a high degree of teamwork and a high level of motivation among its members, and to ensure that the organization was adapted both to its immediate task and to the requirements for change. The principal features of the revised structure were as follows:

(a) decentralization of decision making and control;
(b) associated strengthening of horizontal communications channels;
(c) steps to free senior management from day to day pressures and to encourage longer-term planning;
(d) clear definitions of roles and relationships.

Implementation

It must be stressed that the structural changes which followed shortly after the diagnostic phase was completed were merely the opening moves in the overall programme of organizational development which has continued since and which, at the time of writing, has been in existence for seven years. In addition to further adjustments to the structure, in the light of experience, the programme has included considerable change in the area of management style and in matters such as training and development, innovation in technology and product, etc.

The main difficulties encountered at this stage (apart from the inevitable resistance to change that will be encountered in any long-established family business in a traditional industry) reflected two characteristics of the managing system of the firm which, again, are features likely to be found in most smaller enterprises. These were, first, the relative lack of sophistication of managers in the early stages of the programme and, second, the absence of any slack in the managerial staffing of the concern, which made it difficult to divert people's attention away from day to day tasks to concentrate effort on the management of change. In the early stages of the programme, much effort was devoted—by means of formal training and other, less formal means—to developing new forms of competence among managerial personnel. Not all proved capable of making this adjustment, and some left the firm at this stage, to be replaced—in the main—by more professional managers recruited from outside.

Evaluation

The ultimate test of an organizational development programme lies in the extent to which an organization achieves its objectives. Against this criterion, the Williams Lea investment in organization development has been well justified. When the programme began, the sales turnover was less than £1 million while net profit was £35 000. By 1972, the Williams Lea Group sales turnover was over £3 200 000 while net profit was £204 000.

Between 1964 and 1968, a systematic process of evaluating the effectiveness of the organization development programme, in other than commercial criteria, was pursued. The following four variables were measured by administering a questionnaire to managerial and supervisory staff at two-yearly intervals.

(a) Job Satisfaction:
the percentage liking their jobs 'very much indeed'.
(b) Company satisfaction:
the percentage satisfied with the company as an employer.
(c) Effectiveness of communications channels:
the percentage 'completely in the picture' or 'knowing most of what goes on';
the percentage reporting 'no difficulty' in getting job-related information;
the percentage 'seldom or never' receiving conflicting instructions;
the percentage finding it 'very easy' to get people above them to listen to suggestions to improve efficiency.
(d) Effectiveness of organizational change:
the percentage believing that organization development has made the firm more efficient;
the percentage believing that organization development has made the firm a 'more pleasant place to work'.

The results of these validation studies are shown in Figs. 32.1 to 32.8. The 1964 measures constitute the base line, in that these were taken before the commencement of the organization development programme. The 1966 and 1968 measures reflect the state of affairs as the programme developed. At each stage, all members of the managerial and supervisory staff completed questionnaires; the numbers ranged from 28 in 1964, through 40 in 1966, to 43 in 1968 (reflecting the growth of the company).

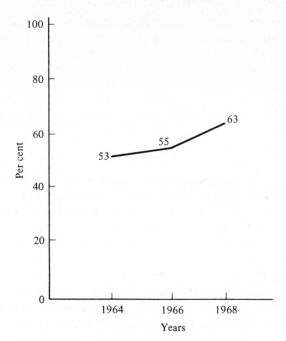

Fig. 32.1. Percentage liking their jobs very much indeed.

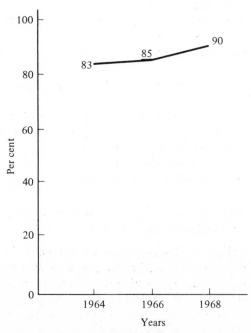

Fig. 32.2 Percentage satisfied with the company as an employer.

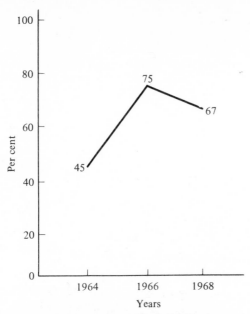

Fig. 32.3. Percentage completely in the picture,
or knowing most of what goes on.

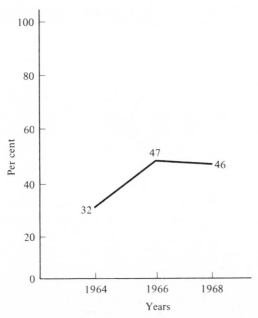

Fig. 32.4. Percentage having no difficulty in getting
job-related information.

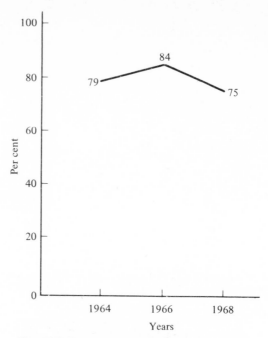

Fig. 32.5. Percentage seldom, or never, receiving conflicting instructions.

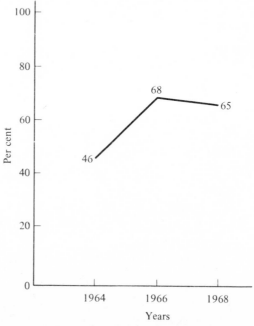

Fig. 32.6. Percentage finding it very easy to get people above them to listen.

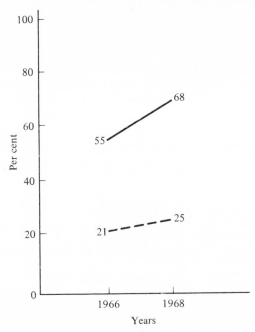

Fig. 32.7. Percentage believing that OD has made
the firm more efficient (solid line) and percentage
perceiving no change.

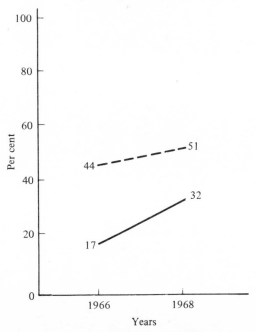

Fig. 32.8. Percentage believing that OD has made
the firm a more pleasant place to work (solid line);
and percentage perceiving no change.

Conclusion

This chapter has drawn attention to the major issues and problems which face smaller enterprises seeking to develop their organizations by means of a planned programme of change, and has shown—by means of an example—that successful organization development is possible in businesses of this kind. The aim has been to demonstrate that, provided there is adequate understanding of the culture of the small enterprise, an organization development programme can work, and that organization development is not an expensive and fashionable management gimmick that only large organizations can afford to play with.

References

1. MILLER, E. and RICE, A. K. *Systems of Organization*, Tavistock, 1967, chapters 9 and 10.
2. SOFER, C. *The Organization from Within*, Tavistock, 1961.
3. BURNS, T., and STALKER, G. M. *The Management of Innovation*, Tavistock, 1962.
4. SADLER, P. J. and BARRY, B. A. *Organization Development: Case Studies in the Printing Industry*, Longmans, 1970.

Suggested Reading

MILLER, E. J. and RICE, A. K. *Systems of Organization*, Tavistock, 1967, chapters 9 and 10.
SADLER, P. J. and BARRY, B. A. *Organization Development: Case Studies in the Printing Industry*, Longmans, 1970.
SOFER, C. *The Organization from Within*, Tavistock, 1961.

33. The role of the consultant in organization development

Geoffrey Morris

'Organization development' is a comprehensive approach to increasing the effectiveness of an organization. It relies less on the imposition of systems than on providing those who work in the organization with the confidence and skill to achieve a better integration of the organization's resources.

Key stages in organization development are: diagnosis of problems and opportunities, with definitions of possible benefits; achieving general understanding of the problems and obtaining commitment to a change programme; training; implementation of improvements. To each of these phases, an external consultant can contribute experience, material, credibility, and objectivity. However, it is important that he works in close collaboration with the organization's own functional specialists and helps them to take a leading role. They must become self-sufficient.

Organization development is fraught with pitfalls—successful programmes have probably been the minority. Among the more frequent cases of failure are: 'behavioural' training out of the business context; inadequate planning of on-the-job follow-up, with the result that euphoria leads to frustration; programmes directed at one section or level of the organization, which consequently become a 'group apart'; lack of clear objectives and criteria for evaluation.

The practicalities of making organization development succeed are illustrated from case experience. While it is essential that each programme should develop its own tools according to the needs of the particular situation, examples are given of documents which have proved successful in context.

The term 'organization development' has been used to cover a broad spectrum of consultant activity. In previous chapters, management styles, Management by Objectives, problem solving and decision making, and job enrichment have been discussed as approaches to OD. Elsewhere, appraisal systems, payment systems, information systems, and group therapy—in fact, a whole gamut of management techniques and almost any application of the behavioural sciences to a work context—have been launched in the guise of OD.

What, then, is the essential nature of organization development? If the process is to be true to its name, it must surely be concerned with the total organization, its purposes and its problems. It will aim to ensure both that the needed skills are present within that organization, and that the skills and efforts of individuals are effectively integrated in the definition and pursuit of corporate goals. As circumstances change, the organization will need to be able to realign itself smoothly and purposefully.

In addition to being directed towards the total organization as such, organization development programmes—in the fullest sense—have two further characteristics: First, they take into account the whole field of management techniques, skills, and resources and bring them to bear as appropriate to the needs of the organization. Thus, while it may be pretentious for individual techniques to claim the OD label, the use of any of these techniques in a total OD context may well be appropriate. Second, OD programmes seek to achieve improvement and change through an organization's own management team and not by imposing instant, consultant solutions. There is a training element.

Such a programme was undertaken by a major subsidiary of a large multinational organization. Target setting on the basis of five-year plans had long been standard practice in this company, and, as early as 1957, a system crudely resembling Management by Objectives was used for the main sections of the business. Long-term strategies were studied in depth from time to time, and, at one stage, an outside consultant was employed to examine the organization and its operating procedures in relation to planned growth.

In 1965, the company formally introduced a system of Management by Objectives associated with profit planning and appraisal. This approach had some success in integrating company operations. Indeed, the importance of establishing objectives for each department, and each manager, became increasingly clear. However, the company's experience illustrated the reality of the problem of management resistance to imposed systems which are not fully understood. In introducing Management by Objectives, the company failed fully to appreciate how important it was to obtain the commitment of managers. Some managers saw objective setting and profit planning as a meaningless chore, and even a threat. In consequence, much time and energy was wasted in producing useless bits of paper.

It was the realization of the importance of management understanding, involvement, and commitment, which led the company to ask itself whether it could, instead of employing consultants or imposing a system, enable its managers to carry out their own regular and systematic review of their operations and make plans for improvement.

In 1967, the board gave a brief to the personnel function to arrive at a means whereby the company could use the experience and skills of all its own managers to appraise overall and group performance on a regular basis and to decide what changes were needed and ensure that necessary changes were brought about. Clearly, this proposition presented certain problems:

(a) the average manager did not have the analytical skills of the outside consultant or in-company specialist department;
(b) it is difficult for a manager to view his own operation objectively;
(c) the process was one of change, and change implies disturbance of routine, extra work initially, risk of unforeseen problems, and interference with the established pattern of status. Managers (the older ones, especially) are therefore apt to fear change;
(d) there was the familiar problem of obtaining commitment to the total process.

Strangely enough, problems (a) and (b) caused the least worry. A great deal could be done towards overcoming them by providing managers with checklists against which they could examine their operations. The resources of excellent in-company service functions were available to management teams. If they would fully use these aids, the teams could set meaningful targets for improvement. However, the whole operation would be doomed to failure unless problems (c) and (d) could be overcome.

The company reached the conclusion that the success of this OD programme would depend very much on an initial, training phase. The broad aims of this phase would be:

(a) to teach managers to understand the problems which can interfere with organizational effectiveness;
(b) to obtain the commitment of managers to tackling these problems;
(c) to attack managerial resistance to change.

When all the members of an actual working team had separately been through the first phase, they would then, and only then, be ready to tackle the second phase.

In this second phase, they would analyse the way in which their work group operated. To do this, they would be helped by checklists. On the basis of their analysis, they would plan how to improve the operations of their group, both as an entity and in its relationship with other groups. Thirdly, a date would be set—three to six months ahead—at which the group would reconvene to examine its achievement of its plans and re-examine its operations. This process would become a permanent cycle.

In reaching the above conclusions, the company had made an extensive study of existing approaches to OD—the Blake Grid, Coverdale, Reddin, Likert, T-Groups, Ergom exercises. Through a small circle of training experts, they gained practical experience of certain of these methods and devised and tested their own approaches.

In-company procedures and events were carefully studied, and account taken of relevant literature and research, varying from the behaviourists (in particular Herzberg, Maslow, and McClelland), through Kepner–Tregoe, to textbooks of OR, marketing, and business economics. The decision was taken to design a programme specially for the company's own situation.

A pilot training phase was run in November 1968 and, on the basis of its success, the board decided to apply the programme as quickly as possible to all members of its management. The first seminar was held in February 1969. By April 1970, almost all members had attended, although seminars are still held at six-monthly intervals to cater for promotions, and newcomers to the company. The training seminars each lasted for one week and were residential. Managers attending worked in four groups which each had the widest possible mix of status, work location, and function.

During this phase, managers were asked to take part in a series of simulated business activities such as report writing, negotiating against another group, making decisions about salaries, or interviewing subordinates. When they had completed the activity, they were asked to analyse what had taken place in order to decide how they might operate more effectively with subsequent activities of a similar nature. In the course of the analysis, they would also tell each other how their individual efforts might be directed more productively.

The sequence of *activity–analysis–individual feedback* was applied to problems which were so designed as to cast light on the basis relationships which form a part of every organization, namely :

(a) interpersonal—at the same level within the same work group;
(b) boss–subordinate;
(c) intergroup or interdepartment.

The effect of a change in group structure was also studied.

As a result of the analysis of their performance in the various exercises, managers became aware of the kinds of behaviour which increased or diminished effectiveness. They learned to look at the way that they themselves, operated rather than to concentrate on criticizing others. Above all, they became aware that the real danger to group effectiveness is not in the 'explosions' which people believe may result when they bring problems into the open, but in the inertia which results from evading problem situations. Openness was encouraged.

Before attending the seminars, individual managers had been asked to provide a brief report on what they believed to be the company's major internal problems. In one of the exercises, each group was asked to write a group report on the company's problems, with suggestions for improvement. The basis for these reports was the earlier reports of the individual managers. Managers found, of course, that their groups contained members from sides of the business which they had blamed, in their individual reports, for some of the company's problems. The interesting result was that groups moved from attaching blame to a mythical 'them' to realizing that the problems involved 'us'.

The whole programme had been carefully geared to preparing managers to make beneficial changes in their normal work operations and, to this end, had deliberately developed:

(a) greater openness in facing up to problems;
(b) increased objectivity in decision taking;
(c) greater commitment to the process of review and objective-setting;
(d) the will to act;
(e) an awareness of the negative effect of seeking scapegoats and shifting blame.

At the end of the seminar, managers were told how it was intended that their learning should be translated into action. In a given work group, this had to wait until all the managers had attended a seminar—in the occasional instances where reviews were held with groups which included one man who had not been trained, the work of the group was considerably slowed.

Part of the logic of creating capacity for beneficial change within the management team was that control of the work group review should be with the normal boss of the group, and that he should run the review in the absence of any outside party. In this way, reviews could become—and, indeed, have become—a part of normal management activity which is regularly repeated.

The task of the trainer in this process was, in conjunction with the boss, to provide a checklist for the review and to act as a general adviser. He also had a role in prompting the groups to fix dates to meet. A typical checklist included the headings:

The taking of decisions affecting the group as a whole.
Communication within the group.
What happens to new ideas.
Relationships with other work groups.
The setting and execution of operational objectives.
Cost–benefit awareness.
Planning.
Commitment to group decisions.
The allocation of responsibility and authority within the group.
Frankness between group members.

Individuals were asked by the boss to record their views before the review meeting, making factual notes, as to how the group actually operated and how it ought ideally to operate, and to consider how changes might be made. With this work as background, it proved possible within two days at the most, depending on the size of group, to carry out a full review and arrive at objectives for making real improvements in two or three high pay-off areas. Vitally important, the date of the next meeting was fixed for about six months later, in order to review progress towards the objectives and to set fresh ones. With few exceptions, all members of management had attended a training seminar by April 1970. The first workgroup review was held at the end of 1969, and by December 1970 fifty-five working groups had passed through this phase. These were largely in senior groups, including the board of the company.

Various measures have been taken of the effectiveness of the total organization development programme and its various parts. Such measures include:

(a) reports by all managers on the seminars they have attended;
(b) questionnaires on attitudes to the seminars 'before and after';
(c) surveys of attitudes to boss, colleagues, and company at various stages of the programme.

These measures have proved gratifying and positive. However, the all-important question is the effect which the programme has had on the performance of the actual working groups who have been through phase 2. To test this, thrity-eight managers who had taken part in phase 2 activities in the senior management groups of the company's six factories were interviewed. With one or two exceptions, they felt that the programme had paid off well. The results which they commonly reported were:

(a) action had been greatly accelerated. Problems which had been discussed but allowed to go unsolved had now been dealt with;
(b) the objectives of meetings and other activities had been defined and examined. Much wasted activity had been eliminated;
(c) there had been a real tendency to 'put one's own house in order'. Discussion of problems usually ended in a plan for action; allocation of responsibility; and provision for checking that the action had been completed;
(d) many interpersonal stresses and strains had been aired and, in some measure, resolved;
(e) some cash figures were put on results, and these exceeded the cost of the programme several times over.

Other effects of the programme which were commonly mentioned were:

(a) the greater participation of managers in the general affairs of the factory;
(b) deeper analysis of problems;
(c) better decisions;
(d) less repetition of errors;
(e) the recording of systems and plans;
(f) better planning and longer lead-time;
(g) decrease in trivia;
(h) more tolerance of the foibles of others;
(i) standardization of procedures;
(j) a more formal information flow;
(k) greater punctuality.

490

Most managers felt that the time spent in meetings had been cut by amounts which averaged 40 per cent. Many referred to behavioural changes, chief among which were:

(a) improved interpersonal relations;
(b) tendency among people to listen more to others;
(c) more spontaneous reaction of subordinates;
(d) greater involvement at all levels;
(e) reduction in interdepartmental competitiveness;
(f) more responsible management behaviour;
(g) more systematic analysis of problems;
(h) more explanation and tolerance from bosses;
(i) a reduction in the frequency of crises.

A striking result of the programme has been the commitment of managers to objective setting in the MBO sense. The pressure for meaningful objectives has come from all levels of management and not from the personnel department as tended to be the case in the past. The purpose of objectives is clearly seen to be the integration of effort, and the consequent improvement in effectiveness. Better appraisal is seen as a by-product and a means to improving performance, not as an end in itself.

It may seem strange that this case history should be quoted in a chapter on the role of the consultant, since outside consultants are conspicuous by their absence. However, it is pertinent to look more closely at the thinking behind the programme. What the company wanted was a programme tailored specifically to its own needs, and this it achieved. The problems on which the managers worked during the training seminar had a clear relevance to situations with which they were familiar. The 'for instances' used in plenary sessions had been collected within the company. General behavioural points were linked to specific company policies. Procedures—in particular, the company appraisal and management development procedures—were put into a meaningful light and subsequently amended in line with the thinking being developed during the OD programme. The work group review checklists were designed in the context of company needs and problems; often to meet the special problems of specific groups. In short, the whole programme was clearly set in the context of the business.

All this was very different from simply using a standard consultant package whose material was necessarily generalized. The central theme was not one behavioural model—several models were introduced, to the extent that they were useful and appropriate to illustrate a point—but the workings of the formal and informal groups which made up the company's own organization.

It may appear, then, that the moral is that an in-company OD team should use outside consultants only as a source of ideas on which a self-made programme can be based, and as trainers of the in-company team. However, there are certain clear advantages which a company can gain from an ongoing relationship with one OD consultant. First, by contributing his experience to the programme, an outside consultant can save money and time, and prevent mistakes. To buy in staff of the necessary calibre, and train them to develop and test material is a lengthy and expensive process. In the case history quoted, the development time was at least eighteen months. Even at the end of this time, polishing remained to be done and mistakes were made, which, fortunately, were not irretrievable.

Similar programmes, both in the UK and on the continent, have profited from the experience gained in this case, and these have been implemented more smoothly and swiftly.

Second, the consultant can reinforce the credibility of the company's own OD resources. Of course, in the past, many consultants have had the opposite effect by acting as advisers to the board quite independently of in-company service functions. If the aim of OD is to achieve improvement through the management team, it is equally true that the role of the OD consultant is to achieve results through the service function. He is well advised to bear in mind the maxim that there is nothing he cannot achieve as long as he ensures that someone else receives the credit or, at least, his due share of it.

Third, a consultant can give an objective view which is not clouded or resisted because of an involvement in the company's power structure.

As I understand it, OD is a process which goes to the heart of an organization. To be successful, it must fully involve the highest levels of management. Its impact can be dramatic. The position of any employee who guides the process is influential, and it is not uncommon, therefore, to find that an in-company OD team is itself involved in the sort of political struggles which it seeks to regulate in the rest of the organization. A consultant can spread some calm over such troubled waters.

A consultant who is to make a contribution of this kind will have the following characteristics:

(a) his thinking will be orientated towards the purpose of organization rather than to the use of a particular technique. Theoretical knowledge will be backed by experience as an organization employee;
(b) he will have a battery of techniques, analytical tools, information, and training material at his disposal but will adapt these to the circumstances which he finds;
(c) he will work with and through the in-company service managers and be concerned for the personal development of these managers.

The OD process can be divided into four activities:

(a) diagnosis of the problems and opportunities for improvement, with a definition of likely pay-off;
(b) achieving general recognition of the true nature of the problems and obtaining commitment to a change programme;
(c) training programme;
(d) introduction of improvements.

Within a full-scale OD programme, the overall activity will almost certainly follow this sequence. However, individual improvements, e.g., an industrial relations policy, a management development scheme, structural changes, may well have to precede the overall training programme, which may then have as an objective the winning of commitment to these innovations.

It is now useful to examine the consultant contribution to each activity.

Activity 1—Diagnosis of Problems and Opportunities, and Definition of Pay-off

This process is similar to that described in Chapter 40. It involves both a consideration of data which should already be available—turnover, return on capital, market share, structure, manpower costs, plans, planning procedures—and the collection of information and opinions on the way in which the organization actually operates.

The standard company data can usually be obtained from one or two senior sources. Information about the way in which the company actually operates can most usefully be collected by discussion with a cross-section of employees, ranging from top management to shopfloor, and by interviews with users of the organization's services—whether they be customers of a business enterprise, the patients of a hospital, the clients of a social service organization, or the students of a college. In practice, there are often revealing differences between the internal and external view.

Clearly, the information must be collected systematically, and carefully specified in advance. Failure to do this leads both to inefficiency and loss of credibility. Therefore, a major role of the external consultant is to advise on the composition of the various questionnaires. An example of a questionnaire used with a cross-section of management is given in Chapter 40. Some of the questions which were posed to a cross-section of former, long-standing, new and potential customers of a company are set out in Fig. 33.1.

The design of the questionnaire asking for standard data is at least as important as that of the others. Gaps in information are highly significant, and anyone who is a part of the organization's own structure may well not realize that certain information ought to be present. It is surprising how

---

Customer questionnaire (selected questions)

1. What are the main factors which determine your choice of ... ?

2. What procedure do you use for purchasing:
   (a) Capital equipment generally?
   (b) ... in particular?

3. Who would you consider to be the principal suppliers of ...? What are your views on each of them?

4. What are the weak points of the service provided by company X (named for the first time)? Examples?

5. What are the strong points of the service provided by company X? Examples?

6. What is your opinion of the equipment supplied by company X?

Fig. 33.1. Customer questionnaire (selected questions).

many companies do not know the ratio—over the years—of their salary, wages, and other manpower costs to their turnover or profit. Even basic market information can be missing.

Experience has shown that there is little value in putting the questions in writing. They must be the basis of a structured interview carried out by someone skilled in teasing out objectively the information which is relevant. The interviewer must also 'sell' the relevance and importance of his project to the interviewee, thus laying sound foundations for subsequent activities.

An obvious interviewer is the consultant himself, and he should certainly be used wherever the use of an in-company man might inhibit the interviewee. However, these interviews represent a good opportunity to establish the partnership between the consultant and the in-company service managers. If the latter are to carry out some of the interviews, their full involvement is guaranteed, and their personal skills can be developed. Indeed, an approach whereby in-company managers carried out all the interviewing, while the consultant remained in the background as an adviser, has proved very successful. When all interviewing is complete, the consultant should be involved in the process of analysis, report writing and definition of pay-off areas. It may well be, of course, that a full scale OD programme is not the first priority, is not right at a particular time, is not needed at all or is not cost justifiable. Though the cases in which a successful programme directed at the total management team will not repay an organization many times over are more rare, the real risk is that it may be impossible to achieve the degree of top-level involvement which will ensure the success of a well-planned and executed exercise.

Activity 2—Achieving Recognition of the True Nature of the Problems. Commitment to a Change Programme

This step is probably the one in which experience is least obviously necessary, yet, in fact, is most necessary of all. The credibility of an adviser is also vital. Unless experience and credibility are present, there is every risk that an organization will fall into one of three dangerous traps:

(a) An 'experimental' project may be set up in one group. While such projects often prove successful in welding that group together, they are usually disruptive of the total organization in that they create an elitist pocket, out of step with the surrounding culture.

(b) A programme may be designed to train the lower levels of management and may omit the higher levels, whose faults will consequently appear greater in the eye of those whom they control. This is a good way of producing rebellion.

(c) Less frequently, top management may become involved in behavioural activity which looks like hocus-pocus to those beneath.

How, then, does one achieve a real recognition of need? Clearly, the first step is to know the symptoms for which an OD programme can provide the remedy. These are:

(a) frequent complaints of poor communication;
(b) much blaming of other departments;
(c) open hostility between departments or management levels;
(d) failure to make systems work;
(e) duplication of effort;
(f) indecision, compromise, and even stagnation, because of conflicting interests;
(g) frustration, and resignation on the part of some of the better managers;
(h) poor industrial relations at all levels;
(i) cynicism about the possibility of improvement.

The latter can be particularly discouraging to those who do not realize its natural part in the pattern. To the enthusiastic company trainer, nothing is more discouraging than to be told: 'We know the problems, but it's no use trying to do anything. We've been through all this before.' In fact, this is the very key to the door, for once a break from the old, frustrating pattern can be established, the commitment to the programme will grow.

Several strategies are possible at this stage. Among them are, first, to hold a conference of all managers above a certain level. At such a conference the problems discovered during the first activity can be stated, and the conference asked to make comments and suggest solutions. Usefully, the conference is preceded by structured preliminary work, and is arranged so that views are formulated in cross-functional working groups. Such a conference should not, incidentally, be expected to replace a training programme. At most, one can expect to achieve some temporary easing of conflicts generally, a clear mandate for one or two pieces of action, and a realization that something more radical is needed. There may be some increase in frustration.

Second, a pilot training seminar can be set up for a cross-section of management, including board members. In the second one, the board should be well briefed in what is involved, and be committed to following up the first seminar quickly if all goes well.

Whatever strategy is used, it is essential that clear pay-off objectives are established, evaluation points agreed, and that the progress and purposes of conferences and seminars should be well communicated. In particular, no manager should attend a seminar without a full briefing.

Activity 3—The Training Programme

The history of OD is littered with cases in which apparently successful training programmes have led to little real follow-up and the eventual abandonment of the activity. Typically, managers leave their training seminars in a euphoric haze—having at last brought into the open the real problems of the organization, and 'levelled' with each other. However, this haze soon turns to deep disillusionment when things go on the same way as ever in the 'back home' situation. This euphoria–disillusionment pattern can be attributed to one of several causes or, every often, to a combination of them:

(a) trainees have been led to believe that increased understanding or organizational problems and, even more so, the development of interpersonal frankness can, in themselves, provide the solution to the problems perceived and discussed. This, of course, in the tenet of Freudian psychoanalysis, and much T-Group work is based on this belief. However, managers trained in this way can become involved in probing personal and interpersonal problems to an extent that is detrimental to their real business of producing results.
(b) Expectations have been raised too high. No training programme, even with good follow-up is a panacea. Achievement will only be won through perseverance; without it newly created standards of organizational behaviour will slip back towards the old. Constant review is essential.
(c) Evaluation points have not been built into the programme. In consequence, managers will often think about what they have failed to achieve, instead of remembering the positive effects. The provision of positive information can result in a powerful reinforcement to further action.
(d) The follow-up has not been clearly foreseen in designing the training stage. In fact, many programmes have been launched in the pious hope that some benefit must surely follow if the seeds of wisdom are strewn. Sometimes this is true, but is the pay-off maximal?

The above are some of the major pitfalls round which the consultant must steer his client.

A company's needs were carefully diagnosed, and goals for a programme established as follows:

(a) demonstrable cost-savings/profit improvement (the 'demonstrable' would of course, be less than the actual);
(b) speedier action and change;
(c) meaningful objective setting;
(d) better appraisal and development of people;
(e) increased motivation at all levels;
(f) better planning and greater commitment to it;
(g) control of manpower strength;
(h) less destructive competitiveness;
(i) greater consistency in management action;
(j) improved employer–employee relations;
(k) better communication.

Objectives such as these clearly depend on the active involvement of managers at all levels. Alternative strategies for achieving this are the result of permutating the answers to two questions.

First: Are the training and application both to take place within the work groups or is an off-the-job training phase to precede work group application? The former approach has immediacy and directness in its favour; the latter means that, during training outside their normal environment, managers will feel far more free to take risks and are, therefore, emboldened to take a more thoroughgoing approach to the work group phase.

Second: 'Is the work group review to be catalysed by a consultant trainer; observers chosen from the group members; or a checklist; or is it to be left to its own resources following a training phase?' The first of these four alternatives has the advantage of greater insight into group workings but means that the group may either become dependent on, or resistant to, the outsider. The second has the same advantages and disadvantages, though in milder form, but adds the disadvantage of the group being incomplete as a work team. The third approach, it may be argued, may not achieve the same depth in understanding its processes, but has the great advantages that the group is not reliant on outsiders, functions as a normal entity, and that responsibility for both the results and the process is clearly in the hands of all group members. Only a few groups are likely to succeed in carrying out a completely unstructured regular review process on a basis of preliminary training, and the fourth approach is unlikely, therefore, to have the pay-organization impact which is desired.

While the choice of strategy must depend on situations, and while most of the possible permutations have been used with some success, the strategy, which provides for radical review yet maintains group independence—circumstances permitting—is that in which stranger group training precedes on-the-job applications, using a checklist.

If such a strategy is chosen—or any other strategy—the training phase must be designed strictly in line with the total strategy and the goals of the programme, e.g.,

(a) if a checklist without 'stranger' intervention is to be used in the application activity, a checklist ought to be used in the training activity, and the trainers must stay out of the groups—however frustrating they may find this. (To 'feel' the groups and help them in such circumstances is a skilled operation);

(b) the underlying plan of the training activity, and the problems used, must be geared closely to the programme goals (the consultant must adapt tested material and techniques to organization need);

(c) the work group activity must be introduced during the training activity and be seen, clearly, as the planned follow-up;

(d) all analysis of process must be strongly linked to action plans for improvement.

Finally, it is of vital importance that the evaluation points—e.g., those described in the case history discussed earlier—are clearly defined before training begins.

Activity 4—The Introduction of Improvements

We have said, from the first, that a key characteristic of OD programmes is that improvements are generated from within an organization's own members, from within the group in whose area the subject for improvement will normally fall. Sometimes, the improvement may indeed lie in resolving the issue of who is responsible for a particular subject.

In this activity, the consultant's first role is to help the in-company OD team to catalyse the various working groups individually and to coordinate their review activities in the context of the total organization. In some strategies, as we have said, he may sit with a seminar group, to help to make problems overt and bring the group to decisions to which there is commitment.

	Actual ranking	Ideal ranking	Notes
As an individual, rank the sentences below so as to reflect the way in which the group actually operates and the way in which it ought, ideally, to operate: **Cost–benefit awareness**			
(a) Activities are seldom or incompletely evaluated in financial terms			
(b) Cutting costs is more important than seizing potentially beneficial opportunities.			
(c) Past, present, and potential activities are regularly examined in terms of the value which the company is getting for expenditure.			
(d) Concern for local, group, and individual costs and budgets is often detrimental to company interests.			
(e) Though costs and profits are discussed, many ventures are undertaken without giving full consideration to cost implications			

Fig. 33.2. Cost–benefit measurement.

INDUSTRIAL RELATIONS POLICY CHECK LIST

Rank the following statements according to the way in which they best state the actual and ideal situations.

	Actual	Ideal	Notes
Wage rates			
(a) The company keeps its wage rates as low as the workers will tolerate and delays increases as long as possible.			
(b) The company does not initiate new wage rates but responds quickly and equitably to worker demands.			
(c) New wage rates are negotiated toughly, at prescribed intervals.			
(d) The company tries to ensure that wages are linked to living costs, profits, and local rates.			
(e) The company buys peace at any price. Those who shout loudest get most.			
Discipline			
(a) Discipline is the sole prerogative of line management. Authority depends on strong, independent action.			
(b) Disciplinary action is discussed in advance with the appropriate works representative.			
(c) Management is too soft because it fears the unions.			
(d) Clear disciplinary policies and procedures enable managers to act consistently. In doubtful cases, suspension with pay gives time for consultation.			
(e) Management too often has to retract from its decisions.			
(f) Levels of disciplinary authority are not clear.			

Fig. 33.3. Industrial relations policy checklist.

PROCESS ANALYSIS

Under each of the following headings which follow decide:

1. As *individuals*—which statement best describes the way that the group has operated so far.
2. As a *working group*—which statement best describes the way that the group has operated so far.
3. What remedial action the group needs to take.

	Individual	Group
	(Circle as appropriate)	

Objectives
The objectives of the review are:

completely clear	a	A
very clear	b	B
clear	c	C
fairly clear	d	D
not clear.	e	E

Relevance
The relevance of discussion has been:

complete	a	A
high	b	B
fairly high	c	C
moderate	d	D
low	e	E

Use of time
Use of time has been:

efficient	a	A
reasonably good	b	B
fair	c	C
involved 50 % wastage	d	D
very poor	e	E

Participation
The level of participation is such that:

relevant contribution have been made and listened to	a	A
there have been occasional examples of bulldozing	b	B
bulldozing and talking down have occurred fairly frequently	c	C
a large number of potential contributions have been supressed	d	D
members of the meeting were clearly divided into those who dominate and those who recede into the background	e	E

Tolerance
Examples of intolerance of other people's views have been:

Non-existent	a	A
rare	b	B
few	c	C
frequent	d	D
A dominant feature of the activity	e	E

Frankness
Group members are being:

completely honest with each other	a	A
more frank than usual	b	B
tactful	c	C
guarded	d	D
highly political	e	E

Commitment
The group's commitment is:

complete	a	A
very high	b	B
high	c	C
moderate	d	D
low	c	C

Fig. 33.4. Process analysis.

In the checklist approach, the key lies in the design of the lists and in helping the boss of any group to use the process. Figure 33.2 gives an example of one item from a checklist which has been successfully used to examine the operation of a work group. This technique can be used not only in the basic analysis of a group's workings but, for example, to clarify a management team's attitude to industrial relations. Examples of two items in such a checklist are given in Fig. 33.3. It is useful that groups undertaking such review activities should also review the way in which they are operating on that task—a list to this end is presented in Fig. 33.4. This list stresses the purposefulness of the review process.

At the end of the day, the vital issue is that group objectives, individual objectives, timings, and a date to review progress should be clearly recorded. The consultant must ensure that the whole process is geared to this, and he must help the in-company OD team to help managers to keep to their intentions.

Emerging from the process is almost certain to be a call for specialist help in many areas—planning, objective setting, work study, new financial approaches. To all these, the consultant must finally contribute his knowledge of outside activity.

As might be expected of a process as total and radical as OD, its implementation is a highly complex and skilled operation. Experience, credibility, and a battery of tools and techniques are all vital to its success. These the outside consultant can supply. However, he diminishes his chances of success, and will certainly not be true to the concepts that he seeks to introduce, unless he is prepared to tailor his thinking and material to the organization's particular needs, and work as a part of the 'in-house' functional teams for whose development he must be concerned. The acid test of the OD consultant is whether he can leave behind him an organization which has become self-sufficient.

Suggested Reading

BECKHARD, R. *Organization Development: Strategies and Models*, Addison-Wesley, 1969.
BENNIS, W. G. *Organization Development: What It Is and What It Isn't*, Addison-Wesley, 1969.
FORDYCE, J. K. and WEIL, R. *Managing with People*, Addison-Wesley, 1971.
LIKERT, R. *The Human Organization*, McGraw-Hill, 1967.

Part 5. Planning and organization

34. Organization change and organization planning

Wilbur M. McFeely

During 1971 and 1972, in-depth interviews were held with executives at different levels in fifteen different companies— large and not so large—that have experienced major organization changes. The companies are engaged in such varied fields as banking, the retail trade, insurance, and the manufacture of industrial and consumer goods. To supplement these depth observations, numerous interviews were also held with organization planning specialists—many of whom are, or have been, members of The Conference Board's Organization Planning Council.

The interviews proceeded on two levels: first, straight fact-gathering of past experiences in planning and implementing organizational change—with the emphasis on how results differed from plans. Second, from these and previous studies, a concept began to emerge of the organization as a living system. The interviewees were asked to re-examine and review their experiences in terms of this concept. Their inputs further refined and fleshed out the concept.

There are times in the history of every institution when what seems needed is a major overhaul—a marked change in the strategic structure of the organization. Retrospectively, the organization changes that result are recognized as landmarks in the life of the organizations. The periods between such changes are evidently thought of as epochal.

Changes of this nature, almost without exception, have involved a major shift in the structure—in the architecture—of the corporate organization. In recent years, for example, this has most typically taken the form of shifting from a functional organization to a divisionalized company. For ease and convenience of classification, this concept includes the whole array of semi-autonomous 'profit centres' and such designations as 'free-standing companies'.

Implicit in this structural change are important changes in the relationships among individuals and groups. The reporting relationships of some organizational components may be changed, the influence of others may be enhanced or lessened—but, in any event, there are recognizable changes in roles.

It follows, logically, that such major changes in structure, relationships, and roles bring about significant changes in what might be called the mode of management. Management mode connotes a particular, recurring, and relatively enduring pattern for managing institutional activities. Obviously, management mode varies widely. At any point in time for any company, it reflects the different personalities that make up the group, the facts of ownership, traditions of long standing, and outside influences impinging on the institution. But, most of all, it reflects the personality of the chief executive. His management style has an immediate impact on his subordinate peer group. And this impact, modified by other personalities and functional roles throughout the organization, is to some extent felt throughout the entire organization.

In short, for purposes of ensuing analysis, a major significant organizational change is one that modifies the strategy of the enterprise, alters the structure, necessitates the development of a different character of relationships among the principal components of the organization, and dictates a change in management mode. This kind of change does not postulate an earthquake—but it is of the magnitude that leaves historical records in the top-drawer archives of the institution.

In an exploration of how companies plan and implement major organizational change, The Conference Board had no difficulty in gaining the cooperation of many executives whose companies have been through such massive changes.

Whether the company affected was a bank, an insurance company, a steel company, a chemical company, or a textile company, each was able to depict the approach to the organization change in fairly traditional concepts and technical aspects of organization planning.

They spoke of a new game plan—including more specification in the area of goals, objectives, and targets; of increased organizational effectiveness through new grouping of functional activities; of guidelines for delegation of authority; and of improved relationships, vertical and horizontal, vital to the success of the planned change.

Thus, implementation of the organization change was to follow a well thought out, finely honed plan. Retrospectively, however, each conceded that the finely honed plan became a point of departure. Much occurred that was unexpected and unanticipated. Indeed, in retrospect, there was a question as to whether the overall hoped-for results were being realized. A few comments may suffice to document the variety of unanticipated developments:

> We all recognize that the business of a bank is warehousing money for the convenience of the customer. So, I thought it would be easy to reorganize a bank, but I found out that it wasn't.

504

Our new president, in an effort to develop a more participative style of management, started a weekly meeting with the senior vice-presidents, all of whom are divisional operating heads. But, as a result, some of the vice-presidents reporting to them feel downgraded. The new chief does not deal as directly with them as his predecessor did. It is, of course, partly a question of visibility.

Ours is not much of a 'political organization' but when we learned that there were going to be two men at the top, instead of the single position of chairman and president, pressures developed on behalf of a man who had come with one of the larger acquisitions.

When it became known that we were going to search on the outside for a new president, resistance points developed based upon the usual fear of the unknown.

One thing we have learned from this massive reorganization change is that people will adhere to a new organization with the same tenacity that they clung to the old. We now have people who have become so fond of this one that they deplore any effort to make any further change in it.

We had a *status quo* attitude. This attitude permeated the principal officers of the corporation and was prevalent among the directors as well.

The president had allowed too much of the real power to become vested in the corporate staff groups.

Fear and trepidation were the principal inertial factors that had to be overcome. This was the first time some had ever participated in any cross-divisional activity.

These testimonies, each from a principal officer of a nationally known company, could be multiplied many times over. They document an often-repeated point about organizational change; change affects each person differently—there are different perceptions as to the need for it, the benefits from it, and the impacts of it.

Possibly of greater significance, however, is that while the situations, and the words and phrases used to describe them, are common and easily recognizable, each executive was describing a unique and highly sensitive socioeconomic institution. It has been said that the problem of ecology is that 'every part of nature is attached to every other piece in the universe; therefore, you tamper with one piece with peril'. Somewhat the same is true, evidently, about each socioeconomic institution that bears an organization label. Indeed, the experience of these company executives underscores the fact that an organization is not simply a structure, nor even a strategy, but a kind of closed biosystem, or living system—a multi-institutional system of response.

In this context, 'system of response' connotes people responding to events, situations, policies, and plans, and to other people. 'Multi-institutional' implies that an organization is not monolithic or homogeneous. Rather, there are ingrained and recognizable cultural patterns that characterize internal subsystems of the overall system. And while planning for organization change may be in terms of structure or even strategy, the realities of organization change, and the possibilities of effective change, are keyed to the depth of understanding of the character of the multi-institutional system that is the organization.

Organization as a System of Response

An organizational system can be defined as a series of components so interfaced and interrelated that they work together towards the achievement of the worthy and legitimate objectives of the enterprise. This definition is not meant to convey an organization free of stress, differences of opinion as to what needs to be done in a specific situation, or even outright conflict. But it does imply that, in viable organizations, these differences are effectively managed so that there is a reasonable unity of thrust within the various organizational components.

Although the idea of an organization as a system refers to the functional whole, it is also clear that the vitality or effectiveness of this system is dependent upon a series of highly interdependent elements. For purposes of this analysis, it is possible to discern and identify seven:

Linkage

This refers to the essential network of group and interpersonal relationships which are the very foundation of an organization.

Here, the first consideration is whether the linkages essential for optimum performance do, in fact, exist. In one company, for example, an analysis of the way in which a vice-president spent his time showed that he repeatedly visited those divisional headquarters where he 'felt comfortable' but seldom, if ever, paid attention to those groups where he did not feel immediately 'at home'.

The head of a small division of another company, who found that his 'business' was being sold to another corporation, complained: 'Look, the only contact I have had with the parent company was when the treasurer called me up to send him some money. Beyond that no one paid any attention to me, except the time I asked for help when some union organizers came to the plant.'

In another case, the chief executive of a major heavy goods company realized that, under his functionalized form of organization, he was the only level that could bring manufacturing and selling together; that he was the lowest level that could control profit. He found, also, that there was a great deal of rivalry between manufacturing and selling. He wanted to push profit responsibility lower and at the same time get these people together. He gambled that a move towards a more divisionalized and decentralized structure would change the character of the linkage between these two key functional groupings.

It seems clear, especially in large companies, that the linkages prescribed by the organizational structure are not necessarily viable. This has important implications from the standpoint of organization response.

506

The second criterion of the effectiveness of organizational linkage is the character of the system of management information and feedback. Reflecting on his own organization's experience, an OD consultant summarized the problem this way:

> Most information systems are like a vacuum cleaner. Vast amounts of information and data are sucked up from all parts of the organization. Somewhere up top it is sorted out, digested, analyzed, and acted upon. But the evaluation of these data are not always shared with those down the line in a truly constructive way.
>
> An information system needs to be more like a horseshoe in contour. The information that is sucked up needs to be fed back on terms that have clear actionable implications. But, in spite of all that is said, this is not true of many information systems.

Other testimony indicates that the existence of sound linkages depends on the responsiveness of those in positions of power. Giving people information is not enough; it is evidently the extent to which individuals or groups are heard, and can influence the course of events, that affects the vitality of linkages. Some organizational experts talk about mutual support as the key factor in relationships. But it is apparent that mutual support stems from mutual influence. Support is difficult to obtain if there has been no opportunity for the individuals and groups affected to be of influence. The ability to influence is, in many ways, the precondition of mutual support and another test of effective organizational linkage.

Finally, there is a strong feeling among many participants in this study that an important aspect of sound linkage within an organization is the willingness to face stress or conflict openly and directly. This is in contrast to the feeling observed in many organizations that tension, or conflict between organizational components, is something that should be brushed aside, repressed, or simply be treated as though it did not exist. Tension, stress, and conflict can be the source of creativity within an organization. The innovative handling of these forces within an organization is one aspect of sound linkage.

Balanced Emphasis

In the context of an organizational system, balanced emphasis refers primarily to the relative weight given the long versus the short term; to the relative attention given various functions within the organization. The term is somewhat innocuous; the implications, most company executives attest, are not.

For example, the response of an organization is clearly related to the degree to which the key power structure of an organization is able to maintain a balance of emphasis between the long-term and the short-term objectives of the company. From the view of those inside, almost anything a management does solely in the interest of short-term gains tends to be inimical to the long-term welfare of the enterprise, and vice versa.

'We have decided that for the time being we can live with the level of our theoretical technology,' says the vice-president of a leading company in the field of instrumentation. 'We hope that the need to improve our current position will not hurt us in the future. We shall simply have to be smart enough to recognize when we must again bet on fundamental research.' Here, clearly, a company has opted to improve current earnings in ways that may impair its long-term future—but it hopes that it can achieve both objectives successfully. Examples could be given of companies that have deliberately penalized current earnings to establish planning activities that were not expected to have any short-term benefit but were seen as essential to the companies' long-range viability.

Just as a balance of emphasis between long- and short-term goals is essential, so is an even-handed administration, or attention to the various functional activities of an enterprise. This postulate is accepted readily in principle but apparently is much more difficult to achieve in practice.

For example, the chief executive of the heavy goods company referred to above, in moving from a functional structure to a divisionalized, decentralized scheme, found an impediment in that he had 'a huge hierarchy of people who were specialized in manufacturing or marketing, but very few business-men who could oversee all the essential functions of a business'.

What happens when there is an absence of reasonably balanced attention to all the essential functional areas of an organization? Experience indicates that those who see themselves in veiled sanctuaries tend to develop an attitude of undesirable aggressiveness towards the less-favoured compo-nents in the organization. Those units, on the other hand, that tend to feel neglected often develop an apathetic attitude. They accept for themselves goals that are unambitious and without challenge. In both instances, the organizational system of response suffers.

Balanced emphasis does not imply that the key persons in an organization should not move in aggressively on the problem areas, even if this means short-term de-emphasis of other areas. Various segments of an organization are used to, and can readily accept, this short-term preoccupation. But, this is quite different from a long-term bias.

A final aspect of this element of the organizational system is the degree to which management sees the need for working towards a congruence between the goals of the individual and of the organization. There is mounting evidence from research that an organization functions best when it is able to organize the work, the work situation, and the conditions of work in ways that, while maintaining efficiency, encourage the individual to develop his own capacities and to achieve his own ambitions. The observation is not new—but that such a state of affairs has not been a characteristic of many organizations is readily conceded by competent internal and external witnesses.

Paths of Decision Making

The key point of this element of an organizational system is the effectiveness of the delegation of authority. Organizational analysts are quick to point out that delegation of authority goes beyond organizational structure—it

508

seems to be equated with a particular philosophy of management—it is a basic ingredient of management style. In this context, the extent to which authority is delegated appears to be an index of the degree of trust or confidence that key managers have in those who report to them. And this 'confidence factor' is far more important than the authority that is theoretically vested in a position as spelt out by the organization manual.

In this element of the organizational system, it is impossible to ignore the 'informal' organization. 'The chief executive,' says the vice-president of a major drug and biological products firm, 'works within a formal and an informal organization system. And in matters of major or strategic decisions the informal system may be, and often is, the most important path of decision making.' Therefore, a consideration in measuring the effectiveness of an organization is the extent to which the informal system eases decision making or becomes a bottleneck.

For many executives, the fact that an organization, like nature, abhors a vacuum is a factor of vital importance in any consideration of the path of decision making. Thus, apparently, in almost any organization there are units in which the problem of how to overcome, or bypass, pockets of incompetency is a continuing preoccupation.

Closely related to this problem is what many see as the technique of 'defensive hold-ups' on decision making—and by this they mean what they consider to be an improper use of committees, study groups, and other mechanisms that, under the guise of further fact finding, simply put off the day of reckoning. Those who take this position admit, quite readily, that the distinction between a productive exploration in fact finding and what they consider to be an unfortunate delay is a close line. But they continue to emphasize this as a problem in organizational efficiency.

The Reward System

The ostensible purpose of the reward system is to reinforce all elements of expected behaviour. This encompasses both tangible and intangible rewards. Thus, in a system of response, the system of rewards is clearly a prime element.

Yet, in spite of the thousands and thousands of words that have been written about reward systems in industry, many thoughtful observers question their efficacy. Those who hold this view take the position that the basic value system of the individual is what shapes his performance and that the reward system, at best, touches only a fraction of this universe.

Thus, for example, one company in an effort to stimulate sales offered a special bonus for sales of given items in the line—a common practice. Interviews of both salesmen and sales managers revealed that in this specific case only one out of ten saw any value in this sales bonus. 'I think it is nonsense, but if they want to pay me a bonus for doing what I am already paid to do, I'll take it,' said one regional manager. Another regional manager, referring to the same contest put it this way : 'It is the best thing they have done.'

Those who have attempted to tailor compensation systems realize that the variables in the value systems of individuals, together with other organizational considerations, make it virtually impossible for a reward system to be really discriminatively responsive to the distinctive needs of various individuals. But this does not negate the fact that the system of rewards is one of the basic essential elements of an organizational system.

Administrative Constraints

Every objective, plan, or policy, of an organization is, in a sense, a constraint that affects the speed with which the system can respond to threats, problems, and opportunities. This is not necessarily a negative connotation—these organizational mechanisms are recognized by all the managers interviewed, as one of the instruments required to transform random behaviour into organization 'performance'.

The question raised is not whether these constraints are needed but, rather, which are relevant. Here, the most frequently expressed concern relates to policy limitations on capital expenditures and compensation adjustments at various levels in the organization. The greater sophistication of equipment and price inflation seem to have outdated existing policy limitations in many companies, and this hampers the ability of managers to take timely action.

Far more subtle are what some participants refer to as the 'creedal policies' of an organization. These are the widespread understandings that permeate an organization. They may have no basis in any written policy or communication, yet they significantly influence management action.

As an illustration, the vice-chairman of the board of one company reported with some excitement that a task force of younger supervisors had successfully challenged one of these time-honoured understandings. In this particular company, 'everyone knew' that it was useless to recommend the building of additional warehouse facilities because at some long-ago time, the chief executive had said: 'There is no profit to be made in bricks and mortar to store goods.' This attitude had prevailed during his twenty-year tenure.

Rather than challenge this creedal policy, some division managers simply rented outside warehousing facilities. These costs tended to be hidden in operating expenses. Then, a task force of young managers was appointed to study warehousing procedures. They knew nothing of the general understanding that capital expenditure for warehousing could not get approval. The questions raised by their model for determining the return on investment of warehousing facilities brought into the open the unwritten but compelling policy. It was revised.

The illustration is not atypical. Many a chief executive has created binding policy through a casual statement, and most managers in companies examined could cite creedal constraints of unknown heritage.

Cultural Constraints

To distinguish between administrative constraints and cultural constraints is, admittedly, somewhat academic. They flow from each other. But, in this context, where 'administrative constraints' refer to the creedal or common law of the organization, 'cultural' refers to the habits, attitudes, traditions, outlooks, and patterns of interaction that either develop internally or are part of the behaviour pattern that people bring to their roles with them.

The cultural factors in an organization are undoubtedly the most complex of the elements of the organizational system. The ability of an organization to anticipate the flow of events seems to be particularly related to its cultural heritage. Here, the evidence suggests that the greatest problem is that the habits and attitudes that led to success in the past become enshrined in the present, and tend to freeze the array of coping responses. Thus, there is repetitive evidence of organizations that, when confronted with difficulties, tend to resort to the remedies found successful in the past, even though the problems are quite different. Indeed, in some cases, an organization in difficulty simply seems to redouble its efforts to do much more efficiently those things that led to its trouble in the first place.

Just one example of such an experience is that of a leading soft goods company that, over the years, achieved a well above average profit growth by manufacturing 'commodity'-type goods. This period of the company's success was characterized by very tight control over every aspect of the manufacturing process. Its leadership was based on its ability to be the lowest-cost producer of commodity-type goods.

Then the markets changed, influenced by imports on the one hand, and new technologies on the other. In response, the screws were simply tightened more and more on controls. The company turned more introspective—it wound a tighter and tighter web of control—when many of its key executives saw the major problems as being largely external.

This company was slow to opt in favour of new fabric technologies, largely because it clung to the traditional view that the lowest-cost producer of any product line could hold on, and still turn in good profits. As a result, it was forced to play 'catch-up ball' in many areas of the markets.

In terms of cultural orientation, instead of being present/future in its outlook, its dominant patterns of response were past/present. This time frame is evidently one of the more important cultural traits that conditions response to problems and opportunities.

Another cultural 'norm' involves the question of authority. Traditionally, authority has been vested in a person by reason of his position, and the legitimacy of his authority was seldom, if ever, questioned. Evidently, however, many organizations are experiencing a cross-current in which authority, to be legitimate, must be earned on the basis of knowledge and expertise—it does not necessarily flow automatically from role. Moreover, it is situationally earned, and must, therefore, be earned over and over again.

Thus, in many problem-solving situations, respondents see authority gravitating towards the person perceived by the group as being the most capable to decide. And this may or may not be the boss. But because of the growing complexity of problems and the sophistication of problem-solving technology, many organization analysts see this trend as adding to organizational effectiveness, even as it challenges traditional cultural patterns.

In somewhat similar vein is the thought that behavioural 'norms' within an organization are more effective when they are 'owned' by the group rather than prescribed or imposed on it. It follows that these standards should be changed also only by consent of the group.

Further, in these days when stability is not the mode of organizational life, the ability to live with risk, anxiety, and ambiguity become important vectors of an organization's culture. Closely coupled with this is the capacity for managing fantasy projections. Today, for example, the rate of change in all aspects of corporate environment leads to a rise in the number of suggestions, proposals, and recommendations for management action—each seen by its ardent supporters as the sure road to New Jerusalem. Yet, now, as in the past, the ratio of proposals that simply will not 'go' to those with a high probability for success remains high. Thus, the number of negative responses heard throughout the organization tends to increase, and, consequently, the task of keeping an organization 'turned on' is clearly an essential part of the culture of an innovative, forward-moving organization.

Self-correcting Mechanisms

This element of the system underscores the need for individuals, groups—the entire organization—to be self-correcting: to adjust to the realities of the organization's experience and environment in ways that preserve its forward momentum. Acts of self-correction, of course, also find expression in the other elements of the organizational system. But, here, the emphasis is directed towards various activities or mechanisms that seem to support, encourage, and define paths for self-correction.

When related to other system elements so far discussed, a primary mechanism of self-correction appears to be the quality of the continuing explorations of the organization's role and aspirations. This is the essence of organizational strategy. It requires specification of not only goals or objectives but of means and spirit—what some have called the 'organizing images of the enterprise'—and the accompanying plans and programmes.

When the chairman of an international food product company speaks of what his company must accomplish in the future, he speaks first of the need to preserve the spirit of the atmosphere created by the founder. This would mean conserving a zealous, nearly evangelistic, sometimes old-fashioned faith in the ability of the individual to impose mind on matter and to accomplish what he wants. It is a tradition but not a constraining one since the tradition is self-correcting.

'The bigger you get the tougher it gets to make the idea work,' he said. 'You have to battle every day to keep the spirit alive.'

Perhaps, realistically, he should have added that his efforts will be effective to the extent that these aspirations become 'internalized' within the employee group, particularly among his key managers. For this ability to internalize the goals of an organization, and, therefore, for people to become both mentally and emotionally involved in their achievement, seems essential for meaningful self-correction.

Many respondents indicated that although appropriate mechanisms for communication and feedback throughout the organization are essential to the development of sound 'linkages', they are also requisite to self-correction. Thus, given good interpretive feedback, individuals and groups are able to understand what their impact is on other people around them and on the situations that they are trying to influence. With this knowledge, they are in a position to make suitable self-corrective adjustments that preserve the desired organizational thrust.

In this context, activities such as manpower planning and management and organizational development may be considered within the frame of self-correcting mechanisms. All are designed to enhance the ability of an organization to maintain a high level of competency over a long period of time and under a variety of circumstances. Thus, they are expected to help individuals, groups, and the entire organization, to be continuously self-correcting in an ever-changing environment.

This synoptic review of the elements that are seen as comprising an organization as a system of response underscrores the interrelatedness of all aspects of an organization. Nothing happens in an organization in isolation—everything impinges somehow on everything else. Thus, a major skill of the analyst is to have some insight into what may happen throughout the organization when a significant action is taken with respect to any one element.

The Multi-institutional Nature of an Organization

The difficulties of grappling with the elements of the system are compounded by the fact that no organization is homogeneous or monolithic. An organization, particularly a large organization, is multi-institutional in nature. These internal institutions are, in effect, constituencies identifiable most clearly by the character of their functional roles within the organization. But each constituency also tends to develop a common envelope of attitudes, outlooks, and patterns of actions, interaction, and influence that are of the nature of discrete institutions.

An analysis of the problems of organizational change indicates that within the management group most affected by change, there are at least three recognizable internal institutions.

To suggest that these three internal institutions are like the plies of a laminate would connote too rigid a stratification. Yet the analogy is useful as a vehicle for examining the nature of the three internal institutions and the relationships among them. Thus, an organization may be thought of as a laminate of three plastic plies—with the emphasis on the use of the word 'plastic' as an adjective. The bonding agent consists of immeasurable amounts of communication, work flow, authority, and patterns of mutual influence and support, and, in effect, the facets of the system already discussed.

The key point in the analogy is the distinctive nature of each ply. As has been indicated, each has a characteristic jargon, work focus, and approach that sets it apart from the other plies.

The label given to each ply describes its central role or thrust. Other terms could be used. Alternative suggestions for names of the plies, advanced by those who have examined the concept, are included in parentheses:

ideational (philosophical, ideological, perceptive);
synergistic (transactional, catalytic, enabling);
process (technological, technocratic, operational).

Admittedly, the hypothesis of the three-ply nature of an organization has hierarchical overtones. But it is not simply another way of saying top management, middle management, and lower management. These terms, themselves, have no common basis of definition—for each organization they seem to exist in the eye of the beholder. In the three-ply concept, differences among the plies flow from their packet of traits rather than their hierarchal position. As one executive put it: 'I have the status and prerogatives of membership in the ideational ply but I am actually in the synergistic ply.' Others attest, similarly, that the organizational chart is not necessarily a reliable guide to membership in a ply. It is the cultural differences within the plies that inhibit or frustrate, foster or encourage, organizing for change.

What is most distinctive about each ply seems to be the idiom that characterizes the ply.

Ideational Ply

The idiom reflects its orientation towards the long-range view, the big picture. Apparently, it is also responsive to 'buzz words', 'trigger terms', and other style-setting expressions currently employed by thought leaders among corporate executives. This is evident from examples of the prevailing idiom:

corporate objectives;
long-range planning;
Management by Objectives;
market orientation;
profit centres;
free-enterprise system;
free-market economy;
decentralization;
centralization;
liquidity;
environmental influences;
public affairs;
company image, identity, character;
stockholder reaction;
government policy;
international competition;
results oriented;
team building.

514

The idiom is obviously very generalized in character and may have different shades of meaning in different companies. It reflects broad concepts, ideas, notions, and promptings of strategic policy-making executives.

Synergistic Ply

The idiom of this ply is quite varied and is sprinkled liberally with the jargon of specialists. There are certain common denominator words:

system;
study;
policy statement;
programme;
development;
action goal;
research;
analysis.

These words come with a great variety of objectives—financial, budgetary, cost, engineering, value, process, market, product, pricing, legal, personnel, organization, community, public, information, control. The working language emphasizes also the experiment, the tentative approach, the provisional try, contingency, and search: 'What would happen if we tried this?' 'Here is something that might prove useful!' 'What do we really want to accomplish?' 'What further data do we need?' 'If this doesn't work, we won't lose much!' 'Where do we go if this just doesn't work?'

As the label of the ply suggests, the idiom reflects a wide variety of disciplines in both the arts and the sciences. It is the language of the enabler, the catalyst, and of the persons who are charged with the responsibility for fleshing out broad concepts and making them operational.

Process Ply

The idiom of this ply reflects its concern with technology, processes, and mechanisms that in an economic or accounting sense result in vaue added to the product. It is concerned with the organization's 'throughput' of goods and services:

schedules;
methods and standards;
standard costs;
predetermined costs;
over/underabsorption;
raw material availability and quality;
waste control;
quality specifications and control;
orders;
shipments;
inventory levels;

house-keeping;
maintenance;
job training;
turnover;
absenteeism;
grievances;
personnel practices;
contract provisions;
safety.

Some participants have called this the 'real gut world'. It deals primarily with what is happening here and now. Clearly, however, it keeps its eyes peeled for developments in processes and technology that may have a future impact on its operations.

In terms of organizational change, the implications of the different idioms are fairly clear. There is nothing new in the thought that if people are to grasp a thought or an idea it must be expressed in a language they understand. The same idea may have to be couched in different terms to make it meaningful to different audiences. This truism is underlined in the three-ply concept of organization. The idiom that has a clear meaning in one ply may have no operational counterpart in another. For example, an executive of a telephone company, in reviewing efforts of his company to control operating costs within the traffic department, states:

> The difficulty, in part, is that our top managers think and speak in terms of dollar budgets. At the operating level, however, the emphasis is on load. It is a problem of manning: How many persons are needed to provide adequate service at various loads, on various holidays, or days of the week? They think in terms of dollars only peripherally. Their primary job is to provide a level of service that will keep them out of trouble both with customers and top management. They are, of course, really managing dollar budgets but that is not how they think in terms of their jobs.

A junior bank officer puts it this way: 'Our senior officers talk about increasing the average return of the portfolio—but what does this mean to the small branch office bank manager? Does it mean that he should try to get another eighth of a percentage point on Mrs Jones' loan?'

From the standpoint of managing change, these varying idioms, reflecting as they do differences in work orientation, present more than a communications problem. They may actually mask important considerations inherent in a proposed change. As a result, hindsight shows that some factors that should have been included in the planning for change are not given sufficient consideration, or are overlooked completely.

As an illustration, the chief executive of a metal-processing company, in reflecting on a recent organization shift, offered this comment:

> The three-ply concept touches several sensitive areas and highlights some things we overlooked in a recent problem area. We discussed with our key managers the changing character of our markets. This means that in many of our product lines we must use alloys containing more exotic metals. But, although we must have these

specialized products in our line, the orders for them are relatively small. At the process level, it means more set-ups and shorter manufacturing runs. I see now that in our product planning we did not give enough consideration to its impact on manufacturing, and, further, our incentive systems were not changed to reflect the new conditions—so no one wants to run these exotic metal alloys. We have spent many years trying to develop corporate incentive systems. My guess is that our standards people either did not see clearly the impact of these changes, or did not want to bring out how they impacted upon the corporate plan. We just did not make clear that these market changes would, of necessity, cause changes in our traditional manufacturing orientations and their support systems.

In this instance, the chief executive was thinking and acting in terms of market requirements. He assumed that when the manufacturing and systems people saw the need for a new market orientation, they would understand the implications in terms of their functions and adjust to them. But inertia remained, apparently because many persons—though they hear about the changes to come—tend to think and act in terms of their own work focus and institutional bias. In short, each ply tended to respond in terms of its traditional patterns of reaction and outlook.

Three examples, from among many similar expressions of executive concern, will serve further to document this notion. An outside director of a major soft goods manufacturer expressed his concern in these terms:

I guess, in terms of this model of organization, I would have to say that we really do not have a viable ideational ply. Our chief executive came up through operations and is still in most respects a member of the process ply. Moreover, many of the executives in the company see him as being too heavily influenced by those with the same bias—they keep saying we are a mill-oriented organization at a time when market considerations are the first priority. We, as a company, suffer from lack of exploration in any depth of such questions as 'what are we' and 'what should we try to become, say within the next five years'. It is in this sense that we do not have an ideational ply. We have several very able younger men who keep pushing in this direction. But they are in the synergistic ply and this presents a problem. The chief executive listens to them but really believes they are too theoretical and, perhaps even more important, he sees them as not having any real sense of institutional accountability. So, it is very difficult for them to induce any significant change in direction. One of the repeated reasons given for younger men leaving the company is the lack of any clearly stated, strategic objectives.

This director's testimony points to perhaps the most important characteristic of the ideational ply—its structure, work delegations, and patterns of communication and of influence tend to be a reflection of the chief executive officer. It reflects the way 'he wants to go'. It tends to be an extension, indeed, an expression of his management style. If, therefore, his style does not furnish leadership for the vital functional role of the ideational ply, the health of the organization may deteriorate.

Again, this is not simply another way of saying that the configuration of the ideational ply is synonymous with 'top management', even though the leadership of the chief is the key to its functioning properly. A member of this ply is one who plays a decisive part in the functional role of the ply irrespective of his hierarchical position.

To many observers, the most difficult aspect of organizational planning and development is that of assuring the vitality of the ideational ply. For some, the core problem is what they believe to be the inherent tendency of most organizations—to get hardening of the mental and attitudinal arteries. And, further, these sclerotic tendencies almost inevitably lead to organizational changes that are the other side of crises rather than orderly, ongoing adjustments to change.

Others, though accepting the 'crisis renewal' aspect of most significant organizational changes, ascribe other causes to the problem. For them, the fundamental consideration is that it is very difficult for anyone to perceive the apocalypse—to have a viable image of the grand design of the future and to believe in it. So, it is easy to pretend that it will not happen and to ignore the portents. And, in this process, organizations get out of step with the realities of the changing scene. Those who take this position point to the number of fractious problems that organizations have been dealing with in the past decade on an *ad hoc* or piecemeal basis because of their failure or inability to stay 'out front' in the problem area.

Either perspective, obviously, supports the thesis that ensuring an effective ideational ply is one vital key to planning and implementing organizational change. By the same token, however, this ply does not stand alone. Each of the other two plies has its own place in the sun and cannot be allowed to bask in the shade if an organization is to maintain its competency.

By way of further illustration, the president of a medium-sized family controlled, manufacturing company saw his problem in terms of the character of the synergistic ply. 'I see now,' he said, 'that our tradition of putting "good men" who have outlived their usefulness in their present positions into staff jobs—into the functional areas of the synergistic ply—may catch up with us one of these days. They may not be able to give us the push and expertise we shall need.'

This executive pointed out that this practice had become ingrained as a consequence of the company's philosophy of 'taking care of its own'. The consequence, however, was that a necessary organizational role was in danger of being seriously short-changed, and, if timely corrective measures were not taken, the long-range competency of the organization could be threatened.

'The more I think about it,' he continued, 'the clearer it becomes that when everyone else is overwhelmed, or at least preoccupied with the here and now problems, these are the guys who are practically the only ones continuing to search for tomorrow's better alternatives. They are paid to search when others are not.' This remark brings into sharp focus one vital role of the synergistic ply that evidently should not be overlooked in organizational planning.

Another senior executive saw the major problems of his organization as stemming from the relative neglect of the process ply. 'Our trouble began,' he observed, 'when we became so future oriented that we forgot to mind the store. We found ourselves delegating responsibilities right and left to production people who did not know how to manage.' This company had grown very rapidly through an imaginative and aggressive marketing effort and by a series of acquisitions. Its earnings per share of common stock, however, had not risen at anything like the same rate, and this disparate trend prompted the chief executive to take a careful look at what was happening within the organization.

In short, experience indicates that, in the planning and implementation of organization change, the need for having each ply competently staffed in terms of its distinctive role cannot be overemphasized.

A second, and highly interrelated planning consideration, is the fact that the orientation of the three plies—the three internal institutions—is not congruent. At times they are, but at other times they may be quite different—even to the point of being in opposition.

Further, it seems evident that, in managing change, the most critical problems are likely to arise in those areas in which there is the greatest divergence in norms, customs, and values among the plies. Conversely, it is reasonable to assume that where there is little or no difference, evidence of inertia, or of opposition to the proposed changes, will be minimal.

This divergence of orientation among the three internal institutions is a function of many complex variables within an organization. Of these causative factors, two seem to be particularly important as a frame for planning and implementing organizational change. The first is clearly the work focus, or the central thrust of the dominant tasks that characterize the ply. As previously indicated, the distinctive nature of each ply is most vividly reflected in its idiom. These dissimilarities among the three constituencies nurture differences in perception regarding the nature and worth of the contribution each ply makes to the organization as a whole.

To this is added what appears to be the other major influencing factor—the perceptions of each constituent group are constantly being shaped and modified as it participates in the processes and work flow throughout the entire organization. Thus, the patterns of interaction, or of response among the three plies of the organizational laminate, are neither fixed nor rigid: the motive power of an organization is not transmitted through fixed gears, but by a fluid drive. Nevertheless, each ply has a fairly consistent and endurable, and, therefore, recognizable envelope of attitudes and outlooks—of us/them perceptions—that are highly important to any consideration of organizational change.

These us/them perceptions are, in effect, the bonding agents between the plies of the organizational laminate. And the ability of a management to effect change is influenced by its capacity for managing these differences in perception.

Thus, for example, people in the other two plies see the ideational ply as being highly peer oriented, both inside and outside the enterprise. 'What the chief hears from another chief tends to be more credible than anything he hears from anyone on the inside' is a typical comment. Members of this ply often disagreed at first with this perception of them, but on further reflection conceded that the tendency may be real. But, whether real or fancied, this perception is bound to have some influence on the attitudes of the other two plies towards proposals for change.

Clearly, also, those who are part of this ideational ply see themselves as setting the pace, mood, and mode of corporate leadership. They want to project the image of a well-coordinated, smoothly functioning, aggressive, cohesive team. They are also highly conscious of their role of establishing and maintaining the 'character' of the company, and wish to project the same identity to significant groups outside the enterprise—the community at large, financial institutions, government agencies, customers, and stockholders. This leadership role seems to underlie the great emphasis placed on teamwork.

This perception coupled with the dominant role of the chief executive within the ideational ply, tends to make the members of the ply highly compatible in terms of language and individual managing styles. This does not, however, connote conformity. But executives who see themselves as parts of this ply do suggest that one of its characteristics is relatively low tolerance for disagreement within the group. There is room for discussion and differences of opinion during strategic explorations, but no room for the heretic—and for most observers this is consistent with the concept of the final accountability of the chief executive.

These characteristics and outlooks are, of course, not confined exclusively to this ply. Each of the other two plies could be described in part, in the same way. However, observers see these characteristics as being the more determinate elements that define the institutional nature of the ideational ply.

An examination of the synergistic ply—the inner ply of the organizational laminate—offers some further insights of significance for the planners of organizational change. This ply has some traits that are peculiarly its own, but the nature of its us/them perceptions are clearly conditioned by its constant interaction with the other two plies.

The members of this ply, at times, see themselves as being part of the ideational ply because they are often involved in the management processes of that ply. This participation is essential to the synergistic ply's role of taking broad ideas and concepts and translating them into operational realities. This involves a variety of transactions, catalytic roles, and some trade-offs.

But involvement with and membership in a ply are two different things. For, after its involvement with the ideational ply in developing strategy, the synergistic ply is left with the difficult task of implementation. And 'left with' is an apt term for what the synergistic ply sees as characteristic of its role. It sees itself as standing alone. There is often the feeling of being let down. The ideational ply may now be seen by members of the synergistic ply as not having a real depth of commitment, and as not giving its full support to the new strategy or programme. As one organizational analyst puts it: 'They now feel they have been given inadequate support and unrealistic time schedules.' Evidently, this can go so far as to develop into a credibility gap.

Somewhat this same circle of moods describes the relationships between the synergistic ply and the process ply. At times, their members embrace each other and tackle problems as though they were members of a single ply. At other times, however, those of the synergistic ply tend to feel rebuffed, and, as one executive put it: 'During these periods, the reaction is often both thermal and sonic.'

The synergistic ply is also the world of multiple loyalties. 'I am bothered sometimes,' says a personnel vice-president, 'that often I feel much more loyal to my profession than to my company.' Much the same statement could come from the scientist, accountant, or computer technologist. At other times, these same individuals exhibit an intense loyalty to their companies. Either of these loyalties may be accompanied by a kind of missionary zeal, as members of the ply see themselves as vital change agents. On the other hand, they are pictured by some as having 'Civil Servant' mentalities.

An inherent function of this ply is to be a channel of communication between the other two plies, to be a conduit for ideas and needs, and, at times, to be a buffer. Implicit in this function are potentially serious difficulties. Obviously, if this ply wishes to avoid any major unpleasantness or confrontation with either of the other two plies, its interpretive presentations may be highly filtered.

In a sense, the synergistic ply is somewhat amorphous. The multiplicity of its roles and the nature of its involvement with the other segments of the organization make it so. And it is this attribute that becomes an important consideration in the management of change.

The process ply tends to be somewhat rigid psychologically, which is a reflection of the ply's environment. Its world is very stable and resistant to change.

Those within the process ply, for example, may participate in discussions, or receive memos concerning new strategies and plans, new concepts of management, and other forecasts of vital things to come, but their world does not seem to change. Tomorrow, as today, they are under pressure to get out a given quantity of product, of a specified quality, and at a predetermined cost. There is almost always a time lag between the formulation of new marketing or product development plans and their impact on the process ply. Further, some of the ideas for product development, or market penetration, never do come through and, consequently, this ply remains relatively untouched.

Some managers report that this time lag—and, more important, the fact that not all plans can be brought to fruition—tends to develop within the process ply a credibility gap towards the other plies. A typical comment made about this ply: 'We have seen them come and go.' Managers take much that they hear with the proverbial grain of salt.

This ply is reportedly highly ambivalent in its attitude towards the synergistic ply. This ambivalence appears to be at the root of many organizational problems. Thus, the process ply embraces the synergistic ply when it is seen as a buffer between itself and the ideational ply, or when it is really needed to help solve a pressing problem. At other times, the efforts of the synergistic

Elements of an organization as a system	Internal institutions of an organization			Desired environment
	Ideational	Synergistic	Process	
Linkage	*Internal*: heavy and directive; pattern setting; continuous *External*: heavy with peer and interfacing groups on economic, political, and social issues affecting company; stockholders *Within ply*: relationships reflect style of management of chief executive; cohesive in terms of that style	*Internal*: heavy in response to request or own initiatives; intermittent, and short term; probing *External*: medium to light with professional and peer organizations *Within ply*: fragmented as result of multiplicity of roles and disciplines; no common denominator of style	*Internal*: heavy, but short-term around problem areas or process studies *External*: medium to light with peer groups and suppliers *Within ply*: cohesive and stable; tendency towards low tolerance for disagreement	Effective network of relationships: Existence of effective linkages throughout the organization Appropriate system of communication and feedback Power that is responsive: a system of mutual influence and support Open and direct handling of conflict rather than suppression or avoidance
Balanced emphasis	Emphasis on long- and/or short-term corporate goals, and performance against goals Functional balance of emphasis tends to be an extension of chief executive style	Enabling, catalytic, transactional inputs Emphasis on trends in fields of disciplines	Short-term emphasis: mechanisms, processes, techniques to optimize value added to goods or services	Balance of emphasis between long-term and short-term objectives Even-handed attention to various essential functional areas Congruence between organizational and individual objectives
Paths of decision making	Establishes, modifies, and sustains decision-making paths in both the formal and the informal organization on questions of objectives, strategy, organizational structure, and performance	Involvement heavily dependent on initiatives of other two plies Initiates recommendations for action	Heavily within own ply and on short-term concerns—emphasis on throughput of goods and services	Effective delegation Minimal incidence of bottlenecks of incompetence or detours through the informal organization No defensive 'holdups' on decision making by improper use of committees, study groups, referrals

Reward systems	Industry norms; individual status; overall performance of company	Industry norms; status; quality of professional inputs into system, status of those who 'listen'	Industry norms; status; efficiency of throughput of goods and services; actual v. expected performance	Tangible and intangible system of rewards that reinforce all elements of expected behaviour
Administrative constraints	Establishes parameters of organizational constraints concerning directions and magnitude of growth of enterprise; its 'character' or identity, and renewal mechanisms; through the formulation of, and control over, objectives, plans, and policies	Conforms to patterns of constraints established by the ideational ply Recommends changes designed to increase effectiveness of organizational response Sets parameters of constraints within own ply in areas not covered by formulations of the ideational ply	Conforms to patterns of constraints established by the ideational ply Recommends changes designed to increase effectiveness of organizational response Sets parameters of constraints within own ply in areas not covered by formulations of the ideational ply	Objectives, plans, policies, procedures, and practices, which are enabling, with only those constraints that are essential for performance, rather than random behaviour Absence of inhibiting 'creedal' policies
Cultural constraints	Highly peer oriented—internally and externally Sets tone of attack by its perceptions of vectors of threats, problems, and opportunities Projects itself as a solid 'team' setting the mode, mood, and pace of leadership for entire organization Projects 'character' image of enterprise: internal/external Management styles an extension of style of chief executive	Multiple loyalties: profession and institution Circle of moods: missionary zeal, defensive retreat, civil servant response Ambivalent attitudes towards other plies Amorphous in nature by reason of multiplicity of roles and nature of involvement	Cohesive, internally disciplined group; tendency towards rigidity Ambivalent in attitude towards other plies Creative in process methodologies Influential by reason of its economic role	Present/future orientation rather than past/present Authority that is earned rather than inherited or merely vested by hierarchal position Standards or norms of behaviour that are 'owned' by the groups rather than imposed or dictated Ability to live with anxiety, risk, and ambiguity Ability to manage a climate of innovation or creativity Ability to manage fantasy projections

[continued overleaf

Fig. 34.1. A matrix of organization.

Internal institutions of an organization

Elements of an organization as a system	Ideational	Synergistic	Process	Desired environment
Self-correcting mechanisms	Creates and maintains, in accordance with its perception of the forces of technological and social momentum impinging on the company, processes for a continuous redefinition of corporate role identity, and aspiration Personal development Creates and supports an organizational climate that encourages personal development of others	Personal development Updating of theory and practice of various fields of functional specialization within the company	Personal development Product, process, and equipment development to retain competitive position Productivity increases by all means consistent with the safety, health, and dignity of the individual employee	Ability to specify organizational aspirations that are timely and appropriate, and to internalize them Individuals and groups that are self-correcting; they know what their impact is on people around them and on situations they are trying to influence, to make corrections that sustain forward thrust Appropriate programmes of manpower planning, and of manager and organizational development

Fig. 34.1. A matrix of organization. (continued)

524

ply to be 'helpful' may be resisted as 'meddling' into the affairs of the process ply.

When others look at the process ply, they see a highly cohesive group with a relatively low level of tolerance for disagreement, and with a kind of tenure in the ply that tends to foster institutional rigidities. Despite this psychological set, however, this ply retains an innovative thrust in the areas of technology and process techniques, and because of its vital economic role it exerts strong influence within the other plies of the institutional laminate.

Organization Change—Reconsidered

The organization, to those pragmatic executives who live in, and with it, emerges as basically an instrument, a mechanism, a means for solving problems and implementing decisions. The health of an organization, to the practical executive, is measured not in terms of its promises but by attained results. The health of an organization can be equated with its ability to formulate and achieve objectives that are both timely and appropriate; to maintain a suitable internal structure and work environment; and to respond fittingly to the relevant external environment—economic, political, and social. In short, organization health is virtually anonymous with organization change.

Abundant experience of company executives suggests that, in every organization, there is an elusive balance between fear of change and the hunger for change. Looking at the organization as a multi-institutional system of response helps to clarify the systemic elements of environment that those who hunger for change would modify. And it underscores that the responses to planned change are heavily flavoured by certain ingrained patterns of outlook and attitudes associated with each ply of the organization.

In this sense, this schema of organization as a multi-institutional system of response is a diagnostic tool for describing and analysing the health of the organization. More significant, so far as executives with whom this was discussed are concerned, is its possible use as a prescriptive tool in planning and implementing organization change.

Descriptive Tool

When arrayed in a matrix—with the systematic elements forming one axis, and the ply elements the other—executives find little difficulty in describing how any particular systemic element manifests itself relative to a given ply. The resulting matrix (Fig. 34.1) provides a basis for analysing the existing organization.

Prescriptive Tool

In the very process of characterizing the elements as they apply to each unit, the executives who shared in this exercise—drawing on hindsight—

were also able to see what might have been: if only .... Adding up the 'if only' comments produces an extra column on the matrix: the desired environment.

Thus, this column of the matrix does not describe any existing organization. What it does is to set forth goals or standards that provide a basis for auditing an existing organization and for planning changes that will improve the quality of life within an organization.

35. Manpower forecasting: estimating demand for and supply of managers*

A. R. Smith

Manpower forecasts are part of a planning process which is essentially the provision of the best possible framework of information for decision making in conditions of uncertainty. Forecasts of future manpower needs (demand) should take account not only of established trends and relationships between organizational objectives and staff needs, but of developments which may break those trends and relationships. Forecasts of manpower supply usually depend on statistical methods or models which treat manpower as a dynamic system with 'stock' determined by 'flows' of recruitment, promotions, wastage, etc. The underlying concepts are described, and some problems and limitations discussed.

Manpower planning is no longer the neglected topic in management literature that it was until the mid-sixties. Today, there is probably no need to dwell on the importance of manpower as a resource, nor upon the nature of effective planning. For that reason, I shall merely restate, very briefly, these *raisons d'être* of manpower forecasting.

Management is essentially a continuous process of making decisions about the acquisition, use and disposal of resources, with a view to achieving certain objectives. The time span under consideration in this decision-making process may be a few hours or weeks, or many years, but in every case it is concerned with the future. The future involves uncertainty—uncertainty about future political developments, market conditions, costs,

* The views expressed in this chapter are those of the author and should not be assumed to represent the views of the Civil Service Department. The author wishes to thank Mr J. J. Burke of the Treasury Board of Canada, and Professor D. J. Bartholomew, both of whom kindly read and commented on his manuscript.

competitor behaviour, union strategies, and so on—and when decision makers look to the future, implicit or explicit assumptions are made about the relative likelihood of very many trends and events. Decisions are more likely to be good decisions if they are based on the best possible information about the future than if they are based simply on hunch or intuition. Hence, the case for systematic planning. The planning process is essentially the provision of the best possible framework of information within which decisions can be taken. And an organization which has a good information system for planning will be more likely than others to be able to adjust successfully and quickly to changing circumstances and unforeseen events as they arise. That, briefly, is the case for planning.

Because it is not like any other resource, manpower needs special treatment in this planning process. It cannot be owned by an organization (at least in our kind of society), no matter how cogently the human resource accounting exponents may argue. Manpower has a will of its own, and can change its value to an organization in any number of ways if it does not like a decision (or lack of a decision) taken by management—it can resign, strike, or simply not bother to work effectively. Manpower needs to be treated with due regard for human values, and this includes planning to try to ensure reasonable recognition of aptitudes, potential, and aspirations. Moreover, in many cases, manpower of the kinds needed by an organization cannot be acquired easily and at short notice. Knowledge and skills peculiar to the organization may be necessary, and can perhaps be acquired only during several years in the organization. Even where this is not so, there may be national or local shortages which limit the chances of recruiting to replace losses or feed growth. And there are good social, economic, and political reasons for not seeking to keep the human resources of an organization in line with its needs simply by adopting a 'hire and fire' policy. Hence, the need to plan manpower so that the needs of the organization, of the people who compose it, and of the society in which it exists, are met in the most satisfactory way. That, basically, is the case for manpower planning in employing organizations.

In most cases, it seems to be useful to think of company manpower planning as being made up of three aspects. First, there is the task of trying to estimate how many people of each kind will be needed at various stages in the future to enable the organization to meet its objectives. Despite objections from economists, it is a reasonably well-established convention to call this stage the 'demand' side of the manpower equation. Second, there is the task of estimating the future 'supply', by reference to the likely trends in recruitment, training, development, promotion, retirement, and so on. Third, there is the task of taking decisions which will increase the chance of bringing the demand and supply into balance at the most desirable levels in the future, bearing in mind the desirability of minimizing the likelihood of redundancy; violent surges in recruitment and training needs; unduly high costs; sudden loss of too much experience; promotion stagnation; and so on.

528

A basic assumption in elementary 'old-style' economics is that demand and supply will automatically be brought into balance at the 'right' levels by allowing price to move freely. Put crudely in manpower terms, a threatened shortage of particular skills will be covered by raising salaries or wages. In practice, this is rarely a useful concept in manpower planning. The 'price' can rarely be altered with ease in a manipulative sense, because of the complex systems of internal and external relativities, union pressures, political considerations, and so on. Moreover, it is even more difficult to lower the 'price' when a shortage, in the course of time, threatens to become a surplus. Obviously, every manpower system is also an economic system, but, in practical manpower planning, price manipulation rarely has a central place (although price is a central factor in assessments of costs of manpower policies) and, throughout most of this chapter, it will be ignored.

It should be obvious that the task of keeping demand and supply in reasonable balance will be greatly eased if flexibility and adaptability are built into both sides of the equation. Subject always to the overriding need to get work done as effectively and efficiently as possible, jobs should not be allowed to become the preserve of any one highly specific class of employee if they can be performed as efficiently by a wider range of people. Similarly, people should be encouraged to be adaptable, and to acquire a wider range of skills by training or retraining, or learning on the job. Part of the task of manpower planning should be to seek out opportunities for widening the range of options. It remains the case, however, that not all jobs can be done by everybody, and no one person can do any job. Moreover, the needs of individuals for collective security, and the power of unions and professional bodies—plus the practical management problems of large organizations—are bound to impose real restraints on flexibility.

It follows that manpower in any sizable organization should be classifiable into occupational groups or categories and into hierarchical levels, grades, or ranks. These provide the latitude and longitude for manpower planning. In highly structured organizations such as the armed forces or the Civil Service, these groupings will tend to be explicit (though, sometimes, misleadingly so when the established labels persist after the nature of work has changed). In firms in which no systematic classification has been developed, a fair amount of diligent inquiry may be needed before manpower can be classified and manpower planning work begun. In some cases, the use of sophisticated statistical techniques,[1] e.g., cluster analysis, may help to establish or improve the classification methods, but these techniques are beyond the scope of this chapter.

Among the occupational groups and hierarchical levels will be a number—perhaps even a majority—which can be described collectively as managerial. No attempt is made in this chapter to define the word 'manager'. Others have tried to do so; I shall merely refer to a recent report for NEDO,[2] in which it is said: 'In the real world of management there can be no precise and general definition and there is no point in recapitulating rival definitions'. The reader, then, is free—if he wishes—to apply what follows to any part of the manpower of an organization other than to those people who have, and need, no skills. It can be applied to managers, but it can be applied equally well to other categories.

Demand

In any organization which has been in being for any length of time, there will be established relationships between the nature, tasks, and objectives of the organization on one hand, and the structure and numbers of its management force on the other. The first can be described or analysed in terms of organizational components, and the second classified into various kinds of management posts, each identified as belonging to particular organizational components and put into the form of statistical tables. These will provide a starting point for a forecast of future demand.

It may be that the established relationships between work loads and staff numbers are not optimal. For example, top management may feel that there is a degree of overmanning which ought to be eradicated. Alternatively, some areas (often the newer and innovative ones) may be undermanned. Any corrections to the demand picture will be among the factors to be taken into account in preparing statistical tables of future, required manager numbers corresponding to the starting-point ones.

Apart from corrections of these kinds, the job of converting the starting-point tables into a series of future tables—one for each of a series of future dates—will, initially, be a matter of examining each task and objective, and getting the best possible information about how it is likely to change over time. To some extent, it may be possible to use statistical techniques, either to help predict changes in tasks or to predict staff changes consequential upon changes in tasks. For example, if one of the objectives of an organization is to maximize sales of a particular range of products, then analysis of trends in past sales, and statistical market research techniques, may be useful for forecasting sales; further analysis may show that there is a statistical correlation between area sales and sales-management and production-management staffs which may be expected to continue to apply in the future. Similarly, in the public services, an objective may be to provide a certain minimum range of welfare services for old people, disabled people, single-parent families, and so on. Demographic statistical techniques[3] may be used in such cases to establish the best possible forecasts of the numbers and distribution of people for whom services have to be provided, and, hence, forecasts may be made of the staff required to manage such services.

Statistical techniques of these kinds have a useful part to play in forecasting future manpower demand—but this is not the whole picture. Generally, statistical techniques identify and measure trends and relationships which have been established in the past, and project into the future on the assumption that these trends and relationships will continue. But due allowance must be made for changes which may break these established trends and relationships. These changes may result through planned policy changes in respect of management organization, tasks, or objectives; foreseeable changes in the economic, social or political environment of the organization; technological change; and so on.

There can be no simple rule-of-thumb method for translating such changes into changes in the numbers and kinds of managers needed. The only rules are that the forecasting should be tackled systematically and analytically, and the best-informed people in the organization should contribute to the translation process. The best-informed people will include top management, who may have tentative plans for growth or a change in direction for the organization as a whole; research and development staff who may be able to see revolutionary changes in technology ahead; marketing men who may be able to foresee new opportunities; and so on. The bringing together of all these contributions to forecasting cannot be expected to be easy, but is probably most likely to be successfully tackled by establishing an effective corporate planning activity within the organization, and establishing very close links between it and manpower planning activity. (My opinion is that the manpower planning activity should never be allowed to be subsumed by a corporate planning staff, but should be closely associated with personnel management where the human factors and the practical politics of staff relations will not be overlooked.)

In many organizations which have established an acceptable routine framework for forecasting manpower demand, a common pattern seems to have evolved. First, there is a close link between corporate and financial planning and manpower planning. Second, the time span of the forecasts is more often than not five years ahead or, in some cases, ten (depending on the lead-time for capital projects). Third, the forecasting process is carried out in full once a year and 'rolled forward', and modifications are made between annual reviews as new decisions are taken or circumstances change. Fourth, there is systematic feedback from the planning process to the contributors to it, to allow each to adjust his own assumptions and plans to accord with the total picture, i.e., to ensure that the plans of the component parts of the organization are in line with each other, with top management policies and objectives, and within resource availabilities. In this sense, the annual planning process may involve cycling through several stages before all the ingredients are mutually compatible and accepted by top management.

Much systematic forecasting, as we have said, looks ahead for five years, or possibly ten. But for any organization which aims to provide careers for its staff, rather than depend on 'hire and fire' the time span for career planning could be as much as forty years. Desirably, for example, the number of administrative trainees being selected in 1975 by the UK Civil Service Commission should bear a reasonable relationship to the numbers of Under Secretaries and higher grades that the Civil Service might be expected to need in the years 2000–2015. In practice, no one can possibly foresee needs so far ahead, and any substantial and costly effort to forecast long-term needs is hardly likely to be regarded as justifiable. However, the occasional attempt to produce appreciations of possible long-term developments may well be worthwhile. These attempts might take the form of bringing together top management and other key people in the organization, together with one or two well-informed people from outside, for 'think tank' sessions. Any thinking ahead of this kind should concern itself not only with how many 'top people' will be required by the organization in the long-term future, but also, with what they are likely to have to do, and what mix of skills and abilities is desirable. Generally, however, and bearing in mind the very many uncertainties, the best safeguard against long-term surplus or shortage is the deliberate cultivation of flexible attitudes.

A great deal of effective forecasting work can be done, not by posing the question 'how many?' will we need in the long-term but, rather, by posing a range of questions of the form 'what if?' the number that we need remains unchanged, increases by x per cent per annum, reduces by y per cent per annum, and so on, and by considering the consequences in terms of forecasts of supply.

Supply

The supply side of the equation is well catered for in terms of useful statistical methods for forecasting. Most of these methods depend on the fact that bodies of manpower can be conceptualized as dynamic systems in which the 'stock' at future dates will be determined partly by the size and composition of the present stock, and partly by various 'flows' which will occur between now and the future dates. The flows in very small organizations may not be large enough to exhibit a regular pattern, and in such organizations, common-sense and simple arithmetic may be more relevant than statistical methods in forecasting. (I shall return to this point later.) But in organizations of any appreciable size, the flows—which will be, in the main, recruitment; casual wastage; transfers; training throughput; promotions and retirements—are likely to lend themselves to statistical treatment. Given that the numbers in the system are reasonably large, then examination of past statistical data should reveal regularities in the patterns of the flows which, when linked with knowledge of personnel management policies and practices, should provide a reasonable basis for forecasting. This is best explained by considering some of the flows in more detail.

It is convenient to think of wastage as being made up of three components: retirements related to age or service, redundancy discharges, and all other losses bracketed together under the label 'casual wastage'. Redundancy discharges are usually a once-for-all type of loss, as opposed to a regular flow, and will usually occur as a result of substantial, unforeseen change in demand, or because of a failure to plan the supply adequately in the past, or just because there is inadequate planning generally. Redundancy, if necessary, will emerge as an output from the manpower planning process rather than being an input of data. Generally, an organization which has a well-established manpower planning programme will be less at risk of redundancy than one which has not, because it is more likely to foresee risk in time to moderate the consequences by exploiting natural wastage and adjusting recruitment and retraining programmes.

In contrast, casual wastage will tend to conform to 'natural laws', and exhibit the same kinds of regularity as the statistics on mortality or road accidents. Provided that the composition of the payroll, in terms of age, sex, occupation, and so on, remains reasonably constant, the wastage rate will remain reasonably constant—the crude wastage rate being defined as the number of losses in a period of time divided by the number of people 'at risk', which in turn will be, say, the average number of people on the payroll during the period in question, or some reasonable approximation to it. But in practice, the composition of the payroll is liable to change, and, in any case, a single wastage-rate figure for the whole payroll is not likely to be of much use for forecasting because the forecaster will be concerned with individual occupations and grades. Separate wastage rates will be needed for each relevant category of employee, for each geographical location—if locations need to be forecast separately—and for each sex if the sex composition is likely to change.

Beyond that, the need for further refinement will depend on the particular case, but it is almost certain that it will be necessary in most cases to calculate the wastage rate for each length of service (e.g., by single years of length of service), or age where it is reasonably safe to assume that age is closely associated with length of service. Very many case studies have shown that wastage rates are much higher for people who have recently joined an organization than for those with longer service. This means that an expanding category of people will tend to suffer higher wastage *numbers* than a constant-sized or contracting one because it will contain more recent recruits, even though the wastage *rates* (properly measured in terms of length of service) may be the same. This, in turn, means that the recruiting and training effort needed to sustain a significant expansion is substantially greater than might be thought at first, and, conversely, the reduction in payroll which can be effected by simply cutting back on recruitment is smaller, or the cut-back more severe or more prolonged, than might at first sight be thought.

To sum up, casual wastage—if properly measured by examining past data—will yield rates which can be used for forecasting purposes, by applying them to numbers 'at risk', in a reasonably reliable way. Casual wastage rates will change, but, usually, they will change only slowly over time, or fluctuate within fairly narrow limits (provided that the numbers with which we are concerned are reasonably large), and be good enough for most practical forecasting purposes.

Retirement data can usually be handled by using much the same approach. There may be a fixed retirement age, in which case forecasting is no problem. Alternatively, retirement may take place within a range of ages. Within the relevant age or service-length band there will be numbers 'at risk' of retirement, for whom there will be appropriate rates derived from statistical

Length of service (years)	Wastage rate (% per annum)	Case 1 Strength at start of year	Wastage in year	Case 2 Strength at start of year	Wastage in year
0–1	20	50	10	150	30
1–2	10	50	5	100	10
2–3	6	50	3	50	3
3–4	4	100	4	50	2
4–5	2	150	3	50	1
all		400	25	400	46
Overall casual wastage rates, i.e., excluding 'retirements' at end of five years		$6\frac{1}{4}\%$		$11\frac{1}{2}\%$	

Note: Service-specific wastage rates are defined in these cases as the losses during a year, expressed as a proportion of the corresponding strength at the beginning of the year. For simplicity, employment is assumed to be terminated after five years, but similar pictures would emerge if careers were assumed to last for many more years.

Fig. 35.1. Wastage rates: hypothetical cases.

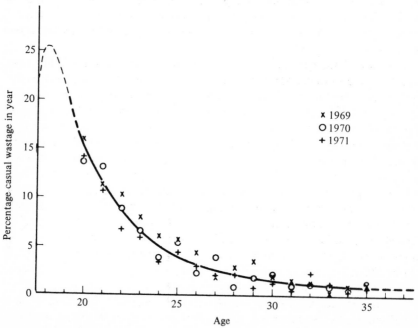

Fig. 35.2. A free-hand curve drawn through the pattern of wastage rates for each year of age among men of one category of junior managers, for each of the years 1969–71. (Losses were counted by year of birth, and expressed as a percentage of the average strength of men with that year of birth. The average was the simple average of the numbers at the beginning and end of the year with that year of birth.) Above age 35, the wastage rates remained reasonably steady at less than 1 per cent until retirement age was reached. Below age 20, a more complicated analysis was necessary. This was because a substantial proportion of recruits to this category were aged 18 or 19. In such circumstances it would be better to analyse the figures relating to the under-20s in terms of length of service, preferably month by month. (A corresponding picture in respect of women would show wastage rates declining much more slowly, from about 20 per cent at age 20 to about 8 per cent at age 30, before falling to about the same rates as for men after age 35.) Many case studies have shown that standard statistical curves, such as the log-normal curve, will fit wastage patterns of these kinds, and can be used for analysis and forecasting.

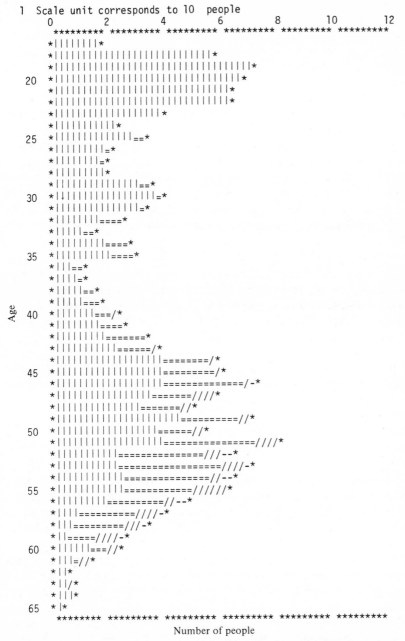

Fig. 35.3. Manpower data analysed by computer. Example of data in respect of one manpower category, analysed by age and grade: an age/grade distribution computer print-out. Grades are identified by varying the type of symbol printed by the computer.

data in respect of earlier years. Unless management has some change in retirement policy in mind, forecasts of retirement numbers can be made by using the appropriate rates and applying them to the numbers still employed who have already passed the minimum retirement age, and to those who will shortly reach that age. If a change in policy is in mind, the change can be allowed for in the forecasting process. It is common for organizations, when they first start to engage in forecasting, to find that they fairly soon observe quite dramatic changes in the numbers of retirements, because of marked peaks or troughs in the age and length of service distributions of their staffs (attributable to marked changes in recruitment many years before, e.g., during the Second World War). These changes in retirement numbers can have serious consequences in relation to the availability of adequate skills and experience, promotion opportunities, career development plans, and recruitment and training needs. It is in giving management more time to plan to ameliorate the consequences of these peaks and troughs that the introduction of forecasting is likely to show the most obvious early benefits.

Although most organizations would claim, with reason, that when selecting people for promotion they simply 'select the most suitable people' or 'select by merit', promotions in organizations of any appreciable size do seem to exhibit statistical regularities, in that the age, or length of service, or seniority distribution of annual batches of promotees tends to be stable from one year to another, and the proportion of each cohort (or age, or length of service, or seniority group) of people 'at risk' of being promoted, who will in fact be promoted, also tends to show stability. The word 'tends' is important here because these two aspects—the distributions of promotees, and the rates of promotion—can appear to conflict with and distort each other, usually because the natural tendencies of rates to remain constant will be thwarted by the fact that the number of vacancies (determined by demand as much as supply factors like retirement and wastage) vary from one year to another.

There is no *simple* statistical method or model which allows one to forecast promotions realistically in such a way that changes in numbers of vacancies, changes in numbers eligible for promotion, and any possible changes in policy can all be adequately allowed for. But there is a range of statistical models, mostly too complex to be explained here, which enable managements to take all these factors into account and examine, realistically, the consequences of continuing their current promotion practices or policies, or of adopting any changes in practices or policies which they may have in mind.

In the most simple applications of manpower forecasting, it may seem adequate merely to regard recruitment numbers as an 'output' from the forecasting process. This will be the case when the role of the forecast is seen merely to be to estimate vacancies during the next year. In such a case, the recruiting need will represent the difference between the demand that is forecast for one year hence, and the present stock (which may be a positive or negative difference), allowing for forecast wastage and net promotions or transfers from the category with which we are concerned; this presupposes that recruits do not need training before they can fill posts; if they do, allowance also has to be made for the time taken in training and for trainee wastage.

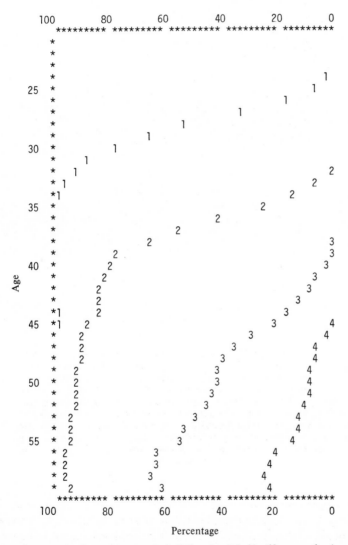

Fig. 35.4. An example of a computer analysis designed to help identify promotion 'norms'. In this case, everyone in the trainee grade is in the early 20s. By the age of 50, about 10 per cent have reached the highest grade, 40 per cent the next highest grade, and so on. The age at which promotion hopes are probably at their highest occurs where the line of digits is nearest the horizontal. About 20 per cent of trainees who survive can expect, if these patterns persist, to reach the highest grade, and virtually all can expect two promotions. More sophisticated manpower models can be used to establish what the size of each grade would need to be if these patterns were to persist, and to establish how the pattern would need to change to match any forecast of demand.

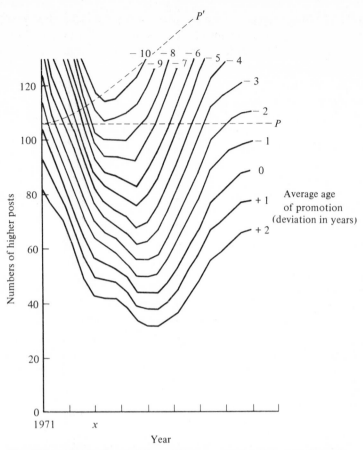

Fig. 35.5. A visual aid to decision making—one of a number, each illustrating a specific point, produced from computer forecasting models. In this case, a substantial run-out of senior managers is forecast, as an 'age block' reaches retirement. If the number of posts remains unchanged at level P, it will be necessary (given a range of other stated assumptions) to lower promotion ages on average by nearly nine years between 1971 and year x. If the number of posts increases to the extent indicated by P', dramatic changes in promotion and recruitment practices may be necessary. The decision maker will then need to take into account the reversal of trends after year x, as indicated in the figure.

Such a simple approach is rarely appropriate, however, in organizations of any appreciable size and complexity. In most cases in which 'managers' are the category being forecast, it will not be sufficient merely to gear the number of recruits to the short-term forecast of vacancies arising; one has to take into account the longer-term needs for experienced and more senior people which the short-term future recruits can in due course become. At first sight, it may seem that this raises a perplexing problem: the short-term and long-term needs may conflict, in which event the possible long-term may well have to be ignored in favour of the near-certain short-term.

538

But, in most cases, it should be possible to reconcile the short-term and the long-term by regarding recruits as being several distinct flows rather than a single flow, each of the flows having distinct characteristics in terms of wastage, promotion expectations, and so on. Examples of distinct streams would be high-quality fast-stream university graduates, middle-quality school leavers (high-school graduates in the US), older people joining after experience in other organizations, transfers from other parts of the organization, etc., with the sexes regarded as distinct streams—at least for the younger types of entrant.

In the more sophisticated types of computerized manpower model, not only the recruits, but the people already in the system, will be divided into distinct streams or substreams in this way, and the balance between short-term and long-term recruiting needs struck at an acceptable level by manipulating the size of each stream within the total. (These streams need not exist as a matter of explicit policy: they need only exist as a matter of fact and be identified by analysis.)

Streaming of this kind is often also necessary for resolving potential incompatibilities between promotion opportunities and the expected numbers of posts at each level in the hierarchy. For example, if an organization appears to management to have too few posts in the upper reaches of the graded structure to appear attractive enough to people at the bottom of the pyramid, it may be practicable to classify a proportion of the posts (if only for forecasting and planning purposes) in the lower grades as being earmarked for late-age promotees from non-management categories, or for short-term contract staff, or late-age recruits, and so reduce the number of posts to be filled by high-potential staff in the lower grades early in their careers to a number compatible with the promotion opportunities. It is with these possibilities in mind that some of the more sophisticated computerized manpower forecasting models have been, and are being, developed.

The cost of developing complex computerized manpower forecasting models can probably only be justified in very large organizations (and in university departments where work in this field is appropriate to the teaching and research roles). But once developed and tested in practical management situations, these models tend to be of fairly general application. Even in large organizations, the models are only of real value if they can be used for a variety of problems in a variety of manpower subsets or subgroups, each of which will tend to differ from others in the number of grades, streams, promotion practices, and so on; so the development tends to be towards generalized models. These models, by virtue of their generality, should be usable in many medium-sized organizations also.

Such models are not of great value in small organizations, or in small highly specialized subsystems of larger organizations, largely because the statistical regularities on which the models depend will not, in such cases, be identifiable in a reliable way. Retirement and promotion numbers may be so small that it does not make sense to express them in terms of statistical probabilities, but, rather, to express them in terms of the precise ages, assessed abilities, and, perhaps, the intentions of individuals. (Statistical probabilities, of course, also depend on these things, but it is the aggregates of these characteristics for many individuals which form the regularities of the statistics. These cannot often be deduced from small numbers, or applied to small numbers.) Where the focus is necessarily on individuals, then the systems concepts outlined in earlier paragraphs will still be relevant as concepts, but the actual forecasting will be much more a matter of simple arithemtic, intelligent interpretation of available information, and career succession planning. Computers and advanced statistical methods will not be relevant. Between the large organization and the very small will be a hazy border area where other kinds of statistical/computer models may be relevant, e.g., simulation models tailored to small numbers.

A prime requirement for any forecasting of manpower supply is a good data base, derived from reliable information about each individual in the organization. This will usually consist of a set of personnel records—held perhaps in a card index in a small organization, but, almost essentially, in a computer in large organizations—showing all the relevant stages through which the employee has passed, with the dates in each case, and other relevant information such as qualifications. From such a record will be derived all the necessary forecasting information about stocks and flows. Personnel records are notoriously difficult to maintain in an accurate state, and, for that reason, there is much to be said for having personnel records maintenance closely associated with payroll. For large organizations, the ideal is probably an integrated computerized pay and record system, with the record for each individual printed-out, then checked for accuracy by that individual at least once a year, and with the records mounted on a computer which is also suitable for applying the manpower analysis and forecasting models.

References

1. CLOUGH, D. J., LEWIS, C. G., and OLIVER, A. L. *Manpower Planning Models*, English Universities Press, 1974.
2. LEGGATT, T. W. *The Training of British Managers: A Study of Need and Demand*, Report by the Institute of Manpower Studies for the National Economic Development Office, HMSO, 1972.
3. Department of Employment, *Company Manpower Planning*, HMSO, 1968.

Suggested Reading

BARTHOLOMEW, D. J. and MORRIS, B. R. (Eds.) *Aspects of Manpower Planning*, English Universities Press, London, 1970; Elsevier, New York, 1970.
SMITH, A. R. (Ed.) *Models of Manpower Systems*, English Universities Press, London, 1970; Elsevier, New York, 1970.
BARTHOLOMEW, D. J. and SMITH, A. R. (Eds.) *Manpower and Management Science*, English Universities Press, London, 1971; Heath, Lexington, Mass., 1972.
LEWIS, C. G. (Ed.) *Bibliography of Manpower Planning*, English Universities Press, London, 1969; Elsevier, New York, 1969.
SMITH, A. R. (Ed.) *Some Statistical Techniques for Manpower Planning*, CAS Occasional paper no. 15, HMSO, 1970.

STAINER, G. *Manpower Planning*, Heinemann, 1971.
Institute of Manpower Studies, *Bibliography of Manpower Studies* 1969–73 (to be published).
Institute of Personnel Management, *Company Practices in Manpower Planning*, 1972.
Various articles in *Personnel Review*, **1**, 1–3, 1971–2.

36. Management manpower planning

Derek Walker

This chapter deals with the essential process of planning a company's management manpower, identifying the significance of the management role, and defining manpower planning in relation both to the general utilization of human resources and the satisfaction of personal objectives.

It describes a system of planning based on a management development programme which takes account of the fundamental fact that people develop faster under 'forcing' circumstances, and that they require constant answers to two questions: 'What business are we in?' and 'Where do we intend to go?' It deals with the role of managers and their subordinates within this system.

The essential steps necessary to launch such a management development scheme are described, indicating the close relationship to overall business planning. The problems involved in operating such a programme are discussed, as are specific areas of benefit, the most important of which being the machinery that the programme provides for training through work *itself.*

Finally, future trends are discussed, stressing that management manpower planning—as well as all other—is going to be of prime concern in the world's fast-changing economic, political, and social scene.

The management of an enterprise has always been a critical element in its success. Trite though this statement may seem, the *full* meaning of the truism is often overlooked, and companies are slow to take action to ensure the effectiveness of management teams. The creation and maintenance of a truly effective management group should be high on any company's list of priorities.

The necessity for more effective management manpower planning can easily be demonstrated by looking at executive wastage and redundancy, and the costs involved in hiring and firing. On the reverse side of the balance sheet, we can look at benefits to be gained, such as improved morale, company performance, and profitability.

Given that an enterprise has a future and, more important, an expanding one, then forward planning has to be added to the essential thinking to ensure a continuing and viable management team. From this comes the planning of *management* manpower as a part of overall manpower planning needed to ensure the growth and, thus, the future of the company. It is only recently that attention has been focused on this issue, and any real consideration given to the importance of planning in the human resource area of business operations and the fact that such planning should be an essential, integrated part of total corporate planning.

Before proceeding further, it is worth defining what is meant by management and manpower planning. So far as the former is concerned, it is important to have this definition in that it assists in clarifying the role of managers within the managerial group. Management is essentially a continuous process of making decisions about the acquisition, use, or disposal of resources, with a view to achieving certain objectives. Bound up with that process is time, and one of the more remarked-on phenomena today is the rapidly increasing rate at which events in the business, commercial, and technological world are changing. Alongside this, there is the very significant rate of change in society as a whole, bringing with it changing attitudes towards the conventions and practices of the past.

Turning now to manpower planning, this can be defined fairly simply by saying that it is an activity or process which involves the planning of a desired future in terms of both the effective utilization of human resources and the satisfaction of the personal objectives of the individual. It has often been thought that manpower planning was simply a 'numbers' exercise or, alternatively, a matter of statistics. It is true that analysis of management manpower planning in these terms, such that a view of the basic supply and demand equation can be established, is very necessary to the establishment of a corporate plan. However, particularly in the area of management against the background of the definitions previously given, it soon becomes clear that it is very much more than this. Emphasis must be placed on the establishment of objectives, the resource planning necessary to the achievement of those objectives, the decision making again necessary for the attainment of those objectives, and a continual reference to change in all its forms—not forgetting attitudinal change.

Business today, more than ever, demands effective management, whether by the individual manager or the management team. In this situation—which is becoming ever-more critical—the need becomes apparent for a system or method which effectively meets the requirement with the degree of flexibility necessary to accept the dynamism of a fast-changing world.

Description of a System

In many companies today, management manpower planning is approached through a comprehensive management development programme which lays emphasis on the development of a management team, consistent with the objectives of the company and the business plans developed from them. What follows, outlines such an approach.

The guiding principles for a management development programme which will be good for the business, and for the employees in it, are as follows. Every business is a 'living organism' with its own traditions, climate, opinion and special make-up, and, therefore, management development for that company must be a tailor-made affair. In this way, it will take into account the thinking and attitudes of the people within it, and their circumstances. However, people develop faster under 'forcing circumstances', and, thus, it is necessary for them to be faced with the right kind of challenges. Additionally, before devising any scheme of management development for a business, the top management would be well advised to ask two fundamental questions: 'Exactly what business are we in?' and 'Where do we intend to go?' The answers can provide an effective base for determining the nature of a management manpower plan and an appropriate management development programme. Inevitably, there are a number of other more detailed questions that must be answered; some of these are below:

(a) What is the current organizational situation and has it any weaknesses?
(b) In answer to the question 'Where are we going?' have we the strategies and policies necessary for the fulfilment of our ideas in this direction?
(c) Given those strategies and policies, have we the practical operating plans for getting there?
(d) When will the results be achieved, and what will be the rates of progress, the build-up of resources, programmes, schedules, stage by stage targets, that should form part of those operating plans?
(e) Who is going to be affected? The answer to this question is to be expressed in functional terms as well as in terms of individual managers.
(f) What changes will this mean to the organization structure and the assignment of tasks and responsibilities to people?
(g) What will be required in the way of resources? And is it possible? Although the aim is higher, if we attempt to achieve what we ought to go for—is the thinking sound, the risk justified, the return on resources employed going to be acceptable? Most particularly, in human resource management terms, are the people fully competent to meet the challenge? If not, how long will it require for them to come to that degree of competence, or will there be a necessity to inject fresh blood? We have said that people develop faster under 'forcing circumstances' but, if the fresh thinking on organization, communications and the programming of events produce undue strain, this will produce inefficiency, and the objectives that we originally set will never be attained.

As stated earlier, the purpose of questions like these, and those that can be derived from them, is to ensure that an all-encompassing scheme for the development of management may be devised, which will be appropriate to the needs of the business.

Launching a Management Development Scheme—The Major Ingredients

In considering how to launch a management development scheme, it is essential to bear in mind the objectives and criteria outlined previously, but the steps that need to be taken can be stated fairly simply:

(a) The clear communication to all concerned in the company of the intentions, applications and benefits of management development with appropriate help and support in follow-up with individual managers, as required.

(b) The universally known, unequivocal leadership and practical support of the scheme by the managing executive.

(c) The appointment—if the business is large enough to warrant it—of a senior executive who will ensure the health, dynamism, and relevance of the scheme throughout the business as time passes, together with ensuring enthusiastic, yet sensitive and intelligent implementation by managers as part of their everyday life.

(d) The clear, sound construction of organization charts for functions and the business as a whole, showing all management posts and those immediately subordinate.

(e) The construction of job descriptions and man specifications—thus gearing recruitment and selection into the management development scheme in a realistic manner.

(f) The establishment of policies, criteria, objectives and targets, together with clear means of measuring performance.

(g) The conducting of performance reviews against targets.

(h) The provision of training, guidance, or experience to fill the 'competence gap' between what the job demands *currently*, and what the job holder is able to do.

(i) The selection of people for training, guidance or experience who appear to have the *potential* for further development beyond the current job.

(j) Organization planning and the assessment of manpower requirements.

(k) Preparing management succession plans and career paths.

(l) Planning and implementing development programmes for individuals, the aim of which is to fit them to fill more responsible posts within the given time.

Figure 36.1 is a systems diagram which provides an overall view of the total management development approach. It shows its sequence, the inter-relationship of its component parts, and the way that it integrates with the normal running of the business to produce improved results. The on-going sequence is shown in solid lines and arrows, and the most vital of the feedback loops in dotted lines (these dotted lines therefore represent output of the current cycle of operation, becoming input to both modify the present cycle and contribute to the next). Company policy, corporate and marketing strategy both determine, and can override, all other plans and objectives. For this reason, it is not good enough for policy to 'exist' or 'be known';

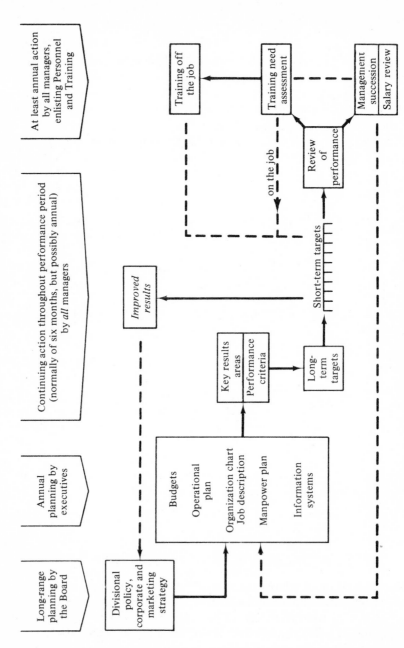

Fig. 36.1. Management development: system and summary.

it should be committed to writing and communicated as far down the organization as security allows.

The annual planning by senior executives of the four main resources—finance, manpower, time, and information—is easily recognized in budgets and operational plans, though the need for planning manpower and information is less widely acted upon. All four are fed from the output of the previous cycle of performance, and this includes salary review. Training is related to management succession planning and to the needs of the current job and, whether carried out on or off the job, is followed through by targets in the form of appropriate projects.

Implementation

In implementing any such approach to management development and planning, inevitably there are problems as well as benefits. So far as problems are concerned, they originate—in the main—from any failure of management support. It is fundamental to the success of a management development programme that it receives strong on-going *top* management support. As no doubt will have been appreciated, such a programme prescribes an approach to management itself, which may well differ from that which had gone before. This is particularly true if the approach to management generally tended to the pragmatic. Inevitably, there is a definitive requirement for planning, both in the short- and long-term, even recognizing that planning is—and should be—a dynamic process. Where a return to pragmatism occurs, either the system dies and withers away or, worse still, carries on in the sense that managers complete the paperwork because they think it is the 'policy' but, as they have no real belief in it, the paperwork and the discussions and actions that flow from it have little or no relevance to the business. It cannot be overemphasized that strong support from the top is essential, and that periodic checks or audits must be made to ensure relevance.

The benefits to be obtained from the introduction of planning, in the whole area of management manpower—via a management development programme—can be manifold. The management development scheme may, therefore, be said to be a kind of machine by which resources are converted through work into results.

Figure 36.2 attempts to show the need for optimizing four basic elements of such a machine or system and to recognize that each affects, and is affected by, the others. These elements are as follows:

(a) The organization of related people and functions avoids gaps, overlaps, and friction, and changes such potential waste into cooperation.
(b) Information on objectives, and on the measurement of results, provides both direction and a control or 'steering' facility.
(c) The capability of the individual has a strong influence on determining business objectives, just as organization structures cannot really be designed in a vacuum from some set of theories. In practice, rightly or

547

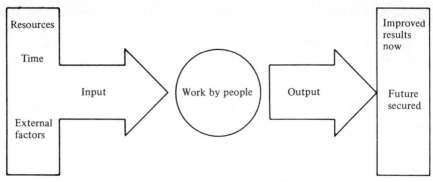

Fig. 36.2. The structure of work.

wrongly, individuals in a company tailor its objectives to their own strengths, weaknesses, and inclinations.

(d) Above all, motivation is increased through involvement in determining objectives, personal identification with company objectives, and commitment to their achievement. This motivation boosts the force, power, or effort applied to work and sustains it through time. This is one way of looking at the benefits that can emerge.

Now, to point to specific areas of benefit:

(a) The company has the means of continuously ensuring that it has an organization structure apposite to its business.

(b) There is an ability available to ensure more effective recruitment and selection, since the base data for job descriptions and man specifications are readily available.

(c) There is a planning tool readily available—the apparently innocent formalization of good management practice puts pressure on management to think through the most fundamental issues of running the business; by definition, only the most critical and important business objectives are selected for this concentration of effort. Not only annual operational objectives for each job holder, but even organization structures, call for the strategy and policies themselves to be examined, clarified, and often modified as a result.

(d) Participation in establishing objectives helps managers to identify with those objectives and be totally committed to achieving them. Thus, sound ways of measuring success or failure have to be discovered, and management information systems overhauled. This creative approach both stimulates quality and innovation and harnesses the energy needed for sustained pressure. Work, like exporting, needs opportunity and minimum restriction to be fun.

(e) The system proposed undoubtedly contributes to the cost effectiveness of training by:
(i) throwing up apparent individual needs which are at least based on operational performance;

(ii) encouraging assignments, projects, evaluation and follow-up of formal training.

However, its most significant effect on the training and development of managers is that it provides the machinery for training *through work* itself. Such training is almost costless, can be carried out frequently and constantly, can ensure the 'transfer' and application of any formal training received, and can actually benefit the superior simultaneously.

Future Trends

There can be no doubt that management manpower planning, approached through management development, or some such similar system will increasingly make its contribution to the overall planning within the business. Inevitably, because of developments in Europe and elsewhere, there will be a need to look carefully at the way that organizations are structured. Indeed, organization development and design is becoming a subject in its own right. Management development and the whole management manpower planning process provide the data base from which such work can proceed with objectivity.

Related to this particular point is that of future developments in the area of job descriptions which will come about as a result of the work on job design. Equally, there is much to be done on the question of performance criteria. Many managers find it extremely difficult to provide performance criteria that are really pertinent in the case of staff jobs. Inevitably, therefore, it is essential that work should be done in this area because it is all a part of the control and 'steering' mechanism mentioned earlier.

Another area that demands attention is appraisal—and whether the existing methods of appraisal are in fact viable. More important, whether there is a link—a link that should be used—between appraisal and salary assessment and review. There is a school of thought that suggests that there should be an on-going appraisal system, for only then can one objectively, and fairly, link such appraisal systems to salary assessment.

The future must also require management to work harder towards the provision of viable data base information, which will permit improvements in the whole area of training cost–benefit analysis.

There are many other aspects that will be looked at to gain improvement in the system, but the severest challenge to a planned approach to management nearly always comes about when there is a fundamental shift in philosophy or style. In the weeks, months and years to come, managerial philosophy and operating style are certainly going to change by reason of the political and social pressures—both national and international—within the business environment. The question, then, is, how to ensure that the planning system reacts to such dynamism.

Suggested Reading

Institute of Personnel Management, *Company Manpower Practices*, 1972.
Department of Employment, *Training for the Management of Human Resources*, HMSO, 1972.

Department of Employment, *Industrial Relations Code of Practice*, HMSO, 1972.
WAGHORN, C. Five Barriers to Company Planning, *Director*, Mar. 1972.
McGREGOR, D. *The Human Side of Enterprise*, McGraw-Hill, New York, 1961.
GELLERMAN, S. *Motivation and Productivity*, American Management Association, New York, 1963.

37. The organizational review: assessing the business and its management

Neville Osmond

In this chapter, the organizational review is related to the business as a whole, and to its development over time. While the assessment of the managers and key employees is often the key concern in carrying out any review, unless this is founded upon the business realities it will have limited validity. Strengths and weaknesses must be judged in this overall context, whether they stem from people, technology, markets or structure. More importantly still, it is for top management to judge the limits of any organizational review, and to decide whether, and how, it evolves into a programme of managed organizational change.

It is usually difficult to generate enthusiasm and imagination when first faced with the prospect of an organizational review, whether one will be leading it or contributing to it. Clearly, any such exercise must be thorough if it is to be of value; patently, it will be complex; probably, it will prove to be painful or upsetting to many people. So why undertake it? Among the most common reasons are:

(a) the emergence or intensification of a business crisis;
(b) the identification of a substantial business opportunity;
(c) widespread organizational pains—business growth, inefficiencies, poor employee motivation, rising employee expectations, etc;
(d) problems of management continuity and succession;
(e) changes in ownership, or in owners' expectations.

Thus, the impetus for organizational review and change can be positive and creative, or reactive and defensive, and very often is a mixture of the two. It is important to know which is the case, and to recognize this.

Whatever the motive, each review should be designed and managed within a broad perspective. The key factors may appear to be sited in the business environment in one instance, whereas the organizational structure may be the critical factor in another, while the abilities and personalities of a few key people are seen to be the cornerstone in a third. But whatever the immediate and central focus of attention, it must be related to all the other organizational factors. This is because the business and its component parts, its environment and markets, its people, resources, purpose and priorities, and its organizational fabric are each interdependent and inter-acting. Therefore, any organizational review, whatever its impetus and motives, must cast its net widely and relevantly.

However, this need not prove a disincentive, despite the investment of time and effort involved. Any review can, and should, produce far more than the catalogues of people and procedures required to justify or facilitate key decisions, which may have already been taken on the principle of: 'My mind is made up, don't confuse me with the facts.'

In contrast to this approach, a well-designed and well-led review provides an invaluable opportunity to achieve the following creative and dynamic objectives:

(a) the identification of alternative courses of action, and varied oppor-tunities;
(b) securing a better overall balance within the business, between it and its members, and between it and its environment;
(c) the identification, development, and full and flexible use of its strengths, human and other.

So far as organizational reviews are concerned, the reader can find specific references[1,2] to the practical tasks of organizational analysis, design, and change. Meanwhile, Fig. 37.1 outlines a general and summarized framework for designing, planning, and carrying through an organizational review. Central to this is the need to match organizational capacity to the organiza-tional tasks. At the same time, while the scope and performance of those tasks is obviously limited by the current organizational capacity, the very performance of new and different tasks will dynamically build up that capacity.[3] Equally, the various changes in market needs, shareholder expectations, product performance, employee teamwork, etc., all inter-act with each other. They produce new problems and opportunities, new tasks aimed at matching resources and needs, and new demands on top management, who must set fresh priorities and lead others towards their fulfilment.

The various areas which need to be researched, assessed or reassessed are set out in Fig. 37.1. It is, of course, essential that each one is investigated in an appropriate way. This will probably involve an interdisciplinary or interfunctional team effort. Figure 37.2 shows the sort of checklist which can be used, provided that it is specifically designed for the particular situation and the individuals concerned.

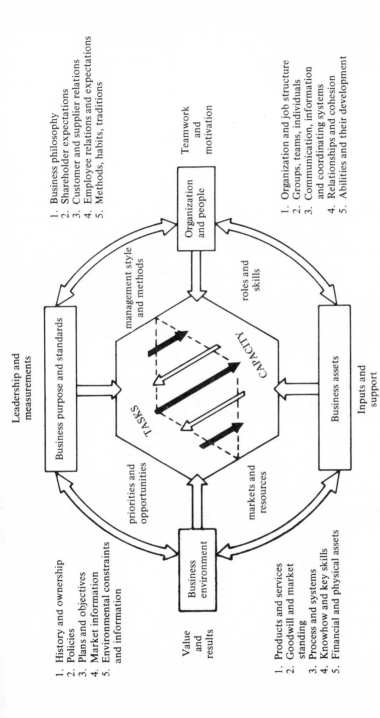

Fig. 37.1. Framework for organizational review.

Leadership and measurements

1. Business philosophy
2. Shareholder expectations
3. Customer and supplier relations
4. Employee relations and expectations
5. Methods, habits, traditions

Teamwork and motivation

Organization and people

1. Organization and job structure
2. Groups, teams, individuals
3. Communication, information and coordinating systems
4. Relationships and cohesion
5. Abilities and their development

Business purpose and standards

management style and methods

roles and skills

CAPACITY

TASKS

priorities and opportunities

markets and resources

Business assets

Inputs and support

Business environment

Value and results

1. History and ownership
2. Policies
3. Plans and objectives
4. Market information
5. Environmental constraints and information

1. Products and services
2. Goodwill and market standing
3. Process and systems
4. Knowhow and key skills
5. Financial and physical assets

Areas reviewed	Key questions

1. Products, services
2. Technical processes, systems
 	
Make an overall assessment
Are the organization's structure and systems, and its members' skills and attitudes, matched to the technical reality, diversity and trends, and vice versa?
Are the varied resources of products, services, processes, and systems giving full value to the customer and to the business alike?
What opportunities have been, are, or will be, overlooked or underexploited
 	
Try not to:
Confuse products with services or processes
Overlook process developments
Ignore the less 'visible' elements of systems and services
	1. For each distinctive product, range, process, etc.
	    Strategy: focused on product or market
	    Product strength: article, service
	    Product life: max min., scope for renewal or extension
	    Process: strength, obsolescence, renewal
	    Product/process: investment, payback, contribution to profit
	2. Overall
	    Process diversity, compatability
	    Product range completeness, duplication
	    Systems: fragmented, coherent, or unified
	    Human implications: jobs, skills, careers, productivity
	    Financial aspects: investment, payback, contribution to profit

Fig. 37.2. Organization review: extract from checklist.

The term 'management audit' has, despite its overtones, been applied in many cases to situations where a review has (knowingly or unknowingly) been carried through, either for limited purposes or with limited validity. It has been used to describe the rapid one-sided assessment of managers and management systems which has often accompanied merger negotiations or takeover inquiries. More often, it has been undertaken with a genuine concern for management development and management succession, but with surprisingly little relation to the future needs, realities, or direction of the business.

In short, the organizational review must be broadly balanced in the present, with full participation by all levels of management, and should—wherever feasible—provide a dynamic basis for future business development. This is the theme which will run through the rest of this chapter, since it links with the main concern of this book: the performance, motivation, and development of managers. This, in turn, has necessitated a selective and terse approach to the whole area of organizational review, change and development, and the reader is therefore asked to follow up the annotated references and the reading list as appropriate.

More important, each area must be related to the problems or opportunities on which the review is focused. As information is built up, however, that focus may itself shift, and unforeseen opportunities open up. Thus, the organizational review must be regarded as an exploratory process, and managed as such.

It will rely on the unique experience and knowledge of many people, at all levels of the business, as well as outside it. By drawing upon their contribution, management will be more able to motivate them to play a creative part in subsequent organizational changes and development, which should prove more realistic and workable as a result. Of course, the more information and ideas which are unearthed and evoked, the greater

554

is the need for integrative viewpoints and skills, and for leadership and shared effort.

To sum up the argument so far, in reviewing its organization any top management faces a basic choice between:

(a) a limited exercise which aims to provide immediate answers to specific, short-term problems;
(b) a wider exercise concerned with the profitable balanced development of the business and its people over a period.

Unless the key problems are indeed short-term ones, or the rate of change of the business is so continuous that planning and development efforts are not practicable, the second course, despite its challenges, is far more profitable and worthwhile.

Business Development and Organizational Change

Whether the organizational review has been triggered off by business problems or by human factors (if the distinction is accepted for the moment), it is important to take a number of bearings in order to establish where the business has come from, where it is at present, and where it is going. Of course, the very process and evolution of the business' development, and the opportunities and problems that this generates, frequently dominates the review and the way it is carried through.

Whether the changes which flow from the organizational review are designed to boost or facilitate a predetermined programme of business development, or whether they involve a recognizably new departure or phase, they need to be carried through with understanding of the situation, the alternatives, and the effects on people. This equally applies to the project management of the organization review itself: if it becomes clear during its course that radical changes or developments are likely to be necessary, there is often an opportunity to test alternatives, to sound out attitudes, and to prepare the people concerned.

There have been several noteworthy attempts to produce a structured framework and rationale of business development, its character and its phases. Some, notably Chandler,[4] have centred on historical studies of large-scale industry. Chandler himself was concerned about the interaction between strategy, resource accumulation, and structure. Others, including Lippitt and Schmidt[5] and Bos,[6] have concentrated on the managerial tasks, skills, and styles, as well as the organizational systems, which are appropriate to the various stages between the pioneering-style birth of the business, and its integrated (but not necessarily diversified) maturity. Each tends to relate his argument to a model which is more or less evocative and helpful to the individual reader. There is as yet no consensus, nor is there likely to be one.

Greiner[7,8] has, in particular, emphasized that organizational change is a messy, disjointed, and reactive process—if left to itself. He has also, albeit in a somewhat overstylized fashion, made the point that organizational change is uneven, whether or not it is well managed, and that the organization's history contains both the clues for its successful development and, if they are neglected, the seeds of its downfall.

There are, of course, many tangible examples of an organization trying to adapt to, master, or exploit the business realities which it faces. One is the continual adjustment between centralization and decentralization,[9-12] although these are relative and not mutually exclusive. It is often necessary, as new tasks arise and the business grows, both to centralize and decentralize at the same time, and to define jobs while loosening them up. Each is a matter of degree, and requires the matching of the men to the situation.

Another regular theme is the choice between the functional forms of organization, the product or project forms, and the matrix which hovers between them.[13,14] Though there are many factors involved, there is a general evolution towards the product and project forms, as the organization experiences greater diversity and change in its environment and markets, and to the functional forms in simpler, quieter circumstances.

Then there is the whole question of size. As an organization grows with the business it serves, it becomes increasingly relevant to know, or judge, whether the growth is due to simple enlargement of a single business (coal mining, copper mining, etc.), or to diversification—whether by internal inventiveness or by acquisition. Organizationally, it is important to decide whether there is diversity or interdependence between the component businesses.[15,16] Though currently in short supply, the skills required to manage and lead conglomerates are nevertheless distinctive, and will become increasingly important.[17] There will always be the conundrum that Edith Penrose stated: growth is good, but extreme size tends to be bad.[18,19] The solution can only be one of effective delegation, if not the hiving-off of selected businesses.

Yet another perspective can be obtained by relating the central management tasks of coordination, control and development to the business' technology on the one hand, and to its market and environment on the other. Woodward[20,21] and her colleagues have built up studies which relate the organizational characteristics of varying types of technology to appropriate product markets, managerial skills, and control systems. The most persistent and intractable problems are centred in the areas of greatest complexity and uncertainty: large batch/mass production and mixed production systems. Nevertheless, they can be contained, or overcome, by perceptive and co-ordinated business management.

Much of the uncertainty and complexity experienced by the business is, of course, a product of the environment and markets in which it operates. Lawrence and Lorsch[22] have carried out studies which show how, according to varying market circumstances, an efficient firm will either be able to delegate important operating decisions down the line, and thus release top management for business planning and development, or will be forced to retain day to day control at the centre.

Developmental Stage	Critical concern	Knowledge	Skills	Attitudes
Birth	To create a system	Clearly perceived short-range objectives in mind of top man	Ability to transmit knowledge into action by self and into orders to others	Belief in own ability, product, and market
	To survive	The short-range objectives that need to be communicated	Communications know-how, ability to adjust to changing conditions	Faith in future
Youth	To stabilize	How top man can predict relevant factors and make long-range plans	Ability to transmit planning knowledge into communicable objectives	Trust in other members of organization
	To earn a good reputation	Planning know-how and understanding of goals, on part of whole executive team	Facility of allowing others a voice in decision making, involving others in decision making, obtaining commitments from them, and communicating objectives to customers	Interest in customers
Maturity	To achieve uniqueness	Understanding, on part of policy team, of how others should set own objectives, and of how to manage subunits of the organization	Ability to teach others to plan, proficiency in integrating plans of subunits into objectives and resources of organization	Self-confidence
	To earn respect and appreciation	General management understanding of the larger objectives of organization and society	Ability to apply own organization and resources to the problems of the larger community	Sense of responsibility to society and mankind

Fig. 37.3. Requirements to meet crises. (Reproduced with permission of the *Harvard Business Review*.)

Whatever the particular circumstances of business change and development, there can be no doubt about the inhibiting and dispiriting effect of managerial obsolescence, particularly at the top. Figure 37.3, reproduced from the paper by Lippitt and Schmidt,[5] shows how the knowledge, skills and attitudes, that have been essentially important in one phase of business development, may become an impediment in another. This is a major concern to all those in top management who seek to ensure managerial continuity.

People in Relation to Evolving Tasks

However, this concern with line-managerial competence and continuity must first be related to the many factors which decide the degree to which an organization's employees, as a whole, match its tasks, within the great variety of situations which can occur or evolve.

Figure 37.1 indicates that the business, in the form of its ownership, management and history, both sets its own tasks and provides the capacity to meet them—and, hence, it provides its own opportunities and its own limitations. Any failure of the business to define and redefine realistic market opportunities will lead to its eventual, and more or less sudden demise—just as will its failure to build, match and exploit its capacity, both human and technical. The overall dynamics must always be borne in mind: not only the dependence on the environment, but the scope for change. So must the variety, for if ever it is true that 'there is no one best way', this is the case with the management and development not only of individuals and teams, but also of groups and organizations. The part of will power, purpose, and imagination must also be remembered.

It is not just a question of self-development, job design and redesign, the evolution of teamwork, and the selection of appropriate management systems and styles—essential though usually these are to the matching process. Rather, it is the realization that while one can learn from others' experience and situations, it is not a matter of simple acceptance or rejection but of analysis, working through, and adapting to one's own situation. This, in turn, depends on people's shared experiences and/or perceptions of the business situation and purpose, in its many aspects. Morse and Lorsch[23] have convincingly established that, since the purpose and the tasks pursued by the particular business in its overall situation will vary, as will its people and their skills, we must expect very different patterns of organization, decision taking and management style to be relevant and acceptable to the people concerned. Theory 'Y' is thus a model which is no more or less helpful than theory 'X', although the use of the term theory 'X' is usually pejorative and non-analytical.

People will accept decision and leadership styles,[24,25] job design and task organization which often cannot, in any way, be regarded as approaching the ideals of theory Y, because by and large they make sense to the individuals concerned, i.e., they fit the needs of the situation which the individual perceives. Of course, this begs many questions concerning appropriate selection, training, job improvement, communication, etc., as well as the whole matter of self-selection, alienation, apathy, excessive staff turnover, and so on. It does, however, make the main point.

The matching of people to tasks over a period of time is, equally, more than a matter of organizational design and management. It has to do with the whole question of the individual career,[26] whether this is planned or unplanned, straightforward or discursive. It is largely worked through by means of, and in the context of, individual jobs and of groups.[27]

There are many references elsewhere in this book to the detailed aspects of individual self-development, training, and organizational change. Here, the emphasis can usefully switch to the parts played by top management. For top management are themselves a miniature organization; their perceptions and ambitions influence and guide or impede the whole process of organization and business development. Not least they, crucially, decide whether, and in what way, any organizational review and change programme shall be undertaken and carried through.[28,29] Thus, their own appointment, training, development, management style, and means of succession can often be decisive; not only for business development but for the whole health and spirit of the organization.[30]

Top Management, Its Organization and Style

Any business or organizational review is an invaluable occasion for a balanced consideration of the future managerial needs and resources of the company in the context of its total development. This aspect of the review often centres on top management, its structure, performance, skills and continuity.[31] By 'top management', we mean the management levels which together determine the day to day operation and coordination, and the development, of the business. This can in practice include (or exclude) all, or most, of the board of directors. Alternatively, it can include many managerial echelons or individuals who would not be considered as part of the 'top' in hierarchical terms, but where knowledge and skills are in fact depended upon: this is particularly the case in the smaller firm.

Every organizational review must pose, develop, evaluate, and answer the basic question: 'What are our key strengths and limitations?' This questioning must be the task of the management team, and must be particularly applied to themselves. It is, however, only meaningful in the context of a clear, evolving organizational purpose, and with an open view of markets, people, technology, etc. Thus, an organizational review, even if not triggered off in whole or in part by specific problems at the top, may (if badly handled) actually give rise to them. How is this to be avoided or resolved? Largely by a combination of:

(a) the full involvement of the chief executive;
(b) teamwork at board level or executive team level, in oversight and guidance of the review;

(c) involvement of, and contribution by, a balanced and representative cross-selection of managers and employees;

(d) realistic and energetic project management of the review.

The tasks involved have been set out elsewhere,[32-35] but the hard and imaginative work must be obvious to the reader, from this outline description. This means that any organizational review must have a clear objective and pay-off, which simultaneously applies to:

(a) the business as a whole;

(b) top management, collectively and individually;

(c) other employees, collectively and individually.

We are therefore concerned with the motives of top management in launching a review and taking it forward. They need to be clear about this, to themselves as much as to others. Above all, whether its main thrust is one of restructuring or of development/evolution, it needs to be flexible and exploratory in style and design, for all the reasons indicated.

If we take this theme of flexibility and exploration further, beyond the immediate phase of the organizational review, there are additional implications for both the structure and style of top management and middle management. Is the structure to be rapidly crystallized within a short time, as an outcome of the review? Or is it to evolve, but with the advantage of the information and insights gained during the review?

The Chloride Group provides an interesting case study of one particular strategy, whereby management teams are progressively formed and re-formed within a framework of policy and Group-level teamwork, and thus the overall and individual organization structures evolve and develop.[36] Moreover, the sequence and interdependence of such factors as individual skills and experience, teamwork, policy, structure, procedures, and techniques is illustrated in the Group's selective development of MBO.[37]

This is only one example, among many others regularly recorded in business books, newspapers,[38-41] and journals, which illustrates the interaction between the business, its history, ownership, markets, structure, and people—and how, sooner or later, this is worked out at top management level, as it must be elsewhere in the organization.

Coordinating Organizational Change

It was earlier argued that top management has, in embarking on an organizational review, to choose between a relatively limited exercise focused on specific short-term problems, and a broader one concerned with integrated business development over a period of time. In reaching its conclusions at the end of the review, and in implementing its plan of action, top management now faces another choice. Since organizational change is continuous, and the business situation and strategy is (hopefully) clearer than before, should they not manage and oversee a continuous programme of organization development within the overall context of business development?

An approach to organizational change and development has been described elsewhere.[42] It is concerned to generate improved organizational options, by means of the coordinated management of planning and review activities on the one hand, and design and development activities on the other, within an overall policy and plan for the business. This approach constitutes:

(a) *Planning and Review*
     business
     manpower
     management succession
     organization
     management performance and potential
     key employees' performance, etc.

(b) *Design and Development*
     organization
     jobs and tasks
     business controls
     communications
     incentives and employee motivation
     management skills
     other key skills, etc.

The inevitable adjustments to, and balances within, the organization (regrouping, promotions, transfers, recruitment, training and retraining, salary changes, etc.) become progressively more creative and effective as the improving information and the development of resources interact. This provides the means for better operating control and organizational adaptation, plus the fuller exploitation of opportunities—thus, the more profitable and secure development of the business and its organization.

It is for top management progressively to decide:

(a) whether an organizational review is both necessary and feasible, and what its objectives, management, and scope will be; and thereafter
(b) whether it will become the first one of a regular set of organizational reviews, matched to the needs and development of the business; and/or
(c) whether any review will itself lead on to a continuous process of planned, coordinated organizational change and development.

It can easily be seen how this links with several major themes in this book: management development, succession and training; organization planning; and organizational development. It only remains to emphasize that, like each of these activities, the organizational review itself must be grounded upon a realistic and broad knowledge of the business and its total situation, allied to a respect for, and knowledge and use of, the strengths—and thus the development—of the people within it.

References

1. DRUCKER, P. F. *The Practice of Management*, part 3, 'The Structure of Management', Pan, 1968.
2. OSMOND, C. N. Organization development series, *Management Matters*, no. 28–31 and 33, MSL Group, 1970–71.
3. PENROSE, E. *The Theory of the Growth of the Firm*, Blackwell, 1959, chapters 4 and 5.
4. CHANDLER, A. D. *Strategy and Structure*, Doubleday Anchor, 1966.
5. LIPPITT, G. L. and SCHMIDT, W. H. Crises in Developing Organizations, *Harvard Business Review*, Nov.–Dec., 1967.
6. BOS, A. H. Development Principles of Organizations, *Management International*, **9**, 1969.
7. GREINER, L. F. Patterns of Organization Change, *Harvard Business Review*, May–June 1967.
8. GREINER, L. F. Evolution and Revolution as Organizations Grow, *Harvard Business Review*, Jul–Aug. 1972; and 'Letters', Sept.–Oct. 1972.
9. HILL, R. New Mould for a Glass Company, *International Management*, Sept. 1972.
10. HILL, R. The New Shape of Germany's Hoechst, *International Management*, Nov. 1971.
11. INGERSOLL, R. Germany's Rheinstahl Forges a New Form, *International Management*, Jan. 1972.
12. OATES, D. Finding the Right Balance at Plessey, *International Management*, May 1972.
13. WALKER, A. H. and LORSCH, J. W. Organizational Choice: Product vs. Function, *Harvard Business Review*, Nov.–Dec. 1968.
14. GALBRAITH, J. R. Matrix Organizational Designs: How to Combine Functional and Project Forms, *Business Horizons*, Feb. 1971.
15. DRUCKER, P. F. *The Practice of Management*, Pan, 1968, chapter 18.
16. OWEN, K. Why Honeywell Was Split in Two, *The Times*, 10 Oct. 1972.
17. BIRD, N. A. What's Different About Conglomerate Management, *Harvard Business Review*, Nov.–Dec. 1969.
18. PENROSE, E. *The Theory of the Growth of the Firm*, Blackwell, 1969, chapter 11.
19. HILL, R. Are Firms Getting Too Big to be Efficient?, *International Management*, May 1971.
20. WOODWARD, J. *Industrial Organization: Theory and Practice*, Oxford University Press, 1965.
21. WOODWARD, J. (Ed.) *Industrial Organization: Behaviour and Control*, Oxford University Press, 1970.
22. LAWRENCE, P. R. and LORSCH, J. W. *Organization and Environment*, Richard D. Irwin, 1969.
23. MORSE, J. J. and LORSCH, J. W. Beyond Theory Y, *Harvard Business Review*, May–June 1970; and 'Letters' Sept.–Oct. 1970.
24. HELLER, F. A. *Managerial Decision Making*, Tavistock, 1971, pp. 111 *et seq.*
25. SADLER, P. J. Executive Leadership, in *Industrial Society*, Pelican, 1968.
26. SOFER, C. *Men in Mid-Career*, Cambridge University Press, 1970.
27. DAVIS, L. E. and TAYLOR, J. C. (Eds.) *Design of Jobs*, Penguin, 1972.
28. ZIMMERMAN, A. Task Teams Help Beat Inertia, *International Management*, Apr. 1972.
29. MACKENZIE, E. Employees Redesign their Jobs in Norway, *International Management*, Aug. 1971.
30. DRUCKER, P. F. *Managing for Results*, Pan, 1967, chapter 14.
31. OSMOND, N. Top Management: Its Tasks, Roles and Skills, *Journal of Business Policy*, **2**, 2, 1971–2.
32. DRUCKER, P. F. *The Practice of Management*, Pan, 1968, chapter 14.
33. STIEGLITZ, H. *The Chief Executive and His Job*, The Conference Board, New York, 1969.
34. OSMOND, C. N. Organization Development: Guidelines for Top Management, *Management Matters*, no. 34, MSL Group, 1971.
35. SCHOONMAKER, A. N. How Should Companies Reorganize?, *International Management*, Sept. 1972.
36. CHAMBERS, P. Fluid Style Aids New Company Structure, *International Management*, Dec. 1972.
37. EDWARDS, M. The Tip of the Iceberg, *Management by Objectives*, **1**, 1, 1971.
38. PALMER, D. BP Management Changes: How the Structure will Operate, *Financial Times*, 9 Oct. 1970.
39. VAN MUSSCHENBROCK, K. Cash Conscious Unilever, *Financial Times*, 8 Aug. 1972.
40. TRAFFORD, J. Decision Taking: the Loner versus the Team, *Financial Times*, 4 Oct. 1972.

41. HILL, P. *Towards a New Philosophy of Management*, Gower Press, 1971.
42. OSMOND, C. N. Organization development series, *Management Matters*, no. 35, MSL Group, 1972.

Suggested Reading

DRUCKER, P. F. *The Practice of Management*, Pan, 1968.
OSMOND, C. N. Organization development series, *Management Matters*, no. 28–31, and 33–35, MSL Group, 1970–72.
STEWART, R. *The Reality of Organizations: A Guide For Managers*, Macmillan, 1970.
STIEGLITZ, H. *Organization Planning*, The Conference Board, New York, 1962.
PENROSE, E. *The Theory of Growth of the Firm*, Blackwell, 1959.
LIPPITT, G. L. and SCHMIDT, W. H. Crises in Developing Organizations, *Harvard Business Review*, Nov.–Dec. 1967.
GREINER, L. F. Patterns of Organizational Change, *Harvard Business Review*, May–June 1967.
WALKER, A. H. and LORSCH, J. W. Organizational Choice: Product vs. Function, *Harvard Business Review*, Nov.–Dec. 1968.
LAWRENCE, P. R. and LORSCH, J. W. *Organization and Environment*, Richard D. Irwin, 1969.
MORSE, J. J. and LORSCH, J. W. Beyond Theory Y, *Harvard Business Review*, Sept.–Oct. 1970.
FRANK, H. E. (Ed.) *Organization Structuring*, McGraw-Hill, 1971.
WOODWARD, J. *Industrial Organization: Theory and Practice*, Oxford University Press, 1965.
WOODWARD, J. (Ed.) *Industrial Organization: Behaviour and Control*, Oxford University Press, 1970.
THOMPSON, J. D. *Organizations in Action*, McGraw-Hill, New York, 1967.
STIEGLITZ, H. *The Chief Executive and His Job*, The Conference Board, 1969.
OSMOND, N. Top Management: Its Tasks, Roles and Skills, *Journal of Business Policy*, **2**, 2, 1971–2.

38.   The establishment and organization of a company training centre

R. A. Godsall

The first half of this chapter discusses elements in the problem of deciding whether or not a company should invest in its own management training centre. It goes on to examine many of the important factors to which the manager attending a course is typically subjected, and from this examination suggests the necessary features for environment and learning. The author argues that 'tutorial staff and delegates must have silent, unobtrusive, flexible support from the centre's administration'. He therefore devotes the second half of the chapter to considering problem areas and details which may need to be provided for in the organization's system. In doing this, he also offers helpful guidelines and an insight into the minutiae which allow smooth operations.

Looked at purely as a training space resource, there are few good reasons for any company having its own centre today. Excellent facilities are increasingly available for hire, through hotels, universities, and organizations created specifically to satisfy this market. Moreover, from the cost point of view, the use of these facilities is generally much less expensive overall than the maintenance of an owned unit, and avoids the associated problems. Certainly, no competent and determined training team will find it impossible to carry out a planned programme for want of secured training space. What, then, are the factors which should be given consideration in the decision whether or not to create an owned or, at least, a sole-user management training space facility? There are probably only four initially: the importance placed by a board upon management and management training in its company, or the impetus that the company wishes to give to its acceptance; the volume and continuity of the training programme; flexibility;

and privacy. Naturally, other factors emerge, not the least being cost, but these should only be given full consideration once the necessity for such a training centre has been established.

The first factor mentioned—essentially a declaration of intent—is obviously political and psychological rather than practical, but its importance can be greater than any other. Indeed, its consideration must be continuous, since it relates to secondary factors such as size and type of space/building, location, equipment, etc. The creation of a centre against this factor is to provide solid evidence that investment in training is important, that managers and their development are important, and that the company believes in it. Undoubtedly, the provision of such an asset against a relatively large investment can have an impact on employees and, if properly exploited, can commit management towards the training goals. It can, at least, cause them to be more prepared to listen to arguments in support of training.

The desirable volume and continuity of the training programme probably only become of major significance when the company—and, therefore, the number of managers involved—is large, and when the envisaged programme of development is planned to span a number of years. To give some indication, the relative volume would need to be approaching at least 600 manager training weeks per annum over four or more years. Beyond this level the difficulties associated with finding suitable locations, pre-booking hired space, etc., can become great enough to endanger continuity and planning of the programme and therefore cause an owned or controlled unit availability to ease the burden considerably.

Reasonably, as any programme planned involves more managers and spans a longer period, the more likely it is that modifications, additions, or deletions are necessary to keep the programme appropriate and on schedule. Undoubtedly, this is where the flexibility potential of an own-space resource can aid the training team significantly. With the best will, no organization in the facility hire business can usually adapt to clients' changing demands, or provide space, without substantial notice or without charging a cost penalty. The one requirement is usually impossible, and the other obviously undesirable.

The final item mentioned as one of the four prime factors was privacy. The importance of privacy is often overstated. However, it does need consideration when training programmes are likely to involve the display of company information in rooms which may be left unattended, where discussion on internal issues is likely to continue in bars or over dinner, or where persons of some eminence are likely to be gathered together. Certainly, where the trainer would like the participants to be as relaxed as possible, their consciousness that they are not likely to be seen or overheard by others can be an important influence.

Secondary Factors in Establishment

Once it has been decided to create one's own management training centre, other factors—mainly affecting investment cost—must be assessed. Of these, perhaps the foremost is the environment that it is seen necessary to create, a factor which immediately relates back to the importance which the company places on the training of its managers. 'Environment' will include location, facility style, accommodation, furnishing, and services.

Experience has shown that a training/development programme has little chance of being successful if any element of the environment in which it takes place is unacceptable to the participants. It seems that dissatisfaction —even unconscious—over any of these items quickly transfers itself to dissatisfaction with the training programme, its methods, materials, tutors, or company.

We should be concerned, then, to study something of the psychology of learning, and of the feelings that managers are likely to have when subject to a course. By considering these factors, guidelines for the creation of a conducive environment will emerge.

In management development, we are mostly occupied with prompting people to examine their experience, assess new concepts, sharpen their awareness, broaden their outlook, or improve certain necessary skills rather than merely absorb information. In other words, the balance is heavily weighted towards exercise and development of existing inputs rather than feeding in more. Yet, for most of these people, the use of that time of their life which has been devoted to learning—usually school or university exclusively—was weighted largely in the other direction. Moreover, this time, which even at age 40 still represents more than a third of total life experience, was spent in an environment where the 'student' was under relatively strict discipline and routine and in very much a subordinate role to the 'tutors'. This environment may, arguably, be appropriate for information absorption but it is doubtful if it is for our purposes.

Since man typically prepares himself for, or reacts to, situations in a manner based on experience, it is likely that the manager attending the infrequent training course will mentally anticipate the environment and experience that one-third or so of his life has taught him to expect. He may therefore, be prepared for the schoolroom and its associations, and, as a result, apprehensive and in a state of mind unsuited to the necessary receptivity.

Moreover, since 'being sent' on a course could be construed as a demonstration that his superiors are not satisfied with him, these feelings, and those of disquiet, may be compounded. Thus, a resentment of the course as perceived can build up even before he arrives. Naturally, this must be quickly dispelled—particularly, when a course is short—since it presents a further barrier to relaxation and, therefore, opening the mind.

These pre-course barriers, generated through insecurity, apprehension, feelings of inadequacy, or resentment often cause the delegate to compensate by becoming more conscious of his dignity of office or status. It is important, therefore, to give him no grounds to feel that this is also being threatened. Indeed, it is important to help him emphasize it, since by this reassurance the other barriers may relax a little. Thus, by implicit recognition of his position through providing surroundings at least as good as those he basically believes to be proper to a manager, we may help him—whether or not his normal working environment meets these standards. Moreover, if he finds that his surroundings more than match his expectations he will also feel that the company recognizes training as valuable.

We have, then, two guidelines for creating the appropriate environment, both intended to help the delegates to become less tense. The first is that it should be as obviously 'unschool-like' as possible, and the second, which is consistent with the first, that it should match the delegates' concepts of managerial surroundings. These two criteria alone eliminate prefabricated huts, works canteens, or temporarily modified offices, etc. for course purposes. On the other hand, the criteria reinforce the need for comfortably furnished, well-decorated surroundings with good service facilities supporting the teaching/learning space. Such facilities as are necessary will, of course, depend on whether or not it is believed that training should be carried out on a residential basis. To consider this point, it is essential to return to the issue of relaxation and the removal of barriers to learning. At the same time, location can be considered since it, too, has a bearing.

Our continued concern for relaxation is essential to generate receptivity. We also wish to ensure that, once relaxed, the delegate can concentrate, particularly since the course will be short and he will take time to settle anyway. We need to break an existing pattern and to replace it temporarily with one more appropriate to learning. Going home in the evening is part of the existing pattern and only reinforces it, since it is 'normal' and throws the 'artificial' day which the course represents into further unsettling relief. Moreover, the home environment will either cause the delegate to switch off from the new problems he is facing during the day or, at least, make it difficult for him to think about them by reason of interruptions or the mental dichotomy of being at home and normal or at home and unusual. Additionally, the non-residential course also loses one of the most prized opportunities to the trainer—that of enabling the delegates to mix in the pseudo-relaxed atmosphere after formal course work is over for the day. The fact is that they do not really relax but feel that they do. As a result, much valuable work is produced during periods in the bar, or lounge, or at dinner.

Similar arguments support provision of a course location at least one or two hours' journey from the delegates' work place and home. Far enough away to protect him from the dangers of thought-interrupting work queries by nervous superiors, far enough away to help him feel about any problems he left: 'Well I can't do anything about it anyway.' Far enough away to make the trainer's need for residence seem natural by reason of distance rather than by the actual reason.

In assessing the foregoing arguments to be considered in establishing a training centre, what kind of picture does the reader get? A fairly remote, comfortably furnished country house with good residential and working accommodation, pleasant lounges, bar and dining rooms, all supported by competent service and set in fine grounds? If so, then the author would not disagree—the picture fits, despite the 'knocking' which this has been subject to in recent years. Nonetheless, we should be reminded that this only provides the right background for training. The quality of the training contents depends entirely on the competence and dedication of the staff.

Internal Organization

An indication has been given of the environmental background in which a delegate can feel that every consideration has been given to catering for his needs to an acceptable standard, and in which he can concentrate on the demands of the course without undue distractions. It must be the main purpose of the organization of a training centre to maintain this atmosphere.

In its control, function and staffing, the detailed organization will depend on the size of the centre and on the company policy, but there are four main areas which have to be covered and coordinated:

(a) liaising with, and processing the delegates;
(b) providing for their needs;
(c) supporting the tutors;
(d) maintaining the common services and essential business routines.

Provision and Processing of Delegates

For a company with a strong central training organization and an acceptance of the training provided by the centre, the nomination of delegates becomes a normal reaction to the publication of the dates and purpose of a course with, perhaps, an allocation of places to the different parts of the company. In other cases, some marketing effort may be required by the centre, to fill the vacancies. Whatever the method, at the centre an organization is required to record and acknowledge bookings, in some cases checking their suitability for the particular course and, as the start date approaches, in liaison with the tutorial staff, for the issue of joining instructions together with any pre-course work and a request for arrival times and transport requirements. Once this information has been received, course lists can be prepared, bedrooms allocated, and the catering staff warned of meal requirements.

Discrepancies, either through clerical errors or late changes, often appear in the course lists, and it is desirable that arrivals are checked against the list to ensure subsequent accuracy, modify catering arrangements, and investigate and account for any who do not turn up.

If fees are paid to the centre, it benefits the centre's cash flow if these can be paid in advance, a process which also has the advantage of discouraging late withdrawals from the course. Where payments are not made in advance, the attendant problems of post-course invoicing have to be met. Accounting efficiency will also be increased if personal accounts for extras can be settled before the delegate leaves.

Reference back to previous courses may be required for a number of reasons, e.g., checking attendance from any company or division, or ascertaining previous attendance by individuals—and to provide the information readily, complete cross-referencing between individual, company/division, and course is important.

At the end of a course, the opinion of the delegate on the course itself, and the administrative services provided, monitors the effectiveness of the tuition and his reaction to the environment; this can be greatly enhanced by a further feedback some weeks or months later.

Reception

First impressions are, as ever, important and the arrangements for the reception of delegates and guests should be as complete as possible. Besides being met and shown to their rooms, the new arrivals should be told when, and where, they are next required to assemble and where they can relax in the meantime. It is helpful if a booklet with all the centre's facilities explained can be sent with the joining instructions; amplification or alteration, only, will then be necessary on arrival. As part of the introduction to the course, an opportunity to question and explain the administrative arrangements should be provided, either by the tutor himself or by a member of the administrative staff. What to do and where to go for help in any difficulty or emergency and how any request or complaint can be made should be explained. The facilities for telephoning and for transmitting incoming messages for delegates are particularly important.

Domestic Facilities

In providing a service to delegates, the domestic organization must be based on the requirements and timetables of the courses. Flexibility to meet last-minute changes and to deal with reasonable variations from the norm is, however, essential if the vital confidence and cooperation between tutorial and domestic staff is to be maintained.

From the kitchen and dining-room staff, fast and cheerful service will enable studies to be renewed with the minimum of delay and can be exploited to encourage punctuality with the promise of hot and freshly cooked food. In keeping with the environment being created, the cuisine needs to be at least of a good home-cooking standard, well varied and substantial enough to sustain hunger generated by mental stimulation, yet not so heavy as to affect concentration shortly after. The ability to provide for particular diets, both medical and religious, must not be overlooked.

Some organizers of conferences and courses may wish to hold course dinners segregated from other centre activities, and while a centralized dining hall probably provides the best general service, the facility to be able to lay on special meals in a private room is much appreciated. Similarly, separate rooms where courses may hold cocktail parties are often in demand, though this in no way detracts from the need for a general bar where opening times are related to normal course working hours; prices must be competitive enough with those of local hostelries to encourage delegates to remain at the centre, where valuable work can continue over a drink.

Instructional Facilities and Tutorial Support

The management training/development staff may be concerned with the organization of training only, or may themselves tutor the courses, as well as calling in speakers from outside the centre. To fulfil their functions, they will require office space and, by nature of their work, many will seek privacy both for concentration in the preparation and development of their programmes and to have a place where they can discuss, without interruption, their plans and theories with their colleagues. To assist in their researches, to keep up to date and to support their courses, they will require access to the latest books and periodicals; this makes a library and abstract facility essential. A film library or hiring function can be incorporated with this, since the use of films continues to be an important aid in the training field.

In producing a course, considerable work is involved in the preparation of notes, handouts and case studies, with the attendant requirement for typing, duplicating, collating and storage. While a course is running, assistance is needed to prepare for the later sessions while the tutor is occupied with the current ones and to generally relieve him of day to day chores; also, for dealing with individual administration problems of the delegates. Thus, a very competent secretarial service is necessary, with additional peak-load help and a variety of reprographic services readily available.

Course organizers and tutors will have their own ideas on how they wish the conference rooms to be laid out with the instructional equipment they need, and the centre staff should be prepared to meet their wishes to the utmost. It is not always possible to ascertain beforehand the full requirements, which may, in any case, change at short notice; it may therefore be advisable to adopt a standard layout that meets fairly general approval in default of instructions but to be prepared to respond quickly to any later demands. As ever, flexibility in meeting the requirements will maintain the goodwill of the tutorial staff.

The types of instructional equipment on the market are proliferating, and it would be impossible to stock everything. Fashions change, and in recent years the popularity of such aids as film strips, slide projectors, overhead projectors, flipcharts, etc. has waxed and waned. A balance is necessary, and with a full outfit of currently popular types, a selection of older equipment, which can be produced on demand, should be kept available. New requirements may be highlighted as courses are developed, and if the future need appears to justify the outlay, new equipment must be acquired— on hire at first perhaps, until the need is confirmed. Inevitably, in this electrical/electronic age, ample power points will be essential to support such equipment, and ring mains for CCTV and telephone sockets for computer terminals are also desirable.

All this equipment represents a considerable capital outlay, and as much of it is used only occasionally, it can deteriorate in store if not properly and regularly maintained and checked. Breakdown and damage can be minimized if trained operators are always employed, but this may not be feasible when course hours do not remain within normal staff working hours; arrangements thus have to be made to instruct tutors and their assistants in the use of equipment, and steps taken to ensure that it is carefully checked before being put away after use.

Cinemas where courses assemble to view films should be considered and, in providing an excuse to move to a different room, may be desirable, but generally it would seem more advantageous to be able to project in the conference room in use, preferably from an insulated soundproof booth where a whole, or part of a film can be integrated into the presentation without the distraction of a move to another room.

As projectors and similar equipment are so often in use when maintenance staff are not on duty, a ready-to-use supply of lamps and fuses should be available, and its whereabouts known to course organizers.

Maintenance of Buildings and Grounds

The problem of maintaining the fabric of the buildings and their internal and external appearance is no different to that of any other building used by a large number of people to whom it does not belong. The higher the standard at which it is kept, the greater the respect in which it will be held and treated by visitors—if the centre looks unkempt and second rate, it will be treated as such. How much can be done depends on the money available and the current state of the buildings. A planned programme for redecoration over several years is necessary, with provision for the renewal of soft furnishings before they begin to deteriorate or become outmoded.

As most courses are short and intense, breakdowns of services cannot be tolerated since delays and interruptions may not easily be recoverable, and lowering of standards—even temporarily—causes distraction and loss of confidence in the efficiency of the centre, with a deterioration of the environment which it has been striving to create.

Planned preventive maintenance by contract for heating systems, kitchen equipment, and cleaning or washing machines is probably the most suitable way of ensuring adequate routine maintenance and quick breakdown service, but this is an expensive method for minor day to day work on plumbing and electrical systems or for general running repairs to furniture and fittings. A good handyman and, if the establishment is large enough, a resident engineer or mechanic will provide the immediate 'first aid' to reduce the delays and embarrassment which can arise when services break down at inevitably awkward moments, as well as reducing the need to call on the services of outside tradesmen, who are rarely immediately available, for minor work.

Although closely related to the provision of general domestic facilities, the cleaning of offices, lecture rooms and public rooms may have to be treated as a separate maintenance problem and, possibly, put out to contract as the times when this can be done without interference to instruction rarely fit in with normal domestic routines. Early-morning cleaning before classes start is probably the most satisfactory, but if this is not possible, it must be arranged after the afternoon sessions and before evening work starts. It adds to the image of the establishment if conference rooms can be neatened, ashtrays emptied, and water carafes replenished, etc. during breaks in sessions.

Attractive and well-kept grounds are an asset which assists greatly in creating a pleasant atmosphere, in contrast to so many of the work places of the delegates, and provide mind-relaxing moments between work. Their maintenance is labour intensive and a constant target for economies. Mechanization reduces the manpower requirements but brings problems of capital expenditure and maintenance.

Some outdoor recreational facilities may be provided for delegates, but should be of a short-duration nature, since most courses leave little spare time for leisure.

Coordination

To provide a proper and efficient service all the activities of the centre must be coordinated; the formulation of long-term forecasts with detailed plans for the immediate future calls for the close cooperation between training and administrative staffs. The effective implementation of the plans, with a friendly and cooperative attitude to delegates and visitors, should make the company and the delegates feel that their training centre is a valuable asset which adequately fulfils its purpose.

The above is only an outline of the necessary details which must be given full attention in a training centre. Sufficient should have been given however for the reader to note the central theme—the uninterrupted comfort of delegates and silent, unobtrusive, flexible support for the tutorial staff to work with. Given that all these elements are present, only the training staff's capabilities limit the opportunity for a successful training programme.

39. Developing management development trainers

John E. Henriksen

Throughout this chapter, the word 'trainer' refers both to personnel specialists—here, named MD specialists—and to the other managers of the company who must undertake MD training.

The importance of cooperation between the professional MD specialist and all the managers of the company is stressed. Of course, the job does not present the same aspects to the top executive as it does to the foreman, but what they have in common is the opportunity to contribute to the best obtainable standards of the other managers of the company.

This chapter describes the development possibilities for managers and MD specialists, suggests objectives for management development, and emphasizes the importance of an organic learning programme.

As stressed in other chapters, companies are in a process of development, the acceleration of which is steadily increasing. This makes heavy demands on the persons in charge of the development of present and potential managers who are to fill higher-graded positions in the future. Who are these people? The answer must be that, first and foremost, company managers should be considered management development trainers. It is important that any leader should fully understand that it is part of his everyday work to contribute to the training of other leaders and enable these potential executives to acquire the background and education needed for top positions. This might be, after all, the most important task for a manager. In his line job, the manager should take part in the development of the present and future leaders; as he makes his way to the top of the pyramid, the importance of management development increases. Top executives should consider the task vital for the company.

Too many firms make apparent commitments to development efforts without an awareness of possible consequences. They send executives to 'school' for development training and expect a change, or improvement, to occur. If top management is not willing to make policy decisions and commitments in the areas discussed—preferring instead to go through the motions of development by participation in college and intracompany programmes—then they must recognize that improved performance is highly unlikely. Development then takes the same form as extracurricular activities. Such activities may, of course, be highly satisfying to the participants, but such satisfaction might be obtained more economically by using other techniques.

Whenever the subject of management development trainers is discussed, people tend to think in terms of the professional personnel specialist who acts as a consultant to the top team, sets up programmes for job rotation and management training, and who participates in planning the company's management succession programme, career development, and all the staff development programmes. What kind of development does this man need? To specify more clearly how to recognize the possible management development trainers among the staff, the following factors need to be considered.

Training Officers

The professional training officer, who plans the entire training programme for the company, is a key figure in management development. The organization of special training programmes, including professional training, basic training, and staff development in general, may be his whole job or only part of it, depending on the size of the company. However, whether he is directly or indirectly involved in management, his functions are of great importance to the company's management development programme. Many leaders are drawn from the line of specialists, i.e., accounting, marketing, EDP, etc. and it is important that they, in addition to their specialist background, achieve a 'helicopter view' of the company and its problems, in order to find out where they fit into the organization as a whole. To a high degree, the trainer function can develop an efficient management development programme through a combination of professional training and the 'helicopter view'.

The Line Manager

The line manager's attitude is the key point in management development. It is important that he gives his full support to, and participates in, the development of the future leaders. In his day to day work, the line manager can identify numerous situations which he could exploit to support the management development programme. Valuable possibilities for potential leaders to gain practical experience arise from decentralization, or when the manager is away on vacation or courses, or has sick leave. Also, job rotation programmes need full support from line managers.

Top Executives

A successful management development programme is entirely dependent on the attitude of the top executives. Career progression, replacement plans, rotation programmes, and development of everyday work presuppose a positive and constructive attitude and participation at the top executive level.

The Management Development Specialist

Large companies, in particular, make use of specialists who can act as advisers to the top executives, do the planning, and carry out management development activities in cooperation with the other managers of the company. These staff organizations can provide substantial assistance to line management in identifying development needs and methods to satisfy these needs. However, the establishment and maintenance of a challenging and stimulating climate for development must, ultimately, rest with line management.

In his report of a one-year field study sponsored by the Harvard Business School, Miles Mace has concluded that the 'creation of a satisfactory climate (for development) depends upon factors of much deeper significance than open doors or amenities of social exchange'. He found that, in those companies where developmental projects seemed to be most effective, top management maintained an active interest and participation in a vigorous on-going developmental programme. Where top management engaged in its own developmental programmes, conferred with equivalents in other companies, required annual or semi-annual reviews of progress and personnel (coupled with frank and realistic discussions), maintained personal interest in subordinates, and consistently held a conscious 'coaching attitude', greater satisfaction was reported by those interviewed in the survey.

Critical Aspects of Coaching

The most critical aspects of coaching as an integral part of development are: personal knowledge of subordinates' strengths and weaknesses and the assignment of tasks which develop skills and reduce weaknesses; creation of an atmosphere of trust and truthfulness, in which an employee will feel free to discuss his progress; and acceptance of the executive role as a supportive coach, as well as a director and controller. To be effective, this climate must include the physical, intellectual and psychological availability of the executive to his subordinates. Because the executive is in a position of daily interaction with the subordinate, he has major control over the atmosphere for development. In effect, every executive is his own personnel officer. Personnel departments may be adept at augmenting training and development programmes, but 'affirmative coaching is the responsibility of the line manager, not the management specialists' responsibility.'

Top Executives' and Management Development Specialists' Needs for Development

A cursory study of modern literature on management may leave one with the impression that management is a well-defined and unambiguous activity. But management is not static and universal; it is dependent on the employees of the firm in question, and on the structure of society as it manifests itself at a given point of time. Accordingly, the list of general requirements for developing top executives and MD specialists is by no means unambiguous and complete. The relative pressure of each individual need has to be correlated with the actual situation. Therefore, this chapter does not claim to give a standard description of the general needs for the development of all top executives and MD executives but, rather, it is an attempt to pinpoint those areas in which needs can usually be expected. It is obvious that top executives' and MD specialists' needs depend, to a great extent, on their personal identity. Are they new to the job, what kind of education do they have, what kind of experience have they gained, and what kind of company do they work for?

The everyday life of the company offers great opportunities for development. Managers must concern themselves with the company as a whole (cf. the above-mentioned 'helicopter view'). A thorough knowledge of the entirety makes it possible, by means of a diagnosis of the company's social system, to acquire a profound insight of the company's MD problems, including the capacity of other managers in the organization and, particularly, of those colleagues capable of becoming the future leaders. It is obvious that it is not always possible to obtain such knowledge on a personal basis, because information on the employees in larger companies often comes from assessment forms, etc.

Exchange of Experience Between Colleagues

Conferring with managers from other companies in order to exchange experience on management development is an inestimable help today, when things move so fast that nobody is able to gain sufficient knowledge through personal experience. Participation in meetings of management associations, and visits to other companies, helps the personal development of top executives as well as MD specialists.

Personal Studies

A study of descriptive theories will provide a theoretical ballast that can be utilized in discussions with other professionals from the company. Today, a huge number of theoretical structures are being erected, together with descriptions of practical examples of management development (see 'Suggested Reading' list). It is a characteristic of the efficient top executive, the line manager and the MD specialist that they are always in a process of learning. One way to improve the MD standard is to form study groups (syndicates) of people from the company, or colleagues from other companies. It is probably wise to arrange such syndicates so that the participants are well equipped, through preparatory studies, to minimize the risk of the discussions turning into 'small talk'. It is necessary to discuss practical experiences but, also, to obtain a knowledge of new theories. Most of the knowledge achieved through a basic education becomes obsolete in a few years, and this is true of management education also. The established top executive may find it particularly difficult to keep up his theoretical studies, and to him, participation in such syndicates may prove to be an inspiration.

Use of External Consultants

The use of management consultants in the company's management development programme may contribute new knowledge and prevent stagnation of the company due to an inbreeding of methods. Throughout the world there are experienced management consultants available. Most of the larger companies can well afford to arrange regular short seminars for their managers and MD specialists and to invite European or American management consultants to provide the company with an input on MbO, organization renewal, job enrichment, Grid OD, matrix organization, creativity training, mix organizations, etc. Firms are often somewhat reluctant to invite foreign management consultants because of cultural barriers, but this obstruction does not need to be insurmountable. An adaptation to unfamiliar attitudes and ideas can prove beneficial.

Discussions Through Groups, Committees, etc.

Regular meetings with groups concerned with MD problems, makes it possible for the young leaders, the established leaders, and other collaborators to voice their views of the company's MD programme. Those leaders who participate in the programme must, as a matter of course, be given the opportunity to express their opinion of the support that they receive from the top executives, the line managers and the MD specialist.

Participation in Group Training

MD trainers need a certain amount of insight in human psychology. If attitudes, skills, and behaviour are to be changed effectively, it is necessary to make use of a participating group technique. The members of the group must be actively engaged in its activities, must be given the opportunity to verbalize and show their present attitude and behaviour, to compare them with the other group members' reaction to them and, moreover, be given the opportunity to experiment with alternative ways of conduct and attitudes before an actual change can be expected. Sykes[1] concludes that such a training is most effective in group environments where a number of participants work together on the common problems in any human relationship. The environment must be of a sort that offers support, even when the group members reveal their own weaknesses and problems. This climate will, in its turn, act as an incentive to a more open and honest expression of feelings.

In the organization itself, it is important that MD trainers contribute to the development of an open climate. In this process, the leaders also play an extremely important part and, in the organizing system, one must admit that the education which a leader has received, and the assumptions on which it is based, has a considerable effect on his mental picture of the organization; moreover, it will influence the attitude of many other members of the staff and, thereby, the entire organizing system.

Teamwork between top executives, senior managers, and other managers and MD specialists in their daily work across the different personal functions —whose limits are defined by tradition—is all-important for an atmosphere of cooperation in the company. The value of highly specialized selective procedures, highly specified for work descriptions, and highly specialized training procedures seems to be much less than the value of the connection between the organizing functions through an extensive cooperation between leaders and colleagues. A worthwhile MD programme is based on a close connection with a programme for organizing development and improvement.

Group Dynamic Training or Sensitivity Training

When undergoing this kind of training, the members work in unstructured groups. The purpose is for them to acquire a knowledge of their own attitudes in relation to that of the group member—this can be of the utmost relevance in MD training.

At a Cornell University conference on management development in New York City, Odiorne severely criticized sensitivity training and said that it was not 'training', since the objectives and process have not been well defined, and are not well understood as yet, and are not within the control of the instructor, and it has been known to result in serious mental disturbance for the participants. Odiorne reports having witnessed a serious mental breakdown precipitated by participation in a T-Group training programme. In rebuttal, Argyris said that there have been only four nervous breakdowns among 10 000 participants, and 'all of these people had previous psychiatric histories'. He stated further, that 'a trainer can only go so far in preventing destructive experience'. The important thing is that people 'can decide how much they want to pay psychically' for what they are learning.

Argyris maintains that sensitivity training is not psychotherapy, though it does aim to change behaviour. 'Openness and trust are what we want to develop'. However, he agrees that the technique ought not to be conducted for lower supervisory levels, for, as one member of the conference suggested: 'Wouldn't this mean stripping a man of his defences in the areas he needs them most?'

Management development trainers can develop their own maturity through participating in sensitivity programmes and personally assess its significance in training managers.

Participation in the Use of Simulation Models

Business games mainly offer simulation. Described or constructed situations will most often form the basis of the game (see Chapter 16). Used properly, they offer a good training in estimating the consequences of actions from a given amount of advance information. At the same time, as the result of one's actions appears, the theory of decision making can be studied. Of course, it is an essential requirement that the basic material is sufficiently realistic for the participants to take the game seriously. The game must not be arranged in such a way that abnormal actions lead to good results.

Establishing MD Objectives

Together, the top executives and the MD specialist have to establish the necessary objectives, and this can be done according to the following criteria :

(a) agreement with organizing needs;
(b) coordination with the organizing planning;
(c) conversion into quantitative units of measure whenever possible. Qualitative objectives can be used too, if they are carefully supported by premises;
(d) making sure that objectives do not conflict with the expectations of organization members.

Further, they can ensure that the time element of the MD programme correlates with the other development plans of the company.

Gearing Objectives to Organizational Needs

The qualitative aspects of the development objectives should be established so that the desired changes in managerial skills and efficiency reflect the organization's actual needs and current problems. Many development programmes have failed because the objectives established were merely mirror images of development objectives commonly used in industry. For example, it will be useless to train an industrial supervisor in general principles of discipline if what he really needs to know is how to apply the specific rules of his company.

A logical first step is to diagnose by making an inventory of current problems. This inventory can be based on interview sampling of opinions at all levels of management and employees. Once the major, and most pressing, problems of the organization have been identified, it will be easier to determine how a development programme can contribute to their solution. Where the problems stem from lack of knowledge or understanding, a development programme can make a substantial contribution. However, when the problems stem from poor communication from top management, incompetence in selected key positions, or inadequate technical factors, such as budget and control systems, other approaches may be required. Under such circumstances, methods such as managerial replacement, reassignment of responsibilities, increased use of controls, and/or closer supervision might be used. Most frequently, the effective solution of major problems will require some combination of several of these approaches. Using development as an exclusive means for solving major problems and bringing about change will be effective only when the key members of the organization are already receptive to change. After the major problems are recognized, the method of their solution must be devised to supply those relevant organizational factors which are missing.

The development programme must be designed to assist the organization in meeting its long-range plans and goals. For development efforts to be geared to plans and goals, the strengths, weaknesses, and development needs of participating managers must be assessed, together with the abilities of present managers to attain long-range objectives. Trouble frequently results because many programmes are established without consideration of these factors. For example, it is unrealistic to teach the benefits of participative decentralized management in an organization which is already headed by an authoritarian executive who insists on centralized controls and who has no intention of changing.

Two planning areas in particular should be reviewed during the formulation of the development objectives. First, the relevant external factors concerned with future market conditions: sociological, economic, and technological trends affecting the organization. This requires a careful review of factors such as:

(a) the organization's current and expected position within the industry;
(b) general industrial, economic, and sociobusiness trends;
(c) current and expected product and labour market requirements;
(d) current government regulations and regulatory trends;
(e) expected technological change that may be relevant to the organization's economic progress.

Second, the organization's immediate and long-range plans.

A careful review of the following factors is required:

(a) the specific managerial behavioural patterns required to meet the organization's long-range plans;
(b) the projected cash outlay involved in meeting the development objectives;
(c) the cost on organizational efficiency of committing key executive time to the development of the objectives and the subsequent programme;
(d) the potential problem areas that may arise as a result of the organization's transition from its current operations and practices to the revised methods necessary to meet future external requirements;
(e) the present trends that may change the existing environment within the foreseeable future.

Having identified the major problems of the organization and the requirements anticipated in the future, we can compare the strengths and weaknesses of present managers with these requirements, and estimate their ability to meet the long-range objectives of the organization. The result of this analysis should provide an organization with realistic plans for meeting its internal requirements in relation to its current and expected market position.

Compatibility of Change with Expectations

In addition to meeting definite needs determined by considering plans and goals, development objectives must also be in a certain accord with the personal goals of the participants. Conflict between programme goals and participant goals creates barriers—particularly, slower motivation to learn and a resistance to change. Development objectives which deal with an individual's performance must also be compatible with his supervisor's expectations. When the boss expects behaviour which differs from what has been learnt in a development effort, problems may arise. The manager who sends his subordinates to 'get developed' may, in fact, be their chief deterrent to job improvement.

Stating Objectives for Development

A precise statement of the development objectives, although a technical consideration, is crucial to the design of the entire management development programme. When objectives are specified in advance, the necessary conditions can be spelt out, specific reinforcements ascertained, and methods of instruction determined. Specific objectives should be stated in the following areas:

Knowledge. The knowledge objectives, if stated precisely, describe the responses which the participant should make in reply to requests for information taught in the programme.

Attitudes. Objectives concerned with attitudes state the beliefs, convictions, and emotional responses expected of the participants as a result of the development. Questionnaires, interviews, and direct observation can be used to measure attitude change.

Skills. Objectives concerned with the achievement of skills describe the actual behaviour which the participants can exhibit under learning conditions. Skill objectives fall into two broad categories—intellectual skills and social skills. Skill achievement can be measured by the use of classroom assignments which simulate actual working conditions. Examples of such assignments are role playing, in-basket techniques, management games, and case studies.

Job Performance. Objectives concerned with job performance state the desired responses to actual job situations and problems. Performance change can be measured through direct observation by the participant's associates, superiors, and subordinates.

Operational Results. Finally, objectives concerning results specify desired changes in productivity, cost, employee turnover, group cohesiveness, grievance frequency, and the like. The first four objectives, when achieved, serve as intervening variables to bring about improved operational results. Operational results are stated as organizational output rather than individual performance. When records are maintained for areas of managerial responsibility, and when responsibilities are clearly defined and separated, operational results can be measured by the use of managerial performance standards.

Management Development Trainers and the Organic Learning Process

It is important that management development trainers are well grounded in the principles of learning. The organic learning process aims at giving the employee more self-confidence and at helping him to obtain a high degree of self-acceptance. Through an effective organic learning process, the employee is taught how to accept other people by learning how, fully, to accept himself. Frequently, attitudes are changed and this can lead to a more open, confident, and sincere relationship with other people. People acquire an awareness of their own potential abilities and become more capable of making use of hitherto unexplored creative abilities.

Organic learning takes place without assistance from others, but the MD trainer is able, for instance, to assist other leaders through counselling. Naturally, it is extremely difficult to change the opinion that a person has of himself, often he clings to a distorted picture with the utmost stubbornness. Nietzsche once said: 'A man may despise himself, but yet respect himself for his own self-contempt'. Although it is difficult to change these attitudes, the MD trainer can be a big help to his colleagues by helping them to develop a more precise picture of themselves, if he is able to establish a helping relationship. This relationship is decisive for the kind of counselling that he is to carry out—this should not entail setting himself up as a judge of his colleagues' actions. The one who tries to help must be understanding and more than professionally interested in the other person. This does not necessarily have to be an acceptance of what the other person does, but the counsellor should act as a mirror that reflects the other person's strengths as well as his weaknesses.

This helping relationship demands from the MD trainer a personal, sincere and honest investment in the other person. Indifference, exaggerated professionalism, or manipulation easily destroys the relationship. It is difficult to imagine that a person should try to acquaint himself with his own behaviour unless he first admits to himself that apparently his own behavioural pattern is not satisfactory, and that this is due to something on which he, himself, has no influence. The recognition of the existence of a problem, and the awareness of its possible consequences to oneself, is often alarming and may cause ambivalent feelings towards the actual situation, and may create anxiety, confusion and uncertainty. All this can make the learning process extremely difficult and place the colleague in a defensive position once he starts considering the trainer to be a threat to him.

One of the best forms of organic learning is to create possibilities for the self-development of the employee. This means that the person in question should be allowed to choose the hour and the pace of learning instead of being placed in a controlled learning situation where his behaviour is narrowly supervised and more or less conducted by others. The person who approaches the trainer to discuss his problem is *en route* to a solution. Learning via experience in non-controlled situations where the employee assumes full responsibility is the way of organic learning. Of course, there is a risk that the employee will not succeed or will make an error in these circumstances. However, during the learning period, the collaborator must not be subject to sanctions and, ultimately, the line manager must be the one responsible.

The Importance of Effective MD Trainers

In this chapter, it has been pointed out that the actual MD trainers are the top executives and the line managers, and that the MD specialist is a staff and service function to these. If, as often happens, leaders do not take this part of their work seriously, it is probably due to the lack of attention shown by companies to the systematic development of leaders. By permitting collaborators free scope for their abilities by coaching and support, an interest in the company's objectives and identity is aroused, and its employees identify themselves with the company and cease to be mere wage earners.

References

1. SYKES, A. J. M. The Effect of a Supervisory Training Course in Changing Supervisors' Perceptions and Expectations of the Role of Management, *Human Relations*, **15**, 3, 1962.

Suggested Reading

ODIORNE, G. S. *What's Wrong With Sensitivity Training*, Paper, Cornell Conference, New York, 1963.
MACE, M. L. *The Growth and Development of Executives*, Harvard University Press, 1950.
SCHEIN, E. H. and BENNIS, W. G. *Personal and Organizational Change Through Group Methods*, *The Laboratory Approach*, Wiley, New York, 1965.
BENNIS, W. G. A New Role for Behavioral Sciences: Effecting Organizational Change, *Administrative Science Quarterly*, **8**, 2, 1963.
BENNETT, W. E. The Lecture As A Management Training Technique, *Personnel*, **32**, 6, 1956.
HORNSTEIN, H. A., BUNKER, B. B., BURKE, W. W., GINDES, M., and LEWICHI, R. *Social Intervention*, Free Press, 1971.

40.   The analysis and costing of management training

John Talbot

This chapter reviews analysis and costing as a means of ensuring that training is effectively managed in a business context. Emphasis is on the analysis of problems and financial control, rather than detailed techniques of training needs analysis. Examples are based on a simple questioning approach that has been proved in practice. The respective roles of trainers and managers are discussed in terms of close collaboration and involvement. Training is seen as a positive, live and continuous process inextricably linked with the mainstream of business activity. Effective analysis is described as a means of helping training to influence change, as well as react to it.

Analysis and costing provides a practical basis for managing management training. It is concerned with the on-going clarification of the role and purpose of training, and ensures that vital questions are considered and answered. Too often, links with genuine business problems are not clear, and the consideration of costs and financial return is vague. Objectives are in training terms—sometimes called behavioural terms—when they should be in business terms.

The basic questions of analysis and costing are:

How does the training relate to business problems?
What is the financial justification for investment in training?
Are there any financial measures and controls—or even estimates?
Is training regularly and critically reviewed in terms of meeting real needs at reasonable cost?
Has there been adequate evaluation before, during, and after the training?

This chapter looks at some current approaches. Much has been said and written about many of the techniques, particularly those associated with the assessment of training needs. To avoid duplication, emphasis is placed on the perspective of training needs, and techniques of problem analysis and financial review.

Training Needs in Perspective

Training needs are often considered purely in terms of skill and knowledge requirements resulting from change or expected change. They are reactive needs. Where this approach is dominant, it can have a fundamental influence on the scope of training and the role of the training officer. Excellent training activities may flourish, but the depth of training thinking may be surprisingly limited. There may be a curious separation of training and management thinking. Managers will take decisions and set objectives and then refer to the trainer, who is expected to react in training terms. He is seen essentially as an instructional technician, however sophisticated the techniques may be. The result may be superb courses or learning programmes in computer knowledge, corporate planning, finance, control systems, behavioural science, and so on. They may all be useful, relevant and seen to be successful, and yet the training operation may, in fact, be going off at half cock. Training needs are not just concerned with correcting faults and deficiencies in the present situation. Future needs do not just arise as a result of change. Training is also concerned with shaping the future. The role is one of change agent as well as agent of change.

If this role is to develop, there can be no separation of management and training thinking. The trainer must be involved and influential at the formative and development stage. This involvement will be helped by systematic problem analysis before any detailed review of training needs. The needs will then include positive development needs. The trainer's role will be to help in the development of analytical and critical thinking, decision taking, personal relationships, creativity and management style. He will be concerned with developing the skills, the approaches, and the rethinking necessary to shape and control future policy.

A recent study of training needs in the retail area clearly demonstrated the differences of emphasis. The main preoccupation had been with how changes such as the development of supermarkets and hypermarkets and entry into the EEC, etc., would affect skill requirements. Only a small number of traders saw their training needs in terms of developing the skills that would enable them to shape their industry and influence the trends. Among these, promotion of flexible skills and management thinking in small shops—geared to personal service and real customer needs—was recognized as a means of retaining a highly profitable small-business sector. Similar skills and rethinking were seen to be contributors to better margins on certain supermarket lines. The successful blending of training and management thinking, in this way, has now lead to a broader recognition that both reactive and development needs must be considered. For many managers training is now a live and primary consideration, rather than a mechanical and secondary one. Trainers are expected to help change and to be concerned with the fundamental business issues involved.

In helping change, trainers will be involved in strengthening those factors which promote effective change, namely:

(a) increased objectivity;
(b) better problem diagnosis and decision taking;
(c) better facing up to problems;
(d) the development of a common language and approach for problems;
(e) commitment to objectives and associated training.

They will also be concerned with a deliberate attempt to attack those aspects of management behaviour which impede change and effective training, e.g., tradition attitudes, thinking and approaches; lack of frankness; incomplete involvement; unwillingness to recognize conflicts and destructive competitiveness; the habit of blaming others.

The analysis of training will be seen as a continuous and living process of:

(a) challenge and questioning;
(b) problem recognition;
(c) rethinking and skill development;
(d) definition of secondary learning needs;
(e) formal training;
(f) challenge and questioning.

Within this process, links with business thinking and financial priorities will promote a realistic view of training from the cost viewpoint, in terms of expense and cost control, cost effectiveness, cost benefit, and investment control.

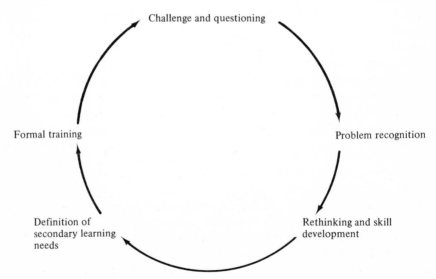

Fig. 40.1. The analytical process.

586

When problems have been identified, and cost and pay-off taken into account, needs can be defined in terms of learning needs and knowledge gaps. In most cases, lack of knowledge and skill is easy to identify, but a more important question is the significance of such lack. Lack of ability to use available knowledge is often much more important than acquiring more. Major gaps will usually be filled by individual managers without much prompting, if these are a real barrier to their success. Immediate recourse to training should always be critically questioned. Probing the problems behind the situations will help to keep the needs in perspective. Training thinking will be challenged and questioned in business terms.

Problem Analysis

Challenge and Questioning

Disillusion with standard approaches to training is now very widespread. This is because problems are continually changing. It is essential that methods should be geared to the scale and type of problem, and that the aims of questioning and analysis are clear. Some, or all, of the following aims may be appropriate:

(a) to sound the organization on the ways in which change, training, and development could be profitable;
(b) to review major problems and barriers to improvement;
(c) to establish areas of common ground related to problems, skills, and objectives;
(d) to establish priorities for action in business and training terms;
(e) to establish a framework for the on-going recognition of problems and opportunities.

Question patterns which have been used as part of an initial examination of major problems are illustrated in Figs. 40.2 and 40.4; these are best used as a basis for a structured interview.

Problem Analysis in an Industry

In analysing an industry situation, some thirty to forty questions of the kind illustrated in Fig. 40.2 provide the background against which more detailed training needs can be discussed. There are a number of stages involved:

(a) the recognition of problems;
(b) the identification of managers involved—and their views;
(c) the definition of change and development areas;
(d) the recognition of barriers to progress and their links with management skills;
(e) the establishment of major knowledge and skill requirements;
(f) the definition of priority areas in terms of the impact of managerial skill on major problems.

1. What is the present structure of the industry in terms of:
   size of companies
   organization patterns
   numbers of managers?
2. Are any changes planned?
   What are they?
   Who is involved?
   How will they be brought about?
3. Are any changes considered necessary?
   By whom?
4. What are the major problems facing the industry?
   What action is planned?
   What additional action should be taken?
5. What problems most impair the effectiveness of:
   companies
   industrial sectors
   managers or groups of managers?
6. What are the major opportunity areas?
   Does anything inhibit the greater exploitation of these areas?
7. What are the most significant recent technological changes?
   How do these affect:
   organization
   management responsibilities
   training?
8. Are there any major knowledge, understanding, or information gaps?
9. Are management roles and responsibilities clearly defined?
   Are they changing?
10. Has there been a systematic analysis of management skills?
11. Is management training:
    effective
    accepted?
    What are its main purposes?
    Are changes necessary?

Fig. 40.2. Problem analysis in an industry.

If this questioning procedure is carried out with a cross-section of key managers in the industry, the result is likely to be a clear recognition of training needs linked to priority problems and developments. Involvement in the analysis process will encourage commitment to the training solutions. The necessary finance is then likely to be made available in line with the true investment priorities.

Training needs emerging will be of two kinds. Firstly, those centred on company or industry problems, or opportunities for development. Organization and industry development programmes, industrial relations training, engineering training, and computer training are activities related to needs of this kind. Secondly, those centred on individuals whose skill requires improvement, either to make them more efficient in their present job or to prepare them for future tasks crucial to the industry. These needs can then be grouped in an assessment of overall training needs which indicates:

(a) the major problems to which training can make a contribution;
(b) anticipated developments and training implications;
(c) the extent of individual training needs;
(d) the costs of providing the training;

588

(e) the priorities;
(f) the expected benefits;
(g) a plan of action.

Each part of the plan can then be thoroughly reviewed on an on-going basis in line with the kind of assessment illustrated in Fig. 40.9. A summary of training needs established on an industry basis is shown in Fig. 40.3. This covers all levels of training, although the major priorities concern management, and all the activities involve management.

Large companies	Smaller companies
1. Training for objective setting providing a basis for massive change in management approach, and large-scale measurable results.	1. Training of managing directors—including training in a problem-centred approach to training.
2. Industrial relations training—contributing to major performance and relationship improvements.	2. Training concerned with pricing and basic sales techniques—a key profit area.
3. Training in engineering troubleshooting—an area of biggest potential return within the industry, especially when related to new machines.	3. Training in market analysis and buying strategy—vital to the full realization of profit.
4. Operator training—especially when linked to machine utilization, yield, quality, or transport.	4. Training in merchandizing and shop marketing techniques.
	5. Training concerned with key financial ratios and controls.
5. Training for innovation and creativity—particularly important in developing measurable results, as well as contributing to new product development.	6. Training related to the economic use and maintenance of vehicles—a key cost area.
	7. Training in the recognition and development of entrepreneurial skills as an overall priority.
6. Group training for clerical work.	

Fig. 40.3. Industry training needs: priority areas.

Problem Analysis in a Company

Initial analysis may follow a similar pattern at company level. Figure 40.4 illustrates a questionnaire used with a group of senior managers. The basic stages of questioning are the same as at industry level, although more emphasis has been placed on the needs and contributions of individuals. The framework also allows for the specific assessment of training needs.

Once the initial assessment has been carried out on a problem-centred basis, it is often helpful to analyse requirements by means of a skill-centred assessment. An illustration of a simple checklist used in this context is illustrated in Fig. 40.5. The danger with this type of approach is a failure to recognize real priorities and to assume that deficiencies are needs. Every activity should always be checked against the changing pattern of business objectives and opportunities for increased financial effectiveness.

589

Preamble

Explain the concepts of:

1. Sounding the company on the ways in which change could be profitable.
2. Helping the management team to devise and implement its own strategies for improvement.
3. Providing a training back-up which will pay off on the job and which will be deliberately applied on the job.

Questions

1. (a) What are the company's major external problems at this time?
   (b) What additional action should it be taking to cope with these problems?
2. (a) What external problems do you foresee?
   (b) What action is being taken?
   (c) What additional action should be taken?
3. (a) Are there any opportunities which the company is failing to grasp?
   (b) What do you suggest the company should do?
4. (a) What are the company's major internal problems?
   (b) What action should be taken?
5. (a) What are the most important features of your job?
   (b) What are the most important features (qualities and skills) of someone in your job?
6. (a) What problems most impair the effectiveness of your own department?
   (b) In what ways could the effectiveness of your own department be increased?
7. (a) What are the major cost areas within your control?
   (b) Are there any problems in controlling costs?
8. (a) What are your major opportunity areas?
   (b) Does anything inhibit greater exploitation of these areas?
9. What are the most important attributes of those who work for you?
10. (a) What are the main aspects of your department's policy for the next twelve months?
    (b) Do you have objectives?
    (c) What are your key result areas?
    (d) When were job descriptions last rewritten? By whom?
11. (a) What training have you received over the last two years, and how do you rate its effect on your performance/its use in practice?

Training/Course	No harmful effect	Beneficial	Very beneficial

    (b) What comments do you have about the relevance and application of training?
12. What training, if any, could make you more effective now?
13. (a) What training do your subordinates need?
    (b) How would they use it?
    Man_________ Need_________ Use_________
14. What is your view of appraisal?
15. How do you see your own future prospects?
16. What motivates your subordinates?
17. What frustrates your subordinates?

Fig. 40.4. Problem analysis in a company. Format for structured interviews with a cross-section of management.

Involving Managers in Analysis

Where groups of managers are involved, and problems are concerned with organizational relationships and systems, it is helpful to involve managers much more directly in the analysis process. This can link the main stages of the analytical process by providing managers with a structured framework for reviewing and challenging their present situation, defining their problems, rethinking their approach, and setting targets—including training targets—for improvement, which may be part of a broader organization development process.

	1	2	3	4
1. Satisfactory skill or knowledge level 2. Sound basic knowledge—not fully up to date 3. Little knowledge or skill 4. No knowledge or skill Tick as appropriate, or indicate if not applicable				
Training need area	1	2	3	4
Value-added taxation			√	
Planning and control of working capital		√		
Computer use		√		
Industrial relations law	√			
Industrial relations policy		√		
Corporate planning		√		
Appraisal and counselling		√		
Management by Objectives		√		
Employment law			√	
Motivation techniques			√	
Organization skills		√		
Stock control	NA			
etc.				

Fig. 40.5. Management training needs checklist.

Figures 40.6 to 40.8 illustrate approaches which have been used in analysing organization problems, information systems, and manpower costing requirements. Using the 'gap theory', managers compare their actual situation with the ideal. Groups of managers first review their situation as individuals and then attempt to arrive at a group understanding and agreement. Instructions to managers are normally on the following lines:

Under each of the column headings (Figs. 40.6 to 40.8) are listed five alternative ways in which the organization may operate. All or most of the statements have probably been true of your own situation to some degree at some time. Under each heading, mark the statements in the order (1 to 5) in which they best describe the situation in your own organization, and the situation which should ideally obtain in your organization.

	Actual ranking	Ideal ranking	Notes
1. Information channels are clogged. There is too much form filling and paperwork.	————	————	
2. There is a sound balance in the information system which facilitates effective control and decision taking. Frequency and detail of communication is appropriate to the organization needs.	————	————	
3. Formal information channels are strictly observed. Adequate information flow is achieved by tight administrative control.	————	————	
4. Information flow is haphazard and largely informal. Key data is often difficult to obtain.	————	————	
5. Information flow is hampered by questions of politics and power.	————	————	

Fig. 40.6. Organization information.

591

Differences between the actual and ideal will indicate organization needs and pointers to training needs stemming from these.

Where a number of managers have been directly involved in the analysis in this way, there will also be a direct training and learning impact and high commitment to training geared to the problems involved. The examples are selected from checklists covering the following areas:

Organization

    organization information (Fig. 40.6);
    strategic planning;
    decision taking;
    communication;
    review;
    objective setting;
    responsibility;
    commitment;
    cost–benefit awareness;
    relationships between groups.

Information Systems

    work group information;
    organization information;
    strategic planning information;
    control information;
    operational information (Fig. 40.7).

Manpower Costing

    awareness;
    allocation;
    measurement (Fig. 40.8);
    system.

	Actual ranking	Ideal ranking	Notes
1. The type of operational information varies from department to department. Consistent standards are lacking.			
2. Frequent mistakes and delays occur through lack of basic data.			
3. Although widely accepted systems exist, many errors occur as a result of clerical inefficiency.			
4. Consistent and well-established systems exist throughout the organization. Those concerned are trained to use them effectively and consistently.			
5. A standard approach to records and data systems is achieved by centralized control. Data handling is a specialized function.			

Fig. 40.7. Operational information.

	Actual ranking	Ideal ranking	Notes
1. Expenditure is logically controlled by a system of budgets and establishments, but not always directed to areas of greatest need.			
2. Expenditure is loosely controlled and strongly influenced by departmental, group, and external pressures.			
3. Finance is allocated in line with a system of controls geared to obtaining the best returns from investment in human resources.			
4. Manpower expenditure is out of control and overshadowed by other financial considerations.			
5. Manpower budgets and controls exist, but are confined to limited areas of direct expenditure such as wages and salaries.			

Fig. 40.8. Measurement.

An application in the industrial relations field is included in Geoffrey Morris's chapter on the role of the consultant in organization development.

All the examples quoted have been used in practice. They have succeeded in providing a basis for the identification of training needs. They have done this in a situation where:

(a) there has been a thorough probing of all the possible problems;
(b) immediate and obvious needs have been put in perspective;
(c) managers concerned have been involved in a number of ways and are likely to be committed to the training which follows.

In many cases, rethinking and learning will have been part of the process of challenge and problem recognition. Training, in a positive development sense, will have started as an integral part of management thinking, concerned with influencing change as well as reacting to it.

Against this background, specific secondary training needs can be identified in context, and costing and financial thinking will form a natural part of the process.

Training Cost Control

Training has often been seen as an extension of the educational—schoolroom—process within business. This is linked to the instructional technician view of training. Learning has been expected to take place outside business or, at least, 'off the job'. The fact that most learning is clearly inextricably linked with development within the job has been conveniently ignored.

This distortion has had drastic implications, not least in the field of training investment and cost control. Business measurements have been applied to easily defined off-the-job activities. This has produced a facade of control techniques, without any real control. The separatist view of training has been given an aura of accounting respectability, with highly unfortunate results for both training and industry. The calculations are often basically irrelevant in any broad sense, and the outcome is that the real contribution and nature of training is not established and that management fails to recognize the impact, in terms of investment, of one of its key resources—manpower.

Training is neither a science in which the results of action can be accurately predicted nor a separate activity which can be given clear financial boundaries. This brings difficulties in terms of achieving control and assessing contribution, but it also brings reality. Training is an integral part of business, and the process of learning is a continuous one. It follows that the responsibility for training and for examining its cost and usefulness rests squarely with the operating managers of the business. The trainer's job is to ensure that this happens by establishing a systematic basis for considering training in financial terms and estimating costs and benefits as far as is reasonably possible. The costs of running specific training sections or activities may be easily recognizable, but result from decisions made by the operating managers. It is, therefore, essential that any costing system is related to individual and group needs viewed as business priorities. Careful budgeting of specialist training activities is essential for control purposes, but there are a number of dangers:

(a) that the training specialist is seen as fully responsible for the training cost;
(b) that the line manager's thinking, in terms of the financial implications of training, is limited;
(c) that training costs and contributions are not seen in relation to the real priorities of the business.

Against the background of these difficulties and the need for integration and realism, what are the basic factors to be considered in establishing effective training cost control?

Definition

Training costs have been defined as 'the total monetary sacrifices, made by firms as a result of the training function. They are the sum of all increases in expenditure and all decreases in income, which stem from the decisions which management have taken about the training activity'. In a purist sense, this definition is true but, on its own, gives a negative impression. Costing is a basis for measuring contribution, as well as expense. Before deciding on a control system, it must be put in perspective. It is impossible to obtain a completely accurate picture of total training cost since many of the items are interwoven with other costs. A number of basic questions should be asked: What training costs can be recognized? How are they caused? How significant are they in terms of:

a. *Cost Effectiveness.* Whether the training method is economical compared with other methods.

b. *Cost Benefit.* How training relates to likely benefits.

594

c. *Investment Appraisal.* The validity and importance of training as an investment in manpower. Will it depreciate or appreciate? Is the pattern of investment logical? How valuable is it to record each type of training cost?

Basic Cost Evaluation Questions

As a step towards an overall appraisal of investment in management training, the vital questions are: Has the training succeeded—on the basis of appraisals, questionnaires, attitude surveys, output, sales and quality figures, etc.? (*Validation.*) How much did it cost—in relation to budgets, cost reports, time, loss of output, etc.? (*Cost assessment.*) What were the benefits—on the basis of output, sales and quality figures, learning times, waste, flexibility, organization improvement, etc.? (*Cost–benefit analysis.*)

These are apparently simple questions, but, without reasonable answers to them, management training cannot be effectively managed. Often, the questions are not asked, or are asked singly rather than together. They are sometimes avoided because answers which inevitably include general estimates and indications of trends are thought to be of little value. It is assumed that if analysis is not precise it is not valuable. This confuses the needs of academic evaluation with the normal guidance requirements of managers. In fact, it is often surprising how clear the answers can be. The more the questions are asked, the more numerous and helpful the answers are likely to be.

Like all other analysis questions, it is vital that they are asked at the right time—before the training, during the training, and afterwards. A simple checklist designed to help management trainers in this whole process is illustrated in Fig. 40.9. This may, of course, be amended to fit particular situations, but it does provide a working basis for asking the key questions and drawing the necessary facts together. Alongside the questioning approach to problems and training needs, it provides the trainer with essential on-going data for balanced training decisions in a business and financial setting; involves management in the process by systematic probing; stimulates rethinking in training and operational terms.

Measuring Performance

It is sometimes said that many of the questions about benefits and results cannot be answered at management level because of the impossibilty of measuring impact on individual managers. There are difficulties, but three important factors should be borne in mind:

(a) the questioning process can help to clarify management thinking, irrespective of the ability to measure precisely;
(b) as has been said, intelligent estimates can be produced as a valuable basis for management decisions (estimates which are often at least as good as in other areas);

1. *Cost Assessment*

At planning stage		While training is in progress		When training is completed	
Questions	Cost	Questions	Cost	Questions	Cost
What costs will be incurred in the following areas?		Are costs in these areas at variance with budget? If so, reasons		What was the final cost? Was the plan realistic? Reasons for variance Changes for the future Is there a cheaper way?	
1. Course fees					
2. Exam fees					
3. Equipment: books, etc.					
4. Travelling expenses					
5. Accommodation					
6. Subsistence and meals					
7. Trainee's pay					
8. Trainee's employment costs					
9. Instructor's pay					
10. Instructor's employment costs					
11. Appraisal costs					
12. Assimilation costs					
13. Loss of business					
14. Loss of output					
15. Training materials					
16. Training equipment					
17. Training staff pay					
18. Training staff					
Employment costs					
19. Bought out-training					
20. Hire charges (specify)					
21. Administration costs					
(perhaps apportionment)					
22. Depreciation					
23. Other costs					
Any significant cost ratios to be used? e.g. relationship to NSV or total salaries					

[continued overleaf]

2. *Validation*

At planning stage		While training is in progress		When training is completed	
Questions		Questions		Questions	
What standards should be set for measuring success? How are the standards to be expressed?		Are notes of progress satisfactory? Are standards proving realistic?		Have standards been met? (a) In full? (b) In part? Should standards be revised?	
Is improvement expected, and if so, how is it to be measured?		Is the rate of improvement being maintained? Reasons for results better or worse than expected?		Have improved standards been maintained?	
Are there any other factors which can affect measurement? e.g., changes in market? raw material? opportunity to learn? organization? methods of payment? basic ability of trainees?		Are any outside factors affecting performance or measurement? Can they be eliminated? Can they be allowed for?		Have any other factors affected results? Can the contribution or detraction be measured or assessed? Can they be eliminated for future trainees?	
Is group improvement expected? How is group performance measured?		Can improvements related to training be recognized? Are they satisfactory?		Has group performance improved? Can training contribute to further improvements?	

3. *Benefit analysis*

At planning stage — Questions	While training is in progress — Questions	When training is completed — Questions

Skills: Will the training contribute to:
1. Introduction of new
  (a) market?
  (b) products?
  (c) processes?
  (d) systems?
  (e) equipment?
2. Improved skills?
3. Total company expertise?
4. Keeping pace with technological change?
5. Job security?
6. Other?
	Is the introduction of new markets, etc. proceeding satisfactorily?
	
	Are skills being improved?
	
	Is the company keeping pace technically?
		Has training produced desired result?
		
		Were aims too high? too low?

Finance: Will training contribute to:
1. Sales
  (a) Increased total?
  (b) Increases in particular lines?
  (c) New lines?
2. Operating costs
  (a) Raw materials usage?
  (b) Labour utilization?
  (c) Plant utilization?
  (d) Unit costs?
  (e) Working capital employed?
  (f) Stock holding?
3. Increased output?
	Are sales improving in areas chosen?
	
	Are there progressive changes in the reduction of operating costs?
	
	Can the effect of training be isolated?
		Has the desired contribution been made?
		
		Any improvements in the future?
		
		What were the major areas of financial impact?
		
		What is your estimate of financial impact?

Are other benefits likely in such areas as: 1. Objective setting? 2. Organization effectiveness? 3. Personal relations? 4. Morale? 5. Recruitment? 6. Other? Will any of these have an effect in any other area?	Are there interim measures of benefit in these areas? Are there any other effects?	What planned benefits were achieved? Any others? If so, why? Can they be planned in future?

Fig. 40.9. Management training: cost assessment; validation; benefit analysis.

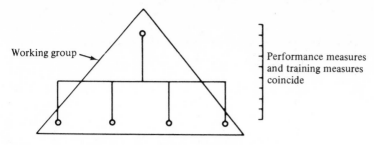

Fig. 40.10. Measuring management performance.

(c) a group of managers, e.g., a department or sales team, is often the logical basis for measurement and, therefore, the logical target for training, rather than the individual. Performance of these groups is usually already measured, and, despite other variables, the impact of training can often be clearly assessed (Fig. 40.10).

Investment Appraisal

The final outcome of the whole process of analysis is the provision of a thorough assessment of the total situation as the basis for management decisions about training investment. Many of the threads can be drawn together from the kind of material already reviewed, but this is not the whole picture. Once managers have started to think about training in these business terms, financial logic is likely to be applied on a much broader scale. A few examples illustrate this kind of total investment thinking.

Alternative Policies from an Investment Viewpoint

Figure 40.11 illustrates alternative approaches to investment in management training. Too frequently, investment is in an individual manager in terms of a course or training project. Heavy investment is put in at the training stage, but little into follow-up consolidation. The result is 'transfer barrier' with little of the investment being put to use in the company. Apart from the basic difficulties of introducing new ideas once the manager returns from a course, there is often marked antagonism within the working group to the intrusion of anything remotely new. There has been no investment in preparing the group to accept change, which is the underlying objective. In many cases where this happens, the individual may well realize that, although the company is not capitalizing on its investment, he can now easily do so himself. He has been made marketable because the training itself was valid and successful. He, therefore, leaves and the company not only fails to use its training investment, but loses a valuable human resource. By any kind of logic, this approach is clearly a waste of money and bad investment policy. The alternative is either direct investment in group training, so that change and new ideas take root regardless of turnover, or nominations for individual training which allow for an easy exchange of

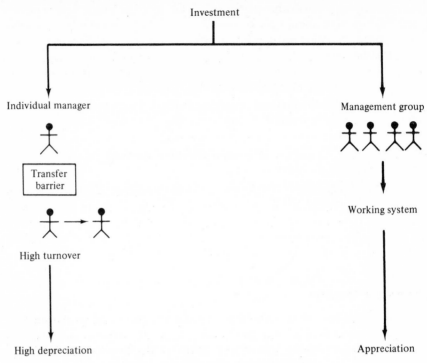

Fig. 40.11. Investment in management training.

ideas afterwards. This can be done by clusters of nominations from one group in a short period rather than by nominations from all over the organization, on the sole basis of individual need. It is interesting that this is in contrast to many well-accepted management development routines which focus attention purely on individual talent.

Costs of Inconsistency

Figure 40.12 illustrates the danger of an inconsistent investment at horizontal levels in the organization. Many training activities are aimed at middle management or supervisors and often introduce styles of management

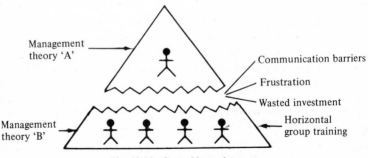

Fig. 40.12. Cost of inconsistency.

inconsistent with those above or below. The result is reflected in reactions such as 'my boss should have gone on this course', the build-up of dissatisfaction with other parts of the organization, and frustration at inability to apply the new and fashionable teaching. This is interesting training for revolution, but not for integrated organization. Communication barriers are enhanced, and more problems raised than solved. One glance at this waste of investment in financial terms is usually enough to lead to a rigorous review of training in terms of value for money.

Investment Curves

A useful check on management training is a simple comparison of investment at various levels or in various parts of the organization. Figure 40.13 shows a normal investment curve. This simple check can very often illustrate a

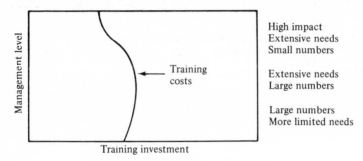

Fig. 40.13. Management investment curve.

number of clear inconsistencies in terms of failure to invest where needs are greatest, or pay-off most likely. A checklist of basic questions about investment appears in Fig. 40.14. Investment curves in some companies could well be completely reversed.

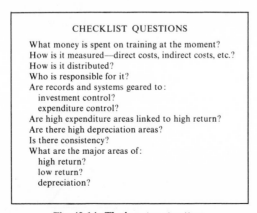

Fig. 40.14. The investment pattern.

All these examples are simple illustrations of the appraisal of management training in investment terms. They show the ways in which the systematic and detailed review can be supplemented by basic questions as to whether investment is appreciating or depreciating, or whether the investment is logical. They help to present a total picture of training, and answers to the questions posed at the beginning of the chapter. They are part of the business-like basis for managing management training which systematic analysis and costing can help to provide.

Suggested Reading

BOYDELL, T. H. *A Guide to the Identification of Training Needs*, British Association for Commercial and Industrial Education, 1971.

Food, Drink and Tobacco Industry Training Board, *Assessing Your Company's Training Needs*, 1971.

OTTO, C. P. and GLASER, R. O. *The Management of Training*, Addison-Wesley, Reading, Mass., 1970, chapters 7 and 10.

GARBUTT, D. *Training Costs*, Gee, 1969.

TALBOT, J. R. and ELLIS, C. D. *Analysis and Costing of Company Training*, Gower Press, 1969.

BASS, B. M. and VAUGHAN, J. A. *Training in Industry—The Management of Learning*, Tavistock, 1966. chapter 6.

41.   The use of attitude surveys in management development and training

Robert M. Worcester[*]

Many management development courses today, and perhaps most training courses, have end-of-course examinations that provide an evaluation of the impact of the educational material on the student. Rarely do such tests measure attitudes. Attitude surveys are used to measure concerns and motivations. This chapter suggests how they can enhance the effectiveness of management development and training; why they are useful; and gives a general indication of procedures that may be employed. Further, a case example is provided showing how one organization used attitude surveys to evaluate the effectiveness of its management development programme.

What do attitude surveys have to do with management development? We are trying to build our management team for the future by developing our managers' skills. We are training them to do a better job. We are not conducting a morale exercise, nor are we trying to measure the effectiveness of our internal communications or development programmes. So, what do attitude surveys have to do with us, what use can they be to us in management development?

Most people consider themselves experts on education because they have all spent a healthy proportion of their lifetime in an educational environment. In a way, this is the bane of every executive responsible for management development and training—he is 'second guessed' at every turn. In addition, he has to combat the general assumption made by most people that once their schooldays are over, and any other job training that immediately follows has been learnt, then education as such is over for the rest of their lives. Many people do not expect to go back to the classroom

* The author wishes to acknowledge the assistance of Miss Angela Mais in the preparation of this chapter.

again and frequently find it difficult to recognize the need, in later years, to take lessons which will be of benefit to them. Those who are already executives feel they have 'made it' and those selected for management development courses feel they are 'on the way'.

In the classroom situation, everyone has experienced the immediate challenge of examinations, which tend, generally, merely to test the short-term impact of the sessions. Rarely is there a longer-term evaluation of the absorption of the content of the course, or any questions on topics outside the immediate curricula, such as creature comforts, the length of the course, and the like.

Many management development courses today, and perhaps most training courses, have end-of-course examinations that provide an evaluation of the impact of the educational material on the student. These examinations tend to be held at the end of a course and are primarily used to award kudos to the top 10 per cent and to provide evidence of the need for some hard talk to the under-achievers when they get back to the job. Rarely are tests used to measure attitudes. Tests measure what was taught and learnt or, alternatively, what was not learnt because it was not taught at all, it was taught badly, or, for some other reason, was not absorbed by the student. In a training situation, such tests are of value. In a development situation, it is also useful to measure motivations and feelings which can be done by conducting an attitude survey.

How does one define 'attitude surveys', and how do they relate to management development? Attitude surveys are, basically, a statistical measure of people's feelings, concerns, awareness, and motivations. They provide a baseline from which to determine what action should be taken in order to improve operating methods, working and/or living conditions; to increase effectiveness and productivity; to create a greater degree of satisfaction and to meet the needs of those surveyed. Frequently, attitude surveys are repeated over time; this enhances their usefulness, for it provides an on-going measure of employee attitudes, thus measuring the before-and-after effect of actions taken or events that have occurred.

Over the past decade, managements in the US, and increasingly in other countries have used the results obtained from attitude surveys to improve communications with their employees, to correct specific grievances, raise morale and to increase general employee satisfaction. This was the original purpose of employee attitude surveys. The scope of such surveys is, however, increasing, and the technique is now applied in order to obtain from employees, at all levels, a researched view of how the company can improve its effectiveness in dealing with external publics, and how the company can—both through its employees and advertising and other communications media—be seen to be a good 'corporate citizen' by the public in general, and by the groups that it comes into more direct contact with through its management and employees.

How do attitude surveys relate to management development and training? Management development and training can be approached in a number of

604

ways. On the development side, managers are frequently sent on courses and lectures outside the firm itself or receive instruction while actually at work; both these methods are often used. It is less usual, except in very large companies, for management development lectures and courses to be conducted within the company. On the training side, instruction is usually provided while the trainee is actually at work; and occasionally, trainees are given a course of instruction either within the company or, less frequently, attend lectures and courses outside the company.

Managers attending development courses bring with them the basic skills of their job. The purpose of the development course is usually not so much to improve these skills as to bring managers into contact with new ideas and techniques of managing, to show how they can improve their performance as managers, and to help them to do a better, more effective and valuable job. At the same time, some courses attempt to show managers how to improve their relations not only with employees but also with the outside publics with which they come in contact. Their reactions to such a course can be constructively measured by an attitude survey, rather than by an end-of-course test which will merely tell us how much of the educational material has been absorbed. A test will not give a measure of how the managers felt about the course, whether it was of any use to them, how it will affect the way they do their job, what they would wish added or subtracted from the course, and the like.

General Procedures in Employee Attitude Surveys

As the uses to which employee attitude surveys can be put increases, so the general procedure for conducting such a survey will have to be adapted. However, the basic structure will, most likely, remain the same. An outline of this structure follows, then we go on to describe its use, with some adaptations, in a particular case study.

The goal of an employee attitude survey, as stated earlier, is to produce an accurate and detailed photograph of employee satisfactions, as well as their dissatisfactions; their knowledge and understanding of the company and its operations; any road blocks which may be limiting employee productivity, etc. In recent years, the research procedures have increased in complexity.

The normal employee attitude survey is now at least a two-step research project. In the first stage, intensive depth interviews are conducted with top managers and with a small sample of employees from the group under study. In the second stage, a quantitative measure of employee attitudes is obtained via a questionnaire.

The Developmental Phase

To develop the necessary understanding of the company's employee relations practices and objectives, to discuss current operating problems and to explore employees' ideas as to 'what the survey really should cover', it is normal to conduct preliminary interviews with members of management, both staff and line, who have responsibility for the group under study, and with representative employees from the group itself. These interviews are conducted by personnel highly trained in the techniques of depth interviewing. The interviews are unstructured. The interviewer follows a general questioning guide, but is free to develop any leads encountered in the course of the interview. Among the areas which are usually explored in detail are: communications, working conditions, working relationships, attitudes towards supervision, knowledge of the industry, its economics and its special problems.

Since these interviews are not designed to produce quantitative information, it is not necessary to obtain an exact cross-section of all employees. However, it is desirable to distribute the interviews broadly throughout the organization and to obtain representation from all major departments, all job levels, etc.

The Quantitative Survey

Depending on such factors as the number of employees who can be taken off the job for the survey, and the budget available for obtaining and processing the data, the procedure may be:

(a) to survey all employees—a survey based on 100 per cent coverage takes maximum advantage of the morale-building potential of employee attitude research. It also permits detailed analysis of results department by department or unit by unit and an analysis of the thinking of small groups of employees whose functions or problems may be deemed especially important;

(b) to survey a representative sample of employees—the sample can be so planned that an adequate number of interviews is obtained from both supervisory and non-supervisory employees and that enough interviews are taken in major departments to permit separate analysis of the results for key employee groups.

In either case, normal procedure is to notify employees in advance that a survey will be made and to assure employees that the results will be anonymous and that management honestly seeks their frank opinions.

The survey itself can be conducted either by personal interview, at home or in the office, by post or, preferably, by self-completion interview. In any case, usually pre-coded, structured questions—frequently of the multiple response or scaling variety—are used, as well as open-ended questions which allow the employee to answer 'in his own words'. Following completion of the survey, open-ended questions are coded, the questionnaires key-punched and data-processed, and the results analysed.

It is, of course, impossible to specify a specific structure for any single attitude survey, but the procedure is readily adaptable depending upon the nature of the group being surveyed and the specific results that the company hopes to obtain from the survey. In the case study that follows, an example is provided that illustrates how one very large organization used attitude surveys to evaluate their management development programme.

Barclays Bank: A Case Study

Most British managements have been slow to take employees into their confidence. Companies who would not consider entering a market without soundly designed research on likely consumer reaction nonetheless launch new employee benefits, curtail employee communications programmes, and conduct training and development programmes without consulting those most directly affected. Many British executives go about their business with the smug assumption that 'all employees care about is more pay for less work'. These executives are overlooking a most valuable asset—the minds of their employees. Some companies' executives have come to realize the value of monitoring employees' attitudes, and the work done for one company provides a suitable illustration of the use of attitude surveys in management development and training.

Several years ago, Barclays Bank—Britain's largest bank with some 60 000 employees—had been conducting a series of $2\frac{1}{2}$-day business development seminars for branch managers. The success of the programme, together with the recognition of its limitations, led the Bank to agree to a substantial investment in time and money to expand the seminars into a programme entitled 'Spectrum'.

Spectrum, an expansion of the business development seminar idea in both time and content, began in the autumn of 1972 and continued until 1975, by which time all branch and assistant branch managers had attended the week-long course. The objective of the programme was to equip the Bank's branch managers and assistant branch managers with a sufficient knowledge of marketing to enable them to set and achieve meaningful targets under the Bank's MbO programme. Further, and perhaps stated in a more concrete manner, the end objective was to change managers' attitudes towards marketing so as to encourage positive business development.

The Bank recognized the desirability of assessing the effectiveness of the course in two ways, tactically and strategically; the former to include course content evaluation and to determine shortfalls in provision of proper creature comforts; and the latter, longer-term 'strategic' aspects of attitude change and changes in actual behaviour while at work.

The Bank employed outside consultants because they did not feel that the necessary expertise was available among the Bank's own personnel; in order to ensure that the effectiveness of the course was measured over time; to eliminate any bias; and to provide respondents with the assurance that their responses would be anonymous. During the period of time over which the Spectrum programme is running, it was proposed that two parallel studies be conducted. The appraisal of course content (tactical) study is discussed first, followed by an outline of the plan for the attitude (strategic) study.

607

1. When you were first told about Spectrum did you think the course was...?

Circle *one* number   (15)

1. A very good idea
2. A fairly good idea
3. Neither a good nor bad idea
4. A fairly bad idea
5. A very bad idea

2. How interesting did you feel the seminar would be?

Circle *one* number   (16)

1. Very interesting
2. Fairly interesting
3. Neither
4. Not very interesting
5. Not at all interesting

3. How useful did you think the seminar would be to you in your job as a manager?

Circle *one* number   (17)

1. Very useful
2. Fairly useful
3. Neither
4. Not very useful
5. Not at all useful

2.   Session organization

4. How would you rate the following?

Circle *one* number for *each* item

	Good	Fair	Poor	
Content of the sessions	1	2	3	18
Sequence of the sessions	1	2	3	19
The films shown	1	2	3	20
The session leaders	1	2	3	21
Balance of the curriculum	1	2	3	22
The case studies	1	2	3	23

4a. If you rated any as poor, please tell us why, and what should be done. Please make it clear which item you are commenting on.

3.   Creature comforts

We feel that your personal comfort during the seminar is important.

5. How do you rate the following aspects?

Circle *one* number for *each* item

	Good	Fair	Poor	
Acoustics	1	2	3	24
Hotel accommodation	1	2	3	25
Meals	1	2	3	26
Temperature	1	2	3	27
Seats, seating arrangements, etc.	1	2	3	28
Informal dress	1	2	3	29

5a. If you rated any as poor, please tell us why, and what should be done about it. Please make it clear which item you are commenting on.

6. How would you rate the duration of the following?

   Circle *one* number for *each* item

	Too long	About right	Too short	
The seminar overall	1	2	3	30
The length of the day	1	2	3	31
The breaks for meals, coffee, etc.	1	2	3	32
The sessions themselves	1	2	3	33
The case studies	1	2	3	34

7a. If there were any particular sessions which—in your opinion—need considerable improvement, please say which they were, and why improvements need to be made.

	35
	36
	37
	38
	38
	39
	40

7b. Are there any comments or suggestions you would like to make?
    (Please write in)

	41
	42

5. Back in the branch

8. How easy or difficult will it be to put into practice what you have learnt?

   Circle *one* number   (43)

1. Very easy
2. Fairly easy
3. Neither
4. Fairly difficult
5. Very difficult

9. Has the seminar changed your attitude towards any of the following?

   Circle *one* number for *each* item

	Has changed a great deal	Has changed a little	Has not changed	
Your staff	1	2	3	44
Your customers	1	2	3	45
Your job	1	2	3	46
The Bank overall	1	2	3	47

10. What are the two or three most important changes, if any, you will make when you get back to the branch?

	48
	49
	50

[continued overleaf

609

11. Having attended the seminar what do you think your job will be...?

Circle *as many* numbers (51)
as you feel apply

1. Easier
2. More interesting
3. More rewarding
4. More of a challenge
5. Remain the same
6. Some other difference (write in)

7. Don't know

12. How would you summarise your overall impression of the seminar both favourable and unfavourable? (Please write in.)

Favourable impressions:

Unfavourable impressions:

	52
	53
	54
	55
	56
	57

6. Personal details

We need a few details for analytical purposes; please do not sign your name.

13. Which of the following age groups do you belong to?

Circle *one* number (58)

1. Under 35
2. 35–44
3. 45–54
4. Over 54

14. What is the size of your branch?

Circle *one* number (59)

1. 10 staff or less
2. 11–24 staff
3. 25 or more staff

15. Which of the seven regions is your branch in?

Circle *one* number (60)

1. London
2. South-east
3. South-west
4. East Midlands and East Anglia
5. Wales and West Midlands
6. North-east
7. North-west

16. What position do you hold?

Circle *one* number (61)

1. Branch manager
2. Deputy manager
3. Assistant manager
4. Submanager
5. Trust officer
6. Other (write in)

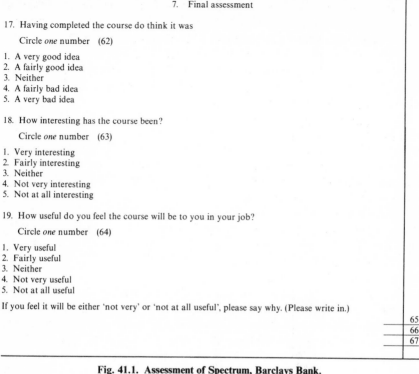

Fig. 41.1. Assessment of Spectrum, Barclays Bank.

Tactical Study

The purpose of the tactical study was to enable the course managers to evaluate the mechanics of the course as it proceeded and to sharpen the focus of course content and to uncover any problem areas that existed in the form and/or quality of the instruction, physical facilities, or other similar concrete matters. Also, the intention was to ask subjective, attitudinal questions as well, although it was recognized that the answers would be suspect, taken, as it were, in the *bonhomme* euphoria of end-of-course good feeling. Indeed, one of the advantages of the two-stage approach is the ability this provides to measure the 'decay-rate' of such enthusiasm as it is dampened down by the shock of re-entry into the system (to mix metaphors).

The questionnaire was developed from the experience gained from use of the appraisal forms from the business development seminars, from other course appraisal forms, and from the agency's experience. Once developed, it was discussed with those attending the first course or two so that it was certain that all pertinent question areas were covered with a maximum of clarity and a minimum of wastage. Following piloting of the first 150 or so attendees, the questionnaire was finalized, printed in its final form, and made a part of the course materials kit (see Fig. 41.1).

After introducing the purpose of the questionnaire and stressing the absolute confidentiality of the replies, the course leader left the room, allowing respondents to fill it out then and there. The procedure recommended was for questionnaires to be distributed at the end of the course by a member of the class who then collected them after they had been completed, and posted them in a pre-addressed envelope to the agency's offices. The names of respondents did not appear on the questionnaire, so as to assure that the results of the survey would be anonymous and that the frank opinions of the respondent were honestly sought.

Once returned to the agency, the questionnaires are sorted, key-punched, and processed to a standard format. Each question is analysed in the same way, allowing for analyses such as size of branch, type of branch, the position of the respondent, the specific course attended, and other characteristics, including attitudinal measures such as expressed initial scepticism or enthusiasm for the Spectrum idea.

At the same time that the computer analysis takes place, the agency extracts verbatim responses to the open-ended questions, both to provide the 'flavour' of honest replies to season the statistics and to enable the individual thoughtful respondent to communicate a good sound idea to the managers of the course.

The end-result is a report of the responses—both in statistical and in written form—to the Bank, together with a memorandum highlighting significant findings and making comments about the implications of the findings as the agency sees them.

Early in the programme, the course director began to use the research tactically, to restructure the organization of the sessions, to eliminate some elements and shorten others, to take care of overheating in the class-room and to crack down on the unsatisfactory catering at one location. Having the same course given at seven different locations allows the research to look across locations (horizontally) so that normative data is automatic (the odd man out is conspicious); at the same time, having a new set of students at the same location every week allows the data to be examined longitudinally so that the effect of corrective methodology is that it is a census of all students, and, thus, there is no sampling error to contend with.

The survey results were tabulated on a month by month basis for the first (autumn 1972) series, and are thereafter analysed thrice yearly. In addition, every six months a 'workshop session' is held at which the regional seminar leaders are given a presentation of the study findings and trends and discuss ways of improving the course.

Strategic Study

The purpose of the proposed strategic study was to enable the Bank's management to assess the effectiveness of Spectrum in changing attitudes and behaviour of the branch managers and assistant branch managers. The plan for the study was to survey a sample of approximately 500 branch managers and assistant branch managers twice each year, a different sample each time, so that at the end of four years all 3200 would have been sur-veyed.

The questionnaire for the proposed survey is unrelated to the course *per se*, but instead, queries attitudes of the respondent to his job and to the Bank, and it attempts to measure attitude change in the group before and after attendance at Spectrum. In order to accomplish this, an indirect measure is required, employing a control group. It was proposed that, every six months, a survey of a sample of branch managers and assistant branch managers be conducted, ensuring that a subsample of Spectrum attendees is included in each survey. In this way comparisons of attitudes and behaviour could be made in three ways:

(a) in ordinary ways—by size of branch, type of branch, region, and other characteristics;
(b) by measuring the extent of differences between those attending the Spectrum course (and those attending a specific series) versus those who are 'unexposed';
(c) over time, to see how recent attendees' attitudes 'decay' and whether one-time exposure is sufficient or whether repeat or refresher courses are necessary or advisable.

The mechanics of the study were that the Bank would be responsible for sampling, i.e., providing a properly drawn sample of respondents, for distribution of the questionnaire, and for 'chasing' non-respondents to the survey to ensure a high response rate, a requirement especially crucial to the satisfactory completion of the study. Sample sizes being small so as to minimize costs, it is essential to obtain, as near as possible, 100 per cent completion of questionnaires so as to eliminate any potential margin of error.

The agency would be responsible for the design of the sample, for development and testing of the questionnaire, for receipt, processing and analysis of the questionnaires, and for reporting the results to the Bank. Reports of findings, together with summary highlight memoranda and comments on implications would be sent out semi-annually. In the end, however, events superseded this plan. Instead Barclays commissioned a wide-reaching staff attitude study that covered many aspects of employees' attitudes among all employees. This exercise, conducted in 1973–74, of course included all branch management. Questions designed to evaluate the strategic, longer-term effects of Spectrum were included in the questionnaire and analysed to meet the objectives outlined above.

Conclusion

While it is not possible to set up a *pro forma* survey able to be universally applied, it might be useful to conclude with a few principles about the use of attitude surveys in management development and training. It is important, at the outset, to recognize the difference between 'tests' and attitude surveys; tests are designed to measure learning, attitude surveys are ideally used to measure shifts in attitudes and motivations. If changes in behaviour result from changes in attitude and motivation, then it is important to determine what factors combine to cause these changes. In a management development programme a survey can be used to measure change over time and to discover what the students feel about the course and its value to them. At each stage, the data can be analysed not only by itself, but in comparison with previous surveys, thereby providing guidelines along which to change, adapt, and develop the programme so that it is of the greatest benefit to the greatest number attending.

Bad research is frequently worse than no research at all. It is important to get the mechanics of sampling, questionnaire design, and analysis right. Thus, the Reading List which follows is composed of books dealing with the application and techniques involved in attitude surveys. These, coupled with the basic outline given here, form the tools required for conducting an attitude survey to evaluate management development and training programmes.

Suggested Reading

ERDOS, P. L. *Professional Mail Surveys*, McGraw-Hill, New York, 1970. Especially: chapter 6, Questionnaire Construction; chapter 16, Checking in Returns; chapter 17, Data-processing; chapter 19, Editing and Coding; chapter 20, Card Punching and Machine Tabulation; and chapter 21, Recaps and Calculations.

MOSER, C. A., and KALTON, G. *Survey Methods in Social Investigation*, second edition, Heinemann Educational, 1971.

SELLITZ, C., *et al. Research Methods in Social Relations*, Holt, Rinehart and Winston, 1964. Especially: appendices B and C.

WORCESTER, R. M. (Ed.) *Consumer Market Research Handbook*, McGraw-Hill, 1972. Especially: chapter 3, Sampling; chapter 4, Questionnaire Design; chapter 9, Mail Surveys; and chapter 20, Corporate Image Research.

MAINWARING, G. and STUBBS, R. Spectrum: A marketing seminar, *European Research*, Jan. 1974.

Bibliography

Neil R. Hunter

The bibliography consists of references to books, reports, theses, journal articles, and other bibliographies published from 1965 to date. For books, the place of publication is usually indicated, unless it is the United Kingdom. In some cases, where the title is not indicative of content, a brief indication of subject matter is given in parentheses after the bibliographical details.

Contents

1. Management development and training—general.
2. Management development and training in particular areas of management activity (e.g., the public services), specific departments (e.g., marketing), or individual firms.
3. Management development and training for new recruits and junior managers.
4. Management development and training for senior managers.
5. Management education and the business schools.
6. Management development, training, and education in countries other than the United Kingdom and the United States.
7. Evaluation of management development, training, and education.
8. Bibliographies.

1. Management Development and Training—General

ADAIR, J. *Training for Leadership*, Macdonald, 1968.
American Management Association, *Making the Most of Training Opportunities*, AMA, New York, 1965.
American Society for Training and Development, Proceedings of the 23rd National Conference, *Training and Development Journal*, **21,** 9, Sept. 1967 (whole issue).
ARGYRIS, C. *Management and Organizational Development—The Path from XA to YB*, McGraw-Hill, 1971.
ARONOFF, J. and LITWIN, G. H. Achievement Motivation Training and Executive Advancement, *Journal of Applied Behavioral Science*, **7,** 2, 1971.

615

ASHALL, R. D. *Participative Exercises for Management Training*, International Textbooks, 1969.

BARRY, A. Improving Managerial Effectiveness, *Personnel and Training Management*, Mar. 1968.

BERGER, M. L. and BERGER, P. J. *Group Training Techniques*, Gower Press, 1972.

BINNIE, J. H. Management Development, *Training Officer*, **4**, 6, 1968.

BIRIEN, J.-L. Votre Fichier 'Formation Continue', *Management*, Apr. 1972.

BLAKE, R. R. and MOUTON, J. S. *Corporate Excellence Through Organization Development*, Gulf, Houston, Texas, 1968.

BLAKE, R. R. and MOUTON, J. S. *The Managerial Grid: Key Orientations for Achieving Production Through People*, Gulf, Houston, Texas, 1968.

BLAKE, R. R. and MOUTON, J. S. Work Team Development, *Training in Business and Industry*, **5**, 6, 1968.

BLAKE, T. Management Training and Development, *Industrial Training International*, **5**, 8 and 9, 1970.

BOCHET, E. Les Cadres Devant le Perfectionnement, *Management France*, Feb. 1972.

BRECH, E. F. L. *Management: Its Nature and Significance*, Pitman, 1967.

British Association for Commercial and Industrial Education, *Three Case Studies in Management and Supervisory Training*, BACIE, 1969.

British Institute of Management, *Company Information on Management Development and Training: Some First Results*, British Institute of Management, 1968.

British Institute of Management, *Making a Success of Management Development*, British Institute of Management, 1968.

British Institute of Management, *Making Management Development Effective*, British Institute of Management, 1965.

British Institute of Management, *Management Development and Training: A Survey of the Schemes used by 278 Companies* (by R. Somers), British Institute of Management, 1969.

British Institute of Management, *Questions of Management Development: A Checklist*, British Institute of Management, 1965.

BROOKS, R. Industry Loosens the Old School Tie, *Industrial Management*, Mar. 1971.

BURKE, W. Perfectionnement des Dirigeants et Développement de L'Organisation, *Synopsis*, Mar.–Apr. 1972.

BURSK, E. C. and BLODGETT, T. B. *Developing Executive Leaders*, Harvard University Press, 1971.

CAMPBELL, J. P. *Management Training: The Development of Managerial Effectiveness*, Richardson Foundation, Greensboro, North Carolina, 1966.

CARROLL, S. J. and NASH, A. N. Some Personal and Situational Correlates of Reactions to Management Development Training, *Academy of Management Journal*, **13**, June 1970.

CARSON, I. Computer Helps Train Better Managers, *International Management*, **27**, Feb. 1972.

CASEY, D. Individual Growth in a Company Context, *Personnel Management*, **3**, 10, 1971.

Challoner Management Appointments, *Management Development and Training: A Survey*, 1966.

CHASE, P. H. Creative Management Workshop, *Personnel Journal*, **51**, Apr. 1972.

CLARK, D. G. *The Industrial Manager: His Background and Career Pattern*, Business Publications, 1966.

CONNELLAN, L. The Identification and Development of Entrepreneurs, *Journal of Business Policy*, spring 1972.

CONNELLAN, L., EGAN, D., and GORMAN, L. *The Use of Behavioural Science Findings in the Training of Entrepreneurs: A Research Project with Small Industry Owner-managers*, Irish Management Institute, Dublin, 1973.

CONNELLAN, T. K. Management Development as a Capital Investment, *Human Resource Management*, summer 1972.

COOK, F. P. Management Development in Times of Change, *Personnel Management*, **47**, 371, 1965.

COOPER, C. L. and MANGHAM, I. L. *T-Groups: A Survey of Research*, Wiley, New York, 1971.

COOPER, G. Changing Employees into Men of Action, *International Management*, July 1971.

CRAIG, R. L. and BITTEL, L. R. *Training and Development Handbook*, McGraw-Hill, New York, for the American Society for Training and Development, 1967.

CROTTY, P. T. *Professional Education for Experienced Managers: A Comparison of the MBA and Executive Development Programs*, North Eastern University Bureau of Business and Economic Research, Boston, Mass., 1970.

CROZIER, M. Theory, Training and Practice in Management, *International Social Science Journal*, **20**, 1, 1968 (whole issue).

DALEY, P. and McGIVERN, C. The Ongoing Management Situation as the Training Vehicle, *Industrial and Commercial Training*, Mar. 1972.

DELINCOURT, B. La Formation Mal Entendue, *Management*, Dec. 1971.

Department of Employment, *Survey of Management Training and Development*, HMSO, 1971.

616

Department of Employment and Productivity, *An Approach to the Training and Development of Managers*, HMSO, 1967.

Department of Employment and Productivity, *Training and Development of Managers: Further Proposals*, HMSO, 1969.

DESATNICK, R. L. *A Concise Guide to Management Development*, American Management Association, New York, 1970.

DHIR, K. S. The Problem of Motivation in Management Development, *Personnel Journal*, **49**, 10, 1970.

DOVE, M. I., SUTCLIFFE, J. K., and RITCHIE, R. P. Value Analysis as a Contribution to Management Development, *Works Management*, Apr. 1967.

DUBRIN, A. J. Management Development: Education, Training or Behavioural Change, *Personnel Journal*, **49**, 12, 1970.

ECKHARDSTEIN, D. VON. *Laufbahnplanung für Führungskräfte*, Duncker und Humblot, Berlin, 1971.

FARNSWORTH, T. Management Development: Establishing a Policy, *Industrial and Commercial Training*, **2**, 11, 1970.

FARNSWORTH, T. Planning a Manager's Development, *Personnel Management*, **1**, 6, 1969.

FERGUSON, L. L. Better Management of Managers' Careers, *Harvard Business Review*, **44**, 2, 1966.

FOREMAN, W. J. Management Training in Large Corporations, *Training and Development Journal*, May 1967.

FOSTER, G. Making Managers—Executives on the Grid, *Management Today*, Apr. 1966.

FOY, N. The Maverick Mind of Reg Revans (Action Learning, a New Approach to the Training of Managers), *Management Today*, Nov. 1972.

FRANZ, E. and LUDEKENS, B. OD, Management Development and 'Future Shock', *Industrial Training International*, **7**, 9, 1972.

GARBUTT, D. Management Training Needs: A Typology, *Management Education and Development*, Jan. 1972.

GOODSTEIN, L. D. Management Development and Organizational Development: A Critical Difference in Focus, *Business Quarterly*, Oct–Dec. 1971.

GRUNENFELD, L. W. Personality Needs and Expected Benefits from a Management Development Program, *Occupational Psychology*, **40**, 1 and 2, 1966.

HACON, R. J. *Conflict in Human Relations Training*, Pergamon, 1965.

HACON, R. J. *Management Training—Results, Not Responsibility: Achievements, Not Activities*, Institution of Training Officers, 1967.

HAGUE, H. R. P. Defining Management Training Needs, *Industrial and Commercial Training*, Oct. 1971.

HAGUE, H. R. P. The External Catalyst in Management Training, *Industrial and Commercial Training*, **3**, 1, 1971.

HAYES, F. C. Training for the Management of Human Resources, *Industrial and Commercial Training*, Aug. 1972.

HEAVISIDE, G. C. Starting a Scheme of Management Development: The Command Group Training Approach, *Industrial and Commercial Training*, **2**, 8, 1970.

HEFFNER, R. W. Training and Development from Management's Perspective, *Personnel Journal*, **46**, 9, 1967.

HERMAN, S. M. Towards a More Authentic Manager, *Personnel Administrator*, Nov.–Dec. 1971.

HESSELING, P. Using a Communication Exercise for Training Managers, *British Journal of Industrial Relations*, **3**, 1, 1965.

HINRICHS, J. R. Two Approaches to Filling the Management Gap: Management Selection vs Management Development, *Personnel Journal*, **49**, 12, 1970.

HODGSON, R. C. Career Development for Managers, *Business Quarterly*, autumn 1972.

HOUSE, R. F. Leadership Training: Some Dysfunctional Consequences, *American Sociological Quarterly*, **12**, 4, 1968.

HOUSE, R. J. A Commitment Approach to Management Development, *California Management Review*, **7**, spring 1965.

HOUSE, R. J. *Management Development: Design, Evaluation and Implementation*, University of Michigan Bureau of Business Research, 1967.

HOUSE, R. J. Managerial Reactions to Two Methods of Management Training, *Personnel Psychology*, **18**, autumn 1965.

HUMBLE, J. W. *Improving Business Results*, Management Centre Europe, Brussels, 1967.

HUMBLE, J. W. *Improving Management Performance*, British Institute of Management, 1965.

HUMBLE, J. W. Improving Management Performance, *Personnel Management*, Sept. 1965.

HURLEY, J. R. Science and Fiction in Executive Training, *Journal of Applied Behavioural Science*, **7**, 1971, pp. 230–3.

KENNY, T. Growing Pains of Management Development, *Personnel*, **1**, 12, 1968.

KOHN, V. *An Assessment of Participants' Reactions to Management Development Meetings*, American Foundation for Management Research, New York, 1968.

KOHN, V. and PARKER, T. C. The Value of Expectations in Management Development, *Training and Development Journal*, **26**, 6, 1972.

KRAUT, A. I. Hard Look at Management Assessment Centers and Their Future, *Personnel Journal*, **51**, May 1972.

KREITZ, H. J. *Méthodes d'Appréciation des Cadres*, Editions d'Organisation/Editions Eyrolles, Paris, 1971.

KROLL, A. M. *Career Development: Growth and Crisis*, Wiley, 1970.

KRUPPA, M. *Systeme betrieblicher Ausbildung des Führungsnachwuchses*, Duncker und Humblot, Berlin, 1970.

KUBICEK, T. Some Issues in Training for Development of Professional Managers, *Cost and Management*, May 1968.

KURZMAN, P. A. Developing the Industrial Statesman, *Training and Development Journal*, **23**, 4, 1969.

LAZORKO, L. Junior Boards Train Managers, *International Management*, Jan. 1972.

LEHRER, R. N. *The Management of Improvement: Concepts, Organization and Strategy*, Reinhold, 1965.

LEIGH, D. R. Development or Developers? Developing Others as a Management Development Method, *Training and Development Journal*, Nov. 1966.

LESCAR, L. La Révolution de l'Éducation Permanente. *Hommes et Commerce*, Sept. 1971.

LEVINSON, H. *The Exceptional Executive*, Harvard University Press, 1968.

LOCKWOOD, J. Management Development by Objectives, *Management Decision*, **1**, 3, 1967.

LORD, D. Internal versus Outside Training, *International Management*, Nov. 1971.

LUNDBERG, C. C. Planning the Executive Development Program, *California Management Review*, autumn 1972.

McCLELLAND, G. Executive Development within a Manpower Plan, *Business*, July 1966.

McKIBBIN, L. E. A Comparison of the Effects of an Executive Development Program on Owner-Managers and Employee-Managers, Ph.D. thesis, Stanford University, 1968.

McLARNEY, W. J. and BERLINER, W. M. *Management Training: Cases and Principles*, Irwin, Illinois, 1970.

McNULTY, N. G. *Training Managers: the International Guide*, Harper and Row, 1969.

MANT, A. *The Experienced Manager: A Major Resource*, British Institute of Management, 1969.

MARKWELL, D. S. and ROBERTS, T. J. *Organisation of Management Development Programmes*, Gower Press, 1969.

MARSH, J. International Man and Management Development, *Canadian Personnel and Industrial Relations Journal*, Jan. 1968.

MARSH, J. The Managerial Convolution, *Management Today*, Sept. 1971.

MASON, J. G. *How to Build Your Management Skills*, McGraw-Hill, 1965.

MENDLESON, J. L. Manager Goal Setting: An Exploration into its Meaning and Measurement, Ph.D. thesis, Michigan State University, 1967.

MILLER, R. D. A Systems Concept of Training, *Training and Development Journal*, **23**, 4, 1969.

MILLS, G. J. Management Development, *Office Management*, **19**, autumn 1965.

MORGAN, T. Developing Interactive Skills, *Industrial and Commercial Training*, Apr. and May 1971.

MORRIS, R. Turning on Latent Business Talent, *Industrial Training International*, Nov. 1971.

MORSE, G. E. Mandate for Education and Training: Focus on the Individual, *Personnel*, Nov.–Dec. 1971.

MUMFORD, A. *The Manager and Training*, Pitman 1971.

MUMFORD, A. Self Development for the Manager, *Personnel Management*, **4**, Jan. 1972.

NASH, M. M. Intelligent Reading for Self Development, *Personnel Journal*, Nov. 1971.

National Economic Development Office, Management Education Training and Development Committee, *Comparisons of UK and US Management and Qualified Manpower* (by A. D. Little Ltd), NEDO, 1970.

National Economic Development Office, Management Education Training and Development Committee, *The Training of British Managers: A Study of Need and Demand* (by T. W. Leggatt), HMSO, 1972.

ODIORNE, G. S. *Training by Objectives: An Economic Approach to Management Training*, Macmillan, 1970.

OLDFIELD, F. E. *The Making of Managers*, Mason Reed, 1967.

PAGE, D. J. A Facelift for Executive Development, *Industrial and Commercial Training*, Sept. 1972.

PALMER, W. J. Integrated Program for Career Development, *Personnel Journal*, **51,** June 1972.

PARKER, T. C. *The Anatomy of Organization Development*, American Foundation for Management Research, New York, 1968.

PARLOUR, R. R. Executive Team Training, *Academy of Management Journal*, Sept. 1971.

PAUL, O. A. Grasping at Straws or Diving for Pearls? *SAM Advanced Management Journal*, Jan. 1971 (an analysis of management development programmes).

PEARSE, R. F. Certified Professional Managers, *Personnel*, Mar.–Apr. 1972.

PIREE, M. La Formation Permanente, *Etude du Travail*, Dec. 1971.

PODNOS, I. The 'Consultative Method of Training', *Personnel*, Sept.–Oct. 1971.

RAKES, G. K. and WHEELEN, T. L. Preparation for Leadership, *Public Utilities Fortnightly*, **89,** 11 May 1972.

REEVES, E. T. *Management Development for the Line Manager*, American Management Association, New York, 1969.

REID, A. M. An Approach to Leadership Training, *Training and Development Journal*, **21,** 6, 1967.

REVANS, R. W. Action Learning—A Management Development Program, *Personnel Review*, autumn 1972.

REVANS, R. W. Managers as Catalysts, *Personnel Management*, **2,** Nov. 1970.

REVANS, R. W. *The Theory of Practice in Management*, MacDonald, 1966.

REYNOLDS, M. The Effects of Training Interventions on Management Relationships, *European Training*, Jan. 1972.

RICE, A. K. *Learning for Leadership*, Tavistock, 1965.

RIGG, R. P. *Audiovisual Aids and Techniques in Managerial and Supervisory Training*, Hamish Hamilton, 1969.

ROBERTS, T. J. *Developing Effective Managers*, Institute of Personnel Management, 1967.

ROBERTS, T. J. Training Managers to Make Decisions: The In-basket Method, *Personnel*, **42,** 5, Sept.–Oct. 1965.

Role of Trainer and Manager in Situational Management Training, *Industrial and Commercial Training*, Jan. 1972.

ROOD, A. *Realising your Executive Potential: Job Strategy for the Management Career Man*, McGraw-Hill, 1965.

ROTHSCHILD, W. E. The CASE Approach—A Valuable Aid for Management Development, *California Management Review*, Oct.–Dec. 1971.

SALBERG, J.-F. Une Formation Personnelle pour les Cadres, *Chefs*, Apr. 1972.

SAMPSON, R. C. *Managing the Managers: A Realistic Approach to Applying the Behavioural Sciences*, McGraw-Hill, 1965.

SCHEUPLEIN, H. Guiding Factors for the Group Work in Management Training and Business Management, *Management International Review*, **2,** 1966.

SCHMUCKLER, E. The Establishment of a Management Development Programme, *Personnel Journal*, Oct. 1971.

SCHWARTZ, F. C., STILWELL, W. P., and SCANLAN, B. K. Effects of Management Development on Management Behaviour and Subordinate Perception, *Training and Development Journal*, **22,** 4 and 5, 1968.

Sensitivity Training in Action, *Industrial and Commercial Training*, Jan. 1972.

SHETTY, Y. K. Ownership, Size, Technology and Management Development: A Comparative Analysis, *Academy of Management Journal*, **14.** Dec. 1971.

SIEGAL, G. B. Management Development and the Instability of Skills, A Strategy, *Public Personnel Review*, **30,** 1.

SINGER, E. Overlooking Coaching, *Personnel Management*, **1,** 7, 1969.

SLEVIN, D. P. Assessment Center: Breakthrough in Management Appraisal and Development, *Personnel Journal*, **51,** Apr. 1972.

SMITH, E. P. *The Manager as an Action-Centred Leader*, Industrial Society, 1969.

Social and Cultural Factors in Management Development, *International Labour Review*, **94,** 2, 1966 (whole issue).

SORENSON, P. F. Management Development Under Conditions of Change, Ph.D. thesis, Illinois Institute of Technology, 1971.

SPALTON, L. M. *Management Development and the Industrial Training Boards*, British Institute of Management, 1968.

SPEAR, H. C. *Training for Management: Today's Top Priority*, Institute of Personnel Management, 1971.

619

STEWART, V. and STEWART, A. Beginning Appraisal Training, *Industrial Training International*, July 1972.

STILL, M. Determinants of Management Training Policies, *Journal of Business Policy*, summer 1972.

STOLZ, R. K. Executive Development: New Perspective, *Harvard Business Review*, May–June 1966.

TANNEHILL, R. E. *Motivation and Management Development*, Auerbach, Princeton, 1970.

TERRY, P. and KNIBBS, J. Reality-centred Management Development, *Industrial Training International*, **5**, 8 and 9, 1970.

THOMPSON, N. Creating a Management Style, *Industrial and Commercial Training*, **2**, 10, 1970.

THOMPSON, N. Do It Yourself Management Training, *Industrial Society*, Mar.–Apr. 1971.

THORLEY, S. Management Training—Is It Worth It? *Personnel Management*, Jan. 1971.

TIMBERS, E. Motivating Managerial Self-Development, *Training Directors Journal*, July 1965.

TOFFIN, J. Formation: Générosité Bien Ordonnée, *Informations*, 27 Mar. 1972.

TOSI, H. and HOUSE, R. Continuing Management Development Beyond the Classroom, *Business Horizons*, **9**, 2, 1966.

Training for Management, *Bankers Magazine*, Aug. 1966.

Trends in Management and Management Training, *Industrial Training International*, **1**, 9, 1966.

TRUTTER, J. T. Playing Management Improvement for Keeps, *Management Review*, **61**, Apr. 1972.

United States Civil Service Commission, *Self Development Aids for Supervisors and Middle Managers*, Civil Service Commission, Washington, 1970.

VATIER, R. La Période Sauvage de la Formation Continue, *Management*, Feb. 1972.

VETTER, E. V. Manpower Planning for High Talent Personnel, University of Michigan, Graduate School of Business Administration, 1967.

WAKELY, J. H. and SHAW, M. E. Management Training—An Integrated Approach, *Training Directors Journal*, **19**, 7, 1965.

WERNHAM, R. Getting the Measure of Management Training, *Personnel Management*, Mar. 1972.

WEST, J. P. and SCHROEDER, K. V. Management Development, *Training and Development Journal*, **22**, 12, 1968.

WILCE, H. Managers Learn How to Lead, *International Management*, July 1971.

WILLINGS, D. R. *How to Use the Case Study in Training for Decision Making*, Business Publications, 1968.

WILSON, A. T. M. Some Sociological Aspects of Systematic Management Development, *Journal of Management Studies*, Feb. 1966.

WILSON, J. E., MULLEN, D. P., and MORTON, R. Sensitivity Training for Individual Growth—Team Training of Organisational Development? *Training and Development Journal*, Jan. 1968.

WILSON, S. R. Incentive Approach to Executive Development, *Business Horizons*, **15**, 24, Apr. 1972.

WINDSOR, J. B. Training for Whom or What? *Industrial Training International*, **4**, 9, Sept. 1969.

WOODWARD, J. Organizational Change and Management Development, *Personnel Practice Bulletin*, Sept. 1967.

WREN, W. H. Management Development Through Planned Job Transfer, *Factory Management*, Oct. 1970.

YOUNG, J. P. Practical Techniques of Executive Development and Advancement, Sydney, Australia, Rydges Business Journal, 1965.

ZANER, R. Action Research in Management Development, *Training and Development Journal*, **22**, 6, June 1968.

2. Management Development and Training in Particular Areas of Management Activity

BEAHAN, P. H. A Case of the Offensive, *BACIE Journal*, **21**, 4, Dec. 1967 (Management Training in the Hospital Service).

BERNIKLAU, V. V. *Management Development of Scientists and Engineers in the Federal Government: An Analysis of Basic Behavioral and Systems Considerations*, National Technical Information Service, Springfield, Virginia, 1970.

Bettignies, H. C. de and Weinshall, T. D. Formation des Cadres pour les Sociétés Multinationales, *Management International Review*, **11**, 4 and 5, 1971.

Bowman, D. O. Executive Development for Public Utilities, *Public Utilities Fortnightly*, **89**, 15 Mar. 1972.

Brenner, M. H. Management Development for Women, *Personnel Journal*, **51**, Mar. 1972.

Business International Corporation, *Developing Management for the Worldwide Enterprise*, BIC, New York, 1965.

Byars, L. L. Management Training in Public Utilities, *Public Utilities Fortnightly*, **88**, 9 Dec. 1971.

Civil Service Department, Training and Education Division, *Civil Service Training*, 1967–1968, HMSO, 1969.

Dawson, V. Aspro's Effective Executives, *Personnel*, **1**, 12, 1968 (Aspro's Management Development Scheme).

Department of Employment, *Training for Marketing*, HMSO, 1972.

Department of Employment, *Training for Purchasing and Supply*, HMSO, 1972.

Department of Employment, *Training for Transport and Physical Distribution*, HMSO, 1972.

Department of Employment, *Training of Training Officers: Introductory Courses*, HMSO, 1966.

Department of Employment, *Training of Training Officers: Pattern for the Future*, HMSO, 1967.

Dunsire, A. and Alderman, R. K. *Management Training Survey: A Report on the Association of Municipal Corporations*, Association of Municipal Corporations, 1967.

Ford Motor Co. Ltd. *Management Development*, Ford, 1965.

Hill, P. *Towards a New Philosophy of Management: A Study of the Company Development Programme at Shell UK Ltd*, Gower Press, 1971.

Hurley, F. G. *Training Retail Managers: A Symposium*, Institute of Personnel Management, 1971.

Institute of Bankers. *Bank Management—Recruitment and Training*, 1969.

Jefford, R. E. Training in Management and Supervision for Staff of the Hospital Service in England and Wales, Ministry of Health, 1967 (unpublished report).

Jordan, H. The Training of Training Officers—An Educational Viewpoint, *BACIE Journal*, **22**, 2, June 1968.

Keeling, D. Central Training in the Civil Service, *Public Administration*, spring 1972.

Keeling, D. The Development of Central Training in the Civil Service, *Public Administration*, spring 1971.

Leonard, W. M. Management Training at AMPOL, *Personnel Practice Bulletin*, Mar. 1966.

Lord, D. Uniroyal Trains Managers by Moving them Around, *International Management*, Apr. 1972.

National Economic Development Office, *Management Training in the Distributive Trades*, HMSO, 1969.

National Health Service, *A Report by the National Staff Committee on Recruitment and Management Development of Administrative Staff in the Hospital Service*, 1967.

Oates, D. Littlewoods Gears Its Managers to a New Era, *International Management*, **26**, Nov. 1971.

Passett, B. A. *Leadership Development for the Public Services*, Gulf, Houston, Texas, 1971.

Sherwood, F. P. *Selected Papers: Executive Development and the Federal Executive Institute*, Civil Service Commission, Washington, 1971.

Smith, B. C. and Stanyer, J. Administration Developments in 1970, *Public Administration*, winter 1971 (Civil Service and Local Government).

Stait, N. H. Management Training and the Smaller Company, *Industrial and Commercial Training*, July 1972.

Taylor, N. *Selecting and Training the Training Officer*, Institute of Personnel Management, 1966.

Treasury. *Management Training in the Civil Service: Report of a Working Party*, HMSO, 1967.

Turner, B. T. *Management Training for Engineers*, Business Books, 1969.

Turner, B. T. Production Management Training, *Production Engineer*, **46**, 1, 1967.

United States Civil Service Commission, Bureau of Training, *Employees Training in the Federal Service, Fiscal Year* 1971. Washington, 1972.

United States Department of Transportation, *Management Development Study*, Washington, 1970.

VAN DER VLIET, J. A. Management Development in an International Company, *Works Management*, **19**, 3, 1966.

WEINSHALL, T. D. Formation des Cadres pour les Sociétés Multinationales, *Management International Review*, **2** and **3**, 1971.

3. Management Development and Training for New Recruits and Junior Managers

BAILEY, M. Laying the Foundations of a Graduate's Career, *Industrial Society*, July-1971.

BARRY, A. Developing Tomorrow's Managers, *Personnel Magazine*, Jan. 1966.

BYHAM, W. C. Assessment Centres for Spotting Future Managers, *Harvard Business Review*, July–Aug. 1970.

BYHAM, W. C. Assessment Centres: The Place for Picking Management Potential, *European Business*, **35**, July–Sept. 1972.

DRUCKER, P. F. *Symposium on Preparing Tomorrow's Business Leaders Today*, Prentice-Hall, 1969.

EVANS, R. W. The Management Apprentice, *Management Decision*, winter 1967.

FITZGERALD, T. H. and CARLSON, H. C. Management Potential: Early Recognition and Development, *California Management Review*, **14**, winter 1971.

FLOOD, R. J. L. The Graduate Problem, *CBI Review*, June 1972.

HENEMAN, H. G. Developing Tomorrow's Managers Today, *SAM Advanced Management Journal*, Oct. 1970.

KURILOFF, A. H. Identifying Leadership Potential for Management, *Personnel Administration*, **30**, 6, 1967.

LESTER, T. The Reluctant Graduate, *Management Today*, Nov. 1970.

LUSHER, B. Graduates: The Raw Material, *Industrial Society*, Oct. 1971.

MANSFIELD, R. Inducting Graduates in Industry, *Management Decision*, summer 1972.

MUSE, W. R. Identification and Development of Tomorrow's Managers, *Personnel Journal*, Jan. 1972.

National Economic Development Council. *Management Recruitment and Development*, HMSO, 1965.

REVANS, R. W. The Management Apprentice, *Management International Review*, **8**, 6, 1968.

RODGERS, R. P. Developing Young Managers: An Individualized Program, *Personnel*, Nov.–Dec. 1971.

ROGERS, T. P. G. and WILLIAMS, P. *The Recruitment and Training of Graduates*, Institute of Personnel Management, 1971.

SKERTCHLY, A. R. B. *Tomorrow's Managers*, Staples Press, 1968.

SORRELL, M. Finding Tomorrow's Managers, *Management Today*, Dec. 1966.

STESSIN, L. and RODGERS, F. P. Developing Young Managers, *Personnel*, Nov.–Dec. 1971.

4. Management Development and Training for Senior Managers

ANDREWS, K. There Are Some Tricks Only Old Dogs Can Learn, *Columbia Journal of World Business*, **1**, 4, 1966.

GLICKMAN, A. S. *Top Management Development and Succession: An Exploratory Study*, Collier-Macmillan, 1968.

GREEN, W. H. Developing Key Personnel, *Management Accounting*, **53**, June 1972.

GWILT, J. R. Leadership and the Succession, *Personnel Management*, **47**, 371, Mar. 1965.

HICKS, R. L. Developing the Top Management Group in a Total Systems Organization, *Personnel Journal*, **50**, Sept. 1971.

RAPOPORT, R. N. *Mid-career Development: Research Perspectives on a Developmental Community for Senior Administrators*, Tavistock, 1970.

SOFER, C. *Men in Mid-career: A Study of British Managers and Technical Specialists*, Cambridge University Press, 1970.

WILLIAMS, A. P. O. The Managerial Grid: Phase Two, Case Study of a Top Management Team, *Occupational Psychology*, **45**, 3 and 4, 1971.

5. Management Education and the Business Schools

ALBERT, P. and JACQUELIN, P. Les Seminaires au Banc d'Essai, *Management*, Dec. 1971.

American Association of Collegiate Schools of Business, Annual Meeting 1969, *Proceedings: Entrepreneurship and the Dynamics of the Educational Process*, 1969.

ARNDT, H.-J. Weiterbildung wirtschaftlicher Führungskräfte an der Universität, Econ, Düsseldorf, 1968.

BAKER, E. I. Business Studies—Past, Present and Future, *BACIE Journal*, June 1966.

BAKER, H. C. The Role of the Universities in Management Education, *Commerce*, Oct. 1969.

BERGER, F. The Truth about MBA's, *European Business*, 29, spring 1971.

BERRY, D. F. *Gardens and Graveyards in Management Education*, (research paper no. 56), INSEAD, Fontainbleau, 1971.

BLACK, S. Thoughts on Management Education, *Industrial Relations Journal*, winter 1971.

BRIDENNE, A. and TEJTEL, M. Cultural Revolution in Business Schools, *European Business*, 36, winter 1972.

British Institute of Management, *Business School Programmes: The Requirements of British Manufacturing Industry* (by T. Owen *et. al.*), 1971.

British Institute of Management, *Management Courses in the United Kingdom: A Select Guide*, Management Publications, 1970.

British Institute of Management, *Management Education in the 1970's*, Management Publications, 1970.

BURGOYNE, J. Business Schools and the Development of Managerial Attitudes, *Management Decision*, summer 1972.

Business Graduates Association, *British Industry's Attitudes to Business Graduates and Business Schools*, Business Graduates Association, 1971.

Business Graduates Association, *The Business Graduate in Britain*, Business Graduates Association, 1968.

CARSON, D. Problem Schools of Management, *Management Today*, Aug. 1967.

CARSON, I. Business School with Big Ambitions, *International Management*, May 1971.

CHERRINGTON, P. Management Education in Britain, *Adult Education*, **38**, 1, May 1965.

CHERRINGTON, P. *Wider Objectives in Management Education*, Industrial Education and Research Foundation, Occasional paper no. 8, 1970.

COLEMAN, R. W. Current Conflicts and Problems in Collegiate Schools of Business, *Rivista Internazionale di Scienze Economiche e Commerciali*, **17**, 1970, pp. 237–57.

Consultative Council of Professional Management Organisations, *Professional Management Education and Training*, Consultative Council of Professional Management Organisation, 1968.

Conference on Education for International Business, *Business Schools and the Challenge of International Business* (Edited by S. A. Zeff), Tulane University Graduate School of Business and Administration, New Orleans, 1967.

CORLETT, E. N. Some Problems of Management Education in Britain and a Proposed Solution, *Management International*, **6**, 1965.

DANIEL, W. W. *Business Education at 18+: A Survey of HND Business Studies*, Political and Economic Planning, 1971.

DARLINGTON, T. I. G. Behind the Diploma in Management Studies, *Personnel Magazine*, Apr. 1967.

DIEHL, P. Les Quatorze Semaines Sabbatiques du PDM d'Harvard, *Hommes et Commerce*, May 1972.

DUDLEY, P. D. Management Studies, *Trends in Education*, **13**, Jan. 1969.

DUNN, M. *Industrial Society*, **53**, Aug. 1971 (training of executive secretaries at Strathclyde University School of Business and Administration).

EDWARDS, R. *Universities and the World of Business*, British Institute of Management, 1969.

FARNSWORTH, T. After the Course is Over: Dynamism of Despair, *Personnel and Training Management*, Feb. 1969.

FARNSWORTH, T. How to Select External Courses, *Industrial and Commercial Training*, **2**, 6, June 1970.

Foundation for Management Education, *Education for Management: A Review of the Diploma in Management Studies*, Foundation for Management Education, 1968.

GARBUTT, D. The Wilderness of Mirrors: Education for Management, *Accountant*, 20 Jan. 1972.

GARRATT, R. Towards a Reform of Management Education, *Management Education*, May 1972.

GILBERT, O. *Arbeitsstudium und Management*, I. H. Sauer Verlag, Heidelberg, 1971.

GOLD, B. Adjusting Teaching Methods to Changing Objectives in Management Education, *Management International Review*, **1**, 1966.

GOLD, B. Re-organising Management Education: A Case Study, *Journal of Management Studies*, **2**, 1, 1965.

GOLDMAN, M. Marketing Education: The Real Needs of Business, *Advertising Quarterly*, autumn 1971.

GOODING, J. 14 Weak Pressure Cooker for Tomorrow's Top Managers, *Fortune*, **85**, Feb. 1972 (Harvard's management development programme).

GORE, T. Management Education—The Need for a Reappraisal, *Industrial and Commercial Training*, Jan. 1972.

GREGOIRE, R. The University Teaching of Social Sciences: Business Management, UNESCO, 1966.

GRUBEL, H. G. The MBA Education Myth, *Journal of Business*, **42**, 1969, pp. 42–9.

HAGUE, D. C. *What Should the Business Schools Teach?* Manchester Statistical Society, 1965.

HALL, N. *Academic Freedom in Management Education*, British Institute of Management, 1966.

HANDY, C. B. Exploding the Management Education Myth, *European Business*, spring 1971.

HARVEY, N. Comparing Package Management Training Courses, *Industrial and Commercial Training*, **3**, 10, Oct. 1971.

HENDERSON, A. *Policies for Management Education*, Association of Teachers of Management, Occasional paper no. 3, Blackwell, 1966.

HENDERSON, A. Private Network, *Management Education and Development*, **2**, 3, Jan. 1972 (establishment, by the Association of Teachers of Management, of a network for the exchange of ideas on management education and development).

HESTER, M. US Business Schools: A Cautionary Tale, *Management Decision*, spring 1968.

HILL, A. H. C. Teaching Business Concepts—A Businessman's View in Brief, *Management Education and Development*, July 1971.

Irish Management Institute, *Education and Training for Management*, Dublin, 1971.

JONES, D. Management Education: A Few of the Facts, *Management Education and Development*, Aug. 1972.

KEMPNER, T. *A Guide to the Study of Management*, Association of Teachers of Management, Occasional paper no. 6, Blackwell, 1969.

LIANDER, B. *International Study of Marketing Education*, International Marketing Federation, 1967.

LING, C. C. *A Seminar for New Deans*, series II, American Association of Collegiate Schools of Business, St. Louis, Missouri, 1970.

LIVINGSTONE, J. S. Myth of the Well-educated Manager, *Harvard Business Review*, **49**, Jan.–Feb. 1971.

LOASBY, B. J. The Substance of Management Education, *District Bank Review*, 160, Dec. 1966.

LORD, D. Hiring and Handling Business Graduates, *International Management*, **27**, Feb. 1972.

LOWE, P. M. *Business Studies Courses for the Sixth-form Leaver*, Careers Research and Advisory Centre, 1965.

LYNN, R. *The Universities and the Business Community*, Industrial Education and Research Foundation, 1969.

MCCLELLAND, W. G. Myth Squared, *Management Education and Development*, Oct. 1971 (Myth of the Well-Educated Manager, see Livingstone above).

MCLENNAN, K. Education and Training for Managerial Jobs, *American Journal of Economics and Sociology*, **28**, 1969, pp. 423–36.

MADISON, R. *Institute for Minority Business Education: Final Report*, Washington, Howard University, 1972.

Management Education Review Conference, London, 1970, *Management Education in the 1970's*, British Institute of Management, 1970.

MANN, J. *Management's Responsibility for Management Education* (Fourth Urwick Lecture), British Institute of Management, 1968.

MANT, A. Management Teaching's New Horizons, *Management Today*, Nov. 1972.

MARGERISON, C. Management Education—Its Content and Presentation, *Management Decision*, summer 1972.

MARRIAN, J. Marketing Education: A Review, *Marketing*, May 1971.

MAXWELL, S. R. The Business School: Strengths and Weaknesses, *Journal of Business Policy*, autumn 1971.

MINER, J. B. *Studies in Management Education*, Springer, New York, 1965.

MORRIS, J. F. Management Training at Manchester, *Management Decision*, **2**, 4, winter 1968.

MOSSON, T. M. Business Schools in Britain, *Management Education and Development*, **3**, 1, 1972.

MOSSON, T. M. *Teaching the Process of Management*, Harrap, 1967.

MUSGRAVE, P. W. The Educational Profiles of Management in Two British Iron and Steel Companies, with some comparisons, National and International, *British Journal of Industrial Relations*, **4**, 1966, pp. 201–11.

National Economic Development Office, *Survey of Student Finance on Full-time Postgraduate Type Management Courses* (by D. G. Clark), NEDO, 1968.

National Economic Development Office, Management Education, Training and Development Committee, *Education for Management: A Study of Resources* (by D. Jones, K. Ball, and M. Shellens), HMSO, 1972.

National Economic Development Office, Management Education, Training and Development Committee, First Report, NEDO, 1961.

National Economic Development Office, Management Education, Training and Development Committee, Second Report, NEDO, 1971.

National Economic Development Office, Management Education, Training and Development Committee, First Report on the Supply of Teachers for Management Education, NEDO, 1970.

National Economic Development Office, Management Education, Training and Development Committee, Second Report on the Supply of Teachers for Management Education, NEDO, 1972.

National Economic Development Office, Management Education, Training and Development Committee, *Management Education in the 1970's: Growth and Issues* (by H. B. Rose), HMSO, 1970.

National Economic Development Office, Management Education, Training and Development Committee, *Marketing Education in the UK*, NEDO, 1971.

Organisation for Economic Cooperation and Development, Statements delivered at the Symposium on Management Education, 2 and 3 June 1971, Paris, OECD, 1972.

OTTESON, S. F. *Internationalising the Traditional Business Curriculum in Accounting, Business Policy, Finance and Marketing*, Indiana University Graduate School of Business, Bureau of Business Research, 1968.

PACK, L. *Ausbildung und weiterbildung von Führungskräften an amerikanischen und deutschen Universitäten*, Gabler Verlag, Wiesbaden, 1969.

PETERSON, R. B. Chief Executive Attitudes Towards Education: An International Comparison, *Journal of Management Studies*, Feb. 1972.

PITFIELD, M. and REES, F. M. Can Team Teaching Aid the Integration of Management Education? *Management Education and Development*, Aug. 1972.

PUGH, D. *The Academic Teaching of Management*, Association of Teachers of Management, Occasional paper no. 4, Blackwell, 1966.

QUARTANO, R. Attitudes of British Business: The BGA Survey, *Business Graduate*, **1**, 5, Oct. 1971.

REID, W. Rethinking the Business Schools, *Management Today*, June 1971.

REVANS, R. W. *Developing Effective Managers: A New Approach to Business Education*, Longman, 1971.

REYNOLDS, M. Aiming for Relevance in Management Courses, *Personnel Management*, Feb. 1972.

ROBERTS, K. The Emergence of a British Harvard, *Personnel and Training Management*, Jan. 1968.

ROBERTSON, A. Business Schools—Is the Backlash Justified? *Management Decision*, **4**, 3, 1970.

Role for Industry in Management Education, *Personnel Management*, Jan. 1972.

RYAN, D. Management Education—Why? *Management*, Nov. 1971.

SCHEIN, E. H. Attitude Change During Management Education, *Administrative Science Quarterly*, **11**, Mar. 1967.

SCHUTTE, T. F. *A Directory for Graduate Education in Marketing*, American Marketing Association, New York, 1968.

SIMMONDS, K. Businessmen in Business Schools, *Management Today*, Oct. 1971.

SIMONDS, R. H. College Majors, Grades versus Business Success, *Business Topics*, **14**, summer 1966.

SIMS, G. D. and BLOODWORTH, C. G. University/Industry Partnership, *Trends in Education*, **13**, Jan. 1969.

625

SMALLBONE, D. W. Developments in Marketing Education, *Vocational Aspect*, **17**, 38, 1965.
SPIEGBERG, A. Business Schools Under Fire, *Chemistry and Industry*, **29**, 17 July 1971.
STUART, C. *Education for Business Management*, Pergamon, 1967.
SWANSON, E. A. *New Media in Teaching the Business Subjects*, National Business Education Association, Washington, 1965.
TAYLOR, B. A Seller's Market for Management Education in Britain? *Management Decision*, summer 1967.
TONNE, H. A., POPHAM, E. L., and FREEMAN, M. H. Methods of Teaching Business Subjects, McGraw-Hill, 1965.
Tulane University Graduate School of Business Education, *Business Schools and the Challenge of International Business*, papers presented at the Conference on Education for International Business, 1968.
VANCE, S. C. Higher Education for the Executive Elite, *California Management Review*, **8**, summer 1966.
VIZZA, R. F. A Study of the Education and Formal Management Training of Chief Sales Executives of Large Industrial Goods Firms, Ph.D. thesis, New York University Graduate School of Business Administration, 1967.
WHEATCROFT, M. *The Revolution in British Management Education*, Pitman, 1970.
WHEELAN, T. H. The Market's View of the MBA, *Business Quarterly*, **35**, winter 1970.
WHEELER, G. E. Present Position of Courses for Managers, *Works Management*, Oct. 1970.
WHITAKER, G. *T-Group Training: Group Dynamics in Management Education*, Association of Teachers of Management, Occasional paper no. 2, Blackwell, 1965.
WILLIAMS, E. and MARSH, P. Sandwich Course in Management, *Industrial and Commercial Training*, Jan. 1972.
WILLIG, J.-C. Business School Graduates, *European Business*, autumn 1970.
WILLIG, J.-C. Send the Bosses Back to School, Complain Young MBA's, *European Business*, **28**, winter 1970.
WINGO, W. *Pattern for Success*, World's Work, 1968 (Harvard Graduate School of Business Administration's advanced management programme).
YODER, D. Business Schools: The Academic Smorgasbord, *Personnel Administrator*, Mar.–Apr. 1972.
ZALAZNICK, S. The MBA—The Man, The Myth and The Method, *Fortune*, **77**, May 1968.
ZOLL, A. Z. *Dynamic Management Education*, Addison-Wesley, 1969.

6. Management Development, Training, and Education in Countries Other than the United Kingdom and the United States

ADLER, J. and CHERRINGTON, P. *Management Education in West Germany: A Short Study of Post Experience Courses made in 1965–6*, Administrative Staff College, 1966.
AGARWALA, A. N. *Education for Business in a Developing Society*, Michigan State University Institute for International Business and Economic Development Studies, 1969.
ARNDT, H.-J. and FASSBENDER, S. *Management-weiterbildung im betrieb: erfahrung in Feldstudien in Deutschland*, F. Knapp Verlag, Frankfurt, 1971.
Centre d'Etudes Industrielles, *Doctoral Programs in Nine European Countries: A Survey*, Geneva, CEI, 1970.
DOUGIER, H. From Confusion to Fusion: Assessing Management Education in Europe, *European Business*, Oct. 1969.
European Association of Management Training Centres, *A Handbook of the Association and Its Member Centres*, Brussels, 1970.
European Association of Management Training Centres, *Management Training Programmes Organised by Member Countries*, Brussels, 1970.
EVANS-VAUGHAN, G. F. *Management Education in Spain*, Administrative Staff College, 1968.
EVANS-VAUGHAN, G. F. *Management Education in the Netherlands*, Administrative Staff College, 1966.
INOUE, K. La Formation Interentreprises au Japon, *Revue Internationale du Travail*, July 1968.
LESTER, T. Making German Managers, *Management Today*, Feb. 1971.
Management Centre Europe, *Attitudes of European Managers Towards Their Job and Towards Management Training*, The Centre, 1972.
Managers Soviétiques à l'École Capitaliste, *Problèmes Economiques*, 16 Sept. 1971.

626

Mosson, T. M. *Management Education in Five European Countries*, Business Publications, 1965 (Belgium, France, Italy, Spain, and the UK).

Ormsby, G. A. G. *Management Education in Belgium*, Administrative Staff College, 1965.

Revans, R. W. *Final Report of the Senior Research Fellowship*, 1965–68, European Association of Management Training Centres, Brussels, 1968.

Richman, B. *Management Development and Education in the Soviet Union*, Michigan State University Graduate School of Business and Administration, 1967.

Smith, H. Management Development in 'New' Countries: Perspectives from Russia and America, *Management International*, 5, 1966.

Summerfield, P. J. Management Training in Europe Today, *Works Management*, May 1968.

Wall, A. Europe's Business Schools Under Fire, *International Management*, May 1968.

Willatt, N. Europe's New Management Medicine, *Management Today*, Oct. 1972 (deals with European business schools).

Willig, J.-C. Organizational Man or Entrepreneur: Europe's 'Business School' Manager, *European Business*, 27, autumn 1970.

7. Evaluation of Management Development, Training, and Education

Andrews, K. R. *The Effectiveness of University Management Development Programmes*, Graduate School of Business Administration, Harvard University, 1966.

Belasco, J. A. Training as a Change Agent: A Constructive Evaluation, Ph.D. thesis, Cornell University, 1967.

Catalanello, R. F. and Kirkpatrick, D. L. Evaluating Training Programs—The State of the Art, *Training and Development Journal*, May 1968.

Cone, P. R. and McKinney, R. N. Management Development Can Be More Effective, *California Management Review*, 14, spring 1972.

Cowell, D. An Approach to the Evaluation of Short Post-experience Courses in Marketing, *European Journal of Marketing*, spring 1972.

Cowell, D. Evaluating the Effectiveness of Management Courses, *European Training*, Jan. 1972.

Deutzer, B. A. Measuring the Effectiveness of a Selected Management Development Program, Ph.D. thesis, Ohio State University, 1967.

Ference, T. P. and Ritti, R. R. Evaluating the Functions of Management Education, *Personnel Journal*, 49, Aug. 1970.

Ferrari, S. The Open Problem of Management Training Evaluation, *Management International Review*, 4 and 5, 1970.

Hand, H. H. The Mystery of Executive Education: Effectiveness Requires Evaluation, *Business Horizons*, June 1971.

Harmon, F. L. and Glickman, A. S. Managerial Training: Reinforcement Through Evaluation, *Public Personnel Review*, Oct. 1965.

Hepworth, A. Evaluation Research in Perspective, *Management Education*, May 1972.

Hesseling, P. *Strategy of Evaluation Research in the Field of Supervisory and Management Training*, Van Gorcum, Assen, Netherlands, 1966.

Jerkedal, A. *Top Management Education: An Evaluation Study*, Swedish Council for Personnel Administration, Stockholm, 1967.

Kohn, V. and Parker, T. C. *Management Development and Program Evaluation: Partners in Promoting Managerial Effectiveness*, American Foundation for Management Research, New York, 1969.

Kohn, V. and Parker, T. C. Some Guidelines for Evaluating Management Development Seminars, *Training and Development Journal*, 23, 7, July 1969.

Luthans, F. Evidence on the Validity of Management Education, *Academy of Management Journal*, 12, Dec. 1969.

MacCallum, K. Appraisal and Its Place in Management Development, *Industrial Training International*, 6, 3, Mar. 1971.

MacNair, J. S. C. Evaluation of Management Training, *Management Education and Development*, Dec. 1970.

Revans, R. W. The Evaluation of Management Courses, *Bulletin of the Association of Teachers of Management*, June 1966.

Rose, H. C. A Plan for Training Evaluation, *Training and Development Journal*, May 1968.

SPAUTZ, M. E. A Survey of the Effectiveness of Management Development Programs, Civil Service Commission, Washington, 1971.

STIEFEL, R. T. Die Evaluierung in der Management-Schulung, *Unternehmung*, July–Sept. 1971.

THORLEY, S. Evaluating an In-company Management Training Program, *Training and Development Journal*, **23**, 9, Sept. 1969.

THORLEY, S. Evaluating In-company Management Training by Assessing the Performance of Groups, *Training Officer*, **7**, 3, Mar. 1971.

TRACEY, W. R. *Evaluating Training and Development Systems*, American Management Association, New York, 1969.

WARR, P., BIRD, M., and RACKHAM, N. *Evaluation of Management Training: A Practical Framework*, Gower Press, 1970.

WHITELAW, M. *The Evaluation of Management Training: A Review*, Institute of Personnel Management, 1972.

WHITELAW, M. The Methodology of the Evaluation of Management Training, M.Sc. thesis, University of Bradford, 1971.

WILLIAMS, R. Can We Evaluate Management Training? *Industrial Training International*, **4**, 3, Mar. 1969.

WILLIAMS, R. and BERGER, M. The Evaluation of Management Development, *Management Education and Development*, May 1972.

8. Bibliographies

Department of Employment, *Glossary of Training Terms*, HMSO, 1971.

Department of Employment, *Training Research Register*, HMSO (annual).

Eric Clearing House on Adult Education, *Management Development and Supervisory Training*, Current information sources no. 26, ECH, Syracuse University, New York, 1969.

Eric Clearing House on Adult Education, *Management Development*, Current information sources, ECH, Syracuse University, New York, 1968.

Institute of Personnel Management, *Personnel Management—A Bibliography*, Institute of Personnel Management, 1969.

KOHN, V. *A Selected Bibliography on Evaluation of Management Training and Development Programs*, American Foundation for Management Research, New York, 1969.

PERRY, P. J. C. *BACIE Bibliography*, 1960–1970, British Association for Commercial and Industrial Education, 1971.

Index

Abilities, resourcefulness, 110–12
Absenteeism, 378, 429, 458
Abstract games, 221
Abstracting services, in training centres, 570
Acceleration, manager development, 13
Accountability of superior, in MBO, 406
Accounts, in entrepreneurial courses, 145–6
Achievement, need to feel, 104, 107
Action, urge towards, 210
Action-Centred Leadership (ACL), Chapter 30
  and manager development, 445–6
  and mergers, 444, 445, 446
  and MBO, 444, 445
  and organization development, 444–5
  assessment in, 451
  assessment of, 452
  case studies, 451
  course content, 450
  development programme, 450–1
  exercises, 451
  gains from, 446
  group needs, 448–50
  need for training, 443–5
  objectives, 450–1
  programmes, 452–3
  results, 452
  role, 445
  tutor's role, 451
Action learning projects, Chapter 15
  essentials of learning, 204–6, 212
  operational model, 211–12
  programme, 207, 212
  theory into practice, 207–10
Activities and skills, diagram, 176
Adair, John, 444, 445, 453
Adjournments, industrial relations, 362
Administrative constraints, 510
  matrix, 523
Administrative Staff College, Henley, Chapter 14
Administrative Staff College of India, 151
Administrative trainee programme, Civil Service, 531–2
Administrator development, 151
Administrator and manager contrasted, 150–1
Admirable Crichton, The, 448

Adult education, 12
Advertising for job applicants, 92
Advisers (*see* Consultants; MBO Advisers)
Affective changes in learning, 183
Africa, influences on its development, 151–2
Age of managers, 99–101
  effect, in small firms, 137
Age (*see also* Younger generation)
Age of Discontinuity, 110
Agents, job filling, 92
Agreements, industrial (*see* Negotiation)
Agricultural method, of selection, 86
Aid, foreign, 152, 156
Alexander the Great, 126
Alienation, sources of, 90
Alternatives, in decision making, 318–9
Ambition, 111, 112
America (*see* United States)
American Board of Professional Psychology, 258
American Group Psychotherapy Association, 243
American Management Association, 44, 49, 219
American Telephone and Telegraph Co (AT&T), 43, 44, 64, 67, 73
Analysis, life goals, 353–4
  of key issues, MBO, 414
  of tasks, approach to management education, 174–5
Analytical skills, in management, 172
  lack, in managers, 487
Andretta, Thomas, 53, 62
Anstey, E., 94, 98
Anthropologists, in organization development, 372
Anthropology, 171
Apathy to business, factor in planning, 330
Appley, L. A., 13, 21
Applicants for jobs, obtaining, 92, 94, 106
Application forms, of candidates, 94
  use in executive assessment, 45
Appointments (*see* Applicants for jobs)
Appraisal: component of management development, 36
  concept, in MBO, 406
  diagram, 37

Appraisal:—*cont.*
  future of, 549
  of future managers, 13, 19–20
Appraisal interview simulation, 80
Appraisal systems, 486
Apprenticeships, 104, 184, 185
Aptitude tests, 95
Ardennes offensive, 219
Argyris, C., 129, 134, 381, 382, 384, 578
Aristotle, 432
Armed forces, and resourcefulness, 124–5
  business attitude to, 120
  groupings of staff, 529
  influence on developing countries, 151
  influence on syndicates, 191–2
  officer training, 43
Asch, S. E., 375–6, 383
Asia, influence on its development, 151–2
Asian Institute of Management, Philippines, 156
Asian Institute of Technology, Thailand, 156
Asian Productivity Organization, 152, 156
Assembly-line, and job enrichment, 438
Assessment: combination of methods, 49–50, 61
  in Action-Centred Leadership, 451
  of executive potential, Chapter 4
  of individuals, 41–2, 69–70
  promotion based on, 475
  techniques, 40–50, 51–61
    determination of, 42
Assessment centres, 43–4, 50, 53, 58, 64, Chapter 5
  accuracy, 64–5
  as training experience, 66–8
  choice of participants, 73
  costs, 68–9
  dimensions to be assessed, 73–6
  exercises, 76, 77, 78–80
  foundation, 70–1
  job levels, appropriate, 71–3
  nature, 63–4
  objectives, 70–1
  problems, 78
  small organizations, 69
Assessors, benefit of assessment centres, 66–7
  training of, 66–8, 71, 76
Assignments, individual, career planning, 120–1
Assumptions, need for information on, 334
Attack mechanisms, against organization development, 122
Attitude surveys: Barclays, 608–11
  case study, 607–13
  definition, 604
  developmental phase, 605–6
  in job enrichment, 436
  in management development, Chapter 41
  in organization development groups, 490
  in Organization Renewal, 459

  procedures, 605–7
  quantitative survey, 606–7
Attitudes, 175
  and communication training, 306
  add MBO, 408–10
  and management development, 7–8
  changes in, 7–8, 306, 374, 582
  development programme, 581
  diagrams, 176, 179
  factor in planning, 329
  international management education, 179–80
Audio-visual aids, and management, Chapter 18, 273–4
  defined, 262
  in case studies, 187
  know-how, 263–6
  nature, 262–3
  production, 266–7
  in sensitivity training, 241
  software, 264–5
  in syndicates, 202
  South Africa University, 289
  in training centres, 570–1
  types, 266–73
  value, 260–2, 265
  workshop, illustration, 264
Authentic relationships, sensitivity training, 243
Authority, factor in planning, 329–30
  in firms, 475, 511–12
  in managers, 210
  national differences, 6
Autocracy in small firms, 473–4

B & B electronics game, 78
Bach, 234
Back-up (*see* Support)
Background case, 186, 189
Background interview, assessment centres, 78
Balanced emphasis, in organizations, 507–8
  matrix, 522
Bales, R. F., 233, 375, 383
Bangladesh and management development, 152
Barclays Bank Ltd, attitude surveys, 607–13
Barnard, C. I., 406, 427
Barrie, J. M., 448
Bass, B. M., 46, 602
Battle games, 219
Beckhard, R., 373, 383
Beeching, Richard, Baron, 113
Beer, S., 119, 125
Behaviour: in communication training, 306
  individual, 376–7
  problems, and managers, 41
Behavioural changes, after O D courses, 491
Behavioural school of thought in management, 171
Behavioural sciences, areas of, 373
  conflict and resolution, 379–80

Behavioural sciences, areas of—*cont.*
  contribution to organization development, Chapter 26
  definition, 373
  individual behaviour, 376–7
  organization structure, 373–6
  organizations and change, 377–9
  reservations, 373
  techniques in organization development, 380–3
Behavioural sciences (*see also* Human relations)
Behavioural scientists, 46, 379–80, 430
Behavioural skills and international managers, 8
Belgian Inter-University Programme, 208–9, 213–15
Belgium, use of Revans model, 123
Bennis, W. G., 110, 248, 258
Biographical data forms, in assessment, 45, 50
Biographies, value of, 125, 142
Bird, Charles, 447
Blackboards, 189, 202, 267
Blake, R. R., 320, 373, 377, 381, 382, 384, 487
Blue Skies planning exercise, 282
Board of directors, and company training, 490, 495
  and planning, 336–7
  (*see also* Top management)
Body movement analysis, 94
Bonuses (*see* Financial incentives; Rewards)
Bos, A. H., 555, 562
Boulding, K., 379, 384
Brainstorming, 75
  in job enrichment, 436
Branch games, 221
Breakdown in organization, 119, 123
Bridge, contract, 220
Briefing, in MBO, 411
  of executives, 339
Brigham Young University, 343
Britain (*see* United Kingdom)
British colonial influence on developing countries, 151–2
Budgeting, 148
  for training, 593–5
  in entrepreneurial courses, 145–6
Budgets, need for information on, 336
Bureau of Internal Revenue, 54
Bureaucratic organizations, 475–6
Burma, management development in, 152
Bushido, 101
Business and family conflict, 474
Business analysis, 142–4, 145–6, 147
Business development and organizational change, 555–8
Business environment, future, 3–4
Business games (*see* Management games)
Business goals, life planning, 343
Business hierarch, 155

Business leadership, 277
  (*see also* Leadership)
Business results (*see* Results)
Business schools: bibliography, 623–6
Byham, W. C., 43, 62

Cadbury Bros Ltd, 473
Campbell, J. P., 40, 50, 61, 89, 98, 247, 258
Canada and organization renewal, Chapter 31
Candidate bank for appointments (PER), 94
Capabilities, need for information on, 335
Capital, lack in small firms, 137
Career counselling, 67, 107
Career development and resourcefulness, 112–9
Career development plan, and counselling, 107
Career planning, 119, 170, 545, 559
  attacks as bureaucratic, 109
  problems, 109–10
Career progression, 575
Careers, types, 113
Carter, C. F., 115, 125
Case history, compared with case study, 182
Case method in management training, Chapter 13
  (for headings *see* Management training syndicates)
Case studies: compared with case histories, 182
  audio-visual media, use of, 187
  development programme, 581
  in Action-Centred Leadership, 451
  in Life Goals Planning, 345–50, 357–8
  in management training, 185–90
  in Organization Renewal, 455–7
  in sensitivity training, 242
  in small firms, 476–9
  in South Africa University, 281, 284
  industrial relations, 365–8
Cash budgeting, 148
Cash planning, in entrepreneurial courses, 145–6
Caterpillar Company, 43
Cause-effect chain, 320
CCTV (*see* Television)
Central Management development service (*see* Management development service)
Central Training Council, 130
Centralization, 20, 556, 574, 580
  of decision-making, 15, 21, 137
Centre for Economic Development and Administration, Nepal, 151
Chain of command, 475
Chandler, A. D., 555, 562
Change, and MBO, 407, 408
  and Organization Renewal, 455
  attitudes towards, 409
  commitment to, 494–5

Change, and MBO—*cont.*
   compatibility with expectations, 581
   direction of, in small firms, 474–6
   factors promoting, 586
   factors affecting planning, 329–30
   factors in society, 99, 103, 543
   in organizations, 377–9, 503–5, Chapter 34
   managing, Chapter 34
   need for, in Action-Centred Leadership, 444, 445
   problems of, 487
   resistance to, 129, 378, 393–4, 599
   response to, 330
   udderstanding, in Organization Renewal, 463
Change strategy, in organization development, 488–9
Checklists: aid to analysis, 487, 489, 497, 498–500
   industrial relations training, 363, 498
   in preparing job specification, 89
   in problem analysis, 589, 591
   in setting up management selection, 97–8
Chess, 218
Chief executive officer (CEO), effect of, 504, 517
   involvement, 559
   responsibility for planning, 337–8
Chloride Group, 560
Chorafas, D. N., 5, 11
Church, The, and irrationality, 124–5
Cinemas in training centres, 571
Cinevision, 269
CIOS, 152
Citrine, Walter, Baron, 361
Civil Service (British), attitude towards, 120
   administrative trainee programme, 531–2
   groupings of staff, 529
   influence, in developing countries, 151
   selection methods, 85, 95
Civil Service Commission (US), selection by, 51–61
Classification, of managerial jobs, 114–19
   of occupations, 93, 529
Classroom situation, 48
   (*see also* Learning at school)
Client-centred consultancy, 129–33
Closed circuit television (*see* Television)
Cluster analysis, 529
Coaching in management development, 575
Codot, 92–4, 98
Coercion-power values, 392
Cognitive changes in learning, 183, 184, 185
Cohen, B. M., 43, 62
Cohen, K. J., 223, 238
Cohesiveness and group size, 375
Cohorts, age groups, 100
Collectivist values in Japan, 178
Collins, O. F., 155, 164

Colonial influence in developing countries, 151–2
Command, appetite for, 210
Commitment, to change, 494–5
   to fundamental values, 111, 112
   to MBO, 486, 487, 491
Committees, value in management development, 577
Communication, Chapter 20
   ability needed, in sensitivity trainer, 254
   administration of, 307
   barriers, 299
   by attitude surveys, 604
   by management, 295–9
   criteria, 297
   defined, 294
   evaluation, 308
   factors affecting, 297
   failures, 297–9
     symptoms, 300
   future, 308–9
   implementation, 303–8
   importance, 293, 294
   improvement programme, 302–3
   in learning, 260–1, 273–4
   in Organization Renewal, 463
   management by, 296–9
   meaning of, 293–4
   media diagram, 303
   need, in international managers, 8
     in planning process, 333
   objectives, 305
   of job vacancies, 106
   plan, 304–8
   problems, causes, 300
   process diagram, 298
   programme, 306
   role, 295
   schedule, 305
   types, 301
   views on, 296
Communications department, 274
Communicators, training of, Chapter 20
    (*for sub headings see* Communications)
Company data, 493
   (*see also* Information)
Company games, 220–1
Company training centres, Chapter 38
   administrative services, 568–72
   coordination, 572
   domestic facilities, 569
   environment, 565–8
   equipment, 570–1
   instructional facilities, 570–1
   maintenance, 571–2
   organization of, 568–72
   reasons for, 564–8
   staffing, 570–1
   (*see also* Training centres)

Compensation Committee assigned role group discussion, 79
Competance, international, 7–8, 10
  output of Management development, 7–8
  problem in family firms, 472, 474
Competition, 444
Competitiveness, 474
Complex case, 186, 189
Computer analysis of manpower data, 535, 537, 538, 539
Computers, in business games, 185, 219, 222
  in decision-making, 326
  in training centres, 570
  mathematical school of thought, use by, 172
  personnel information, use in, 52
  South Africa University, use in, 282
Concentration of human resources, 404
Concentrations, 3, 135
Conceptualization in learning, 242–3
Concern, for people, 385–6
  for production, 385–6
  in business relations, 381–2
Conditions of service, management development, 36
Conduct of meetings, 361–2
Conference Board, 503, 504
Conference rooms, training centres, 570
Conferences on company problems, 495
Conferences (see also Courses)
Confidence factor, in organizations, 509
Conflict, and its resolution, 379–80
  in groups, use of, 449
  in management development, 5
  in organizations, 379–80, 393–4, 507
  job inclination analysis, 90
  key to decision-making, 317
  management of Managerial Grid, 395, 396
Conformity (see Norm setting)
Conglomerates, 3, 556
Connections between jobs, 119
Conseil International pour l'Organization Scientifique (C I O S), 152
Consensus-Insight values, 392–3
Conservatism (see Change, resistance to)
Consonance index in management games, 233–5
Constraints, administrative, 510
  as part of MBO, 404
  matrix, 523
  cultural, 510–12
  matrix, 523
Consultants, 12, 409
  as interviewers, 494
  characteristics, 492
  client-centred, 129–33
    problems of, 133
  contribution to change programme, 494–5
  contribution to diagnosis, 493–4
  contribution to improvement plan, 498

contribution to training programme, 495–7
defined, 126, 129
in Organization Renewal, 457
motivation, 131
on job filling, 92
rarity, in developing countries, 159
relations with in-company staff, 491–2
role, 491–500, Chapter 9
  choice of, 128
  in organization development, Chapter 33
skills of, 130–1
training needs of, 129–30
types of work, 127–8
training trainers, use of in, 577
Consultants' appraisals, executive assessment, 47, 53
Consumer orientation of firms, 371
Context training, 130
Continuity, communications training, 305
Contract bridge, 220
Contracts of employment, 430
Control, and MBO, 405
  concept, 406
Control system in organization, 119
Controlling inspectors, 21
Cooperative education programmes, 105
Coordination, role of management development service, 29–30
Coordinator, role in Managerial Grid, 391
Cornell University, 578
Corporate planning, and management education, 173
  and manpower planning, 531
Corporate resources and management development service, 31
Corporate strategy, 114
Corporations, 3
Corps of General Administrators, 55, 60–1
Correlations, use in validation, 96
Correspondence courses, 276–7
Cost-benefit measurement, in organization development, 498
  of training, 594–5, 598
Cost control of training (see Training cost control)
Cost effectiveness of training, 548–9, 594
Cost factors in training, 586–7
Costs, hidden, in small firms, 137
  of assessment centres, 68–9
  of courses for entrepreneurs, 145–6
Counselling, 21, 86, 107, 340, 582
  (see also Career counselling)
Couples, in life planning, 343
Course members' records in syndicates, 200–1
Course objectives and game characteristics, 224–5
Courses, in training centres, 568–72
  length, for small firms, 138–9
  length, in sensitivity training, 254–5
  material, South Africa University, 280–1
  objectives, management games, 224–5

Courses, in training centres—*cont.*
  only part of the story, 20
  pre-course barriers, 556
  types, in developing countries, 159–60
  (*see also* Conferences; Education)
Coverdale, 320, 487
CPA (*see* Critical path analysis)
Creativity, management development services
    as sponsors, 32–3
  nature, 310–11
  need for, 20–1
Creativity growth groups, 247
Creativity training, 577, Chapter 21
  excursion into, 313–14
Creedal policies of organizations, 510
Cresap, McCormick and Paget Inc., 158,
    164
Crises, reason for review, 551
  requirements to meet, 557
Crisis renewal, 518
Criteria of manager selection, 96
Critical incident case, 187, 189
Critical mass, 394, 396
Critical path analysis (CPA), 209
Cross-cultural management, Chapter 1
Crown princes, family firms, 473
Cultural constraints, 510–12
  matrix, 523
Cultures, national, effect on management, 6
Curriculum, South Africa University,
    280–1

Darwin, Charles, 310
Data (*see* Information)
Davies, J. G. W., 98
Davies report, 85, 98
Davis, S. M., 104–5, 108
DCF (*see* Discounted cash flow)
De Bettignies, H. C., x
Decentralization, 20, 556, 574, 580
Decision analysis, 318
Decision analysis matrix, 323–5
Decision case, 186, 189
Decision-making, 171–2, 485
  and the future, 527–8
  base, in MBO, 407
  computers in, 326
  conflict, as key, 317
  in assessment centres, 77
  in management games, 231
  in management selection, 95
  in South Africa University, 281
  paths of, 508–9
    matrix, 522
  training in, Chapter 22
    applications, 324–6
    definitions, 318
    difficulties, 318–24
    future, 326–7
    misconceptions, 318
    process, 318–24

Decision-making process, centralized, 15, 21,
    137
  variations in countries, 6
Decisiveness in decision-making, 318
Defence mechanisms against Organization
    development, 122
Delegates in training centres, 568–9
Delegation, 556
  effectiveness, 508–9
  lack in small firms, 137–8, 145
  need in planning process, 333
Demand curve, 146
Demographic statistical techniques, man-
    power planning, 530
Department managers, courses, 139
Deployment, component of Management de-
    velopment, 36
DeSatnick, R., 49, 62
Developing countries: Management develop-
    ment, Chapter 11
  bodies concerned with, 161–4
  civil service influence, 151
  content of courses, 159–60
  emergence pattern, 157–8, 160–1
  entrepreneurship in, 155–6
  goals, 153–5
  present status, 156–60
  problems, 151–3
  types of courses, 159–60
Development, diagram, 38
  component of Management development
    system, 36
  in Inland Revenue Service, 58–60
  of executives, in assessment, 48–9
Development Dimensions Inc., 76n, 77
Development functions, 118–19
Development plan, manager improvement,
    401–2
Development posts, 120–1
Development programme, 580
Developmental administration, developing
    countries, 159
Diagnosis of development needs, 64
Diagnostic observer, sensitivity training, 251
Diagnostic training concepts, 251
Dialogic learning, 278–9
Dicostanzo, F., 53, 62
Dimensions, definition, 75
  list, 77
  obtaining, 74–6
  to be assessed, 73–4
Diplomatic service, 10
Direct costs, 146
Direct teaching method, South Africa Uni-
    versity, 286–7
Directors (*see* Board)
Discipline in decision-making, 317
Disciplines in education, 15
Discontinuity, factor in planning, 329
Discounted cash flow (DCF), 209, 326
Discussion leader, aims, 189

Discussions (*see* Group discussions; Seminars)
Disputes, industrial, 430
Dissatisfaction (*see* Job satisfaction)
Diversification, 556
  in small firms, 471
Division of labour, 475
  and sensitivity training, 246
Divisionalization, 444, 503
Domestic facilities, in training centres, 569–70
Drive for effectiveness, 111, 112
Drop-outs in correspondence courses, 277
Drucker, P., 110, 125, 402, 404, 415, 427
Dunnette, M. D., 46, 62, 89, 98, 247, 258
Duplicating facilities, 202, 570
Dynamic case studies, South Africa University, 285
Dynamic training, 578

Eastern Europe, influence on developing countries, 152
ECAFE (*see* Economic Commission for Asia and the Far East)
Ecology, 505
Economic climate, 444
Economic Commision for Asia and the Far East, 152
Editing department, 274
Education, adult, 12
  and training process for planning, 339–40
  higher, failures of, 207
  improvement, implications for industry, 429
  objectives, 170–5
  programmes, matrix approach, 174
  relation to management education, 156
  steps in Managerial Grid, 387
  systems, discussions, 149
Educational records, analysis of, 44
EEC (*see* European Economic Community)
Effectiveness, drive for, 111, 112
  implication of, 175
  through manpower planning, 542–3
Efficiency and human factors, 433
Egalitarian base of synectics, 314, 315
Egypt: action learning programme, 208, 209, 213, 215
  use of Revans model, 123
Einstein, Albert, 310
Elitism, 310
Emergent behaviour, 373, 374–5
Emotional life in T-Groups, 380
Emotional resilience, 111, 112
Employee attitude surveys (*see* Attitude surveys)
Employers' associations, 359, 362, Chapter 25 passim
Employment concept, 429–30
Employment, Department of, 93
Encounter groups, 242, 247
Engineering function, 371
Enlightened self-interest, in MBO, 407
Entrepreneurial approach, 112

Entrepreneurial firms, 473–4
Entrepreneurs: development of, Chapter 10
  in developing countries, 155–6
  identification, 136
  programme of development, 139–40
    content, 140–8
    structure, 141
Environment, and behaviour, 374–5
  need for information on, 335
  of training, 565–8
  of training centres, 14–15
Equipment in training centres, 570–1
Ergom exercises, 487
Esalen, 242
Europe, US influence on, 152
European Economic Community (EEC): size of firms, 135
Europeanization, 444
Evaluation, in Life Goals, 355–6
  in Managerial Grid, 387
  of management development: bibliography, 627–8
  of performance of syndicate, 195
  of sensitivity training, 246–7
Evans, E. O., 364n
Examinations, in management development, 604
  of successful learning, 206
Exchange of experience between managers, 576
Executive briefing sessions, 339
Executive potential: testing, Chapter 4
Executive system, federal (US), 51, 53–61 passim
Executive training, 42
Executives, US Government service, 51–61
Exercise case, 186, 189
Exercises (*see* Tests; Examinations)
Exit interviews, 89
Expectations bargain in MBO, 410
Experience, as weight, 209–10
  exchange of, between managers, 576
  in learning, 242–3
  indicator of executive potential, 44–5
Exploitation of opportunities, 115
External consultants (*see* Consultants)
External system in organizations, 374–5

Fact finding, assessment centres, 77
  (*see also* Information)
Family businesses, 470, 471–3
  conflict in, 474
  need for changes, 474
Fayol, H., 12
Federal executive system (US), 51, 53–61 passim
Feedback, in learning, 183
  of information, 400–1
Fees in training centres, 568
Festinger, L., 234
Film projectors, 269–70

Films, in Action-Centred Leadership, 451
    in role play cases, 187
    in training centres, 570
Finance, in-put of knowledge, 145–6
    in small firms, 137
    use of knowledge, 147
Financial analysis exercise, 79
Financial function, 371
Financial incentive, 431, 443
Financial measurement, figure, 593
Financial participations, 3
Financial planning and manpower planning,
    531
Firms, size of, 135
    (see also Family businesses; Organizations;
        Small firms)
First-generation entrepreneurial firms, 473–4
Fisher, Barbara, 343
Five-year forecast, diagram, 35
Fixer style of management, 115–6
Flannelgraphs, 267
Fleischman, E. A., 382, 384
Flexibility, in international managers, 8,
    178
    in planning process, 333
    in resourcefulness, 110–11
Flipcharts, 202, 267, 570
Florida, University of, 43
Forcing circumstances for growth, 544
Ford Foundation, 152
Ford Motor Co., 67, 308, 361
Forecasting, component of management de-
    velopment, 36
Forecasting, Manpower (see Manpower fore-
    casting)
Forecasts, five-year, diagram, 35
    routine, in manpower planning, 531
Foreign agency, 10
Foreign aid, 152, 156
Foreign environments, 9
Formality in organizations, 475, 509
Forms, use in executive assessment, 45
France: employment, 428–9
    incentives for management development,
        ix–x
Frank, I. D., 243, 258
Franks, Oliver Shewell, Baron, 113
Free-standing companies, 503
French colonial influence, 151–2
Freud, Sigmund, 310, 432, 496
Functional divisions, of organizations, 117
Functional forms, of organization, 556
Functional games, 220
Functional leadership, 444, 446, 448
    model, 449
    (see mainly Action-Centred Leadership)
Future (see Change; Prediction)

Games, educational use, 219–20
    (see also Management games)
Gap theory in analysis, 591

General Electric Corporation, 43, 64, 66
    and orientation, 105
General Motors: job monotony, 314
General schedule system (US), 52–3
Generations, different, 99–103
German army, 219
Germany: size of firms, 135
Ghana, management development in, 152
Ghiselli, E. E., 89, 98
Gibb, Jack, 247, 258
Goal-setting exercises, 144–5
Goals, and constraints, 404
    business, and life planning, 343
    development programme, 581
    long- versus short-range, 507–8
    need for information on, 335–6
Greiner, L. F., 555–6, 562, 563
Gresham's law, 210
Grid (see Managerial Grid)
Grid seminar individual training, 387–8
    compared with T-Groups, 388
Grievances, industrial, 430
Grounds, of training centres, 571–2
Group assignments, South Africa University,
    284–5
Group development projects, career planning,
    121–4
Group discussions, in management develop-
    ment, 44, 63, 77, 577
    of cases, 188–9
    participation by top management, 16
Group experience in sensitivity training, 253
Group reviews in organization development,
    489–90
Group tasks, for applicants, 94
Group therapy, 486
Group training and management develop-
    ment trainers, 577–8
Groups, and Action-Centred Leadership,
    448–50
    concepts, 244
    make-up, sensitivity training, 255
    membership of, by trainer, 252–3
    and sensitivity training, 244
    (see also Management training syndicates;
        Teams)
Growth: problem in small firms, 474
Guidance (see Support; Counselling)

Habits of companies, 510–12
Hagen, E. E., 6, 11
Hague, Hawdon, 130
Hajra, S., 158, 164
Handwriting analysis, 94
Harvard Business School, 182, 208, 344, 373,
    575
Harvey, William, 311–12
Hawrylyshyn, Bohdan, 9, 11
Hawthorne experiments, 374

Heinicke, C. J., 375, 383
Helicopter mind, 85, 111, 574, 576
Henley (*see* Administrative Staff College)
Herzberg, F., 377, 384, 428, 430–2, 440, 488
Hierarchies, 375
  classification of occupations, 529
Hierarchy: levels of management skills, 174–5
  of needs, 376–7
Higher education, failures, 207
Hire and fire policy, 528
Hogan, Daniel, 257–8, 259
Homans, George, 373, 374–5, 377, 383, 384
Home environment, effect on training, 567
House, R. J., 4, 11, 246, 258
Human factor, in change, 444–5
Human relations (*see* Behavioural sciences;
      Communications; Relationships)
Human relations laboratories, 240
Human resources, and leadership, 443
  characteristics, 528
  importance, 31
  no longer pliant, 429
  (*see also* Manpower; Work force)
Human skills, needed in management, 171
Human values in training, list, 345
Humble, John, 400, 402, 427
Hygiene factors, in companies, 31–2
  in jobs, 377, 431–2

IBM, 43, 64, 108
Ice breaking, Life Goals, 350–1
Ideas, handling in management, 115
Ideational ply in organizations, 514–15, 517–
      18, 519–20
Identification of potential (*see* Assessment)
ILO, 92, 152
Immigrants in employment scene, 429
Impersonality, in firms, 475
Improvement, and consultants, 129
  (*see also* Job improvement; Results)
In-basket exercises, 43, 63, 66, 67, 68, 70, 77,
      79, 186–7, 189, 190, 387, 581
Incompetence, 433
  in family firms, 472, 474
Inconsistency in training investment, 600–1
India, and Management development, 156,
      158
  public servants and managers, 151
  young workforce, 101
Individual assessment, with schedule, 69–70
Individual assignments, career planning, 120–1
Individual behaviour, 376–7
Individual manager development, 5, 10–11,
      387–9
Individuals, and sensitivity training, 244
  interaction with organizations, 344
  needs of, 449–50
Induction programme (*see* Intern programme)
Industrial bureaucracy, 475–6
Industrial relations training, Chapter 25,
      362–4, 372, 444

case studies, 365–8
conduct of meetings, 361–2
content, 361
exercises, 364
nature, 360–1
participants, 359–60
policy checklist, 498
purpose, 359–60
strategy, with checklist, 362–3
Industrial relations officers, 359
Industrial Society, The, 444, 452, 453
Industrial training boards, 130, 131
Inertia (*see* Change, resistance to)
Inflation and small firms, 137
Influence and sensitivity training, 246
  management as process of, 6
Informality in organizations, 475, 509
Information: collection, 493–4
  fact-finding, assessment centres, 77
  feedback needed by manager, 400–1
  needed by planner, 330, 333
  needed by staff, 21
  in organizational review, 554–5
  pollution of, 30
  role of management development service, 30
  standard categories of, 334–6
Information explosion in planning, 329
Information systems, 486, 592
  analysis, figure, 591
  character, 507
  lack, in small firms, 136, 142–3
  manpower planning, 528
  setting up, 148
Initiative, 111, 112
Innovation, and MBO, 403
  management of, 114
  Management development services as spur
      to, 32–3
  need for, 21
  small firms, 474
  (*see mainly* Change)
Innovation process, with diagram, 311–12
INSEAD, 9
Insight-consensus values, 392–3
Institut Européen, d'Administration des
      Affaires (INSEAD), 9
Instructional facilities, training centres, 570–1
Instrument laboratory groups, 255–6
Instrumented team learning, 394, 396
Intelligence, in planning, 329, 333
  in resourcefulness, 110–11
Intelligence tests, executive assessment, 47–8
Interchange (*see* Communication)
Intercultural competence, 7–8, 10
Interdepartmental planning of management
      development, 17
Interest tests, executive assessment, 47–8, 50
Intergroup development, 389
Intergroup exercises, sensitivity training,
      242
Intern programmes, 103–5

Internal Revenue Service (US), 53–61 passim, 64
Internal study groups, 409
Internal system, in organizations, 374–5
International aspects of Management development, Chapter 1, 177–80, 577
  lack of attention, 5–6
International Association of Social Scientists, 258
International Business Machines (IBM), 43, 64, 108
International Labour Office (ILO), 92, 152
International know-how, 178
International management, 3–4
Interpersonal changes in learning, 183
Intersyndicate activities, 196
Inter-University programme (see Belgian Inter-university programme)
Interview sampling of opinions, 579
Interviews, appraisal, simulation, 80
  exit, 89
  in assessment centres, 66
  in assessment of executives, 45–6, 50, 66, 69–70, 74–5, 77, 78, 80
  in attitude surveys, 606
  in problem analysis, figure, 590
  of applicants, 94–5
  to gain company data, 494
In-tray case (see In-basket exercises)
Inventories: in executive assessment, 45, 47
  Life Goals, 353
  of current problems, 579
  of personnel, 42, 45
  US government service, 52, 53
Investment, lack in small firms, 137
Investment appraisal: training costs, 595, 599–602
Investment curve, 601
Investment pattern, 601
Involvement (see Commitment)
Ireland: incentives to Management development, ix–x
Irish Management Institute, Chapter 10 passim, 135, 138, 148
Irrationality in life, 124–5
IRS (see Internal Revenue Service (US))
Issigonis, A., 115
Issue commitment in Organization Renewal, 464

Japan, comparison with US management, 178
  size of firms, 135
  use of management, 6
Japanese: assignment programmes, 104–5
  youth of workforce, 101
Jay, Antony, 124, 125
Job analysis, assessment centres, 74–5
Job applicants (see Applicants for jobs)
Job capacity, 89–91
Job content, 431–2
Job context, 431–2

Job descriptions, 42, 400, 545, 548, 549
  criticism, 130
  (see also Job specifications)
Job enrichment, Chapter 29, 371, 486, 577
  case studies, 436–40
  caution needed in timing, 434
  value of trials, 434–5
Job improvement: diagnosis of needs, MBO, 421–2
  planning, with figure, 414–6
  statement of objectives, 423
Job improvement plans, 411
Job inclination, 89–91
Job level, in assessment centres, 72, 74
Job monotony, 314
Job performance (see Performance)
Job review, 404–5, 410
Job rotation, 20, 48, 65, 170, 574, 575
Job satisfaction, with table, 431–2, 443
Job specifications, 88–90, 92
  steps in preparation, 89–90
  (see also Job descriptions)
Jobs: connections, 119
  invention of new jobs, 119
  managerial, classification, 92–4, 98, 114–19
  versus careers, 113–4
  (see also Employment)
Joint ventures, 3
Judgement, effective, 111, 112
Jung, C. G., 204, 205, 432
Jungle method of selection, 86
Junior boards, 170
Justice, need for, in companies, 32

Kepner, C. H., 319, 320, 321, 325, 327, 488
Key areas in MBO, 402, 410
  list of, 404, 413–14
Knowledge: diagram, 175, 176
  changes through Management development, 7, 8
  communication training, 305
  development programme, 581
  in international management education, 178–9
Koontz, H., 405, 427
Kriegspiele, 219
Kuriloff, A., 380, 384

Laboratory methods, 240, 241–2, 380–1
  (see mainly Sensitivity training)
Labour force (see Work force)
Laird, Dugan, 53, 62
Land, Edwin, 115
Lateness of staff, 429
Latin America, influences on, 152
Lawrence, P. R., 119, 125, 556, 562, 563
Lawton, Esther C., 84–5, 94
Leadership and communication, 273–4
  and human resources, 443
  and sensitivity training, 245, 246
  in business, 277

Leadership and communication—*cont.*
  in study groups, 284
  in syndicates, 200–2
  need for, 442–3
  of groups, case study, 189
  redefined, 446–50
  style (*see* Management style)
  training (*see* Action-Centred Leadership)
Learning, at school, 429, 566, 603–4
  barriers to, 566
  comparison with training, 593
  contrived, 183–4
  essentials of, 204–6
  goals, 383
  motivation, 204–5
  natural, 182–3
  objectives, diagram, 179
  organizational, 4–5, 10–11
  over long period, 104
  processes (*see* Learning process)
  social process, 205–6
  theory into practice, 207–10
Learning by doing, 8, 10
Learning experience, sensitivity training, 251
Learning manager, Managerial Grid, 394
Learning process, and correspondence courses, 276–7
  and Management development trainers, 582–3
  assessment, with diagram, 10, 175–7
  design, international, 8–11
  in communications training, 306
  in creativity, with diagram, 311–12
  in sensitivity training, 242–3
  international context, 8–11
  of management development, 7
  organic, 582–3
  pyramid, diagram, 261, 262
  table, 212
Learning situation and training centres, 566–8
Lectures, few in Action-Centred Leadership, 450
  in study groups, South Africa University, 285
  printed, at South Africa University, 285
  use in education, 266
Leggatt report, 529, 540
Levels of abstraction, 319
Levels of management, needs for skills, 174
Levels of purpose, decision-making, 319–20
Levinson, H., 344, 358, 405, 427
Levinson Institute, 344
Lewin, K., 379, 384
Lewis, Martin, 204
Libraries, 188
  in training centres, 570
  South Africa University, 282
Life Goals Planning, Chapter 24
  case studies, 345–50, 357–8
  content, 350–5

evaluation, 355–6
  feedback, 355
  form, 354
  history, 343
  model, figure, 351
  nature, 343
  processes, 350–5
  purpose, 343–4
  survey of, 347–50
  value, 344–5
Life styles, younger generation, 101–3
Likert, Rensis, 31, 246, 258, 373, 377, 382, 384, 487
Line managers, and industrial relations, 359–60
  communication needs, 302
  responsibility for development, 13, 15–16
  responsibility for planning, 338
  role in management development, 574, 575
Link department, 274
  central management service as, 28–9
Link trainer, 184
Linkage, in organizations, 506–7, 513
  organization matrix, 522
Lippitt, G. L., 345, 358, 555, 558, 562, 563
Listening to clients, by consultants, 130–1
Location factor, in isolation of Top management, 14–15
  of training centres, 14–15, 19
Logic, management games, figure, 227
Looseleaf books for planning information, 333, 335
Lordstown, 314, 315
Lorsch, J., 119, 125, 556, 558, 562, 563
Love-trust values, 392

McBer and Co., 140, 148
McClelland, D. C., 136, 148, 488
McGregor, Douglas, 240, 258, 377, 382, 384, 400, 427
Mace, M. L., 575, 583
Macy's Department Store, 43
Magnetic boards, 267
Malaysia, 102
  management development in, 152
Malaysian Institute of Management, 157
Management, 17
  and new media, 273–4
  and public administration, comparison, 150–1
  as influence, 6
  concepts, factor in planning, 340
  cycles, 21
  mode, and change, 504
  national characteristics, 6
  of innovation, 114
  principles, 6
  problems, 79
  process, 16–17
  role in sensitivity training, 256
  structure, 21

Management associations, developing countries, 159, 161–4
Management audit, 36, 39, 554
Management by Objectives (MBO), 89, 173, 320, 340, 394–5, 396, 452, 485, 491, 560, 577, Chapter 28
  advisers, 411, 420–1
  and Action-Centred Leadership, 444, 445
  and attitudes, 408–10
  and innovation, 403
  and life goals, 344
  and management development, 17, 20
  application, 399–400, 407–8
  at Barclays, 607
  background, 400–3
  beginning, 412
  concepts, 403–7
  eclecticism of, 403
  factors in success, 411–12
  features, 408–11
  framework, 412–14
  individual control, 416–18
  planning improvement, 414–16
  policy clarification, 419–20
  problems, 486
  progressing action, 415–16
  rationale, 399–400
  response to change, 330, 332, 403
  results, 416–18
  time factor, 411, 420, 426
  training of advisors, 421
  user companies in UK, 399
Management development, and Action-Centred Leadership, 445–6
  and manpower planning, 543–4, 545–9
  and organization development, 4
  appraisal, 19–20
  as improver of effectiveness, 170
  as monitor of learning process, 10
  bibliography, 615–22
  definitions, 4, 13, 15–16, 150
  department, isolation possible, 14–16
  evaluation by attitude surveys, Chapter 41
  evaluation: bibliography, 627–8
  impact, 4–5
  in-company courses, 605
  incentives towards, in Europe, ix–x
  in developing countries, Chapter 11
  in family firms, 473
  international operations, Chapter 1
    bibliography, 620–2
  learning system, 8–11
  nature, 4–5
  objectives, 322, 579–82
  outputs, 7–8
  overseas, Chapter 11
    bibliography, 626–7
  policy responsibility, Management development service, 25–6
  problems, 4–5
  programme, reason for existence, 23–5

questions on the organization, 544
relativity of principles, 5–8
role of top management, Chapter 2
  (*for headings see* Top management)
schemes: extent in UK, x
  steps in, 545
service (*see* Management development service)
specialists (*see* Trainers)
system: components, 36
tasks, 156
Management development service, and corporate resources, 31
  as advisor, 26, 28
  as coordinator, 29–30
  as information disseminator, 30
  as motivator, 30
  components of management development system, 36
  environmental awareness, 28–9, 32
  essentials, 24–5
  evaluation, 33
  innovation, 33
  isolation, possible, 14–16
  model, 24
  monitoring, 31–2
  operational role, 28
  policy responsibility, 25–6
  relationships, 26–8
  review, 33
  role, Chapter 3
  standardization, 32
  staff, 28, 33–4
  tasks, diagram, 25
Management education: aim, 169
  and business schools; bibliography, 623–6
  approaches, 170–5
  conceptual framework, Chapter 12
  extent, 12–13
  growth of, 12–13, 372
  integrative model, 175–7
  international aspects, 177–80
  objectives, 170–5
  (*see also* Management development)
Management games, Chapter 16, 67, 77, 578–9, 581
  categories, 220–3
  characteristics, 224–5
  comparison with other methods, figure, 236
  computers in, 185, 219, 222
  definition, 217
  developments, 217–19, 237–8
  educational use, 219–20
  evaluation, 229, 232–7
  history, 217–19
  in decision-making, 231
  information, 229–30
  international management education, 179–80
  limitations, 223
  logic, 227

Management games—*cont.*
management of games, 228–31
operation, 227, 228–9
participants, 228, 232
reports required, 231
situational stress, 230
South Africa University, 282, 284–5, 286
special assignments, 231–2
team composition, 228, 232
Management guide in MBO, 417, 424–5
Management information (*see* Information)
Management intern (MI) programmes (*see* Intern programmes)
Management job descriptions, 400
(*see also* Job descriptions)
Management levels, and need of skills, figure, 174
bibliography, 622
Management manpower planning, Chapter 36 (*for headings see* Manpower planning)
Management reviews, 36, 39
Management selection, Chapter 6
approaches, 84–6
control, 95–6
decision-making, 95
development, 95–6
establishment of, checklist, 97–8
policies, 86–7
techniques, 87–95
validation, 96
Management seminars, 338
Management simulation (*see* Simulation)
Management style, 20, 115–17, 474, 485, 504, 517, 558
and sensitivity training, 246
change by MBO, 410
responsibility for, 337
Management thinking and training gap, 585–6, 593–4
Management trainees: analysis and costing, Chapter 40
investment appraisal, 599–602
measurement of performance, 595, 599
needs of training, 585–7
problem analysis, 587–93
training cost control, 593–5
Management training (*see* Management development; Management education)
Management training syndicates, Chapter 14, 188, 576–7
accommodation, 202
audio-visual aids (*see* Audio-visual aids)
case methods, Chapter 13, 188–90
types, 185–8
chairmen and secretaries, 200–2
composition of, 193, 199–200
construction of, 193, 199–200
discussion after, 188–9
equipment, 202
evaluation of performance, 195
features, 193

feedback, need for, 190
future developments, 202
in learning process, 198–9
inter-syndicate activities, 196
learning, types of, 182–5
management of, 194–5
mix, 193, 199–200
objectives, 170, 189–90
relevance, need for, 190, 197
resources, need for, 188
size of syndicates, 195–6
staff role, 196–8
tasks, 193–4
(*see also* Groups; Teams)
Manager identification, Chapter 4
Managerial Grid, Chapter 27, 377, 381–3, 487, 577
comparison with T-Group, sensitivity training, 388
dynamics, 392–5
evaluation, 385, 387, 395–6
operation, 385–7
programme, 387–92
Managerial jobs, classification, 114–9
Managerial lag, in planning, 329
Managers, and problem analysis, 590–3
and resourcefulness, Chapter 8
as trainers, 573–5
behaviour problems, 41
development as people, 20–1
identification, Chapter 4
manpower forecasting, Chapter 35 (*for headings see* Manpower forecasting)
needs, 400–1
reserve of talent, 20
selection (*see* Management selection)
self-knowledge, 8
Managing by communication, 296–9
Managing change, Chapter 34
Manchester Business School, 121–4
Mankind: problems, 153–4
Manpower: characteristics, 528
needs in developing countries, with table, 158–9
(*see also* Work force; Human resources)
Manpower costing, 592–3
Manpower forecasting, figures, 35, 36
characteristics, 528–9
classification, 529
data base, 540
demand, 528, 530–2
framework of, 531
need, 527–30
of managers, Chapter 35
outflow of staff, 532–3
staffing for, 531
supply, 528–9, 532–40
Manpower planning, Management, ix, Chapter 36, 513
and management development, 543–4, 545–9

Manpower planning—*cont.*
  benefits, 548–9
  defined, 543
  description, 543–4
  future, 549
  implementation, 547–8
  ingredients, 545–9
Mant, A., 133, 134
Manuals, looseleaf in planning, 333, 335
  use in teaching, 266
Manufacturing method of selection, 86–7
Mao Tse-Tung, 432
Map manoeuvres, 218–9
Marathon groups, 247
Marginal costing in small firms, 146
Margulies, N., 379, 384
Marketing, 118
Marketing conditions, 580
Marketing era of business, 371
Marketing experts and manpower planning, 531
Maslow, A. H., 373, 376–7, 383, 488
Massachusetts Institute of Technology, 208
Massey-Ferguson, 361
Mathematical models in decision-making, 326
Mathematical school of thought in management, 171–2
Matrix of organization, 522–6
Matrix organization, 577
Maturation of learners, 183, 184
MBO (*see* Management by Objectives)
Mead, Margaret, 101, 108
Measures (*see* Assessment; Evaluation; Performance measures)
Media: diagram, 303
  (*see mainly* Audio-visual aids)
Meetings, conduct of, 361–2
Mental ability tests, executive assessment, 48
Mental breakdown, possible, in sensitivity training, 247, 578
Mental stimulation, goals, 352–3
Mergers, 3
  and Action-Centred Leadership, 444, 445, 446
Metaphor: root of creativity, 310–11
Metrication, 444
Middle management: syndicate training, 192–3, 199
Military (*see* Armed forces)
Mind stimulation, Life Goals, 352–3
Misconceptions, factor in isolation of top management, 15–16
Mix organizations, 577
Mobility, increased, 107
  internal, 106
Model building in management, 172
Modernization problems, 153
Moffitt, W., 343
Money (*see* Finance; Payment systems; Salaries)
Monitoring (*see* Control)

Monotony in jobs, 314
Morale in assessment centres, 78
Morocco, and management development, 158
Morris, Geoffrey, 593
Morse, J. J., 558, 562, 563
Moses, Joel C., 43, 62
Motivation: factor in planning, 340
  in sensitivity training, 245
  increase, by manpower planning, 548
  lack in small firms, 138
  of entrepreneurs, 136
  of learning, 204–5
  of personnel, 372, 376–7
  role of management development service, 30
  sources of, inclination analysis, 90
  surveys of, 613–14
  understanding, 171
Motivators, 377, 432, 436, 440
Mouton, Jane S., 373, 377, 381, 382, 384
Muller, H., 111, 125
Multicultural training, Chapter 1
Multinational companies, 10
  and life styles, 102–3
Multinational management, 3, 135
Multinational teams, learning in, 177–80
Multiple appraisals, 50

Nadler, D. A., 108
NALGO, 364n
National Alliance of Businessmen (US), 107–8
National and Local Government Officers Association, 364n
National development (*see* Developing countries)
National dress, 102
National Economic Development Office (NEDO), 529, 540
National Freight Corporation, and OD, 122
National Institute of Development Administration, Thailand, 151, 156
National Research Development Corporation (NRDC), 115
National Training Laboratories, 241, 343
Natural learning, 182–3
NEDO, 529, 540
Needs, human, 431–3
  hierarchy of, 373, 376–7
Needs, training and consultants, 129–30
Negotiation, training for, Chapter 25
  definition, 359–60
  (*for headings see* Industrial relations)
Nepal Centre for Economic Development, 151
Nepotism (*see* Family firms)
Network of relationships in organizations, 506–7
New media, use in management training, Chapter 18
  (*for headings see* Audio visual aids)
New opportunities, seeking, 136
Neitzsche, F., 582

Nigeria, management development in, 152
Non-computer games, 223
Non-stochastic models, 222
Norm setting, 374, 375
Norms, 389, 512
NRDC (*see* National Research Development Corporation)
NTL (*see* National Training Laboratories)
Numeracy, over-stress in management games, 223

O and M, 409
Objectives: communications training, 305
  decision-making, 318–19
  development programme, 581
  geared to organizational needs, 579–80
  in MBO, 408, 413
  lack in small firms, 137, 145
  need for information on, 335–6
  of management development, 16–17
  of organizations, 548, 549
  setting, MBO, 414–15
  setting, problems, 486
Objectivity, difficulty of securing, 487
Observation of behaviour, assessment centres, 66
Occupations, classification of (CODOT), 93, 114–19, 529
Odiorne, G. S., 240, 258, 578, 583
Office of Population Censuses and Surveys, 92
Officer training (*see* Armed forces)
Open system of learning, 278–9
Openness, 475, 488, 489
  and Management Grid, 388
  encouragement by organization development, 488–9, 577–8
  in sensitivity training, 243
  needed in international managers, 8
Operational functions and development specialisms, 117–18
Operational information, figure, 592
Operational intelligence, planning factor, 340
Operational results, development programme, 581–2
Operations Research (OR), 326
Opinion surveys, of MBO, 412
  checklist for, 421–2
Opportunities, exploitation in management, 115
  need for information on, 335
OR (*see* Operations Research)
Organic learning process, 582–3
Organic organizations, 475–6
Organismic organizations, 475–6
Organization and Methods (O and M), 409
Organization culture, 393
Organization development, 10–11, 121
  and Action-Centred Leadership, 44–5, 445
  and Managerial Grid, 389–92
  (*for headings see* Managerial Grid)
  and MBO, 403

and people power, 455
contribution of behavioural sciences, Chapter 26
  (*for headings see* Behavioural sciences)
definition, 372
diagnosis and critique, 391–2
effect of, 490–1
evaluation, 490–1
growth of interest in, 372
improvement of effectiveness by, 170
in small firms, Chapter 32
  (*for headings see* Small firms)
nature of, 486
process, activities of, 492–3
values underlying, 392–3
Organization man, 155–6
Organization planning and organizational change, Chapter 34
Organization Renewal process, 577, Chapter 31
  assessment, 458–9
  case studies, 455–7
  definition, with figure, 455–6
  evaluation of organization, 460–1
  feedback, 463
  goals, 458, 460
  implementation, 464–5
  in Canada, 465–8
  internal-external mix, 457
  performance, 458–9
  workshop, 459–64
Organizational capacity, 552
Organizational change, and business development, 555–8
  and organizational planning, Chapter 34
  coordination of, 560–1
  descriptive tool, 525
  prescriptive tool, 525–6
Organizational inventory, figure, 461
Organizational learning, 4–5, 10–11
Organizational review, Chapter 37
  and people, 558–9
  and top management, 559–60
  approach to, 561
  business development, 555–8
  checklist of, 554
  coordination of, 560–1
  framework, diagram, 553
  objectives, 552
  perspective, 552
  reasons for, 551
Organizational tasks: model, 114–19
Organizational theory, 119
Organizations, and sensitivity training, 245–6
  as multi-institutional systems, 505–6, 513–25
  as systems of response, 506–13
  characteristics, 373–6
  communication needs, 301
  definition, 406
  dynamics, 373–6

Organization, and sensitivity training—*cont.*
  information on, analysis, 591, 592
    need, 336
  interaction with individuals, 344
  matrix, 522–4
  needs and objectives, 579–80
  problems leading to review, 551
  size, 556
  specification, 88
  structure, 373–6
Organizers, separation in management struc-
    ture, 21
Orientation, 105, 108
Output of organization, 7
Outside consultants (*see* Consultants)
Overhead projectors, 268–9, 570
Owen, Bill, 343
Owen, Robert, 12
Owner managers, Chapter 10 passim
Oxford University Department for External
    Studies, 363, 364n

Papaloizas, A., 237, 238
Participants: impact of assessment centres, 67
Participation: factor in planning, 330
Participative management, 330, 444
  and MBO, 410
Participative methods, in skill development,
    177
Paternalism in family firms, 473, 474
Pathology and sensitivity training, 243
Pay records and manpower planning, 540
Payment (*see* Bonuses; Financial incentives)
Payment systems, 486
Pedagogy (*see* Learning)
Penrose, Edith, 556
People, and tasks, 558–9
  as corporate resources, 31
  concern for (*see* Concern)
  development of, 13–14
  (*see also* Behavioural sciences; Manpower;
    Personnel; Work force)
People power, 455
PER (*see* Professional and executive recruit-
    ment)
Perceptions, changing, in organizations, 519–
    20
  (*see also* Attitude surveys)
Performance, 7, 46–7
  as predictor, 49
  development programme, 581
Performance appraisal process, 66, 170
Performance evaluation, 46–7, 49, 549, 595,
    599
Performance levels, and MBO, 409, 411
Performance measurement, of training, 595,
    599
Performance review, 401, 411, 545
  role of external consultant, 127–8
Performance standards, determination of, 418
  in South Africa University, 287–8
  types, in MBO, 418

Personal counselling (*see* Counselling)
Personal inventories (*see* Inventories)
Personal security, need, sensitivity trainer, 253
Personal studies, by managers, 576–7
Personality tests, in assessment, 48
Personality training (*see* Sensitivity Training)
Personnel auditing, 87
Personnel changes (*see* Mobility)
Personnel departments, 372
Personnel interviews (*see* Interviews)
Personnel inventories (*see* Inventories)
Personnel officers, 12
  and industrial relations, 359
Personnel records, manpower planning, ix,
    540
Personnel selection, decision structure, 91
PERT, 209
Peter principle, 345
Philippine Executive Academy, 151
Philippines, 156, 158
Photocopying facilities, 202, 570
Physical world and resourcefulness, 111
Pilkington Brothers Ltd, 473
Pilot seminars, 488–91, 495
Pittsburgh, University of, 43
Placement, Internal Revenue Service, 59–60
Plan implementation, Managerial Grid, 390–1
Planned changes, 4, 504, 555, Chapter 34
Planners, 21
Planning, in entrepreneurial courses, 147–8
  lacking in small firms, 138
Planning council, 338
Planning exercises, South Africa University,
    282
Planning folder, entrepreneurial courses, 143
Planning management, and Top management,
    17–18
Planning, Manpower (*see* Manpower fore-
    casting; Manpower planning)
Planning process, 334
  and manpower planning, 528
  factor in planning, 340
Planning skills: benefits, 330–2
  categories of information, 334–6
  change factors, 329–30
  changes, 328
  characteristics, figure, 331
  developing, Chapter 23
  dynamic, 331
  purpose, 330–2
  response, 330
  responsibility for development, 336–40
  specifications, 333–4
  static, 331
Planning specialists, 334, 338–9, 340
Plans, of organizations, 580
Plessey, and organization development, 121–2
Policies, need for information on, 336
Policy clarification in MBO, 419–20
  checklist, 420
Post-and-bid system: job mobility, 106

Post Office, and Organization development, 122
Potential, of entrepreneurs, 144–6
of executives : methods of testing, Chapter 4
Potential problem analysis, 324
Power-coercion values, 392
Practice-based learning (see Simulation)
Pragmatic school of thought in management, 171
Prediction, in case study, 187
in decision-making, 326
management selection as, 86
of behaviour, 61
Predictors in selection, 87, 96
Prestige (see Status)
Pretoria University, 276
Price manipulation, manpower, 529
Probability in decision-making, 326
Problem analysis, 321, 587–90
in a company, 579–80
in an industry, 587–9
management and, 590–3
Problem-solving, 44, 485
aid to learning, 206
in Managerial Grid, 389
(see also Creativity)
Problems in management : list, 495
Procedures and MBO, 408
Process analysis : organization development checklist, 499
Process chart, with figure, 419–20
Process examination, 241
Process ply, in organizations, 515–16, 518–19, 521
Product-contribution analysis, 146
Product forms of organization, 556
Production, concern for, 385–6
Production process, 371
Productivity and unemployment, 428
Productivity bargains, 361, 407
Productivity centres in developing countries, 159
Professional and Executive Recruitment (PER), 92, 94
Professional training and sensitivity trainers, 253–4
Profit centres, 21, 503
definition, 444
Profit planning, 486
Profits, motivation, 136
Programmed learning, 282–3
Programmes, for international management development, 4, 8–11
need for information on, 336
Project Evaluation Review Techniques (PERT), 209
Project forms of organizations, 556
Project groups, 107
Project studies, South Africa University, 282, 284
Project teams, 121, 124, 170, 180

Projectors in training centres, 570, 571
Promotions, manpower forecasting, 528, 532, 536, 537
based on assessment, 475
Prussia : war games, 239–40
Psychoanalysis, 496
Psychological elements in work contract, 429–33
Psychological growth, 432–3
Psychological tests, executive assessment, 44, 47–8, 65
Psychologists in executive assessment, 46, 69
in organization development, 372, 376
industrial, 430
Psychology, and organization development, 372
as a study, 171
Psychology, educational, 220
Psychometric standards, of data gathering, 94–5
Psychomotor changes, in learning, 183, 184
Psychotherapy, sensitivity training, 243–4, 578
Public administration, 150–1
Public support of business : planning factor, 330
Punctuality, lack of, 429
Purchasing method of selection, 87
Purchasing power, of small firms, 137–8

Qualifications, 42, 56, 184
Qualities of leaders, Action-Centred Leadership, 447
Quantification, 136
Questionnaires, for standard data, 493–4
in assessment, 43
in business analysis, 142–4
in Managerial Grid, 388
in organization development seminars, 490
in problem analysis, 587, 588, 590
to determine dimensions, 76

Raia, A. P., 379, 384
Ramakrishnan, P., 158, 164
Randell, G. A., 89, 98
Rationalization, 444
Rationality, in life, 124–5
Reception in training centres, 569
Recommendations, in executive appraisal, 47
Recruitment, component of MD system, 36
of managers, Chapter 6
(see also Manpower planning)
Reddin, W. J., 403, 427, 487
Redundancy, and manpower planning, 528, 532–3
Re-entry to firms, from external courses, 16, 19
from foreign training, 102–3
Reference materials in case studies, 188, 190
References, in executive assessment, 47
Regional cooperation, management development, 152, 157

Regional Institute of Higher Education and Development, Singapore, 156–7
Relationships, and resourcefulness, 111–12
  between levels of management, 401
  in sensitivity training, 243
  network of, 506–7
Relativity of principles, international operations, 5–8
Remuneration, in management development system, 36
Renewal (see Organization Renewal)
Renewal stimulator, 457–8, 463
Replacement plans, 575, 579
Reports, in management games, 231–2
Reprographic services, training centres, 202, 570
Research, in sensitivity training, 246–7
  in South Africa University, 281
  on evaluation of South Africa University, 288
  on types of organizations, 475
Research and development staff, manpower planning, 531
Research budget individual fact-finding and decision-making exercise, 79
Research proposals: South Africa University, 284, 287
Research work, 115
  and job enrichment, 438–9
  by managers, 576–7
  by younger people, 102
Resignations: manpower planning, 378
Resilience emotional, 111, 112
Resistance to change (see Change, resistance to)
Resourcefulness, developing, in managers, Chapter 8
  and career development, 112–19
  approaches, 119–24
  defined, 110–12
Resources, need for information on, 336
Response, organizations as systems of, 506–13
Results, and MBO, 407, 408
  attitude to, 408–9
  improvement, 408
  needed in manager, 400
  pragmatic school of thought, 171
Retail trade: training needs, 585
Retirement data, manpower forecasting, 532, 533, 536
Revans model, 123
Reviews, for planning process, 338
  of work groups, 489–90
Reviews, job (see Job reviews)
Rewards, for managers, 401
  in selection system, 87
Reward system, 509–10
  matrix, 523
Risk-taking in business, 136
Roethlisberger, F. J., 374, 383
Rogers, Carl, 242

Role, defined, 126
Role models, lack of, 105
Role play case, 187–8, 189
Role playing, 43, 48
  in Action-Centred Leadership, 451
  in industrial relations training, 361, 363
  in sensitivity groups, 242
  programme, 581
Rotation of jobs (see Job rotation)
Rubenowitz, S., 94, 98
Russia (see USSR)

Salaries and assessment review, 549
Sales force, and job enrichment, 436–8
  assessment, 64, 73
  manpower planning, 530
Satisfaction (see Job satisfaction)
Scanlon plan, 146
Schedules, need for information on, 336
Schein, E., 129, 134
Schelling, T. C., 379, 384
Schmidt, W. H., 555, 558, 562, 563
Schon, D. A., 110, 125, 129
Schools (see Education)
Schools of thought: approach to programme design, 171–3
Search and analysis, MBO, 414, 416
Sears Roebuck, 43, 64
Seashore, C., 242, 258
Seashore, S. F., 375, 383
Secretarial services, in training centres, 202, 570
Section managers' in-basket (see In-basket exercises)
Seiler, J. A., 380, 384
Selection, of managers, Chapters 4 and 6
Selection for courses, by top management, 18, 38
Selection process, in Internal Revenue Service, 56–8
Self-analysis of entrepreneurs, 142, 144–5, 146
Self-confidence, needed in sensitivity trainers, 253
Self-control, in MBO, 406
Self-correcting mechanisms, 512–13
  matrix, 524
Self-criticism, in organization development, 488
Self-development, 20–1, 582–3
Self-discovery, sensitivity training, 243
Self-esteem, need in managers, 401, 410
Self-examination, Managerial Grid, 387
Self-fulfilment, laboratory training, 241
Self-knowledge: output of management development, 8
  sensitivity training, 245, 253
Self-selection of job applicants, 88
Self-study: problem of evaluation, 282
  South Africa University, 282–3, 286
Semantic parallelogram, 304
Semi-State organizations, 147

Seminars, Management, 338
  (*see also* Grid seminars)
Seniority and executive potential, 44–5
Sensitivity training, 8, 171, 180, 320–1, 380,
    Chapter 17
  and leadership, 245, 246
  and therapy, 243–4
  assumptions in, 242–3
  beginning, 257
  case studies, 242
  conditions for, 248
  criticism of, 578
  defined, 242
  evaluation of, 246–7
  factors affecting, figure, 250
  groupings, 255
  in South Africa University, 279, 286
  internal-external, 256
  issues, 254–6
  length of, 254–5
  qualifications of trainers, 253–4
  participants, 244–6, 252–3
  research in, 246–7
  responsibilities of, 248–51
  risks, 247, 256–7
  role of management, 256
  role of trainer, 251–3
  subtlety of, 248
Sequential case, 187, 189
Sequential selection, 87
Shell International Petroleum Co Ltd, 308
Shephard, Herbert, 343
Silber, M., 128, 134
Silberer, P., 94, 98
Simon, H. A., 404, 427
Simplicity needed in planning process, 333
Simulation, 48, 77, 133, 171, 175, 177, 185,
    488, 578–9
  activities and armed forces, 120
  business management games, figure, 226
  in decision-making, 326
  Managerial Grid, 387
Singapore, 102
Singapore Institute of Management, 157
Situation case, 186, 189
Situational approach in Action-Centred
    Leadership, 447–8
Sizes of firms, 135
Skills, 175–7, 179
  acquisition, sensitivity training, 243
  changes, through management develop-
    ment, 7
  development programme, 581
  in communications training, 305–6
Slide projectors, 267–8, 570
Small firms, and assessment centres, 69
  case studies, 476–9
  changes in, 474–6
  development, 138–9
  diagnosis, 476–7
  evaluation, 479–83

implementation, 478–9
  objectives of organization development, 474
  organization development in, Chapter 32
  prescription for, 478
  types of, 470–4
Smith, Norman, R., 155, 164
Snake in the tunnel, MBO as, 404
Social abilities, resourcefulness, 111–12
Social mixing, training centres, 15
Social value systems, national variations, 178
Society: change factors, 99, 103, 543
Society games, 221
Sociologists, in organization development, 372
Sociology, study of, 171
Sociometric techniques, assessing manage-
    ment games, 233
Software: audio-visual aids, 264–5
  South Africa University, 280–2
Solid style of management, 115–16
Solvay, E., 12
South Africa, University of, Chapter 19
    passim
  activities, 282–8
  curriculum, 278
  evaluation, 288–9
  future, 289
  learning basis, 278–9
  school's objectives, 277–8
  software, 280–2
  students, 279–80
  study groups, 283–6
South African Association of Business Leader-
    ship, 276
South-East Asia, and Management develop-
    ment, 152, 156–7
  needs, 157, 164
Special assignments, 170
  in management games, 231–2
Specialists, 575
  dangers, in Management development ser-
    vice, 28
Specialization, and Top management isola-
    tion, 14
  lack in small firms, 137
Specific games, 221–2
Spectral analysis, diagram, 179
Spectrum, Barclay's Bank, 607–13, 614
Staff, of training centres, 570–1
  role in Action-Centred Leadership, 451
  role in communications training, 307–8
  South Africa University, 281
Staff College, 191–2
Staff meetings on problems, 144
Staff officers, responsibilities for planning,
    338
Staff recruitment: difficulty, 137
  role in sensitivity training, 242
Standardization and Management develop-
    ment, 32
Standards, maintenance, in sensitivity train-
    ing, 251–2

Standards—*cont.*
  (*see also* Assessment; Constraints; Evaluation; Objectives; Performance measurement)
Standards of living, 444
Stanford University, 247
Statistical techniques, manpower planning, 530–1, 532, 536
Statistics of costs, entrepreneurial courses, 146
Status, individual, 378
Status groups, 374
  (*see also* Hierarchies)
Status problems, and organization development, 123
  and sensitivity training, 246
  in assessment centres, 71–2
Stewart, M., 378, 384
Stiefel, R., 237, 238
Stochastic models, management games, 222
Stock, manpower, 532
Stock, D., 246, 258
Strategic modelling, 389–90
Strategic objectives continua, diagram, 321
Strategic plan, 17
Strategies, in management games, 219
  need for information on, 336
Streaming, manpower planning, 539
Stress, in management games, 230
  in organizations, 507
  in T-Groups, 247
Stress situations, 94
Students, South Africa University, 279–80
Study groups, 121, 124, 576–7
  internal, 409
  leadership in, 284
  South Africa University, 279, 283–6
Style (*see* Management style)
Sublimation, discovery of, 310
Success, needed in development programme, 139–40
Succession problem: family firms, 472–3, 474
  planning, 545, 547
  small firms, 137, 145, 474
  table, 39
Sudan: management development, 152
Supergrades, 52
Supervisors, courses for, 139
Support, in managers, 401, 404–5, 406, 575
  in organizations, 507
Support facilities, for organization development, 122–3
Survey of needs approach to management education, 173
Sweden: employment, 428–9
Sykes, A. J. M., 577, 583
Syndicates (*see* Management training syndicates)
Synectics Education Systems, 310–16
Synergistic ply, in organizations, 515, 518, 520–1
Syria, action learning project, 208, 209

Systems analysts, 409

Takeovers (*see* Mergers)
Talks (*see* Lectures)
Tannenbaum, R., 242
Tape-slide systems, 267–8
Target-setting, 452, 486, 545, 590
  in small firms, 138
Targets, limitations of, 433
Tarmac, and organization development, 121–2
Task forces, 107, 170, 338
Tax (*see* Internal Revenue Service)
Taylor, F. W., 378
Teachers: shortcomings, 263
Teaching methods: diagrams, 176, 179
Teaching problems, and audio-visual aids, 262
Teaching techniques: correspondence courses, 277
Team building, 380
Team development: Managerial Grid, 388–9
Team effectiveness analysis, 462–3
Team training, 255
Teams, in management games, 228
  composition, 232
  (*see also* Groups; Syndicates)
Teamwork, and MBO, 402, 407
  concept, 406–7
  emphasis in firms, 475
  in management development, 578
Technical abilities, resourcefulness, 111
Technical journals, 147
Technology, modern, in small firms, 138
Teletuition, Chapter 19
  (*for subheadings see* South Africa, University of)
Television, audio-visual aids, 270–3, 570
  illustrations, 266, 271–2
  in assessment centres, 66
  in Malaysia, 102
  in role play cases, 187
  values, list of, 273
Tension, between groups, 389
  in organizations, 507
Testing, combined with assessment, 49–50
  executive potential, Chapter 4
  of applicants, 94
  (*see also* Assessment)
T-Groups, 244, 246, 247, 254, 380–1, 487, 496
  Comparison with Grid seminars, 388
  criticism of, 578
Thailand, 151, 156, 158
Thailand Management Association, 157
Theoretical ideas, factor in isolation, 15–16
Theory of games, 219
Theory presentations: sensitivity training, 242
Therapy and sensitivity training, 243–4, 486, 578
Theses, South Africa University, 283
Think-tank sessions, manpower planning, 532
Thinking as communication, 302
Third world, 102

648

Timing of assessments, 73
Toffler, A., 110, 125
Top management, and autonomous M.D., 20–1
  and ideational ply, 517
  and Managerial Grid, 395
  and manpower planning, 531
  and programmed Management development, 16–20
  communication failure, 301
  development of, 576
  function, in management development, 12, 13, 16
  isolation, 14–16
  organization and style, 559–60
  role in management development, Chapter 2, 573–4, 575
Top management games, 221
Total enterprise games, 221
Towne, H. R., 12
Trade fairs, 147
Trade unions, 359, 362, Chapter 25 passim
  and manpower planning, 529
Traditions: attitudes, 586
  in family firms, 474
  of companies, 510–12
Trainers, and Management development objectives, 579–82
  and organic learning process, 582–3
  development of, Chapter 39, 576–9
  importance of effectiveness, 583
  specialists as, 575
Training, analysis of, 586
  and top management, 17–20
  as change agent, 585
  component of MD system, 36
    diagram, 38
  continuity, in centres, 565
  control, 19–20
  duration, 18–19
  environment, 565–8
  factors in centre, 565
  flexibility, 565
  for industrial relations negotiators, Chapter 25
    (for headings see Industrial relations)
  for communicators, Chapter 20
    (for headings see Communicators)
  for managers to understand youth, 107–8
  implementation, 303–8
  importance seen by firms, 565
  in-company, figure, 34
  in learning process, 184–5
  in perspective, 585–7, 588–9
  nature of, 593–4
  needs, 299–302
    gap between needs and training, 585
    list, figure, 591
    summary, figure, 589
    of executives, 48–9
    organization of, 19

  privacy of, 565
  selection for, 18
  specific versus general, 17–18
  to improve effectiveness, 170
  use in assessment, Internal Revenue Service, 58–60
  volume, factor in centre, 565
Training (see also Education)
Training boards, industrial, 130, 131
Training centres: isolation, 14–15, 19
  availability of facilities, 564
  (see also Assessment centres; Company training centres)
Training cost control, 593–5
  checklist, 596–8
Training director, sensitivity groups, 256
Training element, in organization development, 486
Training officers, 574
Training programme in organization development, 495–7
  goals, 496
  pitfalls, 496
Training skills in sensitivity trainer, 254
Transfer barrier, 599
Transfer problem, learning process, 170, 184
Transfer values, 21
Transfers, staff, 378, 532
Transparencies, 267–9
Treasury Department (US), 53–61 passim
Tregoe, B. B., 319, 320, 321, 325, 327, 488
Trial situations, as predictors, 85
Trouble-shooting by managers, 114, 120
Trout basin theory of talent, 20
Trust-love values, 392
Turkey, management development in, 152
Tutorial support, training centres, 570–1
Tutors (see Staff)

Uncertainty in management, 527–8
UNDP, 152
Unemployment in UK, 428
Uniformity (see Standardization)
Unions (see Trade unions)
United Kingdom, incentives towards MD, ix–x
  invasion of, 219
United Nations, 151
United Nations Development Programme (UNDP), 152
United States: employment, 429
  comparison of management styles, 178
  entrepreneurship, 155–6
  influence on developing countries, 151–2
  lead in management research, x
  size of firms, 135
United States Agency for International Development (USAID), 152
United States Civil Service Commission, 51–61

United States Government Service: assessment techniques, 51–61
   intern programmes, 104
United States Naval Academy, 219
United States Steel, 104
United States Treasury Department, 53–61 passim
Urwick, L. F., 126–7, 134
USAID, 152
USSR: influence on developing countries, 152
   invasion of, 219

Vacancies: table, 39
Vail Group, 343
Validation, of selection procedure, 96
   of training, 595, 597
Values, acquisition, sensitivity training, 243
   fundamental, commitment to, 111, 112
   in OD Managerial Grid, 392–3, 396
Variables, stochastic, 222
Videotapes (see Audio-visual aids)
Visual aids (see Audio-visual aids)
Von Reissewitz, 219

Wage claims, 428
War chess, 218
War games, 219
Warburtons of Bolton and OD, 122
Wastage rates, manpower planning, 532–4, 536

Welfare and job enrichment, 434
Welfare services: staffing requirements, 530
Weschler, I., 242, 243, 258
Westinghouse Electric Corporation, 43
Weyerhaeuser Company, 343, 345
Weyerhaeuser Management School, 343, 345–50
Whitehead, T. N., 374, 383
Whyte, W. F., 378, 384
Will to achieve, 205
Williams, B. R., 115, 125
Williams Lea: case study in OD, 476–9
Wills and Co, 473
Woodward, J., 556, 562, 563
Work force: age table, 101
   youth of, 100–1
Work structure, figure, 548
Working conditions, 315, 345
   physical changes, 374
Working parties, 121, 124
Writing analysis, 94
Writing exercises, assessment centres, 77

Yale University, 343
Younger generation, and managers, Chapter 7
   current practices, 103–6
   different ideas, 429
   trends, 106–8

PRINTED BY J. W. ARROWSMITH, BRISTOL, ENGLAND, BS3 2NT